REAGAN'S AMERICA

Books by Garry Wills

REAGAN'S AMERICA: INNOCENTS AT HOME

CINCINNATUS: GEORGE WASHINGTON AND THE
  ENLIGHTENMENT

LEAD TIME

THE KENNEDY IMPRISONMENT

EXPLAINING AMERICA

CHESTERTON

POLITICS AND CATHOLIC FREEDOM

ROMAN CULTURE

JACK RUBY

THE SECOND CIVIL WAR

NIXON AGONISTES

BARE RUINED CHOIRS

CONFESSIONS OF A CONSERVATIVE

INVENTING AMERICA

AT BUTTON'S

REAGAN'S AMERICA

INNOCENTS AT HOME

GARRY WILLS

HEINEMANN : LONDON

William Heinemann Ltd
Michelin House, 81 Fulham Road, London SW3 6RB
LONDON   MELBOURNE   AUCKLAND

First published in Great Britain in 1988
Copyright © 1985, 1986, 1987 by Literary Research, Inc.
Reprinted 1988

British Library Cataloguing in Publication Data

Wills, Gary
Reagan's America: innocents at home.
1. Reagan, Ronald   2. Presidents—United States—Biography
I. Title
973.92′092′4   E877

ISBN 0 434 86623 ⌐ (hardback)
ISBN 0 434 86625 3 (paperback)

Printed in Great Britain by
Mackays of Chatham Ltd, Kent

To Ken McCormick
gentleman, editor, friend

CONTENTS

INTRODUCTION

These wells that shine and seem as shallow as pools,
These tales that, being too plain for the fool's eyes,
Incredibly clear are clearly incredible—
Truths by their depth deceiving more than lies.

—G. K. Chesterton

The geriatric "juvenile lead" even as President, Ronald Reagan is old and young—an actor, but with only one role. Because he acts himself, we know he is authentic. A professional, he is always the amateur. He is the great American synecdoche, not only a part of our past but a large part of our multiple pasts. That is what makes many of the questions asked about him so pointless. Is he bright, shallow, complex, simple, instinctively shrewd, plain dumb? He is all these things and more. Synecdoche is just the Greek word for a "sampling," and we all take different samples from the rich store of associations that have accumulated around the Reagan career and persona. He is just as simple, and just as mysterious, as our collective dreams and memories.

He is capacious, surrounding contradictions. Different worlds cohabit the man—"Death Valley Days" and Silicon Valley, Des Moines and the District of Columbia, Sacramento and Eureka. Nor has he simply passed through these places as points of travel—he is still there, at each point. Return him to Eureka College, and he looks instantly at home. He is perfectly suited to the most varying scenes of his life, yet his manner never changes. He is the opposite of a chameleon: environments adapt themselves to him.

He spans our lives, culturally and chronologically. Born in the year the first studio opened in Hollywood, he reached that town just two years after Technicolor did. His second term as President runs through 1988, the two-hundredth anniversary of the ratification of the United States Constitution, and his life spans over a third of that history of constitutional government. His career as a public figure was already a fourth as long as the national government's in the year he went to the White House. Born eleven years into the twentieth, he is scheduled to leave the White House eleven years from the twenty-first century.

He began his regular radio career the year Franklin Roosevelt delivered his first fireside address. An adult during the Depression and World War II, he has known union crusades and corporate worries, spoken for civil liberties and for red hunting. He has been a Hollywood success and a Las Vegas flop. After two victories by wide margins in California, he went down to two defeats as a presidential candidate. He died for victory as the Gipper and won personal glory in the defeat of Barry Goldwater. We have been through it all with him. The GE "House of the Future" he lived in, and Star Wars for the outfitting of space. War movies, and real war (well, almost) in Grenada. Death from prop six-guns, and John Hinckley's real bullets. Reagan runs continuously in everyone's home movies of the mind. He wrests from us something warmer than mere popularity, a kind of complicity. He is, in the strictest sense, what Hollywood promoters used to call "fabulous." We fable him to ourselves, and he to us. We are jointly responsible for him.

He is aware of his own prototypical status, yet that awareness neither galls us nor discommodes him. It is simply "All-American" in his eyes for him to be all America; so, in his eyes, he is. His vast claims are made in ways that convey modesty, not megalomania. One psychobiographer has tried to trace Reagan's political views and actions to a deep insecurity derived from his father. But what must strike the candid observer is the President's almost preternatural security, the lack of inner division that he maintains despite so much contained diversity.

Self-assurance reassures others, and that has not been the least of Reagan's gifts to us, at a time when the nation needed some reassuring. President Carter had discovered such disorientation in the country, or in himself, that he scolded his countrymen for the crime of "malaise." More voters understood him to be the cause of this complaint than its cure; but there can be no doubt that it was a serious charge to bring against any American. Carter spoke of limits, of lowered goals as well as thermostats, of accommodation with the Russians and other unpleasant realities. That is not only demoralizing in a country that defines itself in terms of growth; it stirs a subtle panic, a claustrophobia, that has haunted the American consciousness all through this century. When the Census Bureau declared the frontier closed in 1890, it seemed to be announcing a doom upon the nation. What would we be without the frontier? It had shaped, conditioned, defined us, said Frederick Jackson Turner in 1892. A frontierless America would be non-America. So, once the physical line had been removed from our maps of the continent, we had to engage in metaphorical cartography, tracing "new frontiers" of various sorts, inner or outer, microfrontiers in the laboratory, macrofrontiers in space.

Beneath the spacial anxiety expressed in modern America, there is an even deeper *temporal* fear, that of aging. What if the New World should turn out no different from the Old? Progress may be our most important product, but youth is our oldest boast. As we passed through the various "birthdays" of the 1970s and 1980s, a litany of bicentennials, it should have been harder to maintain our political infancy. Yet, if we did *not* maintain it, what were we to make of claims that this alone preserved us from the gentle decrepitude or active corruption of our European forebears? We are now ruled by the oldest written constitution governing in any nation. Our plight resembles that of Mr. Crummles with his Infant Phenomenon, or Mary Pickford doing Polly-anna—we need an indulgent audience to make the act work.

Yet the rebound from malaise was accomplished in what seems, at first, a perverse way. We regained our youth by electing the oldest President in our history. Four years after the electorate had declared that it was worse off than it was in 1976, one could hardly distinguish Ronald Reagan's stunning re-election victory from the flags and gold medals of the 1984 Olympics. The young athletes seemed to draw strength from their aging leader, not the other way around. In the famous exchange after John Kennedy's death, journalist Mary McGrory said, "We will never laugh again," and Patrick Moynihan answered, "No, we will laugh again; but we will never be young again." Reagan's success of 1984 was "big magic" by any measure: he made us young again.

How did he pull it off? It is not enough, I think, to say that he resummons our youth because he remembers it, as if anyone sufficiently old would do. Nor is Reagan like the other old men we have used, paradoxically, to sym-bolize America's youthful spirit—the wise old birds with white hair who seemed to defy the calendar: Mark Twain, or Thomas Edison, or Henry Ford. Those were progeny of Benjamin Franklin, men remembered for a youthful exploit they enacted or described so as to make it timeless—Frank-lin walking the streets of Philadelphia with his bulky inadequate bread rolls, Twain's eternal haunting of the youth gangs in Hannibal, Edison with his chemicals in the boxcar, or Ford in his workshop. They spoke for and out of a boyhood legend of themselves, authenticated by the fame and wealth such boyhoods led them to. Each, besides, was a genius (or was held to be one) who did not speak the language of the specialist, confirming our picture of America as natively shrewd yet naive. They offered us brilliance as an every-day matter, pairing wisdom with innocence.

Reagan has no archetypal boyhood achievement like Franklin's labor at the press or Ford's at the combustion engine. He has neither an author's nor an inventor's originality. He does not even have the warrior's glow that quickened Dwight Eisenhower's foxy-grandpa popularity. The key point is, precisely, that we do not think of Reagan as grandfatherly (no matter how many grandchildren he may have). Though he was only briefly a leading man on the screen, he has since acquired romantic luster in what passes for real life. He did not age gracefully into character roles, like Jimmy Stewart finally playing Lassie's owner's grandfather. Failure at the box office spared Reagan that honorable second and third life of the fading star who still finds work.

But the alternative to such lessened grandeur is normally even worse—to become a fading nonstar, a Sunset Boulevard relic, the frail lacquered icon of an earlier self, as "ageless" and as unconvincing as Mae West. How did Reagan avoid all these traps? He did not age gracefully; he managed somehow not to age at all, at least in symbolic terms. Part of this, of course, is the luck and discipline of physical health. He took good care of himself. But so did Mae West. Reagan, however, was not seen as pampering himself, pickled in adulation for what he did before. He directed his and others' attention from himself to the principle of America as a politically rejuvenating phenomenon. This was accomplished by a mysterious access of Reagan's believing self to our own springs of belief and desire to believe. That is: no one has undergone a more thorough initiation into every aspect of the American legend than Reagan has, and no one has found so many conduits—so many channels, open and indirect, associative, accumulative—for bringing that legend to us in the freshest way. He is the perfect carrier: the ancient messages travel through him without friction. No wonder he shows little wear or tear.

Much of this access derives from Reagan's long familiarity to us in radio, movies, television, and then again on the radio. This is both an obvious and an unexamined fact about Reagan's political life. Early attempts to dismiss him as "just an actor" misfired so badly that more thoughtful attention has not been given to the fact that he *was* indeed an actor, along with everything else. His own first handlers tried to minimize the importance of his Hollywood days, and so have later analysts of his policies. Reagan, with surer instinct, cheerfully emphasizes what others feared to bring up. He understands that a show-business background is part (though only part) of his political resonance. He was never a boy genius, but he was in the place where legends of boy geniuses were fabricated. He was dying as the Gipper while Mickey Rooney played young Edison.

He is an icon, but not a frail one put away in the dark, not Norma Desmond gone brittle on celluloid, her reality decomposing. He is a durable daylight "bundle of meanings," as Roland Barthes called myth. Reagan does not argue for American values; he embodies them. To explain his appeal, one must explore the different Americas of which he is made up. He renews our past by resuming it. His approach is not discursive, setting up sequences of time or thought, but associative; not a tracking shot, but montage. We make the connections. It is our movie.

PART ONE

HUCK FINN'S WORLD

CHAPTER 1

Jack

There warn't no home like a raft, after all.
—Huckleberry Finn

Ann Sheridan writes in the snow, "Happy New Year." Ronald Reagan, over her protests, whisks out the last word: "Happy New *Century,* Dummy!" It is 1900 in Kings Row, and Erich Korngold's music confects a sugary future.

Mark Twain took a dourer view of the new century. He dated its inception from January of 1901 and realized, halfway through the year, that the nation's lynching rate (eighty-eight so far) would surpass the preceding year's (one hundred and fifteen for the whole twelve months).[1]

Ronald Reagan calls his childhood "one of those rare Huck Finn-Tom Sawyer idylls" (Hubler, p. 18). The Twain novels he refers to are chronicles of superstition, racism, and crime. *The Adventures of Huckleberry Finn,* in particular, takes place almost entirely at night, as a series of panicky escapes from one horror to another:

> I ain't agoing to tell *all* that happened—it would make me sick again if I was to do that. I wished I hadn't ever come ashore that night, to see such things. I ain't ever going to get shut of them—lots of times I dream about them . . . Jim warn't on his island, so I tramped off in a hurry for the crick, and crowded through the willows, red-hot to jump aboard and get out of that awful country. [Ch. 18]

Huck mainly "lights out" in terror, not in joy. "One is bound to remember that at eight Samuel Clemens found a stabbed body on the floor of his father's office one night, and at nine he witnessed a murder, of which the perpetrator was acquitted. Huck wants to get away from everything rather than into adventure."[2]

Twain already suspected, in 1901, that the twentieth century offered no haven from nightmare. Ronald Reagan's parents moved to his birthplace, Tampico, Illinois, in 1906, during a wave of revivals in the area, a matter of timing that would greatly influence their son's life. But just a month after

their arrival, the small village paper ran a lurid tale with three large headlines:

HANG AND BURN THREE NEGROES

MOB AT SPRINGFIELD, MO., REVENGES ATTACK MADE ON WHITE GIRL

Rope Breaks Precipitating Victim Into Burning
Embers of Pyre Where Two Others Had Preceded Him,
But Crowd Is Relentless

The man who fell into the fire was retrieved alive and hanged again. The
account shows no sense of outrage, or of irony: "The victims were strung to
the Goddess of Liberty statues on the electric light tower in the public
square at the courthouse."[3] New century or old, the country was still living
through Huck Finn-Tom Sawyer dreams, which were never as idyllic as
Reagan remembers.

Reagan is not the only person, of course, who has filtered out the darker
aspects of Mark Twain's work; but there is a special poignancy in his superficial gesture toward Huck Finn, since there is much of Twain's Mississippi in
Reagan's background. His father, Jack, was born, grew up, and married on
the Mississippi; in fact, Twain first steamed up the northern Mississippi, past
Fulton, Illinois, just one year before Jack Reagan was born there. Like Huck,
Jack Reagan was orphaned, had to leave school, and led a drifting life. The
Rock River, from whose current Ronald saved many lives, is a tributary of
the Mississippi, and it became an important part of the big river's canal
system early in this century—a fact that explains Ronald's birth in Tampico.
The future President got his first job after college working on the Missis-
sippi, and for a man more improbable than any character to be found in
Twain. The Reagans were under the spell of the Mississippi, of all the
muddy bright promises it meant to break.

Twain's mood as he approached Fulton in 1882 was one of optimism,
induced by a sense of release. He had just revisited his dear benighted South,
the source of his life's troubled dreams, home of a fictitious "chivalry" and a
very real racism. Like his own Huck, he was "lighting out" from the horrors
—but not to the Territory, not westward. Paradoxically, he traveled north to
a "new frontier" of industrialism and reason. "In Burlington, as in all these
upper-river towns, one breathes a go-ahead atmosphere, which tastes good in
the nostrils."[4] Northward, it seemed, no more lynchings.

Twain had begun *Life on the Mississippi* with memories of a youth caught
in the falling and the rising arcs of two technologies, when the rough era of
keelsmen and large rafts was yielding to the tailored expertise of steamboat
pilots. He expressed a nostalgia for the age of rafts, but felt an overriding
excitement at the discoveries of his own time. The Mississippi book ends
with a similar crisscrossing of old and new technologies: the steamboat is
dying, the railroads are taking over. Twain's sympathies are again divided;

he regrets the lost splendor of the pilot, but hopes for enlightenment from the smokestacks of the rational north.

> Hour by hour the boat plows deeper and deeper into the great and populous Northwest; and with each successive section of it which is revealed, one's surprise and respect gather emphasis and increase. Such a people, and such achievements as theirs, compel homage. This is an independent race who think for themselves, and who are competent to do it, because they are educated and enlightened; they read, they keep abreast of the best and newest thought, they fortify every weak place in their land with a school, a college, a library, and a newspaper; and they live under law. [Ch. 58]

This is Huck in reverse, "lighting out" for "sivilization" and schoolbooks and the law. Twain is able to keep some of the mythic value of the frontier, in the Eden he imagines along the upper river, by treating it as fresh and "virgin" in a chronological sense: "This region is new; so new that it may be said to be still in its boyhood. By what it has accomplished while still teething, one may forecast what marvels it will do in the strength of its maturity."

Twain was reading Francis Parkman's account of the early discoverers of the northern river, as part of his research for *Life on the Mississippi*, whose opening section draws on Parkman's *La Salle and the Discovery of the Great West*, that book of magical style which had appeared just thirteen years before. The rhythms of Parkman, in which terrifying encounters with Indians alternate with peaceful moments of camping or canoeing, are similar to those of the novel Twain was working on while he finished the Mississippi book. (He used each of his own tasks to prod the other forward). And there is remarkable similarity between the moods of release achieved on the river in Twain and in Parkman. In those moments, at least, it was a happy new world. In Parkman's fifth chapter, the Jesuit Marquette (of all people) seems to prefigure Huck:

> They had found what they sought, and "with a joy," writes Marquette, "which I cannot express," they steered forth their canoes on the eddies of the Mississippi . . .
> Again they were on their way, slowly drifting down the great river . . .
> They resumed their course, and floated down the interminable monotony of river, marsh, and forest. Day after day passed on in solitude . . .

In chapter 20, La Salle is the voyager "floating prosperously down between the leafless forests that flanked the river":

> They followed the writhings of the great river on its tortuous course through wastes of swamp and canebreak, till on the thirteenth of March they found themselves wrapped in a thick fog . . .

After pushing his canoe down the whole river's length to the Gulf of Mexico, La Salle later tried to reach the river's mouth from the Gulf, but could not distinguish its marshy outlets: "Now every eye on board was strained to detect in the monotonous lines of the low shore some token of the great river. In fact they had already passed it" (Ch. 24). La Salle, swept on to Texas and his murder, is in the plight of Nigger Jim when the raft drifts past Cairo. The river deceives even those who think they are initiated into its secrets.

But Twain let himself think, when he saw the upper river submit to railway bridges, that industrialism was bringing rationality to the Midwest. The spread of railroads pollinated towns. Fulton had not even been a village when, in 1852, it was marked for a railroad landing. By the time the first train pulled in, three years later, it was opening the largest hotel west of Chicago, the Dement House, and had incorporated itself as a village.[5] A year before that (1854), Jack Reagan's father, the President's grandfather, was born in Fairhaven, Illinois.[6]

When Jack was orphaned in Fulton, at the age of six, he went to live part of his time with an aunt across the Mississippi, in a town that was actually younger than he was at the time. Bennett, Iowa, named for the railroad purchasing agent who dealt with local spokesmen, was called into existence in 1884. For a while, at least, the trains seemed to act like Hank Morgan in *A Connecticut Yankee at King Arthur's Court* (1889), raising towns and schools and workshops across the countryside. But by the time Twain finished the Connecticut Yankee book, he had become as disillusioned with the "rational" North of Colt Factories as with the superstitious South.[7] By the time Neil Reagan was born, in 1908, Twain was cursing the whole "damned human race."

The farmers of the Northwest were quicker than Twain to resent the railroads they had bid for so eagerly.[8] But they looked deceptively prosperous as Twain, in 1882, glimpsed Davenport (scene of Ronald Reagan's first radio job), "another beautiful city, crowning a hill" (Ch. 58). Farther north, his boat swung with the river around "Cromwell's nose" as Twain watched the Iowa side, the lumberyards at Lyons, instead of Fulton lying just across the river, quickly hidden by its channel island.

Twain talks about opera houses and other great works going up near the river, but he neglects the real cathedrals of the railway age in the Midwest— the tall grain elevators, self-painted continuously by the fine stuff they take up into conspicuous hiding. These perpendicular structures unite the flat lands stretching behind the river's bluffs. In them the work of the seasons is slowly gathered and raised, to be released in quick showers when the train stops. Rural and urban rhythms are joined here, the rumble of the trains beneath, the quiet tower above.

John Michael Reagan, the President's grandfather, worked in Fulton's grain elevator; but the only year for which we have a record of his service, 1880, shows he was out of work for a third of the year.[9] This might have been for health reasons—he died young—but there was a slow depression inching over the Northwest even while the trains gave a surface chatter of life. In fact, the rapider movement of foodstuffs went along with a sharp decline, in the 1870s, of farm prices.[10] The new grain cathedrals were old already, but they did not know it. For farmers along the Mississippi, the great depression of the 1890s was already, insensibly, on its way. The same year Jack Reagan was born to the elevator worker in Fulton, Illinois, William Jennings Bryan, who would become the voice of farmers' anguish, finished law school in Chicago. Bryan was better at articulating that anguish than at mitigating it: "His public life was devoted to translating a complicated world of public affairs he barely comprehended back into those values he never questioned."[11]

Ronald Reagan remembers his father as an organization Democrat during the Depression of the 1930s, given patronage jobs by the New Deal. But the formative years of Jack Reagan were also spent during a national depression, this one blamed on the Democrats. Jack was eleven in the depression year of 1894, the year of Coxey's army, the Pullman strike, and Populist elections. Coxey's army, which moved on Washington from all over the nation, used Chicago as its staging area. In Iowa, the Northwestern Railroad banned marchers from its line and threatened, if a train was seized, to speed a riderless engine down the track to meet it.[12] Wheat, which had sold for $1.22 a bushel in 1881 was now going for $0.45.[13] Third parties were formed, to express discontent with past politics. Elements of the Prohibition Party went into the new Populist Party. When the "ritualistic" Democratic Party tried, against its ethos, to absorb the radicalism and pietism of this agrarian movement, it suffered a crushing defeat in 1896.[14]

Jack Reagan, an Irish Catholic, was one of the old Democrats, nonpietistic and "wet," not an agrarian radical. His forebears had always been farmers, in Ireland and America, but he was a decidedly urban man, with no interest in owning land. When, in 1937, Ronald brought his parents to California and gave them the first home they had not rented, Jack's wife wrote her friends in Dixon with surprise that Jack found he liked keeping the little garden in their yard. It was his first sign of interest in growing things. We have no record of his ever having worked but at urban white-collar jobs.

When John Michael and Jennie Cusack Reagan both died in 1889, they left four children, all of school age (Jack was the second youngest at six).[15] John Michael had two, and possibly three, living sisters in the area, who must have shared the task of raising, educating, and finding work for their nieces and nephews. One of these sisters, Margaret, was married to Orson G. Baldwin, who kept a department store in the new town of Bennett, Iowa, fifty miles from Fulton. It is certain that Jack lived sometimes with them, but uncertain for how long at any one time. He was surely there in the summer of 1897, when he managed the first boys' baseball team in Bennett, and in 1898, when he was photographed on the town baseball team.[16] In 1900, he was playing for a neighbor team, and the Cedar County Census for 1900 lists him as a Bennett resident whose occupation (at sixteen) was "dry goods salesman."[17] On the other hand, he registered in the Bennett Hotel as a visitor from Fulton in 1898—and as a visitor from *Bennett* in 1898![18]

By 1901 the local paper (Tipton *Advertiser)* reported that he was in Bennett to visit relatives.[19] He must have moved around from one relative's home to another, like his siblings, according to the school seasons and the presence of jobs for the parentless children. The family base throughout was Fulton, where Jack's grandmother was still alive. It should be noticed that Jack retained his Catholicism, and there was no Catholic church in little Bennett.[20] When Jack moved to Tampico in 1906, the paper there said he had been working at Broadhead's Store in Fulton for eight years.[21] This seems to conflict with the Census Report that places him in Bennett as late as 1900. But he could well have worked seasonally in both towns as he shifted places with his brother or sisters from his aunts' to his grandmother's house. He was still in his teens for five of the eight years at issue. Just before he moved to Tampico, he and his wife had been living with his grandmother.[22] This mode of life probably resembled Huck Finn's too literally, and the only other boy among the children—Jack's older brother Bill—may have been hurt by such a rootless adolescence, since he later led a life of hard drinking, depression, and commitment to institutions.[23]

The skills needed to survive as the perennial guest or charitable boarder are those of adaptation and ingratiation. Jack seems to have been better at developing these arts than was Bill. Jack was a blarneyer, a josher, a cutup. Ronald Reagan, a connoisseur in the matter, calls him "the best raconteur I ever heard" (Hubler, p. 14). In Twain's novel, Huck is orphaned over and over, when his father is reported dead but lives, or is thought to be living but is not, or is finally identified with the "gashly" sight Jim saved Huck from seeing too close. Huck invents a new parentage for each new situation, remaking himself to find acceptance. Children who live dependent on others, not their parents, feel they must constantly renew their credentials. The frangibility of their situation, combined with the finality of the deaths that occasioned it, makes for an urgency toward "easiness" with others, sometimes to a self-defeating self-promotion.

Jack Reagan dreamed new selves out of his charming head, which was "burning with ambition," his son tells us (Hubler, p. 13). Jack had to please, impress, show he belonged. He developed a flamboyance displayed in little things, as in the large jaunty signature, "Jack," on his county wedding license. The priest more severely put him down as "John" (and misspelled his last name). At fifteen, he stands out from the other baseball players in the picture of Bennett's team because of his wavy hair parted in the middle[24]— the "aesthetic" fashion Oscar Wilde, his fellow Irishman, had brought to America six years before the picture was taken. It was a style Jack's older son Neil would imitate. The showman appears, as well, in Jack's listing of residences in the Bennett Hotel register—sometimes "Dublin, Ireland," sometimes "Molasses Junction."[25]

Though Jack tried later to specialize in one line of goods, shoes, he worked for a long time as a general clerk, and must have aspired to become a general manager. At the birth of his second son, he was still selling general goods.[26] He gave his occupation, on his wedding certificate, as "clerking in store." He was listed in the Fulton City Directory of 1905–6 as "clerk." He served as a clerk at Baldwin's store in Bennett, Broadhead's in Fulton, Pitney's in Tampico, the Fair Store in Chicago, O. T. Johnson's "Big Store" in Galesburg, and the E. B. Colwell store in Monmouth.[27] Each of these was the biggest store in its respective town. The Bennett building was torn down in the 1960s, and the Chicago one in the 1980s; but the rest survive, each still impressive on its site.[28]

Department stores of this sort, in the small towns where Jack Reagan began, were channels of sophistication arriving from the outside world. They boasted a broad range of suppliers and the rapidest influx of new styles. As early as 1903, Pitney's in Tampico was proclaiming, "We are agents for Ed. N. Pierce and Strauss Bro's Tailor Made Clothing."[29] The dapper Jack could form as well as show off his style in such places, dealing with traveling agents as well as local customers. Eventually, through suppliers, travel, and better jobs, he flirted with the edges of the big time, at least part of the time.

Jack's banter, flair, and ingratiating ways were fitted to the salesman's task. The salesman traffics in hope. As Melville's Mississippi salesman puts it, "Hope is proportioned to confidence. How much confidence you give me, so much hope I give you."[30] The salesman must make his customer confident about the future—about future ability to pay, about the enjoyment that will exceed costs, about the meeting of other commitments after the purchase of just this one more item. He speaks always for the triumph of promise over thrift. He is the one who makes grass look greener beyond a series of pay turnstiles. Like most good salesmen (and many bad ones) Jack Reagan believed in his own gospel of desired things hovering nearer. He jostled to reach for them, maneuvering, preparing himself.

When he moved to Chicago in 1914, Jack Reagan worked for the first department store to open in that city, an aggressive advertiser, the occupant of a Willian LeBaron Jenney building eleven stories high and filling a whole block. Its 55,000 square feet of selling space boasted "Everything to Everybody Under One Roof."[31] When he moved on to Galesburg, in the next year, it was to live on a broad brick street, where Jack eventually rented his grandest, most spacious house, 1219 N. Kellogg Street, in whose attic Ronald found the owners' collections of birds' eggs and butterflies that fascinated him so (Hubler, p. 16).[32]

Monmouth, three years later, was a step down, to judge from the house the Reagans moved to; but they lived there only briefly, not enough time to be picked up between rental directories for 1917 and 1918.[33] Then it was back to Tampico, where Reagan had impressed his former employer with a growing specialization in his selling art. The Tampico *Tornado* could announce that "a graduate of the American School of Practipedics" was now in charge of Pitney's shoe department. Tampico, on this second go-around, is the first place where there are living memories of Jack Reagan's specializing in shoe sales.[34] And this was just the prelude to his most expansive moment—the opening of his own store, backed by Pitney's money. The Dixon paper heralded the arrival of a fifth shoe store in town with a flurry of titles:

H. C. Pitney and J. E. Reagan will open an exclusive store in this city in the building formerly occupied by O. H. Brown & Co. All new, modern fixtures have been installed and the store will be stocked with all new spring styles. The new establishment will be known as the "Fashion Boot Shop." Mr. Reagan, who will act as manager, is an experienced shoe man and also a graduate practipedist, and understands all foot troubles and the correct methods of relief for all foot discomforts having had years of experience in this line in many of the larger cities throughout the state.[35]

The rationalist northern cities of Twain's vision could, at last, boast a scientific approach to foot hygiene, a thing that concerned people in the 1920s.[36] Neil Reagan remembers that his father's store was the first to X-ray feet as a fitting procedure. And Ronald, while revealing that the practipedist was a "graduate" of correspondence courses, says that he "spent hours analyzing the bones of the foot" (Hubler, p. 11). Jack, the Mississippi confidence man, at last had a gimmick, and a tasteful way of exploiting it.

It was as the promising manager of this new store in town that Reagan moved his family to Hennepin Avenue, where people now visit the restored "boyhood home" of the President. But Jack never stayed long in one place. Within four years, he had started the moves to smaller apartments that eventually took him to five different sites in Dixon (four extant). By 1929, not only had the Fashion Boot Shop disappeared, but Reagan was not even selling things, for the first time in his adult life. He had what the local paper called some unspecified (possibly clerical) "position with the Dixon State Hospital," and he had to sublet all but one room of the apartment he was renting on Lincolnway.[37] Then he went to work for one of the other shoe stores in town, with the hope that he would become a manager in one of its branches at Fort Madison.[38] That prospect was quickly blighted; half a year later, he had accepted a job with Redwing Shoes as a traveling salesman.[39] The year after that, he was working in what Ronald calls a "hole-in-the-wall" shoe store in Springfield (Hubler, p. 50).

Practipedist—literally "foot-manipulator"—simply meant "foot loose" for Jack. Shuttled among relatives as a child, he had shifted places as restlessly throughout the first decades of the twentieth century. There was always a new store, a new town—Bennett, Fulton, Tampico, Chicago, Galesburg, Monmouth, back to Tampico, Dixon, Springfield, back to Dixon. Always traveling, sometimes the proverbial traveling salesman, intruding his insider's patter and outsider's new stories into strange company, catching attention, trying to please, peddling bright promise from dingier briefcases.

His loyal wife went with him, and one adoring child, and one who looked quizzically from a distance after finding him drunk one night on the Hennepin Avenue porch (Hubler, p. 12). Ronald, born above a bakery in Tampico, soon moved to à house that faced the grain elevator. After that, he has dim memories of a gas-lit house in the Hyde Park area of Chicago, of attending first grade in Galesburg, of sledding on the Monmouth College campus, of things slowing to an "idyllic" pace in Tampico, and of arrival at his "real" home of Dixon (Hubler, pp. 15–22). Actually, the pace was even brisker than his account would suggest. Between the ages of six and ten (1917–21), he was in a different school every year for four years in a row (Galesburg, Monmouth, Tampico, Dixon), skipping a grade along the way.

The Reagans lived in five different places in Dixon, four different ones in Tampico, two in Galesburg—all rented; always living from suitcases, like actors. The "boyhood home" restored for public viewing in Dixon, is, according to Neil, the wrong one for Ronald's principal memories of the town. He moved from it, and changed schools, in the middle of the eighth grade, then attended North High School on the other side of the Rock River from the present shrine. Neil finished at South High because his friends were there. Both sons were in transit, always. They had no "boyhood home." That was not Jack Reagan's style. He was always the hopeful child of depression years, the orphan charmer, the rural area's "man about town," just returned from travels to some Dublin of the mind, believing in a better deal elsewhere. When he had married Nelle in 1904, it was, after all, a happy new century.

CHAPTER 2

Nelle

And toucht by her fair tendance gladlier grew.

—Paradise Lost *8.47*

The Spirit was moving in Tampico, Illinois, in 1906, the year Jack and Nelle
Reagan moved to town. They arrived in February. In April, there was a
revival at the Christian Church. In June, Billy Sunday addressed a thousand
people at the nearby Prophetstown Tabernacle, and made twelve converts
from Tampico alone. Tampico bought the Tabernacle, to have it ready in
their town for evangelist L. W. Munhall's arrival in August.[1] That meeting
resulted in one hundred converts, nine of them from the Christian Church.
Even before Munhall's appearance, the Tampico paper estimated conver-
sions in the area at 413 souls.[2] There were meetings everywhere, boiling with
excitement and the power to purify. In April of 1907, a Law and Order
League was formed to promote laws "pertaining to the sale of intoxicants,
the desecration of the Sabbath, and the suppression of all social and moral
evils." The very week after this group was founded, a reform ticket was
voted into municipal office; it ended liquor licensing, and imposed a nine
o'clock curfew on children under fourteen. (They were nightly warned off
the street by a whistle at the electric plant.[3])

It was a godly community the Reagans would be living in the next four
years. Vernon Denison, a classmate of Ronald's in the fourth and fifth
grades, said, "We couldn't do much on Sunday, I tell you—no ball playing,
or anything like that." The Women's Christian Temperance Union was very
active and influential—it gave a beautiful stained-glass window to the Christian Church. On October 12, 1906, a WCTU member had to deny publicly
that she could have strayed so flagrantly as to loan money to a man who
kept a saloon.

Nelle Reagan took to this life enthusiastically, and was a leader of Tampico church life by the time she left the town. Indeed, she was baptized in
Tampico, as a Disciple of Christ, by total immersion, perhaps in the Hennepin Canal, on Easter Sunday, March 27, 1910.[4] Because she was an admira-

bly devout, indeed zealous, churchwoman through the years living memory reaches to, it is often assumed that she was pious from a child. But I find no positive evidence of that. Certainly if she had grown up as a Disciple in the 1880s, she would not have become a skilled dancer, as she was by the time she married Jack Reagan in Fulton.[5] Of Scotch Presbyterian ancestry, she seems to have attended the Methodist Episcopal church in Clyde township during her girlhood on a farm.[6] After she had moved to Fulton, she was in a town with a Disciples church; but in the words of the Illinois historian of that faith, published in 1915, "the Church has never secured a firm hold in the community."[7] If she had been a member in Fulton, her admission to the church in Tampico would have been by letter from there, as was her return to the Tampico church in 1919 and her letter for Dixon in 1920.[8]

A strong pietism on her part would have offered obstacles to marriage with a Catholic like Jack Reagan, who did not mean to be excommunicated from his own church. To avoid that, he had to persuade his spouse to have their children baptized and educated as Catholics—a promise Nelle kept with her first child, but broke after her own immersion. Not only was Ronald not baptized at St. Mary's as Neil had been,[9] Neil was rebaptized in Nelle's community after he came of age. (Disciples do not believe in pedobaptism.[10])

Nelle was no more fond than Jack of her farm heritage. Oral tradition, unsupported so far as I have discovered, makes her a clerk at Broadhead's store in Fulton when Jack, too, was working there. But it is certain she worked for Jack's aunt when Orson Baldwin moved from Bennett and Margaret Baldwin opened a millinery shop in Fulton.[11] Nelle was always known as a "smart" dresser, a stylish performer in amateur theatrics, with literary ambitions. Like Jack, she was an urban person from a rural background. She was a child of the River, that great highway of change, the opening to a larger world.[12]

Judging from its later influence on her life, which was not only privately devout but proselytizing, the conversion she underwent in Tampico was profound. She obviously drew no sustenance from her husband's faith—she may, in fact, have found in it an enemy partly explaining her husband's faults. A deep and energizing belief of the sort she later displayed was not the simple fruit of childhood habits. She entered fully into a new community, which welcomed her in Tampico, Chicago, Galesburg, Monmouth, and especially in Dixon,[13] where she became an acknowledged pillar of the church. Much of her life would be bound up in these churches—teaching bible school, distributing tracts in the prisons, putting on morality plays of her own composition.

Ronald Reagan's early life would also be centered in the Christian Church. He worked in it, cleaning it up; he acted in his mother's skits; he dated the pastor's daughter (for eight years); he led the 1926 Easter sunrise service. He went to a Disciples college, socialized with students at another Disciples college (Drake University) in his radio days, and even formed his first set of friends in Hollywood from the same school circles. He was as close to being a "minister's kid" as one can be without actually moving into the rectory. The Rev. Ben Cleaver was a father figure to Reagan, who advised him, helped him get into college, even taught him to drive.[14] "Reagan was in our house all the time," Helen Cleaver remembers.

It was not a bad world to grow up in. The Disciples constitute one of the most distinctively American developments of religion in the nineteenth century. Like all things truly American, they incorporate in their final synthesis materials that are not American. The light came from distant places—from Princeton; ultimately, from Scotland. The heat came from nearer at hand—from the Great Revival that set "Kentucky ablaze" in the first years of the nineteenth century. Barton Stone was an independent Presbyterian who had studied the natural ethics of Princeton's Dr. Witherspoon, from the same lecture notes James Madison used twenty years earlier.[15] Stone was impressed, but puzzled, by the revival preaching of his fellow Presbyterian, James McGready. He became the bemused impresario of the most spectacular camp meeting in American history, the Cane Ridge Meeting of August 7–12, 1801. He wandered through the scene like a sorcerer's apprentice, watching as thousands were "slain" in states of religious catatonia or impelled to athletic feats of worship.

Stone was the most precise observer there. He catalogued the "exercises" —the facial distortions rapidly run through, ventriloquism, suspended or hyperkinetic states—with scientific detachment. "A person affected with the jerks, especially in his head, would often make a grunt, or bark, if you please, from the suddenness of the jerk."[16] His instinct was neither to encourage nor discourage these heraldings of a new age. He believed some mysterious work of God was going forward; but he did not like to force religious experience on people, because of his own inability to achieve the emotional breakthrough of a single conversion moment that McGready preached as necessary to salvation.[17] Thus, in his account of the revival, the dutiful taxonomist becomes another Adam, in a paradise unexpectedly regained, giving names to the frisky but benevolent animals.

Stone remained by temperament and training a New Light Presbyterian, who thought a reasoned belief in the gospel message was enough to save one. He had always had misgivings about the Westminster Confessional, on rationalistic grounds (he objected to the Trinity, predestination, and justification by *substitution* of Jesus for the saved rather than God's direct love of them).[18] But he was open to the added gifts of the Spirit in revivalism. He went to the defense of some enthusiasts, who were disciplined by the Synod after the revival turmoils, and followed them out of the Synod.

One of the frothier spirits in this company, Richard McNemar, decided that the dissident presbytery they had set up was itself too churchy, that Christians should forswear divisive sects. McNemar wrote a witty piece of theological satire called "The Last Will and Testament of the Springfield Presbytery" (1804). Stone went along with this, and with Rice Haggard, who said all denominational titles should yield to the simple and inclusive "Christian." But when, in 1805, the ebullient McNemar took up Shakerism as the next stage of the Spirit's millennium, Stone cried enough, and began to criticize excessive emotionalism as well as credal dogmatism.[19]

Stone had forged a remarkably liberal theology around simple biblicism. He would later be called a forerunner of modern ecumenism, and he did furnish solid grounds for the tendency of "frontier" Presbyterianism, Baptism, and Methodism to join forces in a scattered population underserved with clergy. His belief (he tried to avoid the word "church") was coherent in message yet decentralized in organization. In fact, holding it together within such generous boundaries would be a problem as the community prospered.

In 1832, the Christians coalesced with a similar yet different strain of Presbyterian liberalism formed in America around two Ulster Scots, Thomas and Alexander Campbell, who had been raised in the independent church tradition of the Haldane brothers of Edinburgh.[20] They were "antiburgher secessionists"—that is, dissidents who opposed the support of the established Scottish church by payment of burgesses. In 1807, Thomas Campbell, Alexander's father, preceded his son to America, where the seceding presbytery was the official one; but Thomas soon had to secede from the official seceders for welcoming the antiseceders to communion.[21] In the story of the Disciples, as Campbell's followers would be called, the fate of the unionist is often division.

Alexander Campbell, who followed his father to America in 1809, had already seceded from the seceders in Glasgow before he came. Like Stone, the Campbells spoke for a rational biblicism, but they put more stress on the presumed structure, or lack of it, in the primitive church. Alexander Campbell became the theorist and publicist of the Disciples, a man at once more learned and more narrow than Stone, polemical rather than irenic. It was he whose dogmatic antidogmatism revealed that early church practice did not include pedobaptism—so both Campbells were baptized by immersion in 1812, in what would become the most important and contested rite of a community always somewhat embarrassed by rules of entry and norms of belief.[22]

It was the Campbells' position on baptism that brought them one of the Disciples' greatest evangelists, Walter Scott, a graduate of the University of Edinburgh who came to America in 1818 to learn from American Baptists the true meaning of immersion. He found the Baptists a disappointment, but was entirely taken with Alexander Campbell, whom he met in 1821. Scott developed a popular teaching method that served especially well a movement uneasy with creeds and catechisms. His most famous device was a five-finger exercise explaining the stages of conversion—a homely technique given a sinister touch in the novel and movie, *The Night of the Hunter*, where the preacher's fingers are tattooed with five letters.

As the Stoneites and Campbellites expanded into the Mississippi Valley, from Kentucky and Ohio, they found much in common, and cooperated in their ministries—leading to a formal union of the two groups in 1832 that roughly doubled each member's size. The groups used the names "Christian" and "Disciple" interchangeably—the first names given, by others and by themselves, to believers in Jesus. The leading figure of each camp struck an uneasy truce with the other, retaining his own theological journal and his misgivings. Stone thought Alexander Campbell too divisive in his eagerness to debate fine points. Campbell thought Stone too inclusive in his welcome to possibly uninformed (or unimmersed) brethren.[23] Each was pushing off from his own background toward the other, without ever quite touching—Campbell from "splintery" Presbyterianism, with its contrary love for confessionals proclaimed and individualism preserved, Stone from the spontaneity and improvisation (a "jazz" form of religion) in the camp meetings. It is a tribute to many of their followers that they saw where the two men's thought should meet, though the men themselves did not follow it there. During their period of greatest union, the groups mushroomed—to nearly 200,000 by the Civil War, and to six times that number in 1900. By the time Nelle Reagan was baptized, there were 682 Christian churches in Illinois alone.[24]

The Christians were a strong presence in Mark Twain's Hannibal—in fact his best friend, Will Bowen, was Barton Stone's grandson. Stone often visited the Bowens, and preached while visiting them. In 1844, he died at their home.[25] Twain wrote in his autobiographical notes: "Campbellite revival. All converted but me. All sinners again in a week." The camp meeting led astray by the king in Chapter 20 of *Huckleberry Finn* is Twain's picture of the revival movement after its prime. His own family were "abandoned Presbyterians," and he was able to observe the Christians at Will's house. He claims that he and Will hid their playing cards, when they were almost discovered at that ungodly game, in a preacher's baptizing robe, and the cards floated out on the river's waters the next time the preacher immersed new Christians.

In his early teens, when he was a printer's apprentice, Twain met one of the founding Disciples himself, one whose arrival in Hannibal created "a prodigious excitement":

The farmers and their families drove or tramped into the village from miles around to get a sight of the illustrious Alexander Campbell and to have a chance to hear him preach. When he preached in a church many had to be disappointed, for there was no church that would begin to hold all the applicants; so in order to accommodate all, he preached in the open air in the public square, and that was the first time in my life that I realized what a mighty population this planet contains when you get them all together. [*Autobiography*, 2.279–80]

Despite Twain's satirical view of them, the Disciples respected and encouraged learning, sowing their communities thick with journals, colleges, libraries. What Twain attributed to the North had, in the case of the Disciples, come from the South he treated as a land of ignorance: "They fortify every weak place in their land with a school, a college, a library, a newspaper." Substitute theological journals for newspapers, and that could be a description of the Disciples. They loved print. Twain's own meeting with Campbell came from the fact that fifty copies of the speech in Hannibal's town square were printed up immediately after Campbell delivered it, the largest assignment Twain's print shop had been given to that point. When a fellow apprentice, to save space, printed Jesus Christ as "J.C.," Campbell, after looking at the text, stormed into the office and admonished the printer's boys never to "diminish the Savior's name again." The Disciples not only preached well, they proofread carefully.

John Boles has made the case that the great revival of the early 1800s had more intellectual content than it has been credited with—he emphasizes the social critique of the times and a providential reading of the remedy.[26] What was true of the revival in general was even more true of the Christian-Disciple church that emerged from it, fed as it was directly and indirectly from Edinburgh, by way of John Witherspoon, the Haldanes, Thomas and Alexander Campbell, and Walter Scott. The very doctrine of moral sense, which Mark Twain darkened back toward Calvinism in the form of cultural determinism, was taught by Stone and the Campbells as an alternative to the total depravity of man preached by some revivalists.[27] The Disciples believed that reason applied to the scripture can lead man to salvation—they were condemned as Arminians by the stricter Calvinists for this emphasis on human initiative. The rational confession of faith that precedes baptism could be given only by an adult, which was one of the grounds for condemning pedobaptism. Ben Cleaver, the pastor whose daughter Reagan was engaged to, used to turn away twelve-year-old candidates he thought unready. (I talked to one such candidate in Dixon.) Ronald Reagan, on the other hand, was immersed at the unusually early age of eleven, perhaps because his mother's house was such a good training ground in Christian values.[28]

The Disciples' devotion to education and the word often outran their resources. They founded more colleges and journals than they could support. Illinois Disciples established four colleges, apart from divinity schools and seminaries, of which Eureka alone survived.[29] Texas Christian University is the most famous of the permanent colleges, but the founder of Drake College (now University) in Iowa became the state's governor, and the president of Hiram College, James Garfield, became the first Disciple to precede Reagan to the White House. (Lyndon Johnson was the second.) Journals came and went even more rapidly than colleges, but one magazine, *The Christian Oracle,* first published from Drake College, moved to Chicago and, with a changed name, *The Christian Century,* became the most important ecumenical journal in America.[30]

The polemical skills of Alexander Campbell bred a fondness for debate among Disciples eager to imitate him. He was famed for knockout blows in public argument, not only with divagating nonimmersionists, but with papists and materialists (the most famous of the latter being Robert Owen).[31] A whole chapter of Haynes's *History of the Disciples of Christ in Illinois* is given over to "The Period of Conquest—The Era of Public Discussions" (pp. 68–87), where an even hundred public vindications of the faith are chronicled in Illinois alone. The desire for discussion was secular as well as sacred. When the settlers in Walnut Grove founded Eureka College in 1855, the first extra-curricular group was the Edmund Burke Society, established to discuss literary works.[32] Settlers and pioneers, viewed by "frontier school" enthusiasts as living a romance, were parched for the romance that only books could bring them—the kind of literary adventures that gave Tom Sawyer his fabulating power over Huck Finn and other boys in Hannibal. Mark Twain himself had to escape into books before he could describe, long after, the life he "lit out" from.

The literary and educational ideals of the Disciples must be considered when we look at the impact of religion in Nelle Reagan's life. Though, like Jack, she never went to high school, she had literary yearnings, expressed in her plays and elocution performances. Neil Reagan tells of his appearing onstage before Ronald did—as the baby in a play starring his parents at Burden's Opera House in Tampico.[33] But already, in Tampico, it was Ronald who was featured in the Christian Church's dramatic recitations. Neil's name does not appear. Thus the local paper for May 6, 1920, tells us that nine-year-old Ronald recited "About Mother" at the church, and the June 3 issue says that his recitation of "The Sad Dollar and the Glad Dollar" immediately preceded his mother's reading, "How the Artist Forgot Four Colors." In Dixon, two years later, at the Dixon State Hospital where Jack would later work, Mrs. Reagan and her son "entertained the patients with a short and enjoyable program," she with a banjo and he with "two entertaining readings." This was the first experiment in what became a monthly church program for the patients.[34]

There was never any question, among those who knew Nelle Reagan, about the sincere charity behind such projects. But the kindness took the form it did because of her creative desires. As Ronald himself says, she was "a frustrated actress" (Hubler, p. 20). A cousin of Nelle's next-door neighbor in Tampico, remembers her as having a "theatrical" voice when she called the children in from outdoors.[35] She took pride in her dialect performances. A favorite was "Levinsky at the Wedding," a string of labored ethnic jokes climaxed by the entry of an Irish policeman who says, "I'm cleaning out the Jew wedding."[36] In letters to friends, Nelle dropped into the dialect of this elocution piece for comic effects—not, clearly, to mock Jews, but out of mere literary virtuosity, as schoolboys "talk Wodehouse" or Swinburne's friends used Dickens dialects. A desire for "style" made Nelle change the spelling of her name, dropping the more prosaic Nellie of all her early legal records (as well as the birth record filed in 1943). It was as close as she could come to a stage name. A friend of hers in Dixon called it her "professional poetry-writing name." A similar dramatic feel for "being different" made the parents tell their boys to address them by their first names (though at eleven, in his first known letter, Ronald was still calling Nelle "Mama"). Ronald would later fulfill Nelle's theatrical aspirations by having her appear with him on radio and in film.

The more serious side of Nelle's literary aspiration found regular expression in her church plays, religious poems, and prose prayers. These are not very original works, but they resemble the journals and colleges started by the Disciples with such faith in the importance of godly culture. As Nelle wrote, "To higher, nobler things my mind is bent." In Tampico, in periods when the Christian church was between pastors, she wrote the weekly church notes in the *Tornado*. These reflect her two main concerns, the Missionary Society, of which she had been elected president, and the Sunday school, one section of which she taught.[37] Every week she urged people to attend Sunday school, pleading, citing scripture, varying her appeals, using humor, poetry, passion:

> Jesus said that the Christian is like a light set where it cannot be hid; come out to Sunday School next Lord's day at ten o'clock. Let us all be shining lights.[38]

> We wish we could give you a flying machine,
> To travel about as you wished a la Wright.
> We're sure you'd come sailing right over this way,
> And at the door of the class room would light.
> But since we're unable to hear of the place
> Where free aeroplanes have been put,
> Please make the journey the old-fashioned way,
> And come next Sunday on foot.[39]

In Dixon, Nelle's involvement in church activities was, if anything, even more intense, and she kept in touch with its members over the years, after she joined the Hollywood-Beverly Christian Church by letter on October 10, 1937. Ten years after she had gone to Hollywood, there was a split in the Dixon church, some refusing to support the mission society that Nelle had been active in. She tried to make her influence felt across the continent. In a letter of November 2, 1947, meant for the whole congregation, she wrote:

> I'm broken hearted over the condition of the church and sicker over the ones who followed the teachings of this "Brown" who surely done a nice job of splitting up our dear Christian Church, who wouldn't even vote together on the idea of rebuilding a new Church, in a different spot after the fire.
>
> Am I foolish in believing that maybe God took a hand in trying to draw his children back into love, and harmony, and fellowship, that would bind them in a Unity, which no minister, with false teachings could split, as this Brown did. Perhaps that's why the church caught fire by some bad wiring. "God works in a mysterious way his wonders to perform." If he used disaster at times to draw his children to him again, when they wandered afar, in the old days, I feel he still works in that way, for my Bible says—"The same yesterday, today, and forever."

Those who have turned against Missions have turned against every thing Christ taught—and the very last words he uttered, "Go ye into all the world and *preach* the Gospel, to every creature." Can't they read their Bibles and see how *wrong* this *Brown* fellow is, in what he taught?

I even wish you'd see that this letter was read to every one, for those who don't believe in the Missionary work of the church have surely turned against Christ,—and again[st] his words—"Love thy neighbor as thyself." Please, God, I wish they'd all come back together again.[40]

When she was still in Dixon, her preaching was subtler, tempered by humor. One younger friend of Nelle's described for me a church play she wrote. The woman telling me the story had quarreled with her husband, and the tightly knit church community knew about it. Mrs. Reagan pointedly asked the family to be present at the next theatrical night. There was a playlet on the dangers of family wrangling, in which Nelle played the mother, and Ronald played the father (wearing a cast on his arm after the "fight"). It was taken in good fun, such good will prompted Nelle's ingenuities of succor.

There was another side to the Disciples' dialectical skills which was bound to have some effect on Nelle Reagan. Like most pietist movements of the midwest, the Disciples had a long history of fear and hostility where Jack Reagan's church was concerned. The most famous of the Disciples' debates is remembered in Haynes's 1915 Illinois history this way: "The same mighty champion of the truth [Alexander Campbell] in January, 1837, in Cincinnati, Ohio, met Mr. 'Bishop' Purcell of the Roman Catholic hierarchy, in a seven days' debate."[41] In a study of Campbell's political ethics, Harold Lunger devotes an entire chapter to his treatment of Roman Catholics, and exculpates him from the worst excesses of nativism (partly because he spread his wrath to organized sects in general, attacking "protestant popery" along with the Roman kind). But Campbell's basic position, spelled out in the famous marathon debate in Cincinnati, was that "Roman Catholicism, in any country, is detrimental to its interests and prosperity; and in a republic, directly and positively tending every moment to its subversion."[42]

Campbell did not neglect the charges of moral laxity among Catholics. Repeated forgiveness of repeated sins like drunkenness was a scandal to the Disciples who, with other pietists, had a perfectionist tradition—i.e., the belief that one should try to live, after one's conversion, as if already in the millennial time. This made them the driest of the dries when the ritualists—not only Catholics but German Lutherans—were condemned for their "wet" habits. When Jack Reagan was growing up in Bennett, Iowa, there was an influx of German immigrants condemned by Methodists and others for drinking and dancing in beer gardens.[43] In Tampico, the licensing of liquor was precarious, when not banned entirely.[44] But there was no question where the Disciples of Christ, Nelle's church, stood on the matter.[45] Disciples use grape juice, not wine, at the communion service.

The Disciples were in the forefront of the temperance movement. Carrie

Nation was a Disciple. So were several prominent Prohibition Party candidates, including a president of Drake University, who wrote *Rum, Ruin, and Remedy.* The Disciples set up the American Temperance Board in 1907. In 1914, twenty-six speakers were traveling around the country to argue the temperance cause. The first Sunday in July was set aside as Temperance Sunday in Disciple churches, and the Uniform Lesson Series for children included a quarterly temperance lesson. Liquor was banned from Disciple campuses, including Eureka as well as Drake. The Disciples of Illinois were the most adamant on this issue.[46]

Nelle Reagan was a good Disciple. A friend of hers told me, "Nelle hated liquor." In Dixon, she wrote a temperance play for the church, one line of which is recoverable because it became a running joke in the family of the girl who played the drunkard's daughter: "I love you, Daddy, except when you have that old bottle."[47] This was bound to affect Ronald's attitude toward his father, as contrasted with Neil's different memories of him. By the time he was nineteen, Neil disassociated himself from the church Nelle had rebaptized him into at the age of fourteen. In the Christian Church record of that second baptism ("6/11/1922"), on the righthand page, in space usually reserved for recording marriages, deaths, or moves, there is this entry for Neil: "Reported April 1927, United with Dixon Catholic Church, without notice."[48] Neil has often mentioned that his mother opposed his break with the Disciples. He told Allison Mitchell of *Newsday* in 1980: "I got dissatisfied with the church I was going to. My mother cried."[49] Neil now went to St. Patrick's, with his father, and to the Knights of Columbus affairs. No wonder his mother cried. The Knights of Columbus drank. When Neil decided, belatedly, to join his brother at the Disciples' college, Eureka, Ronald said he was amazed: "I could see him at some large university where a speakeasy wasn't out of reach" (Hubler, p. 40), but not in the dry fraternity dorms of Eureka. There was no Catholic church in Eureka. Yet, despite compulsory chapel for four years, Neil's stay with the Disciples did not make him give up his Catholicism. He remained as much his father's son as Ronald was his mother's.

In the movie *Kings Row,* Ronald Reagan's part is that of the rakish heir-about-town, Drake McHugh, described in the 1940 Henry Bellamann novel: "That overhandsome face of Drake's was not a thinking face."[50] When Drake sows wild oats with the town's wild girls, Poppy and Jinny Ross, "respectable" members of the community cluck, but with a wink. It is different when he crosses the tracks to see Randy Monaghan (Ann Sheridan). The mother of the "nice girl" Drake has been dating muses: "No use bothering too much about Poppy and Jinny Ross . . . Then all at once it was this Monaghan girl from the lower end of the town. Irish Catholic. Railroad people . . . trashy people" (pp. 367–68).[51] The predominantly Catholic censoring apparatus of Hollywood in the forties guaranteed that all such references would disappear from the screenplay made of *Kings Row*. But Reagan says he prepared thoroughly for what he considered—and still does—his biggest and best role. If he read the novel as part of that preparation, he might have recognized some of the social-religious tensions it explored.

CHAPTER 3

Lifeguard

Whither, 'midst falling dew,
While glow the heavens with the last light of day,
Far through their rosy depths dost thou pursue
Thy solitary way?

—*William Cullan Bryant, "To a Waterfowl"*

Kings Row, as a novel and as a movie, is organized (if that is the word) around contrasting friends, Drake McHugh and Parris Mitchell (Robert Cummings). Drake is devil-may-care, Parris dutiful. Both are orphans, Drake with expectations of money left in trust (like Huck, whose fortune is kept by Judge Thatcher), Parris with a cultured grandmother who is eking out her own days and dollars to guarantee him an education. Drake lives recklessly, outdoors. Parris is pasty with study, a skilled pianist: he speaks French, and aspires to medicine. They should not be friends at all, and they go long periods without meeting; but whenever they do, each thinks of the other as some lost side of himself.

Neil and Ronald Reagan were a bit like that, through much of their lives; but Ronald had the other role, Bob Cummings's—Neil was the social scamp his elders connived at spoiling. Leo Gorman, a Catholic schoolmate of Neil's in Dixon told me, "Neil was all boy, Ronald was a momma's boy." In his brother's eyes, Ronald hung around with "sissies."[1] Neil did not mean to be a minister's kid himself, moving in a circle of Disciples. He obviously admired his father's expansive ways and flamboyant style. He imitated Jack's distinctive hairstyle, parted in the middle, so blatantly as to earn him a lifelong nickname, "Moon" (for the comic-strip character Moon Mullins, whose hair was similarly parted). Something of Jack Reagan's irresponsibility showed, too, in Neil's early days. The harder-working younger brother had money to lend him, but notes that Neil "never paid me back any small loan in his life" before they went to Eureka (Hubler, p. 40). Brothers never sorted themselves out more symmetrically in their allegiances or antipathies —Ronald gravitating toward Nelle's elocutionary piety, Neil toward Jack's hyperbolical conviviality.

Neil, the schoolboy leader, followed Reagan to college, into radio, and to California, and has often expressed a kind of resentment that he was seen as dependent on his kid brother. Asked in 1982 whether he was using his brother's influence, Neil told Tom Bates of *California* magazine: "Ronald ran on my coattails for years. It's about time he reciprocated."[2] In his oral history interview for UCLA, he said he resented his brother before he ever met him. Told there was a new boy at his home, he says:

> I wanted to go the opposite direction. I went home, and for two days after I was home, I would not go in the room where my brother and my mother were. I didn't want any part of a brother. I had been promised a sister by my mother and father. That's all I wanted. I guess that shows you how early I determined not to be a queer. [Laughter.] I was strictly a girl man.[3]

In interviewing people who knew the brothers in their youth, or knew their reputations, in Tampico, Dixon, and Eureka, I found them dividing into "Neil people" and "Ronald people." Neil people found him more easygoing than his brother, more fun, more confiding. Bill Major, who was at Eureka with them, even calls Neil "smarter"—and he certainly seems to have been more savvy, or socially poised, for a time. Drake is the one who has to "show Parris the ropes" in the town of Kings Row; and in his oral history interview for the UCLA archives, Neil still takes the role of mentor for his younger brother as late as 1981.[4] One of Ronald's earliest memories is of crawling under a train with Neil (Hubler, p. 15).[5] (Playing near the tracks is one of the pastimes young Drake and Parris share in Kings Row, and Drake loses his leg when he falls under one as an adult.)

Ronald was shyer than the expansive "Irishman" Neil. The younger son expressed himself in roles created for him by his mother at church affairs, or in plays at Dixon High and Eureka, where his onstage leading lady was his pastor's daughter. The earliest letter I know of from Ronald Reagan, written at age eleven, was sent to a Christian church member, Gladys Shippert, who had moved to Wisconsin. It is a charming letter, written on stationery borrowed from a butcher shop, and full of innocent boasting: "Our class at school has got the janitors job at the church and we get $25.00 a month and were plastering our class room and were going to have scouts and our class took the banners for attendance and collection."[6] Earning the money to plaster one's classroom is playing Tom Sawyer backwards—*paying* to do your *own* white-washing. These are not the feats Neil would describe in order to impress a young lady.

Neil stayed around Dixon for three years while Ronald graduated from high school and went off to his freshman year of college in 1928. When Neil joined him in Eureka at the beginning of Ronald's sophomore year, the elder became the underclassman, with consequent misunderstandings about their age years after. They would become, for a while, like leap-froggers tied together—one jump dragged the other to the next jump, in alternate precedencies. Ronald, unable to see a football in the air, had to play on the line, by tactile guidance, where his light frame made him the most dispensable player during his freshman year at Eureka; he was excluded from one group picture because the team was one jersey short.[7] He sat out that season on the bench. Neil, larger and with good eyesight, played end his freshman year and made the most spectacular play of the season:

> At this point of the game Moon Reagan made his appearance. As the moments were dwindling, Cole threw a pass and that same Moon just reached up and got it. He looked around and then kept on galloping up the field for sixty yards to a touchdown.[8]

The last had become first again. But then, typically, Neil dropped out of football his sophomore year and never returned to it, while Ronald became a solid performer at guard in his last three years. Yet Neil regularly tells reporters (with some germ of truth, at least for high school) that he, not Ronald, was the football star.[9]

It was a tug-of-war that would not end, not the least because the ties of affection could bear any strain. The brothers would remain close, if competing, and Ronald could afford to be generous where Neil could hardly avoid being jealous. Neil was, after all, a bright and handsome young man constantly being overtaken by a brighter and handsomer younger brother. Even as a teenager, Ronald became a hometown celebrity, with front-page newspaper stories about his lifesaving exploits. Neil was called the best-looking boy of his class in the Dixon High School yearbook for 1926; but Ronald had the movie-star look long before he was a movie star. Neil was senior class president at Eureka College, but Ronald had been president the year before. Neil began school three years ahead of Ronald; yet by the fourth grade, Ronald was only two years behind, and at Eureka he would be one year ahead.[10] Though his intelligence has been called into question, Reagan has never let it be known that he skipped a grade in school. Nelle would have discouraged any boasting that might hurt Neil's pride—and Ronald has remained sensitive to his brother's feelings.

Neil has even told friends, as he told Tom Bates, "I was a good student— he wasn't."[11] It may be that Neil got better grades at Eureka College where, as we shall see, Ronald did only the minimum studying necessary on the easiest courses available. Neil himself talks about Ronald's skill at last-minute memorizing as practically "photographic."[12] The few grades made public from Ronald's early years indicate that he was a good student when he cared to be. In first grade at Galesburg, he received a 95 percent average, 97 percent in reading.[13] In Monmouth, the local newspaper could report in the 1960s that "his grades were very good" during the year he skipped a grade. The next year, despite his jump ahead, he was one of five from a class of twenty-two cited for excellent individual work. He got A's in reading and mathematics, B's in everything else, and an A in deportment. Neil, in the sixth grade at the time, received a C in deportment, A's in spelling, writing, and reading, D in language, C in arithmetic, three B-minuses and four B's.[14]

The discipline of the young Ronald Reagan shows best in that large part of his young life (six summers, 1927 through 1932) spent as a lifeguard at Lowell Park. The park, three miles above Dixon, is a stretch of wooded hills running down to a beach on one of the lovelier stretches of the Rock River. It lies just below the Walgreen Estate, the lavish country home of the Dixon man who invented the drugstore. Reagan told Hubler, "it was named after the poet James Russell Lowell, who wrote his famous 'Ode to a Waterfowl' in the vicinity" (Hubler, p. 27), but a plaque put up by donors on the beach says it is dedicated to "Charles Russell Lowell, Colonel of Second Massachusetts Cavalry, Brigadier General United States Volunteers, Killed at Cedar Creek, Virginia, October 19, 1864."[15] The park is municipally owned and administered, though the swimming facilities were licensed to a concessioner by the Dixon Park Board. It was a government facility.

Memories and photographs of Lowell Park in the thirties suggest the happy hometown life Reagan summed up as "a Huck Finn-Tom Sawyer idyll"—picnicking in the woods, family groups on the shore, people trying to ride an anchored "tipping disk" in the water, others fighting the mosquitos under floodlights at night, everyone known to everyone, the same lifeguard who had taught one to swim five years earlier still peering through his glasses at the bobbing heads. The proper note of nostalgia is struck by the famous picture of Reagan in his one-piece lifeguard suit with the tank top. But it was a far from escapist life for Reagan. It was a post of great responsibility, and he approached it, from the age of sixteen, with great awareness of the stakes. The concessioners, if nothing else, made sure of that.

Edward and Ruth Graybill were serious people in a serious time. Mrs. Graybill was a member of Ronald's church. A competent and careful lifeguard was necessary for the Graybills to keep their license and maintain their insurance rates. There were some misgivings about taking on such a slight youngster as Reagan was in 1927—his father was consulted, and Mrs. Graybill assures me that "he had taken lifesaving at the YMCA."[16] The Rock River can have treacherous currents, as Union Army supply boats found when they worked their way up it during the Black Hawk War.[17]

It has been suggested that Reagan's famous rescues (seventy-seven in all) are the product of fame and nostalgia infecting each other long after. But the rescues were famous from the outset. The first time Ronald Reagan ever appeared on the front page of a newspaper was August 3, 1928, because the seventeen-year-old had saved a man, after dark, where another rescuer had failed:

It was not until after quite a struggle in the water that [James] Raider was brought to the shore. One of the members of the party who was said to have attempted to rescue him was forced to abandon the attempt when he too was in danger of being taken down. Raider responded to artificial respiration when he was carried to the bank and was taken to his home.

The *Daily Telegraph* noted that "Lifeguard Ronald 'Dutch' Reagan" was "making his twenty-fifth rescue in the two seasons he has served at the popular beach."

This was the summer that Reagan set the record in the annual race across the river and back (two minutes, eleven seconds), a time he could not equal the next year, when first place was taken by Northwestern's intercollegiate backstroke champion.[18] In 1931, Ronald was back on the front page for making his fifty-first rescue. The year after that, an article appeared under this headline: " 'DUTCH' REAGAN HAS MADE FINE MARK AS GUARD—Dixon Youth Has Made 71 Rescues At Lowell Park Beach." The season was not over when that was written (July 23). There would be a few more lives saved, and none lost in the six years, though the paper notes: "During his six years of service at the beach, 'Dutch' has never had an assistant and has watched a thousand bathers in the water at one time."

There was constant responsibility, occasional danger, and little glamor. "On one occasion a Dixon young man slipped from the diving tower and fell into the deep water. Reagan after several dives rescued him."[19] No other lifeguard stayed with the Graybills for anything like Reagan's term of service. Few boys would submit to the grueling hours and duties for so long a time. Reagan worked at least twelve hours a day, seven days a week, throughout the summer, his entire vacation from high school or from Eureka College. He went every morning to the Graybills' home, took their van to pick up a 300-pound block of ice at the ice house, plus hamburger and supplies for the food stand; then he picked up Ruth Graybill for the ride to the park (her husband worked till late afternoon at his insurance office). Once there, Reagan broke the ice into three blocks of a hundred pounds each, and put them in three coolers. In the crowded season, he would double or triple the order of ice.

The park closed at 10 P.M.—but Mrs. Graybill says, defensively, "We always *tried* to get things closed by ten." She resents to this day the fact that the Park Board made the Graybills pay for floodlights and the lights in the bathhouses, but that let them extend their hours till after dark, making the last part of the long day the most exacting for Reagan, especially with his trouble seeing anything even slightly at a distance from him. Two of the rescues described in the *Daily Telegraph* were made after nine-thirty.

His glasses are the most salient thing in early pictures of him. ("I began to hate the big glasses I had to wear; I hate them to this day," Hubler, p. 25.) There have been stories in print that he threw the glasses down on the shore when he had to help someone in the water, then had to recruit people to find them for him afterward. Mrs. Graybill says he used to throw them down and shout to the nearest person to take care of them. But she also says her husband impressed on all his guards the proper doctrine that one should take a *boat* out to save people in a river of swift currents. If that is the case, how could Reagan direct the boat without his glasses? The answer may be, simply, that he parted with his glasses only for children and others in water deep enough to be over their heads but not over Reagan's, and kept them for use in the boat.

At any rate, keeping track of his glasses was another reason for him to avoid going into the water except for his official duties. The first reason, he tells us, was to keep his suit dry: "No lifeguard gets wet without good reason. In my case it really took an emergency because my job was seven days a week, and from morning until they got tired of swimming at night. A wet suit was a real hardship and I was too money-conscious to have a spare" (Hubler, p. 27).

Mrs. Graybill told me that she and her husband did not go to church in the summer; they had to be out early at the park for the weekend. So did Ronald. There was no time for any other life, including any home life. He ate his two major meals on duty. He picked up some extra money (all saved toward college expenses) by teaching swimming lessons for children of guests at the nearby lodge, a resort that brought people mainly from Chicago. Mrs. Graybill says that Reagan was paid eighteen dollars a week, though Reagan remembered it as fifteen (Hubler, p. 27). Since they both have tenacious memories about money in that difficult time, perhaps they are both right: Reagan started out at fifteen dollars and, over five years, worked himself up to eighteen. It is clear that he was earning twenty dollars in 1932, when new concessioners took over for a time (the Stevenses). Reagan spoke of making twenty dollars, the figure Mrs. Stevens remembered, in a 1941 interview.[20]

Mrs. Graybill does not remember seeing Reagan's girlfriend, the daughter of their pastor, out at the shore—he would have been discouraged from neglecting his duties to flirt with her. Nor are there many memories of his brother at Lowell Park. These were not summers of happy lazying in the sun, of playing in the water, of games with those his own age. The most rewarding times he remembers were serious conversations with a man from the lodge whose child he taught to swim. If Huck Finn had shown up, by some miscalculation, at Lowell Park, the coolly estimating gaze of the bespectacled lifeguard would have intimidated him as much as anything there. He would, perhaps, have gone off to find Neil.

Young Reagan as lifeguard was rather censorious. Wits on television would later say that Dixon must have bred the world's worst swimmers for it to need such constant lifesaving. Reagan thought it bred some of the world's worst rule breakers and thoughtless people. The tone of the reporting of one rescue so resembles what Reagan wrote *earlier,* in his high school yearbook, as to indicate he was the reporter's source for the *Daily Telegraph* account: "A large man had entered the water shortly after eating a heavy meal and swimming out beyond his depth became exhausted and was hauled ashore before sinking and drowning."[21] Three years earlier, Reagan had written: "A big hippopotamus with a sandwich in each hand, and some firewater tanked away in his businessman's addition. He'll need watching."[22]

In the newspaper story written about Reagan in his last year as a lifeguard, he obviously gave the reporter these details: "A stranger visiting in Dixon was swimming about 9:30 in the evening. He had been warned repeatedly against entering deep water and responded by cursing the guard. He sank in the deep water and after a struggle Reagan succeeded in rescuing him."[23] Reagan clearly did not approve of the undisciplined behavior of the people he had to save, and they reciprocated this coolness. In a 1941 interview in Hollywood, he remarked on the lack of gratitude felt for his services. Only one person—a blind man—ever thanked him for saving his life. Why was that, the reporter asked: "I believe it's a combination of embarrassment and pride. Almost invariably they either argued they weren't in any trouble or were so mad at themselves they wouldn't admit someone else had succeeded where they had failed."[24]

Despite the "hippopotami" he had to drag out of the river, and the total absorption of his summers in hard work, Reagan has spoken of "my beloved lifeguarding." If the job kept him from his home, that might have been an attraction in years of tension with father or brother. For the rest, he obviously rejoiced in adult responsibilities early assumed. He shared his mother's communal values. In a life that had been geographically adrift, the Lowell Park job supplied what the Disciples' community had—stability, discipline, an authority recognized and not resented. Ronald was on the side of the communal values, at the shore, in Sunday school, in moral plays—he was one of two leaders at the Easter sunrise service in 1926.[25] This was his mother's world, shaped by precept, example, and admonition (as in the friends' family quarrel turned to moral exemplum). Religion and culture joined here, as in Nelle's poems and composed prayers.

Not a Huck Finn world at all. That world Ronald found, one night, on the porch of his "boyhood home," where his father had passed out. At first, Ronald wanted to "light out" from horror: "I stood over him for a minute or two. I wanted to let myself in the house and go to bed and pretend he wasn't there" (Hubler, p. 12). But Reagan is not a lighter-out. "Someplace along the line to each of us, I suppose, must come that first moment of accepting responsibility." It was hardly his first moment, though he presents it as one of his hardest.

This passage is put in the theme-setting first chapter of Reagan's 1965 reminiscences. Later references to his father's "curse" are frequent, and one long episode is devoted to fears that his father will disgrace the family by getting drunk at Notre Dame during the premiere of the movie Knute Rockne—All American (Hubler, pp. 113–15). There seems to be an unspoken assumption that Jack was least to be trusted in a Catholic place like Notre Dame, as if back among his Knights of Columbus friends. On the other hand, drunkenness would presumably be less singular or reprehensible there. Yet this is the one time in Reagan's account of his Hollywood life when he expresses a fear that his father would shame him.

If he was so deeply ashamed of his father, why blazon that shame to millions of people, who would never have known about it but for his book? This has puzzled many people in Dixon, where the extent of Jack Reagan's drinking is debated. Certainly Jack was never a public disgrace like his brother Bill in Fulton. Unlike Noah's sons, Ronald uncovers instead of hiding his father's nakedness. In fact, he does more. He dramatizes it, almost melodramatizes. He gives us scenes from a temperance play.

Reagan claims that his mother taught him to be tolerant of his father's drinking, as a disease he could not be blamed for (Hubler, p. 12). That may have been her overt attitude. But she was a moralizing, tract-distributing, admonition-delivering temperance advocate. Elsewhere she speaks of people bringing their own troubles on themselves—even of fire in the Dixon church as a divine punishment for "straying." Her own and her church's position on drinking could not be very tolerant, where tolerance involved complicity with the devil's work. While his father was still alive, Reagan became a speaker in Des Moines at father-son dinners, where he always ended with a moral exhortation to avoid "drink, cigarettes, and cheating."[26] After telling Hubler he likes wine at meals himself, he adds (about alcohol): "Probably, down underneath, I think the world would be better off without it" (Hubler, p. 67). The lifeguard disliked "firewater" in anyone's "addition."

The dramatic prominence of Reagan's treatment of his father in *Where's the Rest of Me?* led historian Robert Dallek to trace all the politician's later attitudes to the trauma of that night on the Dixon porch. Because of it "Reagan lived in fear of his father's uncontrolled behavior . . . constant fear of dependency or diminished self-control."[27] Out of this insecurity, Reagan treats attempts to make him dependent on outside influence—his own government's or the Soviet Union's—with hostile anxiety. He resents efforts to "help" the poor by keeping them dependent: "The needy remind him of his dependent father, from whom he has tried to separate himself all his life" (p. 104). Yet try as he will to escape Jack Reagan, he is forced to imitate him: "Like the father he largely rejected but understandably could not detach himself from, Reagan plays fast and loose with the facts" (p. 53). This is a remarkably adaptable explanation. It shows why Reagan is strong and independent, and also why he is weak and insecure; why he is severe about conduct, but permissive about the truth. It makes him repress facts out of insecurity, but blab about the point of greatest insecurity. It even explains the behavior of his associates: "If it were possible to probe in depth the psychology of most Reaganites, I suggest that one might find a shared problem with authority stemming from childhood. I speculate that the conservative worldview is based on an inner need that is satisfied by fighting against excessive power and control in government."[28] Did they *all* have drunken fathers? The theme of the book can be put in a single phrase: "In all this there are echoes of his alcoholic father . . ." (p. 53).

In all this, actually, there is a parody of psychoanalytic technique, in which a therapist explores, with a confiding patient, repressed or distorted memories to find their meaning; and *then*—at least in movie stories of analysis—everything is found to hinge on one childhood episode, largely cloaked in dream form or some other evasive tactic of the mind. Of course, the analyst in such a transaction is prevented by professional ethics from sharing this discovery with other persons than the patient, except in scientific papers where the patient's identity is protected.

Professor Dallek, no more than the rest of us, has such access to Reagan's dreams or unguarded confidences. What he is dealing with is an account dictated in 1964 to help launch Ronald Reagan's political career, a book that is revealing because it is still the work of a newcomer to politics, not absolutely certain what tone to strike or what use to make of his show-business past on the verge of a more serious career. Nonetheless, it is a piece of rhetoric, to be analyzed as such; something designed to make an effect on an audience. Clearly Reagan wants us to know about his father, and thinks we will approve of him for his attitude toward him. The attitude he exhibits is wry, regretful, formally forgiving, but both explicitly and implicitly highly critical. He is an unembarrassed moralist.

And why not? That is the way he was brought up. He was moralized at, and he moralized at others. He was a bit of a preacher, like his mother, not only as a sportscaster in Des Moines, but as a defender of the "moral" people of Hollywood. He gets rid of evil by preaching it away from him. This is a genuine part of Reagan, and a genuine part of his appeal—the straight arrow, the Boy Scout, the square. More accurately, the Disciple. He is not the "good bad boy" of the genre that lies behind the stories of Tom Sawyer and Huckleberry Finn, the genre Thomas Bailey Aldrich made popular. Rather he is the "villain" of those stories, the model boy.

One of the things Reagan contains in his multitudes is this sober and responsible, even somewhat puritanical, rectitude; a trait to be respected—in leaders, at any rate, however we might choose our companions for festive occasions. The limits of this character are not evident in Reagan's case—he rarely seems a prig—because it would be balanced by so many contrasting things in his life: the glamor of Hollywood, the easygoing film image derived from deferential "best friend" roles, his unwished-for divorce and his high-life acquaintances. All that, though, would be later. First came rectitude.

Reagan claims he had a happy childhood, and he is telling the truth. It was all the happier for its responsibilities. It was not a time of escape or exploration, but of fulfillment in a prematurely stalled way. He had, in those key years for such things, no free time, on his own or with friends, to test limits, read, rebel, be thoughtful or thoughtless in any combination. He was fixed in a role he liked. He was admired, and admirable; but it was not a youth that stimulated much independence of thought or action. He seems to have sensed something of this himself. Another side of him was revealed in his delayed moment of apparent rebellion at Eureka College.

CHAPTER 4

Eureka

I fell head over heels in love with Eureka.

—Ronald Reagan (Hubler, p. 30)

When, at age eleven, "Dutch" Reagan wrote to impress the older girl who moved from Dixon, he gave her news about Dixon's high school team. Then he mentioned his favorite college team: "monday momma got a letter from mrs. Wagner and she said Garland has made the team at Eureka they played Illinois last week."[1] Though Eureka was a small school in 1922, over a hundred miles south of Dixon, all Illinois Disciples were involved in its fortunes. It was their school, since 1885 the only college the Disciples had in the state. In that year, Abingdon had been merged with Eureka to reduce the financial drain on church communities supporting higher education.[2] The annual meeting of the Christian churches was held on the Eureka campus, in a Mission Tabernacle specially built for this purpose in 1885, the year of the merger with Abingdon.[3] (The Tabernacle was used for Chatauqua programs in the summer.) When the large women's dormitory needed painting in 1954, word was sent out to the communities, and over a hundred volunteers showed up from twenty-six churches to do the job one Saturday.[4]

The school was the meeting place, in many ways, for the village church community (including the faculty) and for the wider network of Disciples across the state. That led, over the years, to problems of doctrinal discipline, since—as church members—board, faculty, and students were equals, no matter what their academic functions. The view of the school that outsiders took can be seen from the fact that its athletic teams were nicknamed the Preachers at the time Reagan was writing his letter about the school.[5] The students themselves had more normal nicknames for their teams ("Golden Tornadoes"), but also called themselves, unabashedly, the Christians. We read in the school paper of a game Reagan played in: "Titan Crew Downs Christians Saturday."[6] Reagan tells us that his mother believed in tithing, though some church members in Dixon doubt she was in a financial position to do so; but Reagan says he inherited that belief and gave ten percent of his first checks as a radio broadcaster to help his brother finish a last term at Eureka, since his pastor assured him that help for the family would count as his tithe (Hubler, p. 66). It hardly seems a problem worth raising with the Reverend Cleaver—giving to Eureka *was* giving to the church.

Despite its small size (it has not much more than twice the number of students now as it had in Reagan's day), Eureka College has many distinctions. It was coeducational from the outset; it has a long and honorable record of racial integration (Reagan played with a black on its football team in the late twenties); its faculty worked for mere subsistence during periods of economic crisis. Though it lost its North Central Association accreditation in 1936, when it could not meet faculty payrolls, and did not regain it till 1961, the sense of purpose in the community has produced results out of scale to its resources. A document prepared for the North Central Association in 1959 made this case:

> Recent correspondence with the editors indicates that Eureka ranks in the upper twenty-five percent of more than nine hundred colleges in the proportion of its alumni listed in *Who's Who in America*. It is currently claimed to be fourth in this category in the state of Illinois. It has provided Presidents for twenty-three colleges and universities throughout the world.[7]

The college and the village were named Eureka to accommodate the government when a post office was opened in the home of the Walnut Grove Seminary's first professor, in 1851.[8] There was already a Walnut Grove on the mail list. Disciples who settled the area were inspired by the example of Alexander Campbell, who had opened Bethany College in 1840. They brought a Bethany graduate to open the Walnut Grove Seminary in 1849, and the state gave this a charter as Eureka College four years after the post office had made that the local name (1855).

Eureka lives in close and easy touch with its own history. In one afternoon, I went from a large stone house just off the Dixon campus, where Bill Major lives, to a large yellow clapboard house, at the crossroads of the village, where Burrus Dickinson lives. Both are Eureka graduates, and great grandsons of the school's founders. Major's grandson attended the college in the 1980s, making that family span the history of the school in six indigenous generations. These are the most obvious symbols of a general stability in Eureka's population. A dozen or so people whose four years at Eureka overlapped Reagan's, or whose families taught or employed him, still live in the small town.

Bill Major played football with Ronald Reagan when Major was a freshman and Reagan a senior. Major also lived near the campus, a part of the college family, and his brother Stanfield was a senior and a fraternity house brother with Reagan; so Bill knew Ronald well—and knew Neil better. Major, who was badly crippled in a car accident after his college years, has a stately lumbering limp, a mischievous air, and ferocious Hugh Griffith goatee and eyebrows. He keeps in his house the correspondence sent back from Liberia by the twelve slaves his ancestor, Ben Major, educated and freed before moving to free country from Kentucky in 1834.[9] Though the Disciples movement was born in the South, and its history was compromised, like our nation's, by the crime of slavery, there was always an abolitionist heritage in the Disciples—in part a heritage from enlightened Presbyterianism of the sort Benjamin Rush exhibited in Philadelphia. Barton Stone and Alexander Campbell both freed their own slaves, and Campbell became a delegate to the Virginia constitutional convention of 1829–30, despite some early Disciple misgivings about political activism among pastors, to support the abolitionists in Richmond.[10]

Ben Major was the principal figure in setting up the Walnut Grove Seminary and planning for its expansion into a college, though cholera felled him before the charter could be granted. His son, like many Eureka volunteers, served in the fight against slavery under the first Illinois President. Along with the letters from freed slaves in Liberia, Bill Major keeps his grandfather's sword from the Battle of Lookout Mountain.

Bill Major is a raconteur and cramped swashbuckler. Burrus Dickinson, in the village, has a quiet lawyerly air, though he has been mainly a newspaper editor and college president in his long successful career. His ancestor was Elijah Dickinson, who settled in Walnut Grove the same year as Ben Major, and whose son received the first Eureka degree. When Reagan came to the college in 1928, Elijah's grandson was president of the Board of Trustees, and took over the acting presidency after the student strike of that year. Burrus Dickinson had just graduated from the college himself at that time, and was in graduate school; he became Eureka president in 1939, and held the office for fifteen years. He was owner and editor of Eureka's weekly newspaper, and of several others, and when I talked to him in the spring of 1985, he had a police radio on the whole time, keeping him abreast of local developments, though he had retired from active editing and was writing the village's history.

Dickinson knows from family tradition, his own study, and rueful experience, what theological stresses the college has lived under through most of its history. He went through a stormy time in the 1940s when the smaller churches who used to be supplied with preachers by Eureka complained that the school had become too secular.[11] This was part of a wider and longer-standing division which had led the more fundamentalist churches, largely southern, to separate themselves in 1906 as the Churches of Christ (normally called Christians) from the Christian Church (Disciples of Christ).[12] The occasion for continuing opposition between these tendencies varied over the decades—open membership (i.e., admission of the unimmersed), instrumental music at worship, doctrinal training of missionaries, contribution to national organizations; but Eureka was always involved in these struggles. The very ties that made it responsive to the larger community made it vulnerable to discontents felt anywhere in it.

In 1908, just after the formal split in the church, the son of a founder, an ex-president of the college who had also served as president of Drake College, B. J. Radford, resigned from the Eureka faculty and issued a public charge of false teaching in *The Christian Standard.* This led to an investigation of all the students in the Bible department, as well as of the entire faculty. Harsher measures were taken against the former than against the latter. The investigating body wrote:

> We recommend, on the part of the Trustees and Faculty, that strict discipline be exercised over the students of the College with regard to their utterances concerning the institution; that all complaints arising amongst the students be submitted by them solely and only to the President or such committee of the Faculty as may be appointed to receive the same; that any student who is found to be spreading complaints and dissensions among his fellow students, or to be carrying such to outside parties, be summarily dealt with. The sacred interest of our College must not be hazarded by hasty and unripe utterances of irresponsible pupils.[13]

Students were obviously reporting back to more conservative churches that new ideas had appeared at Eureka. The problem of disciplining church members as students on campus is obvious, since the school depended on the good will of its contributing bodies. As always in a democratic sect, there were commendable encouragements to meddle, which makes the community vulnerable to cranks; so one can sympathize with the doomed effort to stem "leaks" from the college—not so different from perennial efforts of the same sort at the White House.

The faculty also had a strong self-governing tradition that led to clashes with presidents and boards of directors. In the 1870s, three presidents were fired in rapid succession—the third one so the first could be rehired, as a result of faculty agitation.[14] The third one fired became president a second time—and he is the man who launched the 1908 assault on the faculty for teaching heresy!

By the 1920s a new set of problems had arisen. It was the flapper era for many collegians defiant of Prohibition and in love with jazz. Eureka, which had never even allowed dancing on the campus, was a sanctuary from such moral irresponsibility—it was still dry, required chapel attendance, and was presided over by a local Disciple community and a mainly Disciple faculty. But even its students exerted some pressure for change and "modernization" as the decade wore on, and they found several friends among their teachers, the most important of whom was Samuel G. Harrod.

Harrod was a large fish in a small pond, a man of immense girth and of learning beyond the college's norm. On a campus where academic credentials were frequently sketchy, he had received his doctorate in classics from Princeton. An alumnus of Eureka, he returned to it as professor of languages in 1909, the year after the heresy investigation. In 1923, on the death of a president who had been largely an absentee raiser of funds, Dr. Harrod became the chairman of the faculty, which meant that he had the duties of acting president for almost a year.[15] In that interim he was appointed dean, and soon added the office of registrar. He was the obvious candidate for president, but the board passed him over for a man of no great academic standing but of tested managerial skills, Bert Wilson, then raising funds for the United Christian Missionary Society. The task the board had to address was a financial crisis growing worse every year, despite a Rockefeller grant in 1921 of $135,000 to rescue the college from debt and build up an endowment.[16]

Contributions had not risen, despite the flourishing state of the Disciples in Illinois during this period. The churches in that state sent 2,353 of their children to college in 1929, Ronald Reagan's freshman year, at a time when college was not the expected term of education in rural America; yet only 187 of those Disciples were attending Eureka.[17] Loyalty to the college was bound to be diluted as church members began to acquire different almae matres—Wilson found that a majority of alumni pledges had not been paid.[18] The year Reagan arrived on campus, freshman enrollment was down by sixteen (a drastic matter in a school of only 187 students).[19]

Yet this indebted and shrinking school was offering an ever wider range of courses—including a new one in journalism given in Reagan's freshman year.[20] The small faculty had two teachers of home economics.[21] With a faculty of twenty people, it was offering courses in twenty-eight departments.[22] The aim was to attract people who needed varied training for jobs teaching in elementary and secondary schools, but enrollment figures show the strategy was not working. And the proliferation of "departments" had increased faculty salaries along with titles. Eureka reserved maximum salaries for heads of departments, and fourteen of the faculty members were receiving that in 1928—as was the athletics coach and (minus two hundred dollars) the music teacher.[23] The obvious solution was to consolidate departments and cut nonessential programs—in short, a return to basics. As Bert Wilson said, home economics has no place in a college like Eureka.

But, naturally, the faculty would resist that—and the most powerful member of the faculty resisted most. President Wilson was the board's man, and the board had passed over Sam Harrod when it appointed Wilson at the end of 1923. By the time the plan for consolidation of departments was approved by the board in 1928, there was a history of bad feeling against Wilson going back four years, and of organized opposition to him on the campus over a period of three years. The students would have been involved in any case, since their home churches were the natural avenue of appeal from the board —as the attempt to seal off that channel in 1908 had indicated. But they were directly engaged during Wilson's first term when the issue of dancing on campus came up again. Wilson had little choice on the formal stand he would take. Faculty members had polled the parents in 1921, and eighty-four of the ninety-six respondents had been against allowing the innovation.[24] Wilson told the students that seventy-five percent of the donors to the college felt the same way.[25]

But an editorial in the school paper *(The Pegasus)* for May 1925, urged the students to organize for a change in the rules, and gradually, over the next two years, by taking things into their own hands, they accomplished this. The churches protested, and the board appointed a committee to investigate what had happened in 1928, but the committee said this was best left to the faculty, which was clearly siding with the students.[26] Wilson, without changing his formal stand, made no attempt to stop the practice—in fact, attended affairs at which dancing took place. It is part of the mythology of Eureka College that the ousting of Wilson in 1928 came directly over the issue of dancing—a tale that has been picked up by some reporters.[27] Reagan himself tells us that the issue was settled before he ever arrived on campus (Hubler, p. 40). Dancing was the issue which had led to an alliance, in 1925, between faculty and students against the president and board. But that did not lead to a confrontation until Wilson brought forward his plan to consolidate departments.

He made his preparations carefully. At the July meeting of the board, he asked that a joint committee be appointed to study the problem (Professor Harrod was pointedly included).[28] On November 15, that committee spent an entire day reaching the conclusions to be placed before the board at its meeting the next day. There Wilson argued effectively, from continuing trends in enrollment and debt, that Eureka could not continue to exist under its present plan in its present site. (There had been talk through the years of moving the college to a larger, denser area of Disciple population—Springfield was the alternative most often discussed.)[29] The town of Eureka was small, with about 1,500 inhabitants in the 1920s. It had no daily newspaper. It could supply no jobs to students needing work. Yet this isolated community was thick with colleges—nineteen of them within a radius of a hundred miles, more than in the whole state of Michigan, or Indiana, or Wisconsin. It proved a tactical error for Wilson to bring up the old question of relocating the school. Not only did that disturb alumni whose loyalties were to the buildings and the site; it made the village newspaper (a weekly) his enemy.[30] And it turned local alumni, those with the most access to the students, into his active opponents.[31]

Wilson vainly protested that he had not recommended moving the site. He argued, merely, that such a drastic step would be necessary *if* its departments were not consolidated.[32] This was typical of his general problem. He made his case logically stronger by including a point that weakened his standing with important constituents.

The reorganization itself made eminent sense—though, among other things, it deprived Dean Harrod of one of his offices (as registrar). Wilson argued:

The standardizing agencies require that a standard small college maintain eight departments . . . A study of what students take in liberal arts colleges in over two hundred institutions shows that about eighty-five percent of all their work is taken in eight or nine departments. Eureka student enrollment shows that they take about eighty-five percent of their work in exactly these same eight or nine departments . . . Now by merging physics with mathematics, the ancient languages with the modern languages into one foreign language, and by dropping home economics which does not belong in a liberal arts college, all the majors now being offered could be secured in the nine departments. Music would be ten.[33]

As the student paper reported, Wilson said the college's "offerings to students in their choices of majors will not be affected."[34] The board accepted the plan. It was announced. The matter seemed settled. On the surface, at least, nothing happened for four days—until Tuesday, November 20, when the students demanded Wilson's resignation.

CHAPTER 5

Strike

—and know to know no more.
—Paradise Lost *4.775*

For the sportsminded Ronald Reagan, it had been a freshman year of some disappointment. He arrived tan and fit, from his summer as a lifeguard, to find that there was not even a team in his best sport, swimming—something he would remedy the next year. His inability to see basketballs was confirmed again (Hubler, p. 38). Worst of all, after playing first-string guard for his high school football team, he found that, even on a campus with fewer than a hundred male students, he could not break into the circle of those who played a minute of the regular football season in 1928. As one of the two football players in Professor Wiggins's new journalism class, he was assigned to describe (floridly) half the season's games for *The Pegasus;* but even that was discouraging work—it was a losing season (three, four, one).[1]

But the autumn had its compensations. Thanks to his pastor's influence (Hubler, p. 30), Reagan had moved directly into "Teke House" as a pledge of Tau Kappa Epsilon fraternity, which turned out to be the most interesting place a student could be that fall. It was busy with schemes. It was right across the street from Sam Harrod's house. The Teke president, Leslie Pierce, was the leader of the student demand for Bert Wilson's resignation. "The nerve center of the strike was Teke House," Burrus Dickinson says. Dickinson was home for Thanksgiving vacation during the height of the turmoil, when his uncle, as head of the board, was negotiating the outcome (which left his uncle as acting president when Wilson left). What occurred has usually been called a student strike, as it was in the newspapers of the time. But Dickinson says, "It wasn't a student strike; it was a faculty strike. You can't explain the strike as a student issue. There was nothing important enough for them to have reacted as they did." Why did they? "The faculty was using them." Who? "A number of them. Dean Harrod." Why? "Nobody living today knows exactly how it started."

A student statement issued during the strike declared larger concerns than the consolidation of departments: "The student body, the alumni, and the faculty were not able to work harmoniously with present administration and had not been in harmony the past four years."[2] The Peoria *Star* said of the crisis: "Where a wisp of smoke had trailed for three of his five years' reign as president of Eureka College, flame suddenly burst forth" (November 24). The same article quoted a student on Wilson's "bad moral influence." The day before that, the Peoria *Journal* had written: "The trouble . . . had its origination three years ago when members of the student body formed an organization when ill feeling began to crop out between the students and the head of the college." The Bloomington *Daily Pantagraph* had the same story on November 22: "Wednesday night for the first time the students made public their organization which had its inception three years ago under the leadership of Leslie Pierce [a "Teke"], Walter Radebaugh [Teke], and Robert Sealock. Now Pierce is chairman of the student organization, which claims membership of more than two thirds of the 220 [sic] students." Only Radebaugh, a junior, could have been in on the founding of an organization three years old, since Pierce and Sealock were sophomores. But they, like Reagan, a freshman, could join a movement that had been gathering steam before they arrived on campus. Another student was quoted in the November 22 *Pantagraph:* "Please make it plain for us that this is not hasty but is a dissatisfaction that has been extant for three years."

Howard Short, senior class president at the time, and one of the most active members of the opposition to Wilson, now says: "We made a great mistake. We didn't know what we were doing. Bert Wilson was a very good man, but he was not a good college president. He later went on to work for our pension fund in Indianapolis" (Short is a Disciple pastor, professor emeritus of divinity, at one time editor of *The Christian*). "He was an excellent person in that field. But we had a grudge against him for some reason. It wasn't the dancing, because we had already won that one. We picked on little things—like the time when Wilson went to Cape Girardo to a meeting, we heard he played tennis, and we said he was not using his time for school business."[3]

Reagan's account of the grievance is straightforward:

Like so many small colleges with church affiliations, Eureka was perpetually broke . . . The new [sic] president of Eureka tripped over the panic button and announced a plan for saving the college. He favored a plan which called for such a drastic cutback academically that many juniors and seniors would have been cut off without the courses needed for graduation in their chosen majors. Needless to say, the faculty would have been decimated and Eureka would have lost its high academic rating . . . He had persuaded the board of trustees to go along without any thought of consulting students or faculty [faculty were included on both committees that drew up the plan].[4] They, knowing this was equivalent to cutting out the heart of the college, responded with a roar of fury [Hubler, p. 33].

Not actually with a roar, but with a scurrying silence. The statement on reorganization was released Friday the sixteenth. Its tenor was known beforehand, from the joint committee meeting, attended by Dean Harrod among others, on the fifteenth. Reagan says that the students first presented a counterproposal, before demanding the president's resignation. But the counterproposal came later, as a response to the resignation, as a further argument for it. The first official statement from the students came on Tuesday, the twentieth, and was a simple petition to the board that it demand Wilson's resignation. It was signed by 143 students.[5] The weekend had been very active. Howard Short, who was a student preacher at the time, remembers coming back Sunday from giving a sermon in a neighboring church to find friends buzzing about a strategy meeting already in progress.

No threat was spelled out in the petition to the board, but strike plans were already being laid. They were discussed openly enough to be reported in the nearby newspapers: there would be a "walkout" if Wilson tried to stay on, the Bloomington paper reported the day after the petition was released.

Trustees on the scene agreed to meet with representatives of the students on Thursday. At a Wednesday night meeting, twenty students were chosen, and they took a legal advisor with them.[6] It was a long meeting, in the village court house, with neither side giving way. That night, some parents arrived for the celebration, on Friday, of "Dad's Day," with a football game against Illinois College. When the game began, few of those present knew that President Wilson had issued his resignation. Early copies of the evening Peoria paper, rushed to Eureka, told them about it late in the game. As *The Pegasus* wrote: "Copies of the *Journal,* Friday night, appearing on the football field, demoralized interest in the Dad's day game between Eureka and Illinois College." Morale cannot have been very high even before the papers circulated: Eureka lost, 19–0.[7]

Wilson resigned in order to free the consolidation plan from squabbling over him. He issued a long statement repeating the arguments for reorganization. It is clear that he saw the faculty, not the students, as the real source of resistance.

My administration has been handicapped from the very beginning because of this [curricular] spreading out process, and because vested interests of teachers have withstood any attempt to make revisions in the program. The board, in order to avoid friction and not disturb the status of the teaching staff, has put off this evil day which all the members have known, sooner or later, had to come. Now that the issue has been clearly faced and action taken, the inevitable revolt has come. If blame and criticism come in large or small degree it had to center on some personality. There can be no escape from that. I am willing to accept full responsibility for all that I have suggested and recommended. Now, you gentlemen, at the very beginning of a sounder academic organization, are face to face with a temporary problem, dealing in personalities rather than giving your constructive and creative thought to the real problem for which you are responsible. Your big problem is most perplexing and most complicated. It is because of your loyalty to me, and my ardent hope that you may be entirely free and unhampered in the solution of your real problem that I am suggesting a course of procedure which may help. Since this unfortunate misunderstanding has arisen not one of you, in Eureka or out of Eureka, has suggested or even hinted that I take the course I am now about to propose. I am, therefore, handing to you [the executive committee of the board] and through you to the board of trustees, my resignation as president of Eureka college.[8]

The students had reason to know that the trustees were not disposed to accept Wilson's resignation, and they spent Saturday increasing the pressure against him. Some called for an immediate return to the situation that prevailed between the death of the former president and Wilson's appointment —i.e., to making S. G. Harrod the acting president.[9] The main student meeting was held at night, and it issued a statement attacking Wilson for loss of faith in Eureka and pledging student support for the college. The statement was signed by Robert Sealock. On the same day, resident alumni issued a statement saying Wilson did not have belief enough in the college to guide it further.[10] This was the theme picked up by the student paper on Monday. The line, now, was not so much that the reorganization plan was wrong as that Wilson's arguments for it were dispiriting:

Newspapers are not to blame that it was broadcasted [sic] in headlines all over the state that Eureka is confronted with a dark future. The source of their information is responsible. The effects of such advertising will not be to the advantage of the school or the town. Prospective donors will be hesitant about giving gifts to any institution proclaimed shaky by its president. Prospective students will be alarmed in the same degree. By questioning Eureka's fitness for "riding the storm," he has, in the minds of everyone, lost mastery and control of the situation.

The same editorial came up, only *after* the resignation, with the "counterproposal" Reagan remembers as having been offered and rejected before. The students would save the school by more energetic recruiting of freshmen:

The undergraduates have assumed the burden of proposing an action which will, in their opinion, provide the only solution for the present problem. If their suggestion is accepted, they are directly responsible for its immediate success. They are honor bound to support their convictions with all energy and enthusiasm. The trustees, upon admitting the demand of the students, should, in turn, charge them with the duty of booming the school's stock. It is the only move that can encourage those hundred and twenty press agents [the strikers] to produce the kind of publicity Eureka needs.[11]

That night, President Wilson replied to the alumni and students that he had faith in the school, but felt it must take prudent steps to strengthen its position.[12]

Tuesday, the twenty-seventh, would be a long, tiring, exciting day for everyone involved. The full board had agreed to meet that day. Heretofore, students had argued that the reorganization plan was never official policy because it had been approved by a board sitting without three (of its twenty-four) members.[13] That argument would not be available by the end of the meeting on Tuesday. The trustees began their session in Burgess Hall at 9:00 A.M. When they broke for lunch and walked to the cafeteria, there was hostility bristling around them. Howard Short remembers one of the trustees ("the state secretary of the churches") shaking his fist at him. There was talk of violence if the trustees did not meet the students' demands. Football players were given peacekeeping assignments.[14] The acrimony of the situation can be assessed only when we remember that many of the participants—trustees, faculty, students, resident alumni—knew each other in church circles as fellow Disciples. That is how the ministerial student and the secretary of churches recognized each other across the invisible barricades.

The meeting dragged on through the afternoon and into the evening. Local alumni were heard; it is clear from later actions that a counteroffensive of some sort was considered against the people who had engineered the attack on Wilson. The students themselves seemed to take it for granted that there would be no weakening in the board's support for Wilson. They had already moved from questioning the validity of the board's November 16 session (with twenty-one members) to the view that "the trustees were responsible to the student body and the alumni for the manner in which the affairs of the College were administered"[15]—a position Ronald Reagan would hear again as Governor of California thirty-five years later.

The trustees broke for dinner and returned to their debate. The resident alumni who had been in the meeting were making angry reports to students that Wilson was sitting with the board, and that the trustees were supporting him and mocking the alumni. The question was not whether Wilson's resignation would be accepted, but whether the board would take punitive action against faculty or students or both. The suspense was not relieved until 11:45, when the marathon session broke up with a brief announcement—the president's resignation was not accepted. The prearranged signal—a bell that had been taken out of the chapel building and hung in a shelter on campus—rang, disturbing the village's sleep.

For those who have not been to Eureka, it is important to emphasize the scale of the arena for this tiny conflict. One can hardly talk of town-gown division where the entire village-school complex is so small. We have to remember the intimacy of those involved, the many family and church ties crossing student-administration barriers. Howard Short, for instance, was dating one of Bert Wilson's daughters at the same time he was working to organize the strike. Before going to the midnight meeting, he asked Wilson if

he would like a report on the outcome. Wilson said he would be asleep by
then; would Short put a note in his window? Short said yes and went off to
vote against Wilson; then, two hours later, he dropped the note off at his
house.

The student meeting was called to order in the chapel, Leslie Pierce presiding.[16] Reports were made by the alumni who had been in the trustees'
meeting. According to the Bloomington paper, "numerous student speakers
were heard." The meeting lasted till 2:30.[17] At one point, as various proposals were being put in form for presentation to the crowd, Professor Gunn of
the Voice Department quieted the audience with a performance of Negro
spirituals.[18] The contending proposals were for the student body to leave
Eureka en masse at the end of the semester (a plan that sat ill with the earlier
statement of loyalty to the institution), or to go on "strike" in some fashion
or other. The latter proposal was voted through by 1:45, according to the
Bloomington paper: "We the students of Eureka college, on the twenty-
eighth day of November, 1928, declare an immediate strike pending the
acceptance of President Wilson's resignation by the board of trustees."

It was at this meeting, as one of the "numerous" student speakers, that
Reagan made his one known contribution to the strike. Howard Short says:
"We put Reagan on because he was the biggest mouth of the freshman class;
he was a cocky s.o.b., a loud talker. Dutch was the guy you wanted to put up
there." Reagan has a different explanation: "It had been decided that the
motion for putting our plan into effect should be presented by a freshman,
because the charge could be made that upper classmen had a selfish interest"
(Hubler, p. 36). But Leslie Pierce, a sophomore, was presiding over the
meeting. Robert Sealock, a junior, had signed the "faith in Eureka" statement. Only those two and another junior were mentioned in print as targets
for the board's reprisal. Howard Short, a senior, says there was never any
attempt to hide the fact that upper classmen were running things. Reagan
spoke as a freshman because numerous students of the different classes,
fraternities, and sororities were called on to express the joint purpose. But
Reagan makes it sound as if his speech initiated and concluded the discussion:

I'd been told that I should sell the idea so there'd be no doubt of the
outcome. I reviewed the history of our patient negotiations [the
counterplan he claims was made before the demand for a resignation]
with due emphasis on the devious manner in which the trustees had
sought to take advantage of us [not consulting the faculty, though they
had]. I discovered that night that an audience has a feel to it and, in the
parlance of the theater, that audience and I were together. When I came
to actually presenting the motion there was no need for parliamentary
procedure; they came to their feet with a roar [as he said the faculty had
after the announcement of reconsolidation]—even the faculty members
present voted by acclamation. It was heady wine. Hell, with two more

lines I could have had them riding through "every Middlesex village and farm"—without horses yet. [Hubler, pp. 36–37]

It is not surprising that Reagan felt at home in a chapel preaching to fellow Disciples. He had acted in his mother's morality plays in the church at Dixon. He obviously felt the same moral urgency about his strike speech, delivered in a similar setting. The moral fervor of his later political talks is more understandable if we consider how easily he could move from an antitemperance speech in the Church of Christ to a denunciation of the morally evil Bert Wilson in the chapel of Eureka College. (He tells Hubler he "later" decided that Wilson was sincere in his plans for the college—he did not even give him credit for that at the time.) The unattractive side to rectitude, so rarely shown by his mother, or by Reagan himself, is the presumption of vice in those disagreeing with one's consciously righteous position. Virtue was no stranger on the Eureka campus—and neither was righteousness. But there can have been few times when the righteousness quotient ran quite as high as on the night and early morning of November 27–28, 1929. "It was heady wine."

According to Reagan, public discussion of the terms of the strike was precluded by the roar of approval when he first expounded them. But the proceedings involved participation at more levels than that. (He never mentions the alternative plan that was put up and rejected.) Would students stay on campus? Run the newspaper? Continue athletic events? Attend chapel? They would do all those things, it was decided—all but go to class. They would abstain from the one thing that (he admits) interested Reagan less than drama, sports, and fraternity life. Hardly a self-denying ordinance. To rub salt in the wounds of the administration, the students would hold a *dance* every afternoon in lieu of classes (Hubler, p. 37). But Reagan says there was discipline to go with the indulgence:

Not once did we neglect our studies. To have done so would have been to contradict the whole spirit of what we were fighting for. The committee set up regular study hours and enforced them; we concocted our own assignments, and worked them out (and in some cases were ahead of the regular study schedule). [Hubler, pp. 37–38]

I asked Howard Short, the divinity student, if he recalled any such regimen. "Maybe some people studied. I didn't."

There was little time, in any event, to set up a regular schedule of study, much less to get ahead of it. The student meeting broke up in the early hours of Wednesday, the day before Thanksgiving, when students were allowed a long weekend to go home (where events at the Disciples' college were bound to be the talk of each Sunday gathering at Christian churches around the state). When the students returned on Monday, they began the two class weeks the strike would last; but they had little time for studying, after all the extracurricular activities, exhortations, recriminations. Every fraternity and sorority joined the strike except Phi Omega, the sorority with two of Bert

Wilson's daughters in it—and some in Phi Omega were bitter that their group did not join the rest.[19] There were comings and goings in the village, of trustees, and alumni, and peacemakers. A negotiating center was set up at Byron Colburn's house. The task was to establish a formula for settlement, and recruit sufficient support for it, before the board reassembled on December 4. The issue was no longer the consolidation plan, but the terms of surrender on either side, the board's and the faculty's (with students manipulated between the two). Some favored dismissing Dean Harrod for his role in the affair, along with selected student leaders. (Reagan was in no danger.) The students, presumably, would not submit to any outcome that involved Wilson's retention. But the board would not let him leave under fire, as if the students' complaints had been vindicated. At length, the broad terms of a deal were shaped.

The possibilities were spelled out in a meeting the night before the board's session, attended by some board members, faculty, alumni, and students. Here the possible reprisals were revealed, and various pleas—including one from President Wilson—were made to compose the community's differences. This meeting obviously sobered the students.

A member of the student committee reported Thursday night that this organization had obtained information to the effect that board members would be led to accept the resignation of President Bert Wilson, which was refused more than a week ago, and at the same time demand the resignation of Dr. Samuel G. Harrod, and Prof. James Compton of the faculty and to request Robert Sealock, Walter Radebaugh, and Leslie Pierce, admitted ringleaders of the fight to oust Wilson, to leave school.[20]

After the board went into session Friday morning, the students assembled, with Dean Harrod playing an active part, and voted a retraction of their demand for Wilson's resignation. This was in the board members' hands before lunch. It was clearly a surrender on which some faculty jobs depended. The students ate all their brave words:

In view of the fine spirited statement made last evening by President Wilson before a group of trustees, faculty, alumni, and student representatives, we instruct our leaders to withdraw our petition . . . We are fully aware of the fact that questions of such vital importance to the life of the college as are those sent out in the petition must be decided by the board of trustees. We do not presume to dictate what their action should be in matters affecting the policy and program of the school.[21]

Even with the students' retraction before it, the board's meeting was long and heated. The hottest subject seems to have been whether Harrod should be fired. He was put on probation instead. The Peoria *Star*'s subhead said, "Prexy Leaves, Dean is Upbraided," and the story began, "A stinging rebuke was administered Dean S. G. Harrod, registrar, by the board of trustees of Eureka College following their acceptance last night of President Bert Wilson's resignation."

> After a hectic session which lasted all day the trustees decided to accept the resignation Wilson insisted upon, although the members of the student council at noon voted to withdraw their demand for ouster of prexy as a step toward reconciliation . . . Dean Harrod came under fire after the board had reached agreement, and his resignation was demanded, to be effective on the instance of further campus disturbance. Although Dean Harrod was present at the student meeting yesterday and is understood to have been ardently in favor of a peace pact between the clashing factions, the demand of the trustees indicates they held him particularly at fault in exciting the near riot.[22]

S. G. Harrod lived on many years as dean and teacher at Eureka, a benign imposing figure to later generations of students—so the official history of the college draws a merciful veil over his part in the strike and the probation period it earned him. But Bill Major adds, significantly, "Harrod never did get to be president." That seems to have been the real issue all along.

The man who displayed grace and charity through the crisis was Bert Wilson—though his eight daughters were estranged from Eureka ever after. Howard Short told me, "When I was a young pastor in Akron, Bert Wilson —who was then with the pension fund—said, 'Howard, you have to get into the pension fund.' I said I knew it, but I couldn't pay for it—it was Depression time. He said, 'I'll take your note for three months.' He paid my fee himself—after what I had done to him. He was a good Christian man."

What did the entire experience mean to Reagan, who lived at its most intense point of focus, so far as the students were concerned? There is nothing in his account about the student retraction, or Harrod's rebuke and probation; nothing about the adoption of Wilson's consolidation plan after all. In fact, the curriculum was reduced to eight departments instead of the nine Wilson had suggested.[23] On the declared object of the strike, which Reagan said would "cut out the heart of the college," the students clearly failed. But Reagan walks away from it and says he won:

> In the end it was our policy of polite resistance that brought victory. After a week [sic], the new [sic] president resigned . . . The marks of the strikers were not notably improved by our layoff [why not, if they scrupulously kept up to schedule, and sometimes ahead?], but we found we achieved a lot more personal attention—plus an education in human nature and the rights of man to universal education that nothing could erase from our psyches. [Hubler, p. 38]

Almost everything factual about the strike had been erased from Reagan's mind by the time he dictated those words; but an elation clearly survived. The students had brought down a president. It was heady stuff for them, and it seems to have had a special importance for Reagan. He had always been a model boy. Now he combined that moralism with the forbidden pleasures of the rebel. In joining the overwhelming sentiment of the students and the immediately involved alumni, he was a dissenting conformist. Twain makes the reader complicitous in the discomfiture of the model boy, Willie Mufferson, when Tom Sawyer gets the Bible prize ahead of him by sharp dealing. Reagan lived, he tells us, in Huck Finn's world; but he was never Huck. He was Willie. But Reagan managed to remain a Mufferson while acquiring a touch of "bad boy" glamor—Huck's, or Tom's. Or even Paul Revere's, rattling every Middlesex village and farm. He could attack authorities by the community's authority, a wonderful combination of traditionalism and innovation. He had been a leading follower in a conformist rebellion, the kind he would always prefer.

The complexity of the problems involved in the strike, the long background of the controversy before Reagan arrived on campus, the way the faculty was using the students, the economic and pedagogic case Bert Wilson made (which proved to be irresistible even without his continued advocacy) —none of these matters had any weight with Reagan in his later account, (or, so far as we know, at the time). He had no respect for the density of the real and vivid piece of history he was living through. He converted it into a "historical" symbol, Paul Revere on the ride. As he liked the resounding name of Lowell, but never learned which Lowell was really involved in the park where he worked, Reagan would embody great chunks of the American experience, become deeply involved with them emotionally, while having only the haziest notion of what really occurred. He has a skill for striking "historical" attitudes combined with a striking lack of historical attentiveness. What he wanted was a side to stand on, the right side, from which to denounce evil, to preach it away—as he had chosen his mother's side, making him a model boy in the first place. He was too busy hugging the strike experience, up close, for him to hold it, at least for a moment, at arm's length for inspection. He felt confident he could follow his instincts, because they were so attuned to sermon, tract, and morality play. He brought passionate conviction to right behavior, without much awareness that rights can ever be in conflict or in doubt. He was trained to rectitude, not to questioning. He was what the period called a muscular Christian, an independent Disciple, the Paul Revere of piety. He did not exaggerate, later, when he said this was a foretaste of his later union crusades.

PART TWO

PAP FINN'S WORLD

CHAPTER 6

Depression

*Dawson's Landing had a week of repose, now, and it needed it.
But it was in an expectant state, for the air was full of
rumors of a new deal.*

—*Twain*, Pudd'nhead Wilson

After the strike, Reagan's three and a half years at Eureka were a happy blur
of many activities—performance in seven plays, letters in two sports (cheerleader in the others), president of the Booster Club, president of the Senate,
one year on the school paper, two on the yearbook, jobs on and off campus,
washing dishes, serving food.[1] By his own account, studies rarely intruded
on this breathless schedule. Returning for an honorary degree, he joked, "I
thought my first Eureka degree was an honorary one." Playing it safe, he
majored in economics—Archibald Gray was the most notoriously easy
grader on the campus.[2] (Later, in the White House, Reagan would assure
Time magazine reporters that he understood economics because that was his
college major.)

True to the strikers' pledge, Reagan did work to recruit new students; and,
unlike most of them, he had some success—he brought his brother back with
him the year after the strike. As president of the Booster Club, he was
responsible for the school's public relations. An article in the school paper
shows him back at the scene of his strike speech two years later:

ANNOUNCEMENTS WERE ON CHAPEL PROGRAM

The chapel program Tuesday morning consisted of the usual devotional
exercises, and very interesting and important announcements by Presi-
dent Lyon and Ronald Reagan, president of the Eureka Booster club
. . . "Dutch" Reagan's announcement concerned that great week-end,
Homecoming. He explained that all students are members of the
Booster club, and he asked them for cooperation in making this year's
Homecoming a big success for everyone concerned.

But it was uphill work. By the time Reagan became President of the
Booster Club, the Depression had settled over the nation. Even with cut-

backs going beyond what Bert Wilson called for, the school was tottering.
Reagan paints a rosy picture of the morale on campus: "The four classes on
the campus [during the strike] became the most tightly knit groups ever to
graduate from Eureka. Campus spirit bloomed. A remarkably close bond
with the faculty developed" (Hubler, p. 38). The students were no doubt on
their best behavior. The terms of Dean Harrod's probation made his job
depend on there being no further disturbances. But various notes in the
school paper indicate that school spirit was not always "blooming." In the
very next issue of *The Pegasus* after Reagan's pep talk to his fellow boosters,
we read: "Mac [the football coach] said that the team wasn't fighting, and
that the Eureka spirit was somehow lacking. What it must have cost him to
say these words we will never know."[3]

Reagan was still not in the starting football lineup at the beginning and
end of his sophomore year,[4] but he saw a good deal of service in the interval,
while Neil was having his successful freshman year. He was a letter-winning
swimmer (a member, therefore, of "the E Tribe"), though the school had
only a small and poorly ventilated pool in the basement of its Pritchard
Building. Apart from swimming, Reagan's most consistent success at school
was on the stage. When the Eureka troupe went to the Chicago area to
compete at Northwestern University, it came in third as a team and Reagan
received an honorable mention for his role in *Aria da Capo*.[5]

Reagan pays tribute to his drama teacher, Ellen Marie Johnson, the third
of his mentors in theater, after his mother and the Dixon High School coach,
B. J. Frazer. Miss Johnson was obviously energetic and involved in many
productions. It is part of the academic spread Bert Wilson deplored that, of
the two teachers who made up the English department, one was also teaching Reagan journalism in his freshman year, while the other, Miss Johnson,
was directing him in his first college play, *The Brat*.[6] Miss Johnson was
herself only two years out of college at the time,[7] and Professor Wiggins, the
head of the English department was, in Howard Short's words, "rather
passive." So the educational basics, later supported by Reagan's secretaries
of education, were endangered in the school Reagan refers to as a model in
his fond reminiscences.

Though Reagan says he always wanted to attend Eureka (Hubler, p. 30),
the fact that his high school sweetheart, Margaret Cleaver, was going there
gave him a further incentive. Yet he tells us that he fell in love with his
leading lady in *The Brat* during his second term as a freshman.[8] She was a
senior, however, unattainable; he returned to "Muggs" Cleaver for the rest
of college, and their engagement was one of those that led the college president to vary "the ivy ceremony" at graduation. Seniors held a long strand of
ivy unwound from the two principal buildings, while the president snipped
off each person's portion. Engaged persons stood together, and were separated as a unit from their classmates. The Reverend Ben Cleaver, who had
moved from Dixon to become pastor of Eureka's church in 1931, was a
respected local resident as well as a leader of the Disciples in the state. It was

with his blessing that his daughter made a public commitment to Reagan, with a nurturing community to cheer. Reagan was never more integrated into the Disciples than at this moment of disjunction, though it was understood that marriage would have to yield to economy for a while. Margaret had a high school teaching job arranged. Ronald, who had not prepared himself academically for such work, had to go back to Lowell Park as a lifeguard. When the park closed in September, he would have no job for five months—his first experience of unemployment, during one of his father's hard spells.

Opportunities for work, in this fourth year of Hoover's presidency, were constricted. Four months after the conclusion of the strike in Reagan's freshman year, Hoover had been inaugurated at the crest of the "roaring twenties" with the boast: "I have no fears for the future of our country. It is bright with hope." A year after that, unemployment was at four million, and those on relief had shot up by 200 percent in the four months since the crash. By the year Reagan graduated, there were thirteen million unemployed.[9] And those who still had jobs—three quarters of the population—were, many of them, working at cut wages or hours or both.

Even with all his lifeguard money saved, swimming tuition help, and steady work at school (sometimes two jobs at the same time), Reagan had needed a loan from a Disciples organization to get through college, himself, and his brother's last year was jeopardized. In fact, Eureka was about to go under. Though Reagan served on the yearbook committee in his senior year, the school was too broke by the spring to produce one. Senior-class biographies were scattered through late issues of the school paper.[10] The president brought in to replace Wilson was by his own confession not a money raiser, and in October 1931, exactly four years after the board approved the cutback that set off a strike, far more drastic steps were taken, including "the Eureka Plan," by which every student would be required to work, eliminating all staff expenses. This meant not only student work in traditional areas —the cafeteria, library, research, etc. Students also did the heavy maintenance of heating and other services, and worked the farms owned by the school, milking cows, harvesting strawberries, doing intensive work in seasonal spurts (to which classroom hours would have to be tailored). Reagan told Hubler that Eureka was always "hard up" and this forged a feeling of togetherness, "much as a poverty-stricken family is bound" (p. 33). But the Eureka Plan, which was in effect during Neil's last year there, shows that poverty does not always elevate. By 1936, when the school lost its accreditation, the official history concludes: "The Eureka Plan had done very little for campus morale. In fact, the Plan added to poor self-image of students. An editorial in *The Pegasus* deplored the lack of college spirit and blamed everything from food to football."[11]

It is strange that Reagan should talk of poverty binding families together when he is describing the period when his own family was most separated, according to him, by poverty. While the boys were both at Eureka, Jack had moved to Springfield, 150 miles from Dixon, to manage a cheap shoe store (Hubler, p. 50), while Nelle stayed in Dixon. It is hard to understand why, even with Nelle's sewing work for Mrs. Sipe at her clothes store, living in two places was more economical. Money seems to have been only one of several strains on the marriage. If Jack Reagan was vagrant, it was as much from his temperament as his pocketbook; it was the Mr. Crummles in him. Ronald, with all his other responsibilities as a senior at Eureka, saved fifty dollars from his dishwashing to send to Nelle (Hubler, p. 51), suggesting there was at least a time of nonsupport from the absent Jack.

Many people in Dixon have wry things to say about Reagan's "talking poor."[12] "They were not worse off than anybody," Leo Gorman told me. "Jack and Nelle were always well dressed," Mary Emmert says. They had two boys in college during the worst part of the Depression, and both sons completed their course. From stores they had worked in, the Reagans could get shoes and clothing at lower rates, and Nelle did her own sewing. Still, the family future must have looked very dark in 1932. The summer job at Lowell Park was a temporary stay, but there was a finality to the approach of September that had never threatened Ronald before.

Fewer vacationers were at the resort than in the carefree days when Reagan began to work at the park in the mid-twenties. Classmates from high school days were able to come by since they had no work. It was a summer in which despondency seemed the last check to rebelliousness. Shortly before Reagan's graduation, the "Bonus Army" of veterans had passed through Illinois on its way to Congress, recreating the struggles of Coxey's army in the last great depression of Jack Reagan's youth. For two months, the Bonus Marchers were shabbily encamped in Washington, trying to get a hearing from Congress or the White House. After police shot two of the marchers on July 28, President Hoover ordered them cleared from Pennsylvania Avenue by the United States Army. General Douglas MacArthur, disobeying the President's commands, crossed the Anacostia River in pursuit of them, and precipitated the burning of their huts.[13] MacArthur, sure he had put down a Communist attempt to take over the government of the United States, felt himself the personal object of Moscow's wrath ever after: "It was the beginning of a definite and ceaseless campaign that set me apart as a man to be destroyed, no matter how long the Communists and their friends and advisors had to wait, and no matter what means they might have to use. But it was to be nineteen years before the bells of Moscow pealed out their glee at my eclipse."[14]

Discontent with Hoover embarrassed the Reagans' largely Republican friends in 1932, but all the Reagans were Democrats. Mary Emmert's father used to kid Nelle after church affairs, "I could really take a liking to you if you weren't such a terrible Democrat." And Ruth Graybill remembers "Dutch" arguing politics with her Republican husband at the beach. The Democrats, gathered at the end of June for their Chicago convention, took a step that would not please at least two of the Reagans. The combined factions of Al Smith and Jack Garner drafted a plank to repeal the Eighteenth Amendment. Otherwise, the platform (written by A. Mitchell Palmer) did not offer much relief from the Depression—it promised to cut government spending by a fourth, balance the budget, and remove the federal government from all fields of private enterprise except public works and conservation.[15] When the convention chose its candidate, Franklin Roosevelt, he pledged to support the platform "one hundred percent."[16]

It was not Roosevelt, but Sid Altschuler, who gave Reagan hope during that ominous summer. Altschuler, a Kansas City visitor to the lodge near Lowell Park, had struck up an acquaintance with the serious and responsible lifeguard who taught both his daughters to swim. In earlier summers he had promised to help Reagan find work after college. Since he failed to do that, it is difficult to see why Reagan expresses such gratitude to him, and makes him a pivotal figure in his career. When Reagan told Altschuler he wanted to become a radio broadcaster (not telling him that this was simply the most accessible-looking branch of show business), the older man apologized: "Well, you've picked a line in which I have no connections" (Hubler, p. 54). But he assured him it was a wise choice, since radio was a young and growing industry, in which there would be expanding opportunities once he entered it at any level: "Take any kind of job, even sweeping floors, just to get in." It was advice Reagan tried to follow through the unnerving months of unemployment that followed his last closing of Lowell Park, months when his father lost his job and Neil's ability to stay at Eureka came into question. Since Altschuler did not actually do anything for Reagan, his importance must have been the encouragement he gave at a time of despondency. Reagan remembers him as sounding "literally the first note of optimism I had heard about the state of the nation" (Hubler, p. 52). Reagan, who would praise optimism all his life, apparently needed some when Altschuler became the second father he clung to (after Ben Cleaver, who was no longer in Dixon).

Before beginning his job hunt, Ronald went back to Eureka, to pledge new "Tekes," and to say goodbye to Margaret Cleaver before she began her year of teaching. Then, leaving Neil to begin his senior year, Ronald hitchhiked to Chicago, where he stayed with a Eureka alumnus while going the rounds of radio stations. Chicago was then the center of the radio industry, but it had no openings for a man whose principal experience was as a lifeguard.

Jack Reagan was back in Dixon now, and he let Ronald borrow his old Chevrolet for a day to canvass the stations in and around Davenport, Iowa, seventy miles to the west. At Station WOC-WHO, Reagan was told there was no opening; but he was given his first audition, as a sports announcer. If he wanted to come back four times during the football season, he would be allowed to do some coverage of the Iowa University games, as "righthand man to Gene Loffler, WOC announcer."[17] He made $35.00 from the season, his only income between the closing of Lowell Park and February of 1934. But Reagan stayed true to Altschuler's advice. He was getting some experience. He had his foot in the door. The WOC program director, who drove him to Iowa City for the games, was encouraging. Between Davenport and Dixon he rode the bus those four times.

Reagan's chronology is confused for this period. He has Roosevelt elected in November of 1932, and Jack Reagan giving out New Deal relief by Christmas of that year (Hubler, p. 65). Roosevelt was not inaugurated until March 4, 1933. Even then, though he made a whirlwind beginning, it was not till May 31 that the first relief program began to function.[18] Illinois was, indeed, one of the first seven states to be given relief grants.[19] But even if Jack Reagan had been the first man in Illinois to go to work for the FERA, Ronald could not have remembered his coming home daily and describing over dinner the people on relief (Hubler, pp. 63–64). By June of 1933, Ronald was in Des Moines, 250 miles from Dixon, having moved there from Davenport in May. Any stories he heard about Jack's relief work were told him on visits.

Reagan's chronology is confused because he formed a natural memory cluster—his college graduation, Roosevelt's election, Roosevelt's rapid initiation of the New Deal, Jack Reagan's relief work, Ronald's own last Christmas at home—and associated it all with 1932. Any memory he has of his father's frustration with those opposed to work relief (Hubler, p. 65) could hardly come before his Christmas visit of 1933, since the Civil Works Administration did not begin its operation until November 9 of that year.[20]

It seems likely that, just as Reagan has confused the Christmases of 1932 and 1933 in his memory, he has done the same thing with the Christmases of 1931 and 1932. His "1932" has become a happy cluster, connected with Roosevelt and the New Deal. The 1931 memories are of tragedy on a melodramatic scale—a Christmas Eve special delivery notice that Jack was being fired (Hubler, pp. 50–51). This blow descended when "we were all home together for Christmas that last year of mine in college." No doubt being fired at any time close to Christmas would have the emotional impact of being fired on the eve of the holiday. The real question is, *which* Christmas is at stake? Jack is in Dixon when he gets the news, but the special delivery notice could have come from Springfield. Did he come back without a job and remain without one from December 1931 to June 1933? He was, by this time, bitter and irascible, in his son's own description, and had already been on a downward spiral toward the "cheap store" in Springfield. He was becoming temperamentally unemployable in the only work he knew. Ronald indicates this was the end of the line for Jack as a salesman. But could both sons have stayed in college if Jack had been unemployed for so long a period? The Reagans, like most middle-class people before the New Deal itself changed public attitudes, would have considered taking relief shameful, especially if neither of two able-bodied sons was seeking employment.

The solution to those problems appears easy. The firing of Jack occurred near Christmas in *1932*, and has been moved back in Reagan's memory by the intrusion of New Deal memories at too early a date. What Reagan remembers as his last *college* year at home was actually his last year of living in Dixon. This date not only gives us a more convincing chronology, but affords a clearer view of the Reagan family's economic plight by December of 1932. Ronald had no steady employment yet. There was some question whether Neil could finish his last year at Eureka, even with the Eureka Plan in effect; Ronald says some of his first money earned as a radio announcer in the new year went to Neil. Then, in December, Jack lost his last selling job. Ronald was employed in February of 1933,[21] but almost immediately fired (Hubler, pp. 65, 67–69); rehired, temporarily; and successful enough to make the move to Des Moines by May. Then, around June, Jack Reagan's party loyalty was rewarded with work that restored some of his self-respect. It was a tight scrape, and fully explains the fact that Reagan has memories of hard times, though most of his youth was not spent in poverty. There was a severe crisis for a period of six months or so before the New Deal programs came to the rescue. A sense of relief and gratitude at this turn of events has buttressed Reagan's emotional loyalty to Roosevelt through all his later political rationalizations of that tie.

The scale of the rescue brought to the Reagan family by the Federal Emergency Relief Administration (FERA) has not been widely appreciated, because most accounts of the matter say only one member of the family worked for the New Deal. Ronald, in fact, told Hubler: "There was no bureaucracy at Jack's level; he shared an office and secretary with the County Supervisor of Poor" (p. 63). But there was soon another person in that office, fresh out of Eureka College. In November 1933, when the FERA's relief program was expanded into the Civil Works Administration, four men were given new federal appointments in Lee County. Here is the third one:

> Neil Reagan, who has been acting as county auditor for the welfare organizations, has been appointed district representative of the Federal Reemployment Bureau, his territory including all counties of the Thirteenth congressional district and DeKalb county.[22]

The fourth officer is described this way: "J. E. Reagan, who has been in the service at the county relief headquarters for several months, has been named certifying officer for Lee County."[23] Both Reagans had been distributing federal funds to the county under FERA rules—federal employees subsidizing the local relief machinery—at a time when local politicians protested governmental hiring of men from the same family *(and* unmarried men, like Neil) so long as some heads of families were still unemployed.[24]

Illinois received more relief money than any state in the nation except New York and Pennsylvania.[25] This was not only because it was hard hit, but because its politicians were skilled at applying for the moneys that became available in historically unprecedented amounts in 1933 and 1934.[26] Patronage and graft were a problem in any system that worked through the local political organizations, and the CWA had famous problems with corruption.[27] Its director, Harry Hopkins, clashed with Cook County politicians over local patronage appointments.[28] Reagan insists that "There were no boondoggles in Dixon to speak of under the WPA" (Hubler, p. 64), but he neglects to tell us that his brother worked for both the FERA and the FRB through his father's influence in the former.

What Ronald remembers as WPA projects were done by the CWA in 1933, and completed by the FERA in 1934. The grandest project is described this way: "Jack, who was no engineer, figured a way to use the old streetcar rails, torn from our main street, as structural steel in the building" of a hangar (Hubler, p. 64). That makes it sound as if Jack Reagan actually drew the plans himself; but the hangar was designed—very skillfully—by the Evanston engineering firm of Robert H. Humphrey and Company.[29] The hangar was not an engineering coup on Jack's part, though it may well have entailed a feat of "human engineering" made necessary by CWA procedures.

The CWA was meant as a temporary measure to get the nation through the difficult winter of 1933–34. It aimed to put four million people to work in two months. In order to accomplish this—and not to conflict with Harold Ickes' longer-range public works projects (the PWA)—the Administration required that jobs be labor-intensive, involving no great investment in tools or material, and have a rapid completion schedule.[30] Jack's job was to get projects certified (approved) by the Chicago field office of the CWA.[31] When he could not meet the standards set by Washington—e.g., when work on a new high school entailed too much investment in materials—he was turned down.[32]

The Dixon airport, like many CWA projects, was already planned, the ground bought, plans chosen, publicity generated—Major Jimmy Doolittle had flown in to praise the site two months before Roosevelt was inaugurated.[33] This work on the runway could move to rapid completion with the infusion of federal money, so long as it did not entail too much investment in materials. Costs for the administration building were kept down by converting a farmhouse already there.[34] Jack Reagan had already cleared funds for the removal of Dixon's streetcar tracks, as part of the road improvement that took up a third of CWA funds nationwide.[35] It was presumably by making these girders available to the engineers that he kept costs of the material low enough to get federal approval for the hangar. The practipedist had finally made his big sale—as a clever bureaucrat. When the governor of Illinois came to dedicate the new airport, he said:

> Of particular interest is the type of construction of this hangar built, as it is, of old steel rails. This pioneering in the field of engineering may open up an entirely new use of this material and at the same time provide an inexpensive type of construction for buildings of this type.[36]

When it was time, in the New Deal's kaleidoscopic early days, for the CWA to melt back into FERA, Jack Reagan was one of five men from Lee County sent to Chicago to discuss the future of welfare in Illinois. For the first time in the *Daily Telegraph* he is called "director of the county program." Six months later, Ronald would get Neil a job as a radio announcer in Davenport. The bad times had been weathered. The New Deal bailed the Reagans out.

CHAPTER 7

Gabriel

Now, in a black moment of despair, came their leader,
their President, talking to them in their homes as
man-to-man, telling them he knew of their misery and
troubles, telling them that it is in no way their
fault, telling them with conviction and sincerity
that these bad things could and would be righted.

—*T. F. Tweed,* Gabriel over the White House

It is not surprising that Ronald Reagan would remember the New Deal as
arriving in Dixon sooner than it did. When, at last, it reached Washington, it
came like a whirlwind. The nation was begging, by then, for action, almost
any action.[1] Roosevelt had, among his many gifts, a great sense of theater.
The famous Hundred Days of legislative activity were preceded by one hundred and twenty days of suspense. President Hoover, more helpless than
most lame ducks as the banking crisis broke around him, begged Roosevelt
for help; but the new man did not want to act till he had a free hand, even
though some were telling him that delay would leave him nothing to rule in
March but a ruined country.[2] In February, businessmen, including Henry
Ford, refused cooperation with Hoover's Reconstruction Finance Corporation to arrange a loan for Michigan's tottering bank system, and the governor had to close that state's banks.[3] Members of Hoover's administration
bypassed him to ask Roosevelt directly for support of a national bank "holiday." By the eve of the inauguration, banking had been suspended in thirty-
eight states. Hoover telephoned Roosevelt twice, without result. The new
President was not to be rushed.[4]

Roosevelt had a precedent. The nation had been literally falling apart
toward the end of 1860. South Carolina seceded in December of that year;
four more states seceded in January, a fifth in February. James Buchanan
turned to the President-elect, who was keeping his distance in Springfield,
for a bipartisan response to the crisis; but Lincoln held his counsel in the
wreckage of the Union.[5] In fact, he had been silent for longer than one
hundred and twenty days. Since he had refused to give an acceptance speech,

or any campaign speech after being nominated, it had been over a year since he had made a policy statement (his Cooper Union address of February 27, 1860).[6] Lincoln's attitude before his own inauguration was that "a crisis must be reached and passed."[7] Lincoln would not talk military affairs, though secret and open arming was taking place, forts seized and surrendered.[8] Hysteria in Washington focused on apparent conspiracies in the cabinet, and Senator Wigfall from Texas tried to arrange a coup with the Secretary of War to overthrow Buchanan and put John C. Breckenridge in power before Lincoln reached Washington.[9]

In such turbulent times, it is shocking but not surprising that both presidents-elect were the targets of assassination attempts shortly before taking office. Lincoln foiled the plot against him by an ignominious secret journey through Baltimore.[10] The assassin stalking Roosevelt shot Anton Cermak, instead, the mayor of Chicago. This was on February 14, 1933, four days after Ronald Reagan had gone to work at the Davenport radio station. Cermak's death was another Illinois tie to a President who consciously defied party tradition by associating himself with Lincoln, the President whose visits were commemorated in Dixon. It was an association Roosevelt had courted as early as 1929, and one to which he later recruited three Lincoln hagiographers, who set the seal of the Great Emancipator on the New Deal.[11]

The disadvantages of the long interregnum of 1932–33 made the final states ratify the Twentieth Amendment, moving up, for future Presidents, the inauguration date. But this last long wait at the worst time for the economy, the assassination attempt, the banking crisis about to reach its height—all these added to the sense of drama around Roosevelt's jaunty proclamation that there was nothing to fear on March 4, 1933 (which was during the period when Ronald had been rehired "temporarily" in Davenport). Some critics claimed that Roosevelt had deliberately let the nation slide into disaster so he would be granted a free rein by people in their panic. And panic did lead to the immediate passage of the Economy Act as one of the first New Deal measures:

> He began by asking Lewis Douglas, on whom he early settled as his Director of the Budget, to draft for him powers of reorganization no other President had ever been able to wangle from a reluctant Congress. This touched their controls over the administrative establishment in so intimate a way that only the most extraordinary conditions could possibly persuade them to concede it. But those extraordinary conditions were impending and Franklin was determined to have the freedom of action he needed. If his proposal should be approved he could reduce or halt any operation and transfer funds to enlarge others. The excuse could be economy, or efficiency, or even merely "crisis."[12]

Congress was in a mood to give him that and more. So were the people. Something of the atmosphere of the times, its fears and promise, can be recaptured in the behind-the-scenes controversy over, and the near-suppression of, a movie being prepared for release as Roosevelt moved his slow way from election to inauguration. Its appearance in theaters was put off till the end of March, when the newly installed Roosevelt had either prevented or begun (according to one's views) the strongman's takeover of government celebrated in the film.

There was national uneasiness not only over the economy but over what was perceived as a crime wave connected with Prohibition. When Charles Lindbergh's son was kidnapped, even President Hoover felt moved to an exercise that always made him uncomfortable, a radio appeal to the nation.[13] Hollywood, assessing the public's fear, launched a cycle of vigilante pictures. Film historians have included in this context director Gregory La Cava's *Gabriel over the White House*.[14] But that movie had intellectual and political pretensions that made it seem more important, for the moment, than films like *This Day and Age*. *The Nation* shrewdly called *Gabriel* "the most important bad film of the year."[15] For one thing, the "intellectual" young Democrat, Walter Wanger, had promoted the project, and drew publisher William Randolph Hearst into it. Hearst even wrote parts of the dialogue.[16] This was during Hearst's pacifist period of isolationism, and he used the story to denounce war.[17] The movie's President signs a world peace covenant using Lincoln's Emancipation Proclamation quill, and he dies to the strains of the "Battle Hymn of the Republic."

Though Hearst produced his own pictures at MGM, under the Cosmopolitan subcredit invented to give him freedom in arranging Marion Davies's career, Louis Mayer was still head of the studio that would be releasing *Gabriel* into theaters during Hoover's last days at the White House. After seeing a preview in Glendale, Mayer told his henchman, Eddie Mannix, "Put that picture in its can, take it back to the studio, and lock it up!"[18] Wanger defended the film, while it was being vetted by conservative friends of Mayer in New York; it was finally released only after internal controversy, cuts, rewriting, and reshootings.[19]

Since the film shows a Lincolnesque Walter Huston (three years after he played Lincoln) waging a high-minded vendetta against crime, Mayer took it as an attack on the inaction of Hoover.[20] Later viewers have thought it suggested too clearly the fascistic possibilities of direct federal acts of the sort that Roosevelt would soon be taking. In any event, Mayer delayed the film's release until a month after Hoover had left office. Roosevelt ran it several times in the White House, where he enjoyed the fantasy.[21] Walter Lippmann was not as pleased. He wrote a column denouncing its "infantile" vision of politics, where "the nations agree to pay their debts and to disarm," as a mere "dramatization of Hearst's editorials."[22] Hearst was clearly taken with the novel on which the movie is based, especially its defense of the gold standard and its insistence that European war debts be paid—he serialized the novel in his New York *American;* but his favorite parts were de-emphasized in the movie.[23]

Thomas Frederick Tweed's novel, from which the movie was made, though crudely written, with Americanisms lifted from pulp magazines, has H. G. Wells's random-shot accuracy on some of the things to come. As a former confidential aide to David Lloyd George, the English author knew his politics, though he had not visited the Washington he describes.[24] Before the story degenerates into a war between the Chicago underworld and the White House, it is an imaginative exercise in how dictatorship might be introduced into America. Tweed imagines another, larger Bonus Army marching to Washington in the late 1930s, and a President putting himself at the head of it to break the power of corrupt congressmen and state legislatures.[25] With a touch of *Nineteen Eighty-four,* the President manipulates the army of unemployed through giant television screens. This was too futuristic for the movies, which had the President work his magic over radio. The President pushes through a National Emergency Resolution (p. 125). He uses a brains trust: "They were an extraordinary lot. Professors and instructors from some of the universities; journalists whose articles had interested him, and some very palpable cranks and fanatics" (p. 71). He creates a vast public works program, involving a National Reconstruction Corps (p. 144), new dams and hydraulic projects (p. 151), and rural electrification (p. 156). He has plans to pack the Supreme Court (p. 77). In all this he relies on a public relations expert, whose movie celebrating the new administration he covertly subsidizes (pp. 74–75). Then he appoints this propagandist to a new Department of Education (p. 79).

The movie was a box-office success, though it was selling "half-hearted" fascism according to *The New Republic* and plain fascism according to *The Nation.* The film had, it is true, been softened in response to Mayer's misgivings. And the New Deal, despite what Reagan would later claim about Mussolini's contributions to it, was never fascist. Still, even those sympathetic to Roosevelt found aspects of it disturbingly applicable to the new administration. The thing that seemed most relevant was the handling of the unemployed. Bruce Bliven wrote in *The New Republic:*

> Instead of shooting down an army of the unemployed which is marching on Washington, as his Cabinet planned, he [the Huston President] houses them in government tents, walks alone in their midst and promises them a scheme for employment almost exactly like Mr. Roosevelt's "peacetime army" . . . the audience cheers loudly both the promise of jobs for the unemployed and the threat of a big navy.[26]

The sense of crisis and the call for emergency powers in 1933 made it necessary to treat economic matters with the rhetoric of war. This is best seen in the use of the National Recovery Administration's "Blue Eagle" as a symbol for parades, rallies, and "patriotic" display. (In the novel, Green Jackets wage "war" on crime.) If even so pacific a matter as reforming business practices elicited a kind of martial fervor, we should not be surprised that the metaphor went farthur with Attorney General Homer Cummings's crusade against racketeers or Harry L. Hopkins's "army" of unemployed. The mobilization of four million workers within two months was presented as the greatest peacetime recruitment ever accomplished, and was ostentatiously studied by the War Department as a model for the wartime deployment of manpower.[27]

Spending, too, began on a wartime scale. As the man responsible for relief, mainly work relief, Harry Hopkins disbursed nine billion dollars. According to his biographer, "he had spent more than any man ever had in the history of the world."[28] Coming back from the White House with his first assignment from the President (as director of the FERA), "he spent over five million dollars in the first two hours of office."[29] As the head of the WPA, he worked under "the greatest single appropriation in the history of the United States or any other nation."[30]

Yet the man behind the FERA's vast power was unassuming, informal, as devoted to his task as the Lincolnian Walter Huston. Journalists loved Hopkins for his lofty ideals and earthy language, his slovenly ways. He seemed a Damon Runyon character drafted to take over Hull House from Jane Addams. He cut corners, invented new rules, improvised daily. "In his perpetual haste, Hopkins was contemptuous of bureaucratic procedure . . . Harry told the agencies to go to hell."[31] He was surprisingly like one of Hollywood's champions of "the little man," unpretentious yet powerful, just trying to give everyone a break.

This is the man for whom Jack Reagan worked, at FERA and CWA and (perhaps) WPA.[32] His son says Jack never criticized the Washington administration of these agencies, and no wonder. Ronald's own account presents Jack as a kind of local Harry Hopkins, hopscotching from agency to agency, repeating Hopkins's motions on a small scale, improvising, breaking rules, defying the bureaucracy:

> There was no bureaucracy at Jack's level . . . One thing sure, he didn't go by the rule book. It took him only a few weeks to start rounding up every odd job, every put-off chore from raking yards to thinning the woods at Lowell Park for the Park Board. He worked nights arranging a round-robin schedule so that every week a number of the men in the line got jobs for a few days or a week. [Hubler, p. 63]

What Reagan is remembering is the rush to find jobs in November and December of 1933, when Hopkins made money available for four million positions if the local people could justify them. Hopkins, like Jack in Ronald's book, was all for work relief as opposed to direct relief (the dole). So, as Reagan realizes, was President Roosevelt. The Hubler book quotes the State of the Union address of 1935: "To dole out relief is to administer a narcotic, a subtle destroyer of the human spirit. The Federal government must, and shall, quit this business of relief."[33]

Reagan does not give the source for his Roosevelt quote; it is the speech where the President asked for the largest appropriation in the history of the nation, primarily to support the WPA. The scale of this request indicates one problem with work relief—it *cost* a great deal more than the dole, which is one reason conservatives of the time opposed it.[34] Roosevelt, too, worried about the costs, since he was still a fiscal conservative in 1935. It was Harry Hopkins who, time after time, convinced Roosevelt that he should, just for now, throw money at a problem—to get through the winter, to get through the next election, to cope with natural disasters. And it was Hopkins who finally broke down Roosevelt's principled resistance to deficit spending. Rexford Tugwell, who had worked unsuccessfully to accomplish the same thing, gives Hopkins credit for this late conversion of 1938:

> His revulsion against inflation and an unbalanced budget was strong. He tended always to consider them evidence of incapacity; and whenever he surrendered to the necessity for using them, he was under compulsion to explain away or camouflage the action. This was the first time—after four years—that he appears to have accepted, not only theoretically but as a matter of positive governmental virtue, the management of income and outgo as a regulator of the economy. This genuine conversion can be credited to Harry Hopkins as much as to anyone.[35]

Marriner Eccles, director of the Federal Reserve Board, agrees with the timing of Roosevelt's conversion, and with Hopkins's responsibility for it.[36]

So Jack Reagan not only worked for "the New Deal" in general, but for the man and the agencies responsible for the most obnoxious parts of that program in the eyes of conservatives, then and now—vast spending on a permanent basis, government intrusion into the production of goods and services, large federal payrolls with consequent nationwide standards for wages and hours (affecting those of the private market). Reagan's praise of his father for being antirelief and antibureaucracy is paralleled in many descriptions of Hopkins by his friends or advocates. But we must take with some critical reservations Ronald's assurance that "there was no bureaucracy at Jack's level." In the Illinois State Archives at Springfield, I cut open for the first time since they were tied up in 1937 the inventories of Lee County projects approved under the CWA (1933–34). They make up a great deal of paperwork. When Jack Reagan stayed up nights finding new jobs for people, he was filling out forms for the Chicago field office, applying for the certification of projects. If this certification was denied (as the high school construction was) there would be no work for Jack's beneficiaries. What Reagan points to as his father's greatest achievement—the combining of two projects to make the second one possible in the case of Dixon's airport hangar—was a *bureaucratic* maneuver that showed Jack had learned to play well the game of satisfying the field office's requirements. He improvised by knowing the rules well enough to use them to his advantage.

Besides, in this context, being antibureaucratic often means opposing the *other* fellow's bureaucracy. Ronald describes his father as opposed to "the locals," not to the national administrators. It was an attitude Hopkins's troops shared with their leader, who had suffered under the necessity of channeling his early relief through state and local agencies already in place. They worked to escape those confines in setting up the CWA and WPA. (One of Hopkins's objections to state control of FERA hiring—local patronage—did not, presumably, bother Jack and Neil Reagan as much as others.) Conservatives, then as now, sided with local government in the name of states' rights, "federalism," and the distribution of power. In working for federal control, Jack Reagan was on the radical edge of the New Deal, along with Hopkins.[37]

Ronald Reagan identifies only one concrete issue that brought Jack into conflict with the local authorities, the contentious matter of a means test for work relief. For early relief projects, under the FERA, Hopkins had to follow the practice of many local agencies in offering work only to the indigent—i.e., to those who first qualified for relief. When he set up the CWA in November of 1933, he omitted that provision for several reasons—the pressing task was to find four million plausible jobs and fill them as rapidly as possible without quibbling over the workers' qualifications. Much of the CWA labor was going to be temporary makework anyway, as even Roosevelt admitted in his 1935 State of the Union address, when he gave a different rationale for the WPA.[38]

When Roosevelt, against Hopkins's protests, disbanded the CWA after the winter of 1933–34, projects with a forseeable end (including the Dixon hangar) reverted to the FERA, which meant that some people now at work on them were disqualified for employment by the old rules. This led to confusion, some fraud, and some humiliation—people not previously on relief had to sign up for it to retain their jobs for the remainder of the projects' life.[39]

This is the situation Reagan refers to in a somewhat confused way. He remembers that Jack opposed a means test, but he thinks relief *dis*qualified people for work rather than qualified them:

> The day came when Jack, who'd kept right on in his regular routine, told a group he had a week's work for them and they said, "Jack we can't take it." To his stunned surprise, he was told that the last time they took his jobs the new welfare staff had cut them off relief. Then their cases had to be reopened with interviews, applications, and new cards. The process took three weeks and in the meantime their families went hungry—all because they'd done a few days' honest work. [Hubler, p. 64]

Since Reagan was in Iowa throughout his father's service with the New Deal, it is not surprising that he is vague about some of its details. For one thing, Jack did not hand out the work relief jobs; that was the task of the registration officer (in Dixon, Tim Sullivan).[40] When Jack became county director of the CWA, he needed a full-time registrar under him to keep the elaborate work rolls required by the administration (in part as a protection against charges of waste and corruption).

Ronald also makes this conflict occur while Jack was working for the WPA. He lumps all his father's experiences together under that agency's title; but that is particularly misleading here, because Hopkins himself returned to the means test when the WPA was set up in 1935—for the very reason advanced by Roosevelt in the speech Reagan quotes with approval. The aim was to *eliminate relief;* public *work* would have to go to all those who had previously been on relief. Only when that pool had been entirely exhausted would the WPA be allowed to hire elsewhere.⁴¹ Reagan's use of the Roosevelt quote in connection with Jack's work indicates what we would expect in any case—continuing agreement between Jack on the local scene and Hopkins in Washington in 1935. That Ronald thinks of his father as working *only* for the WPA shows that Jack's loyalty, if nothing else, continued into the WPA period, means test or no means test. Even the touchy Jack, his son says, never criticized his bosses in Washington. Least of all the blunt man behind all the relief projects Jack worked on. If the Reagan family was bailed out by the New Deal in general, it was more specifically rescued because Harry Hopkins was, for Jack Reagan, a Gabriel over Dixon.

CHAPTER 8

G-Men

Don't shoot, G-Men!

—Machine Gun Kelly, in the FBI version

Ronald Reagan has described himself as briefly in thrall to the New Deal, giving various dates and reasons for his disenchantment. William Leuchtenburg, sifting the several accounts, established that Reagan's voting loyalty to the Democratic Party lasted at least through the 1950 election, when, as a member of the Hollywood branch of the Americans for Democratic Action, he campaigned for Helen Gahagan Douglas against Richard Nixon.[1] But one cannot say that Reagan entirely gave up his devotion to the New Deal at any time. His personal admiration for Roosevelt is continuing and confessed. But, beyond that, we tend to look back with blinkers at what we call the New Deal, forgetting there were many New Deals, not only relief for the unemployed but social security for the employed, credit for businessmen and farmers, organizing rights for unions, recognition for the arts, and—not the least in its impact at the time—federal protection from crime.

The activist government that came in with Franklin Roosevelt was symbolized by the exploits of the Government Man, the G-Man. In that age of proliferating bureaus, no bureaucrat emerged with greater skill at enhancing his department than J. Edgar Hoover. Indeed, the contrast between the two Hoovers—Herbert C. and J. Edgar—expressed, for many, the whole difference between Republican indifference up to 1933 and Democratic energy afterward. An admiring versifyer in the *Saturday Evening Post* was still boasting of the difference in 1943, calling J. Edgar the bane of

> Spies who double-X this G-Man
> (No relation to the Herbert C. Man).[2]

Because of widespread defiance of the Eighteenth Amendment during the nineteen-twenties, people came to believe that a "crime wave" had swept over the nation. This was probably an illusion, fostered by a few notorious criminals glamorized by the press.[3] But the Republican presidents of the twenties, with their ideological reliance on state and local authorities, were unable to counter the image of national violence with any national response. Treasury agents charged with stopping border and interstate trade in alcohol were insufficient in numbers, training, and integrity. The nascent FBI had been given a bad name by A. Mitchell Palmer's use of it in the 1919 Red Raids and its protection of corrupt members in the Harding administration. President Hoover had no desire to widen its still limited mandate.[4] Meanwhile, the impression of a paralyzed national government, afraid to confront local crime lords, became part of the national mythology. State governments —especially Illinois, which sheltered the "anticapital" of crime, Chicago— were supposed to be entirely in thrall to the mobs.

Thomas Frederick Tweed had a solution for the problem. In his novel, published the month of Roosevelt's inauguration, the President appoints his most successful bureaucrat, who had run the propagandistic Department of Education, to the Department of Public Safety:

> Your new department will undertake the organization of a national force for criminal investigation and the prevention of crime throughout the country. It is a big job, Lindsey, but I know you can handle it . . . I don't expect Illinois, New York and New Jersey to recognize Federal authority for the transfer of their police. Until we have got amenable legislatures in all three States it is too much to expect. But it has always been a Federal obligation to see that a multitude of laws covering interstate commerce, Federal taxation and the sale of liquor are enforced, and this applies to New York and Chicago just as much as to the rest of the United States. It will be one of the earliest tasks of your new department to see to it, in these cities, despite gangsters, corrupt politicians and an intimidated populace, that the law is respected, feared and obeyed [p. 179].

The New Deal, that is, had the same problem in law enforcement as in public works and the dispensing of relief—how to get around obstructive state authorities. The problem was "the locals."

Homer Cummings, Roosevelt's Attorney General, also realized that his first target had to be the heavily publicized gangsters. He believed that an equally publicized effort against them could undo the mischief done by panic. He declared "war" on Machine Gun Kelly and other headline figures:

> It is almost like a military engagement between the forces of law and order and the underworld army, heavily armed. It is a campaign to wipe out the public enemy, and it will proceed until it succeeds.[5]

In the movie *Gabriel over the White House,* gangsters are rounded up and put on Ellis Island for summary execution. Cummings decided to establish a superprison for his supercriminals, an American Devil's Island. The Army obliged him by turning over its military prison on Alcatraz. Cummings predicted that Machine Gun Kelly and Harvey Bailey would be captured and put on "The Rock." Al Capone was transferred there.

Cummings put Joseph B. Keenan, famous for prosecuting Ohio criminals, in charge of his crime war, with J. Edgar Hoover training and directing agents. The emphasis was on science, especially the use of expanded fingerprint files. As Charles Coe wrote in the New York *Times* for July 13, 1933:

> They will have at their fingertips a complete international identification bureau. They will use radio, telegraph, telephone, photographs, fingerprints, Bertillon [body] measurements—use in fact every science known to criminal detection.[6]

The crooks were going to be outorganized. The enlarged fingerprint became an icon of war, so popular that theaters showing crime films set up fingerprinting pads in their lobbies—one could enroll in the war against crime by putting one's prints on record. This was so popular that J. Edgar Hoover made it an official program, promoted in tours of the FBI building and in the authorized books.[7] Applicants for work on WPA projects were fingerprinted as part of the war on crime, to eliminate those with criminal records.[8]

Hollywood, always quick to go to war, had many reasons for joining Homer Cummings's crusade. By glamorizing mobsters in a flood of crime movies during Herbert Hoover's last years in office (twenty-five such films in 1931, forty in 1932), the studios met criticism for "glorifying" crime, criticism which led to the enforcement of the Production Code that had been drafted but ignored in 1930.[9] Warner Brothers had made the most famous and violent gangster films; but now Jack Warner was a friend and supporter of Roosevelt and the New Deal. He brought a train of Warners stars to FDR's inauguration, visited at the White House, fished with the President, made pictures at his request.[10] Already in 1933 Warners was redeeming rebellious youths who fled corrupt cities (in *Wild Boys of the Road*) by "a selling reference to the New Deal arrangement of the Civilian Conservation Corps, serving to take thousands of young men from the streets and freight cars."[11]

Jack Warner also cultivated, and was cultivated by, J. Edgar Hoover. Warner was among the first to realize that, by joining the war against crime, Hollywood could retain its violence and portray it as redemptive. Instead of glorifying the criminal, all one had to do was glorify the criminal's conqueror. In support of the "war effort" against public enemies, the FBI approved an exemption from Code restrictions on the depiction of crime, so long as federal agents were shown prevailing over the crooks.[12]

Warner Bros. repaid the bureau by celebrating the new FBI in *G-Men* (1935), a movie that let agent James Cagney show viewers through the famous laboratories and display fingerprint charts.[13] *Liberty* called it "the first of many pictures of the same patriotic air now in feverish production at all the major studios. *G-Men* is one long, lusty paean in homage to our federal agents."[14]

Cagney is recruited, in the film, by a friend who tells him he will be above local corruption in a federal bureau: "No fat-face politicians telling you what to do.''[15] And the film makes an explicit plea for more federal laws, and more heavy artillery in the hands of the federal warriors. The film's grave director, played by judge-type Addison Richards, tells a Senate committee:

> Give us national laws . . . Make bank-robbery and kidnapping a Federal crime . . . Make it a Federal crime to kill a Government agent and to flee across state lines to avoid arrest . . . [Arm agents] not just with revolvers, but with machine-guns, shotguns, teargas, everything else. This is war.[16]

In 1935, this was a celebration on film of the laws that were passed in Congress, at Cummings's urging, through May and June of 1934. It is a quirk of dramaturgy that the Director of the Bureau has to be seen testifying to Congress and dealing with agents in the field, personifying the war on crime not at the top level—in Homer Cummings, or his assistant Keenan—but in the master of the files, who is proleptically brought before Congress, a role Hoover would make a star turn in his later career. Richard Gid Powers dates the beginning of Hoover's myth—and explains Cummings's displeasure with the movie—from this narrative device.

G-Men did not get Justice Department authorization when it appeared, though Hoover had supported its exemption from the Code. There were probably several reasons for this, beyond the fact that the Attorney General became a nonperson in the film. The FBI was no doubt loath to take credit for outright defiance of the Production Code, or for comments on corrupt local officials. The Cagney charisma, in an organization that emphasized submission rather than initiative, may have been disconcerting so soon after Cagney had made criminals glamorous. The FBI at first imitated the President in *Gabriel over the White House,* who subsidizes a movie promoting his own policy, but does it secretly. By 1949, when the movie was re-released on an anniversary of the FBI, Hoover filmed an introduction for it, and it bore the Bureau's seal. It had always borne it, invisibly.

Warner Bros. was known in the thirties as the studio of "social consciousness," and—more especially—as the studio of the New Deal, one that flashed big posters of FDR and the Blue Eagle during Cagney's dance act in *Gold Diggers of 1933.* There was nothing more typical of Warners, or of the New Deal, than the celebration of the new "feds" under J. Edgar Hoover. As Nick Roddick contends, in his book on Warners and the New Deal, the Roosevelt administration was meant to reassure, and even Warners' most "searing" films tried to strike that note, too, throughout the Depression.[17]

The Warners association with G-Men was a continuing one. In 1937, the year Reagan joined the studio, Warners released an important contribution to the legend of the feds' awesome "Rock" (as it is called in the opening sequence), *Alcatraz Island.* The tough discipline of the place is emphasized by showing the ordeal of a minor criminal sent there by accident. The reassurance comes when his life is saved by an FBI undercover man posing as a prisoner to correct any such lapses in the federal system.[18]

Jack Warner wooed Hoover through the years. But he had heavy competition. The spy-catching FBI man of World War II movies is familiar from late-night television, but we may forget that there was also a scramble to get aboard the patriotic bandwagon during the crime war of the thirties. MGM did a series of anticrime shorts, the Crime Does Not Pay series, that won such approval from Hoover that one was made a feature at his suggestion.[19] Paramount went further: in 1938, it bought the rights to Hoover's ghostwritten book, *Persons in Hiding,* and spun four films from it, including the first film version of the Bonnie and Clyde story (banned under the Code from less authoritative retellings).[20] Since Warners lost the Hoover memoirs, it bought the next-best thing, rights to the files of the only "fed" who could claim some seniority to Hoover. William Herman Moran had been in the Secret Service for fifty-five years, its director for eighteen of them (1918–37).[21] The studio ran its four Moran-based movies at the same time Paramount was doing the Hoover series (1939–40).

The Secret Service is part of the Treasury Department, which had a larger police force than the Justice Department for most of our history. A good deal of its police work involved the evasion of federal taxes, especially on alcohol (Treasury men were the hated "revenuers"), and the department's role in the Prohibition era was not a matter of pride. But the Secret Service, aside from guarding the President, tracks counterfeits of the money printed by its department, and Moran's memoirs were first written up (by Lee Katz and Dean Franklin) as *Smashing the Money Ring.*[22] The material had to be stretched, and shaped into separate plots with a continuing agent as hero. The agent was Ronald Reagan, in his first heroic part. He had, to this point, played in even more fugitive B films, or as sidekick to the lead (to Wayne Morris or Pat O'Brien). Here, for the first time, he would be given his own sidekick. Eddie Foy, Jr., was Reagan's Reagan, called his "stooge" in some of the screenplays.

It was as agent Brass Bancroft that Reagan became what he calls "the Errol Flynn of the B's" (Hubler, p. 96). In 1939, Jane Wyman was serving a similar Warners apprenticeship in the Torchy Blane ("girl reporter") series. Reagan says that the factual accounts behind the Bancroft series bored Bryan Foy, the producer, "so he threw away everything but the title" (Hubler, p. 96). Actually, the first film to be released changed the title—it was now called *Secret Service of the Air*—and there was an attempt to make the governmental background seem authentic. Studio stills showed Moran "consulting" with Reagan on the set,[23] and John Litel—a dignified authority figure—was "Moran" in the movie, the director who recruits Reagan. "Brass Bancroft" is a free-lance aviator who helps capture smugglers bringing counterfeit money and illegal aliens into the country. The second picture, *Code of the Secret Service,* sent Reagan to Mexico in pursuit of counterfeiters. The third used the scriptwriters' first choice of title, *Smashing the Money Ring,* and imitated the plot of *Alcatraz Island*—Reagan goes into prison as an undercover agent to get the goods on a counterfeiting ring. The New

York *Times* review called it "exciting enough to hold the interest throughout."[24]

By the fourth picture, *Murder in the Air*, Reagan's mandate as a government man is larger and vaguer than at the outset. Counterfeiting has dropped from the plot entirely, and Reagan, in the prewar atmosphere of 1940, is searching for the spies that Warners had been the first Hollywood studio to discover within our borders—the preceding year, Edward G. Robinson had been a J. Edgar figure in *Confessions of a Nazi Spy*.[25] Reagan's far cruder film looks farther ahead in spy technology—he must protect from enemy agents an early Star Wars device, the Inertia Projector, which knocks planes out of the air at a distance of four miles.

Though Reagan was formally a T-man in this series, not a G-man as the FBI had popularized that term, he was a *federal* officer, and few in the audience made much distinction.[26] The series was capitalizing on the popularity of energetic government action against crime, spies, and the underworld. In the screenplay for *Murder in the Air*, Reagan's superior tells him: "Our President has planned to coordinate all detective forces of the Treasury, Justice, State, War, Navy and Post Office Departments, in a concerted drive to spike the maneuvers of foreign spies, saboteurs and provocateurs." This extended to foreign agents the war on crime that Homer Cummings had launched so successfully and J. Edgar Hoover continued with such dedication. In this, Reagan was very much a part of the Warners team, and Warners was very much the New Deal studio. It is simplistic to say that even the later Reagan was against active government at the federal level. Certain parts of the federal bureaucracy, including the military and the federal policing and intelligence agencies, continued to have his support; and they were part of the original federal expansion that was effected during the Roosevelt administration. Reagan worked on the screen for one government bureau, just as his father and brother had worked for other bureaus in Illinois. In the 1930s, whatever their earlier or later differences, all the Reagan men were G-men. This was more appropriate for people who had lived along the Mississippi and Rock Rivers than the two younger Reagans seem to have realized, even in the 1930s. There was more government in their history than they knew.

CHAPTER 9

"Govment"

*The West was in large part explored by men who were
acting on commission from one or other arm of government.*

—Richard Hofstadter

Despite Reagan's qualified support for New Deal programs in Dixon, the views he later adopted were those of Huck's father, "Pap" Finn:

> Whenever his liquor begun to work, he most always went for the govment. This time he says: "Call this a govment! why just look at it and see what it's like. Here's the law a-standing ready to take a man's son away from him—a man's own son, which he has had all the trouble and all the anxiety and all the expense of raising. Yet, just as that man has got that son raised at last, and ready to go to work and begin to do suthin' for *him* and give him a rest, the law up and goes for him. And they call that govment! . . . Here's a govment that calls itself a govment, and lets on to be a govment, and thinks it is is a govment, and yet's got to set stock-still for six whole months before it can take ahold of a prowling, thieving infernal, whiteshirted free nigger, and—" (Ch. 6)

Pap, that is, hates the meddling of social workers (Judge Thatcher taking custody of Huck) and of regulators (the Missouri rule against expelling freed blacks instantly). The specifics are not ones that make us admire Pap Finn, who is the principal ogre of Huck's nightmares. But the general headings of Pap's indictment Reagan would subscribe to. The government should stay out of family affairs, and keep its regulations to a minimum.

Yet Reagan was born into a town literally flushed with an infusion of government money. Tampico had a ruddy new street of bricks, a crisp line of brick buildings with ambitious cornices.[1] Ronald was born on the spacious second floor of one building in that row, above a bakery recently converted from a bar when the Tampico laws—coming and going on the issue, session by session—once more outlawed liquor. St. Mary's, the Catholics' gothic brick church, the biggest church in the county, was dedicated two years before Jack Reagan moved there.[2] Tampico was differentiating itself from the "wood towns" of Twain's youth—including the one ironically called Bricksville in *Huckleberry Finn.*

Tampico even had its own new trolley, which farmers could flag as it corkscrewed through twelve miles of their farms, veering where it could coax right of way from land holders. The HTY (Hooppole, Yorktown, and Tampico Railroad) made one regular run a day, and special trips to collect and return people for fairs, dances, or other large events in town. It made six runs on the Fourth of July in 1910, its first year of operation. The train was called "the Dummy" since it had no turntable for the engine, which had to back up the whole length of track in order to go forward again. This is the train that often stood in front of the Reagans' house on Glassburn Avenue, at a time when Neil and Ronald played under the railway cars.[3]

The train went into operation in 1910, the year of Mark Twain's death, and it seemed to justify his prediction of mechanical wonders and prosperity along the upper river. Its construction involved seventy teams of horses and mules, providing over two years of jobs and ancillary services to what at Reagan's birth was a boomtown. And this was just the beginning. Plans were already made to electrify the trolley line (that is why it had no turntable) and extend it north from town as well as south. Lou Cannon has written that Tampico was so small in 1911 that it lacked a doctor, but in fact it had four.[4] It had two hotels, one just two doors away from the Reagan home on Glassburn. In the very year Jack Reagan came to town, the citizens felt prosperous enough to raise a granite monument seventeen feet tall to honor the soldiers of the Union Army, though Tampico did not even exist during the Civil War.[5]

What had made this small farming center of 1,500 people blossom in the early years of the century? Tampico had not been a town when the railroad decided to make a stop at John Glassburn's grain elevator in 1871. It became a post office stop in the same year, and was incorporated as a village four years later.[6] The town acquired a bright future, as the twentieth century was opening, because of the lure of the Mississippi, just twenty-seven miles away from Tampico.

Since the founding of the nation, the dream of threading the continent with canals had been considered an urgent national task. The immediate model for such a project, England's extensive canal system, had been based on private enterprise; but there was never any question of waiting for the accumulation of capital in private hands that this would entail in America.[7] The state of New York financed the Erie Canal, completed in 1825, and the federal government itself became a partner in building the Chesapeake and Ohio Canal.[8] Jefferson's Secretary of the Treasury, Albert Gallatin, proposed in 1808 a national ten-year plan for interconnected roads and canals.[9] By 1835, when the railroads had laid barely 800 miles of track, there were already 2,000 miles of canals.[10]

But no beginning had yet been made on a scheme contained in John

Calhoun's national plan for canals of 1816—the linking of the Great Lakes with the Mississippi.[11] Work on that started the next year, 1836, financed by bonds issued on the credit from 300,000 acres of land granted to the project by Congress. The resulting canal system "made Chicago the metropolis of the Mississippi valley."[12]

Water passage from America's greatest inland lakes to its greatest river had seemed within tantalizing reach from the time when Louis Joliet reached the Mississippi by way of the Wisconsin River (1673) and Louis Hennepin reached it by the Illinois (1679). But each had to begin his trip from Lake Michigan with portages. Joliet's was the more difficult. He went up rapids to Lake Winnebago, and needed Indian help to make his way through a watery maze to the Wisconsin. Francis Parkman, the patient retracer of Joliet's steps, who felt the lure of the Mississippi himself, and influenced Twain's descriptions of it, recounts the problems:

> The river twisted among lakes and marshes choked with wild rice; and, but for the guides, they could scarcely have followed the perplexed and narrow channel. It brought them at last to the portage, where, after carrying their canoes a mile and a half over the prairie and through the marsh, they launched them on the Wisconsin, bade farewell to the waters that flowed to the St. Lawrence, and committed themselves to the current that was to bear them they knew not whither . . .[13]

Father Hennepin, who started down the Illinois with La Salle, but preceded him down the Mississippi in 1679, had less initial difficulty; but he and La Salle also left their ship, *The Griffin*, in Lake Michigan, never to be retrieved, and carried their canoes inland:

> They soon reached a spot where the oozy, saturated soil quaked beneath their tread. All around were clumps of alder-bushes, tufts of rank grass, and pools of glistening water. In the midst, a dark and lazy current, which a tall man might stride, crept twisting like a snake among the weeds and rushes. Here were the sources of the Kankakee, one of the heads of the Illinois. They set their canoes on this thread of water, embarked their baggage and themselves, and pushed down the sluggish streamlet, looking, at a little distance, like men who sailed on land.[14]

The Illinois, slanting across the entire state with the same name, was the more promising thoroughfare, but a way would have to be found to tap directly into Lake Michigan, bypassing the river's spongy beginnings. The canal begun in 1836 ran from the mouth of the Chicago River, and picked up the Illinois ninety-six miles on its course, at a town named for the explorer, La Salle. The freight traffic down it could serve the whole lower Mississippi; but, since the mouth of the Illinois is just north of St. Louis, one would have to go far south and churn north against the Mississippi's current to reach the upper towns whose prosperity Twain was predicting in the 1880s—this despite the fact that these towns are closer to the Great Lakes than to St. Louis. The solution seemed obvious: a second canal, downstream from La Salle, to connect the Illinois to a more northern point on the Mississippi. If it could meet the Mississippi where the Rock River runs into it, a plentiful supply of water for the canal's locks seemed assured. That meant the canal would go to Moline, which faces Davenport across the river.

We are now in the Gilded Age of suspect federal largesse; so there was no question of the state's building its own canal, or getting mere land rights from Congress. In 1890, half a million dollars in federal funds were directly allocated to the canal, and the United States Army Engineering Corps began excavating in 1892; thus a great public works program—the last major inland canal to be built in America—came just in time to alleviate the blow of depression in the 1890s. Partly with that in mind, Congress expanded the plan in the worst year of the depression, 1894, adding a feeder canal to tap water into the main canal from some higher point on the Rock River.[15] New technology gave the canal great promise. It would be the first one with locks anchored in poured cement, built with techniques later used on the Panama Canal.

There had been the usual war of competitive surveys, influence, and trips to Washington, to decide where, on the Rock River, the feeder should originate. The two favored sites were Dixon and Sterling. Two men from Sterling, C. C. Johnson and C. L. Sheldon, went to Washington to influence the Secretary of War, Redfield Proctor, and their city won.[16] In 1898, work on the eleven-mile feeder canal began, and this is the section that ran just to the east of Tampico, which had its own landing on the canal. Frances Aldrich Rakow, who attended the fourth and part of the fifth grades with Ronald Reagan, preserves her grandfather's diaries, which recall how men were lodged in the town and horses cared for at Mr. Aldrich's stables during the building of the canal. There was a coming and going of sales agents, surveyers, and laborers for the next decade. Jack Reagan, moving into town a year before the system formally opened, had come to the center of action. His move from Fulton followed that of the steamboat *City of Winona,* which used to run people from Fulton to Davenport and back, until, in 1904, there was better business to be had plying the Hennepin.[17]

The prosperity induced by the canal system did not last. The Hennepin was a governmental anachronism, a grand canal system in the age of railroads, and it never did the business expected of it.[18] Jack Reagan moved on, and so did much else—in time the hotels, the trolley, the canal boats, the newspaper. But the point of the story for Reagan's life is that he was born into a world that might fairly be described as Pap Finn's nightmare—one in which "govment" was everywhere, the Army surveyors and engineers, the bureaucrats, the bought officials, the boondoggles that people welcomed because they put others to work, including Jack Reagan at the Pitney Store.

Nor was this an isolated instance of federal influence over the region. Inland Township, where Bennett, Iowa, was laid out shortly after Jack Reagan's birth, was founded by settlers who had acquired their land with the federal scrip issued to veterans and the heirs of veterans. "A check of the original patent sales of Inland land showed that of 269 parcels sold, only 28 were purchased with cash. All others were bought with land warrants."[19] There was a market in these warrants, which were traded as food stamps would later be; but the warrants were more valuable. The economic importance of such warrants, and the political usefulness of issuing them, is made vivid in the case of the first Illinois President. He served for eighty days as a volunteer in the Black Hawk War of 1832, with these veteran's benefits from that slight military experience:

> Lincoln received a lump payment in 1833 of $125. In 1852 he got a land warrant for 40 acres in Iowa (which he sold during the Civil War) and in 1856 another warrant for 120 acres in Illinois. Land sold for $1.00 an acre when it came on the market and appreciated rapidly. Therefore it might be argued that Abraham Lincoln made more money per diem as a volunteer in the war than he did in any other job before or after, exclusive of the presidency.[20]

The Black Hawk War is important to Reagan's Illinois background, since two of the early towns he lived and worked in—Dixon and Davenport— were founded on federal grants resulting from it. The war was also an example of the federal government's protection of citizens' questionable claims to Indian lead mines and farms. Black Hawk, not a chief, was the leader of a resisting faction within the Sauk tribe. Sauk chiefs, in alliance with Fox leaders, were conducting the most advantageous retreat they could contrive against the advance of white men into their farming and burial grounds. (They already had to move west for their seasonal hunting and trapping seasons.) By the 1830s, the next line to be yielded in Illinois was the Mississippi shore. The government claimed that it had won rights to the land in 1804, but left the Indians free to live in prescribed areas. The Indians denied that they had surrendered their rights, but withdrew to the designated places.[21] Meanwhile, the governor of Illinois, under pressure from constituents who wanted the land and the lead mines, was demanding that Indians no longer remain in the state.

The state of Illinois, only fourteen years old in 1832, was clamorous for hegemony over what the citizens considered their territory. Governor John Reynolds complied with their wishes. The Sauk leaders, negotiating through their council spokesman, Keokuk, tried to receive compensatory advantages in the next line of fallback, Iowa. But Black Hawk, whose village was at the conjunction of the Rock River with the Mississippi (where the Hennepin Canal would have its western terminus, across from the future city of Davenport), came back from his hunting season in 1831, and tried to repossess the village whites had already moved into.[22] The militia was called out to prevent a repetition of this in 1832—Black Hawk would be stopped when he tried to cross back from his trapping season west of the Mississippi.

The federal army, fearful with good cause of the militia—which was made up of undisciplined Indian haters, and made more trouble than it settled—

tried to place regular army troops between the contending factions.[23] But
when the troops arriving at Rock Island from St. Louis seemed inadequate
to the reports (which proved false) of support for Black Hawk growing in
other tribes, the militia was hastened forward, and precipitated the needless
"war" by getting drunk, murdering an Indian ambassador, attacking Black
Hawk where he was encamped with only part of his band, and getting part
of itself "massacred."[24]

This had occurred up the Rock River, above what became Dixon, since
the federal troops were in their fort on Rock Island, facing the site of Black
Hawk's village. Instead of trying to return to his village in 1832, as the
whites had feared, Black Hawk crossed the Mississippi south of it, and
joined the Prophet, a charismatic young Indian seer, who offered to share his
Rock River village. (The site, present Prophetstown, is eight miles from the
place where Reagan was born.) The Prophet convinced Black Hawk, from
visions, that there was British support to be won for his resistance movement
farther up the Rock River. By the time Black Hawk found that these dreams
were false, and was ready to surrender, the incident with the militia had
occurred. Now he had to take his band of a thousand, half of it women and
children—it was always a homing party, not a war party[25]—and try to escape across the Mississippi by Joliet's route, along the Wisconsin to the
north.

But by this time the continued defiance of Black Hawk was an embarrassment to the Jackson administration in the midst of an election year. The
President decided to rush troops from the East Coast, under General Winfield Scott, for a swift elimination of this nuisance.[26] The soldiers, entrained
from Forts McHenry and Monroe, ran into a cholera epidemic spreading
from Canada and became its carriers.[27] The local military, under pressure to
accomplish the task itself, intercepted Black Hawk when he crossed the
Wisconsin, and tried to kill his whole band at "the Battle of Wisconsin
Heights"—an outcome prevented only by Black Hawk's brilliant evasive
tactics. Forced north overland with a dwindling band of followers, out of
supplies, Black Hawk tried at least twice to surrender, but could not cheat
the pursuers of their prize.[28] He was finally trapped on the Mississippi shore
just above the government fort at Prairie du Chien, which sent out a warship
to cruise the river and stop the Indians' passage.[29] The Sauk were butchered
as they dispersed and tried to hide in swamps. Some warriors slipped across
the river and were scalped by Sioux warriors the government had recruited
for this purpose. Of the one thousand who had returned to Illinois four
months earlier, only about one hundred and fifty (Black Hawk among them)
survived into captivity.[30]

It was to serve in this glorious episode that Abraham Lincoln, with an eye
on his first candidacy as a state legislator, enlisted in the militia.[31] He treated
the experience, afterward, with proper irony.[32] He had seen no fighting, but
was part of the force that reached the Rock River at the abandoned village of
the Prophet. A modern antiquarian in Prophetstown took strange pride, and

liberties with truth, in boasting that he lived in a town once put to the torch by the great President.[33] The citizens of Dixon were more reverential to the man who served at Dixon's Ferry, the main military post on the Rock River during the first stage of the war, the place from which the earliest group of militia went out to start the war in partial stupor.[34] Lincoln returned to Dixon in the 1850s, after Dixon's Ferry had become a town, and stayed at the Nachusa Hotel, a decrepit building now housing the elderly. But the statue of him on the town's riverfront shows him as a young captain of militia, wearing a sword—though he says he owned none at the time.[35] There is now a proposal among the citizens of Dixon to raise a companion statue to their other "local" President—who, it must be admitted, saved more lives along the Rock River than Lincoln, or any other militiaman, could lay claim to.

Dixon's Ferry, as it was called when Lincoln arrived with his fellow soldiers, was named for the army supplier who traded at the ferry, John Dixon, who was rewarded for his services in the war with a land grant he laid out as a town in 1834. In 1840, Dixon relied on the good relations he had established with officers at Rock Island, including Lieutenant Jefferson Davis, when he went to Washington and lobbied successfully to have the Land Office of the area moved from Galena to Dixon.[36] The city Reagan would grow up in was put on the path to prosperity by government action, interference, influence, and subsidy. Federal help not only added a few improvements in the 1930s, when Jack Reagan organized New Deal projects— the river-front park Jack's son praises, the airport, etc. The government supplied the very ground and means of subsistence from the outset of Dixon's history.

The history of Davenport is similar to Dixon's, but played on a larger scene, since it is a Mississippi town. George Davenport, like John Dixon, was a military supplier. He worked from Rock Island, now Arsenal Island, the large site Twain visited (to marvel at the munitions factory) in 1882. By the time Black Hawk was delivered up, and the authorities were ready to dictate future terms to the Sauk council, soldiers from the East had reached Rock Island with the cholera panic; so negotiations took place on the Iowa shore facing the island. Here Davenport was rewarded for his services, and here he helped set up what was to become the town named for him.[37]

Here, too, using the island as a stepping stone, the first railroad bridge was thrown across the Mississippi, to the panic of steamboat operators. As soon as the bridge was completed, in 1856, a river pilot, backed by shipping interests, sued the Illinois Central Railroad for obstructing navigation and causing an accident to his boat, the *Effie Afton*. The railroad hired the best legal talent available in Illinois, including Abraham Lincoln of Springfield, who came back to the locale of his Rock River military exploits, twenty years later, to inspect the scene of the accident, test currents, and study the bridge's construction. In the Chicago trial, he defended the right of east-west traffic *over* the Mississippi against the north-south flow *along* it; defended all that railway bustle Mark Twain would hail with grudging approval as his outmoded steamship slid under the thickening web of bridges. Lincoln was, in fact, consolidating the ascendency of the transportation center in Chicago against river cities like St. Louis—a point that did not hurt Lincoln's chances for nomination at the 1860 convention held in Chicago's new "Wigwam."[38]

Illinois calls itself on car licenses the "Land of Lincoln"; and the places where Reagan grew up have special connections with the first Republican President. In Galesburg, where Reagan first attended public school, Lincoln delivered what some think his finest speech in the Lincoln-Douglas series. The plaque commemorating that event helped bend the thoughts of a Galesburg native, Carl Sandburg, to his lifelong fascination with Lincoln.

Lincoln served in the state's last frontier against the Indians, waged along the Rock River—at Prophetstown near Tampico, and at Dixon's Ferry, where his fellow militiamen launched the war that federal troops had to resolve. He helped save the bridge over the Mississippi to Davenport, where Reagan became a radio announcer. Later, when Lincoln expanded federal power more than any President before him, Illinois showed the zeal of a new member of the Union for crushing the "states' rights" that protected slavery. Before that, Lincoln had been an ardent promoter of federal power to underwrite improvements for the West. He first sat in the Illinois legislature in 1835–36, when that body set Illinois on a course of canal development that was the most extravagant in the nation; and he defended the improvement bills when they came under fire.[39] This placed him against the policy of Andrew Jackson and on the side of railroad developers—principally those of the Illinois Central, from which Lincoln derived the largest fee of his legal career.[40] Since Stephen Douglas had introduced in Congress the bill giving the Illinois Central the nation's first federal land grant for a railroad, Lincoln had to show he was even more supportive of the program in his 1858 campaign against Douglas, which was largely waged in or near cities on the Illinois Central line, cities that had benefited from the railway much as Tampico would later benefit from the canal built there in Jack Reagan's days.[41]

If we seek Ronald Reagan's roots, we shall not find them in "a land made great because it was free from big government." Rather, the land grew by the influence of a government that was itself growing in the extraordinary effort at incorporating the whole West. Jack Reagan's move to his sons' birthplace repeated a history of people crowding near the federally guarded Mississippi, then the 1830s canal route, then the 1850s railroad line. The Hennepin Canal was a delayed last chapter in this story of governmental frontier blazing. Despite its modern technology, it looked back as well as forward. In its waters, the Disciples of Christ were baptized, reuniting them with the zeal of the Kentucky revivals from which the Christians were born. The Hennepin was truly a water of transit for them, in the hopeful first years of this century. The ritual of incorporation into the people of this land was one that looked two ways, backward to communal solidarity and forward to technological abundance. The conduit between the two was laid out by federal surveys, constructed by the Army Corps of Engineers, and rescued in a time of national depression by the Congress of the United States. Much as he tries to deny it, Ronald Reagan was cradled in the arms of "govment."

CHAPTER 10

Individualism

If one can't handle this, two won't do any good.
—*Ronald Reagan,* Law and Order *(1953)*

Reagan, who grew up on (and in) the Rock River, displayed no interest in that artery as the scene of earlier trade and conflict. Like most of us, he derived his first image of Indians from cowboy movies, and it remained his working concept. He told Hubler that he yearned to film an "outdoor epic" (p. 234), as part of Hollywood's "cavalry-Indian cycle" (p. 245), because of his feel for the historical period being celebrated:

> I was a "cavalry-Indian" buff. I thought then, and think now, that the brief post-Civil War era when our blue-clad cavalry stayed on a wartime footing against the plains and desert Indians was a phase of Americana rivaling the Kipling era for color and romance. Evidently someone else thought so too: Hollywood started making cavalry-Indian pictures and John Wayne, saber in hand, rode right into the number one box-office spot. Ray Milland took sword in hand; so did Gregory Peck. Everyone rode into the sunset behind fluttering guidons (pp. 233–34).

Reagan is describing the era when, while Warners kept giving him parts with Eve Arden or the postpubescent Shirley Temple, he yearned for the heroic roles he would achieve later, outside his own studio. When those later movies failed, he could blame it all on timing—the Westerns were "wearing thin, due to overexposure" (p. 245).

Actually, he had done one large-scale cavalry movie at Warners, Michael Curtiz's *Santa Fe Trail* (1940); but he did not count that, since he had to yield to the lead actor, Errol Flynn, who repeatedly shouldered him off-camera and stole his lines (Hubler, pp. 112, 121–22). Reagan was forced to play George Custer to Flynn's Jeb Stuart, characters anachronistically joined in duty guarding the overland trails of the 1850s. *Santa Fe Trail* was ludicrous as history, but not wrong in showing the importance of federal troops to the development of the West. During the 1850s, the time purportedly represented by the film, ninety percent of the federal army was stationed in the seventy-nine posts west of the Mississippi.[1] And this was just the beginning of the "govment" role in creating that frontier West celebrated by the cavalry and cowboy myths Reagan rightly (if revealingly) considered a Kipling era of empire.

After the Civil War, the Army's presence became far more important, as federal subvention of railroads made the settlement of the entire continent possible. Henry Adams concluded that the government had mortgaged the nation to the railroads, even before one considered all the ancillary subsidies given to them—the carrying of the mail, the protection of the cavalry, the ministrations of the United States Navy at the Pacific end.[2] All this was in sharp contrast to the hesitant attitude on "improvements" prevalent from the Jackson era to the beginning of the Civil War.[3] The national resources were stretched to their utmost, including those of the cavalry. Tactics forged in the clotted battles for annihilation favored by Lee and Grant were hard to apply on the thinly populated plains.[4] As John Hutchins has argued: "The northern cavalry made its mark during the latter days of the Civil War as a well-armed and well-supplied force of mounted infantry—with dismounted combat as its primary battlefield function—rather than as the galloping, saber-wielding array popularly depicted."[5] Cavalrymen stationed in the West "fought the last war" in terms of tactics—which meant dismounting by fours, in order to use rifles, while one man held the horses. Besides reducing firepower by a quarter, this required a discipline of trust in the horse holder and confidence in the officers that was hard to maintain in isolated units poorly trained during the rush to supply the frontier with soldiers. Since Indians also dismounted in order to use their weapons, horses operated in western battle as chariots do in the Homeric poems, as taxicabs taking people to the scene of the encounter.[6]

The range of good taxi service was limited, since horses operating out from a supply train were forced to burn up energy, carrying heavily armed and provisioned soldiers, where pasturage was doubtful:

> The big grain-fed "American" horse with which cavalry units were generally provided was not the type best adapted to a long campaign, in which an animal's capacity to make rapid marches of perhaps many days' duration with little or no grain had a vital bearing on the outcome. Considerable specialized knowledge and constant attention were needed to husband the strength of grain-fed horses so that they might not flag. In a mounted unit operating deep in Indian country, the tempo of the march could be no more than the pace of the slowest member. It often happened that a unit, because of a few broken-down horses, had to abandon the field altogether.[7]

Thus the federal presence in the West had to be massive in order to be effective—dragging with it a heavy technological "tail" of supply, communication, and transport. This kind of war did not rely on individual heroics of the Errol Flynn sort.

Western communities petitioned for federal protection against Indians and other perils, so that "overlanders persisted in regarding the frontier army as almost their sole guardian and protector."[8] But where the feds were unavailable, according to the myths Reagan absorbed and wanted to re-enact, the lone lawman stood up to forces of disorder. Thus, when cattle drives swept by towns along the Kansas trail, it was important to have a gunslinger of reputation to face down unruly drovers. Ray Billington, often called the dean of frontier historians, perpetuates this myth in his standard textbook: "Seldom did a group of drovers leave without contributing to the population of boot hill."[9] When Marshall Frame Johnson, played by Ronald Reagan, brings the Durango Kid back to town under arrest, in Law and Order, the Kid looks at Boot Hill and asks, "You shoot 'em all?" Reagan answers, "Only those that didn't get hung." But Robert Dykstra, investigating the period of legendary drives through the towns of Kansas, found that places like Dodge City and Abilene averaged only one and a half murders per year, often having nothing to do with cowboys, and usually unconnected with "shootouts."[10]

Nor was a lone marshall hired to stand up to mobs of men. In Law and Order, when a deputy offers to help the marshall handle a lynch crowd, Reagan dismisses the offer: "If one can't handle this, two won't do any good." Similarly, when Reagan sets out to capture his wild brother, the heroine (Dorothy Malone) pleads with him to take others along for help. Reagan just says, "I'm going alone." "Why?" she asks, and the comic sidekick of this movie (Chubby Johnson) tells her, "That's the way he is." But in fact, the towns relied on small armies of law enforcement: "In no case did any cattle town depend upon a lone marshall for its law enforcement. Police bodies of up to five men—carefully ranked as marshal, assistant marshal, and policemen—customarily supervised cattle trading seasons."[11] The average cowherd was driven by only eight to ten men, some of whom had to watch the cattle when others went to town; and those entering the towns had to come disarmed, since it was against the law for anyone but law enforcement officials to carry a gun.[12] Thus a confrontation with drovers was a contest between men well armed and disciplined, operating on terrain they knew with the support of the citizenry, against a small number of unarmed outsiders. It is no wonder, under these circumstances, that gunmen as famous in legend as Clay Allison, Doc Holliday, and Bat Masterson never killed anyone in a cattle town.[13] In fact, a reform mayor of Dodge City twice ran former lawman Bat Masterson out of town as a troublemaker. The second time, in the bloodless "Dodge City War," Wyatt Earp was forced out with him.[14]

Not only were citizens in frontier towns determined to keep peace. Far from cowering until rescued by the lone marshall, they were quick to resort to vigilantism.[15] The word "outlaw" itself means "one outside the protection of the law."[16] The mayor of Dodge City expelled Masterson and Earp by forming a large posse of citizens. Nor was there any nonsense about giving outlaws a "fair chance to draw." They were beyond the pale, driven out of the civilized community to live like wild beasts, and shot like beasts if they fought back. Pap Finn lives thus, and is described thus by his own son, who knows his father is not only outside "govment," but on the other side of barriers erected around common humanity: "He was most fifty, and he looked it. His hair was long and tangled and greasy, and hung down, and you could see his eyes shining through like he was behind vines."[17] The real West had little use for the lone outlaw *or* the lone lawman, in situations where the survival of human values depended on communal purpose.

It was in the interests of the railroads and of other business investors to make settlements safe.[18] And in fact there were extraordinary pressures toward conformity on the "individualist" frontier. Not only was gun control widely practiced, but Kansas adopted prohibition statewide in 1881 (local communities had tried it earlier).[19] Dodge City even outlawed dance halls in 1884.[20] The dynamics at work were the same ones that made western territories prize "gentility" so highly that they were the first to adopt women's suffrage. Kansas let women vote at the municipal level in 1887. Wyoming, which had already adopted it as territory law in 1869, became the first state with female suffrage in 1890. It was followed by Colorado (1893), and by Utah and Idaho (1896).[21] Alan P. Grimes notes that "the actuality of woman suffrage came out of the West when the ideology of the movement came out of the East."[22] Suffrage was just one of several reform movements with a common puritan strain that had great appeal in the West. "By 1917, eight of the eleven western woman-suffrage states were 'dry' (Kansas, Washington, Oregon, Colorado, Arizona, Idaho, Montana, Utah)."[23]

Americans do not think of the West as a puritan place. But we are not used to thinking much about the West at all. Instead, we shuffle "frontier" images, as Frederick Jackson Turner did. We picture the space, and the sparse numbers of original settlers defined against it. We think this conjunction must make for innovation, individual initiative, a break with tradition. But comparative study of frontier conditions indicates that the very reverse of these traits is more often produced. Those really without "govment" want it badly; in fact, go and beg the authorities for it—as American frontiersmen, from the time of Bacon's rebels or the Paxton boys, begged for government troops in their midst. Governor John Reynolds asking President Jackson for an army against Black Hawk was just one in a long line of independent people wanting to become dependent in a hurry.

William H. McNeill argues that comparative study shows "frontier conditions ordinarily provoked not freedom but a social hierarchy steeper than anything familiar in Europe itself."[24] There are a number of economic and social reasons for this. In the first place, precarious living conditions, scarce resources, and danger make for communal discipline and willingness to submit to authority—the reaction that calls for martial law in an emergency. "Free and equal nuclear families scattered thinly over the landscape are in a poor position to protect themselves."[25] The urge to band oneself with potential allies is a very strong one where "trials brought solidarity."[26] Settlers in a wilderness live in a large and lonely world; but, as passengers on a ship live in the ocean, they tend to live very close or they do not live at all. Ships are places where discipline is prized. Drunkenness is especially dangerous in a ship's crew, though it may be especially tempting there; so grog control is an important point of discipline—as prohibition was quick to come to cattle towns.[27] The phrase "we are all in the same boat" conveys a great deal: one does not sink or swim as an individual while making an ocean voyage. Individuality is the luxury of the secure, not the offspring of frontier need.

The clustering instinct had a great deal to do with the popularity of those camp meetings from which the Disciples of Christ took their origin at Cane Ridge, Kentucky. Loneliness and the need for society brought people in from very large areas, and stirred them to extreme expressions of social solidarity. Emotions ran contagious from person to person, fusing them in a single experience.[28] Religion also supplied authority figures willing to impose the rites of order on communities that desperately wanted them—e.g., the observance of the Christian sabbath.[29] One of the most successful frontier communities was that of the Mormons, whose hydraulic organization of society was enforced by a rigorous social discipline.[30] Alan Grimes compares them to the original puritan settlers of Massachusetts, close religious communities with a sense of mission and a high degree of conformity.[31] We have already seen that other western communities followed the Mormon lead in granting female suffrage. They also strove for a high degree of conformity, so that Mark Twain, who traveled west as a federal agent, and was repelled by the authoritarianism of the Mormons, soon found the "wild west" too monotonous for him: "Not only was the milieu of a frontier community, even the most sophisticated frontier communities, confining in a social and economic sense; it seems to have ceased nourishing his imagination. It did not give him enough to write about."[32]

The Mormons' success came from their technological achievements, which depended on careful planning and a complex division of labor. The development of the successive American frontiers—beginning with those first established on the eastern seaboard—are now seen as part of the outer rim of a world-wide capitalist expansion in the sixteenth and following centuries.[33] This expansion was made possible by a technological superiority to the cultures being engulfed, which were set to slave labor, or extruded, or annihilated.[34] Turner could not place the United States in this historical context; his belief in the "self-limiting framework of American uniqueness" precluded comparison with other frontiers, even those nearest the United States.[35] He neglected or played down prior Indian possession, the government seizure of land by conquest or treaty or purchase, and the speculative mania that set up baronies with an agrarian class of wage workers.[36]

The conquest and domination achieved by superior technology created an umbilical connection back to the core of the capitalist order, a dependence often resented, but one the peripheral figures had to maintain, nervously, day by day. Settlers needed guns, horses, ammunition, picks, shovels, plows, drilling and mining equipment, canals, telegraphs, railroads, barbed wire, transit for their produce, credit, cash—all in an ascending technical spiral, along with the skills and discipline to work these instruments of domination.

What was new on the frontier came from adapting old structures to new circumstances, not from the indigenous culture's triumph over its conquerors. Some American Indians were forced to become Christians; Europeans did not become worshipers of the Indian gods. Often, it is true, forces already coming to birth in the core areas of expansion were given freer reign to develop in the new circumstances of the settlers. Owen Lattimore pointed this out with regard to English Whig tendencies in America: "England itself was already beginning to transform itself from a society dominated by the landed nobility and gentry into a society at first commercial and then increasingly industrial; but this could be done only slowly because of the weight of vested interest. The Americans, because of the institutions they had left behind them as well as those they brought with them, and not merely because of the free land and abundant raw materials of the frontier of new settlement, were able, once they had thrown off their disabilities, to move ahead in time in the same direction as the British, but even faster."[37]

Similarly, as the frontier moved west in America, reform ideas that had taken shape in the East were at times more easily adopted in the new constitutions being written by western states (just as women's suffrage came more readily there). But the dominant note of the experience was established by the culture out of which the settlers were moving, not imposed by the nature of the geography they met. A good example of that can be seen along the contiguous frontiers of southern and northern America, where obvious disparities came from the nature of the settling cultures: "Why was it that the Spanish and French frontiers in America (especially the frontier in Canada, so close geographically to New England) did not create societies more like that of the United States—except, significantly, in Canada west of Quebec, where the settlers were British?"[38] From evidence of this sort Lattimore draws "one of the old rules of frontier history," that "new frontiers were shaped less by geographical and material conditions than by the cultural momentum and impact of those who created them."[39] Later studies have confirmed what one might have expected in the first place—that the tools and methods making for expansion and conquest were wielded with a cultural pride in the carriers of those tools. No doubt there were strains between the East and West in white America, as the push to bring a whole continent under technological dominance tested the nation's resources, psychic as well as material; but these tensions were nothing to the superiority felt over black, Indian, Mexican, coolie, Filipino, and Polynesian workers made to serve the arriving capitalist order. And the settlers worked as rapidly as possible to replicate the conditions of the culture from which they had set out—its religious rites, political offices, printing presses, schools, and forms of entertainment.[40]

The undoubted rigors of the trail-blazing efforts of the American frontier, of that rapidly moving first line of danger and the several stages of insecurely established conditions that followed it pace by pace, led to a self-flattering image of work done by the few who were, momentarily, on the exposed outer edge of the whole culture's advance. We still pay homage to individual "astronauts" who sit on the rockets made and fueled and guided by a vast capitalistic-technological effort of the whole community (an effort funded by the government). But space as such is not conditioning the men trained in the ways of laboratories, under the psychic regimen of American patriotism and scientific-industrial discipline. In the same way, Turner's magic "free land" did not work a transformation in the minds of those who came to extrude the Indians and plant the practices they had learned during their enculturation in the widening base of capitalist expansion and control.

The West's very uneasiness about being "backward" in the advanced luxuries of culture was a sign of its imitative tendency. Mark Twain was a typical mediating figure in his early career. He made his literary name with that most "genteel" of practices—the European grand tour, followed by lectures on the cosmopolitan world he had been exposed to. Admittedly, in *Innocents Abroad* (1869), he made fun of the pretensions of the tour as a way of covering his own awkwardness. But he was playing on, and profiting from, the typical western device for keeping up with the East. He repeated the technique, but with Pacific island travels and lectures, in *Roughing It* (1872), and then did Europe again in *A Tramp Abroad* (1880). It was only when he was safely ensconced in the most genteel of literary compounds, Nook Farm, with neighbors like Harriet Beecher Stowe and Charles Dudley Warner, that he was able to remember with fond hyperbole his life on the Mississippi, meanwhile writing to a man who still lived on the Mississippi: "I think I comprehend the position there—perfect freedom to vote just as you choose, provided you choose to vote as *other* people think—social ostracism, otherwise . . . Fortunately, a good deal of experience of men enabled me to choose my residence wisely. I live in the freest corner of the country."[41] He was describing the credit capital of Hartford.

Twain strove to have the best of both worlds. Long after he had become a world traveler and student of languages, a stickler for pure English usage and a scholar of dialects, he liked to present himself as the untutored voice of "natural man," shrewdly warbling his wood notes wild. He pretended to less acquaintance with the high culture than he possessed, while taking advantage of the most sophisticated marketing techniques for his own literary and other projects, in which he had collaborators like President Grant and Andrew Carnegie.

Twain, by leaving Nevada City to seek a more cosmopolitan world, first in San Francisco, then in Hartford, was enacting the recurrent tale of adventurous Americans who escape the conformity of small towns, in which all the community's members know where all the others are and what they are doing. The discipline of the garrison is relaxed in the partial anonymity of the metropolis. Ronald Reagan would, in his own way, repeat Twain's flight. He was determined from an early age to get out of Dixon to a center of show business—to Chicago, in his first attempt; then, by way of Des Moines, to Hollywood. But Reagan, by the roles given him—as the voice of midwestern baseball, as the best friend of the star, as the plain-spoken hero of horse epics —was also repeating an American instinct to claim a simplicity his circumstances belie, to remain with the innocent at home even as he escaped his home. With Twain, the pretense was artful, highly conscious, used for cultural satire. With Reagan, the perfection of the pretense lies in the fact that he does not know he is pretending. He believes the individualist myths that help him play his communal role. He is the sincerest claimant to a heritage that never existed, a perfect blend of an authentic America he grew up in and of that America's own fables about its past. Americans' early days are spent playing cowboys and Indians—as Huck Finn's days were spent enacting Tom Sawyer's adventure-book fantasies. Fake Huck-Finnery is the real American boyhood, one that Reagan never had to give up. And now, through him, neither do we.

PART THREE

RADIO

CHAPTER 11

Davenport

and fansie that they feel
Divinitie within them breeding wings
—Paradise Lost 9.1009–10

If, in 1932, you were walking up from the river rather than taking the trolley, in Davenport, Twain's "beautiful city crowning a hill," you would have to move briskly not to be overtaken by a coiled little man with blossoming cravat. He always moved fast. "A rolling stone gathers no moss," he liked to say, "but it gains a damn fine polish."[1] He would greet you and expect to be recognized; be shocked, in fact, if he were not, and eager to repair your ignorance. Even an audience of one was always an audience for him. His liquid eyes compelled, framed as they were in a dark halo of hair— he washed it once a year, but fine-tooth-combed it clean incessantly.

B.J. would be using his fine hands persuasively, manipulating arguments in the air, and you with them. His father had literally been a mesmerist before settling into the soberer trade of chiropracty—a trade B.J. took away from his father, with acrimony and accountants. Before long a third character would be introduced into the conversation: "Innate," B.J. informs you, told him to buy this or sell that. If you ask about this intimate advisor to B.J., he answers: "Innate is an individualized portion of the All-Wise usually known as spirit." Innate was B.J.'s divinity within him, and it bred the gaudiest wings. Innate was especially helpful in the remodeling of his mansion, which sits on the ridge of the hill. He walks you past it, toward the garden crammed between his home and his chiropractic school. The garden is, a sign tells you, "A Little Bit O'Heaven." He is not embarrassed to collect from you, deftly but firmly, the admission fee of fifty cents—his son used to do that, but now he is becoming a chiropractor himself in the school next door, while acting as business director of the radio station on its roof, and running the cowboy lounge on its north side. Earlier this son had put a roller rink on the second floor of the college; later he would replace the cowboy lounge with a root beer stand. Before that, Dave Palmer tended the alligators in the Little Bit O'Heaven. "Had to get rid of those, though—smell was too strong when we put them in the basement for the winter."

B.J., showing you about his garden, would tell you where, in his world travels, he purchased each treasure, and what he paid for it. If the stationary objects—Buddhist shrine, Japanese temple gate, Greek statues—did not awe you sufficiently, B.J. might show you his leather cigarette case. He had it specially made from a South Sea island girl's breast (notice the nipple?).

Thanks to Innate, the man is still vigorous at fifty. Innate told him to sleep always with his head to the north pole, so earth's currents would flow through him unimpeded. But his life has not been just vigor and bits of heaven. The envy of doctors so pursued him through his early career, his official biographer tells us, that "B. J.'s mind was cracking under the injustice and persecution."[2] Friends recommended a vacation as therapy, but work in building "A Little Bit O'Heaven" became the true restorative. The gardener who collaborated with him on the rock structures later said, "This had been an insane asylum to B. J."[3] By coincidence, one of the businesses B.J. was operating then was an insane asylum. So, while he was maintaining paying customers in the asylum he owned, he figured a way to charge others to visit the asylum he inhabited. B.J. put everything to multiple uses. Innate might give him the most preposterous notions, but he had a way of jiggering them earthward toward a prosperous outcome.

He is straight out of *Huckleberry Finn*. We hear the Duke talking, purest Mississippi River projects: "Early to bed, early to rise; work like hell *and advertize*—makes a man healthy, wealthy, and wise." Though Bartlett Joshua Palmer had been expelled from the seventh grade and he disowned, for a while, his only son for going to college, he became an author and lecturer, speaking on such subjects as "Inductology Versus Deductology" or "Is Chiropractic?"[4]

The basis for everything else—the printing press, the radio station, the dance hall and roller rink and restaurants—was the Palmer School, which he wrested from his father and thrust upon his son. It is still in business, and honors the three Palmers with Soviet-style colossal busts, appropriate monuments when one considers the Palmer history of succession by deposing predecessors. Students are now taught to refer to the elder Palmer ("D.D.") as "Old Dad Chi" (or "Chiro," short for "Chiropractor"). But B.J. usually treated his family as cheap labor. His wife, after one year at medical school, wrote the Palmer textbook on anatomy, and taught that subject thenceforth. Her father and brother were also appointed to the faculty. In the early days of the radio station, various Palmers were announcers.

In his childhood, Dave Palmer, who could never intrude on his mother's work at the school or finish his own around the mansion, got away from his father as often as possible to live with relatives. His love-hate attitude toward the mansion, stuffed as it is with bizarreries, is evident from its largely untouched present state—his father's clothes still hanging in the closets, his own boyhood pennants on the wall. The caretaker told me, "The late Dave could never bring himself to sort through this material for what was valuable, or to let me throw it out." Dave, who lived elsewhere when he inherited the school, tried once—briefly, after his divorce—to move into the house, but lost his nerve at the last moment.

This was the establishment for which Reagan went to work in 1932. B.J. was his employer. Dave—only five years Reagan's elder, and pursuing a leisurely course through the college while running the cowboy lounge—was the station's business manager. Reagan worked on top of the building to whose wall the heavenly Buddhist shrine was affixed, and went down through the school every afternoon and evening to eat with students and faculty in their basement cafeteria. The studios from which Reagan broadcast his first shows bore, like everything else about the place, the unmistakable B.J. touch. "The broadcasting studio has been made after designs of our own. The furniture is rustic. In this room are logs overhead containing snakes and animals and birds looking down as though from the sky over the head of the artists."[5] The original call letters of the station, WOC, stood for World of Chiropractic, and its entire operation promoted in various ways the Palmer School. The sign-off Reagan had heard in Dixon in the twenties went this way:

> This is station WOC, owned and operated by the Palmer School of Chiropractic, the Chiropractic Fountainhead, Davenport, Iowa, where the West begins and in the state where the tall corn grows, broadcasting by authority of the Federal Radio Commission, using a frequency of 1000 kilocycles, signing off at exactly five seconds of twelve o'clock, Central Standard Time. Good night.[6]

After B.J. put the radio station on the roof of his school, he kept thinking of new ways to integrate it into the school's program. He wired every classroom to the studio for announcements. Some lectures to the students were broadcast to the radio audience as well; some radio programs were aired in the classrooms—e.g., Coolidge's state of the union address.[7] When the school formed a band, it broadcast from the studio; simultaneously, B.J. had the music carried in an auditorium below, cleared for dancing, for which he charged admission. Few pennies dropped through the cracks of a Palmer operation.

The station was only ten years old when Reagan arrived at it. B.J. boasted that he was the first to move a station over state lines without government permission. He bought a "Radiophone 9-BY" from an amateur who had been operating it across the river in Rock Island. He also said, "Our first microphone was an ordinary telephone receiver, set in the middle of an ordinary kitchen wooden chopping bowl."[8] B.J.'s stories tend to sprout one nipple more than is absolutely necessary; but it is true that the station was a pioneer. It went from a 500-watt transmitter at the beginning to a 5,000-watt signal in 1924. It was one of the first stations to relay broadcasts from New York, as part of the development of NBC in 1927. In 1929 it merged with station WHO in Des Moines, and in 1931, the year before Reagan began working for it, became the seventeenth station in the country to be licensed for a 50,000-watt power station.[9] There were plans for further expansion when Reagan applied for a job, which explains why the program director encouraged him to keep coming back, though there was no steady work available that year. Radio, like movies, was a growth industry during the Depression.

In 1932, B.J. badly needed the income from his radio station. The Depression had almost as severe an impact on the school underneath it as on Eureka College. From expansion days, when the student body numbered in the thousands, enrollment had dropped to under two hundred, about the size of Eureka. Dave Palmer, a recent graduate of the Wharton School of Finance, was firing faculty and inventing ways for students to raise money for their schooling—he manufactured mops, which students sold door to door for credit on their tuition. Meeting payrolls was a problem, and the Palmers signed no contracts with their employees, even at the station (a fact from which Reagan would shortly benefit). When I asked Lucille Mauget, the accountant in Reagan's time (and for many years thereafter) what payroll records might survive from the period, she said, "None; all payments were in cash."

Radio and the movies flourished in the Depression for the same reason that cheery songs did—escapism. People out of work faced the music, and danced—which meant that some people got paid to do the dancing. As Roosevelt realized, people wanted to be told they had nothing to fear. They needed the message Sid Altschuler had given Reagan. They needed confidence; and, as Melville realized, the Mississippi River is the main historical thoroughfare for America's confidence men. Melville's dispenser of Omni-Balsamic Reinvigorator is also "the Happy Bone-Setter."[10]

The Palmers relied much on confidence. Their method was to make people relax and let nature take its course. As B.J. put it in one of his books:

> INNATE is the ONE eternal, internal, stable, and permanent factor that is a fixed and reliable entity, does not fluctuate up and down scales to meet idiosyncrasies or caprices to puff the ego of educated theorists or doubting Thomases, or to violate its own self-made laws. The same internal natural intelligence which knows when to sneeze, to blow your nose, urinate, or defecate, blink your eyes, how to heal a cut or mend a fractured bone, raise a blister when skin is burned, grow hair, finger nails and toe nails, tells you when you are thirsty, hungry, tired, and sleepy, that causes you to scratch when you have an itch—this and more is the same capable INNER VOICE that is capable of getting any sick organ well.[11]

Some of the rhetoric of the Palmer School must have seemed familiar to Reagan. Jack Reagan, the "graduate of the American School of Practipedics," who "spent hours analyzing the bones of the foot," was the first salesman in Dixon to X-ray people's feet, as B.J. had been the first man to use X-rays in chiropracty. Like D.D. and B.J., Jack was a man without any high school education, but good with words. Dave Palmer says of his father what Ronald Reagan said of his—that each was the best raconteur either son had heard. Jack Reagan used words to create trust, to sell things and grow rich. He had confidence in himself, though not quite on the staggering scale of the Palmers; and confidence breeds confidence. As one of Ronald Reagan's favorite authors from a later time writes:

Concentration on the manipulation of ideas and words (like concentration on the manipulation of paints or musical tones) probably induces an exaggerated notion of the world's plasticity and also of human powers, since the only limits on artistic or intellectual creation are those imposed by imagination, creativity, and skill.

But this brings us to one of the most curious anomalies of the Reagan career; for those words are Jeane Kirkpatrick's, from her attack on "the New Class" of "symbol specialists" for infecting politics with dreams and ideals, mocking the practical people who produce things and meet payrolls.[12] This was an analysis Ambassador Kirkpatrick shared with many Reagan supporters of the 1970s and 1980s. It explained their feeling that "the professoriate" (her term), the media, and the more educated levels of the bureaucracy constituted a kind of "knowledge industry" both new and baneful in the way it affects politics.

It is an interesting thesis, with an interesting (largely Marxist) past that will call for our study in connection with Reagan's later politics. But it is fascinating, at this stage, to notice that Reagan was a part of this "nonproductive" verbal new class from the beginning of his career. He was a supplier of entertainment, comfort, distraction, and healing symbols; entirely a creation of the media, and of B.J.'s media at that. If he did not play his way through the Depression, he traversed its roughest stretch reporting on the ball teams that did. From sports he went into that principal symbol generator of the thirties, the Hollywood studio. Then, keeping pace with the technological revolution, he moved to television. When he went to work for GE outside the television studio, he was not producing electrical products, but giving pep talks to the men who produce them. He was still being hired to entertain, cheer up, and give confidence to others by telling stories, polishing his oratory, encouraging effort. Then he became a radio commentator again, this time as a political pundit, the only other job he has had outside politics. His ranch was an avocation and tax shelter. His union activities, according to the staff member closest to him at the Screen Actors Guild, he ran as some lady bountiful would run a charity.[13]

There is nothing wrong with any of these activities. But it is strange that they should make up the sole background of a hero cheered by critics of mere "symbol skills." The tendencies Kirkpatrick deplored in her 1976 book were victorious in the presidency she came to serve in 1981:

It is not inevitable that American politics should be dominated by symbol specialists or highly educated professionals, but *the importance of public relations image and style assures that communications specialists will play a significant role. And the adoption of presidential and delegate selection processes that make success dependent on self-presentation gives communication skills a special value, so does the salience of ideology and style in politics* [italics and grammar of the original].[14]

The Republican convention in Dallas of 1984, rousingly addressed by Kirkpatrick herself, was almost a revival in its open religiosity and adulation of moralizing candidates. As she had written four years earlier: "The ideological—or rectitude-based—organization is singularly dependent on the agitational skills of its leaders to state and reiterate the purposes that are its raison d'être."[15]

Even before he went to his first radio job in Davenport, "the Great Communicator" had some acting skills nurtured over many years, first by his mother, then by his drama coaches, B. J. Frazer and Ellen Marie Johnson. Kirkpatrick says that the New Class politics will be moralizing and "rectitude-based," drawing on the persuasive skills of those trained for the law and the churches.[16] Reagan grew up in and out of the house of the Reverend Ben Cleaver, who was a second father to him. His own mother was an amateur preacher, as well as a poetess and playwright. The faculty, board, and alumni visible at close quarters around Eureka College were largely led by preachers. Reagan, for that matter, spent his childhood in the home of two great persuaders, one of the yarn-spinning variety, the other an urgent moralizer. His parents, without high school education, had moved from rural to urban expectations and behavior. Ronald and his brother moved from urban to cosmopolitan life, and to great wealth. They had that passport of Kirkpatrick's new class, a college education. Even forty years later, forty percent of the delegates to the presidential conventions did not have a college degree, that sign of mobility both Reagan brothers acquired in the depths of the Depression.[17] It is a success story, but also the story of Kirkpatrick's new class struggling to be born. Reliance on deft public relations sets the tone of her new class,[18] and both Reagan brothers have been in that line of work all their lives, Ronald since his Booster Club days, Neil as the advertising agent for sponsors like Boraxo. Ronald was a public relations man at GE, and made numberless publicity appearances for his radio, movie, and television studios. His presidency has been a triumph of communication at the peak of the media age (though "media" is itself a swear word to many of his followers).

In Davenport, Reagan was going to work for a man with a genius for promotion and an abiding interest in its techniques. One of Palmer's many maxims on the subject was: "Only the mints can make money without advertising." Everything he touched turned into a device for boosting his school. A great fan of vaudeville and the circus, for whose performers he had an understandably fraternal feeling, he persuaded the visiting troupes to mention his school by giving free orthopedic adjustments to the acrobats and tumblers. When Black Hawk's grandson came through town on his way to Washington to ask for better treatment of Indians, B.J., who had compared his techniques to the nature magic of medicine men, invited the Indian to stay at his mansion, and had a costume made so he could dress exactly like his "brother." Even in Davenport, founded as a result of the Black Hawk War, a place where the warrior's name is constantly used, this was exotic behavior—as one can see from the photograph of B.J. in full headdress on page 155 of *The Palmers.* B.J. said that the government needed to draft legislation to recognize the despised chiropractors, so he and the chief had similar grievances. He arranged for fellow chiropractors to feed and board Black Hawk's grandson as he traveled from Davenport to Washington.

To advertise his school's annual "Lyceum," B.J. had a huge model of the human spine made of papier-mâché and paraded through town. Since he called WOC the station marking the point where tall corn grows, he sponsored a tall corn contest to be won by the person who could bring in the highest stalk. B.J. even wrote a book called *Radio Salesmanship,* though Reagan was in Hollywood by the time it appeared (1942).

It was on a point of advertising that Reagan was fired, shortly after being hired, in Davenport. Stories among old friends in Eureka tell of some Disciple resentment at Palmer's station for advertising liquor or places that sold liquor—something that would not appeal to the Reagan who gave temperance talks to boys' clubs in his radio days. Iowa Disciples were historically adamant about alcohol. But the Eighteenth Amendment had not been repealed when he was in Davenport; if there is any truth to those stories, they must relate to his time in Des Moines. Still, his own account of the incident in Davenport shows some moral aversion to the crasser side of the Palmer operation. "My dramatic instinct rebelled at mentioning a mortuary in connection with 'Drink to Me Only with Thine Eyes,' so on this night we got the music and the mortuary got left" (Hubler, pp. 67–68). By omitting a chance to advertise, Reagan had violated everything B.J. held sacred. He was instantly dismissed. He does not say by whom, only that the program director who had hired him, Peter MacArthur, had nothing to do with it. I asked the accountant, Lucille Mauget, who would have been MacArthur's superior in those days, and she said, "Only B.J." But B.J.'s son had the title of business manager, and was by his own account firing faculty members despite his youth. He seems the most likely candidate. Reagan never mentioned Dave, and refers to "Colonel [sic] B. J. Davenport" just once as the founder of WOC.[19] This was not because of B.J.'s retiring nature. The grotesque surroundings of the mansion, garden, and school (all in one complex) are also omitted from the Reagan memoir—the Palmers seem to be an unpleasant part of his life he would rather dismiss.

Reagan reproached the man who fired him for not giving him any prior training or advice—though that presumably would have been MacArthur's duty, for whom Reagan has nothing but affectionate memories. (Actually, he presents MacArthur as taking him to his first football broadcasts in the role of mentor, and as giving him good advice on a range of subjects over the years). Whatever the precise terms of his attack on the nameless boss who fired him, there was doubtless a rich choice of grievance in working for B.J., whose own son says he made cruel demands on his employees (who included most of his relatives). Reagan, as is his custom, concentrates on the cheerful aspects of his new life, calling MacArthur "one of the most unforgettable characters I would ever know" (Hubler, p. 57). B. J. Palmer was the most unforgettable character he would ever forget.

Yet it was B.J.'s sharp practice that saved Reagan at what must have seemed a most desperate juncture. The experienced man brought in to re-place Reagan was experienced enough to ask for a contract. Only the reader who knows more than Reagan is telling can appreciate his deadpan state-ment: "WOC was not in the habit of giving contracts" (Hubler, p. 68). The new man refused to work on those terms, so "they would keep me on until they could find someone else." It is at this point that Reagan says he "blew his top" for lack of better "instructions." MacArthur may have helped turn the temporary reappointment into an extended one. If Reagan could hang on for just a few weeks, he would escape the Palmer School when WOC moved to its sister station in Des Moines.

Since Reagan began his regular work at the station on February 10, and left for Des Moines by the middle of May, he lived in Davenport only three months—though he had been given tantalizing glimpses of the odd Palmer compound on his five trips to see MacArthur and do football games the preceding fall. He also made a trip in January for a final audition in Daven-port.[20] Now he moved there. Davenport was the first large city he had lived in, not counting Chicago, where he had been an infant. From his radio station, and from the apartment house where he stayed, one could see the Mississippi in his day. Davenport, like Twain's Dawson's Landing, "stretched itself rearward up a gentle incline." The Perry Apartments, on the rise of the hill, were just beyond (and to the side of) the Black Hawk Hotel. The apartment house is solid but dingy today—and scheduled for demolition. But it was palatial in 1871.[21] The grand corner suites had been lived in by Sarah Bernhardt, Al Jolson, and other stars of the vaudeville circuit that ran through Davenport. As one of the big river cities, this had always been a center of entertainment. Until well into this century the Streckfus Line of steamboats brought jazz groups up from New Orleans, entertaining at the major stops. In 1919, young Bix Beiderbecke heard Louis Armstrong play on one of those boats at the Davenport landing.[22] One of the biggest news events in Davenport the year before Reagan started traveling there on football Saturdays was the funeral of Bix in his hometown, after his death at twenty-eight—another symbolic burial of the roaring twenties. WOC had devoted the whole day to Bix's records.[23]

Reagan says he daily passed street beggars on his six-block walk uphill from his apartment to the Palmer School. Reagan had a meal ticket for all of his meals at the School cafeteria, and he sent some of his first money to Neil in Eureka; but he says he always had something for the first brother who asked if he could spare a dime (Hubler, p. 66). He could afford to be generous at his new job. There were signs of radio's power to survive the Depression, and to thrive. In Reagan's days, the "Amos 'n' Andy" show was so popular that Davenport movie theaters turned off their films for fifteen minutes to broadcast the show's "Madame Queen" segment. In fact, the Depression was filling radio studios with out-of-work vaudevillians, the new entertainment form feeding off the old.[24]

Reagan had been working in Davenport for five days when Zangara tried to assassinate Franklin Roosevelt. He was still there when, a month later, the new President told Americans they had nothing to fear but fear. Speaking of 1933 a year later, H. G. Wells wrote: "The radio had been dominated by the President, and a certain hopeful imaginative generosity prevailed."[25] The field young Reagan had chosen was the arena of the political future already in this, his first year at the microphone. Like others, many others, Reagan was soon mimicking the patrician diction that Roosevelt somehow made endearing with his penetrating tenor voice. Two months later, Reagan was packing for the move to Des Moines. The large transmitter authorized in 1931 was built now, and the two stations sharing it could consolidate their staff at the larger studio. Reagan was listed as one of the two announcers from Davenport being led by Program Director MacArthur to WHO, where Reagan would still be working for the Palmer family, but not under its immediate scrutiny.[26]

B.J. figured prominently in the move to Des Moines. He had been making a series of speeches there to launch the new broadcasting operation—a talk to the Chamber of Commerce, a description of his upcoming African trip, an announcement that he would give the opening words on the combined stations.[27] Harold Risser, an engineer at the station, says, "Dr. Palmer would come around with those big piercing eyes and blow smoke in your face."[28] Reagan arrived in the wake of his boss, and Myrtle Williams, the music director at WHO, says he profited by the contrast. Almost anyone might look preferable next to bombastic B.J., bustling Dave, and theatrical Peter MacArthur of the Scottish burr. But she says it was more than that. "Dutch sorta stood out. He didn't seem as aggressive as the others. He understood this was not easy for the rest of us who had been there for a while."[29]

The Davenport station would reopen after a year. During the period when the Palmers were hiring with a view to this development, Ronald managed to get Neil an audition. Neil was hired as an announcer in September and sent back to Davenport in October, where he worked for years above the "Little Bit O'Heaven." Neil was not as effective on the air as Ronald, though he showed managerial and advertising skills; so the Palmers made him program manager at the beginning of 1936.[30] It was this period that gave Neil the training for his later life in California advertising firms. Though the New Deal had rescued the Reagan family at its worst economic crisis, the greater

part of the family money earned throughout the Depression came from the
odd empire B.J. had built. There the Reagan brothers were apprenticed as
salesmen, advertisers, product spokesmen. The arrangers of others' dreams.
Somnipractors.

CHAPTER 12

Des Moines

whose fruit burnisht with Golden Rind
Hung amiable, Hesperian *Fables true.*

—Paradise Lost *4.249–50*

Reagan was edging westward. From Dixon to Davenport had been a move of sixty-five miles. But Des Moines is a hundred and fifty miles west of the Mississippi. It seems a small step on the long way to California; but, edgewise, it took him almost there. He moved out of Chicago's orbit, and into a regional world of show business that looked to California for fulfillment. He would make his first movies in Des Moines—as narrator to a local newsreel series. The Hollywood success of performers from his radio station encouraged him to make his California trip.

Thus the great transition, when it came, was an easy one, not abrupt; Reagan could carry so much of the past with him because he never had to break away from it. Des Moines, despite its size (145,000 people in the thirties), was cut from the same pattern as the smaller towns of Reagan's youth. It was another river town, named for its river; a town that developed from a fort in Indian farmland. Indeed, the same tribes, Sauk and Fox, that were extruded from the Rock River in 1832 found themselves forced, in grudging bargain, to yield the Iowa heartland just ten years later.[1] Fort Des Moines was raised in 1843, where the Raccoon River joins the Des Moines.[2] Once again, it was the army trader—W. Alexander ("Alex") Scott—who became the key figure in the transition from fortress to town. He laid out the town, ran the ferry, built the first bridge. He had been the man on the scene with large amounts of cash to buy land when the territory was opened to settlers in 1845, the man who used government patronage to move the state capital there (from Iowa City) in 1857. What John Dixon and John Davenport were to their eponymous towns, Alex Scott was to Des Moines.[3]

When Iowa became a state in 1846, Congress granted lands, on the canal precedent, to improve the navigation system of the Des Moines, Iowa, and Cedar Rivers.[4] By 1850, Fort Des Moines was incorporated as a town, and became a major way station for those on the way to California as part of the gold rush—people like Reagan's great great uncle, Daniel Blue, from Clyde Township, who lost his two brothers in the quest for gold.[5] Citizens of Des Moines liked to claim that many who came through, in quest of gold, were impressed with the thriving new town and stayed. But some natives were lost to gold fever, including the founder himself: Alex Scott, in debt by now, died on the trip to Pike's Peak in 1859.[6]

In the depression of 1894, there was a rush through Des Moines in the opposite direction, of veterans to swell the protesting ranks of Coxey's army —though in Des Moines they were known as Kelly's army, from their leader Charles T. Kelly, who, warned off the railways, had his men build rafts and float down the Des Moines to the Mississippi.[7] Des Moines had loved the military since its fortress days, and President William Howard Taft came in 1903 to open a cavalry post, the new Fort Des Moines, with celebrations commemorated long after. During Reagan's time there in the thirties, Regimental Day was one of three principal events in the annual calendar of Des Moines.[8] The other two were the Drake Relays and the Iowa State Fair. Reagan became a performer of sorts at all three events.

The Iowans had told the gold seekers of the 1850s that they need go no further, gold was under their feet; and they were right. The lands the Indians left support an almost oppressive uniformity of yield, where few breaks in the terrain distract the eye or divert the plow. As if in testimony to the tassled wealth extracted from the ground each year, Des Moines raised a monument of splendid vulgarity in the Gilded Age state capitol of 1884. But in Reagan's time, even Iowa's fertility was crisped and shrinking from the drought that created the dust bowls. During the 1936 campaign, President Roosevelt took his Great Plains Drought Committee on a railway tour of the stricken states, culminating in a conference of all the affected states' governors in Des Moines. Alf Landon, that year's Republican candidate for President, and the governor of neighboring Kansas, had to drive up from Topeka, to be outshone by the President at the climax of his "rainmaking" tour.[9] This was the one occasion when Ronald Reagan saw his hero. Myrtle Williams (now Mrs. Norman Moon), who worked with him at the radio station, remembers Reagan's excitement as they rushed to the window and watched Roosevelt drive by the station in his open limousine, waving to the crowds along Walnut Street.[10]

By this time—September 4, 1936—Reagan was a celebrity himself, not only his voice but his face familiar to everyone in Des Moines. He was a frequent speaker at civic occasions, an attraction at the State Fair, a man valued by the sponsors of his baseball broadcasts, and the sports columnist of the Des Moines *Dispatch*. Just eight months after his glimpse of Roosevelt's passage through Des Moines, Reagan would travel west, on a journey that took him eventually to the White House. His farewell party was broadcast over WHO, and the mayor of Des Moines showed up to wish him well.[11]

Though Reagan did all kinds of announcing at WHO, he was best known for his sportscasting, which he preferred to other assignments. And he became especially associated with baseball, the game he had never been able to play, or even to watch in a big league town. "I had never seen a major league game" (Hubler, p. 77). In fact, he was not even seeing the games he described in vivid detail to a growing audience through the baseball seasons of the Depression. He was three hundred miles away from the Chicago games he reported "live," working from a telegraph relay:

> Looking through the window I would see "Curly" (complete with headphones) start typing. This was my cue to start talking. It would go something like this: "The pitcher (whatever his name happened to be) has the sign, he's coming out of the windup, here's the pitch," and at that moment Curly would slip me the blank. It might contain the information S2C, and without a pause I would translate this into "It's a called strike breaking over the inside corner, making it two strikes on the batter." If the Cubs were in the field, I would continue while I waited for the next dot and dash, saying, "Hartnett returns the ball to Lon Warneke, Warneke is dusting his hands in the resin, steps back up on the mound, is getting the sign again from Hartnett, here's the windup and the pitch." [Hubler, pp. 77–78]

Over six hundred times Reagan went through this elaborate creative process (Hubler, p. 60). The daily demands of such a "think-out-loud technique" (Hubler, p. 77) called for quick wits as well as painterly imagination. That is the point of Reagan's most famous radio story:

> I saw Curly start to type so I finished the windup and had Dean send the ball on its way to the plate, took the slip from Curly, and found myself faced with the terse note: "The wire has gone dead." I had a ball on the way to the plate and there was no way to call it back. At the same time, I was convinced that a ball game tied up in the ninth inning was no time to tell my audience we had lost contact with the game and they would have to listen to recorded music. I knew of only one thing that wouldn't get in the score column and betray me—a foul ball. So I had Augie foul this pitch down the left field foul line. I looked expectantly at Curly. He just shrugged helplessly, so I had Augie foul another one, and still another; then he fouled one back into the box seats. I described in detail the red-headed kid who had scrambled and gotten the souvenir ball. He fouled one into the upper deck that just missed being a home run. He fouled for six minutes and forty-five seconds until I lost count. I began to be frightened that maybe I was establishing a new world record for a fellow staying at bat hitting fouls, and this could betray me. Yet I was into it so far I didn't dare reveal that the wire had gone dead. My voice was rising in pitch and threatening to crack—and then, bless him, Curly started typing. I clutched at the slip. It said: "Galan popped out on the first ball pitched." Not in my game he didn't —he popped out after practically making a career of foul balls [Hubler, pp. 78–79].

These baseball games, which gripped audiences with their drama, were Reagan's creations in the most entire sense—tailored to the radio, to his role, to the audience's taste. He went to Chicago, to construct the mental arena in which he would work his spell. The brother of an acquaintance "took me into the press box so that forever after I had engraved on my mind the picture of how it looked" (Hubler, p. 78).

With the "vasty fields" of Wrigley and Comiskey "crammed within the wooden O" of his broadcast booth, Reagan spent day after summer day playing ball games in his mind. On August 3, 1934, the Des Moines *Dispatch* saluted this achievement:

> To millions of sports fans in at least seven or eight middlewestern states, the voice of Dutch Reagan is a daily source of baseball dope. Every afternoon at 2:00 o'clock "Dutch" goes on the air with his rapid-fire, play-by-play visualization of the home games of Chicago's major league baseball teams, the Cubs and Sox. By the conclusion of the 1934 season, Sept. 30, more than 150 baseball games will have been broadcast over WOC-WHO . . . Evidence of the popularity of Reagan and his "Wheaties" broadcasts come [sic] to WOC-WHO every day in the form of hundreds of letters of thanks and praise . . . Another sports feature to which listeners have become accustomed to listening to regularly, are Reagan's twice daily "Teaberry Sports Reviews," which go on the air every afternoon at 5:25 P.M., and every evening at 10:10 P.M.

Reagan was able to use his imaginative gifts to better purpose than the entertainment of so many people. At the end of his very first summer in Des Moines, Reagan had gone to bed early (11:00) one night in his boarding house, just four blocks west of the river, when he heard an argument on the city street outside. A man had come up behind a young nurse, poked a hard object in his coat pocket into her back, and told her to give him all her money without turning around. She had little money, so she did turn around and started arguing with him. Then, she says, Reagan shouted out the window: "Leave her alone or I'll shoot you right between the shoulders." The man scuttled away, and Reagan told her to wait while he put on a robe and slippers. In that attire, he escorted her the short walk to her hospital. Melba Lohmann King says she already knew Dutch Reagan by his radio reputation, though he had been in town less than six months.[12]

Many years later, as President, Reagan told the editors of *Sports Afield* that it was lucky he had a gun that night. But he also said the robber had a gun, and Mrs. King says she never saw one; he did not take his hand out of his pocket to end the argument. Nor did she see a gun in Reagan's hand when he leaned out of the window.[13] Reagan is not, like some of his followers, a person who grew up hunting and fishing, with guns in hand from his boyhood. His eyesight was too bad for hunting. Besides, Jack Reagan was a determinedly urban man. B. J. Palmer liked to collect and carry weapons, but that would not have been a recommendation to Reagan. Mrs. King says that the streets in Reagan's neighborhood were not considered unsafe, and

Reagan was young, strong, and self-confident, not in need of protection himself. By the time he joined the cavalry reserves, at Fort Des Moines, he might have had the use of a pistol, but the summer of 1933 is too early for him to have joined the reserves. Later in his life, when threats were made against him for his union activities, Reagan submitted with a reluctant sense of "melodrama" to police advice that he carry a gun, and the police had to supply him with a Smith and Wesson (Hubler, p. 200).

Two aspects of the professional skills he was acquiring in Des Moines seem to have come into play, at different times, around Reagan's rescue of Mrs. King. First there was Reagan's quick use of his imagination to cope with emergencies, like a "holdup" in the telegraphic connection when he was "visualizing" ball games: if he could make up a whole ball game, surely he could make up a little thing like a gun. Second, there was the desire to please whatever audience he is addressing at the time—the gun-using editors of the sporting magazine would like to think he had depended on a gun rather than his wits, so he accommodated their desire. Even his genuine heroism is woven into a life of professional pretense.

Saving lives was nothing new to Reagan. In Des Moines he swam at Camp Dodge, the National Guard property—where, by habit long instilled, he spotted a girl going under and rescued her.[14] Reagan was often at Camp Dodge and Fort Des Moines, the two sites that made Des Moines "the focal point of military activity in Iowa."[15] At Fort Des Moines, though it was still a cavalry post, the emphasis by the 1930s was on motorized units.[16] Some horses—those not pampered for the officers or for Sunday polo games—were in danger of neglect, so civilians were allowed to ride them. Myrtle Williams liked to ride, and taught Reagan how. "We used to go ride those old plugs," she said.[17] Reagan apparently liked the military surrounding as much as the riding. He admired discipline, obedience, and dedication, and the cavalry seemed to offer those, with a bonus of romance; so, after becoming a horseman on his own, he faked an eye test, joined the reserves, and became a second lieutenant in the Fourteenth Cavalry Regiment (Hubler, pp. 79–82). This meant, among other things, that he could use the fort's large riding hall during Iowa's long winters. He recaptured some of his Lowell Park environment, but as a year-round drill.

In Des Moines, Reagan for the first time had a considerable degree of independence, money, and fame. But here, as at every juncture of his career, there was an overlapping of new circumstance with stable elements from his past. For one thing, there was Nelle. Myrtle Williams Moon remembers that Nelle was often in Des Moines, staying with friends who had moved there from Dixon. She (Myrtle) and Ronald picnicked with her. Sometimes Jack was there too, but most often Nelle came alone. With Jack and Neil working for the government, and Ronald making more money than either of them, she would have the leisure and train fare to visit her son in his new splendor. Reagan was always glad to have her—as we shall see, he moved his parents to California at the earliest opportunity.

Neil Reagan remembers, as the occasion of his getting a job at the Des Moines radio station, doing a favor for his brother—driving Ronald's car there. Ronald had chosen the Nash convertible he wanted in Des Moines, but ordered it from a classmate working for a car dealership in central Illinois.[18] Neil seems to have taken Nelle with him from Dixon, either when delivering the car or when returning to work in Des Moines, since Ronald remembers that his mother helped Neil get the job (Hubler, p. 72). At any rate, there was a continuing Dixon presence in Des Moines.

Nelle was loved by Ronald's friends not only at the radio station but elsewhere. She and Myrtle became close, and Nelle traded poems with the wife of Peter MacArthur, who had become a third father figure to Ronald (following Ben Cleaver and Sid Altschuler): "I've no way to measure the value of his teaching, his philosophy, or how much it still means to me. I know that this man, with troubles beyond our comprehension [from arthritis and failing eyesight], was still the one person you went to when your own problems were too much to bear" (Hubler, p. 74). No doubt much of MacArthur's fascination for Reagan lay in his vaudeville background; Reagan was still thinking of radio as an entry into larger fields of entertainment.

Reagan's friends from outside the radio station formed an even closer set with Nelle. They all came from a Disciples college (Drake), and some of them from Reagan's fraternity (Teke) on the Drake campus. Iowa Disciples had incorporated Oskaloosa College in 1856, but it did not begin teaching at the college level until after the Civil War. In 1880, a series of disputes arose —a debt crisis, faculty resentment, an attempt to move the college to some more promising city, stout resistance from the local Disciples community.[19] A legal injunction was sworn out against the move, but the faculty went ahead with its plans. The key was $20,000 offered for relocation in Des Moines by the wealthy Disciple banker and railroad man, Francis Marion Drake.[20] The state convention of churches politically approved colleges in both places, Oskaloosa and Des Moines, but it was a meaningless concession, since all the faculty but one left Oskaloosa for Des Moines.

George T. Carpenter, the leader of the migrating faculty, had large ambitions. He quickly revived a defunct law school and threw together a medical faculty from local doctors, making Drake a university from its first appearance on the new site in 1881, an auspicious year that saw the inauguration of Disciple President James Garfield.[21] Carpenter instantly began the large brick-gothic administration building that is still the historical center of the campus, an ambitious structure that rose on the west of town while the even grander capitol was going up to the east.

Reagan had heard of Drake throughout his youth, for the same reason that he had heard of Eureka. The younger institution originally drew heavily on Eureka for its faculty. Carpenter, the founder, was a Eureka graduate. So were two other early presidents. But Drake had gone on to greater success, not least in sports, and was eight times the size of Eureka in 1933. Ronald Reagan's first trip to Des Moines, a month before his move there, had been to cover the Drake Relays track event for WOC-WHO in Davenport (Hubler, p. 69). After he settled in Des Moines, he was hired by the university as field announcer for Drake football games. Drake had just installed a new radio program in its journalism department,[22] and Reagan came to know several of the "J students."

He first met Hubert "Pee Wee" Johnson—who would organize his Escondido campaign office when he ran for governor of California—in the Gus Morales tailoring shop. They were each being fitted with a tuxedo for the all-fraternity dance at Drake. Johnson, like most of Reagan's friends from Drake, did not come from the Teke house but from ATO.[23] They formed a close circle of friends that endured over years—including Will Scott, who was Reagan's best man at his wedding to Jane Wyman; Walt Scott, Will's brother; Glen Claussen, who worked for a while answering Wyman's fan mail; Leroy Austin, later of the Los Angeles *Times;* Ed Morley and Walt Roddy. They used to go after dances or ball games to Cy's "Moonlighter," a kind of rustic speakeasy in these last days of Prohibition. "We sang midwestern fight songs around the piano—'On Wisconsin,' that kind of thing," says Claussen.[24] They even took Nelle when she came to town. Much as she hated liquor, she told Myrtle Williams, "It's just a kind of a family place."[25] Johnson, who had dropped out of Drake, acted as Reagan's football spotter, identifying the Drake players, while Reagan strode up and down on the sidelines with his microphone. He was a campus hero, much pursued by local beauties. But it was in Des Moines that he heard from Margaret Cleaver that their engagement was over, and he seems not to have been serious about any of the dates he danced with. One equestrienne who met him at the riding field and dated him for a long time told relatives her Catholicism offered some obstacle to the marriage.[26] But Reagan does not seem to have been interested in marriage at this point. He was not going to stay in Des Moines. He had his eye on California.

As if the gold rushers had left some tropism behind them, Iowans have felt an extraordinary gravitational tug toward California. Hundreds of thousands of them have flooded into Southern California. Carey McWilliams attributes this historic outpouring to Iowa's late development as a state (after the Civil War) and its rapid rise to agricultural prosperity during the railroad boom, when younger sons who would not inherit the farm did not just move a state away but as far as the train would take them.[27] They were encouraged by a deliberate concentration of California advertising on Iowa, more specifically on Des Moines and the Des Moines *Register.*[28] Those who migrated formed Iowa Clubs, celebrated Iowa Day, boosted the first Iowan who became governor of California (Frank Merriam), and lured friends or relatives after them.[29] When anyone from Iowa was accepted by the movies, the studio sent a flood of promotional material to his or her hometown. When a Warner Brothers talent scout saw a promising young actress from Sioux City at the Pasadena Playhouse and offered her a contract, the Des Moines *Register* ran two stories on her, on January 3 and 11 of 1937: "Sioux

City Girl on Her Way Up" and "Stardom Is Seen for Helen Valkis." When Reagan returned to Des Moines from his own screen test, and was asked who were the most beautiful stars he had seen in Hollywood, he loyally said "that Iowa girl" was as beautiful as any. Valkis had appeared with him in his screen test. "It really was an all-Iowa affair," Reagan told the *Register*. The woman in Los Angeles who took him to an agent was Joy Hodges, a singer he knew from her performances at WHO. And his new agent "manages among others, Kea Ray, a former Drake co-ed."[30] After Reagan's arrival in Hollywood, the Warners studio sent long "letters" from him to the Des Moines *Register*. It was a self-fueling process.

Reagan had been yearning for Hollywood all along. He persuaded the station to send him to Los Angeles for spring training of the Chicago Cubs in 1937—and described, in his sports column, how he wandered about Catalina Island staring at the pictures of the baseball stars.[31] He had taken his first airplane flight to the island, in a small plane on a choppy day. He swore he would never fly again, and for almost three decades, despite considerable inconvenience to his career, he kept that resolution.[32] Though he served throughout World War II in the Air Force, making training films for pilots, and played airmen in four films (*Secret Service of the Air, Murder in the Air, International Squadron,* and *Desperate Journey),* he had no experience of flight at that time beyond his brief trip from Los Angeles to Catalina.

Reagan really went to California, not for the Cubs, but determined to make a screen test. By this time, with growing fame and sponsor support, Reagan was cultivating a romantic image of himself. He had bought the Nash convertible he yearned for, and chose his pipe and jacket colors to match its beige tone.[33] He was chosen by his Wheaties sponsor, General Mills, to address a meeting of sports announcers in Chicago on April 16, 1937.[34] When General Mills heard about the Hollywood offer, it made a counteroffer to keep Reagan in Des Moines at least through the 1937 baseball season.[35] He was giving up something assured and satisfying for a long shot—the studio had just given him its standard six months contract with option to renew.[36] But Reagan knew where he wanted to go. The radio station bought him a large suitcase as his farewell gift, and presented it on the air at a party for him, where celebrities bade him farewell. Friends in Dixon gathered at their radios to listen, and the hometown paper reported it.[37]

Reagan had met Iowans in California, and would soon be joined by a further influx of them he helped to cause. Pee Wee Johnson, Will Scott, and Ed Morley followed their friend to Los Angeles in 1937. In 1938, Glen Claussen, Walt Roddy, and Walt Scott joined the Drake crew, and another WHO announcer, Dick Anderson, showed up as well. Ronald helped pay their rent and Nelle served them all Sunday dinner. Reagan was able to keep his midwestern easiness of manner because he took so much of the Midwest with him, moving in a cocoon of his own making, one the years would not abrade.

CHAPTER 13

Journalist

*All over the country a little band of pioneers were
[sic] as famous as the great teams and athletes they
described: Graham MacNamee, Ted Husing, and Pat
Flanagan.*

—*Ronald Reagan (Hubler, p. 54)*

Reagan's gifts and failings as a politician are often attributed to the fact that
he "began as an actor." Actually, he began as a journalist. His first year-
round employment, his first professional training, his first broad reputation,
came from his work as a reporter of sports events. For four intense years, he
was not merely an announcer, but an interpreter. During the baseball season,
he broadcast twice-daily commentaries which gave listeners what the Des
Moines *Dispatch* called "baseball dope," the real story, the inside stuff. In
the sports column he wrote, he was something of a muckraker, offering
readers the facts behind the sham—the dynamics of football bowl competition, for instance, behind all "that 'guff' the Pasadena Chamber of Commerce spreads."[1]

Two months later, Reagan was suggesting that the fight between Joe Louis
and Bob Pastor might have been fixed: "One week ago the inhabitants of
Slug-Ugly Lane faced into the wind and sniffed a choice odor. It was a
vaguely familiar but very unpleasant whiff, reminiscent of sporting mud
holes like the Black Sox Scandal, the grunt and groan racket, and one or two
horse races John Public lost his shirt on . . . Of course, it's only sheer
coincidence that he [Pastor] laid a golden egg right in the gambler's [sic]
collective lap . . . Joe seems surprisingly indifferent about his failure to
corner Robert."[2] Reagan wonders whether Pastor was allowed to go the
distance if he agreed not to fight, or whether he just lacked fight in the first
place. "Joe Louis won a ten round decision from Bob Pastor, a young Jewish
lad whose mother spent her life battling slums and social injustice. (Maybe
Bob doesn't know about that kind of fighting)." This column ends with the
perennial sports lament, for vanished giants of the past.

Reagan was young to be lamenting the past, but his picture, run with the

column, was meant to make him look as old as possible. It showed him in a
reflective pose, pipe taken from his mouth for a moment's pontificating. The
layout of the feature, as well its style, reveal the model. The column was run
on the top left corner of the sports page, his picture to the column's right,
exactly as Grantland Rice was presented to daily readers of the Des Moines
Register. Rice was still going strong in the thirties, though his glory period
had been the twenties, when he forged the heroic epithets, often alliterative,
that defined an era—the Manassa Mauler, the Galloping Ghost, the Four
Horsemen. Reagan had been a disciple of Rice from his high school days,
when he wrote a prose variation on "Alumnus Football," the Rice poem that
ends with the famous lines:

> For when the One Great Scorer comes to mark against your name,
> He writes—not that you won or lost—but how you played the Game.[3]

Reagan's essay, called "Gethsemane," appeared in *The Dixonian* for his
junior year. It tells, like the poem, the story of a quitter who comes back.
Reagan ends by quoting the poem's conclusion, and his descriptions are
clearly taken from the saga style Rice used in his columns: "An early harvest
moon made ghostly figures of the milky mist tendrils, that hung over the
deserted gridiron like spirits of long dead heroes."[4]

As an adult columnist, Reagan turned off the mist machine. But he still
worked at the "kennings" Rice had made obligatory—we get "Saccharin
Saucer" instead of Sugar Bowl in the *Dispatch*. Rice loved metaphors, and
scrambled them with a certain infectious energy. Reagan mixes his more
tentatively: "All the diplomatic back-stabbing of Europe's 'Heiling' heels has
been relegated to the penny ante table by the crisis precipitated in this land
of swing time and 'bowls' and the bowls have it—I mean the bowls are the
battlefield where the crisis will grow more critical."[5]

Rice used overblown language because the surface details of sports engagement were merely the signs of a larger moral epic, in which destiny and
free will worked out man's fate. All the metaphors were justified because
sports is itself a metaphor for life. So, after airing his allegations about
criminality in the Louis-Pastor fight, Reagan concludes with a moral condemnation of Pastor and "how he played the game." Pastor did not have the
heart to stand and take his licking. "Mr. and Mrs. American shell out to see
the Old College try, they paid to see Bob at least go down trying. He didn't
try and most of us still raise an eyebrow when we wonder why he didn't."[6]

The preliminary murkiness about fact and absolute certainty about the
moral is typical of sports writing at the time, and of much sports writing in
general. What Thorstein Veblen wrote in the 1890s remained applicable long
afterward:

> In athletic sports there is almost invariably present a good share of rant
> and swagger and ostensible mystification—features which mark the his-
> trionic nature of these employments. In all this, of course, the reminder
> of boyish make-believe is plain enough. The slang of athletics, by the

way, is in great part made up of extremely sanguinary locutions borrowed from the terminology of warfare. Except where it is adopted as a
necessary means of secret communication, the use of a special slang in
any employment is probably to be accepted as evidence that the occupation in question is substantially make-believe.[7]

The bellicose language, the moralism, the open partisanship of sports writers, all come from reporters' entry into the "spirit" of the games they cover,
addressing the concerns of the fan, voicing those concerns, stirring them up.
What this means is that Reagan began his career as a journalist, all right, but
in the corner of journalism where accuracy is least expected and often excluded. The relationship of the reporter to the athlete has often been that of
promoter if not exploiter, protector if not adulator—the mutual mythologiz-
ing of Howard Cosell and Muhammad Ali. Long before television, the newspapers actively promoted sports. The Chicago *Tribune,* to take just one paper, not only helped launch the Golden Gloves program of the 1920s, but
invented the All-Star Baseball Game in 1933 and the College All-Star Football Game in 1934.[8]

If the press uses teams, teams use the press in return. Local reporters are
recruited as boosters, or punished for failing to be that. Sports reporting
seems, from one vantage, all a story of bans and reprisals—Ted Husing
locked out of the World Series broadcasting booth for life, Westbrook Pegler
kept from the Notre Dame locker room for insufficient reverence to Knute
Rockne, Jim Piersall fired as White Sox announcer for candid remarks about
the team.[9]

Accuracy, already vulnerable to such direct pressures, also suffers from
contradictory defenses—the claim that "it's only a game" (it would be pretentious to lavish scholarly concern on trivial diversions) and the boast that
it has some "higher" meaning (the moral, which can be extracted from
"mere" facts). So, for a variety of conflicting but mutually supporting reasons, sports reporting tends to lack detachment, objectivity, distance. Other
journalists take pride in controlling their reactions even to violent crimes or
natural disasters. Sportscasters are encouraged to lose their equanimity over
a right hook or a forty-yard run.

It was the ability to convey vocal excitement that made stars of those
announcers Reagan took as his models. Radio was essential to making the
twenties a "golden age" of sports. *Radio Digest* claimed that 127 listeners
had heart attacks during Graham McNamee's dramatic broadcast of the
second Dempsey-Tunney fight in 1927:

Graham McNamee, a baritone singer of small repute in New York,
became the first star of the new medium . . . McNamee enjoyed a
remarkable capacity for using his voice to span the gamut of emotions
—of, as a contemporary put it, "becoming audibly excited at crucial
moments, using the popular idiom, putting the spirit of every punch,
every pitch, every run into his voice, speeding up his voice with the
tensions of the play, letting it subside with the aftermath of calm."

Universally hailed as "the World's Most Popular Announcer," he received over 50,000 letters from infatuated fans in the wake of his descriptions of the 1925 World Series.[10]

In such a medium, drama mattered more than accuracy, especially since the listener had no way of checking the report as it ran on:

> McNamee himself was notorious for the absence of precision in his broadcasts. If he asserted that the wrong back was toting the ball in a football game, he would try to correct himself by quickly declaring that the ball had been lateraled to the player who was actually carrying it. After sitting alongside McNamee during his broadcast of a World Series game, Ring Lardner observed that "the Washington Senators and the New York Giants must have played a double-header this afternoon— the game I saw and the game Graham McNamee announced."[11]

Some people, given the choice between the announced game and the real one, found they preferred the imaginary game. They rejoiced in the exclusion of any world *but* that conjured up by the announcer's voice.[12] At any event, the voice of the sports announcer entered America's consciousness. Boys love to play ball, and to play announcer while they are playing—or even when they are not. Reagan had been doing it long before he made his living at it:

> Once at a fraternity stunt show I had supplied the voice from backstage for a supposed football broadcast and, like my ice-cream-scoop patter at the park, I could launch into a rapid-fire routine of "Here they come out of the huddle up to the line of scrimmage, the ball is snapped," as long as anyone would listen [Hubler, p. 54].

Young people play many of the games of life to the inner cheerings of their own announcer. We are allowed to read the thoughts of Mike Doonesbury at his first college "mixer": " 'Mike the Mix,' inexperienced but eager freshman, still looks around for his first score of the evening." And when we look inside the thoughts of a university president, we find that he has not outgrown the habit: "It's more kudos for Yale's Youthful President as he starts out on his morning walk through the colleges to reduce tensions."[13] Sexual encounters can be "announced," too: "In the black pubic hair, ladies and gentlemen, weighing one hundred and seventy pounds, at least half of which is still undigested halvah and hot pastrami, from Newark, NJ, The Schnoz, Alexander Portnoy!"[14]

The voice of the sports announcer is part of the cultural conditioning of most American boys, and the voice speaks as much *to* a fantasy life as *from* an external world of verifiable events. It was Reagan's first professional discipline to reach that life of fantasy with his voice, to create the suspense and drama of a "real" game from the laconic code messages he received over the telegraph wire. In fact, his games were often more exciting than the ones being played far away, a fact that people not only mentioned but admired.

If one did not understand that there was no deception involved, Reagan's account of his famous dead-wire incident could mislead. As he tells the story of the endless fly balls he had to create, keeping the man at bat while he waited for the receiver to come back to life, great issues seem at stake: "My voice was rising in pitch and threatening to crack"—a professional crisis of the first order for a man whose trade *is* his voice. Why is it so important that the audience not know that the line has gone dead? Because they would find that Reagan was not actually at the game?

They knew he was not there. They gloried in the fact. His skill at "visualizing" was praised in the papers. People were invited to the Crystal Palace at the Iowa Fair Grounds to watch him as he invented the game from scraps of paper.[15] There was a complicity in make-believe. What Reagan feared when the line went dead was, at one level, a simple matter of professional pride, that he would not be able to keep up the patter convincingly enough to sustain his reputation as a creator of seamless illusion. But the deeper concern was for what gave rise to those skills, the demand for illusion in the first place. If Reagan had been forced openly to admit (or subtly to convey) the fact that the line had gone dead, he would have broken the continuity of pretense. All those involved knew they were pretending—as we know that the actor onstage is not Hamlet; but we do not want him to stop in mid-performance and remind us of that. We want to finish the dream, though we know it is only a dream.

Reagan was attuned to his audience's needs. That was the condition of his success. He addressed them, in the *name* of a reality (there *was* a ball game being played somewhere), but of a reality about which nice discriminations were not to be made. The real game "went warrant" for the imaginary one, without guaranteeing any of its lively detail. If Reagan had just been inventing games in an empty room, with no wire at all, the game would instantly have lost its appeal. But once the general authority was established, minute-by-minute concern was for the plausible arrangement of satisfactory incident. Thus, there was an ambiguity about the real built into Reagan's professional life from the outset. In some ways, this is a more complex and delicate thing than the separate world of pretense that is formal acting. Plays end; we are no longer in Elsinore. But Reagan was still playing the same role when, after the ball game was over, he did his evening analysis of what had gone on in the world he had described that afternoon. He made up the game, then criticized the performance—not his, but that of the players he called up in people's minds. Was this a step back toward the real players, resting hundreds of miles away after the game, or one step farther into fantasy? Judging from his sports columns, which imposed an overall moral shape on the event, it was a completion of the myth-making process. He gave the ingredients of the afternoon their final rounded shape at night.

To say all this is simply to say that Reagan was a sportscaster of the thirties. People expected colorful and edifying anecdotes, earthy homilies enlivened by conflict. People wanted mythical figures. In creating and protecting those figures, sports writers sometimes came to believe in them themselves—or not to know what they believed. "Red Barber, a renowned baseball broadcaster who referred to every ball player as a gentleman, insisted that he never heard an obscenity spoken on the ball field."[16] That is a harmless enough delusion, if sincerely entertained. But where does one stop flattering the world with such credulity? The whole sports world must have seemed endlessly plastic to the sportswriter with a flair for dramaturgy:

> For nearly a decade, bridging the 1930s and 1940s, Bill Stern, a CBS announcer, hosted an immensely popular program, "Colgate Sports Newsreel," that deliberately falsified reports of athletes and sports events for dramatic effect. From his deathbed, Abraham Lincoln, according to Stern, summoned a nearby general. "Keep baseball going. The country needs it," said Lincoln. The general's name, Stern cried triumphantly, was Abner Doubleday.[17]

Challenged about his stories, Stern admitted they were designed to "lift audiences out of a humdrum, monotonous existence." He recognized some responsibility to the feelings of his audience, none to mere facts. Let facts take care of themselves. He would take care of people. It is, in several senses, an engaging attitude.

Reagan, it is safe to assume, felt deeper responsibilities than did Bill Stern —if nothing else, to "the team," to sports, to the game. When he gathered to sing fight songs with his fraternity brothers at Cy's, his heart was in every line. He believed that sports, which purify, should be kept pure, at whatever cost. Bob Pastor should have stood still, so Joe Louis could knock him out, for the good of the game. For the honor of the fight game, Pastor should "at least go down trying."

But even this higher responsibility does not bind one to mere fact, make one accountable for the truthfulness of stories told to purify the sport or inspirit a team. In a revealing aside, Reagan admits to Hubler that Knute Rockne may have invented the line Reagan spoke as George Gipp in the 1940 movie *Knute Rockne—All American* ("Win one for the Gipper"): "If the story had come out of his imagination, no one—including Bonnie [Mrs. Rockne]—ever knew" (Hubler, p. 109). But he goes on to say that it does not matter, because the story, whether made up or not, spurred the team "to sacrifice their individual quarrels for a common goal" (p. 110).

The Gipper story is an appropriate one for Reagan to use—he devoted the climax of his Notre Dame commencement address in 1981 to a retelling of it. The tale is as good an illustration as one could find of the code of accuracy in sports reporting. The story began, appropriately enough, with the archetypal sports reporter, Grantland Rice. So far as any record shows, he was the first person Rockne told the story of George Gipp's deathbed request. It was eight years after Gipp's death, on the eve of a game against Army, during Rockne's worst season ever. He had just lost the opening two games of the season; he would go on to lose two more that year (the four made up a third

of *all* his losses in thirteen years as head coach). After trying out the story of
Gipp's death on Rice, at Rice's New York apartment, Rockne said of Gipp:
"He's been gone a long time but I may have to use him again tomorrow."[18]

Rockne was known to use anything that worked when firing up his team.
He was baptized a Catholic in 1925 and two days later "refer[red] to his
conversion to motivate players at the halftime of the Northwestern game,
which they were then losing."[19] James Crowley, one of the famous Four
Horsemen, who became a coach himself, told Coles Phinizy about a trick
Rockne used in one game:

> He came into the locker room with a bunch of telegrams from promi-
> nent alumni and said to us, "I have one wire here, boys, that probably
> doesn't mean much to you, but it does to me. It's from my poor sick
> little boy, Billy, who is critically ill in the hospital." Rock was a great
> actor. He got a lump in his throat and his lips began to tremble as he
> read Billy's wire: "I want Daddy's team to win." We won the 1922
> Georgia Tech game for Billy, and when we got home we found out that
> Billy hadn't been sick at all. There was a big crowd to meet us at the
> station, and running around in front of everyone was "sick" little Billy
> Rockne.[20]

When caught in his tricks, Rockne just admitted them, certain that they
were justified if they worked for the team. He even confessed using the Billy
telegram in an article of his own called "The Psychology of Football." He
also boasted that he would pretend to resign during a pep talk to get the
team fired up.[21] Sometimes he was so good at convincing others, with his
heartfelt pleas, that he convinced himself. Crowley heard from Joe Byrne, an
alumnus friend of the coach, how Rockne complained before one game that
he had nothing to use in his pep talk; Byrne suggested that he say some
alumni, plotting against him, might succeed if the team let him down.
Rockne told the story so circumstantially that, after the victory, he told
Byrne he wanted an apology from those alumni. By then he believed in the
improbable conspirators himself.[22]

Rockne believed what he wanted to believe when it came to George Gipp,
a brilliant athlete who came to Notre Dame on a baseball scholarship, and
had Cubs and White Sox contracts waiting for him when he died as a senior
in college (1920). Gipp, unpredictable and self-destructive, smoked, drank,
gambled, neglected his health, attended practice irregularly, attended classes
and exams intermittently, and drove himself to death by the age of twenty-
five. He secretly played professional football.[23] He bet large sums on the
Notre Dame games.[24] He was expelled from school for misconduct, and
spent six weeks hustling pool in South Bend until pressure from fans made
the school readmit him.[25] (As a reciprocal gesture, he played the only three
baseball games of his scholarship.) None of this is reflected in the saccharine
account of Gipp that Rockne wrote for *Collier's* in 1930. Rockne has him
expelled for academic reasons and readmitted after a nonexistent oral

makeup exam. Rockne, himself a convert by then, also talked of Gipp's deathbed conversion. Gipp was baptized a Catholic on his deathbed, though there is no record of his asking for the sacrament, and his mother was opposed to the step.[26]

Since Rockne made up so many legends about Gipp, and was so unscrupulous about the accuracy of things used in his pep talks, it would be surprising if his story of a deathbed request to "win one for the Gipper" were true.[27] Eight years had passed. The legend of Gipp had grown, but no one on the team would have any direct memory of him. (Gipp's teammates, commenting on the story later, said that he never referred to himself as "the Gipper.")[28] At any rate, Rockne used Gipp for the Army game—it was certain that he would, after giving the story to Grantland Rice, who could not resist relaying such a tearjerker in his column. And the story no doubt had something to do with the fact that Notre Dame beat Army—narrowly. (Army was on Notre Dame's one-yard line with the tying touchdown when time ran out.) How much it had to do with winning is disputable, since the witnesses divide roughly equally on whether Rockne told the story before the game began or at halftime.[29] Since the score was 0–0 at the half, and 12–6 at the end, it serves drama better to have Rockne tell his whopper at the half, and that is what the 1940 movie does.

Reagan grew up with Rice's story of Gipp, and told it on the radio station during his evening shows (Hubler, p. 105). Gipp was the first role he actively sought at Warner Brothers, his second favorite role (after Drake McHugh in Kings Row). The movie added further legends to those already clustered around Rockne and Gipp. It falsifies Rockne's own account of the famous Notre Dame backfield shift. Rockne wrote that it was introduced by his predecessor as head coach, after Notre Dame had been defeated by a razzle-dazzle Yale team. In the film, Rockne himself dreams it up six years later, while watching a vaudeville chorus run through its dance routine, so the "Four Horsemen" can introduce it.[30]

When he returned to Notre Dame as the nation's President in 1981, Reagan was happy to have an opportunity for telling the Gipp story again.[31] He wrote his own speech.[32] He was using memories of his sportscasting days as well as of the movie, for whose premiere he and Pat O'Brien (who played Rockne on the screen) had traveled to South Bend.[33] O'Brien was with him on the platform in 1981 when Reagan spoke:

> Now I'm going to mention again that movie that Pat and I and Notre Dame were in for it says something about America. First Knute Rockne as a boy came to America with his parents from Norway. And in the few years it took him to grow up to college age, he became so American, that here at Notre Dame, he became an All-American in a game that is still to this day uniquely American.[34] As a coach, he did more than teach our young men how to play a game. He believed truly that the noblest work of man was building the character of men. And maybe that's why he was a living legend. No man connected with foot-

ball has ever achieved the stature or occupied the singular niche in the nation that he carved out for himself, not just in sport, but in our entire social structure.

Now, today, I hear very often, "Win one for the Gipper," spoken in a very humorous vein. Lately, I've been hearing it by congressmen who are supportive of the program that I've introduced. But let's look at the significance of that story. Rockne could have used Gipp's dying words to win a game at any time.[35] But eight years went by following the death of George Gipp before Rockne revealed those dying words, his death-bed wish.

And then he told the story at halftime to a team that was losing and one of the only teams he had ever coached that was torn by dissension and jealousy and factionalism. The seniors on that team were about to close out their football careers without learning or experiencing any of the real values that a game has to impart. None of them had ever known George Gipp. They were children when he played for Notre Dame. It was to this team that Rockne told the story and so inspired them that they rose above their personal animosities. For someone they had never known they joined together in a common cause and attained the unattainable.

We were told when we were making the picture of one line that was spoken by a player during that game. We were actually afraid to put it in the picture. The man who carried the ball over for the winning touchdown was injured on the play. We were told that as he was lifted on the stretcher and carried off the field he was heard to say: "That's the last one I can get for you, Gipper."[36]

Now, it's only a game. And maybe to hear it now afterward—and this is what we feared might sound maudlin and not the way it was intended—but is there anything wrong with young people having an experience, feeling something so deeply, thinking of someone else to the point that they can give so completely of themselves? There will come times in the lives of all of us when we'll be faced with causes bigger than ourselves, and they won't be on the playing field.[37]

It is the message of Rice's "Alumnus Football" all over again, of "the swirl of Life's big game." A continuity to Reagan's career would exist even without the Hollywood interval. The Reagan of the sports column and commentaries, of the dramatic baseball "re-creations," is the President who is so good at giving pep talks to the whole nation. His gifts resemble Rockne's own. It is interesting that the Rockne pep talk was put to use by corporate executives, who hired him to fire up Studebaker dealers—much as Reagan would be hired to address General Electric workers in the 1950s.[38]

Reagan often conceives his political speeches in terms of the pep talk, using anecdotes and moral examples to draw the nation together, to instill patriotism, without regard for niggling little details about the source or accuracy of his stories. There is one story he has told so often over the years that it seems to have a special meaning for him—the tale of a B-17 pilot in World War II, who told his crew to bail out after his ship was hit. The belly gunner was too badly wounded to move; the pilot, finding him in tears, said, "Never mind, son, we'll ride it down together." After hearing Reagan deliver this story, with quivering voice, in Racine, Wisconsin, during the 1980 campaign, reporters noticed that, if the two men died together, no one could have reported their last words or actions. One of them, Roger Simon, wrote that in the Chicago *Sun Times,* where Mike Royko picked up the tale and made fun of it in a column.[39] But that obvious flaw in the story's credibility bothers Reagan as little as does the idea that Rockne made up Gipp's dying request. The sports reporter is not accountable for such prosaic kinds of truth. Reagan has continued to tell the bomber pilot story with great emotion, and obvious belief, in many contexts.

The power of the bomber story over Reagan himself was demonstrated when he gave it his full emotional rendition in intimate conversation with some fellow actors. Warren Beatty and Diane Keaton had been invited to the White House for a screening of their movie *Reds.* After the show, the President charmed the two with a witty correction of one joke in the movie. "I could tell that Diane was really surprised and really liking him," Beatty said. Then Reagan commented on the subject of the movie:

> Without missing a beat he said: "You know what's really wrong with the Russians? What's really wrong with the Russians is this." He started to tell this long story from World War II, about a plane that is shot down, and the gunner is trapped, and the pilot, instead of parachuting out to save himself, cradles the gunner's head in his arms and they go down together. It must have been the plot of some movie he saw, or made, or something. I kept looking at Diane and she kept looking at me and we kept waiting for the punch line. And there wasn't one. And then we realized that he meant every word he said about the Russians.[40]

Warren Beatty, too young to remember Grantland Rice, does not understand the logic of the pep talk.

CHAPTER 14

Sports

*Then his sobs ceased and he stood up, his face to the
sky, and the ghosts of honored warriors urged him and drew
him from the low shadows. A love and loyalty took the
place of egotism. His hand strayed to the purple monogram
he wore, and as he looked at the curving track, at the
level field, he realized he loved them.*

—*Ronald Reagan,* The Dixonian *(1927)*

Knute Rockne told the Gipper story when he was two losses into his los-
ingest season ever, and he was not a man who liked to lose. But Reagan
assures us, both in his account to Hubler and in his Notre Dame speech, that
Rockne did not tell the story merely to win a game. Why, then, did he use
the story against Army in 1928? Reagan gives several reinforcing reasons:

Rockne did it because the team was divided, a rare thing for a Rockne
crew. Actually, the 1920 winning team on which Gipp himself became an
All-American was fiercely divided, two in the backfield squabbling with each
other and resenting Gipp.[1]

Rockne did it because this was the team's last opportunity to experience
the joys of common effort. Actually, they had six more games to play that
season.

Rockne did it because the team was suffering from lack of inspiration, not
deficient skills. Actually, they lost two more games after the Gipper story is
supposed to have forged them to a common purpose. Rockne's poor record
in 1928 came from "a nightmarish mixture of the results of the anti-shift
rules, injuries, and the team's lack of depth and youth."[2]

Reagan, like most celebrants of sport, is nervously aware of the objection
that "it's only a game." Sports must be justified in the name of something
beyond sports, a higher meaning to the game. Rockne is not just a winning
coach; he has a key role "in our whole social structure." Veblen described
the pressures at work:

There is a strong body of popular sentiment in favor of diversions and
enterprise of the kind in question; but there is at the same time present

in the community a pervading sense that this ground of sentiment wants legitimation. The required legitimation is ordinarily sought by showing that although sports are substantially of a predatory, socially disintegrating effect; although their proximate effect runs in the direction of reversion to propensities that are industrially disserviceable; yet indirectly and remotely—by some not readily comprehensible process of polar induction, or counter-irritation perhaps—sports are conceived to foster a habit of mind that is serviceable for the social or industrial purpose.[3]

Sports are justified because they instill virtues applicable to a wider sphere than the games. Teamwork, in Reagan's words at Notre Dame, becomes the willingness to sacrifice for "causes bigger than ourselves."

The use of sports as a moral paradigm for the young, combined with the fact that athletics are learned at a prepuberty stage and pursued throughout adolescence, associates such games with innocence, moral struggle, and the challenges of growing. When characters in our fiction yearn for a "cleaner" and more innocent world, they turn often to images connected with the sports of their youth: "Where have you gone, Joe DiMaggio?" John Updike's Rabbit Angstrom, behind the wheel of his car, wants solace: "He tries to think of something pleasant. He imagines himself about to shoot a long one-hander . . ."[4] Jeremy Larner's hero in Drive, He Said "had formed himself outwards around the grip he took on the American basketball." Baffled by complexity, he has one moral gyroscope: "In the last thought before he curled into the grip of deepest sleep, he yearned for the clean true feel of a basketball."[5] Hemingway even has his Old Man alter ego, battling with an uncooperative fish, stiffen himself with the thought that "I must be worthy of the great DiMaggio who does all things perfectly."[6]

Athletic innocence and aspiration verge on the religious. In the Hubler account of the Gipper story, Reagan claims that Chevigny "looked up from the stretcher and said, 'That's the last one I can get for you, Gipper.' " Looking up is the proper touch, since the whole story is based on the continuing interest of a dead football player in the fortunes of his team. Sports is not only a life-and-death matter, but a life-beyond-death matter; Chevigny looks to where George Gipp is presumed to be watching from some ghostlier grandstand.

Locker-room piety was a commonplace by Veblen's time: "It is somewhat insistently claimed as a meritorious feature of sporting life that the habitual participants in athletic games are in some degree peculiarly given to devout practices." An evangelical book on Ronald Reagan uses the same kind of language for Reagan's Bel Air pastor, "a college football All-American, big, unpretentious, straight talking," and for King David, "a rough, tough warrior.'"[7] For some reason it is assumed in such literature that "sissies" cannot be Christians. The true Christian is, like Jud Roberts in Sinclair Lewis's novel, "a real red-blooded regular fellow."[8] One reason for the depth of Rockne's appeal to his own time was his fusion of sports and religion. Communities trust the training of their young to people with a certain devout ferocity:

> If a person so endowed with a proclivity for exploits is in a position to guide the development of habits in the adolescent members of the community, the influence which he exerts in the direction of conversation and reversion to prowess may be very considerable. This is the significance, for instance, of the fostering care latterly bestowed by many clergymen and other pillars of society upon "boys' brigades" and similar pseudo-military organizations. The same is true of the encouragement given to the growth of "college spirit," college athletics, and the like, in the higher institutions of learning.[9]

In the Rockne movie, Pat O'Brien tells a rapt congressional committee that the nation needs football because "the most dangerous thing in American life is that we're getting soft."

A sign of the approximation of sports to religion, and vice versa, is the similarity of their homiletic technique. The modern sermon is often indistinguishable from the pep talk, and the sports anecdote is hagiographical in form. As we have seen, Bill Stern was the master of such *fioretti* when Reagan was broadcasting:

> Stern told of a dejected Frankie Frisch, who was on the verge of quitting Fordham University and ending his life. A sympathetic priest saw Frisch and urged him to give his life "to the great game of baseball. And that priest's name," Stern exuberantly shouted, "was Eugenio Pacelli. Yes, the same Eugenio Pacelli who is famous the world over today as Pope Pius." Few doubted; millions listened in wonderment.[10]

Television preachers work similar miracles with history. Dr. Robert Schuller, for instance, the apostle of "positivity thinking," had this to say on his television program "Hour of Power" in October 1983:

> Remember when Hannibal conquered Rome [he didn't], how he brought all of his troops across the Rubicon [Rhone], and just as he got them all across, and the last one had crossed the bridges [he used rafts], what did he do? Burned the bridges. That's right, that's where the old expression comes, "Burn your bridges behind you."

Few care about such mistakes, since the aim of the preacher's art is not demonstration but inspiration. It can even be considered irreverent to draw attention to mere historical details when the religious message is what matters. We give a man latitude when he is writing advertisements for heaven. We may forget, however, that sports writers of the Grantland Rice type thought of themselves as doing the same kind of divine publicity work; license with the facts was taken as a professional privilege.

There is one area, however, where those interested in athletics do demand accuracy. Even Rice knew that, and wrote a poem on the subject ("The Record"):

> But the Scroll is cast
> And the Record waits.[11]

Accurate statistics are demanded from sports reporters, and have been throughout modern times.

> In the 1860s, Henry Chadwick, the dean of baseball publicists, invented the box score and batting averages, marvelous quantitative devices that made it possible for fans to precisely compare present performances with those of the past. Regardless of the unpredictability and turmoil on the front page of the newspaper, fans, from the time of Chadwick on, expected to find on the sports page confirmation of orderliness and continuity.[12]

Another matter requiring accuracy is the rules. Since a game cannot be played at all if its confines are not clearly marked, the sports writer's vaguely imagined events hover over a precise grid of permissable moves. The reverence for rules is so important that Reagan fashioned one of his homilies on the subject.

> I'll never forget one game [of Dixon High] with Mendota. The Mendota team yelled for a penalty against Dixon at a crucial point. I'd been the culprit and I knew they were right. The official hadn't seen the play, however, so he asked me. I was in an awful spot. But truth-telling had been whaled into me, also a lot of sports ethics which, from the storm that incident raised, evidently weren't exactly practical for fatheads. I told the truth, the penalty was ruled, and Dixon lost the game.[13]

The truth whaled into Reagan was of a selective kind precisely *because* it concerned sports ethics. One must observe the rules: Reagan could not lie to this odd official who was letting him make his own call. He could not make up a false story in the game. But he could make up the entire game. The lost game that Reagan described could not have occurred—Mendota never won by one touchdown against a team that Reagan played on.[14] We see in one tale how the sports code is endlessly permissive about narrative enhancements, however stringent it may be about rules and records.

If the true sports fan has an antiquarian's regard for the Record, that is part of the general conservatism of sports. Maintaining a game's existence demands steadiness in the rules, indoctrination of the young, and ambition for the same rewards, generation after generation. Comparison of athletes from different periods, one of the fans' favorite pastimes, depends on relative uniformity in the conduct of the game. This descends, by no accident, to the clothes that are rightly called uniforms. These, even when made of material improved for the rough wear they get, retain or revert to ancient design. Baseball players are the only men around who still wear knickers.

True lovers of the game delay as long as possible, and then denounce, any introduction of novelties, like Astroturf or the designated hitter. Against the evidence of improved nutrition and training, which have gradually leveled all past records, the sports fan continues to believe that performance was better in the past—there were *men* in those days. Mantle just had a peppier ball to hit than Ruth did. Ali did not have the competition Louis faced. Pole vaulters have springier poles, tennis players better-strung rackets, boxers softer gloves, runners more resilient tracks and better shoes. Literally from the ground up, from the Astroturf that replaces mud puddles and snowdrifts and dust swirls of legendary past games to the Astrodome that controls the weather, technological changes in the game—even if, taken separately, they are clearly improvements—must be opposed because they change the standards of comparison.

A heavy incense toward ancestors permeates sports trophy rooms (trophies are themselves an archaism, descended from war plunder, set up to mark the enemy's "turning," which is what "trophy" means). Uniforms are preserved like relics at the shrines in Cooperstown or Canton. Photographs of past teams are icons on the walls of bars. The best writing about sports is most often about the past, or about the sport most drenched in nostalgia, baseball. Hollywood mingles its tears with this incense. Though athletes have been hired at or near their prime to play other roles—Johnny Weismuller as Tarzan, Sonja Heinie as a princess, Jim Brown as a cowboy—the movies expressly devoted to sports tend to concentrate on dead giants from the past (and especially from baseball's past): the Babe Ruth story, the Lou Gehrig story, the Jackie Robinson story. In Reagan's case, the Grover Cleveland Alexander story.

Memory "improves" sports to the heart's desired scale. Sports thus reverse the normal laws of optics, whereby things lessen as they recede from us. The farther off things are in the sports world, the larger they become. Don Miller, one of Notre Dame's "Four Horsemen," confessed as much to Grantland Rice: "It's twenty-nine years since we played. Each year we run faster, block better, score more TDs than ever."[15] The past is everywhere graven on the present, like the great names stamped on basketballs and footballs, bats and rackets. I first played tennis with "a Don Budge Racket," so I remember him as a figure from my youth, though he was famous from the time just before that. Such generational lags are constant in sports, fathers remembering a different generation from that playing today as they try to instill their own "love of the game" in their sons. We play ball with constant glances back over our shoulder.

If technology is resented when it introduces new rules or materials into the game, it is most vociferously opposed when it alters the economic base of sports. There is no greater affront to the fan's values than the agents and contracts, the franchises and trades, that make up the world of high finance in the age of television. The symmetry of games is altered to squeeze them, in segments, between televised commercials. The scale and spatial setting of the games are altered by zoom lenses, closeups, and instant replays. Overexposure dries up careers, teams, even whole sports—as boxing was depleted by the TV screen in the 1950s, or as football is being depleted in the 1980s.

Radio and television expand the audience for sports events, *and* remove the audience from immediate presence at the events, *and* alter the rhythms of those events, all at the same time. Or they blank out certain teams, certain sports. If, say, roller derbies go off the air, it is not necessarily because the audience for such competition is smaller than that for bowling, or rowdier than that for wrestling, but because surveys do not turn up viewers whose buying habits are of interest to sponsors.

Commercial coverage of sports goes forward, therefore, by a studied coupling of things at odds with each other—a rapidly developing economic and technological structure, at the service of games whose ethos is retrospective and archaizing. The clash is as old as our century. If anything, the tension is better concealed now; the incompatibility does not intrude as it did earlier. In order to film the 1899 heavyweight fight between Jim Jeffries and Tom Sharkey, the Biograph film company hung densely banked lights over the ring, which overheated and drained not only the fighters but the electrical equipment as well. Ice applied to cool equipment boxes dripped onto the canvas, where the fighters splashed with growing desperation. Meanwhile, as if to prefigure the competition between three networks for sports coverage, two other film companies—Vitagraph and Edison—brought their camera in to "piggyback" on Biograph's lighting system, and had to fight off Biograph assaults as they filmed. After the fight, the victorious Jeffries sought out the pirates with his toughs.[16]

The Biograph affair is an early example of the way reporting of the event would alter conduct of the event (and perhaps its outcome). Some earlier movies of professional boxing were even more distortive. They had to be made in the "Black Maria" building at the Edison Laboratory, where lighting and equipment were immobilized. Jim Corbett had to prearrange his knockout blow so it could be in focus.[17] This was a kind of "re-creation," the visual equivalent of Reagan's appeal to the auditory imagination in his fictive baseball games.

The technical lag had been shortened, but it still involved a relay, when the first heavyweight championship match was broadcast on the radio in 1921. Since there was no sound booth in the open air arena where Dempsey fought Georges Charpentier, David Sarnoff, using borrowed Navy equipment, strung a wire to a neighboring railroad shack, where a man receiving the account over headphones wrote an abbreviated version of it, which was then read over the air by a third man—essentially, the three-man team that was involved in Reagan's broadcasts: sender, receiver, and broadcaster.[18] Reagan, by his professional longevity, is a link between the pioneering era of broadcast technology and the sophisticated politics of our modern communications industry. His career began in the first age of big-time sportscasting, during the arrival of radio as a political power. His story of the telegraph line that went dead is a perfect example of the tension arising between the fans' desire to preserve the "pure" game and the changes dictated by participation at a technological remove. Reagan's coverage was a hybrid of two techniques, the telegraph and the radio, disguised to represent the "real thing"—presence in the stadium, attention to human little details that did not, in fact, come over the slim wire that was Reagan's only tie to the stadium. "Re-creations" of the Reagan type continued long after they were technologically obsolete because they were an amazingly cheap way to fill air time—if you could find an announcer who held people's interest as Reagan did. The practice came to an end only when a court decreed, in 1955, that stations must pay the teams for use of their game.[19]

It was Reagan's archaizing imagination, formed on Grantland Rice, that bridged the gap between the fans' sports ethos and the radio station's economic strategy. The use of technical gimmickry, literally deceptive, was "absolved" by Reagan's quality as a surrogate spectator—one who shared the fans' loyalty, imagery, and values. Hidden things were happening—some normal, like the link-up itself; some exceptional, like the break in that "feed" —under the illusion of permanency, of the game as one had always seen it, or heard people who had seen it tell their tale. The fabulator's art, based on the nostalgic reliving of the games, supplied the deficiencies of the reporter's information at the moment. This was the first time in Reagan's career, though far from the last, when nostalgia and technology were illogically yoked together, values from the past with instruments eroding past conditions.

CHAPTER 15

Announcer

How cam-st thou speakable of mute?

—Paradise Lost *9.563*

As Reagan's move to Iowa was a long step toward California, so his work in radio carried him partway to the movies. He says he was hired in Hollywood because of his voice. It was the second time he entered movies because of vocal skills polished on the air waves. Burton B. Jerrel, who produced *Iowa News Flashes* as a short feature for Iowa movie theaters, heard Reagan's pleasant baritone voice on WHO and hired him as the narrator of his films.

Here, as in his first try at radio, Reagan was soon fired. Jerrel said that Reagan was used to ad-libbing his baseball coverage, but could not read a script to match the time-cues of film.[1] Reagan would never have been a success as a newsreel announcer of the nineteen-thirties. He lacked the "March of Time" voice we still hear in the news clips of *Citizen Kane*. Newsreels retained to the end the hectoring voice of authority that was common in early radio and movies, the kind that survives in some advertisements that want to seize attention. Reagan was not even as authoritarian as his fellow announcer at WHO, Ed Reimers, who became famous for decades as the man who assured people they were "in safe hands with Allstate."

Nor would Reagan's voice have fit the early days of Hollywood sound, when stage diction, British accents, and a rapid pace were cultivated. Such an insistent and drumming attack did not suit the long hours of radio talk, especially when it was uninterrupted by music, like Reagan's afternoon baseball games. He was one of those radio performers conditioning people to accept relaxed inflections, mid-American diction, and understated drama. You cannot scream three continuous hours of baseball (hard as Harry Caray tries to).

When Reagan started looking for radio work, he went first to Chicago. That was the national capital of broadcasting for the same reason that it was the national capital of shipping, because of its geographical centrality. But an extra consideration for radio was that Midwestern accents were less strange to national audiences than, say, Southern, New England, or Texan accents would have been. Announcers like Reagan accustomed people to hearing everyday vowels from performers. He did not have to follow the path of earlier actors, who went to New York to acquire mid-Atlantic approximations of "correct" British speech. To this day, Reagan cannot sound all the syllables in "government." He has the midwestern pronunciation of words like *"rut* beer" and house *"ruf."* That was no obstacle in the year he went into radio—a year when Will Rogers was payed $50,000 to do seven broadcasts in his winning cowboy drawl.[2]

It is part of the Reagan luck that he did not go to Hollywood till the sound revolution was over, with its long aftermath of frenetic noise and motion. He was a senior in high school when the nation became aware of sound developments, after Warner Brothers' release of *The Jazz Singer.* This was just five years after the introduction of commercial radio,[3] which had also been full of loud doors slammed, sirens screaming, and other attention-getting devices. There was an acoustical *horror vacui* at a time of fading signals and uncertain equipment: the pace of dialogue had to be kept brisk so no pauses made the audience fear something was going wrong with the set. The movies learned from radio's mistakes, but what they often learned was to repeat the mistakes. Sound technicians were lured away, equipment stolen.[4] The pinch of the Depression coincided with the extra costs of sound production and distribution—all theaters had to be wired for sound, and projection crews doubled. Whole job categories disappeared overnight—the gagmen,[5] studio set musicians, theater musicians. Superfluous extras now went back to Central Casting (founded for economy reasons in 1926) instead of hanging around the sets, where they just made unwelcome noise. Visitors were banned from the new sound stages.

The most famous job losses—though not the most numerous, nor the saddest—were in the acting ranks. There is a myth that this had primarily to do with the quality of their voices, and especially with pitch—squeaky tones issuing from vamps or virile lovers. But the problem was usually one of written or spoken *diction.* Good silent-film directors had learned to time their actors' motions to a kind of inner music. Long gazes, the intimate interplay of looks, had been developed according to a special logic the silent movie created for itself. Words paced everything to a new timetable, on a new level of literalness. No matter how good an actor's voice, simply repeating "I love you" while going through the subtle ballet of a silent love scene would be a descent into silliness. Directors had to change their rhythms, invent a new visual vocabulary of "the natural." And actors had to enunciate words without foreign or regional accents—unless "stage British" is a regional accent. Sloppy diction ended careers like Norma Talmadge's.[6]

Even though stage British was the preferred accent at first, it presented problems, too. For some characters it could seem prissy or mincing. Chaplin's British accent, for instance, would not fit his worldwide image of Everyman as a down-and-outer, the Tramp. After he ended his long fight with the inevitability of sound, he pronounced that "the Tramp is dead" and had to invent a new character to go with his diction—Monsieur Verdoux. Chaplin was sensitive enough to the artistry of each picture as a whole to see that early sound films, with their uncertainty of rhythm, their amalgam of various dictions, the alternating pomp and bathos of their dialogue, were wrong in ways that it would take years to put right. It was not simply a matter of a few obvious problems to be solved—the early sound camera immobilized in its box, the actors clustering around a hidden microphone.

Chaplin fought a clever war against sound, using some of its own techniques against itself in *City Lights* or *Modern Times,* garbling voices in a parody of the rapid delivery encouraged in the early sound films. Evelyn Waugh wrote: "Mr. Charles Chaplin, abused everywhere as a 'progressive,' is the one genuine conservative, artistically, in Hollywood. The others allow themselves no time to get at ease with their materials."[7] Something of Chaplin's resentment at the technology of sound entered into his bitter obsession with machinery in general, embodied in *Modern Times.*[8] He seemed innocent of the irony in such a film. He used movies—one of the earliest industries to apply the principles of Henry Ford's assembly line—to attack the assembly line. Besides, the Charlie being ground through a factory's cogs on the screen was simultaneously being fed through the sprockets of a projector. The toy created by the modern world was put to service against the modern world. The gap between nostalgic message and innovating medium was as great as that between Reagan's expansively imagined ball games and their technical underpinning.

Other actors could not afford, like Chaplin, to wait and experiment. They bashed on regardless, into disaster. Whole screen types were abolished by laughter—just as off-screen jobs had been eliminated for economic reasons. If the Tramp was dead, so were the vamp and the flapper. John Gilbert was victimized by three concurring plagues of the time—silent direction in a sound picture, bad dialogue, and an affected attempt at stage British diction.[9] The "colleges of vocal culture"[10] that sprang up in Hollywood overdid their emphasis on elocution. Harold Lloyd had to learn the hard way that comedians cannot be finicky about pronunciation.[11]

If some movie types disappeared, others rose to new life with sound. Horror films, for instance, had their golden age when sound effects were still novel, and semiarticulate or weird speech could be heard—Frankenstein's grunt, Dracula's hypnotic vowels.[12] Musicals became a national medicine during the Depression—Busby Berkeley at Warner Bros., Astaire and Rogers at RKO, Shirley Temple at MGM. The detective story came from the stage, and Warners changed it into the gangster film, with gunfire and screeching tires.[13]

Talking movies were marked for a long time by the traumata of their birth. Since films were only partly in sound for two years, and projectionists were still learning to use the equipment, any lapses into silence were disturbing. Besides, the faster sound camera, speeding the number of frames through the projector's gate, would have slowed speech and movement if actors had not adopted compensatorily rapid delivery. The release of the sound camera from its mobile box led to virtuoso movement. The need for more expository material in talkies, with the inevitable criticism of their wordiness, prodded actors and directors to drive the pace. The early thirties can seem, on film, like one shouting match. Actors tried to outdo each other in energy. Lovers were stuttery with ardor. Heiresses were madcap. Editors were barking, reporters hiccupy. District attorneys were two-fisted. Gangsters fired their words and their guns with equal authority. Blondes were bombshells. Dialogue crackled. Yapping became the new foreplay.

Writers have frequently wondered how Jack Warner could keep Humphrey Bogart in small parts throughout the thirties. But Louise Brooks notices that Cagney just exploded him off the screen in gangster films.[14] Cagney's was the perfect style for that strenuous era—Graham Greene was the first to realize that he *danced* every role he took: "On his light hoofer's feet, with his quick nervous hands and his magnificent unconsciousness of the camera, he can pluck distinction out of the least promising part."[15] Bogart had his one good thirties role, that of Duke Mantee, under the tutelage of Leslie Howard, who was an anachronism playing an anachronism in *Gone With the Wind*, a leaf blown away by the blustery Clark Gable. Bogart would come into his own only when his slurry speech and slow appraising gaze made *him* a romantically doomed anachronism.

The clash between the Cagney and Bogart styles was still occurring in Hollywood when Reagan reached Warners. Reagan tells us about a film he did with Pat O'Brien in 1938, *Cowboy from Brooklyn*. The quick-talking con man was a role O'Brien had done frequently since he made *The Front Page* in 1931, a movie that helped set the trend for loud wisecracking throughout the thirties. Even Rosalind Russell had to yap her way through O'Brien's part in the 1941 remake. Lloyd Bacon, who had begun his professional life taking pratfalls for Mack Sennett, was directing *Cowboy from Brooklyn* in his normal slam-bang style. He often worked with a regular group of actors, "Lloyd's gang," Cagney and O'Brien, Frank McHugh, Allen Jenkins.[16] It was Bacon who gave the pile-driver tempo to many Warner Bros. crime films. Cagney claims one had to be on guard to prevent his shooting a rehearsal as the final take.[17] But rehearsals with Reagan did not go well, this first time he worked for Bacon: "Scene after scene I would discover had been rewritten after one or two of my drawling rehearsals, and the rewrite would wind up with someone else being given most of my lines. I was miserable, too scared to ask the director what was going on, and really beginning to yearn for my old Secret Service pictures where I was a big wheel" (Hubler 101).

Then a character actress took him aside and explained that he was supposed to snap, crackle, and pop like everything else in a Bacon picture: "Pat builds the scene up and with your line you drop it right in the cellar—and he has to try and bring up the tempo all over again." Reagan had been trying to play in casual contrast to O'Brien's aggressive style, and he concludes that was a mistake. So he went out with a carney spiel in the next scene, and won his lines back. He did what Bogart was forced to do in similar circumstances.

Reagan's account misses the real point of that scene. The shouters' day was coming to a close by 1938. O'Brien himself would lower his voice and start playing priest roles later that year. A relaxed style had been making its way into the movies, in large part from the radio, from performers like Will Rogers and Bing Crosby, who seemed to realize that you cannot be as frenzied in the front room as in a crowded theater. Reagan was part of that radio culture, one that owed something to the Fireside Chats of his hero, which took the level of political oratory down a notch from its platform stridency. Cagney, so reliant on intensity, would have to play his strutting type for laughs by the 1940s (*Strawberry Blonde*), leading to the blustery self-caricature of his later comic style (in *Mister Roberts* and *One Two Three*).

Cagney's was a style so *underlined* that impressionists felt they could imitate it. Reagan, by contrast, is a President who has not been successfully mocked by vocal impressionists. He has the good announcer's unobtrusiveness of inflection. He lacks the vocal idiosyncrasy of Presidents Kennedy or Johnson, Nixon or Carter. Even his trademark opening—"Well . . ."—is not John Wayne's "Waal," or Gary Cooper's "Wul," or Jimmy Stewart's up-and-down-the-scale "We-e-e-l." It is just a vocal intake of breath, done as part of Reagan's choreography of candor: "Well"—eyes down, eyes up, smile, slight dip of head to the right, and begin.

Reagan's instinct had been right in his first brush with Lloyd Bacon; and he would rarely, in later life, let people rush or hurry him out of relaxed vocal command of any situation. He never looks silly in his movies because he does not overaccent his lines, but underplays them, letting just enough vibrancy enter his voice not to be dull. This easiness is what kept him from some intense roles he aspired to; but it was his protection as well.

Reagan's use of his voice has been his most valuable professional skill. It took him into radio. It gave dignity to his movie appearances even when his body was stiff or unconvincing. He played a radio announcer in his first two films, and in two more over the next year. He was the unseen radio announcer in *The Amazing Dr. Clitterhouse* and *Boy Meets Girl*. In the Air Force, he was the narrator of training films. He was given released time to be the master of ceremonies for the filming of Irving Berlin's *This Is the Army*. On television, he was host and announcer as well as occasional actor. He acted as master of ceremonies for a nightclub act in Las Vegas and for charitable and civic banquets. As a spokesman for GE, he perfected the speech that led him into politics. As an elected official, his speeches were the high points of his campaigns and his administrations. After his retirement as governor, his voice was on the air with syndicated political opinion five times a week for five years (1975–80). There has been no time since he was hired by the radio station in 1933—over half a century ago—when Reagan has not been earning his living by the public use of his voice. He not only narrated the films about his own life, and about his wife, at the 1984 Republican convention, but filmed an introduction for Jeane Kirkpatrick's speech. Though he has held fewer press conferences than other modern presidents, he is faithful to the schedule of his regular Saturday broadcasts, making him the President who relies more on radio than anyone since Roosevelt.

Reagan was clearly a beneficiary of Hollywood's fascination with radio techniques and personalities. Radio was a rival, but one that could be used. In fact, Joseph Schenck of United Artists had tried out his actors' voices on radio before risking them in talkies.[18] Orson Welles was given unprecedented freedom in making a first picture because of the success of his radio show, "War of the Worlds." Some studios forbade their stars to appear on the rival medium in the thirties;[19] but Louella Parsons, the Hearst columnist, was too important to offend. When she began her radio show, "Hollywood Hotel," for Campbell's Soup in 1934, the stars had to troop over to appear, and the studios found that this was a good way to advertise upcoming films.[20] Warners lent its lead singer, Dick Powell, who made five films for the studio in 1935, to be the regular vocalist on Parsons's show.

In order to make the relationship even more cozy, Jack Warner made a movie out of Parsons's show, with Dick Powell in the lead and Reagan playing a backup announcer.[21] Parsons took an early interest in promoting Reagan's career, since she grew up in Dixon, Illinois, too.[22] In 1941, the two made a visit to their hometown, bringing with them a trainload of stars who could not say no to Louella (Bob Hope, Jerry Colonna, Joe E. Brown, Ann Rutherford, George Montgomery).[23] When she put together a stage version of her *Hollywood Hotel* a year later, and took it on the road for nine months, Reagan was made the master of ceremonies. Joy Hodges, the singer from Des Moines, and Jane Wyman were other members of the troupe, and Parsons took credit for arranging the wedding between Reagan and Wyman.

Radio was for a long time Reagan's mode of entry into the movies. Not only was he often typecast as a radio announcer, his first friend among the movie stars, Dick Powell, was playing the regular announcer as well as vocalist every week on Louella's *Hollywood Hotel,* and the two men met on the set of the movie derived from that show:

> I found myself playing a radio announcer in *Hollywood Hotel.* The star was one of the top box-office figures in Hollywood, Dick Powell, who couldn't have been nicer. Without realizing just how it happened, I found myself in one of the canvas director's chairs usually reserved for the stars and their principals. Dick somehow, easily and smoothly, had drawn me into the inner circle, as if I had more than two lines. [Hubler, p. 100]

Actually, Reagan had no lines at all, and no billing—which makes Powell's generosity more striking; but it was also a favor to Louella.

Reagan's early career is often misconceived by those who, taking Reagan's hint, think of him solely as the Errol Flynn of the B's. His Warners days were far closer to the pattern set by Dick Powell. Reagan says he was hired for his vocal resemblance to Ross Alexander, a Dick Powell look-alike who had committed suicide at age thirty just before Reagan tested at Warners.[24] Alexander took the same kind of light juvenile leads that Powell did, without the songs; and Reagan took, in his later comedies *(The Voice of the Turtle, John Loves Mary, The Girl from Jones Beach)* the kind of roles for which Warners had been training Alexander—and Powell. As we have seen, Reagan's first movie was done to plug the title of a Powell song.

Powell had come to Warners as the singer and MC with a broadcasting band. By 1937, Powell was trying to change his style from the "sissy tenor" roles he had played in Busby Berkeley spectacles. He was slowing his pace and lowering his voice. Like Reagan, he passed through a Warners intrastudio marriage (his to Joan Blondell), and broke with the studio to seek tough guy roles—more successfully in Powell's case. He brought a flip cynicism to *Murder, My Sweet* or *Station West* that Reagan could not match in his later Westerns. But the two men were among the first movie actors to go into television. Powell became a host of "Four Star Playhouse" from 1952 to 1956, Reagan of the "General Electric Theater" from 1954 to 1962. Both men put on cowboy garb, Powell to introduce "Zane Grey Theater" from 1956 to 1962, Reagan to play host for "Death Valley Days" in 1965 and 1966. (When Reagan left the latter show for politics, Robert Taylor took his place).[25] Each man had a vocal discipline that took him into Warner Bros. and somewhat limited him there. Each found ways to put that discipline to use later on.

Reagan's later control of volatile situations comes as clearly from his announcing days as from his film training. His canniness in debates, his handling of potentially embarrassing moments, his coolness in crisis, all show us the quick inventor of stop-gap plays in made-up baseball games. A comic instance of this is the wry preservation of dignity when he served as master of ceremonies for the Overseas Press Club during a tasteless self-display by Jayne Mansfield.[26] A more crucial moment came in the presidential debate against George Bush at Nashua, New Hampshire, in 1980, when the program was invaded by other candidates, the debate was delayed, the audience unruly, and the promoter of the debate tried to cut off Reagan's microphone as he introduced candidates excluded by the promoter's ground rules. "I *paid* for this microphone, Mr. Green," Reagan said, assuming command of the situation. There was no screaming or splutter on his part. He had given Jon Breen the wrong name, but not because he was under pressure —he simply heard it wrong in the first place. The announcer could cope with anything unexpected.

Reagan's years of handling audiences in every conceivable situation gave him an easiness of carriage under stress that touched the heroic in his reaction to being shot in 1981. When a real gun came into play, and real bullets,

Reagan had the flip manner Dick Powell maintained only in *movie* murders-my-sweet. Reagan not only kept his head but reassured others around him. He was as cool as his model, Roosevelt, had been when Zangara shot at him in 1933, the year Reagan became an announcer.

PART FOUR

MOVIES

CHAPTER 16

The Charlie Skid

yet regular
Then most, when most irregular they seem.
—Paradise Lost 5.623–24

Reagan went to the Warners studio at Burbank in June of 1937. Though he had only a six-month contract with the studio, he was confident enough about himself, and thoughtful enough about his parents, to move Jack and Nelle out in September of the same year.[1] That same month, three of his Drake friends piled into a car and headed West. They had talked with "Dutch" in Cy's Moonlighter about life in Hollywood, and they decided to try it with him.[2] They soon discovered a California equivalent of Cy's in which to sing college football songs. Jack and Nelle went along with them to Barney's Beanery (Hubler, p. 104). Reagan remained a good friend and model son. He even tried, in time, to get his brother into movies.[3]

After work on the set, Reagan would go home, where he lived for a while with his parents, or join the Drake gang at the beach for volleyball and body surfing. "We didn't have boards to surf with in those days," says Glen Claussen. There were picnics at the beach and Sunday dinners of the whole crew at Nelle's table, and long drives around the California ocean front, mountains, and valleys. Thus, from the outset, the Reagans had what James Q. Wilson called the two essential things for Southern California living—a freestanding home and a car. The climate that encouraged year-round life and work on the patio, or year-round use of the convertible with its top down, led to a kind of public intimacy in the lives of ordinary people, as well as of movie stars, around Los Angeles.

People moved around freely and in so doing saw how everybody lived . . . There was no anonymity provided by apartment buildings or tenements or projects. Each family had a house; there it was for all to see and inspect. With a practised glance, one could tell how much it cost, how well it was cared for, how good a lawn had been coaxed into uncertain life, and how tastefully plants and shrubs had been set out.[4]

The setting encouraged a strong sense of property in Southern Californians, and a desire to set an individual mark on each house or car or place of business. Jack Reagan was not the first immigrant to Southern California who found a new interest in planting things around his house.

Southern Californians then wandered through each others' lives, in their extraordinarily social cafeterias,[5] in drive-ins, in roadside fruit stands. As Carey McWilliams points out, the region was not settled by hardy pioneers, young and driven by want, but by comparatively old and wealthy people who had to plan their communities because of the need for imported water. [6] Hydraulic demands led to a regular but loose grid of townships, farms, and housing developments, with a density of population neither urban nor rural, one that spread itself thin over the surface of the fundamentally arid substratum, but moved rapidly around on it. The settlers of Southern California came mainly from the American heartland, from rural and small-town areas, but they invented something different, a kind of hick cosmopolis, a blend of the planned and the peculiar, a kind of nosy mobility that kept threading them back through each others' lives.[7]

Reagan, whose loyalties were expressed in terms of great moral urgency ever since the time of Eureka's strike, became a passionate defender of Hollywood, speaking out against its critics on any occasion offered him. The stock speech he gave was reported on a visit back to Dixon in 1950:

> "Dutch" gave a stirring defense of his "new town"—Hollywood. He compared it with other cities in America and pointed out that it leads the nation in church attendance on a per capita basis; that its schools are among the best in the nation; that the divorce rate in Hollywood is far below the national average . . . He explained that it was only a few years ago that "some churches wouldn't even bury an actor." That attitude, he explained, has changed today, because film actors, unlike the Thespians of old, now settle in one place, build homes, have their children attend school and churches and become part of the community. "You certainly couldn't expect an actor who lived out of a trunk to do that."[8]

One day Reagan brought a Warners starlet (not Jane Wyman) and her sister to the beach with him. Pee Wee Johnson began dating the sister and married her. By then Jane Wyman had joined the volleyball games. The fan magazines noticed that dating Reagan was a matter of dating the whole Drake ensemble. For years Wyman would be quoted saying things like this about their courtship:

> Usually his frat brothers would be along, too. Instead of having a date with him alone, I'd be with four boys. They took in all the sports—football, polo matches, horseback riding.[9]

> She knew she was licked, and after that she laid her next campaign more cleverly. Ronnie spent most of his time with a bunch of fraternity brothers. Swimming. Golfing. Riding. To Jane, the beach was a place

where you got a suntan, but a girl can learn. She wormed her way into the graces of two fraternity brothers. All of a sudden she was a bug for outdoors. Ronnie started hearing what a swell scout the Wyman kid was. Before he knew, she was one of them.[10]

Actually, Jane Wyman was a hit with everyone in the Reagan circle, including Nelle, from the very first, and she joined their activities wholeheartedly. Even after her marriage to Ronald, his Drake friends remained her friends. She went to the Disciples church with Nelle, and became a teacher in the Bible school when Maureen and Michael were later entered there.[11] When Pee Wee Johnson and his wife Nancy had a house on the beach at Malibu, the Reagans used to go over and see them on Sunday mornings. Johnson would be the only one up—like Reagan, he is an early riser. "Where do you get your new body every day?" Reagan often asked him. "I buy 'em by the truckload," Johnson answered. After Reagan was shot, Johnson wrote him a letter of concern. "Dutch wrote back saying that for a while he was afraid he might have to borrow one of my bodies."[12]

It seemed to the fan magazines that Reagan was living the all-American life. And it seemed that way to Reagan, too. And in nothing was he more typical than this: Glen Claussen says that the "gang" often ended its day by going to the movies. They had come to the land of America's dreams because they were dreamers themselves. The movies were not only a way to make a living for Reagan, but a way of life. He resisted his political advisers in later years, who wanted him to play down his actor's background, because he felt passionately that his was an honorable calling and Hollywood was the essential America. He accepted the code of the movies as forthrightly as he did the sports ideals of Grantland Rice or the values of Eureka College.

Reagan had not been given as many opportunities to attend the movies as other American children. He rarely got away from Lowell Park in time to see one during his summers as a lifeguard, and Eureka closed its one movie house (for insufficient patronage) when he was a freshman in college.[13] To show that his father disapproved of bigotry, Reagan says: "On the occasion when the early film classic, *The Birth of a Nation,* came to town, my brother and I were the only kids not to see it" (Hubler, p. 13). But that cannot have been a great deprivation, since Reagan was only four at the time of the movie's release. And there were many occasions for him to do what every American child was doing. He went to the Lee Theater in Dixon, during school months, the theater that would show all his films as they came out. His interest in acting and show business made him a regular patron of the movies in Des Moines, during the years when Warner Bros. was fighting crime and the Depression.

In fact, if current politicians have grown up with the movies, few can still say, with Reagan, that the movies grew up with them. The first studio in Hollywood opened in 1911, the year of his birth.[14] When he was eleven, Warner Brothers launched its first great money-making star, Rin Tin Tin.

The next year it began building the Burbank studio. Clara Bow became the "It Girl" when Reagan was sixteen. Jolson and sound made the news during his senior year at Dixon High. The first Academy Awards were given out during his freshman year at Eureka. The year he graduated, Mae West made her film debut and Rin Tin Tin died. A month after he went to work in Davenport, Jack Warner took the first trainload of Hollywood stars to a presidential inauguration. Two years after he became an announcer (and two years before he went to Hollywood himself), the first full Technicolor movie was released. Hollywood movies were born, learned coordinated movement, matured a voice, acquired political awareness, made social experiments, as Reagan was doing the same things. They were a part of his experience from childhood, in a way they had not been for his parents. His was the first movie generation, as children born in the nineteen forties made up the first television generation.

Reagan is perfectly justified in his claim that the movies uphold American values. Despite the continual prodding of technological innovation, the movies have always been creaky with borrowed tradition. Early Westerns were based on nineteenth-century melodrama, as mediated by wild west shows and the dime novel. The first cowboy star, Bronco Billy Anderson, was in fact Max Aronson, a shrewd entrepreneur, the developer of his own company, the man who brought Chaplin over to Essanay from the Sennett studio; but Aronson's screen role was derived from a sappy tale about a bad man turned good by a baby's smiles.[15] From the outset movies were caught in a cross-rhythm of technological leaps and lags. Sergei Eisenstein found in this conflict the pattern of all American movies, and of American culture in general—"the lace doilies that shroud the wonders of modern technique: refrigerators, washing machines, radios."[16] California remains to this day a place of pioneering retrospection. It has moved beyond the industrial revolution in its science, and lagged behind it in social vision. It has microchips that almost think, and they think in Victorian terms.

Much has been made of the fact that the film industry was largely developed by "immigrants," which was often the code word for Jews—for those distributors at the point where entertainment and business met, in vaudeville, when nickelodeons developed into movie houses. And the McCarthy period would find a subversive meaning in this prominence of immigrants, as if the movies, made by people who were not "really" American, were bound to favor un-American views. But movies were always super-American, reflecting an immigrant urgency to belong that is not limited to Jews. Immigrant directors were as quick as Bronco Billy himself to crank out Westerns, the form André Bazin has called "the American film par excellence."[17] Fritz Lang went from the futuristic *Metropolis* in Germany to *Western Union* and *The Return of Frank James* in America. If John Ford was a better director of Westerns than Lang was, that had as much to do with Ford's bellicose sense of his Irish heritage as with his American birth. And the most cornily old-fashioned patriot of them all was an Italian immigrant who came close, in *Meet John Doe,* to killing his adopted country with kindness.

Adolph Zukor, a Hungarian who came to America at age fifteen, was typical of the "non-Americans" who created the movies. Anita Loos remembers a meeting at Paramount's New York office during World War I:

> During our discussion, a military band on the street below struck up the national anthem. None of us was even aware of it except a boy named Adolph Zukor, who stood up and remained rigidly at attention. After an embarrassed moment, the remainder of us sheepishly joined him until the music died away.[18]

The principal ethnic heritage the movies celebrated was a heritage of joining. The moral of Jolson's *Jazz Singer* movie—unlike George Jessel's stage version of the story[19]—was that becoming an American jazz singer is as good as becoming a cantor for the synagogue. The moral of Bing Crosby's priest stories is that crooning is as good as Gregorian chant. Those not allowed to join, like blacks and native Americans, were mistreated by a combination of all the others who had scrambled aboard. A white supremacist, David Wark Griffith, romantic about his Welsh heritage, set the type of the authoritarian father figure at the helm of production in Hollywood.

As for the business methods of the early "magnates," those were the standard dog-eat-dog stuff of American capitalism—Pat Powers was trading dirty tricks with Carl Laemmle all through the worst part of it. Movies were so thoroughly American that they remained properly racist according to the taste of the period. The Production Code forbade miscegenation, and the wholesale production of "good Indians" by Gatling gun was carried on for decades. John Tuska, after his harrowing exposure to more than eight thousand Westerns, wrote:

> Uncle Carl Laemmle kept Chief Thunderbird, Chief Big Tree and All-American Jim Thorpe under contract at Universal for years. From them he got "zany savages" movies by the bushel such as the serials *The Indians Are Coming* (Universal, 1930) with McCoy and *Battling with Buffalo Bill* (Universal, 1931). Uncle Carl's Indians were happy to be working and in their way did their best to put together an exhilarating cinematic story. The preponderance of Jewish management of the films would have, perhaps, predisposed executives to promote tolerance had that been an issue. It wasn't.[20]

It took no methodological breakthrough for anthropologist Hortense Powdermaker to conclude, in 1950, that Hollywood's vision was politically and culturally conservative.[21] It would have been a miracle if that had failed to be the case. The nature of mass entertainment is to share assumptions with its audience. Many of the men responsible for the movies were anxious to achieve public respectability—Joseph P. Kennedy no less than Louis Mayer. They were all businessmen with large ventures to protect. Social and religious organizations monitored their performance. The star system invited a press scrutiny that was always potentially embarrassing. Powdermaker found the film community taboo-ridden; insecure and trying to please; unable to subvert society even if it had wanted to—and that was the last thing it wanted.

This does not mean that the movies could not be unsettling in their social impact, entirely aside from their intent. But Hollywood works at sustaining the illusion that a world totally altered in its technology need not touch or challenge basic beliefs. The camera has been in a rush to show every latest development in the world around it—automats, revolving doors, escalators, the Empire State Building, generations of new cars and airplanes, rockets, and space capsules—and it has shoved these latest marvels into the oldest-fashioned terms imaginable. Let Boeing bring out its jumbo jet, and Hollywood will quickly photograph it in all its awesome scale—then throw a giant Victorian doily of a story over it. We are whisked off by Technicolor to Oz, only to make us end up claiming there is no place like the black-and-white farm in Kansas. We are allowed to dream the wildest things, so long as we do not *think* anything new.

The basic conservatism of the movies lies beyond or below ideology. It does not matter that John Ford liked to work with reactionaries like John Wayne and Ward Bond, or that Chaplin preferred to flirt with leftist circles. Both men were mainly story tellers, and the stories they told were equally antiquated. Chaplin's vision was based as thoroughly on Victorian sentiment and melodrama as Griffith's own. And Ford was still retelling in 1948 *(Three Godfathers)* the story of Bronco Billy's redemption by a baby.

Of course, now we get "frank" movies in the sense that we hear about the *nude* harlot with a heart of gold. But the nudity came onto the screen well after it had been accepted on the stage, on the beaches, and even the streets, of the nineteen sixties. And the story is still the old one, even when "leftist" Jane Fonda is the golden-hearted whore. We may get sad endings now—slow-motion red martyrdoms of the *Bonnie and Clyde* or Peckinpah type, the apotheosis of crazed mini-Lears. "Top of the world, Ma!"—Waco, Texas, as Colonus. But the basic conservatism, the story-telling for a mass audience, remains.

It is an appropriate accident that movie technology is founded on the eye's ability to be tricked, on persistence of vision. This means that we continue to see, for a while, what is not there. We see each picture long enough not to notice the quick mechanical substitution of the next one. In a larger sense, too, movies are based on persistence of vision—on seeing a cultural scene that is no longer present. Much of film comedy seemed, by unconscious inspiration, to take its material from this persistence of vision. The double take, for instance, expresses the fact that a person can walk blissfully on after confronting the anomalous, which does not register until a second take—or, in Harry Langdon's case, a third.[22] Adherence to outmoded techniques was exploited by Buster Keaton—as when his village blacksmith takes on the chores of a car mechanic *(The Blacksmith,* 1922): he is puzzled when the car will not hold up its tire to be changed.

André Bazin has said that Chaplin, falling in love with the rhythms of his own evasive actions, repeats them enough for an opponent to "read" them, so that a feint that first took Charlie out of danger now leads him into it.[23] This is too narrow a concept. Charlie repeats actions that are not even *initially* successful—e.g., his attempts to open the cab door through the cab door in *One A.M.* (1916). The repetition of outmoded actions is a basic element in his characters, even when the act *begins* outmoded. With Harry Langdon, the humor comes from a persistence in *in*activity: "A fraction of a second *after* the car had gone [by], Harry jumped a little jump, as though to get out of its way."[24] The inertia of the old within a new situation is summed up by one simple maneuver Chaplin often used, the Charlie skid—the way he slides when trying to turn corners—skating without skates *beyond* the corner. His original momentum is at war with the new direction he wants to take, making him the prisoner of his own energies. In *The New Janitor* (1914), Chaplin cleverly grabs a gun and trains it on a burglar, *backwards through his legs,* then must continue hopping around in that pose.

Eisenstein understated the matter when he talked of American movies as advanced in their means and conservative in their end. They are conservative in their intent, but revolutionary in their impact—as MGM, trying to heap praise on Judy Garland's Kansas, wooed us fatally away from it. In order to understand the conservatism of Ronald Reagan, we must begin where he did, below ideology, with the Hollywood conservatism of his young dreams and mature working days. He is himself the large effect of a national persistence of vision. He brings the oldest stories back to us in "real life." Basically, his later performance is a graceful political development of the Charlie skid.

CHAPTER 17

Chastity Symbols

and with calumnious Art
Of counterfeited truth thus held thir ears.

—Paradise Lost *5.770–71*

Some, with a Clark Gable in mind, or a Cary Grant, might think it is
stretching the term to call Reagan a Hollywood star. But he insists on the
word, and he is right: *Kings Row* was "the picture that had brought me star
status" (Hubler, p. 127). In the Hollywood of his day, the first test of stardom was take-home pay, and Reagan passed that. Using 1946 figures, Hortense Powdermaker was able to make Reagan an example of the high salaries
given stars. He earned, that year, just a little less than Errol Flynn, and more
than Rita Hayworth.[1]

Even before *Kings Row* was released, just on the basis of sneak previews,
the studio offered him a contract for three times as much money as he had
been making. His agent told him to grab it, not to wait for longer-term
reaction (Hubler, pp. 120–21). Overnight that gave Reagan the negotiatory
heft of a star. Asked, for his next film, to work with Errol Flynn, he recalled
the way Flynn had stolen lines and business from him in *Santa Fe Trail,* and
told producer Hal Wallis, "Of course, I'm in a little better position than I
was the last time we worked together." Wallis had to promise that nothing
would be taken from Reagan's part, and he stuck by the promise despite
Flynn's tantrums. That was another way you proved you were a star—by
facing down a studio favorite. Five years after reaching Hollywood, Reagan
had finally "arrived"—just before he had to leave for war duty.

The star system—the reciprocal workings of money, billing, publicity, and
box-office "draw"—was invented by one man, Carl Laemmle. At first, actors
did not want their names associated with the toy goings-on inside a Kineto-
scope. Even when longer stories were told on film, actors got no billing by
name. They were referred to by their type or character in the movie—the
Boy, the Wild One, the Young Colonel, Little Mary. Chaplin was indulging
his nostalgia when he called his main characters in *Modern Times* (1936) the

Factory Worker and the Gamin. Yet one actress, known to her public only as "The Biograph Girl," tried to use her loyal following to break a Vitagraph contract in 1910. Both Vitagraph and Biograph were part of the Film Trust, which responded to this bid for individual mobility by blacklisting her from all Trust productions. Alexander Walker thinks it is the first industry blacklisting of an actor.[2]

The Trust had not properly estimated the ingenuity of Laemmle, the most agile of its foes, or the publicity flair of his assistant Robert Cochrane. Outdoing the Trust at its own game, these two released a story to the newspapers that the Biograph Girl had died. The Trust was trying to put her out of work; Laemmle would put her literally out of this world—only to reintroduce her as the resurrected "IMP Girl" (using the initials of his company, Indepent Motion Pictures). He boldly refuted the lies he had spread about her untimely demise. He not only used her improbable daisy chain of a real name, Florence Lawrence, but arranged for her to give the first extensive star interview in the history of the movies.[3] Up to this time, movie actors had no publicly known private life—Biograph went so far, in guarding the anonymity of its players, as to give false names when cast lists were required for British release of its films. (Mary Pickford appeared as Miss Dorothy Nicholson.)[4] But after Laemmle's successful press maneuvers, a public private life would be the paradoxical dwelling place for all future stars.

The first of the lasting stars trod with determination on the heels of Florence Lawrence: Mary Pickford, too, went from Biograph to Laemmle in 1910—but she was only passing through. After a return to the stage, she condemned Adolph Zukor to the pleasant misery of keeping her (and her mother) financially satisfied. The trick was to find something impressive to offer her *after* doubling her salary at each negotiation—e.g., a studio "in which no other pictures could be made."[5]

Pickford was typical of those who would come after her. The most obvious point, and the one most often remarked, was the casting restriction that went with financial privilege. Pickford had to hold the little girl pose she had first struck till she was well into her thirties. Also, "giving" a private life and identity to the actors meant constantly monitoring it. Pickford was first married at Biograph, but she had to keep that a secret, even when she went to Laemmle's company. Only when Laemmle took one of his forays outside the Trust's power, into Cuba, did travel arrangements make it impossible to hide any longer that "Little Mary" was Mrs. Owen Moore.[6]

Still, the public did not want her to be Mrs. Owen Moore; so she appeared everywhere with her mother, not her husband. She dressed like a child for her offscreen life, even when she was (by exception) playing a different part on camera. As Zukor wrote in his autobiography, "It was understandable that Mary wished to dress her age and in the height of fashion, but neither of us could afford it."[7] The interplay of pretense and reality became increasingly complicated. Walker writes, "Though a young woman of nearly thirty, she was obliged to keep on switching into children's clothes to be photographed with distinguished visitors to the studio."[8] She would have to stop acting her role in order to "become" Mary Pickford by putting on her "real" costume. Pickford confesses this was an affront to her husband: "Those blond curls down my back didn't help matters either. They must have been a grotesque and daily reminder to Owen that a child headed the family."[9]

The charade reached its touchiest point when her affair with Douglas Fairbanks led to a divorce from Moore. Both Pickford and Fairbanks were Catholic, and for some reason the movie makers were always obsessed with the Catholic church's power. Perhaps the entrepreneurs, many of them from New York, were impressed by Irish political power in that city. Whatever the reason, they invited a Catholic, Martin Quigley, to draw up the Motion Picture Production Code in 1930, and he relied on Hollywood's favorite Jesuit, Daniel Lord, for guidance. (Cecil B. DeMille had Father Lord say Mass every morning while making *The King of Kings*.[10])

Yet Mary was so popular she could defy her own church. Mrs. Owen Moore went the way of the Biograph Girl; what was resurrected, was in this case, a palace at Pickfair, the kingdom of youth and beauty. Building that fabric of illusion was such a demanding labor that few involved in it could imagine the day when its prince would want nothing more than to be free of its confines. Then "Little Mary" became Mrs. Buddy Rogers, establishing another rule for stars, that financial and matrimonial records tend to be broken in concert.

Yet through it all Little Mary managed somehow to retain her movie innocence. We hear movie stars referred to, often, as sex symbols. They are far more often chastity symbols. Pickford was just the first in an endless line of heroines with perpetually recoverable virginity. The other female star of early pictures, Lillian Gish, was forever on the verge of being ravished, till Griffith reached out and saved her. There was titillation in the delay, of course; but rescue was mandatory. Ingrid Bergman's career was ruined for many years when she ceased to be a chastity symbol. In the years 1932–80, only one woman, Doris Day, reached the number one position in box-office returns, and she is the only woman included in the top ten money-makers for the period as a whole (she comes in eighth).[11] Her popularity in the sixties, her time of dominance, came entirely from the exasperating difficulty her screen partners had in bedding her. An even more recent star, Julie Andrews, achieved success as a chastity symbol and has, like Mary Pickford, strenuously been trying to shed that image ever since—with the same poor results at the box office when she strayed from her audience's demand for virtue.

Hollywood's trick is to be sexy, but innocently sexy. The second biggest female draw at the box office (number eleven overall) was Betty Grable. The right combination could be struck with Shirley Temple's prepubescent salaciousness, or with Marilyn Monroe's voluptuous naïveté ("Is *that* what we're doing?"). Even Mae West could be such a blatant "sex symbol" because she was so clearly untouchable, a *pillar* of vice. True slut glamor like Harlow's has been very rare among the stars—the pruriently staid Louis Mayer was unhappy at having to make money from such a person.[12] Howard Hughes shoved Jane Russell as far down into the gutter as the code allowed, but she daintily picked herself up to become Marilyn Monroe's responsible older sister.

There have been male chastity symbols too, starting with Pickford's co-star, Douglas Fairbanks, described by Booth Tarkington as "a faun who had been to Sunday school."[13] Alistair Cooke wrote in 1940: " 'Doug' could breathe freely on the tops of church steeples, hanging from a mountain crag, or diving through a window pane; the only things that choke him are the scent and epigram of the boudoir."[14] Carlos Clarens compared him with another chastity symbol, Pearl White: "Like her contemporary Douglas Fairbanks, she was athletic and optimistic; as with Fairbanks, physical prowess banished sexual implications from the periodic bouts of bondage and discipline."[15] The top star of all time, by far, was John Wayne, who began his real career in *Stagecoach* as the naive cowboy who knows more about horses than girls, and ended up as the Great Protector of Womanhood, more interested in his bottle than in girls. Gary Cooper, looking up at the ceiling and running his finger around his collar when the siren moves in, was typical of male chastity symbols; even wholesome Jean Arthur had to besiege his virtue. Thus Reagan, playing "Cowpoke" in *Tennessee's Partner* (1955), is the only one who does not realize that the "nice place you have here, m'am" is a brothel.

The Production Code had a great deal to do with the way chastity was symbolized on the screen; but the concern for it among producers, and the yearning for it in the audience, clearly antedate and postdate the Code. The box office returns were what condemned Mary Pickford to her uncompleted adolescence, or drummed Ingrid Bergman out of Hollywood, or soured the till every time Julie Andrews stopped being Mary Poppins. As Molly Haskell has pointed out, the public wanted even its flappers to be chaste.[16] Nor, at one level, were Hollywood powers insincere in their devotion to "family values." Joseph P. Kennedy was at one with Louis B. Mayer in this—he might be having an affair with Gloria Swanson, but he fired director Erich Von Stroheim for making her film, *Queen Kelly,* too racy.[17] Mayer's idea of promoting good causes was to keep making Andy Hardy pictures, which he considered his real contribution to America.[18] Herman Mankiewicz described the studios' rules for a screenwriter to Ben Hecht: "In a novel a hero can lay ten girls and marry a virgin for a finish. In a movie this is not allowed. The hero, as well as the heroine, has to be a virgin. The villain can lay anybody he wants, have as much fun as he wants cheating and stealing, getting rich and whipping the servants. But you have to shoot him in the end."[19]

There was hypocrisy in this, no doubt—Norman Mailer perfectly captures Mayer in "Herman Teppis" of *The Deer Park,* seated at his desk with the picture of "Mother" on the wall and a starlet between his knees. She thinks she is working her way up in the industry, and he is thinking how he will punish her for being such a strumpet. But few people in any line of work actually live up to the ideals they profess. Hypocrisy, despite Hortense Powdermaker's claim, is not what makes Hollywood different.[20]

Certainly the actors, whose lives are often rootless or harried, are sincere when they profess a desire for stability and home. Richard Schickel wrote of Mary Pickford: "Like nearly every major movie actor of this first generation (Fairbanks, Chaplin, the Gish sisters, Mae Marsh, Blanche Sweet, Bobby Harron, to name but a few), she was the child of a broken home . . ."[21] Griffith was just the first movie maker to assert a paternal authority over his collection of waifs and strays. He, too, was sincere, even when his love for "his" little girls turned incestuous—even when he was, in his own eyes, corrupting the person while rescuing her screen image.

And there is the problem. In movies, the manipulation of multiple selves is so *public* a transaction, so calculated and commercial. This might, a priori, be considered an advantage in achieving control over the self. There are explicit rules. But more often it leads to diminished control. It is easy to state the problem too simply, as a matter of conflict between the on-screen image and the off-screen reality. Actually there are at least four entities at work in the functioning star of the old star system. On the screen, we had the movie star Clark Gable playing Rhett Butler. Off the screen, we have the person Clark Gable playing the movie star Clark Gable. And all four of these "characters" are present in the minds of the audience. The interplay between roles was recognized in the famous morals clauses in actors' contracts. Cecil DeMille's contract with the actress who played the Virgin Mary in his film *King of Kings* specified not only that she had to observe the public proprieties in her real life but that, for seven years, she could not assume another *movie* role in conflict with her image in this movie.[22] She must, that is, keep playing a virgin, as Mary Pickford had to keep playing a child—because the public's image was an investment not to be defaced. As Zukor said of Pickford's ridiculous off-screen getup, "we could not afford" to change it. In the same way, the movie brawler is expected to be quick with his fists in "real" life, and is frequently challenged—I once watched Paul Newman being subjected to this ordeal by a drunk. "So, you're not so tough after all." Aha, Mary is *not* an adolescent. Ingrid is not Joan of Arc. But they must, even after that discovery, continue being that discarded self, among others. Pickford wrote about the humiliation of being "found out":

> It was while we were shooting a scene of *Pollyanna* at the railroad station in Pasadena that I overheard a child make a remark I've never forgotten. She was a little girl of about seven, one of the many spectators who had gathered to watch us take the scene. "Mama, she's not a real girl," I heard her say distinctly and astutely; "she's got long fingernails." Needless to say I promptly lopped off the incriminating nails.[23]

One of the best studies of this problem is also an example of it. Jeremy Larner's story *The Candidate* (1972) is not about Hollywood, but about politics; yet it derives much of its fascination from the fact that Robert Redford played the hero in his double public role as political activist and movie star. In one scene, Redford's character tries to make his way across a floor crowded with his own supporters, who hold up large placards with his picture on them, the same gigantic expression repeated, magnified, turning and facing itself. The candidate's real and baffled face looks diminished as he struggles through images of himself that block him. That expresses the simultaneous enhancement and reduction that stars undergo—Barrymore reduced to a profile, Grable to legs, Ekberg to breasts.

Idols can become sacrifices to the beliefs of their own worshipers. Little Mary had to keep putting on her curls. "[Pearl] White was forbidden by contract to appear in public without a blond wig; her fairness was emblematic of white womanhood."[24] Ingrid Bergman had to remain chaste in Italy. Rock Hudson was told by his studio when and whom to marry, in order to protect its investment in his masculine image.[25] The disappearance of identity under manipulation is expressed by Evelyn Waugh's fictional Hollywood agent:

Leo made her Spanish. He had most of her nose cut off and sent her to Mexico for six weeks to learn flamenco singing. Then he handed her over to me. *I* named her. *I* made her an anti-Fascist refugee. *I* said she hated men because of her treatment by Franco's Moors. That was a new angle then. It caught on. And she was really quite good in her way, you know—with a truly horrifying natural scowl. Her legs were never *photogénique* but we kept her in long skirts and used an understudy for the lower half in scenes of violence . . . And now there's been a change of policy at the top. We are only making healthy films this year to please the Catholic League of Decency. So poor Juanita has to start at the beginning again as an Irish colleen. They've bleached her hair and dyed it vermillion. I told them colleens were dark but the Technicolor men insisted. She's working ten hours a day learning the brogue and to make it harder for the poor girl they've pulled all her teeth out. She never had to smile before and her own set was good enough for a snarl. Now she'll have to laugh roguishly all the time. That means dentures . . .

Juanita's agent was pressing the metaphysical point; did his client exist? Could you legally bind her to annihilate herself? Could you come to any agreement with her before she had acquired ordinary marks of identity?[26]

The audience knows there is illusion at work. Viewers did not literally believe that Mary Pickford had been frozen in time, just at the preripened stage; but they wanted to pretend she had, and they wanted her to help their pretense by joining it. In fact, the whole structure of pretense was meant to be penetrable by the knowing eye—which soon became too knowing. Once the movie convention was established, "so the children won't know," that a prostitute will be shown as a dance-hall girl, then adults were free to recognize her, always, as a prostitute. But the writers were no longer free to tell the story of a woman who was *just* a dance-hall girl. "Nice place you have here, ma'am," could not be made a compliment, even if they wanted to make it one. The complications of the Code's logic, invented to keep the innocent ignorant, were too clever by half—they decreed technically "pure" relationship where the truly ignorant saw no distinctions. As Evelyn Waugh said, after his brief exposure to Hollywood's moral canon: "It is the spectacle rather than the theme which impresses a child. That is to say, a boy is excited by the use of firearms whether in the hands of a gangster or a soldier; an embrace is equally inflammatory whether between licit or illicit lovers. Americans are devoted to a conception of innocence which has little relation to life."[27] The Production Code, drafted under Jesuit auspices, was more interested in an ideology of "natural law" than in the psychology of human behavior. So it doubled all aspects of moral pretense in Hollywood's performance.

Waugh, himself a Catholic, noticed how this led to an emphasis on the conventions of morality which undermines any real moral message. His own novel, *Brideshead Revisited,* could not pass the Hollywood censors because they wanted to "straighten out" the marriage relationships of his characters, destroying his point. Hortense Powdermaker shows the same process at work on a 1947 movie that Reagan starred in:

> The successful Broadway play, *The Voice of the Turtle,* could not be made into a movie without changing its basic theme. The play was a quite moral tale about two young people who had "been around" and whose love life had been based on the principle of "love them and leave them." In the play, for the first time they find with each other a love that is lasting, and know happiness and life at its best. The moral of the play is that a permanent and monogamous love brings greater happiness than temporary, illicit affairs. In the movie, the whole point of the play and its moral theme is lost, and the picture has really no point beyond that of depicting a very immature and adolescent girl [Eleonore Parker] falling much in love with a returned soldier [Reagan] who is at first not attracted to her, but later falls for her and proposes marriage.[28]

Once it was realized that movies were sending messages over and around the Code, a kind of snide knowingness was required in the intelligent viewer. The question became not is this storm really the Code's code for intercourse, but can there be any storm in the movies that is *not* a sexual spasm? Skill at guying the Code, at coying with it, became a point of pride, "the Lubitsch touch." So "pretend sin" was an equal partner to the movies' "pretend virtue." There was a perpetual oscillation, a forever wavering balance, between the naive and the knowing, between sappy innocence and winking lubriciousness. One falsehood fed the other. As Ben Hecht wrote: "They have learned how to hint at fornication in a hundred masterful ways and so much that I, for one, watching a movie, am ready to believe that all its males and females fall to futtering one another as soon as the scene disolves."[29]

Alfred Hitchcock, with his "naughty boy" aesthetic, took special delight in extending the covert evidences of sexual activity in his films. He even invented, for *Rear Window,* a way of putting masturbation on the screen. The immobilized James Stewart, after watching scantily clad sunbathers from his window, expresses anxiety followed by exaggerated satisfaction when he manages to scratch beneath the cast around his thigh. Thelma Ritter enters and says, "You know, in the old days, they used to put your eyes out with a red-hot poker." She has caught him. Then, for the censors, she explains that she caught him playing the Peeping Tom. But his face told us something different—just as it will in *Vertigo.* Since Hitchcock's basic theme was not "suspense," as his publicists maintained, but guilt, he liked to prove that what passes for American innocence is really a feigned ignorance, a refusal to admit complicity. *"That* can't be what we're doing."

The pressures of the Code were at work on every movie Ronald Reagan made. They can best be seen in his own favorite. In Henry Bellamann's best-selling novel, *Kings Row,* when Parris tells Drake that he has spent the night with Cassie, Drake answers: "Well, for Christ's sake! You—you spent the night with Cassie Tower! Just like that. You spent the night with Cassie Tower. And I was going to take you around and show you the ropes! For Christ's sake!" Naturally, the Code's famous administrator, Joseph Breen would not let Reagan say "For Christ's sake!" Breen was famous for trying to keep the "damn" out of the most famous line from Margaret Mitchell's novel, "Frankly, my dear . . ." So Reagan says, in both places, "For Pete's sake!" This is about as racy as talk was allowed to get then. Since Drake is supposed to be a decidedly racy fellow, he is forced to repeat the phrase constantly throughout the movie. It is our signal that he is "fast." Mr. Breen has removed a phrase in the audience's everyday use and freighted another phrase, silly in itself, with a labored slyness.

But the Breen office had just begun its work on the scene. Parris, of course, cannot say that he has spent the night with Cassie. On the screen, when Reagan asks him what is the matter, he just mumbles, "I'd rather not say." Then, as Cummings looks acutely uncomfortable, Reagan gives a sly laugh to let the knowing part of the audience realize he has recognized the signs of lost virginity. This leering at normal sex has to go on because Breen has been very active on the script elsewhere, removing incest and homosexuality from the story. Naturally, when Parris and Cassie embraced in her father's gingerbread-gothic office, the camera cut to a storm. The novel also has a storm in that scene, since it is largely assembled from other old movies. But the scene's real turmoil comes from Parris's sense that Cassie, like himself, is *not* a virgin, though he cannot think of any other young man she has been seeing. (That she has been sleeping with her father is the big revelation that lies ahead.) The movie cannot touch any of this, but it tries to signal some of it to the novel's many readers by having Cassie become suddenly "forward" just before the stormy embrace. This is an inexplicable development to those not in the know.

In the novel, after Parris tells Drake about Cassie, Drake says: "Go on to sleep, but move over. I've got to sleep with you—if you don't mind, Mr. Mitchell." That had to be changed, too. But what are naive members of the audience, who may have missed the signal about lost virginity, to make of the result? "Pile into bed. Of course, you'll have to bunk with me. I hope you won't mind, Mr. Mitchell." The trouble with constant sexual signaling is that if you miss one wink, you may misread the others. The "bunk with me" passage, along with the deleted reference to intercourse with Cassie, might suggest that these ardently embracing young men are the real lovers of the story. Actually, the homosexuality of the novel involved another character. Or has the homosexuality been *displaced* over to the two main characters? In the novel, Drake does not whisper "Parris" when he realizes he has lost his legs. In the movie he does.

It is the constant stirring of such questions that made the fantasies of Hollywood far from innocent. They were childishly *pre*-knowing in their evasiveness about forbidden things only half acknowledged. It seems unlikely that Reagan would recall his role as Drake McHugh with such pride if it was meant to be a bisexual story in disguise—he resented it when Edmund Goulding, who had directed *Grand Hotel,* tried to make him give a homosexual reading to a line in *Dark Victory.* Reagan plays a tippling social butterfly and male escort surrendering Bette Davis to George Brent:

> I actually believe that he saw my part as a copy of his own earlier life. I was playing, he told me, the kind of young man who could dearly love Bette but at the same time the kind of fellow who could sit in the girls' dressing room dishing the dirt while they went on dressing in front of me. I had no trouble seeing him in that role, but for myself I want to think if I stroll through where the girls are short of clothes, there will be a great scurrying about and taking to cover. I made a mistake I've promised myself will never be repeated. I tried to compromise and give him something of what he saw in the part. We came to our moment of truth near the end of the picture. In the scene George Brent comes to my apartment, desperate because of his failure to convince Bette that he loves her. She, in turn, thinks his love is pity because they both know she is dying. My part in the scene is to tell George she is on her way up to the apartment, and before I disappear I ask him to be kind to her because I love her too. It was a well-written scene, and a nice moment in the picture. I still insist there is only one way to play the scene and that is simply and with great sincerity. Our director hit the ceiling. He demanded, "Do you think you are playing the leading man? George has that part, you know." In the matter of studio standing, I was outweighed. He was a top director, doing only top pictures. I was up in that class on a raincheck. He didn't get what he wanted, whatever the hell that was, and I ended up not delivering the line the way my instinct told me it should be delivered. It was bad. [Hubler, pp. 118–19][30]

It is unlikely, therefore, that Reagan would be proud of his Drake McHugh perfomance if it gave any hint, in his eyes, of a homosexual dimension. On the other hand, even if there is no such implication, it is astonishing that Reagan still considers "the finest picture I've ever been in" (Hubler, p. 119) this leering adaptation of a trashy novel. Did he see none of the snickering over dirty little secrets, or did he just pretend he did not see? That, too, opens a Chinese box of questions. How would we know if he was pretending to pretend? How would he? Reagan was the perfect Hollywood chastity symbol, one whose innocence became indistinguishable from ignorance.

He lived for a while at the center of pretense in Hollywood. He was the protégé of Louella Parsons, who also came from Dixon, Illinois. Parsons had been around the movie business almost from the beginning. Chaplin first met her in 1915 when she was the "script girl" for Essanay, and he was still cultivating her in 1943 to get favorable coverage in the Hearst papers for his wedding to Oona O'Neill.[31] Warner Bros. had been especially deferential to her because Hearst, dissatisfied with MGM's treatment of Marion Davies, moved his Cosmopolitan Productions to Warners in 1934, where Davies made her films till 1937. Parsons's power was so great by 1941 that one phone call from her to Nelson Rockefeller canceled the booking of Orson Welles's *Citizen Kane* into Radio City Music Hall.[32] Movie tycoons so feared what she might do to *their* images after Welles showed disrespect for Hearst that Louis Mayer offered to buy *Citizen Kane* before its release so he could destroy it.[33]

In less cosmic uses of her influence, Parsons fancied herself a marriage broker, though others felt she was as much a marriage breaker. She took an especially proprietary attitude toward Reagan's marriage with Jane Wyman. She had teamed the two people in her touring version of *Hollywood Hotel*. She called theirs an ideal marriage, a vindication of Hollywood, and held the wedding reception in her home. Though it was Wyman's second marriage, the two were made to conform to the Hollywood myth of innocent young sweethearts, in love for the first time and the last. Parsons gushed protectively over the marriage for years:

> Life was very much the way Jane wanted it on a certain day [when] our vaudeville tour [of *Hollywood Hotel*] took us to Philadelphia. Her brown eyes were sparkling and her voice was bubbling with happiness as she told me, "Have I got a scoop for you! Ronnie and I are engaged!" I had known that Jane worshipped Ronnie, but I hadn't realized he was falling seriously in love with her. I announced the engagement that night from the stage and in the newspapers.[34]

Since the Parsons revue was organized around a plot that showed Louella sitting onstage typing out "scoops" while stars and hopefuls dropped in on her, life and art came marginally together when her show made the "news" it reported—as part of the act. Wyman had, in fact, just been waiting for her divorce from Myron Futterman to become final.

Reagan and Wyman were married at Forest Lawn, on ground sacred to satire, in the Wee Kirk o' th' Heather. It was a little bit of heaven. A marriage made in the Hollywood Hotel issued from the very heart of Hollywood feigning. The radio show of that name took listeners to a party of simulated gaiety—behind which the reality, according to a participant, Mary Jane Higby, was one of labor strife, exploitation and blackmail.[35] The stars appeared for no pay, supposedly because they were such great friends with Louella—actually out of fear. The paid actors, who had to rehearse for nothing, described the mythical hotel's opulent interior and named the milling stars, including some who were not there. The level of pretense was that of Reagan's telegraphed baseball games squared—at least there had been a real game played *somewhere* while he described it with details out of his own head.

The labyrinth of illusion cannot be threaded till one realizes that all the power of Parsons (and her imitators) came from an implicit threat to *stop* pretending. Her weapon was truth, but it was a weapon in the sense that theorists of deterrence advocate: it was powerful so long as she never had to use it. She threatened selectively to stop pretending that everyone was her friend, that Hollywood was wonderland, that morals had fled to their last and safest refuge there. She could not pull out many pieces from that fabric of illusion without destroying her own power. But she could ruin others long before the total structure fell on her—so few people called her bluff. David Niven, in his extraordinarily literate and candid memoirs, describes her method and its effect:

Columnist: Who was that girl you were nuzzling in that little bar in the San Fernando Valley at three o'clock this morning?

Actor: It was my mother.

Columnist: You were *not* with your mother, you were with Gertie Garterbelt. I suppose she told her husband you were both working late?

Actor: Well, we were—we just dropped in for a nightcap on the way home.

Columnist: According to my information, you had one of her bosoms in your hand.

Actor: It fell out of her dress . . . I was just helping her put it back in.

Columnist: Rubbish! . . . But I won't print because I don't want to make trouble for you.

Actor: Bless you—you're a doll.

Columnist: Got any news for me?

Actor: Afraid I haven't right now.

Columnist: Call me when you hear anything, dear.

Actor: *(Wiping brow)* You bet I will.

And he would, too.[36]

Thus, through bluff and blackmail, collusion with the studios, and the power of Hearst's papers, Parsons upheld the mythical Hollywood of happy marriages, celebrating home, country, and God.

It was in the name of all these that she tried to save "her" couple when the pretending wore thin:

> No marital separation since I broke the story that Mary Pickford, America's sweetheart, was leaving Douglas Fairbanks, has had the effect of the parting of the Reagans . . . Jane and Ronnie have always stood for so much that is right in Hollywood . . . That's why this hurts so much. That's why we are fighting so hard to make them realize that what seems to have come between them is not important enough to make their break final.[37]

As Parsons's boss, *Citizen Kane,* tells Susan in the movie, "You can't do this to *me.*" The emphasis on what "I broke," on what "we" are fighting so hard for, is not only an expression of Parsons's proprietary attitude, but that of the fans for whom she spoke. This was the audience's marriage, conducted for its benefit.

Reagan emerged from this world of hypocrisy, of illusion, of endangered identity, with surprisingly few scars. But it is important to see how he managed this—by *pretending* that nothing had happened. As Lou Cannon put it, "Reagan acted as if he had not really been divorced at all. He never changed this way of looking at what had happened to him . . . On the lecture circuit in behalf of the film industry soon after the Wyman divorce, Reagan surprised audiences by invariably including a line or two in his speeches about the high success rate of marriages in Hollywood."[38] He survived Hollywood by using its own weapons against it. When Louella Parsons gave her audience a melodrama of tragic breakup, Reagan solved all that by simply not including it in his own mental movie. He believed he was not divorced. For certain stars, at certain moments, the question of a truth test for what one *wants* to believe must not arise. The all-American world of movies was an elaborate structure of feignings. Each performer had to strike his or her private bargain with make-believe. It is clear, from early on, what Reagan's device would be: he pretended there was no pretense. When he had to, he could will his own innocence. That is what chastity symbols are for.

CHAPTER 18

War Movies

with long and tedious havoc fabl'd Knights
In Battels feign'd.

—*Paradise Lost 9.30–31*

World War II deeply engaged the emotions of Ronald Reagan, as was evident from his address on the anniversary of the D Day landings. He spoke on a windy French promontory, to an audience that included sixty-two Rangers who had scaled the cliffs there: "These are the boys of Pointe du Hoc. These are the *men* who took the cliffs."

It was a war Reagan had fought in, even before the invasion of Pearl Harbor—he was a Yank in the RAF for *International Squadron* (1941).[1] For him, even a student strike, even athletics, had been holy causes; but World War II put Reagan's hero, Roosevelt, at the head of an alliance truly directed against an evil empire. Reagan became, at his own level, as passionate a communicator of the war's importance as was the President himself.

Reagan was ineligible for combat—he could no longer evade the eye test he had tricked his way past at Fort Des Moines. He put on his obsolete cavalry uniform, with its spurs (Hubler, p. 127), but was assigned to clerical duties at San Francisco. Even in the short time he was there, he was often called away to support the war by personal appearances, and he was soon back in Los Angeles as part of an Air Force team at the Hal Roach studio in Culver City. His war duty was to make more war movies—*Rear Gunner; For God and Country; Mr. Gardenia Jones.* He was not only an airman on the screen, but an officer in the actual Air Force, though he still would not go up in an airplane.

One of his early assignments at Culver City was to produce fake mistakes. Every year Warner Brothers put together a short film of outtakes—film not used in released pictures, usually because the actor "went up" in his lines— to show at a studio party (Hubler, p. 232). The films were closely held in those days, when the sight of actors swearing at themselves or indulging in salacious asides could hurt the carefully nurtured image of a star. Now they are commercially available, and seem very tame stuff (Reagan and Eve Arden joking about a soldier's "getting any"). But they were a Hollywood legend then, and his superior officer asked Reagan to get one for a party he was planning. Since Reagan could not or would not ask Warners for the real thing, he gathered what actors were in Culver City and had them deliberately create for the camera fluffed lines, missed cues, and collapsing props. Apparently the generals were not sophisticated enough to notice that the actors were not all from Warners. As Reagan says, his faked "bloopers" showed up in later collections of the real thing (Hubler, pp. 142–43). They still do. It took some skill to make the mistakes look "real." But Reagan has often "goofed" to look more natural—broken the grammar of sentences, feigned embarrassment, professionally avoided the appearance of being a professional. It is an important art in democratic politics.[2]

Plausible fakery had to take many forms in wartime. The Office of War Information, when it sponsored a propaganda magazine, presented it as a commercial venture because paid advertising "lends an appearance of authenticity to a magazine." Besides, the magazine, *Victory,* was directed solely to overseas audiences, and one aim of American propaganda was to impress others with the industrial capacity and wealth of America. The mere presence of ads in a magazine devoted to military matters would tell "an exceedingly powerful story of the war effort of American business."[3]

Even what Reagan describes as his major contribution to the war effort entailed an ambiguity about the real encouraged by his profession. Hollywood scenery men, using prewar aerial films of Japan, plus still photos of ground features, built small models of the Japanese islands and made the camera, with various lenses, "fly" slowly toward and over target cities, giving the illusion of sight from cockpits or through bombsights of the terrain at its proper scale and in various conditions of light. Reagan, as the off-screen narrator, "talked the pilot in" to his target, so he would be familiar with the full-scale reality when he encountered it. Here illusion served reality by precreating it. Reagan is justifiably proud of this vindication of Hollywood's skill at make-believe, though he exaggerates a bit when he says that, for secrecy, it ranked "up with the atom bomb project" (Hubler, p. 137).

Illusion is a necessary weapon in war. In combat, it can take the form of camouflage, feint, secret movement, faked "intelligence" to the foe. In politics, it takes all the forms of propaganda. At Culver City, it was training films. Reagan was part of the broader propaganda effort as well. Not only did he travel across town to make *This Is the Army* for war relief, he was often at fund-raising events, bond drives, troop send-offs. Los Angeles was an important military staging area as well as the capital of filmmaking, and Reagan, as the star simultaneously on military duty and in prominent residence, was useful in a number of good causes. At these affairs he developed an enthusiasm for telling stories of military heroism, a taste he took with him to the White House, as Warren Beatty found out. The emotional receptivity to war stories made Reagan lift the Bill Stern deathbed tale onto a higher plane; and the cooling of wartime emotions, over the years, did not reduce Reagan's earnest attachment to the narratives. His emotional investment in them has, if anything, accrued interest every time the bomber pilot has cradled the belly gunner's head in his arms and said, "We'll ride it down together."

Reagan was, after all, involved in a war service based on the principled defense of faking things. Harold Lasswell, the propaganda expert who served as consultant to the Office of Facts and Figures, predecessor to the OWI, said that effective propaganda must have "a large element of the fake in it."[4] Critic Sherman Dryer publicly opposed the Elmer Davis policy at the Office of Facts and Figures, saying his "strategy of truth" would be "a handicap" in the urgent need to "elicit concerned action from the public."[5] At OWI, the journalists who kept up some measure of regard for accuracy were defeated by increasing numbers of advertising specialists, under the leadership of Price Gilbert, former vice president of Coca-Cola.[6] Not that the remaining liberals in the office were above trickery for a good cause. When they criticized the Italian surrender policy, they did so through the words of a fake political commentator.[7]

The aim of propaganda is to mobilize the proper fighting emotions as rapidly as possible—often as crudely as possible. Arch Oboler, an OWI writer, said the department's job was to put "hate on the air."[8] Percy Winner, an OWI official, opposed surrender terms made to Italy because "cautery of a symptom does not cure a disease of the blood stream."[9] Rex Stout, who wrote often for the government, said, "We shall hate, or we shall fail," since there is a "deep-rooted mental and nervous disease afflicting the German people."[10] The racism directed at the Japanese took even more virulent forms, and was given domestic expression in the detention camps for American citizens of Japanese descent.

Apologies for the policy of hate were made in a way that would ease any guilt about venting it. One of the actors in a Norman Corwin show for the OWI said: "We Americans are affable enough. We've never made killing a career, although we happen to be pretty good with a gun."[11] Even Reagan's affability could be used by Hollywood propagandists. An article in *Modern Screen* said Jane Wyman had

> worked for the Red Cross and been wakened by anti-aircraft fire and entertained the boys at army camps. She'd seen Ronnie's sick face bent over a picture of the small swollen bodies of children starved to death in Poland. "This," said the war-hating Reagan between set lips, "would make it a pleasure to kill."[12]

But Reagan was temperamentally better suited to the inspirational fictions of war—the sentimental stories imagined or embroidered about young heroes like Colin Kelly, or the scripting of words that should have been spoken by men now dead ("Send us more Japs").[13] Even better was the creation of an ideal America for which people were fighting, an image as carefully cre-

ated by propaganda agencies as the stars' images were forged by studio
publicity. Thus, though American troops were segregated—even on the
same troop ships, blacks and whites had separate quarters, including separate galleys—filmmakers and others were instructed to present America as
ethnically integrated. *The Government Information Manual for the Motion
Picture,* drawn up by the federal Motion Picture Bureau for Hollywood
guidance in wartime, instructed filmmakers to "show colored soldiers in
crowd scenes; occasionally colored officers."[14] Hollywood endlessly shuffled
its ethnic types in fox holes and barracks scenes, though there were race riots
on the home front during the war.[15] The idealization of our side was extended to allies, and included a defense of the Moscow trials in the movie
Roosevelt personally asked Jack Warner to make, *Mission to Moscow.*[16] The
glorification of the Chinese involved the creation of a pleasant Oriental stereotype, in contrast to the hateful Japanese. *Time* magazine, owned by a
Sinophile, obliged: "The Chinese expression is likely to be more kindly,
placid, open; the Japanese more positive, dogmatic, arrogant."[17]

Reagan's contribution to the war effort was along such lines. He specialized in uplifting, even devotional, tales about young martyrs serving a perfect cause, tales that entered his permanent repertory, undislodgeable by
others' disbelief or by evidence. These are his war stories, and war stories
were his war, his service to the cause, to building morale, keeping up spirits.
They had an honorable purpose, just as the fake little Japan did, which
guided real bombers toward their goal. If this was not contributing, then
Reagan's military career would have been worthless in his own eyes, a fact
that helps explain his stubborn adherence to the tales. Early in the 1976
primary campaign against Gerald Ford, Reagan told one of his favorite
stories:

> When the first bombs were dropped on Pearl Harbor, there was great
> segregation in the military forces. In World War II, this was corrected.
> It was corrected largely under the leadership of generals like MacAr-
> thur and Eisenhower . . . One great story that I think of at the time,
> that reveals a change was occurring, was when the Japanese dropped
> the bomb [sic] on Pearl Harbor there was a Negro sailor whose total
> duties involved kitchen-type duties . . . He cradled a machine gun in
> his arms, which is not an easy thing to do, and stood on the end of a
> pier blazing away at Japanese airplanes that were coming down and
> strafing him and that [segregation] was all changed.[18]

Reporters pointed out that segregation persisted until Truman abolished it in
1948, three years after the war, but Reagan shook his head and said he did
not believe them. Later, he repeated his conviction that the story was true to
Lou Cannon, significantly saying, "I remember the scene. It was very powerful." Where did he remember the scene from? He was not at Pearl Harbor.
No such combat footage exists, that I know of, or could exist—how would it
"tell" you that the black had done nothing but kitchen duty? Reagan is

remembering a movie he saw, or an image he created cinematically in his own mind, perhaps using scenes like that from *Air Force* (1943), where John Garfield, as a grounded turret gunner cradles his machine gun and shoots a Japanese plane out of the sky.[19]

The story of the machine gunner is not easily surrendered. It appeals to Reagan and his followers on many levels. It expresses his dramatic sense *and* his ideology. In dramatic terms, everything turns on the crisis, essentially on one man's moment, his "finest hour," his big scene, his most memorable line. In ideological terms, the story assumes that the individual makes all the difference—there was no need for historical process, social transaction, political pressure, the play of interests, gradual shifts in the climate of opinion, a complicated sequence, to achieve integration of the armed forces. One man stood on a pier "and that was all changed."

So, in Eureka, the story of the student strike was not one with a history stretching back for years, with complicated arguments on either side; it was not the story of an ambiguous struggle with an ironic result. One man— Reagan—stood up, and in one speech changed things. For Reagan, a football game is the story of a play ("That's one for the Gipper"), a team is the story of a player (George Gipp), a business is the story of the boss (Peter MacArthur), a movie the story of one scene ("Where's the rest of me?"), and the Holocaust was the story of one man, Hitler. As President, Reagan has tried to bring real heroes into his speeches, whose story he can tell movingly before the audience. If he tells the story of a black woman who cares for parentless children in New York, that shows that the individual can solve large social problems. As he said of his wife's work with drug centers, in the film made about her for the 1984 campaign: "These [centers] were started not by government but by people."

Like all good propaganda, Reagan's stories directly mobilized strong feelings. The justification for this is the purpose to which the story is put. In war time, it was enough to ask if the story served the war. "Are you with us or against us?" The method personalizes everything; by glorifying the subject of the story, it makes any attack on the story-telling a denigration of the hero being remembered. For Reagan, those who question his segregation story are themselves bigots not willing to give the black sailor his due. He has shown his regard for the sailor, and sticks by him, his protector, against all the sniggering critics.

Even when Reagan has genuine stories to tell, genuine heroes to celebrate, he casts a mythic, even religious, aura over them, and makes complex operations the story of one man. So, at the Normandy ceremony of June 6, 1984, Operation Overlord became the tale of Private Zanatta, told in the moving words of his daughter, who was present on camera. The story ended with a Bill Stern touch: "The anniversary of D Day was always special for her family; and, like all families of those who went to war, she describes how she came to realize her own father's survival was a miracle."[20]

Reagan's war stories are real to him; his war stories were his war, in part because he was acting a role as a soldier himself, "off to war" while at home. And his hometown, Los Angeles, was a strange mixture of real and make-believe war. Hollywood had gone to war, and the war had come to Holly-wood. There was fear of the Japanese Americans until they were forcibly removed. Then GIs in town terrorized Mexican Americans for days in so-called "Zoot Suit Riots." Japanese air raids, or submarine shellings, were expected. There were blackouts, false sightings, air raid drills. Even the Rose Bowl game was shifted to North Carolina, out of reach of Japanese bomb-ers.[21] The studios built sandbagged air raid shelters. A Warner Brothers executive was especially happy to have a *Life* photographer on hand when his stars did an air raid drill.[22]

Since Reagan's popularity was at its peak when he entered the Army, and Wyman's was growing, theirs became the quintessential wartime parting, he to the front and she to keep up things at home. "Now it's real, she thought. Now it's Ronnie's war and mine."[23] When Reagan returned to Los Angeles in a few weeks, for his film work, the fan magazines continued to treat him as "off at war." *Modern Screen* wrote: "It's nine months now since Ronald Reagan said, 'So long, Button-nose' to his wife and baby, and went off to join his regiment."[24] The article describes Wyman's loneliness, the way she looks around to see her man and he is not there. Where was he? *Movie Life* covered Reagan's arrival with Wyman at the opening of his picture, *This Is the Army,* as if he were back in town for the event. Just to add to the make-believe war in town, camouflaged snipers were perched around the entry lobbies.[25]

Reagan had made *This Is the Army* in Los Angeles, where he made all his military movies. He showed up at other events, and the press left it obscure where he was coming "home" from: "Captain Ronald Reagan, former movie star and now serving with the Army Air Force First Motion Picture Unit, today will light the new victory torch of Southern California's women at war. He will report for duty at the Examiner Recruiting Headquarters, 424 West Sixth Street, to welcome the first contingent of women to apply for enlistment."[26] When Reagan went with Wyman to the Hollywood Canteen, *Movie Life* assured its readers he was home "on a short leave."[27] A leave from where? *Photoplay* had been marginally more honest when it said Rea-gan had been "temporarily" returned to Burbank.[28] As late as April of 1944, *Modern Screen* was still writing, "After Ronnie left Jane *and Hollywood* for Army, his fan mail swelled. . . ." (italics added). His wife continued to be treated as the brave one who endures her husband's absence. She was de-scribed as choosing dresses that would match his uniform when he came home on leave.[29] Where was he? Well, on the day that Hiroshima was bombed, he was driving across town to the Disney studio, to narrate an animated short about the war (Hubler, p. 145). Disney's ingenuity in finding new ways to create make-believe war had won much praise. *Fortune* called him a great educator—greater (and more American) than any Ph.D. would be, since he retained "the two essentials of good teaching [clarity and interest]—essentials that have been all but forgotten in the craze for scholarly research with which the German Ph.D. system has cursed American education."[30] Clarity and interest matter in propaganda; facts do not.

Reagan fought so many wars on so many fronts during his time "off to war" that he seems to have forgotten exactly where he was. When he makes one of his rare references to his divorce in the Hubler account (p. 159), he presents it as a war movie: "By the time I got out of the Army Air Corps, all I wanted to do—in common with several million other veterans—was to rest up awhile, make love to my wife, and come up refreshed to a better job in an ideal world. (As it came out, I was disappointed in all these postwar ambitions.)" Where had he been that he could not make love to his wife? They had been in the same town for the last three years. Their only prolonged time of separation was Wyman's tour of the Southern states as part of a bond drive—she got farther from Hollywood than he did. Yet Reagan obviously believes he was "off to war." He was in a never-never land of publicity absences and fan-magazine presence. He was making war, not love, the only way he was allowed. He was in heart and mind with those he glorified. He was "off at war" exactly as he had been inside the Hollywood Hotel.

The disorientation of Reagan about the places of his wartime service lies behind the most astonishing answer he has given to the question where he was during the war. On November 29, 1983, speaking in the Oval Office to Prime Minister Yitzhak Shamir of Israel, Reagan said that he had been assigned as part of his war duties to the filming of Nazi death camps for the Signal Corps. He kept one film, since he felt that the authenticity of the Holocaust would one day be questioned, and sure enough, one day he had to show the film to convince a skeptic. The story was so movingly told that Shamir repeated it in detail to his Cabinet, from which the Jerusalem newspaper *Ma'ariv* printed it. It was carried, from there, in the *Near East Report* of February 10, 1984.

Two and a half months after Shamir met with Reagan, Rabbi Marvin Hier and Simon Wiesenthal were at the White House in connection with the dedication of the Simon Wiesenthal Center, and Reagan told them the same story. Rabbi Hier, after their conversation, told Joanne Omang of the Washington *Post* that the President had photographed the death camps for the Signal Corps. She thought that interesting, but not news—her job was to deal with the Simon Wiesenthal Center.[31] But when she next saw Cannon, Reagan's biographer, at the office of the *Post,* she asked why he never mentioned to her that Reagan had photographed the death camps. Because he didn't, said Cannon; he was never out of the country during the war.[32] Cannon, however, had just seen the *Near East Report* story, so he asked Ed Walsh, at the Jerusalem office of the Washington *Post,* to confirm it with cabinet sources there.[33] Then he printed an account of both meetings in his column.

There is an obvious continuity between this tale and the one *Modern Screen* told in 1942: "She's seen Ronnie's sick face bent over a picture of the small swollen bodies of children starved to death in Poland." Both stories were told "for the cause." Both had their intended effect. Reagan was "at war" in both cases, using images for morale and inspiration, giving a pep talk to a whole country. All his war-making has been in the mind, and he will make it the way he wants. As late as the presidential debates of 1984, Reagan revealed the connection between war and war movies in his mind: "I think the people should understand that three quarters of the defense budget pays for pay and salary—or for pay and pension, and then you add to that food and wardrobe . . ." When he had been in army wardrobe himself, he was off at war, where he could not make love to his wife. He had been somewhere. Perhaps it was Dachau.

Cannon's column set alarm bells ringing in the White House. Cannon says that he has never seen such a retrieval attempt from the Reagan team. James Baker called him to deny his version of the meeting with Wiesenthal and Rabbi Hier. A videotape of some earlier Reagan comments (1981) on the Holocaust was made available to the press. Callers from the White House convinced Rabbi Hier, but not Wiesenthal, that what Reagan had meant was that he had seen Signal Corps films while in the service, and saved one of those.[34] Reagan himself wrote Cannon saying that was his meaning. Wiesenthal's "mistake" was attributed to faulty English. (He has accented, not faulty, English.) Rabbi Hier told Cannon that Reagan may have fallen into "rhetorical excess." There was apparently nothing the White House could do about Yitzhak Shamir. Cannon wrote a retrospective account of the whole sequence in the *Post,* wondering how such intelligent men as Wiesenthal and Shamir could, on two separate occasions and independently of each other, take an unexceptional story (who has *not* seen films of the death camps?) and imagine an *identical* elaboration of it. The last criticism to be made of Reagan's stories is that they are hard to understand. Cannon, a longtime student of Reagan, understands his modes of belief. Reagan, after all, believes he *saw* the integration of the armed services accomplished at Pearl Harbor.[35]

It was this part of Reagan's continuing fascination with war movies that most people did not know about, or had forgotten, when the Bitburg controversy arose early in 1985. In the course of that dispute over Reagan's commemoration of V.E. Day, it was revealed that the West German government had suggested he visit a death camp, but the White House firmly ruled that out.[36] Handlers of the Reagan image, led by Mike Deaver, had made such expert preparations for his photogenic earlier trips to Korea, Ireland, and Normandy that people wondered how they could be so inept as to brush aside the suggestion of a death camp and go instead to a German cemetery (where, it turned out, S.S. troops were buried). One answer is that the Bitburg cemetery is photogenic, and Reagan is good at tributes to dead soldiers. But those who did the initial planning had to remember their strenuous containment of the death camp stories Reagan had already told. They did not want that can of worms opened again. Acute awareness of that

danger helped blind them to other, even greater ones, so wary were they of
the power of Reagan's storytelling ability and the trouble it can cause a
nervous staff. War movies are hell.

Appropriately, it was on the European trip including Bitburg that Reagan
demonstrated again his ability to visit countries without anybody's ever noticing. Heckled in the World Parliament by protestors shouting "What about
Nicaragua," Reagan retorted: "They haven't been there. I have.''' He did it
during the war.

CHAPTER 19

Could He Act?

[Actors] sit on a narrow ledge, and they are preserved by our response, our loving them.

—David Thomson

Reagan described his "return" from war as a postwar movie about the difficulties of a combat veteran in readjusting to civilian life.

> Like most of the soldiers who came back [from where?], I expected a world suddenly reformed. I hoped and believed that the blood and death and confusion of World War II would result in a regeneration of mankind . . . I discovered that the world was almost the same and perhaps a little worse. My first reaction was to take a vacation at Lake Arrowhead. There I could laze around and take time to figure things out. One of the first impulses was to rent a speedboat twenty-four hours a day. The rental proprietor thought I was crazy. "It's all right," I assured him, "I just want to know that the boat is there at the dock any time I wanted to take a drive on the water. I can't walk on it any more." In the end the rental cost more than the total cost of the boat. It was worth it. [Hubler, pp. 160–61]

He also made model boats. "I suppose this was proper therapy."

The trip to Lake Arrowhead may have been therapy for Reagan, who had to recover from making war films so he could make more films (including war films, like *The Hasty Heart*, *Prisoner of War*, and *Hellcats of the Navy*). But for Jane Wyman, the lake trip was work—she was there to do location filming for *The Yearling*, in which she was playing Gregory Peck's wife. Boats were rented by the studio (MGM) to get to and from the shooting site.[1] Reagan was back in a movie setting, with his actress wife and their two children. It is not the lonely scene he described to Hubler. That comes from a postwar movie.

The lake stay may, in retrospect, have become symbolic for Reagan, but not because the world remained unchanged, unredeemed. The real significance of the scene lay in the fact that his wife had changed. While he had not started work on a new movie yet, she was engaged in one of the year's biggest projects for the town's biggest studio. Though Reagan "went off" during the war, and Wyman "stayed home," she, not he, was altered by the experience. She had been making movies for ten years, five years longer than her husband, when Reagan was inducted; but her career had been stalled, for most of that time, among the chorines, "gold diggers," and girl reporters who were as interchangeable at Warners as the three actresses who played Torchy Blane in the reporter series. All that changed during the war.

Some of this transformation may have occurred even without the war. Though she was twenty-eight in 1942, she had always looked younger than her years, and the "button nose" to which fan magazines had reduced her gave a juvenile, even comic, cast to her features. It would be hard to take her seriously till she had aged a little. As the leading lady's best friend—she was to Priscilla Lane what Reagan was to Wayne Morris—she was beginning to be more understanding, less flighty, as the forties began.

But the war gave her important new opportunities. For one thing, it dispersed the Drake circle of intimates around Reagan, the gang of pals for whom Reagan was still "Dutch" the jock and she was the gang's "good sport." These friends—hers as well as his, by this time—went into the army or other work, and would never resume the life they had maintained during their first years in California. Also, the fan magazines that had imprisoned Wyman in her own trivial prettiness now helped shape a different, soberer image—the responsible mother without her man carrying on during the war, a Mrs. Miniver with glamor. (The several servants who took care of her house and children never showed up in fan-magazine pictures or prose.) She was even asked to dress for a new role—as, indeed, all women were, during wartime drives against the wearing of jewelry or other "shallow" decorations.[2] Women, too, had to go into their own kind of uniform.

Wyman, precisely because she was asked to typify wartime woman, was expected to be responsible for larger tasks than charming men. This was one of the many ways "the war transformed the image of American women."[3] As a performer, as well as a mother, Wyman had a serious purpose now. Her public appearances were for the war effort. She stepped out of her chorine character and made articulate appeals to patriotism. It was in this context, after her image had been altered with the changing social situation, that Billy Wilder gave her her breakthrough part. As an alcoholic's fiancée in The Lost Weekend (1945), made while Reagan was still in the Air Force, she was allowed the dignity of worry. Then, in The Yearling (1946), being completed when Reagan was mustered out, she was asked to be Ma Baxter, a sternly tried mother—just what the wartime publicity had made her. She was capable of the larger roles. She won an Academy Award nomination as Ma Baxter. Finally, at age thirty-four, she had the dramatic heft, along with her still-youthful face, to play her best role, the raped teenager, deaf and mute, in Johnny Belinda (1948). This won her an Oscar, and led to two more nominations, deft performances in Hitchcock's *Stage Fright* (1950) and Frank Capra's *Here Comes the Groom* (1951). After singing in the Capra movie, she recorded duets with Bing Crosby ("Cool, Cool, Cool of the Evening"), Danny Kaye, and others.

When she divorced Reagan in 1949, he said wryly: "I think I'll name *Johnny Belinda* as the co-respondent."[4] That seems to have been the attitude of Reagan's sympathizers. It blamed no one. Glen Claussen says: "The divorce was a terrible blow to Nelle [Jack had died eight years earlier], who blamed it on *Johnny Belinda*. She said it changed Jane's whole character." How? "She used to spend days doing nothing but being a deaf-mute." At the divorce proceedings Wyman claimed that Reagan had dragged her off to political meetings that bored her; but California law dictates that the wife must plead extreme mental cruelty to justify a divorce, and allegations made *pro forma* should be read with suspicion. As we shall see, the idea that Wyman was not interested in Screen Actors Guild politics will not hold.

The comments on *Johnny Belinda* indicate the fact that there had always been a gulf in temperament between Reagan and Wyman. She had a fierce professionalism under her flighty first manner. She was never just a "good sport." She suffered through the cute years, determined to transcend them, and she did. She would do whatever she had to in order to become a character different from the doll or toy in the public's fancy. She was trying to escape one of the basic traps in the Hollywood system, where becoming a "starlet" can of itself prevent one from acting. If you evade the trap by acting that is good enough, you become a bigger star, and have to think of new ways to escape—as Marlon Brando's career demonstrated on the grandest scale. Wyman would not work so maniacally at becoming an escape artist. But to cease being a kittenish "Torchy," she was willing to turn her life upside down.

Reagan's attitude toward his craft—as toward life—was quite different. He learned his lines; was winning, conscientious, dependable; but did not agonize over character. For one thing, he likes regular hours. He did not like location shooting because it played havoc with his schedule of rest and exercise. He never aspired to *become* the character he played. Even in what he considers his greatest feat of acting intensity, he emphasizes that he screamed well as Drake McHugh only because he thought of the scene as showing "Ronald Reagan with his legs cut off."[5] Reagan liked the star system; he wanted to be like John Wayne, always the hero walking tall in every role. He played a "bad guy" only once, in *The Killers,* and he regretted that. For him a bigger part meant the lead in a Technicolor Western.

Reagan was frustrated by the studio after the war, but for reasons entirely different from Wyman's. He had reached the A pictures; he was a star in salary and fan attention; he was being given good scripts (adaptations of hit plays by John Van Druten, Norman Krasna, John Patrick). Warners even gave him a Technicolor picture, at last—*It's a Great Feeling* (1949). And Reagan did not mind being typed. In fact, he wanted it. But he felt he was being mistyped. He wanted to be an action-adventure hero. They wanted him in light comedy roles. Shortly after Wyman, three years his junior, played Ma Baxter, Reagan was cast as leading man to a finally nubile Shirley Temple in *That Hagen Girl* (1948).

Which side was right, Reagan or the studio? It is interesting to see how the studio went about making the decision. It used polling techniques similar to those brought to much greater sophistication in the Reagan campaigns and White House. The famous advertiser David Ogilvy, who began his career in the Gallup polling firm, did a "Continuing Audit of Marquee Values" of Reagan for Warner Brothers in 1941–42, when he was still playing the hero's best friend and Brass Bancroft, just before *Kings Row* appeared.[6] It showed that Reagan was more popular with women than with men (in interesting contrast to his presidential polls), and most popular with women in the twelve-to-seventeen age bracket (an important audience at the box office). He was the bobbysoxers' hero, the Tab Hunter of his day. Teaming him with Shirley Temple was no accident. The audit has the wrong profile for a man trying to become an action hero. Cowboy heroes ride on the little-boy imaginings of men in the audience. John Wayne was more popular with men than with women for most of his career.

Reagan thought that *Kings Row* should have changed all that; he took his raise in salary to be an earnest of "manlier" roles. But there was no reason for the studio to agree with his analysis. Reagan was a success in *Kings Row* —though less than has been claimed in retrospect.[7] And the reasons for that success were more likely to confirm than alter the studio's view of him. For most of his time on the screen he is the light and witty fellow of many earlier or later movies *(Brother Rat,* say, or *The Girl from Jones Beach),* his infectious grin made more effective than ever by the gloomy surroundings of the plot and cinematography. One of the studio's ways of clearing up the novel, to get it past the censors, was precisely to cast Reagan as the "wicked" Drake McHugh. If *he* is as naughty as things get in town, then *Kings Row* cannot be so hellish after all. Reagan also benefits by proximity to the picture's nominal lead, Robert Cummings, in a pretentious role whose nobility he makes even more ludicrous. Finally, in the climactic scene, the most important visual element is the return of Reagan's easygoing grin, withheld during a period of childish pouting during the latter part of the movie.

We must take a closer look at *Kings Row,* since many people now (like Reagan himself) make it the test case of his acting ability, and many of them are convinced (like Reagan) that they have watched a scene that does not occur in the movie. The scene in question shows Reagan's character, Drake McHugh, waking after surgery has removed his legs. "Coming from unconsciousness to full realization of what had happened in a few seconds, it presented me with the most challenging acting problem of my career" (Hubler, p. 8). But the movie does *not* show Reagan coming to full consciousness in a few seconds. He is shooting his own movie in his head, not the one director Sam Wood made and which the rest of us see.

"Randy!" I screamed. Ann Sheridan (bless her), playing Randy, burst through the door. She wasn't in the shot and normally wouldn't have been on hand until we [sic] turned the camera around to get her entrance, but she knew it was one of those scenes where a fellow actor needed all the help he could get . . . [Ibid., p. 10]

She "wasn't in the shot"? The whole episode is told from Sheridan's point of view, through her concern. The camera stays with her. The scene is set up as Sheridan, downstairs in her house, lets out the nurse who has sedated Reagan. Her father tells Sheridan she should go out, too; she has had no rest. "I'd like to be here when he finds out," she answers. She and her father discuss the future; then her brother comes down the stairs to tell them, "He's waking up," and she goes to the stairs. She is held there a moment, talking with her brother about Reagan, when she hears the cry "Randy" from above. She runs up the stairs, into the camera, as Reagan, *still off-camera,* shouts his second "Randy." The door is thrown open and we see her face, registering concern, as he shouts his third and last "Randy." All that time, while he was "coming from unconsciousness," we have not even seen Reagan. Ann Sheridan, "not in the shot" according to Reagan, *was* the shot. The idea that Reagan had to convey the realization of where he was, and what had happened, is simply not the director's idea. We have been set up to experience the moment through Ann Sheridan's reaction, which is what we get again after the camera shows him (briefly) shouting in a hoarse voice, "Where's the *rest* of me?" Back to Sheridan. Then Reagan looks up toward the ceiling, says, "It was that accident," and falls back on his pillow whispering, "Parris."

Reagan assures us that he was properly worked up for the scene, and truly felt legless as he shouted; he thanks the director for doing it in one take. But the director clearly did not think of this as a big scene at all, and certainly not as Reagan's big scene. It is short, rapid, and dependent on Sheridan. The Korngold score does not lavish special care on it. (The scene was short and unemphatic in the novel, too, in accord with McHugh's subordinate interest.) The camera does not linger on Reagan long enough for him to go through any such sequence of emotions as his book describes. It does not even show the place where his legs should be, or explore the disorientation of the man in the strange room. It is *not* a strange room to Sheridan; it is her house—and we are sharing her consciousness.

To see how Wood used Reagan's appeal in *Kings Row* we have to look at what *he* intended to be the big scene, which is supposed to tax the skill of Robert Cummings, though Reagan plays a longer and more crucial part in it than in his own favorite sequence. As in much of the movie, Wood is making do with a weird story foisted on him, and with the limits of his two male leads.

There are several old pros lurking in the shadows of this movie—Judith Anderson, Claude Rains, Charles Coburn, Harry Davenport. Maria Ouspenskaya cannot be said to lurk, since she lives in the house brilliantly lit with her sanity by cinematographer James Wong Howe. The most interesting thing in the film is the interplay of different interiors designed by William Cameron Menzies—the sunlit house of Ouspenskaya, who is Cummings's grandmother; the corkscrew staircase in the home of Coburn, the sadistic surgeon; the somber office of Claude Rains, an incestuous doctor (cleaned up for the movie into the caretaker of his insane daughter); and Ann Sheridan's shack, with its cramped loft, cut into by a gable, where Reagan learns to live with his curtailed body.

Howe was working in the very year *Citizen Kane* appeared, with Gregg Toland's dazzling deep-focus shots—e.g., that of Kane entering a distant door while the glass from which Susan drank poison is kept focused in the foreground.[8] Howe equals that when he brings Cummings out of the hall into his grandmother's antechamber: during the whole of his approach, the hypodermic needle that will betray Ouspenskaya's illness is reflected, in the foreground, from a silver basin.[9] The real contrast in the movie is between that silver basin, along with its pitcher, and the conical coffee pot at the center of all motion in Ann Sheridan's kitchen (which seems to be the only downstairs room). When Reagan falls in the railway yard and his leg is bruised by the train's wheel, we see that coffee pot, which Sheridan had carried to the station, crushed on the track.

The novel, and much of the movie's dialogue, had played on a different contrast, one of social geography, the "good side" of town pitted against the other side of the tracks. But we are not allowed to *see* this contrast. At the outbreak of the war, restrictions were placed on the money that could be used for set materials, so no sense of the town's layout or contrasts is ever given. We are not even shown a view of Ann Sheridan's house—just of its loft above some railway cars. The idyllic rich side of town is suggested by a tree against the skyline clearly borrowed from *Gone With the Wind,* which had also been designed by William Cameron Menzies.[10]

The film's climax brings together all that is best and worst in it. While the rakish boy-about-town Drake McHugh was getting his legs cut off, and being nursed by a girl from across the tracks, Parris Mitchell had gone to Vienna, to become one of America's first psychiatrists (the year is 1900, the beginning of a "happy new century"). Returning to his small hometown to visit his friend, Cummings-Mitchell gets involved in a struggle to keep Reagan-McHugh from learning the truth—that his legs were needlessly amputated. Finally, the new love in his life suggests what all his Vienna training could not, that it might be better to tell Reagan the truth after all. Cummings, his cherubic features chalkily made up to suggest long nights with his books, feels he might soften the blow by reciting Henley's "Invictus" to the suffering man. Parker Tyler calls this "the poetry cure for the castration complex."[11]

Wood and Howe shrewdly use the cut-up space of the loft given them by Menzies. Cummings is at the foot of the bed, reciting as if to win an elocution contest. Sheridan flutters, momentarily, between the friends, trying to prevent the confrontation with reality; then she sinks down beside Reagan— we see her across his profile as he sits and absorbs the truth. There is a long pause in which it is Reagan's job *not* to react, to build suspense. Then he breaks the tension with a return of the old Drake McHugh laughter, with-held since he hit bottom. The easy Reagan laughter, returning, leads to some brave new lines: "That's a hot one, isn't it? Where did Gordon think I lived, in my legs?" There is more, but by this time we are not paying much atten-tion to the words, since Erich Korngold's title theme returns to the sound-track like the Life Force, building behind Reagan's words until (the *nerve* of it is breathtaking) a heavenly choir actually bursts into the blessedly indistin-guishable words of Henley's poem—I say blessedly because, if you do listen with care, you find that Korngold, who fancied himself an opera composer, has set the last two lines of Henley's poem (which even Cummings spared us), this way: "I am the mast-*ER OF* my fate, I am the *CAP*-tuh-unh of my-ee soul." Reagan did not have to act much—just pout, then laugh. And even the fact that Cummings could not act does not matter finally. The scene works because the scene is Korngold's.

Korngold is best known for the declamatory signature tunes he wrote for Errol Flynn as Robin Hood or the Sea Hawk, the kind of hero-arriving-in-the-nick-of-time music John Williams would later do for the Indiana Jones films. The *Kings Row* theme is supposed to be classier soap-opera stuff, suggesting that Life Goes On, like Max Steiner's title theme for *Gone With the Wind*.¹² But Korngold's range was not wide, and he gives us music for a Sea Hawk of the Small Town. Since the pasty-faced Cummings does not fit the swashbuckler description at all, Reagan's defiant laughter at the end identifies him finally with the heroic theme: *he* is the Captain Blood of his own soul. He does not have to steal the picture from Cummings. Korngold stole it for him.

Thus *Kings Row,* rather than challenging, confirms the view that Reagan was not an actor of depth or intensity. The desperate nature of any larger claims for his acting is illustrated by the fact that some use his one villain's role to show he could "escape type." But his was a small part in *The Killers* (1964)—seventh ("special") billing—and that was a made-for-television film not released on the networks because of its sadomasochistic treatment of Angie Dickinson, the stylish "Hitchcock" lady whom the men must stand in line to threaten, abuse, beat up, or kill. Reagan's part is to hit her, and to scowl. A squint narrows his eyes, and makeup thins his lips, but mainly he relies on a trick he had used to comic purpose theretofore, the ability to lift his left eyebrow independently of his right.

When he went off to make Technicolor Westerns—several directed by the aging pioneer of Hollywood, Allan Dwan—Reagan proved that the studio had been right all along. He is too light and likeable to have the menace needed for such roles. There is something slightly cautious in the way he moves—perhaps the legacy of a childhood of insecurely oriented movement before his parents realized that he needed glasses.[13] He is ineffaceably nice, as those political foes have discovered who tried to depict him as malevolent. Nelle's boy did not grow up to slap Angie Dickinson, and his regret for the one attempt is apt as well as genuine. He would never change his nature for a role as Wyman did, as great actors do. It is a price that may not be worth paying in the long run, since many great actors leave a trail of human wreckage behind them. Wyman did a dreadful thing to Reagan's life when she left him.[14] It took great strength for him to recover, after staggering. But that strength is not in his acting.

We are dealing with a question people pick at in their various ways. On the one hand, some try to explain Reagan's extraordinary success in politics by saying he gets by because he is "just an actor." On the other hand, we are told he was not even a good actor—which seems to make his political success more mysterious. Which is it to be? Is he just reading lines, following his script, using theatrical skills, as President? Or did a man lacking the depth for great roles in the theater somehow acquire a knack for filling the most responsible role in the world? He spent thirty-three years of his life, most men's most creative years, in the movies. He spent thirty-seven years performing, if we include the first years in radio. As I write this, he has been in politics only twenty-one years. How did a man who could not master his chosen profession, after such prolonged endeavor, pick up new skills late in life? How explain the rise to the very top of politics, and heady triumphs there, after comparatively meager returns on a lifetime of trying as an actor?

There is no single answer to such questions. First of all, to say that Reagan was never an actor of great intensity is not to deny what the studio saw in him—a light romantic leading man, with a good voice, good timing in the reading of his lines, skill in handling dialogue (so give him scripts from plays). He was better than Wayne Morris, who started out billed above him. He was in the league of Van Johnson, Peter Lawford, Rod Taylor, Gig Young—not a bad league; they were solid performers. And it is wrong to say he ever failed in this league. Even the ridiculed *Bedtime for Bonzo* (1951) is a pleasant romp Reagan served well and was served well by. Reagan failed in Hollywood because he was not satisfied with his proper rung, with the range he commanded, but attempted heavier roles he could not sustain. These spiraled him downward from *The Last Outpost* (1951) to *Hellcats of the Navy* (1955), and even to *The Killers* (1964). In his rise, he had been a winner, not a stunner; in his fall, he was a fader, not a loser. But this was no fall from heights.

We should remember that Reagan had three show-business careers—in sports announcing, the movies, and on television. With "General Electric Theater" he returned to his basic strengths—to his voice, his well-timed delivery, his sincerity and likeability, all things that had been important in his earlier successes as in his later one.

Besides, in politics, the weight of office held or run for gives dignity to the role. Reagan does not, any longer, have to struggle against his own feeling that he should be playing a different kind of part, as he did in even his best movies. His sincerity, easiness, and optimism make him approachable without destroying the seriousness of the task. This is not something that he accomplished all by himself, like the individuals in his own anecdotes, outside historical process and social dependencies. He arrived in politics when it was absorbing show-business technique and personnel at an increasing rate. There was preparation for him, along with helpful contrasts at each stage— the contrast of his charm with the rigidity of other Goldwaterites in 1964, with the bitterness of Pat Brown in 1966, with the oatmealiness of Gerald Ford in 1976, and with the fecklessness of Jimmy Carter, the most unpopular President in modern history.

There was a complex interplay of elements at each stage of Reagan's slow Hollywood demise and rapid political rise. It is wrong to think of his life as divisible into neatly differing parts, first show business then politics. He is not "just an actor" in politics, not a failed actor who took up politics as something different, not a person for whom acting was all along a minor form of expression who finally "got it right" or found his voice in the 1966 campaign. All of his life—the good acting period and the bad, the various kinds of performing, the sports reporting, the spells as promoter for SAG and GE, along with the virtues and limits deriving from Dixon and Eureka —all these things are present and discernible, to people who have been exposed to him over the years, in his presidential appeal. Could he act? Of course he could, though not as Jane Wyman could act. He always acted like Ronald Reagan. It is a heartwarming role.

CHAPTER 20

Costarring

that Fruit, which with desire,
Inclinable now grown to touch or taste,
Sollicited her longing eye.

—Paradise Lost 9.741–43

When the movie in which Nancy Davis had her first lead role opened at Radio City Music Hall, Dore Schary, the film's producer, described her as "the girl whom this picture was going to make into a great star."[1] In fact, "two new stars . . . had just been born," Miss Davis and James Whitmore.[2] Schary felt a mission to complete *The Next Voice You Hear,* with its religious message (of unspecified content). He even battled the censor, Joseph Breen, over references to Davis's pregnancy. The movie could *show* her pregnant, but the censor originally blue-penciled a line in which she refers to her own "being big."[3] The Davis career never quite took off as Schary hoped; yet he rightly described her as having an "earnest intent and preparation." In the book he wrote about filming his favorite picture, he described her background: "Nancy majored in drama at Smith College, spent her summer vacations doing stock, and after graduation did supporting parts on the New York stage . . . She was an actress by profession rather than by accident."[4]

Not long ago, a politician who took an actress to wife might have been risking his career. Yet Nancy Reagan has added luster to her husband in the White House. Of course, Reagan was still an actor himself when he married Nancy Davis; but that of itself did not, necessarily, lighten her task. It might have been easier for the first actor President to have a wife who did not also come from Hollywood. We do not give that possibility much attention because Nancy Reagan has so skillfully resolved all dissonances between her past and present roles.

Her example, in fact, has subtly altered the standards for combining the world of politics and entertainment. Ronald Reagan's successor as governor of California was criticized for dating a pop singer; but the attacks were muted by a consideration that his predecessor had an actress for a wife, one who presided with dignity at state functions for eight years. Nancy Reagan has been an important part of the process that merged Hollywood and Washington over the last several decades.

This is not to say that all conflicts have simply disappeared. It would take nice calculating indeed to determine whether Elizabeth Taylor was a greater asset to her political husband, Senator John Warner, during her aberrant time of devotedness to him, than a liability when she returned to her stable condition of inconstancy. The potential for confusion was always there, even when she lived in exile on the Potomac—one wondered, for a start, which body the bodyguards were there to guard. This is the kind of divided attentiveness, the cultural double take, Nancy Reagan had to overcome with her loyally supportive pose near her husband—two steps back, great eyes turned up, feet rooted to the ground in matronly rapture. She had to prove that what Monaco can do, the United States can do—successfully "demote" a Hollywood princess to a ruler's housewife.

It might be said that Mrs. Reagan, unlike Princess Grace, was never a Hollywood princess. She was more a "starlet," just beginning a career—a brief detour from her housewifely destiny—that Reagan rescued her from. It is certainly true that she never achieved the box office status of Grace Kelly —though they came to Hollywood at about the same time, and they made exactly the same number of movies. In fact, Nancy Davis had a longer career in Hollywood than Grace Kelly did. Davis made her first movie in 1949; Kelly made her first in 1951. Davis made her eleventh and last movie in 1957; Kelly had already made her eleventh and last in 1956. Kelly retired in order to marry. Davis acted for ten years after her marriage. (She was in three TV dramas in 1962.)

Not only was her Hollywood career longer than Kelly's; Nancy Davis's Broadway touring company experience had been longer and more varied, as well. As the daughter of actresss Edie Luckett and the niece of a theater manager in Richmond, Virginia, Nancy Reagan grew up with show business. She had a head start on her chosen career, which she pursued from childhood till she was thirty-six years old.

For a studio biography written in her professional days, Nancy Davis forgivably reduced her age by two years.[5] But it is important to restore those years if we are to understand the background of Nancy Reagan. She was born in 1921, the year of the Fatty Arbuckle scandal in Hollywood. This was more a scandal of press exploitation than of real Hollywood sinfulness; but the Arbuckle murder trial, with similar episodes immediately preceding and following it, made the movie studios nervous. Actors were forced to become demonstratively respectable. A glorious exception to this was the circle around Alla Nazimova. She had made her name in New York for her Ibsen heroines—she was the first Stanislavsky-trained actress to play a lead role on Broadway.[6] In Hollywood, at her famous palace (which became the Garden of Allah Hotel), she held seances that awed Rudolph Valentino—he was so impressed that he married, seriatim, *two* of the lesbians from her circle.[7] The second of these, Natacha Rambova (*née* Winnifred Shaughnessy), designed art-deco sets for the Nazimova-Valentino *Camille* that came out in 1921, the year of Nancy's birth. Undeterred by censors after the Arbuckle trial, Nazimova and Rambova made their ostentatiously homoerotic *Salome* the very next year.[8]

All of this is relevant, along with the correct date for Nancy's birth, since Nazimova was Nancy's godmother—in 1921, the year of her appearance as Camille, and just before her scandalous Salome. Nazimova kept her ties with old theater friends in New York, including Edie Luckett. To her goddaughter, Nancy, the screen vamp was always "Zim."[9] Though Nancy grew up just outside Washington, D.C., and went to school inside the District, the presence of both Broadway and Hollywood was felt around her childhood from cradle days. It is appropriate that the woman whose godmother had made such a hit in *A Doll's House* should have her own "real" doll's house knocked together for her amusement by a stage carpenter.[10] Domesticity would always be theatrically conceived in her life.

Edie Luckett had played in Nazimova's Broadway production of '*Ception Shoals* (1917). That was just one of many theatrical associations that proved important to Nancy's childhood and youth. As she grew up calling Nazimova "Zim," she grew up calling Spencer Tracy "Spence." Edie had played with him in *The Baby Cyclone* (1928). When Nancy's New York dates with an MGM executive led, in 1949, to a Hollywood screen test, her mother called Spence to help arrange it—he lined up George Cukor to direct her in a scene from a forthcoming big-budget production, in which she landed a part.[11] Edie had also played with Walter Huston in *Elmer the Great* (1928), and during her adolescence Nancy's family spent summers at the Huston home. She was in touch with a very wide world, through her mother.

But, for some time, she was barely in touch with her mother. She grew up with relatives from ages two to eight, while Edie was on tour in New York. She got only glimpses, on visits, of the glamorous life her mother seemed to lead. She told Bill Libby: "I loved to dress up in her stage clothes, put on her makeup, and pretend I was playing her parts." And she added: "There's a particular 'smell' to backstage that's hard to describe, but its rather musty and to me always seemed glamorous and special."[12] She rarely saw her father, Kenneth Robbins, who had left her mother when Nancy was an infant.

It has been assumed in some accounts, that Nancy gained a mother and lost the glamor of the stage when, in 1929, Edie Luckett married a distinguished Chicago neurophysician, Loyal Davis. But Mr. Davis was attracted to theater people, as one might suppose from his shipboard romance with the actress who became his wife, and he encouraged her to maintain her old ties. She even acted, as Edie Luckett Davis, in *Betty and Bob*, a dramatic series on network radio.[13] Some of her famous actor friends became patients of Dr. Davis, as well as his house guests when they played in Chicago theaters. As we have seen, the Davises summered with the Hustons, and Dr. Davis—a commanding figure in his own operating theater—liked to read roles with

Huston and others. When, after graduating from Smith, Nancy became a "struggling young actress in New York," she was the struggling one Clark Gable dated when he was in town,[14] the one Zasu Pitts put in her road show and Mary Martin in her Broadway show.[15]

She had already served her apprentice years, in summer stock and college plays; with the help of her mother's friends she took the rungs rapidly—New York theater, New York television, Hollywood. At an age when Reagan was still making his name as an Iowa sportscaster, Nancy was on Broadway. When he went to Hollywood, it was to the "cheapskate" studio, Warners, where he put in three years making twenty pictures before Pat O'Brien helped him get his first role in an A film. She made the A film she had tested for, *East Side, West Side*. Reagan did not work with an important director (Michael Curtiz) until his twenty-third film. She began with Cukor, and the next year had the lead in William Wellman's *The Next Voice You Hear*. Reagan's first social circle in Hollywood was drawn largely from Iowa. She was invited to the homes of executives like Dore Schary.

Retrospect picks out, from her eleven films, her last and worst—*Hellcats of the Navy*—as the only one from which scenes can be shown of her acting with the future President. But she had played with actors who were, by the early fifties, bigger stars than Reagan—with James Mason and Van Heflin in *East Side, West Side* (1949), with Glenn Ford in *The Doctor and the Girl* (1949), Ray Milland in *Night into Morning* (1951), Frederick March in *It's a Big Country* (1952).

Yet, though she was appearing in high-budget films, she was gently, against her best efforts, being shunted into subsidiary roles. "Character parts" in Hollywood usually mean older roles, but there is such a thing as a young character part, and she was succumbing to it. She did not have the legs to wear bathing suits, or even short skirts, for cheesecake shots. The camera learned in no time to reduce her body to her face, and her face to her eyes. She was seen as a *responsible* young person, no seductress. She existed in a state of married semipregnancy: "In those first months I mostly played a series of roles in which I was either a young wife with children or about to have a child. I was padded to appear pregnant more times than I can recall."[16] She was the steady woman, with soberer attractions than good legs or glamor: "I remember Bill [William Wellman] didn't want me to wear any makeup in the film or to have a hairdresser. He wanted everything in the film as natural as possible."[17] It is no wonder she recalls with greatest fondness the film that let her break out of this stereotype, "one of the few times I wasn't a wife." *Night into Morning* was her *Kings Row*. Like Reagan in *his* favorite film, she played the second lead, and got her own mate, the other second lead (John Hodiak). But it was clear she had little time or chance left for romantic lead parts. In 1951, the year of her role with John Hodiak, she turned thirty, though she was still telling the studio she was in her twenties. Grace Kelly had arrived, two years earlier, at age twenty-five. Davis, if she stayed at MGM, would graduate easily from young to old character parts—

to the type played by Anne Revere, less horsey of face, perhaps, but unremittingly good. Domesticity was descending on her like a shroud. In 1952, she decided to leave MGM. Anything was better than a permanent semipregnancy.

Reagan had made the same move when he felt typed and held back by Warners. He wanted the lead parts in Technicolor Westerns. But both the Reagans made their clunkers out on their own: *Donovan's Brain* for her, in 1953 (the year after she married Reagan). Four years later, they ended it all together, in *Hellcats of the Navy.* She had tried to relaunch her career with a man who was ending his own. He had gone back to Warners for one picture the year they were married, and it was his last good one—*The Winning Team,* about Grover Cleveland Alexander.

So it is not quite true to say that Nancy Davis, like Grace Kelly, had a brief fling in show business, then married to "get away from it all." Both actresses, of course, married older men—though Prince Rainier was only six years older than his bride; Reagan is ten years older than Nancy. Both women, as it turned out, married rulers. But Nancy Reagan thought she was continuing her movie career, not ending it, with Ronald Reagan. The story often told is that she went to him for help in clearing her name of Communist associations in 1950. But she had many friends in Hollywood, at the executive level or the top of the acting profession, who had no trouble distinguishing her from other Nancy Davises on the books. Dore Schary wrote that he gave her the lead in *The Next Voice You Hear* (1950) because his wife suggested her.[18] Her father and mother were well known to prominent people in Hollywood, and Dr. Davis was famously conservative in his politics. She needed little political help from Reagan. Yet her career needed more professional help than all her mother's friends had been able to give her— more than anyone could give her, as another five years of effort in movies, and on television, would demonstrate. She had not made a brief detour from domesticity into Hollywood. Quite the reverse: Hollywood had thrust on her a housewifely decorum she kept trying to escape—even if it meant recourse to *Donovan's Brain.* Was this the end of Zim's goddaughter?

But Hollywood had done her an unsolicited favor when it typed her. If the movies were to supply us with an image of a President's wife, Anne Revere would be the right one. The face proclaims responsibility, whatever frivolities the story line might impose. That was the instant and accurate judgement of those casting Nancy Davis at MGM. Her eyes, so wide with caring, seemed incapable of narrowing with calculation. She could play a mother, even in her twenties. Well before she was married, the studio tried to create for her an artificial family, assigning contract actors to play her friends when she moved into a new apartment, with cameras watching for a fan magazine.[19] Joan Didion would notice the same element of make-believe when Mrs. Reagan "played house" for reporters as the governor's wife in Sacramento:

"Fine," the newsman said. "Just fine. Now I'll ask a question, and if you could just be nipping a bud as you answer it."

"Nipping a bud," Nancy Reagan repeated, taking her place in front of the rhododendron bush.

"Let's have a dry run," the cameraman said.

The newsman looked at him. "In other words, by a dry run, you mean you want her to fake nipping the bud."

"Fake the nip, yeah," the cameraman said. "Fake the nip."[20]

Mrs. Reagan was shocked that Didion's published account treated the pretense as pretense: she complained of "unfriendliness" in the reporter.[21] She expected political coverage to observe the standards of fan magazines. In the social economy of Hollywood, circular feigning is a necessity, creating a vast ecosystem of self-protective adulation. "Friendship" of the sort Louella Parsons had for her "guests" on *Hollywood Hotel* runs throughout the studio, is diffused by publicity offices, is reflected back from the fans. It is professional death to be excluded from this ecology of omnidirectional feigning. It is an affront to the system not to be friendly to Ronnie, and to Ronnie's friends. Nancy Reagan thought Didion was in her system.

And, in fact, most of the nation has been drawn into that system. The responsible roles she had been assigned in the movies have, when played as politics, received fan-magazine coverage. Her charity work as governor's wife (for the Los Angeles group, the Colleagues) or as President's wife (for the drug centers) was done with just the right air of welcomed burden. There is something about her face that seems to go well with a nurse's uniform. In fact, for wide eyes and sculpted chin, the nurse in *Hellcats of the Navy* is almost interchangeable with the nurse in *The Hasty Heart*, Patricia Neal, another nonseductress destined to supply first one shoulder, then another, for men to lean on. Reagan seems to have preferred the wide-eyed Responsibles—even Jane Wyman became one during the war. They all look so indefatigably understanding. No wonder Reagan, who did not call his mother "Mommy," called his wife that.[22] They are the world's mommies, Anne Revere and all her younger sisters. And what better type to have in the White House than an Anne Revere with just the least offensive touch of class —less horsey of face than Eleanor Roosevelt, but actually less "show biz" than Jacqueline Kennedy.

Mrs. Kennedy has been, in subtle ways, the measure for all her successors. It is hard to estimate the extent to which the brief Kennedy years shaped all our expectations of the modern presidency. Just as each successor President has tried to have his very own missile crisis, so each "First Lady" must have her official concern, her project. We take this for granted now, so that wives of presidential candidates in the 1984 primaries were asked what their project would be if they made it to the White House. (They all had their answers ready.) The Project has become almost as institutionalized a part of government as the national debt. Yet it was invented as recently as 1961. Eleanor Roosevelt was "causey," but from inner urgencies, and her concern could not be channeled into one publicly celebrated good work. In her day, being a "social worker" was as much criticized as praised. Bess Truman and Mamie Eisenhower were innocent of the patron's self-promoting self-sacrifice. Not until the 1960s did the upper-class institution of "the lady's charity" reach America's self-consciously middle-class ruling house. We are talking about one of the distinguishing marks of Veblen's leisure class—the langorous bestirment that marginally consumes but principally advertises a woman's conspicuous leisure:

> Many and intricate polite observances and social duties of a ceremonial nature are developed; many organizations are founded, with some specious object of amelioration embodied in their official style and title; there is much coming and going and a deal of talk, to the end that the talkers may not have occasion to reflect on what is the effectual economic value of their traffic. And along with the make-believe of purposeful employment, and woven inextricably into its texture, there is commonly, if not invariably, a more or less appreciable element of purposeful effort directed to some serious end.[23]

Considered not in the light of its putative object, but in terms of public relations, the first lady's project is a very economical affair indeed. It concentrates the attention on a single, symbolic activity, meant to stand for a generalized concern. Insofar as it shows a woman striking off into her own area of activity, it mollified those who fear that political wives are treated as mere adjuncts to their husbands. Yet it is always a politically safe project, one that reflects traditionally "feminine" preoccupations, either aesthetic or familial.

This was clearest of all in the case of the first modern project—Mrs. Kennedy's redecorating of a house she could not bring herself, very often, to inhabit. What could be more wifely than "furnishing the nest"? Yet she added elements of style (and turned duty to public largesse) by making historical display of her antiques, uniting scholarly research and popular celebration (on her own television show). It is just one example of many victories for the Kennedy style of public relations that, after Mrs. Kennedy, a President's wife could no more afford to be without her project than a President could afford to be without a wife.

Ladybird Johnson pitted daisies against billboards. Pat Nixon sponsored "volunteerism"—a broad but shrewd choice, when one considers that the work, by its very nature, all but requires desultory attendance. Her husband, as was his practice, explained the obvious: "She bridled at the idea that voluntarism was her 'project,' or that her interests had to be compartmentalized. She once said, 'People are my project.' "[24] Betty Ford concentrated on handicapped children. (The Gerald Ford Museum in Grand Rapids is so bare of other excuse for being that it turns its first floor over to a display of First Ladies' Projects, completing the semiofficial designation of this office of government.)

Rosalynn Carter, inspired by Peter Bourne, a man who later became something of an embarrassment to her husband, chose mental health as her project. Nancy Reagan has concentrated on drug abuse, and even appeared on a situation comedy to deliver her serious message—on a warm family comedy, with a lovable black child as its star, so her encompassing maternity was emphasized, along with a slight remembrance of her Hollywood days. The latter image does not jar, after all—she specialized, even during the 1950s, in responsible wifery. In fact, Nancy Reagan seems ideally suited to the White House role that was created by Jacqueline Kennedy. If anything, she is more socially involved, with her drug center visits, than was Mrs. Kennedy in her conferences with curators. Mrs. Reagan has managed, despite her Hollywood background and some flamboyant California friends, to project an even soberer image of the wife as political helpmate. For one thing, she is undoubtedly devoted to her husband, who is undoubtedly "square."

But the cultural significance of our first Hollywood actress in the White House goes deeper than the maternal roles she used to play. And the deepest part of her appeal lies, paradoxically, on that mysterious surface, the human face. I said earlier that the cameraman learned to reduce Nancy Davis's body to her face, and her face to her eyes. Indirectly, in a light but pointed way, she draws attention to her main physical asset in the tapes she made for Bill Libby.

I can remember going into the makeup department for my first day of shooting and how exciting it was for me to be sitting next to June Allyson or Elizabeth Taylor, both of whom later became good friends. Sidney Guilaroff was the famous hair stylist, and Bill Tuttle was head of makeup. As I was being made up the first day, Bill came in to introduce himself and said, "Well, I guess that's all right, but we'll have to do something about her eyes—they're too big for pictures." He was joking, but I was so nervous I thought he was serious, so I went around the rest of the day with my eyes half closed. Finally, George Folsey took me aside and asked me if I was tired, what was the matter? I told him what Bill Tuttle had said, and I thought he'd never stop laughing. Finally, wiping the tears from his eyes, he said, "Nancy, don't you know your eyes can never be too big for pictures?"[25]

It is a nice, if incredible, way of underlining what nature has already emphasized. She had been in the theater six years, and done some work on television, before going to Hollywood. It is a commonplace in the theater that large features, especially eyes, are useful to an actor for projection to the back row; and much of the cult of Hollywood actresses has turned about their large eyes, made even larger by makeup and lighting in publicity shots. It is inconceivable that no one had ever told her before, or she had not figured out herself, that her eyes were her most attractive feature.

She is careful to call them large eyes—she does not really tell us what is distinctive about them, their spacing. That is not as clearly an advantage as mere size—though it is far better to have widely spaced eyes than narrowly spaced ones. The latter condition can consign one to shrew's roles, comic or serious. Witness the career of Agnes Moorehead. But spaced-out eyes can not only be disguised, in profile or three-quarter shots (which Claudette Colbert used to insist on), but exploited. They give that intensity of gaze without specific suggestiveness that the movie stills encouraged, a kind of blank urgency capable of being taken in a number of ways. An indiscriminate soulfulness. Mrs. Reagan's famous stare at her husband was being born.

The Hollywood look developed its iconography from many technical, historical, and aesthetic considerations. Even actresses famous for great figures enjoyed a special concentration on the face that was part of making a Hollywood "goddess." These photographs had almost as much to do with the special status of the early stars as did their actual appearance in the movies —which was made to approximate the publicity photos, fulfilling expectations created by the ideal pose and lighting given the actress in repose. Billy Bitzer, Griffith's cameraman, resented having to attend to Lillian Gish's beauty, moment by moment, more than to the logic of the action; but William Daniels, in his long attendance on Greta Garbo, proved that lens magic is stronger than any logic.[26]

The Hollywood face was the result of accidents creatively exploited. For one thing, the sluggish response of early cameras to light meant that makeup had to be chalky, which unnaturally detached the face from its dark background, giving the floating effect Roland Barthes emphasizes in his famous essay on Garbo's face.[27] Barthes notices a similarity between Chaplin's "floury" face (farineuse) and Garbo's, but does not understand the literally "earthy" reasons for this heavenly resemblance. The makeup, along with the lack of depth focus in early lenses, made the face in a close-up seem like a white saucer on a black sea, the eyes dark ponds within the larger sea. The faces were near yet remote, naked yet artificial, seen with surreal clarity, like the surface of some farther moon studied through the strongest telescope on earth. Barthes calls such a face "the untouchable thing we cannot let go of" (que l'on ne pouvait ni atteindre ni abandonner).

Along with the face's unnatural detachment from its background went a comparative immobility, partly due to scale. When a poster is going to be seen at several times life size, every bleminsh or irregularity must be played down by makeup, lighting, camera angle, expression. The same is true of close-ups in the theater, where the face that looms so large does not have to "project" with energetic contortions. Griffith is famous for "toning down" the facial expressions of stage actors for the screen (telling Gish, in Bitzer's jaundiced version, just to "be beautiful"). Famous faces had a special motive for keeping the serene gaze of their own best effects, where every change in expression must register across an acre or so of screen. Beaudelaire's Géante must not become a jitterbug. Students of Garbo's face rebuked her on the rare early occasions when she contorted her features for a scream.[28] She learned better. Cary Grant had a limited number of facial expressions he made serve all occasions by varying the angle of his head. He tilts, pouring shadows back and forth along the planes of his face, with an expressive minimalism that is very eloquent. The gods and goddesses were not only larger than the rest of us, but less perturbable. The face of the sex goddess, Barthes claims, is "almost desexed" in its deliberate composition of a "snowy loneliness." That kind of *voluntary* beauty is especially suggested by the wide-eyed look, which seems to express simultaneous strain and control, as if the eyes were kept from wandering even farther apart by an act of concentration.

It was so important to keep Shirley Temple wide-eyed that lights could not be aimed directly at her, tempting her to squint. Lights were aimed above her, though most actresses like to be lit from below, and those in a scene with Miss Temple had to submit to the scheme that showed her features to best advantage.[29] Each star was given similar iconographic ministrations. Alexander Walker discusses the construction of Jean Harlow's face: "Her eyebrows were shaven into antennae, perhaps to lighten a too-heavy forehead; the slightly cleft jaw was stubborn and had to be lighted extremely carefully; her mouth was painted slightly above the lip line and up at the corners in a smile of fixed expectation."[30] One of the problems that held up the filming of Orson Welles's second film was the need daily to construct the face of Delores Costello in the lense of Stanley Cortez's camera: "Costello needed special lighting and filters to mask the blemishes on her face. This was not an unusual problem for a Hollywood cameraman, but it gave Cortez a great deal of trouble."[31]

Hollywood achieved an eidetic stability for its great stars. Buster Keaton realized the comic possibilities of combining a maximum constancy of features with the minimum stability of comic action, keeping his face quiet in a maelstrom of its own making. But even the serious actors had to hold more or less "dead pans" for the light to play upon. For one thing, vivid expressions might cause, reveal, or indurate wrinkles. Marlene Dietrich learned from Josef von Sternberg how to treat her face, and later arranged her own lighting. It was not simply a matter of photographing the "good side" of John Barrymore or Claudette Colbert, but of making the eyes glisten in the same way, scene by scene. If the god's luster disappears, the magic is gone. The face itself had become a mask that seemed to reveal, yet veiled. The great still photos reconciled erotic focus and inclusiveness.

There is a kernel of truth in Parker Tyler's description of Hollywood's "love goddesses" as somnambules. Their expressions were designed to combine the intensity and diffuseness of reverie. They have the vividness, yet the inconsequence, of dreams. These faces are themselves dream receivers and dream conveyers, tranquil transmitters of a sexual charge that does not disturb the features as it passes through them. They are entranced inducers of trance. Thus Garbo's face is "a dramatic arrangement of chastity and passion."[32] Her elegance is lit through by lusts that do not stain it. The

Hollywood images, combining surrender and innocence, resemble the *sleeping* beauties of Keats and Shakespeare:

> Her eyes were open, but she still beheld,
> Now wide awake, the vision of her sleep.
> —"The Eve of St. Agnes," xxxiv

So important was the retention of the Garbo mask that her movies are really a series of still poses; the more she stirs, the less sex she exudes.[33] She is only really comic when she tries to dance. Her allure forever borders on a lethargy, and she most compels the heart in her acts of endless renunciation.

> Where like a virtuous monument she lies,
> To be admir'd of lewd unhallowed eyes . . .
> Showing life's triumph in the map of death,
> And death's dim look in life's mortality.
> *The Rape of Lucrece,* 390–91, 403–4

Marlene Dietrich was a gutter Garbo, Mae West a comic Garbo; and in both cases, the women learned to be sexier by moving less. In West's case, the lethargy became inertia. The Hays office apart, one cannot imagine her undressing on the screen—and not only because her dresses become a kind of symbolic flesh in themselves. Taking them off would simply require too much energy. Parker Tyler talks of Mae West in conjunction with the show girl who is "an animated obalisque."[34] But animate Mae West and you get Shirley Temple.

Tyler is as imprecise in other descriptions; but he rightly calls Bette Davis the bitch as somnambule—she twitches involuntarily. Dilute the neuroses and you get Joan Crawford, emptiness passing for restraint. Step up the neuroses and you get Elsa Lanchester. One could work out a larger typology than Tyler does. Thus, lower down from Garbo on the somnambulistic scale, Ann Sheridan is the gutter Ginger Rogers, and Eve Arden the comic version. In all such cases, the goddess descends if she moves too much. The trance is dispelled. The somnambule not only wakes, but winks.

Though Nancy Reagan never became a Hollywood star, she did not waste the eight years she spent trying. She learned a thing or two about the Look. She practices a severe economy of expression that makes three or four compositions of the features cover all necessary social tasks—the smile of delighted surprise at the top of the airplane stairs, the concerned gaze at redeemable druggies, and—most of all—the upward stare at her husband. In photograph after photograph, one finds the same expression, not varied by a centimeter. The mask has been perfected. It takes unsleeping vigilance to remain a somnambule, a political chastity symbol. She is the conduit of feeling for those who jump and demonstrate when Reagan appears or finishes his speech. She must not break the spell; but the voltage of political loyalty travels through her fixed expression, just as surely as sex flowed through the cool white face of Garbo.

CHAPTER 21

Being Up

Such high advantages thir innocence
Gave them above thir foes.

—Paradise Lost *6.401–2*

Is the trance in which Mrs. Reagan watches her husband perform that of the hypnotized or the hypnotizer? In the 1984 campaign, that question focused on an episode at the Reagan ranch, on August 1, when the President stood in apparent thought for a full five seconds, after being asked what America could do to bring Russians to the negotiating table. At last, Mrs. Reagan, after looking up at him, whispered, "Doing everything we can." He lifted his head then, and grinned. "Doing everything we can."[1]

Later Mrs. Reagan denied that she had been prompting her husband. She had just said the words to herself in a musing way, and he—despite his poor hearing—overheard.[2] The President endorsed her version, and said that he had not been pausing to *find* an answer, but *refusing* to answer because this was a "photo opportunity" at which no questions were supposed to be entertained.[3] That would seem to give his wife even more influence—the power to change his stand on a point of principle.

But such prompting from the wings, as it were, is not unusual with the Reagans. People just had not noticed, or had forgotten, that the same thing happened in the preceding campaign. Reagan was asked in Florida if people might smoke less if they used marijuana. His wife did not wait in that case, but poked him instantly, and whispered, "You wouldn't know." "I wouldn't know."[4] Later, on March 23, 1985, when greeting children from the Special Olympics at the White House, the President was asked about the CIA's airlift of Ethiopian Jews, and she whispered to him, "I don't know." This time he varied the wording: "No comment."[5]

It would be easy to make something sinister of this, a kind of reverse Svengali relationship, with the President himself as Trilby. But that would be another case of misunderstanding the Reagans by underestimating their formative years as performers. Helping another actor when something goes wrong, keeping the show going, covering an awkwardness, is instinctive, and shows not domination but the joint effort of the troupe. Reagan has done the same for her, through the years, when a touch of her asperity at the press comes through, and he softens it with a joke.

Mrs. Reagan has immense power, but one should notice its base. She is the one most concerned with getting her husband "up" and keeping him up for his appearances. Her famous run-ins with his aides have almost all been over things they did to throw him off stride, wreck the mood, get him down. Special skills and training are used to "warm up" an audience. It is even more important to warm up a performer. Singers or dancers do this by a drill that loosens their voices or muscles. All of them use some procedure to loosen the nerves. Having people around who will facilitate this becomes important to performers. They develop rituals that others reinforce.

The performing ego is a delicate one. It takes nerve to keep going out before people, to be funny, heroic, graceful, tuneful, or acrobatic, not afraid of the audience yet not defiant of it, respectful but in charge. Too many rebuffs, too many laughs (or too few), sometimes a single boo, can shatter the needed combination of skills, experience, and egotism—a combination that must be reassembled on schedule, and displayed time after time. Even the best suffer agonies, as Laurence Olivier has disclosed. A paralyzing stage fright came over him, late in his distinguished career, and stayed with him for five years. Simply to get onto the stage, or to stay there, became an ordeal for which he needed support:

> Early on in the course of it I had to beg my Iago, Frank Finlay, not to leave the stage when I had to be left alone for a soliloquy, but to stay in the wings downstage where I could see him, since I feared I might not be able to stay there in front of the audience myself. Finally, everyone who had scenes with me had to know what was going on, in order to be able to cope in case of trouble.[6]

The troupe had to rally around. Olivier sought aid, for a while, from tranquilizers. Most performers have been led even earlier to try those, or booze, or heavier drugs, voodoo, hypnotism, strange religions. Those strong enough to refrain from those need even more the stimulant of praise, the narcotic of flattery.

Actors' superstitions are derived in great part from the feeling that you "need all the help you can get" to make it out there and get through a performance. It is comforting to think that there is something special about the place or time or set or costume, some omen or amulet one can fall back on. Actors are often wearing or carrying "something lucky" when they do their routine. Hollywood supports a number of highly paid astrologers who can coax good news out of the heavens for their clients. Something must cheer them on, from the galaxy if not the gallery. Stars rely on the stars.

Since everyone involved in a theatrical project knows that performers can only give their best if they feel confident, they are energetically flattered by those around them. Criticism comes tucked inside the lushest flowers of praise. People live in a contest of superlatives. Simply in order to keep a project going, people semideliberately blind themselves to its flaws—the story told with such insight by Lillian Ross in her account of the filming of *The Red Badge of Courage.* Director John Huston saw the weakness of Audie Murphy in the lead, but had to keep trying to repair it with showers of praise for virtues that would not bloom, however irrigated. Huston himself had to be kept "upbeat." His producer said: "John is like a race horse. You must keep him in a good mood all the time. John is a charmer, you know; but he is really very forlorn."[7] The producer had to kid himself about the first rushes, not to despair of what was already invested in the picture.[8] And so on, in a circle of "greats" and "terrifics," keeping men at the hard task of achieving a mediocre result. Even the producer of Huston's next show is hoping for the success of this one: "I get him next. For *The African Queen.* I like to get him when he is feeling good."[9] Huston, perhaps knowing how he would feel if he waited for the results, went to Africa before the recutting of *Red Badge.*

As a performer, Reagan is far from panicky—as he showed in the Nashua debate of 1980. He is equable in temperament and regular in his habits. His self-confidence and optimism impress everyone who knows him. But if he were not sensitive to audience reaction, he could not play on it so well. If he did not love applause, he would not have courted it so assiduously, in so many ways, over so many years. And you cannot love applause without fearing its absence, or its opposite, in some measure.

No one knows all this better than Nancy Davis Reagan. She came into his life when he was still rattled by "something I never expected to happen to me," the deep rejection of his divorce. She was with him when his movie career went sour, from bad roles to no roles, to the point where there seemed nothing left but the night club circuit—and even there his role would be minor, since he could not sing, dance, or do his own comedy routines. He was a successful master of ceremonies and straight man at Las Vegas; but the late hours, smoke-filled rooms, and drunken clientele were not for him.

This is the point where many actors, including the greatest, go bitter, become caricatures of themselves, live in the past, or otherwise lose touch with a world that is passing them by.[10] It is Norma Desmond time. But Reagan bounced back with "General Electric Theater" (among the top ten television shows from 1955 through 1958) and his corporate missionary work for its sponsor.[11] When he lost both those positions, his brother Neil did him another favor, as the advertising accountant for Boraxo, sponsor of "Death Valley Days."

Nancy Reagan, herself an actress knowing the strain, saw Reagan through this sequence of difficult times. He maintained his jaunty smile and hopeful outlook, but with inevitable effort. And the effort had to succeed: a Reagan without confidence would not be Reagan. It is against this background that we must interpret all tales of Nancy Reagan's "ruthlessness."

Jim Lake, the campaign press secretary, recalled that in 1980, after Reagan had been upset by Bush in the Iowa caucuses, he was very depressed and not up to par in his first New Hampshire appearances. Lake and a press associate, Linda Gosden, went into Reagan's room and told him so. Nancy Reagan was present, and as Lake and Gosden left, she went out with them and told them that was definitely not the way to handle her husband. He needed to be built up, she said, not knocked down.[12]

The upset in the Iowa caucuses came, in part, from the strategy of John Sears, a brilliant political tactician who, not much impressed with Reagan's ability to answer questions, kept his candidate away from Iowa.[13] Rather than get Reagan "up" to perform, Sears was implicitly telling him he could not be trusted to perform—an attitude unacceptable backstage. Disapproval from the other side of the footlights is one thing. Doubt from the wings is forbidden. Reagan let it be known that the squabblings in his troupe were giving him "knots in my stomach."[14] Nancy Reagan stepped in, and Sears had to step out.[15] When it seemed that Sears was being confirmed in his analysis during a period of repeated gaffes on Reagan's part, Nancy Reagan buried her own hostility to publicist Stuart Spencer, whom she had considered a traitor for working with Gerald Ford against Reagan in 1980.[16] She asked him onto the campaign plane, since he had proved in the California campaigns that he could coach Reagan while "reinforcing" him, the accepted word around Reagan for stroking, hand holding, and ego building.[17]

Something very like the Iowa-New Hampshire sequence of 1980 occurred in the presidential debates of the 1984 campaign; and once again there were charges that Nancy Reagan was taking too much power to herself. The first debate was potentially a greater disaster than the Iowa caucus had been—Reagan looked wilted and disoriented against Walter Mondale, who was not normally an imposing adversary. On the flight back from Louisville, the debate site, Mrs. Reagan shared her thoughts with Senator Paul Laxalt, who broadcast her version of the matter: Reagan "was brutalized by a briefing process that didn't make any sense."[18] This was widely interpreted to mean Reagan was crammed too full of facts and figures, since he had tried to use too many statistics in the debate. But Reagan's preparation had in fact been desultory by comparison with 1980, and his briefing book was slim.[19] Apparently what "brutalized" Reagan was a withering performance in the practice sessions by David Stockman, playing an aggressive Mondale with a theatrically released intellectual contempt for Reagan.

When the session finally ended, Reagan shook Stockman's hand. "You better send me some flowers," he said, "because you've been nasty to me."

"Baker made me do it," Stockman answered, flushing a deep red.[20]

Reagan, who has been known to worry at a dead issue (like what others say he said about social security), was still trying to answer Stockman's flow of figures when he faced Mondale. He was "brutalized" because he was not got "up" for the performance but down.

Again, Mrs. Reagan moved swiftly on the reinforcement front. "What have you done to my husband?" she demanded of Mike Deaver, her most trusted ally in keeping the President up. Operation pep talk went into action. The number of practice sessions for the next debate was cut from five to two, old friends were summoned to keep Reagan company, a warm-up rally was scheduled for him to address just before the debate in Kansas City, and Roger Ailes ("Dr. Feelgood")—a man who specializes in coaching business-men and others to speak confidently in public—was brought in to oversee the practice and prepare Reagan psychologically. Ailes sent him out to meet Mondale with a locker-room talk worthy of Knute Rockne:

> "When you see Mondale, remember this guy had twelve years as sena-tor and vice-president and it was a mess. And what he wants to do is get your job so that he can undo everything you spent your entire life doing." For a moment, the room seemed still. Reagan winked at Ailes. "I got it," he said.[21]

Just before Reagan went onstage, James Baker handed him a note saying, "Chuckle again, and have fun out there." All this may seem excessive prim-ing for a professional who has gone before audiences all his life. But it is just because of that background that the importance of psychological atmosphere is so highly rated (sometimes overrated). What happened to Reagan in his first debate with Mondale was a bit like the stage fright that hit Laurence Olivier after decades of dramatic success—and Olivier, too, turned to his fellows for some hand holding. He needed his Iago always in sight, even when he was apparently alone on the stage. Reagan needed Nancy in sight— and his team was careful that he knew where to look for her in Kansas City. Paradoxically, because his presidency is based more than any predecessor's on public eloquence, the raised stakes make him most susceptible to hurt on this point, most in need (a wife will commendably believe) of urgent support. The one thing a performer must always deliver is the *performance.* Other Presidents, of more conventional political background, might be held more accountable on matters of fact and policy. President Nixon was supposed to have a competence, especially in foreign policy, to compensate for oratorical shortcomings. Reagan is judged by lenient standards when it comes to knowledge of policies, even his own. That makes it all the more crucial that he succeed in the area where he has set the highest standards, as the su-preme, and supremely confident, "communicator."

In her desire to keep her husband psychologically prepared, Mrs. Reagan took her most questionable step when, shortly after his operation for cancer of the colon, he had a skin polyp removed from his nose. That was on July 30, 1985. Mrs. Reagan knew by August 1, a Thursday, that a biopsy had found the nose skin cancerous, but she instructed her press secretary, Jen-nifer Hirschberg, to deny that a biopsy had even been performed.[22] Mrs.

Reagan wanted to break the news to her husband carefully, at Camp David, where they were going for the weekend. So that Friday, when they left, the President's spokesman, Larry Speakes, was equivocal on the matter of a biopsy, but Ms. Hirschberg roundly denied one had occurred. In fact, throughout the coverage of this second operation, Speakes and others were as little communicative as possible because Mrs. Reagan had publicly and privately denounced "as a doctor's daughter" the medical details published about the colon cancer.[23] Though the competance of a man with great responsibilities must be scrutinized in a democratic society, she knows the importance of a star's image, and still thinks in terms of the studios' protection of that asset, especially as it effects the star's own optimism and ability to perform.

Actors have to believe in themselves—which means, variously, in their luck, their "star," their destiny, their gods (or God). Listing the attributes necessary to a successful career as actor, Lord Olivier lists in order of importance: talent, luck, and stamina. Then he says of luck: "Though this must vary, it must be good enough to believe in the truth of it yourself. You must see that it has provided you with the right opportunities at the right times."[24] Reagan believes in his own star. He quoted in this connection a prophesy made by a teacher at Eureka, "a French professor with a reputation as a psychic"—which could only be Mary Hoover Jones, a Eureka graduate, Reagan's senior by ten years, the only French teacher on the faculty.[25] She said, of a class he was in, "This is a class of destiny."[26] What is interesting is not that she said it—we do not know how frequently she may have had these insights—but that Reagan remembered it years afterward in connection with his own career and her "reputation as a psychic."

Reagan believed that his mother had psychic powers at times, and that he inherited some of them:

> Some of Nelle's fey quality regarding hunches rubbed off on me. There have been a few moments in my life when I have known, or at least had a positive feeling, that something would happen. One day on Catalina, Charlie Grimm, the Cubs' manager, bawled me out for not even showing up at the practice field. How could I tell him that somewhere within myself was the knowledge I would no longer be a sports announcer? [Hubler, p. 84]

Like many Hollywood stars, Reagan read and was friendly with the astrological columnists:

> One of our good friends is Carroll Righter, who has a syndicated column on astrology. Every morning Nancy and I turn to see what he has to say about people of our respective birth signs. On the morning of the meeting I looked, and almost suspected an MCA plot: my word for the day read, "This is a day to listen to the advice of experts." Cutting out the item, I walked into the meeting and, without even saying hello, asked, "Are you guys experts?" [Hubler, p. 283]

A mystical feeling about oneself comes easily to performers in the spotlight, cheered by so many people; but it becomes most necessary when it does not come easily, when the sense of control is shakiest. In the film shown at the 1984 convention in Dallas, Reagan recounted a visit from New York's Catholic Cardinal Cooke after Hinckley's attempt on the President's life. Reagan remembered how the Cardinal told him "God must have been sitting on my shoulder." After nodding a gracious acknowledgment, Reagan assured the audience that "whatever time I've got left, it now belongs to Someone else."

Some prominent evangelical leaders prophesied, dramatically, that Reagan would be President, though it was ten years before the event. They had come with Pat Boone to visit Governor and Mrs. Reagan, and they closed their meeting in a prayer circle of seven people, holding hands:

"I was just sort of praying from the head," [Rev. George] Otis said. "I was saying those things you'd expect—you know, thanking the Lord for the Reagans, their hospitality, and that sort of thing."

That went on for ten or fifteen seconds, and then it changed. "Everything shifted from my head to the Spirit—*the* Spirit," Otis recalled. "The Holy Spirit came upon me and I knew it. In fact, I was embarrassed. There was this pulsing in my arm. And my hand—the one holding Governor Reagan's hand—was shaking. I didn't know what to do. I just didn't want this thing to be happening. I can remember that even as I was speaking, I was working, you know, tensing my muscles and concentrating and doing everything I could to stop the shaking.

"It wasn't a wild swinging or anything like that. But it was a definite, pulsing shaking. And I made a great physical effort to stop it—but I couldn't."

As this was going on, the content of Otis's prayer changed completely. His voice remained essentially the same, although the words came much more steadily and intently. They spoke specifically to Ronald Reagan and referred to him as "My son." They recognized his role as leader of the state that was indeed the size of many nations. His "labor" was described as "pleasing."

The foyer was absolutely still and silent. The only sound was George's voice. Everyone's eyes were closed.

"If you walk uprightly before Me, you will reside at 1600 Pennsylvania Avenue" . . .

[Otis] later learned from [Herbert] Ellingwood, who had been on the right side of Reagan, that the governor's other hand had been shaking similarly to Otis's. Ellingwood himself recalled years later that he somehow felt a "bolt of electricity" as he clasped Reagan's hand.[27]

On the night Reagan was elected, Pat Boone called Reagan's home and asked him if he remembered "that time we joined hands and prayed, and we had a sense you were being called to something higher."[28] Of course, Reagan did—it was more memorable, surely, than Mary Jones's prophesy, and he had remembered that.

Had a story like that of George Otis's prophesy been told about Jimmy

Carter, it might well have prevented his election to the presidency. There was an initial suspicion of Carter's religion as "kooky." But Reagan is so manifestly a normal American that any signs of his good luck are welcomed like a good horoscope. This does not mean that Reagan is insincere in his religion. The contrast with Carter is not in *degree* of belief but in *what* they believe. There are different theologies at work. Carter's in some ways more modern than Reagan—he had, for instance, enough scientific training not to question the validity of evolution. But he is comparatively old-fashioned in his theology; too old-fashioned, in fact, in the eyes of evangelicals them-selves, who deserted him for Reagan in 1980. Carter's religion is what William James called that of the "sick soul"—a religion of man's fall, of the need for repentance, of humility. In its Calvinist form, this "classical" religion was important in the early history of America.[29]

But America has increasingly preferred the religion James called "healthy-mindedness," which replaces sin with sadness as the real enemy of human nature.[30] The modern evangelicals, beaming and healthy successes in the communications industry, are exemplars of that religion. Their older theological ties—which would have bound them to Carter, a more assiduous member of their historical community—they hastened to downplay in favor of Reagan's personal and national assertiveness.[31] It is actually a pledge of one's religious acceptability, in such circles, to feel one has a lucky star; that the individual, like the nation (or the football team), is favored by heaven. Humility, never a national virtue to strenuous patriots (or football players), is not even a personal virtue now, except in the Reagan sense of affability. To acknowledge limits, like Carter, is to "love misery" and have a martyr com-plex.[32] We would have been leery of a Jimmy Carter receiving George Otis's prophesy precisely because we know that Carter does not pay attention to astrology. We trust Reagan in the same situation because he does.

Reagan not only believes in his own luck. He has been lucky. After two unsuccessful tries at the presidency, he ran at last against his perfect foil—one, moreover, who had brought partway into the mainstream of politics the very people who would desert him for Reagan: the evangelicals. The Reagan campaigns of 1980 and 1984—both directed against Jimmy Carter, the latter through his former Vice President, Walter Mondale—were attacks on "gloom and doom" in the name of healthy-mindedness. After much market testing and public relations wizardry, the campaign committee chose as its 1984 slogan, "America Is Back."[33] George Bush repeated that endlessly out on the stump. America was back, was up, standing tall, number one, star-struck and on the path to glory.

Reagan, though an actor, could enter politics so successfully not simply because of the techniques usually given credit for the process—the way poli-tics has acquired show-business expertise, especially in television. More pro-foundly, the imperative to "feel good about oneself" has become a national and personal priority, not simply a show business necessity. It has become a patriotic, even a religious, duty. Nancy Reagan's job is to get her husband "up" for performances so that he can get the country "up" for its historical destiny. Doctor Ailes had to minister to Reagan so that Reagan could become a "Doctor Feelgood" to the rest of us. The show must go on.

CHAPTER 22

Hollywood on the Potomac

Heav'n ruining from Heav'n.
—Paradise Lost *6.868*

For some people, Ronald Reagan's lacquered pompadour and wide "zoot suit" shoulders are evocative of their own earlier days. For others, too young to remember, they set a new style. Reagan, simultaneously old and new, plays tricks on our sense of historical sequence. This was suggested, appropriately, in some movies made while he was President. In *The Philadelphia Experiment* (1984), a young man is propelled from the 1940s into the 1980s and finds this strange world intimidating. When the female lead finds him in a motel room, he is watching Abbott and Costello on TV. She says, "Oh, I see you found an old movie." He responds, "Yes, it's the only thing I seem to understand around here." But later he switches the TV to a Reagan press conference: "Allison, I know this guy. Is this another movie?" "No, David, this is not a movie."

In *Back to the Future* (1985), time travel is made in the opposite direction, taking the young hero out of the 1980s and returning him to the fifties. After he sees Reagan's name on a theater marquee (advertising *Cattle Queen of Montana)*, he tells a man that Reagan will be President one day. The man asks, derisively, who will be Vice President—Jerry Lewis?

The film devoted to Nancy Reagan at the 1984 Dallas convention had similar time displacements. That film worked into its technicolor wizardry two black-and-white segments from *Hellcats of the Navy,* even accommodating the sweet, undistinguished scoring of Dean Thomas on its sound track. Later we heard but did not see Frank Sinatra singing "Nancy with the laughin' face." It is just the kind of "bobby-soxer" song Sinatra did when he was a band vocalist: "Gee, what a thrill each time I kiss her." In those skinny days he was known as the Voice, much as Barrymore was the Profile and Grable the Legs. Parker Tyler wrote that Sinatra "reverses many a personal chronicle of the screen by having practically originated as a voice and gradually added to it a body."[1]

The personal theme composed for Mrs. Reagan in her film was wispily theatrical, Chaplinesque; and the film ended with the Reagans outdoors, in their ranch clothes, walking away from us like Chaplin and Paulette Goddard at the end of *Modern Times.* As they walk off, Mrs. Reagan gives her husband an affectionate backward kick in the fanny, a Charlie kick. Chaplin's backward kick, delivered as if he were not aware of what his leg is up to, was a staple of his early films. (In one particularly athletic variant, for *The Count* of 1916, he did a *double* backward kick *upside down.)* Mrs. Reagan's kick was perfect. It played to the camera behind her back, even as the convention said that the lovers were strolling alone. It seemed to interrupt the sentimentality, though it was just a subtler form of sentiment. Even Sinatra, still on the sound track, the man who "grew up" from the Voice to be barred from Kennedy's White House for unsavory acquaintances, had regained his innocence in this time-canceling vision of septuagenarian teenagers. We were out of time, in their movie with them.

But, "No, David, this is not a movie." As the lights went up in the convention center after her film, Mrs. Reagan herself came out on the podium. After such a beautifully crafted dream, an entry of the "real" person could easily become a letdown, but she deftly transcended the unreality. Brought out by a band playing "You Do Something to Me," standing there with her instant-sunrise eyes, she underplayed the scene, with pulmonary premonitions of laughter, little puffs of excitement under the pressure of applause and shouts. When, at great length, the band signaled it was ending its last go-around of "You Do," she "conducted" it down to the concluding note with large parody gestures, then thanked the audience simply and graciously, prefacing her remarks with a bemused: "There's no experience like watching yourself on film that you've done thirty years ago." But of course she was simultaneously watching herself on films that were done just weeks and months ago, and all through the years. It was her life on film, up to this moment, all wrapped up in her greatest film, specifically made to *create* the excitement she is shaking her head at now, while she is—again—being filmed. The boundary between her "real" life and a movie life is now as little noticeable as the smooth seam created between the sound track of her Dallas movie and that for *Hellcats.*

She ended her remarks with another movie reference: "Let's make it one more for the Gipper." Because of the size of the Dallas arena, a magnified image of the speakers was thrown on a screen behind them throughout the convention. But after Mrs. Reagan's speech, her image disappeared behind her and we saw that of her husband—in shirt-sleeves at his hotel room—watching her on his television set. We watched him watching her, before she saw that the change had been made. The crowd shouted and signaled for her to turn around, like the audience at a silent movie telling the lovers to go

ahead and kiss. When she responded to their prompting and waved, there
was more signaling to get him to wave back. He did not seem to understand
the situation. People grew urgently clamorous that the two should see each
other *at this moment,* though she had just come from his side and would
shortly be returning there. The union had to be sealed, again, at the crowd's
loud insistence. The satisfied roar when they did wave in coordination made
them keep doing it, to prolong the frenzy of these matchmaking delegates.
Fans had clamored ineffectually, through Louella, for "Ronnie and Jane" to
hug again in the 1940s. Now they were getting their way with "Ron and
Nancy." It was an identical clamor.

Tom Brokaw on NBC called this a giant version of *The Dating Game,* a
television show where the "date" and potential suitors are seen by different
cameras, which feed their images to an audience but not back and forth
between the studio participants until the climactic moment of the show. We
had been swept up, electronically, into the Reagan marriage, through a long
multimedia performance that makes the blend of techniques in *Citizen Kane*
look primitive. Something else was being consummated here—the marriage
of Hollywood and Washington.

It had been a long wooing, each side trying to use the other. William Selig
tried unsuccessfully to get Theodore Roosevelt to include one of his cameramen on an African safari.[2] D. W. Griffith, who used Woodrow Wilson's
biased account of Reconstruction (from *The History of the American People)*
while filming *The Birth of a Nation,*[3] elicited from the President the famous
phrase, "It is like writing history with lightning." Joseph Tumulty, in the
best tradition of presidential press advisers, tried to rewrite the history of
that particular comment.[4] Edward Bernays, the pioneering press agent, decided that Calvin Coolidge could be "humanized" for the 1924 campaign if
he invited a group of movie stars to have breakfast with him in the White
House, but not even Al Jolson could melt the frost around the President.[5]

Louis B. Mayer cultivated Herbert Hoover and William Hearst with equal
ardor, and by similar tactics. He brought into the MGM studio Hoover's
former secretary, Ida Koverman,[6] and Hearst's continuing mistress, Marion
Davies. It was partly by the wheedling of another movie entrepreneur, Joseph P. Kennedy, that Hearst was detached from Hoover for the 1932 campaign.[7] Jack Warner supported Roosevelt; but Mayer remained a bitter foe of
the New Deal, and in 1934 his studio mounted the first major intervention of
Hollywood in an election.

The secret campaign waged by MGM against the Democratic candidate
for governor of California in 1934, Upton Sinclair, was thoroughly despicable, though it was undertaken by that darling of the intellectuals, Irving
Thalberg. Here was pioneered a technique that is in wide use today, and was
put to great effect in the President's film at the Dallas convention—interviews with people on the street, from which only the desired ones are
screened. But Thalberg went further:

Often these so-called newsreels were clips from old movies, such as a shot from a feature film of young hooligans getting off a train which purported to be a crowd of bums lured to California by the prospect of enjoying the beneficence of Sinclair's welfare state. The most notorious one was a fake newsreel featuring an interview with a menacing figure with a beard and broken accent, a caricature of the Jewish anarchist bogeyman.

"For whom are you voting?" asks the interviewer.

"Vy, I am foting for Seenclair."

"Why are you voting for Mr. Sinclair?"

"Vell, his system worked well in Russia, vy can't it work here?"[8]

Challenged about his role in making these shorts, Thalberg shrugged, "Nothing is unfair in politics."[9] Hollywood seemed determined to prove that thesis during its years of propaganda for World War II (heavily racist), and for the Cold War (hysterical about the communist menace at home as well as abroad). But even this subservience was not enough to satisfy Washington, as we shall see when we look at the congressional investigations of Hollywood.

The merger of Hollywood with Washington did not become a real possibility until the presidency of John F. Kennedy. For a brief time, the worlds of entertainment and serious politics looked indistinguishable. Arthur Schlesinger dazzled himself with the idea that he had dazzled Marilyn Monroe. It did not seem to improve her life very much, but it certainly did change his. "Jack" and "Jackie" were as glamorous as the movie stars they mingled with —and were addressed with the same proprietary intimacy by fan magazines. Their marriage belonged to the dreaming public, and to Professor Schlesinger, as the marriage of Ronnie and Jane had belonged to Louella. There was even literal intermarriage of Hollywood with Washington: a member of the Sinatra "clan," Peter Lawford, wed a member of the Kennedy clan.

Joseph Kennedy had used Hollywood to expand his fortune from the time when he bought Film Booking Offices of America in 1926. Kennedy was one of the bankers who, during the transition to sound, imposed a new economic discipline on Hollywood studios—in his case, on DeMille-Pathé, later Pathé.[10] David Sarnoff's Radio Corporation of America, developing the sound equipment called Photophone, bought into both FBO and Pathé before Kennedy arranged a merger of the three that produced RKO, "one of the largest business compacts in the history of the American film industry . . . resulting in the birth of a $300 million corporation."[11] But Kennedy had cultural as well as financial ambitions in Hollywood. In 1927, the year of *The Jazz Singer,* Kennedy shed new respectability on the movie industry by arranging a lecture series at the Harvard Graduate School of Business Administration, where he brought the heads of studios to explain their industry. The series was published as a book, under Kennedy's name as editor. By a single project he impressed his old school, his new business associates, and the publishing world.

Though Kennedy's Hollywood period is often recalled, now, for his affair with Gloria Swanson, fully described in Swanson's autobiography, he promoted himself at the time as a family man interested in promoting family values. He said he hired Red Grange for his studio because his sons wanted to see their football hero in the movies.[12] He became a friend of Will Hays, the public guardian of Hollywood's morals in that time before the Production Code. When he fired Erich von Stroheim as director of *Queen Kelly*, he brought in Edmund Goulding to eliminate the immoralities, though it was too late to salvage anything for American release. (Goulding, whose homosexual direction Reagan resented in *Dark Victory*, proved so accommodating to Gloria Swanson that she asked him to pretend he was the father of one of her illegitimate children).[13]

Although Kennedy left Hollywood at the end of 1928, after making five million dollars in three years, he maintained his ties with the movie industry throughout his life. Even as Ambassador in London, he would show first-run films as the normal way of ending a Kennedy day. His children grew up with a tropism toward the entertainment world that was reciprocated. It would have been a severe blow to Joseph Kennedy's great ego could he have known that Hollywood would later portray him as a villain, John Huston playing the part in *Winter Kills* (1979). But that is only one of many ways the merger with Hollywood turned against its matchmakers. Frank Sinatra and Marilyn Monroe led the way for "radicals" like Jane Fonda, Robert Redford, and Paul Newman, who merged their screen careers and their politics in ways unthinkable in "the old Hollywood." (In 1960, all Sinatra had to do to be liberal on civil rights was submit to the fawnings of Sammy Davis, Jr.) And the anti-Vietnam movie stars helped, in their indirect way, to elect a Republican movie star President of the United States. Each step of show business into politics legitimated other steps, including those of political foes.

The heady days of Hollywood on the Potomac had soured by John F. Kennedy's second year in office. Joseph Kennedy had risen from a background of poverty, and was careful with what he earned. John Kennedy had seen death hastening toward him, and lived recklessly. The father tried to break off his son's wartime affair with a politically suspect beauty queen, Inga Arvad, but the FBI had tapes of the liaison. In the White House, the son was still reckless, especially when suffering from physical pain.[14] His younger brother now had to play the role once played by the father, breaking off the affair with a woman who was also a gangster's mistress.

The source of this trouble was the source of many of the Kennedys' ties to Hollywood, including the Lawford-Kennedy marriage: Frank Sinatra. One of Sinatra's scouts had brought him a woman who looked like Elizabeth Taylor. When finished with her himself, he circulated this prize impartially to his friends—to Sam Giancana in the world of crime, to John F. Kennedy in the world of politics. Then the two worlds, with a harsh jarring, touched. The CIA had hired mobsters to kill Fidel Castro. The FBI, protecting its turf, let the Attorney General know that it was aware of the President's double connection with Mr. Giancana—through the CIA plot and through

Judith Campbell (later Exner). Robert Kennedy ended the White House calls of Miss Campbell, called off the use of organized crime against Castro, and severed the connection with Sinatra.

"It seemed he [Sinatra] almost took a pleasure," Peter Lawford said later, "in flaunting his friendship with Giancana . . . Giancana often stayed at Frank's home in Palm Springs" . . . Sinatra, expecting to entertain Kennedy in his Palm Springs house, had put in a helicopter pad and made other preparations . . . The President then compounded the humiliation by staying at the Palm Desert house of Bing Crosby, not only the rival troubadour of the day but a Republican. The President's action deeply wounded Sinatra. The lovely actress Angie Dickinson told me the next year that she had heard Sinatra say, "If he would only pick up the telephone and call me and say that it was politically difficult to have me around, I would understand. I don't want to hurt him. But he has never called me." I ask Angie about Lawford and Sinatra. She said, "Well, the President excluded Frank, so Frank excluded Peter."[15]

But the man too unsavory for the Kennedy White House became the chairman of the inauguration committee for the Reagans in 1980. He sang "Nancy with the laughin' face" to the new First Lady on inauguration night, and she blew him a kiss. After that he sang at birthday parties for the President and his wife. He specially recorded *To Love a Child,* released in conjunction with the book Mrs. Reagan "wrote" on the Foster Grandparents Program. After the convention film was shown in Dallas, Mrs. Reagan joined Sinatra in her box.

People justly praise men like Richard Nixon for their political comebacks, but Sinatra's is a neglected masterpiece of political recovery. Other performers have come and gone in presidential favor. (Sammy Davis, Jr., showed up, for a while, flickering beside and behind Richard Nixon.) Yet no one but Sinatra has been such an intimate of a Democratic President, then fallen from favor and become even more at home in the White House of a Republican successor. Sinatra's gamy connections with Giancana and Campbell and Kennedy are purged from the public memory. Rather than tarnishing the wholesome image of the Reagans, he has been scrubbed clean by it.

To some it seemed incongruous that Nancy Reagan, who praises oldfashioned values, should sit at a luncheon during the Dallas convention and laugh at the off-color humor of Joan Rivers. But Zim's goddaughter is no stranger to such things. Her own mother was famous for her raunchy stories. Barry Goldwater told William F. Buckley, "Mrs. Davis has told me stories *I* wouldn't tell *you!*"[16] Mrs. Reagan shows an inclination toward those of slightly dingy glitter—Nazimova, Alfred Bloomingdale, Roy Cohn, Sinatra. Ronald Reagan really did enjoy the simple life on his ranch, while Mrs. Reagan preferred the Jerry Zipkin party circuit. Yet she manages a personal exemption from any sordidness associated with such friends. At the Dallas convention, reporters learned that the woman called an "ambassador to the world's children" in her film had not seen her own most recent grandchild, though it had been born over a year earlier. She had not met most of the twenty-eight foster grandparents described in "her" book on them when the book was completed.[17] She spent more time with Sinatra planning, discussing, rehearsing and mounting a joint performance of the title song than she did with any of the foster grandparents.

Mrs. Reagan's enthusiasm for her projects is as expertly confected as the role Mary Pickford kept playing well into her maturity. But there is a crucial difference. The Pickford image, created voluntarily, had to be maintained for financial advantage, even when the actress had grown uncomfortable with it. In Mrs. Reagan's case, the motherly halo forced on her by movie producers in the nineteen-fifties has become a welcome ornament, advantageous in every way. In fact, Mrs. Reagan seems to have solved the problem that Pickford could not. When "Little Mary" became "Our Mary," she lost control over her professional life—what she had been fighting for when she left Griffith, and Zukor, and set up on her own. She would not be Trilby to their Svengalis. But she ended up letting her audience possess *their* Mary in ways that amounted to imprisonment in her doll's finery. Nancy Reagan, forced to be mature too early in her Hollywood roles, has discovered in that borrowed drabbery a kind of perpetual youth. She controls her audience. They are in her movie.

But the same developments that made celebrity an advantage in public life, so that stars make the audience feel "up," can make people illogically punish the stars if they feel "down." The outsized passions of admiration and demand, of envy and disillusionment, that Hollywood calls forth become dangerous by their very urgency. Made up entirely of illusion, they are vulnerable to attack from the oddest *other* kinds of fantasy. As Nathanael West put it in *The Day of the Locust,* "At the sight of their heroes and heroines, the crowd would turn demoniac" (Ch. 27). And the punishing can come even from those who want to protect, whether the protector is Louella Parsons, or a voracious fan club, or one of the series of Svengali directors— Griffith with Gish, Mauritz Stiller with Garbo, Josef von Sternberg with Dietrich. Marion Davies was actually a good light comedienne, but Hearst wanted his mistress to be seen only in pure and dignified roles—he tried to wrest the part of the poetess Elizabeth Barrett from Norma Shearer when MGM filmed *The Barretts of Wimpole Street.*[18] Griffith wanted his heroines to have a nymphet's freshness, so their ravaging would be unthinkably evil. All his projections of a monstrous lust onto black men or lower-class brutes were actually his feelings, publicly forsworn and preached against as he rescued heroines from the ever-closer dangers he dreamed up for them. Louis B. Mayer deplored the use of "sexpots" by his own studio, and sought to woo some "nice" ones for his private delectation—protégées like Ginny Simms. He used to punch men who spoke disparagingly of womankind.[19] The movie makers developed a frustrating desire simultaneously to display and withhold, to keep their chastity symbols untouchably desirable. And they passed these conflicting urges on to fans.

A perfect example of this double drive, toward exploitation and expiation, is the guilty sexuality of Alfred Hitchcock's movies. He deals again and again with the male fantasy of a woman with a cool exterior who is secretly in heat—who, as he put it, would suddenly attack one in the back of a cab.[20] To get this effect, he would sometimes, just before filming a scene, whisper into the ear of one of his refined beauties a shocking obscenity, hoping the "dirty thought" would play through the haughty dialogue.[21] He cultivated a tension between the lungings forward of desire and recoils into respectability —especially in *Vertigo*, where, as Donald Spoto puts it: "The most famous trick shot he devised for the film—the combination of a forward zoom and a reverse tracking shot to achieve the effect of the dizzying elasticity of dimensions—is itself the visual equivalent for the admixture of desire and distance, the longing to fall and the fear of falling."[22] Samuel Taylor, the screenwriter for *Vertigo*, said he watched Hitchcock doing in real life what he made James Stewart's character do in the movie—remake a woman after a vanishing ideal, down to the last aspect of her clothes, hair color, and bodily carriage.[23]

Hitchcock tried to remake Vera Miles and Tippi Hedren, to make each "the new Grace Kelly," signing them to exclusive contracts with him, giving them whole new wardrobes for private life as well as filmed scenes. Like DeMille protecting his religious "Madonna." Hitchcock was a Pygmalion educating women to proper tastes. Vera Miles had to be "toned down" to the proper blond pallor, made another in the series of chilly but sensual Ligeias of this latter-day Poe. The contract he signed with "his" starlets exempted them from cheesecake or "unladylike" promotion of their careers.[24] They were the new somnambules.

Yet each of Hitchcock's ideal ladies let him down—as the woman Stewart is refashioning in *Vertigo* resists him and must die. After a pounding-surf scene with the "first" Kim Novak, Stewart tries to recapture that moment with the second one. He has dressed her, coifed her, arranged her to create the proper mood. Now he kisses her in the garish neon light of the "hotel" where she lives, and the camera circles the couple in a slow 360-degree swing, to Bernard Herrmann's lush love theme. The axis of the couple is meant to be seen as horizontal, according to Hitchcock's constant equation, in this film of depth shots with crane shots, his insistent linking of sex with acrophobia.

During this revolving shot (one of Hitchcock's additions to the anti-Code code for intercourse), Stewart looks up at one point with a baffled expression, and Herrmann returns to the sick merry-go-round music of the title theme, which suggests the fear of falling (it played under Saul Bass's vertiginous credit animations). Then Stewart returns with more effort to the kiss. Immediately after, he must take Novak to the mission tower where false madonnas are revealed, and drag her up the stairs in a frenzy: "I need you. I need you to be Madeleine for a while . . . You're my second chance . . .

He made you over, didn't he? He made you over, just like I made you over, only better." Carried away by his passion, he climbs higher than before: "This was as far as I could get, but you went on." Then, at the top, his face relaxes and he says dreamily, "I made it." The falling he feared was detumescence, and he has overcome it by denouncing the woman he once revered, violence driving out adoration. When the hero of Mailer's *The Deer Park* asks why a particular party is being given in the movie colony, he is told, "Marty made it." But in that case the woman did not have to die.

All Stewart's stagings of encounters with Novak were ways of engineering his own dreams—devices like the "revolutionary uplift" of the brassiere that figures so largely in the opening scene with Barbara Bel Geddes. The tight spiral of his dream woman's golden hair resembles the neat bouquet she holds in the painting—the bouquet Stewart sees, in his dream, open into a terrifying vortex just before he falls. The gilt-madonna hair he had forced Novak to tie up so crisply must be torn loose on the way up the stairs of the tower.

Tippi Hedren wears the same hair style in *The Birds,* and the first gull's assault is against that closed love knot, whose gradual fraying out, until it streams loose in the scene where the birds ravage her body, is the real story line of the movie. The world of "Bodega Bay" is one of predatory women circling a lone male. The story's pair of mothers, one promiscuous, one possessive, is a match for Norman Bates's mummy. Termagants of detumescing force appear regularly in Hitchcock's work, from the one who put out a lighted cigarette in cold cream *(Rebecca)* to the one who extinguishes hers in cold eggs *(To Catch a Thief).* In *The Birds,* the mass assault begins during the eleventh-birthday party of the story's little girl, at the age where innocence gives way to adolescence. (Hitchcock typically claimed he thought of menstrual blood when he looked at wine.)[25]

Hitchcock displayed a genuflecting fury toward his women, the very feeling Tod has for Fay Greener in *The Day of the Locust:* "The sensation he felt was like that he got when holding an egg in his hand. Not that she was fragile or even seemed fragile. It wasn't that. It was her completeness, her egglike self-sufficiency, that made him want to crush her" (Ch. 11). The need to idealize and the itch to degrade are typical of the illusions created on-screen, from Griffith to Hitchcock. In fact, Tippi Hedren's claustrophobic scenes in *The Birds,* where the doors are being forced by lustful violence, recall the prototypical episodes in Griffith of assailants forcing the door open a little more each time on a resisting heroine, while the rescuers have still some distance to ride. The movies enshrine their chastity symbols, and then besiege the shrine.

Martin Scorsese's Travis Bickle, in *Taxi Driver,* is a victim of the very urges Hitchcock put in movie after movie. He seeks surcease from the filth around him in the love of a pure woman. In an *hommage* to Hitchcock, Scorsese has a passenger (played by Scorsese himself) ask Bickle to spy on his wife through a window as theatrically lit and framed as were those on

Hitchcock's famous set for *Rear Window*. Hitchcock had used the custom-ary "shorthand" for intercourse in his films—pounding surf in *Rebecca*, fireworks in *To Catch a Thief*. He even added a mechanically droll literalism —train enters tunnel at the end of *North by Northwest*. Scorsese stretches such ingenuity further. While a passenger is having an orgasm in the back seat of his cab, Bickle drives through the spray from a loosened fire hydrant, his windshield wipers working frantically. (The shot had been prepared dur-ing the opening credits, when the steam escaping from sewers was made a symbol of the city's latent sexual heat.) The hydrant's sudden violent shower from below corresponds with Bickle's tirade, when a politician takes the cab, about the need to "clean up" the city. Images of cleansing and sullying, or purging and fouling, merge throughout the film. Bickle is staring into the blinding white fizz of a seltzer tablet at work as a fellow cab driver says, "Well, some one's gotta do my dirt." Then the same man tries to sell Bickle a bit of dirty Hollywood lore, a piece of Errol Flynn's bathtub: "I got this at his estate, The Pines."

When Bickle sees a woman who works at the politician's campaign office, her appearance redeems the city. "She was wearing a white dress," he tells us in voice-over. "She appeared like an angel. Out of this filthy mess, she is alone. They cannot touch her." (Stewart to Novak in *Vertigo:* "No one pos-sesses you—you're safe with me.") Bickle woos the political worker with the assurance that others do not understand her, do not see her depth as he does. Of her fellow office worker, he says, "I don't think he respects you." Then, after his first success in treating her as "different," he tries to take his god-dess to a dirty film, and she leaves him. "She's just like the others," he tells himself, "cold and distant." But he has just shouted at her, "You're in a hell, and you're going to die in a hell like the rest of them."

Bickle had alienated the woman's political candidate with a similarly gauche directness of admiration during his demented talk in the cab. Now he goes into training to kill the candidate, and the punishment must go along with protection: he finds a new "innocence" to protect, a child prostitute he pursues to her room, with its bank of madonna candles, where he plays the leering mentor, Griffith to her Gish. She, too, is in a hell, but he did not put her there. Thwarted in his attempt to kill the candidate, he settles for killing the girl's pimp in a final cleansing and sullying rain of blood around and on him. After the fire-hydrant scene, we had heard his voice saying that when he returned the cab after night runs he had to "clean the cum off the back seat—some nights I clean off the blood."

When Bickle bought his small arsenal of guns from a hustler in a hotel room, he trained the long barrel of one down through a window at cars moving toward an underpass. The washed-out colors seen through the win-dow, the angle of the barrel, the look of the road are all arranged to suggest black-and-white photographs from the windows of the Dallas Book Deposi-tory. Bickle is seen making himself an Oswald. This is only one case of the movies' using images of recent political horror in an exploitative way.

Dealey Plaza was directly shown in Dalton Trumbo's *Executive Action* (1973). The pietà scene of Robert Kennedy lying in his own blood was suggested in *The Parallax View* (1974), the Patty Hearst bank robbery and the Vietnamese officer executing a prisoner with his pistol held at arm's length for *The Amateur* (1982), the My Lai massacre for *Apocalypse Now* (1979), the Chappaquiddick accident for *Blow Out* (1981).[26] These movies represent an unhealthy union of Hollywood and Washington, in which political shame is tickled and played with for the story's sake. This, too, was a part of the Hollywood pact Joseph Kennedy had not bargained for.

And after Bickle turned himself into Oswald, John Hinckley turned himself into Bickle. It was not Scorsese's fault that, on March 30, 1981, a crazy man wandered into his movie, and brought the Reagans with him. But the man was, like many insane people, following too literally a logic of publicity that makes our moods depend vicariously on the fortunes of the idealized rich or famous, our prosperity a glow derived from theirs, our weakness a reflection of their power. The celebrities who bless can also damn. The adored can be destroyed. It was a movie-driven man who tried to murder our first movie-actor President.

John Hinckley came from a moral, even godly, home. His mother had grown up the daughter of devout Disciples of Christ,[27] and his father had become a born-again Christian in 1977.[28] John's older brother and sister seem to have cared for him and to have found meaningful lives for themselves. But Hinckley, emotionally stunted, had a private life entirely filled with public images—with John Lennon and the Beatles at first. He was drawn like one of Nathanael West's locusts to Southern California. He wrote to his parents, after arriving there in 1976: "I live about three blocks away from the famous Hollywood & Vine corner and two blocks away from Sunset Strip."[29] But there was no further point of entry into his dream, and he did in Hollywood what he had done in Texas and Colorado—went to the movies. That summer, he saw *Taxi Driver* fifteen times during its run at the Egyptian Theater.[30] He bought the book on which the movie was based, and the record of its sound track. He fashioned an imaginary woman he was dating, for his letters home describing her as an actress. He told his parents he was going to New York for dates with his friend, though he went to New Haven to spy on the "real" friend, Jodie Foster, who was enrolled at Yale. (He had learned that fact from *People* magazine.) Hinckley called and wrote Foster, saying he would rescue her.[31] He stalked her in a deadlier *Dating Game,* the near but unseen suitor.

The scene around him in New Haven revolted him. "The students dressed like total slobs . . . Is anything sacred any more?"[32] He was buying an arsenal like Bickle's, eight guns in all, though three were confiscated at an airport scanner and he had to sell two, leaving him with three handguns.[33] Though he did not drink, he toasted the first minutes of the New Year 1981 with peach brandy, Bickle's drink.[34] He stalked political figures (Carter at first) as a way of purging the world of slobs and rescuing Foster, winning her attention and her love by the same act. Afterward he called his murderous act "the greatest love offering in the history of the world," one that linked him forever with his beloved in the distant intimacy of shared celebrity: "I may be in prison and she may be making a movie in Paris or Hollywood but Jodie and I will always be together, in life and in death."[35] David Thomson wrote of him:

> For decades now, media experts have been saying that college freshman have witnessed (or had the set "on" for) 18,000 to 20,000 representations of murder. But all the kids who are not Hinckley have been exposed to just as many enactments of love—I don't mean the love act, but falling in love. It may be there, in that much more normal urge than killing, that we have been most influenced. John Hinckley was in love, and stories had told him love was never denied.[36]

In the movie *Taxi Driver,* Bickle shot the pimp and became a hero, thanked by the prostitute's parents for having saved her. Hinckley expected some such reaction on Foster's part. When, at her deposition for his trial, she refused to recognize either him or his "sacrifice," he threw a pen at her and said he would kill her.[37] The impotent first worship, then rend. *Hommage,* inadvertent, to Hitchcock.

Travis Bickle is presented by Scorsese as a voyeur through the rearview mirror, listening in on life, ignored, invisibly present, unable to face others. As a type, he is all those people put in small, isolated cars to watch outsized people on the giant drive-in screens, bigger than the persons beside them in the car, but no more to be grasped than the fuzzy patches of color on the concrete "screen." Dreams are always tall—and some people they shrivel to the point of desperation.

In *The Moviegoer,* Walker Percy has William Holden walk through the New Orleans of the novel. Because he has always been seen as an image without substance, Holden suddenly drains the others of substance as he passes. He is "realer" than they; they are not in his movie. Everyone he passes is affected, one way or another. Some frankly gush. Others watch the others' reactions. A young man resists the lure, pretends not to know who Holden is, even when the actor asks him for a match. He is "showing" him, declaring his independence by an elaborate pretense of his own, forcing Holden into a movie where the young man is the star. Some people demonstrate that they are not impressed, in similar circumstances, by picking fights with Humphrey Bogart or Paul Newman. Or by demanding that clowns be funny in real life, *become* their dream selves on the spot. Others, the crazies, the Hinckleys, just shoot.

PART FIVE

UNION MAN

CHAPTER 23

SAG: Actors and the New Deal

*I turned really eager and I have considered myself
a rabid union man ever since.*

—Ronald Reagan (Hubler, p. 154)

The New Deal prepared the way for Reagan in Hollywood. It would have more to do with his working life there than it did with his father's and brother's employment in Dixon. Neil Reagan worked only a year for the New Deal, and Jack Reagan for about three years. But Ronald Reagan worked very actively for a quarter of a century in the Screen Actors Guild, which grew out of the struggle over employment codes called for by Roosevelt's National Industrial Recovery Act of 1933, and was finally reorganized in 1937 with the help of the National Labor Relations Board. As so often in his life, "govment" had prepared the arena in which Reagan was to act.

Roosevelt had no single strategy for coping with the deflationary spiral of the Depression, by which prices, production, and employment all drove each other down. He launched separate, contradictory efforts to force each of these back up. The trickiest problem was that of prices, which could not be allowed to rise till there were more goods to sell and more consumer dollars to buy them. Merchants were selling cheap in 1933 because buyers were not solvent, and production costs had gone down as labor was cut in hours and in wages. Under the first New Deal acts, relief was putting money in the hands of consumers. Public works would stimulate production. Prices would naturally rise, and should be encouraged to. But how was profiteering to be avoided? Roosevelt was opposed to federal price controls, and could not have guided them past the Supreme Court anyway. Even a normal rise in prices could result in unfair profits, since failing businesses had resorted to cheap wages, sweatshops, and child labor to stay afloat. If companies kept up cheap labor policies while reaping normal profits, the circulation of money (as wages) back to the consumer—artificially encouraged by the relief infusion—would again be choked off.

Roosevelt asked two main groups of advisers to come up with plans to handle this problem.[1] One proposed that trade associations be encouraged to set their own standards, with the help of representatives of the public and of labor on their boards. Some feared this would give companies the tools for price-fixing and the evasion of antitrust law. (They were right.) The other group called for government regulation through licensing procedures. Some felt this would amount to price controls, and be found unconstitutional in that era. (They were right, too.) Roosevelt told the two groups to lock themselves in a room and not come out till they had forged a compromise.[2] The result satisfied few but Roosevelt and the man he chose to head the National Recovery Administration, Major General Hugh Johnson, the head of the World War I draft effort.

Much depended on the way the Act would be administered. The government was given a vague power to enforce the codes of fair practice drawn up by the NRA, but General Johnson would not test these powers. He preferred the mode of exhortation, at which he was skilled. The whole "Blue Eagle" quasi-war enrollment of business under the standard of fair practices went forward in a mood of euphoria bordering on hysteria.[3] But the businessmen were meanwhile skewing the codes in their favor. Tugwell believes Roosevelt accepted this as inescapable, the minimum he had to give business if he was to extract from it what Senator Robert Wagner, Secretary of Labor Frances Perkins, and the labor leaders were insisting on—that labor's right to organize be recognized in the Act (by Section 7a). As Tugwell puts it, "The unwise codes were bribes."

> A businessman who agreed to enlarge his labor force at once, recognize the union in his plants, raise wages, and renounce child labor could, for the moment at least, be allowed the privilege of restraining trade and increasing prices. It was a good bargain for the public.[4]

The bringing of the NRA codes to Hollywood followed the pattern Tugwell describes: the producers tried to use them as instruments for increasing their control, and labor used them as the occasion to organize. But in the film industry, Hollywood producers already had almost total control over production (as opposed to exhibition). They tried to use the codes to complete their hegemony on the lots. As for labor's organizing, there was already a workers' organization in place—the Academy of Motion Picture Arts and Sciences—which seemed strengthened at first by the codes, but then fell to other guilds encouraged by the NRA's arrival.

Hollywood's treatment of its workers during the onset of the Depression had resembled that of other businesses. The cost of conversion to sound equipment by 1930 had already led to massive cuts in the work force and in wages. As the Depression deepened, the army of extras—always exploited, much as migrant workers were in Southern California's fields—lived under increasingly precarious conditions.[5] Stuntmen received no insurance for injury. Noncontract players were unprotected. Long shooting hours were extended without overtime or the guarantee of rest between assignments. There were plenty of grievances, but the Academy was not militant in addressing them. It was not intended to be.

Currently we think of the Academy as Hollywood's standing committee for giving itself awards—those Oscars called by Evelyn Waugh the community's infertility symbols.[6] But the Academy was set up with a much more practical function in mind: to prevent the organization of unions among actors, writers, directors, and technicians, or to keep the embryo unions of such workers weak. Southern California had a long and bitter history of hatred for all unions. The Los Angeles *Times* made opposition to them a sacred cause after its building was dynamited by radical organizers in 1910.[7] The movie colony was especially feared, as an outside force that might contaminate the local scene through its ties with stage and vaudeville guilds. Producers did not want unions on the lots to cause them trouble. When Actors Equity won its battle for a closed shop on Broadway in 1920, it began to organize in Hollywood. By 1927 it had become a serious threat, and Louis B. Mayer set up the Academy, an elitist company union based on the assumption that directors, writers, actors, musicians, and cameramen were artists, professional colleagues who could work out their differences amicably, without intermediaries from outside the film world itself. Mayer invited congenial spirits from the five branches of production to make up the board, which became self-perpetuating and alone had the power to change the Academy's constitution.[8]

Thus the grounds for keeping Equity out of Hollywood were laid: actors were already represented within the Academy, where they could negotiate for their rights. This had to be more than a pretense if it was to work, so the Academy did negotiate the first standard contract, for actors not under long-term studio arrangements, in 1927.[9] Equity charged that this was insufficient, since it did not limit work hours or provide for compulsory arbitration; but it was enough, in combination with the Los Angeles *Times*'s campaign against "outsiders," to keep the actors quiet for a while.

The transition to sound in the next few years brought an influx of stage actors, eventually reaching over the thousand mark, and these were people who already belonged to Equity.[10] The union saw new opportunities, but the Academy responded with an improved contract of its own, including an eight-hour day and binding arbitration.[11]

This was the situation when the Roosevelt administration took office. The Academy had been handling union matters, largely to the producers' satisfaction, for five years. It seemed in firm command. But studio executives mourned their lack of control over one aspect of the business. Ever since Carl Laemmle had "stolen" Florence Lawrence from Biograph, the star system had been a monster the producers kept building up, only to have it turn on them. The more desirable the studio made an actor at the box office, the more irresistible that star became to competitors, driving up the price of keeping him or her satisfied. Producers had tried to police each other by self-denying ordinances, but agents made this difficult or impossible, playing one studio against another, encouraging stars to hope for better things elsewhere if they did not get what they wanted from their own company. The policy against "raiding" another firm was not enforceable, since the public would not allow one of its favorites to be denied work by all the studios.

The businessmen saw in General Johnson's fair practice codes the answer to their problem. They would get the government to enforce against them-selves what they could not accomplish on their own. The code drawn up by the Academy, with the president of the actors' branch involved in the drafting, had three main provisions, all aimed at breaking the star system. It forbade raiding, limited the authority of agents, and put a ceiling on actors' salaries.[12]

For the first time, the stars had an economic stake in union matters. They felt betrayed by their representatives in the Academy, which had already made some of them distrustful in March of 1933 when the Academy en-dorsed a studio move to halve salaries for two months as a response to the Depression. This yielding to producers' demands disgusted several actors, who set up a dissident organization of their own on July 12—the Screen Actors Guild, with eighteen members, none of them stars of much luster.[13] All that changed with publication of the proposed NRA code in September. There was a stampede of stars out of the Academy and into the Guild, which was able to stage a mass rally for thousands of new members at the El Capitan Theater on October 8.[14] A long telegram was sent from the meeting to President Roosevelt, protesting the code, yet several weeks later General Johnson approved the code. The actors turned to Eddie Cantor, who knew Roosevelt, and Cantor was invited to spend Thanksgiving with the President at Warm Springs, where he made the case against the code. Roosevelt sus-pended the provisions having to do with the star system, using the kind of broad executive discretion the Supreme Court would find unconstitutional in the NRA's operation.

The Guild won another round when it had its proposal for a "five-five" negotiating board written into the code, made up of five representatives from the actors and five from the producers. The actors made their loyalty clear when they elected all their representatives from the new Guild in February of 1934. The producers stalled, refusing to appoint a team of their own five. When, in June, they finally formed a delegation, its instructions were clearly to obstruct. In October, the actors filed a complaint with the NRA that there had been no good-faith negotiating. The producers were trying to create some new equivalent of the Academy, and the actors kept telling them that was no longer enough.[15]

The actors' guild (SAG) had been getting support, in this formative pe-riod, from the writers' guild (SWG), set up a few months before their own, in response to the same grievances; and, like the writers, the actors were seeking broader labor support. They made their peace with Equity in November of 1934, each union granting the other jurisdiction over screen and stage respectively, as a condition of the Guild's entry into the American Federation of Labor. Guild members attended the first national convention of the A.F. of L.—later a forum for Reagan in his union struggles—in 1936.[16]

While the fight went on in the five-five committees, the Academy was trying to reestablish itself as a voice of labor. It negotiated new writers' contracts, dealing with the touchy matter of screen credit, in the summer of 1934, and it won a very favorable actors' contract in February of 1935.[17] But by now the Guild was a body with its own *esprit,* and a determination to win sole negotiating rights for the acting community.

As the campaign of "talent guilds" (Actors, Writers, and Directors) hardened against the Academy over the years, Oscar award night became a battleground. By 1936 the guilds were on the verge of closing Oscar night down by a boycott. They persuaded performers to stay away from the event, and even to turn down the awards. Director Frank Capra, the newly elected President of the Academy, was called on to rescue the show. Capra had swept the ceremony the year before (five Oscars for *It Happened One Night),* and had reason to guard the prestige of his prizes, though he presents his defense of the Academy as a selfless act undertaken to preserve "Hollywood's lone bastion of culture."[18] What he did was a master stroke of theater, appealing to Hollywood's artistic aspirations, nostalgia, curiosity, and loyalty all at once. He turned the night into a tribute to the retired, exiled, retrospectively hailed first "genius" of the movies, D. W. Griffith. Griffith, something of a broken blossom himself by now, was brought back from Kentucky in a weepy pageant of tributes culminating at the award banquet. Not to attend was somehow to dishonor the "father of us all." Few had the strength to hold out against this combination of overdue recognition and self-congratulation, though the writer and director of the night's biggest winner, *The Informer,* did not accept their Oscars—Dudley Nichols and John Ford.[19]

Capra remembers Reagan as the leader of the Guild's opposition to Academy night in 1936; but Reagan was still broadcasting in Des Moines. Capra also thinks the 1936 dinner was simply the most hazardous in a series of embattled ceremonies, when the Academy struggled for its very existence. Actually, by the next year, when Reagan had arrived in Hollywood, the Academy's power as a labor force was broken forever, and the awards could go on pleasantly because they no longer posed a threat to the Guild, which had won a closed shop for actors.

For its final drive toward recognition, the Guild could not rely on any NRA code, since the NRA had been struck down by the Supreme Court on May 27, 1935. Tugwell argues that Roosevelt was relieved to be rid of the Agency, which had proliferated unenforceable codes.[20] But the President, in his desire to launch a new initiative after this apparent setback, reversed his stand on the Wagner Labor Bill and made it a legislative priority.[21] The bill passed quickly, and the National Labor Relations Board was established to determine the genuine representatives of workers in each industry. The Guild applied to the Board for authorization and won it.[22] It was ready now, with A.F. of L. support, to demand a closed shop, and to strike if the studios resisted. The craft unions of the IATSE (International Alliance of Theatrical Stage Employees), with whom the Guild would shortly have a falling out, offered financial support during the strike period.[23] The IA (for short) had just won an important five-year contract for its own workers, and it threatened producers with the ultimate weapon—refusing to man projection booths all over the country in a sympathetic strike with the Guild. Enough stars were pledged to walk out on major productions to close Hollywood down. Faced with these massive threats, the studios granted the Guild a closed shop on May 15, 1937, the time when Reagan was driving his Nash convertible across country from Des Moines.[24] The agreement was signed in June, during his first month on the Warners lot.

Reagan arrived in the first flush of victory for the Guild, in a town where actors as a whole, from stars to extras, had just prevailed after four years of struggle. He likes to remember his time of moral assertion at Eureka as a strike, and he was seeing now the results of a strike threat on a grander scale. Despite all this, he was reluctant to join the Guild:

> I must admit I was not sold on the idea right away. I was doing all right for myself; a union seemed unnecessary. It was Helen Broderick, that fine actress, who nailed me in a corner of the commissary one day at Warner's, after I'd made a crack about having to join a union, and gave me an hour's lecture on the facts of life. After that I turned really eager and I have considered myself a rabid union man ever since [Hubler, pp. 154–55].

One might ask why Reagan was given any choice in the matter, since the June contract was a closed shop agreement. But the producers asked for a five-year transition, during which ten percent of the employees could be nonunion.[25] The more people they encouraged to fill out that ten percent, the more they could argue that the union was not really popular. There lay the significance of Reagan's hesitation. It seems surprising for one who was even potentially a "rabid union man." The explanation may lie in the fact that Reagan's employment experience to that date had been as the sole employee at the Lowell Park concession, favored and even famous though hard-worked, and as a "star" broadcaster who had won his own support after a rocky start in the highly individualistic enterprises of B. J. Palmer. Palmer did not ever give contracts, much less recognize unions.

Besides, Reagan was a believer in his individual destiny. The real proof of this individualism comes not from Reagan's first resistance to the union, but from his final reason for embracing it. He tells us that his conversion came only when he was placed on the board of directors—three years after he had joined the union.[26] "My education was completed when I walked into the board room. I saw it crammed with the famous men of the business. [There was at least one woman there—his wife.] I was beginning to find the rest of me" (Hubler, p. 154). Reagan was star-struck, as he himself tells us—it was the prestige of the people who were giving their valuable time to union affairs that made him think those affairs important:

> It is a damned noble organization: I mean exactly that. It demonstrates in practical terms the instinctive brotherhood which exists in show business. The ones who made SAG work in the early days were the ones that didn't need it: Eddie Cantor, Edward Arnold, Ralph Morgan, Robert Montgomery, James Cagney, Walter Pidgeon, George Murphy, Harpo Marx, Cary Grant, Charles Boyer, Dick Powell—and a hundred other stars who could call their own tunes on screen salaries. They were willing to use their personal power in order to better the lot of their fellow actors [Hubler, p. 153].

One could hardly turn the history of the Guild more entirely upside down. As we have seen, it was born precisely of the stars' effort to protect themselves from the provisions of the 1933 code, which endangered the power to "call their own tune" on salaries. As the first historian of that process put it:

> Spurred by the salary reduction in March, 1933, the free-lance actors created the Guild to protect their economic interests. The stars and feature players who joined in October, 1933, also did so essentially for economic reasons. They distrusted the implications of the salary-fixing provisions of the NRA code.[27]

Reagan interprets the Guild's rise as he did the Eureka strike, which he called the act of altruistic students with no personal stake in the school cutbacks. Faculty members were excluded, as the direct targets of the offensive measures. Even upperclassmen were excluded, as indirectly affected by them. Only the underclassmen were pure enough to speak for the others, who had to depend on an act of rescuing generosity—just as extras depend, in his version of the Guild, on the largesse of the stars. For Reagan, even union affairs must be run like a Western movie—the hero rides out of nowhere, motivated only by the urge to deal out justice; then, after saving the lowly, he rides off.

It is true that movie stars continued their efforts for those less favored, after they had won what they wanted for themselves. Much of this later activity came, no doubt, from personal regard and charitable impulse. But, granting all that, how could the stars have used the grievances of extras, the cooperation of craft unions, the bargaining position of membership in A.F. of L., the ceding of rights from Equity, only for the moment when they needed it, and shown no reciprocal sense of responsibility?

It should be noticed, moreover, that the stars of Reagan's time, while working for a decent level of wages and conditions for extras and free lancers, retained the independent contract powers that had been the basis of their joining in the first place. Somehow, Reagan twists even that into an act of nobility:

> In contrast to the usual union custom where the minimum becomes the maximum, to this day they have kept 90 percent of the membership with their own individual bargaining powers; only 10 percent actually work for contract scale. This is a measure of their integrity; keeping the dignity of the artist intact with the benefits of the craftsman [Hubler, p. 153].

It is clear that, for Reagan, economic motives are justifiable for the individual—people can "better themselves" by their own effort, to the point where stars "call their own tunes" for money. But for a *group* to act from economic motives is somehow sordid and unworthy. The reality at Eureka College involved a faculty guarding its position by joint action and the recruiting of allies. Reagan did not want to face that reality. The only group that could act with real legitimacy was one without a common economic stake. So, in Hollywood, the stars brought not only a necessary power to their fellow actors' plight, but also the cleansing *disinterestedness* required. Reagan, for the same reason, later made a point of the high salaries his governmental appointees were giving up when they entered public service—as if one who needed pay to live on were by that fact disqualified for public life. Even when talking about his own father's government work, he stresses mainly the aid he gave others, not the need he had for help himself—or the fact that he helped his son, Neil, with a job. These were not people giving up high salaries for public service.

Roosevelt himself seems to have been admired by Reagan as a patrician who did good altruistically, not out of any class solidarity with the unfortunates. (Roosevelt was the last major politician in our democracy who could get away with wearing pince-nez glasses.) Even in his view of national motivation, Reagan thinks that the United States must act from higher motives than self-interest, playing the role of an international Shane, rescuing other countries, asserting their rights for them, punishing those who threaten them, all in the most selfless manner.

This high-mindedness of Reagan's may be justifiable in its own terms, and is certainly attractive; but it seems inappropriate in a union man, and even less appropriate in a union leader, one who was president of the Screen Actors Guild longer than any other person. Union solidarity normally presumes common interests, an interdependence for mutual economic stakes, not dependence on outside rescuers, however highly motivated. Yet nothing in Reagan's long union experience ever changed the way he viewed the Guild itself as an extension of the stars' altruism. Jack Dales, the executive secretary of the Guild, Reagan's friend and adviser through all the strikes and policy struggles, was dumbfounded to realize, later in their relationship, how little Reagan understood the dynamics of the organization he was leading, how ready he was to give up the closed shop which was the basis of its being, the thing it had fought to achieve before Reagan came to Hollywood. Dales tells the astonishing story:

> He [Reagan] said, "You know, Jack, the Guild is so well thought of, is so popular, and does such one hell of a job, do we really need a union shop? Why don't we just say, 'If you don't like it, don't be a member. If you want to join, fine; but if you don't like it, you don't have to be a member, we'll still represent you.' "
>
> And I said, "Ronnie, you're out of your bloody mind. Every time any actor got the slightest gripe, he'd quit paying dues, and we wouldn't have a union. Not only that, I can just see it leading to an alternative union. The Teamsters would move in, and say, 'Well, we'll take over where you have to be.' "
>
> He accepted it. But it was just a grandiose idea—"We're so damned good, why do we need a union shop?"[28]

Dales was able to keep Reagan from revealing what he really thought in this case. Later aides, trying to cope with Reagan's voluntarism (e.g., on social security), would be less lucky. At a profound level of instinct, Reagan is repelled by the idea of stable economic alliances based on the confessed interests of the members. That was true even of the alliance he was president of. His own service to the Guild was altruistic. Why couldn't everyone's be?

CHAPTER 24

IATSE: Controlling Exhibitors

You guys paint pictures, too.

—Herb Sorrell

Reagan had missed the preparations for a major strike that gave his Guild sole bargaining rights for actors. The first strike to involve him was conducted by a different body in the A.F. of L. It was a strike he disapproved of, on patriotic grounds, since it was launched before the end of World War II. He says: "The American Federation of Labor—biggest grouping of autonomous unions in the world—gave the United States a no-strike pledge for the duration. The doubtful kudos for breaking that fragile pledge went to the Hollywood unions."[1] The OWI's Bureau of Motion Pictures had instructed Hollywood not to film stories with strikes in them during the war.[2] Yet here was part of the film community actually *going* on strike.

Reagan plunged enthusiastically into the effort to keep the Guild dissociated from the strike. He went back on the Guild's board of directors by July of 1945, first as an alternate for Rex Ingram, then for Boris Karloff.[3] But he worked so hard to keep the Guild dissociated from the strike that he became the principal spokesman at public events, and one of the principal negotiators behind the scenes.[4]

This flurry of activity is at odds with his own account of a postwar period spent making model boats or brooding at Lake Arrowhead. He claimed that he had been away from union affairs for three and a half years. But, as we know, he was in Los Angeles for over three of those years; his wife was still active on the Guild's board of directors; the Los Angeles community was acutely aware of, and divided over, the origins of the strike, whose most violent episodes took place in October of 1945, at the gates of his own studio, Warners. His rapid involvement at the heart of the dispute belies his professed remoteness from it till the moment he was mustered out. "Hollywood, in spite of my being stationed in Culver City, seemed as far away as another planet. I like to pay attention to one thing at a time. At the moment, finishing off the war in Europe and the Pacific seemed all-important" (Hubler, p. 160). As we have seen, Reagan's war was directed at morale on the home front—and possible sabotage. So even as part of his war duty he would have been concerned with a divisive strike in his own backyard.

The 1945 strike was a complicated matter, and Reagan's account of it in his 1965 book is uncharacteristically confusing. Most of that book is vividly simple, a collection of stories polished in their delivery over the years. The jurisdictional, legal, and tactical problems of the 1945 strike are fuzzily spelled out—perhaps the result of Hubler's working from Reagan's notes and memos concerning that period, or of Reagan's going over them in a desultory way with him.

For an understanding of the strike, one must know something of the craft unions' history in Hollywood. The so-called talent unions were of comparatively recent growth. The Screen Actors Guild was typical in this—Equity attempts to organize from 1920 to 1927 were followed by the Academy's assumption of control from 1927 to 1933, the Guild's struggle for recognition from 1933 to 1937, its assured position after that. But the craft unions had come to Los Angeles before the studios did. While movies were still being made in New York and elsewhere, they were already being shown in Los Angeles; and so the first two projectionists' locals were organized in 1908.[5] This reflects the real basis of the movies' economy. We often think of the film industry as synonymous with production—the exotic "plants" in which they are crafted, the huge salaries of writers, directors, and actors, the processing of film once exposed. But these are a minor part of the empire involved. The studios are minuscule in comparison with the physical plant represented by thousands of theaters across the country—many of them, in the thirties and forties, exotic and cavernous. Large productions boasted the exceptional cast of thousands. But the real labor force, almost invisibly dispersed, spent daily hours of regular employment at projection booths, ushers' aisles, ticket booths, popcorn counters, and—before sound—in the orchestra pit. The work force for movie exhibition was approximately 241,000 in 1940.[6] It was always large.

In an organized way from 1919, and continuing till 1948 (when the Supreme Court ordered divestiture), the production and distribution of the movies were vertically integrated by the major companies. Paramount films went to Paramount theaters. The five biggest studios owned an eighth of the theaters in America, including the major houses in the larger cities.[7] The nerve centers of these vast enterprises were in New York, where the "money men" kept an eye on the entire country, not just on their Hollywood production branch. Lillian Ross dramatized this in the very structure of her 1952 book *Picture*. She set out from the office of *The New Yorker* to learn about the movie business in Hollywood. Only at the end of a long and confusing journey did she track the story back to its real springs, where the key decisions were made, in Nicholas Schenck's Manhattan office.

Labor organizers understood the economics of the business. They could only be strong where the work force was—in the vast distribution channels. That was where the companies collected their money; it was the place where money could be collected from them. For one thing, the sheer spread of the operation took distributors onto local turf, social and political, where unions had a say in the rules—unlike the Los Angeles production site, so inhospitable to unions. The most skilled member of the great distribution army, the projectionist, was also the most exposed. Film is flammable. It proved easy to steal or damage during the long hours when it had no keeper but the projectionist. And the companies needed their projectionists. Safety rules, as well as basic knowledge of the equipment, prohibited the use of unskilled labor for this job. By organizing projectionists, unions could balance the preponderance of economic power the studios had. No matter how many pictures were made, and no matter how well, nothing could be paid for seeing them if the projectionists refused to work. That was the fulcrum of the craft unions' rise to power. The projectionists were easy to discipline, and through them the corporations could be kept under discipline. The power this gave them over the studios could be used to organize other crafts, even in Hollywood where the struggling local unions were often overpowered by the out-of-town resources of the projectionists' union.

It was the stagehands' union, the International Alliance of Theatrical Stage Employees (IATSE, known as the International Alliance or IA), that incorporated the movie projectionists in its old stage union—over the objections, to be renewed through the years, of the electricians' union (the International Brotherhood of Electrical Workers).[8] The only union of competing strength in the early days of film was the musicians' union, which lost its countrywide leverage when sound came in. The symmetrical response of the IA to corporate strength in exhibition made it repeat the companies' pattern of absentee leadership for Hollywood. The larger-than-life "moguls" on the studio lots, so menacing to those who worked under their gaze, privately lamented their dependence on New York. Lillian Ross had the good fortune to be writing *Picture* just as the dread Louis B. Mayer was being toppled in favor of Dore Schary by Schenck's decision in Manhattan. In the same way, local labor organizers resented the fact that they had to wait for decisions from the International's president in New York.

Crafts that had tried to organize as part of their trade groups in the A.F. of L.—as carpenters, for instance, or painters—fought off the voracious approach of the International Alliance. Besides, independent companies (like the Disney studio) were outside the arrangements made by the majors with IA bosses, and that left room for new worker alignments. Squabbling over specific areas of craftsmanship—in that complex interplay of skills needed to create the fabric of film dreams—threatened, by 1926, to reduce the IA's bargaining force with the majors; so it made common front with its rivals to demand what became known as the Studio Basic Agreement. This contract, besides improving wages and conditions, set up a five-five committee (model for the one later put into the NRA code by the Screen Actors Guild), on which the five major producers would meet with the presidents of five craft internationals to settle jurisdictional disputes on the set.[9]

The coming of sound, the Depression, and the NRA threatened to break the power of the IA, but ended up strengthening it. In a race to get its claims recognized before the code could go into force, the union illegally struck Columbia Pictures and found Washington blessing the employment of non-IA workers from the clamorous Depression market.[10] On the other hand, the IA's hold on exhibitors, relaxed by the impact of the Depression on theater owners, was tightened by the NRA codes. With the lucrative Christmas season of 1935 approaching, Chicago's Paramount theaters were shut down by the IA—which made the studios themselves require that twelve thousand Hollywood workers join the IA.[11] The producers also paid shake-down money to the IA's collection man, gangster Willie Bioff. (Joseph Schenck, of the producers' organization, would be jailed for being the middleman in these payments.)

During this period of maximum IA arrogance, Hollywood craft locals tried to form leagues to challenge its reign. One of these, made up of several cosmetics specialists (from makeup artists and hair stylists to scene painters and set designers) tried to strike for recognition in 1937, when the Screen Actors Guild was demanding a closed shop. In return for helping the Guild, the IA received a pledge that the actors would not support the challengers' group (though the actors had helped to form it).[12] After the Guild won its independence by such compromising means, the IA tried to split extras off from the Guild as a new union under its own aegis.[13] The Guild fought back by hiring private detectives to investigate Bioff's activities, and gave its findings to columnist Westbrook Pegler. Pegler's Bioff columns won him a Pulitzer prize, and played a part in Bioff's downfall.

Reagan, naturally, presents the Guild's 1939 campaign against Bioff as a form of altruism, an expression of citizens' concern:

> Those responsible for breaking open the B&B scheme were Westbrook Pegler with his anti-racketeering columns, and a continuing campaign in the trade paper *Variety*. Both were vitally aided by information gathered and transmitted by investigators hired by the SAG. One of our first tip-offs on the plot, by the way, came when Ken Thomson, now a member of the SAG office staff, glimpsed a .45 automatic in Bioff's open desk drawer. He wondered how it was going to be used in labor negotiations. When SAG was pressured to contribute to the boodle-kit, we flatly refused. Not only that, we were directly responsible for the ousting of Bioff and Browne from the AFL fold [Hubler, p. 184].[14]

No record I know of indicates that the IA ever tried to shake down "boodle" from the Guild. It was trying to take its members away. That is what made the Guild fight back with private detectives. Writing shortly after the events, Murray Ross described the sequence:

> An extra in the Screen Actors Guild obtained a card in the [International] Alliance. Contrary to guild policy on the strike, she worked as a make-up artist, and the guild suspended her. In reprisal, the Alliance threatened to raid its members. For some time, the Alliance had been eyeing the large extra group covetously. . . . The struggle between the actors and the stagehands stimulated nation-wide interest from Hollywood to Broadway and focused public attention on Bioff, who was still the power behind the Alliance throne in Hollywood. In an effort to embarrass their opponents, the Screen Actors Guild had uncovered a great deal concerning the racketeering careers of some Alliance leaders.[15]

During this fight with the IA (1939), as in the earlier pact with it that helped the Guild win a closed shop (1937), the sympathies of many actors remained with the craft locals. They had a common fear of the IA's desire to complete its control of exhibition by organizing all laborers in production. One of the scrappiest critics of the IA was an ex-boxer who had risen in the painters' union. Herbert Sorrell led and won a strike of the cartoonists against Walt Disney in 1941.[16] Disney was a paternalistic employer who had formed his own company union and bitterly resented independent organizing as a betrayal.[17] Herb Sorrell became something of a personal demon to him, but a hero to those who wanted to keep the craft locals out of the IA's thuggish empire.[18] Sorrell's painters' union became the key member of a new coalition, the Conference of Studio Unions (CSU), whose membership grew during the war to 10,000 (against the IA's Hollywood membership of 17,000). When, in 1943, a local of interior decorators tried to affiliate with the CSU, as their 1942 contract allowed, the IA challenged the validity of its election and producers refused to recognize it. Sorrell took his case to the NLRB and the War Labor Board, and was upheld before them both.[19] The producers neither complied with these decisions nor attended further negotiations, fearing an IA threat to take out the projectionists if the CSU were recognized. As the head of the interior decorators' local said, "The producers' fear of an IATSE threat is greater than their respect for the federal government."[20] It was only after the exhaustion of all these means of recourse that the decorators struck, with the CSU backing them, on March 12. Reagan's account of the process leading to the strike is this: "A highly confusing and nonbinding arbitration was held which favored 1421 [the interior decorators] but was not attended by any stagehand [IA] representatives" (Hubler, p. 156).

One may fault the patriotism of the strikers during wartime. Reagan certainly did, and had every right to. But he also seems never to have understood the economic motives of the conflict. As he puts it: "To prove how easily a witch's brew can be concocted by determined cooks, remember the whole thing involved only seventy-eight decorators" (Hubler, pp. 155–56). The right of the local to choice over its membership in one labor league or the other was at issue; it was the basis for all the concerns—localism vs. absenteeism, independence of the producers vs. complicity with them, organization by crafts vs. industry-wide organization, alliance with the local labor effort in Los Angeles vs. manipulation of the theater chains—that had divided labor for and against the IA. Reagan repeatedly, at the time and later, dismissed the substance of the grievance as merely "jurisdictional," a quibble over who gets to drive what nail into what set. But all the largest issues of union work in the movies had turned on jurisdictional matters— including the one the Screen Actors Guild exploited in order to win its closed shop in 1937. Division of spheres (national vs. local, skilled work vs. unskilled, cooperative vs. competitive relations on the set) went to the heart of working conditions. This had been true from the original labor conflict that set patterns still at work in 1945: "The big craft unions in the A.F. of L. had never completely accepted the surrender of some of their territory to the Alliance. They had watched with annoyance as it absorbed the carpenters, electricians, and projectionists in the theaters. Its attempt to encroach upon the studio work which they considered reserved for their own members exasperated them."[21]

None of these "jurisdictional" factors seemed real to Reagan, since he could not recognize the legitimacy of group economic activity. The official position of his guild was one of neutrality between the IA and the CSU. Reagan, with his moralizing genius, turned this into a peacemaking mission. This put him in de facto alliance with the IA and the producers, who were breaking the strike by crossing its pickets. The strike dragged on for months, into the postwar period. The CSU was gaining sympathizers; Reagan waxed more eloquent against its disruptiveness.

His mandate, he tells us, was a vote of the Guild members—secret and by mail, which guarantees that no voter can be pressured. "Nothing affecting Guild policy can be passed by a vote of the membership at a meeting. It must be submitted to the entire membership for a secret mail ballot. Adopt this in every union and see how many faults of labor would disappear" (Hubler, p. 204). But a vote can be biased by means other than public clamor at meetings. In this matter of the CSU, the Guild's board drafted a letter "explaining" the vote, which gave instructions rather than asked for opinions. (This was sent out before Reagan rejoined the board.) The letter began: "Screen Actors Guild 'A' Ballot: This ballot is sent to you in order to determine what the guild's official position shall be . . ." But it goes on to say:

The board of directors has given serious consideration to the course which it believes the membership should follow. By unanimous action, the board has arrived at the following conclusions which it presents herewith and recommends to the membership. The background and ramifications of this strike are extremely complex. The controversy is between two unions which are both affiliated with our parent body, the A.F. of L. Therefore, the board does not consider it advisable for the guild to take sides in any way in the dispute. . . . Should the guild membership vote to observe the picket lines, and thereby join the strike, it would be a clear violation of our basic contract. This would entitle the producers to terminate the contract.[22]

In the "Instructions for Voting" this note is included: "Since a vote to observe the picket lines would constitute a strike by the guild, this vote is governed by article V, sections 3 and 5 of the guild bylaws. These sections require approval of such a step by separate votes of the A and the AJ members and a 75-percent majority of those voting in each class." One would not have predicted a close vote. By the way, this letter, drawn up in March, nowhere mentions the patriotic consideration that the strike was taking place in wartime.

In an attempt to bring the other side back to the bargaining table, where it won every battle in this war, the CSU decided to concentrate its picketing on Warner Bros. in October. The Burbank and Los Angeles police were present in force; violence broke out, blamed on either side according to the observer. But the leftist Screen Writers Guild sent authorized observers to future confrontations, with a warning to the producers that they would make a report, and the violence disappeared.[23] When the CSU showed it could survive on the picket line, the producers finally had to defy the IA and abide by the NLRB decision on the validity of the decorators' vote to join the CSU.[24] All the "merely jurisdictional" blocks had been raised by the IA, the producers going along with the union that controlled their theaters, and the actors going along with the producers.

That was the end of the most violent postwar strike in Hollywood, but not the longest or bitterest. This was only round one for the CSU and the IA, and no one would be more ardently engaged in the next strike than Ronald Reagan. For him it had become a crusade. It was just like Eureka.

CHAPTER 25

CSU: Hot Sets

Hot. *Associated with or affected by a trade-union dispute. orig. U.S.*

—*Oxford English Dictionary (Supplement)*

After the decorators' strike of 1945, a Jesuit priest, George H. Dunne, then forty years old, went back to Los Angeles to write about the labor situation for a liberal Catholic magazine, *Commonweal.* Dunne had grown up there, running several community papers with his boyhood friend Dan Marshall before he went into the seminary. He went to China as a missionary in 1932, hoping to finish his studies and be ordained there; but superiors called him home in 1936, meaning to send him back after he completed training in international relations. He took his doctorate at the University of Chicago, but by that time World War II had sealed off China, and he was sent to teach political science at the University of St. Louis. Fr. Dunne, an outspoken advocate of civil rights, wrote a famous *Commonweal* article, one of its most frequently reprinted items, "The Sin of Segregation." While he was in St. Louis, he criticized the resistance to integration so passionately that he was sent back to his home province of California. That is what took him to Los Angeles, to Loyola University, in 1946.[1]

Fr. Dunne's main interest was still civil rights. He wrote a play, *Trial by Fire,* about the bombing of a black worker's home in Fontana, California. It was produced in Hollywood in 1947. Bishop Sheil of Chicago subsidized its presentation at any church that would schedule it in his diocese. With his boyhood friend Dan Marshall, by then a lawyer and a prominent Catholic layman, Dunne founded the Catholic Interracial Group, later suppressed by the conservative Cardinal McIntyre. It was Dan Marshall who helped spur Dunne's interest in the unions, since Marshall had represented a local of the IA in the Bioff era, when it was trying to resist the IA's dictatorial procedures. For the *Commonweal* article, Dunne talked to Marshall, Carey McWilliams, and other knowledgeable observers, preparing himself to interview the principals in the 1945 strike. He began with Stewart Meacham, who had written the NLRB decision in favor of the CSU. He took extensive notes for the article, and a year later told a congressional committee under oath that Meacham was troubled in 1946:

> He told me that in his opinion if the producers and the IATSE wanted peace in Hollywood, they could have it following the settlement of the 1945 strike. But he was afraid, from what he saw of things as they were developing, they did not want peace in Hollywood. That it appeared to him that they were determined to destroy the Conference of Studio Unions and he foresaw in this the seeds of great difficulty and strife in Hollywood.[2]

Dunne then talked to Herb Sorrell of the CSU, who told him these fears were exaggerated. He tried to speak with Richard Walsh, the IA president, who was in town but would not return his calls. He finally did get an interview with Roy Brewer, who had replaced Willie Bioff as the IA president's local representative in Hollywood. When he brought up criticism of the IA's "dictatorial" ways—Mr. Walsh was empowered to change the constitution of the union without consulting the members—Brewer explained that "the IATSE was engaged in a war to fight for its existence." The extraordinary powers given to its president were emergency measures taken for the duration of the struggle against the CSU. "Mr. Brewer's talk to me was a war talk, with no possibility of compromise. The IATSE and CSU could not exist together in Hollywood; one or the other must be destroyed."[3]

Stewart Meacham had reason to worry about the prospects of peace. The question of jurisdiction between the craft unions allied with the IA on one side and CSU on the other ran through all departments of the studios. Should cameramen or machinists service cameras, machinists or teamsters service motorized vehicles, film or optical technicians service laboratory equipment? So many boundaries were in dispute that the A.F. of L. would have to appoint an infinite series of boards to adjudicate them one by one. So, at a special meeting held in Cincinnati during the month of October, 1945, a formula for overall settlement was agreed to by local unions, national officials, and the producers. The month of November would be devoted to good-faith attempts to end most of the disputes. Any left unresolved in December would be adjudicated by a three-man committee of A.F. of L. vice presidents, none of them connected with the crafts in dispute.[4]

Few quarrels were settled in November, though an important contract was reached between grips and carpenters, defining the difference between moving and constructing things on sound sets.[5] So the "three wise men"—as they came to be called, sardonically—flew to Hollywood. In eight days of hearings, they listened to the pleas and arguments of seven different unions, then went off to study their findings and make a report before the end of the month.[6] The three men proclaimed their intent, then and later, not to take jobs away or create new work categories, but to confirm established practices. For the most part they succeeded, and both groups of unions acquiesced in their awards. But on one point, by inadvertence, they innovated. Asking for the "historic" basis of the division of labor between carpenters and stagehands, they were shown a 1925 definition of spheres that was referred to in a 1926 settlement (and so is often confused, in later accounts, with the 1926 Studio Basic Agreement).[7] The committee later testified that it was unaware of the fact that carpenters had never ratified the 1925 formula, so it never went into effect—though Reagan calls this dead letter from twenty years back the "traditional guidelines" (Hubler, p. 165).

At issue was the building of new structures on a sound set, a labor that had hitherto been performed by carpenters, and which grips had just conceded was theirs in the agreement successfully signed before the wise men arrived—an agreement shown to the wise men along with the 1925 definition, but one they overlooked. The resurrection of the 1925 text, for which even the IA was not contending with any conviction, clearly went against the criterion proclaimed in the text of the wise men's own decision, that it would enforce only the "division of work designations within the industry patterned after previous agreements, negotiated *mutually* by the various crafts" (italics added).[8] The carpenters had never been party to a mutual agreement on these terms.

Still, when the wise men's decision was issued on December 27, 1945, it allotted "set erection" to stagehands. Pat Casey, labor liaison for the producers, justifiably interpreted this as giving stagehands the right to construct new sets, and the studios fired about 350 carpenters, whose jobs were taken by a newly formed IA union of "set erectors." The carpenters protested Casey's interpretation, saying the wise men's decree should be read in light of their declared intent and the history of the language's treatment over the last decades.[9] But they abode by the decision, while protesting it—especially to the head of their union, William (Big Bill) Hutcheson, who was a vice president of the A.F. of L., and who immediately brought the point up at a meeting of the international's directors in Miami.[10] The authors of the report did not want to get into a series of amendments to their supposedly final decision, but Hutcheson would not let the issue rest, and he had the votes at the next national convention to cause trouble if he took the matter to the floor; so the three men wrote an August clarification to their December decree, saying that by set erection they meant only the "assemblage" of sets, not their construction, which still belonged to the carpenters.[11]

That would seem to settle the matter on its merits. The decree was out of line with its own criterion. The intent of the authors was clear. They admitted they included the specific language from 1925 on the basis of a misunderstanding, believing it was already in force. That was the only point of dispute over the December awards, and the carpenters had protested without work stoppages or the threat of a strike, even though they lost 350 jobs. Now the jobs were restored.

But the producers reacted to this August missive, sent from the President of the A.F. of L., by meeting with IA representatives to formulate a plan for defying it—indeed, for using it as a way to "create an incident," so they could fire *more* carpenters, and many painters as well, all members of the CSU. First, of course, they asked their lawyers to supply a legal excuse for ignoring the August clarification. The lawyers could produce only the flimsiest pretext. The three-man committee, it was alleged, had no power to alter its decree, since it no longer had legal existence—it had been dissolved after performing its task in December.[12] But the producers liked to use the argument, when it suited them, that they could not intervene in jurisdictional disputes between members of the A.F. of L., since adjudication of such matters was entirely in the Federation's hands—and the clarification began with the words "Pursuant to instruction handed down by the executive council [of the A.F. of L.] . . ." After telling the Federation it alone had the authority to resolve its internal problems, the producers were now making an outside decision on what was proper procedure for the A.F. of L.

Informal minutes of the producers' strategy meetings with lawyers and IA representatives, held in August and September, are to the investigation of the 1946 strike what the White House tapes became to the Watergate investigation. By the time the minutes were produced in the Education and Labor Subcommittee's 1947 hearing, several of the participants had already denied under oath that such meetings ever occurred.[13] Pat Casey, who later had qualms about some of the activities he took part in, let the investigators know of the minutes' existence.[14] (They had been taken down during the proceedings by Victor Clarke of MGM.) What emerges from the minutes is a detailed plan for creating an incident at each of the major studios by beginning work on new sets with IA labor, and then—after they had been made "hot" in labor parlance—calling in carpenters and painters to complete them. If they refused, they could be dismissed under the terms of an interim agreement reached less than thirty days earlier, in which all unions had agreed to a moratorium on work stoppages.[15] If other CSU unions joined in a sympathetic strike, as was expected, the IA had assurances from Dave Beck of the teamsters' union that the picket lines would be breached, and the CSU could be broken for good.[16] Joseph Tuohy ran the local operation for the teamsters, and was rewarded by the producers with an executive's job.[17]

Why, it may be wondered, would the studios collaborate in the IA's plan to destroy a competitor? The answer is given in the minutes, and is the old one—IA control of the exhibitors. That might have been challengeable during the March 1945 strike, when the nation was at war, and the attempt to close theaters would have been considered an affront to national morale. But the producers had given in even then. They were helpless to resist in 1946. Richard Walsh. the IA president, was in Hollywood to deliver the ultimatum. On August 22, in the first of the meetings of IA officials with all the major producers, he precluded any move to recognize the A.F. of L. clarification:

[Richard] Walsh advises that any company that makes one single change in the administration of the AFL directive in compliance with the new interpretation will have all work stopped in the studios, *exchanges [distribution centers], and theaters.*[18] [Italics added.]

The producers were thus enlisted in the war on the CSU that Brewer had described to Fr. Dunne. In fact, Brewer's very language of war powers was repeated in the secret sessions: "Brewer feels his organization is in much stronger position to keep studios open than in March 1945. Walsh's power recently conferred gives him added strength."[19] Brewer could, therefore, issue marching orders to the producers:

Brewer said to put IA men on sets so carpenters and painters will quit, provided—
1. IA is advised in advance when and where.
2. Put on enough set erectors and painters in groups for self-protection.
3. Keep procedure quiet so CSU can't gang up at one spot.[20]

The producers agreed to act in concert, with a single mode of procedure, a central command post at the Producers' Labor Office (Pat Casey's office), designated contact men in each studio, a running total and distribution of men laid off and of IA replacements available. Lawyers advised them they must go through the motions of negotiation with the CSU while engaged in this secret war to destroy it.[21] All department heads were to keep within carefully planned operating tactics:

1. Any employee who refuses to perform the work properly assigned to him in accordance with his regular classification of work should be requested to leave the premises.
2. In the event that such employee asks whether he is being discharged he should be told "no."
3. In the event that any such employee asks whether or not he is being laid off he should be told that he is not being laid off, but that he is not wanted on the premises as long as he refuses to perform his customary duties.
4. In the event that any such employee further asks what is his status he should be told that he is requested to leave because of his refusal to perform services requested.
5. He should be paid off to time of leaving.
     If any such employee asks to return to his former job he is to be welcomed back. It was agreed each studio would assign work to carpenters by Monday *to create an incident.*[22] [Italics added.]

Violence was expected, and provided for. "Mannix thought someone or group should meet with the sheriff, district attorney, and the chief of police to explain the situation, and arrange for necessary protection."[23] Elsewhere we read: "Be sure to have police near each set when IA erectors or painters are working."[24] It was anticipated that the police action would not be edify-

ing. "Somerset thinks it advisable to not have stars see the picket line broken
—but to hold them somewhere until they can enter studio peacefully."[25] The
source of that last suggestion is as interesting as the suggestion itself. It came
from Pat Somerset, assistant to Jack Dales on the executive staff of SAG.
Members of the Guild took part in the planning of this war on the CSU,
while its board was pretending neutrality between the contending unions.

Events took the course that Walsh and Brewer had planned. Carpenters
and painters refused to work on the hot sets. Other CSU personnel were
called from workshops to replace them—some who had not worked on sets
for years—in order to clear them out. CSU locals went on sympathetic
strike, and Brewer had IA replacements on hand for all of them. The only
charitable interpretation of Reagan as a union leader in the ensuing months
is that he knew nothing of the plans that had been concerted to break the
CSU by defying the A.F. of L. leadership, though there were ample signs of
what must have preceded the actions, signs easily read by acute observers
like Carey McWilliams. Besides, Reagan's later account of the strike, given
to Hubler in 1964, came after the revelation of the conspiratorial meetings to
the House Subcommittee (the Kearns Committee) in 1947—obviously, Reagan did not care that one union was acting in concert with management to
break another union (the latter being the more democratic of the two).[26]

The SAG board's aim was to maintain a neutral stance, which allowed its
actors to keep crossing the picket line and working. But the best way to
maintain a neutral pose, in the face of protests over the high-handed actions
of the IA, was to feign intervention. This "intervention" mainly took the
form of "fact finding," calls for improved arbitration procedures in the future, and vague appeals to peace, which amounted to de facto support of the
producers. The permanent staff leaders of the Guild constituted its institutional memory and created its longer-range policies. The actors, after all,
worked for the Guild only in their spare time. The day-to-day business of the
union was managed by the personnel who had made this their career—
which means Jack Dales and Pat Somerset were the makers and implement-
ers of policy; and we have already seen that Pat Somerset was helping the
producers "handle" the actors while keeping the picket lines up. The rest of
the Guild's activity was mainly cosmetic.

Reagan excelled at this kind of work; no one could bring quite the conviction to it that he could. It was during the strike that Reagan was chosen by
the board to fill out Robert Montgomery's term as Guild president (Montgomery had to resign because he became a producer himself that year) and
was then elected to his own term by the membership. He had helped lead the
delegation of stars that descended on the A.F. of L. convention in Chicago
and threatened to send celebrities around the nation denouncing the Federation unless an improved negotiating procedure was set up for future use.
(The convention meekly voted the grand gesture through, and that was the
end of it.)[27]

Reagan not only broke off work on a picture to go to Chicago; he and Jane

Wyman had to take extra time to get there and back by train, since he was still not flying. While the Hollywood delegation was in town, it engaged in its own "fact-finding" mission. It would find out at last what the wise men really meant. Reagan "found out," and relayed to a large public meeting back in Hollywood three main things:

1. The August clarification meant nothing. It was extracted from the wise men by the carpenters' boss, Big Bill Hutcheson, who just wanted "a basket of words" his men could quibble over.[28]

2. The wise men had resented the pressure, and all three had written resignations in their pockets if Hutcheson tried to bring any further force to bear, or take the issue to the floor. (Reagan admits Hutcheson had the votes to prevail if he did take it there.)[29]

3. Thus Hutcheson was the one man defying the A.F. of L., whose sole legitimate directive was issued in December and gave set construction to the stagehands (Hubler, pp. 172-73). Reagan neglects the fact that the executive council of the A.F. of L. issued the clarification as well as the directive, and the body of the A.F. of L. was ready to back it up, wise men or no, if it went to the floor.

A year later, Reagan would repeat these three points in his testimony to the House subcommittee. There all three wise men denied Reagan's major contentions under oath. All denied using the term "basket of words," experiencing any illegitimate pressure, writing their resignations, or saying that Hutcheson had acted in defiance of the A.F. of L. council.[30] (He had no need to defy the council; it was on his side.) The defiance of the A.F. of L. was on the part of the IA and the producers.

When, back in Hollywood, Herb Sorrell challenged Reagan's version of the wise men's views, saying he had received a different story when he consulted them in Chicago, Gene Kelly suggested that a delegation of union members fly east in the CSU plane and confront the wise men with these differing versions. Reagan refused, pleading his fear of airplanes, and suggested a telephone conference call instead.[31] The call was arranged for the next day. Unfortunately, the best-informed of the wise men, who had kept the notes for the committee, had gone directly from the Chicago convention to Europe. But the other two were found, in Indianapolis and Kansas City, and the schedule set for the three-city hookup.

Sorrell was so certain that Reagan and his fellows were distorting the committee's statements that he agreed to end the strike if they were vindicated by the call. But he insisted on having a transcript of the conversation —which is fortunate, considering what Reagan makes of the call in his later accounts. Edward Arnold began by trying to get the wise men to answer a loaded (and inaccurate) question: "Now, were you of the mind in your decision that the construction work went to the IATSE because they had had it for so many years?"[32] Reagan and George Murphy pursued this line. Then a CSU spokesman tried to ask his own leading questions from the text of the August clarification. One of the men at the other end of the line did not have a text of the clarification, and as the other one began to read from his, it had a slightly different first line from the one sent to Hollywood by William Green, President of the A.F. of L. This broke up the phone call in confusion; but the next day the CSU claimed a victory because the man reading from a different text, Mr. Birthright in Indianapolis, telegraphed the true text, and it was identical with the one Hollywood had received in August.[33] Reagan does not mention this telegram at all in his account. And his distortions are not confined to the omission of points embarrassing to his thesis. He makes an accusation that is not only false, but whose falsehood was clearly established during the Kearns hearings.

Why was there a different text of the August clarification in Hollywood and in Indianapolis? Reagan leaps to a triumphant conclusion:

> It [the clarification that had been sent to Hollywood] was a clear phony, evidently invented by someone in Hutcheson's office. What the four-hundred-dollar telephone call meant, in simple terms, was that the "clarification" which had set off labor rivalry in Hollywood was a deliberate fraud: a lie and a hoax. We did not know—or care—who had done it [though he has just accused Hutcheson's office of having evidently invented it]. We only knew it had been issued by the authority of someone who wanted the strike settled his way, regardless of how many people were thrown out of work. We figured that at long last, to anyone of good will, the strike was over. We were wrong [Hubler, pp. 178–79].

That was the story Reagan was still telling in 1965, though the mystery of the two texts had been cleared up in 1947, on the same day Reagan himself testified to the Kearns Committee. The three wise men, testifying together under oath, described how they wrote their clarification in the anteroom of the executive council's meeting at the A.F. of L. convention, taking the draft in and reworking it with the whole committee, so there were several drafts.[34] The one sent out had come from the proper authority, and was the final one, not a "phony," but an instrument drawn up in accord with its own first words—"Pursuant to the instructions handed down by the executive council . . . ." Hutcheson was not the one defying the A.F. of L. The producers were, with their odd argument that the Federation could not decide for itself what were its own statements. Reagan seems to recognize this indirectly in parts of his narrative, as when he admits that Hutcheson had the votes to win on the floor if appeal were to be made to that. He won in executive council, and could have won on the floor. What other forum was there for appeal to the A.F. of L.? The producers were excluding any right of appeal while piously claiming to uphold it. Reagan himself told the committee that "the record of the American Federation of Labor in the present Hollywood strike does not reflect glory on the organization."[35] He means that it did not agree with him or the producers.

After the conference call, Reagan became fierce in his own war against the CSU. The Screen Actors Guild, he would claim, had acted with impartiality to establish the facts and settle the strike, and its peacemaking mission had been rebuffed by men of bad will determined to make trouble. Yet, in the months ahead, the CSU tried to place the issues before any truly impartial arbiters—an interfaith council that offered its services, the Catholic archdiocese, the NLRB.[36] It even offered to submit its case to the new arbitration machinery voted for in response to the Guild's motion at the Chicago convention. But Reagan, who made the motion, refused to consider using the machinery for a matter he considered closed. He took the producers' line that "you cannot arbitrate an arbitration."[37] The unyielding party was the IA, which had come into the fight to destroy the CSU, and would hold the producers' feet to the fire to the end.

Father George Dunne, who began his work on the *Commonweal* article before the strike broke out, was well prepared to observe its first days, and was entirely convinced that the IA and the producers had planned this development as part of the war Brewer first told him about—a view that would be confirmed a year later by the Kearns Committee, before which he testified. Abandoning the article, he became a public defender of the CSU, on the radio and at rallies. The union voted to send him as its spokesman to get Congress interested in the strike—he talked in Washington with Senator Hartley, chairman of the Labor Committee, who sent the Kearns subcommittee to Hollywood the next year.[38] During this trip, Fr. Dunne stopped off to talk with W. C. Birthright, one of the wise men, in Indianapolis, and confirmed that the committee of three did not realize the 1925 agreement had never been put into practice.[39] Birthright, who was present when Dunne testified before the Kearns Committee, later said on the stand that Dunne had represented their conversation accurately, while repudiating entirely Reagan's account of his dealings with the three.[40]

In March of 1947, Fr. Dunne made an attempt to break the stalemate by asking the CSU to surrender its claim based on the clarification. Since Reagan and others had thoroughly obfuscated that issue, Dunne persuaded the CSU to abandon it and base its case solely on a fair reading of the December directive before a panel of arbitrators.[41] The IA said no. No forum could be found where they would go. They had gone into their trenches for the war, and there they stayed.

Reagan's role in the strike is best seen in his reaction to Fr. Dunne. Dunne was felt as a threat to the producers. If he was right, Reagan was not a union man speaking for labor, but a strikebreaker doing the will of the producers. Here is how Reagan put it in 1965:

> A particularly upsetting incident involved a Roman Catholic priest, a teacher of political science at Loyola University, Father Dunne. He took to the air waves and blasted the SAG and all opponents of the CSU eloquently and with vigor. The papers reported also that he appeared on the platform at CSU rallies. George Murphy and I decided he must be the victim of a snow job. We knew he had never been exposed to the Guild side of the contro· ··· and he was saying some pretty

harsh things about us. We called and asked if we could see him, and then went down to the university one evening armed with our records. We were a little taken aback when he introduced us to his lawyer, and coldly informed us he had asked the lawyer to sit in on our meeting [Hubler, p. 208].

It was a homecoming of a sort for Reagan. Loyola had stood in for Notre Dame six years earlier when Warners filmed *Knute Rockne* there (Hubler, p. 108). Fr. Dunne, who now lives in retirement in the Jesuit community at Loyola, described the meeting for me thirty-seven years later. More important, he described it shortly after it occurred for the Kearns Committee.[42] The Guild actually sent a four-person delegation to cope with Dunne— Reagan, Murphy, Jane Wyman, and Jack Dales, the head of staff. And they did not come "armed with our records." The day afterward, they sent over to Dunne a transcript of the meeting where Reagan told his version of the Chicago convention and a transcript of the conference call. Dunne, who had a thorough acquaintance with the history of the strike, was not convinced by this "documentation." Neither was his friend Dan Marshall, the lawyer Reagan refers to, who had represented an IA local and often visited Fr. Dunne in connection with their joint work on the Catholic Interracial Group. Marshall, a member of the board of directors of Loyola, just happened to be on the campus when the actors arrived. He was not there as Dunne's lawyer. At Dunne's several appearances before the Kearns Committee, he took no lawyer with him.

The producers had not silenced Dunne with a delegation of stars, so they turned to economic muscle. Prominent benefactors of the diocese let the Cardinal's office know that this Jesuit in their midst was a nuisance. Dunne was summoned to the archdiocesan chancery to give an account of himself, and he did. His superiors were supporting him until, one night, he was told his classes would be taken over by someone else, and he was expected to report at the upstate Jesuit novitiate the next day. It was the second time, and would not be the last, when Dunne's outspokenness for justice led to his exile.[43]

Several years later, when Fr. Dunne was working in a parish in Phoenix, Arizona, he came across an old foe on the golf course—the affable executive hatchetman for MGM, Eddie Mannix, who asked: "What are you doing here?" "I think you had something to do with that," Dunne answered. "Well, you were getting in the way, you know," Mannix grinned.

Ronald Reagan does not want to be denied his part in this producers' victory. He ends his story of the visit to Fr. Dunne at Loyola with a sly boast: "It was a short meeting. The next night he was back on radio kicking our brains out. But not for long: someone else began to teach political science and he was on the other side of the country" (Hubler, p. 208).[44]

CHAPTER 26

HICCASP: G-Men II

. . . professing next the Spie

—Paradise Lost *4.948*

Despite his deep engagement in the Hollywood strike that began in 1946, Reagan's later account of it is confused when not false. This was not because of bad faith, any more than his misjudgment of President Bert Wilson's policy had been in 1928. His grasp of particulars was sketchy because he thought them unimportant. He quickly isolated a symbolic moral point, and devoted all his energies to enforcing that. Details were left to others. He took Jack Dales with him to the A.F. of L. convention and to his session with Fr. Dunne, as he took Pat Somerset with him to testify before the Kearns Committee—staff men who could supply him with dates and documents. He had to delay his testimony to get a sequence of meetings straightened out by Mr. Somerset.[1]

This is not surprising. Reagan always maintained that the problems of union jurisdiction were mere quibbles, a pecking at word baskets. And, even more fundamentally, he shied from group expressions of economic interest as somehow unworthy or illegitimate. He acted—he assures us (and, surely, himself)—from a motive outside the petty tangle of competing interests. He sought only peace and equity. He did his foes the favor of thinking that they, too, acted from motives not immediately selfish or petty. They, too, were altruists of a different (and a hateful) dream. They were Communists.

He had evidence, some of it good, for thinking so. It made him careless or contemptuous of the facts disputed by people who did believe in immediate "petty" motives. I have delayed, thus far, consideration of the ulterior motives assigned to his enemies, partly out of deference to those who (like Fr. Dunne and Carey McWilliams) did believe in the immediate issues, but mainly because it is so easy for the grander charge to obscure facts once it has been introduced. That happened in Reagan's own mind; and those who believed, with him, that Hollywood was on the verge of a Communist takeover will naturally be impatient with nice distinctions between constructing and shifting stage properties on a sound set.

The Red menace was a vivid presence in Southern California from the beginning of this century, and it was intimately linked to union activity, especially after the dynamiting of the Los Angeles *Times* building in 1910. The combination of migrant workers and Hollywood exotics always looked explosive to California "natives," who had arrived the day before yesterday rather than yesterday. The exploitable poor and cosmopolitan radicals, considered dangerous singly, were especially menacing in combination; and the Depression seemed to be inundating the Los Angeles area with both kinds. The introduction of sound in the movies had brought a wave of English actors and German technicians to town, and the Depression had made the newcomers harder to employ. In 1934, half the state's unemployed—250,000 people—were in Los Angeles County.[2] That was the year Irving Thalberg made his propaganda movie of bums and radicals descending on the state to take over if Upton Sinclair won the governor's office.

Two years later, when the Screen Writers Guild was working for recognition as the scriptwriters' sole bargaining agent, Thalberg called them "a bunch of Reds" and organized a company union to oppose them, the Screen Playwrights. John Lee Mahin's collaboration with Thalberg on this project gave Budd Schulberg part of his plot for Sammy Glick's launching of the Association of Photodramatists in *What Makes Sammy Run.*[3] Mahin later admitted: "Yes, we were a company union, formed by the workers themselves. We were cloak-and-dagger, and we found out all the leading, hard-working guys in the [Writers] Guild were members of the Party . . . Frankly, we spied on them."[4] Later, when the producers finally gave in to the NLRB's authorization of the Screen Writers Guild to represent screen writers, members of the company union (like Morrie Ryskind) shifted their anti-Communist activities to the Motion Picture Alliance.

In 1939, when IATSE unions were discredited by the Bioff-Browne scandals, the CIO tried to take Hollywood's unions away from the A.F. of L. Though the CIO's industry-wide organizing philosophy offended the craft orientation of the CSU, Herb Sorrell took the help of Harry Bridges's longshoremen's union and Jeff Kibre's fishermen's union, both of which were later expelled from the CIO for being under Communist influence.[5] From this point on, the IA's customary response, whenever it was accused of gangsterism, was to point to a greater evil—the CIO's international Communist connections.

In 1941, when Sorrell won the Disney strike by involving Technicolor workers, Walt Disney ran an advertisement in *Variety* claiming: "I am positively convinced that Communistic agitation, leadership, and activities have brought about this strike."[6] This charge attracted the attention of the California legislature's Jack B. Tenney. The composer of the 1923 hit song "Mexicali Rose," Tenney had become president of Local 47 of the musicians union, but he was defeated in 1939 because of corruption charges.[7] Tenney had been a radical himself; had, in fact, called for the abolition of the Dies Committee when it investigated communism in Hollywood. But by 1939 he blamed his defeat on Communists within the union, and began a lifelong vendetta that made even devoted anti-Communists like Roy Brewer conclude he was irresponsible in his hatred of unions as well as of "Reds." In 1952 he ran for Vice President of the United States on the anti-Semitic ticket of Gerald L. K. Smith.[8]

In the California legislature, Tenney turned his Joint Fact-Finding Committee into the most aggressive of all the anti-Communist committees. (Ironically, in the light of his previous opposition to the Dies Committee, his became known as the "Little Dies Committee.") One of Tenney's first investigations was of Herb Sorrell, and there a purported Communist Party card for "Herbert Stewart" was produced, with the testimony of handwriting experts that it had been signed by Sorrell.

Sorrell denied the card was his to the Tenney, Kearns and Thomas committees, and he was a man known for his touchy honor about his word. Even Pat Casey, the producers' representative who was Sorrell's opponent in the 1946 strike, had this to say of him to the Kearns Committee:

> I will take his word for anything he says in a deal. He has never broken it with me. What he might have done with something else, I know nothing about. As far as I am personally concerned, that is the situation. Now, I will go further. I have heard of a lot of the CIO fellows being Communists, and I think they probably have proven so. I think this reference to Conway, who was referred to in the testimony yesterday—he is the head of the Newspaper Guild—probably is correct. I think Leo Gallagher, a lawyer out there, and who is probably as bright and smart a fellow as the Lord ever put breath into—he does not deny he is a Communist. But so far as anybody in the A.F. of L. movement that I have ever had business dealings with, I do not know of one that I would say was a Communist.[9]

Sorrell, of course, was in the A.F. of L. and had many dealings with Casey. Casey was denying the allegations by Brewer and others that Sorrell was a Communist.

Radicals thought Sorrell naïve in his sense of pride, the way he gave his word to class enemies like Casey.[10] People serious about revolution would not pledge, as Sorrell did, to call off a strike if his version of a conversation with the three wise men could be proved false. Sorrell was an impulsive man, friendly and bellicose at the same time, not controlled by others, even his friends, and obviously outside Communist discipline. John Cogley concluded that, when Sorrell and the Communists ended up on the same side, it was because they followed him, in his days of popularity, rather than from his submission to them:

> The Communists for their part treated him with uncommon care. When Sorrell disagreed with a Party decision, several ex-Communists have

testified, the Party tried to adjust itself to his positions . . . Sorrell became a kind of folk-hero to those who regarded the IA as a corrupt, reactionary force.[11]

Sorrell posed a special problem for the Party when he called the 1945 strike supporting the interior decorators. The Party line was to support the common war effort with Russia and forbid all strikes. Sorrell was obviously as little impressed by that as by the A.F. of L. pledge to avoid strikes (a position that was unpopular with the lower ranks of labor in much of the country). Cogley's report continues:

> The Communists were embarrassed when the strike was called. For some time they had been losing patience with Sorrell, who was giving increasing evidence that he was not in their pocket. They opposed the strike because of their all-out support of the war. Yet they were loath to cut off the support they were getting within the CSU. Inside the party, a controversy raged on the question of the strike. *The People's World,* Party paper on the West Coast, ran an editorial about Sorrell called "A Good Guy Gone Wrong."[12]

On April 19, *The People's World* accused the CSU of "wasting forces needed for making that new world for which the President gave his life." On May 19, it called the continuation of the strike "a disgraceful situation."[13]

It was only after the fall of Earl Browder as the head of the American party in June of 1945 that Communists could rejoin others of leftist sympathy in supporting the CSU strike. *The People's World* finally came out for it on September 24. Browder had taken advantage of the popular front caused by support for the war, for Roosevelt, and for the New Deal to integrate the Party into a broader left movement, even changing its name from the Communist Party of the United States to the Communist Political Association. But as tensions developed between Russia and the Truman administration, and with special speed after the atomic bombs were dropped, Browder was denounced by the international leadership of the Party as having gone soft and liberal. A series of vindictive disciplinary moves was instituted to shake up the dilettante leftists of the film community. The humiliation of screenwriter Alfred Maltz early in 1946 was the most famous of these.

Liberals who had worked with Communists, knowingly or not, in the Roosevelt campaign of 1944, or war rallies, or opposition to wartime strikes, noticed the postwar Communists' shifts of opinion *en bloc.* One of those liberals was Ronald Reagan. Despite his Air Force commission, he had been very much on the Hollywood scene throughout the 1944 election, when the Motion Picture Alliance was set up to denounce the New Deal for giving cover to Communists. The MPA not only opposed Roosevelt's election to a fourth term but called for a congressional investigation of Communists in the film industry. Several friends of Reagan were involved in the MPA from the outset—Sam Wood, who had directed *Kings Row,* became its first and most zealous president. But Roosevelt was still Reagan's idol, and support for his administration of the war seemed a patriotic duty to Reagan, as to most citizens. Furthermore, he did not like the antiunion bias originally shown within the MPA, and he always shared the producers' desire to keep Congress away from legislation for the movies. There were many reasons for him to join Democratic party groups, labor groups, and civil rights groups opposed to the MPA in 1944 and 1945. One of these, the Hollywood Democratic Committee, changed its name on June 6, 1945, to the Hollywood Independent Citizens Committee of the Arts, Sciences and Professions (HICCASP). This was just before the fall of Browder, and Communists who belonged to the organization would be put through some revealing contortions in the next few months, at the very time when Ronald Reagan was asked to serve on HICCASP's board of directors, along with other non-Communist Democrats like James Roosevelt, Dore Schary, and Olivia de Havilland. HICCASP was infiltrated, but not controlled, by the Party, whose internal quarrels would disqualify it from effective manipulation in this period.

The FBI was busily spying on Communists, real or suspected, and everyone who dealt with Communists. J. Edgar Hoover had used the war to expand his mandate, budget, and activities in ways that did not shrink after the war. For the first time he had been given charge of espionage throughout the American hemisphere, and the man who made his reputation in the Bureau by compiling dossiers on Reds for A. Mitchell Palmer did not let the wartime alliance with Russia blunt his suspicion of the Communists. In fact, Hoover told his Hollywood friend, George Murphy, that the Communists had engineered Roosevelt's New Deal.[14]

Hoover was especially sensitive to the propaganda of Hollywood movies—he had used them to promote his own agency, after all. The number of aliens concentrated in Hollywood, the generally gossipy nature of the place, and Hoover's willingness to use people like Hedda Hopper and Louella Parsons to collect and disseminate views, meant that a clandestine movement had little chance of escaping notice—especially when its members were reacting so uniformly to a punitive line directed as much against them as against the society they were supposed to be overthrowing. In Hollywood, the first response to personal or professional trouble was to take out an ad in *Variety*.

One of the many spies recruited by the Bureau was none other than Neil Reagan, who had veered to the right earlier and more ardently than Ronald. He warned his brother against HICCASP, then secretly spied on its meetings.

He [Ronald] was in an organization that was as bad as you could get: Hollywood Citizens Committee of Arts, Sciences, and Professions. And I used to beat him over the head, "Get out of that thing. There are people in there who can cause you real trouble. They're more than suspect on the part of the goverment, as to their connections that are not exactly American, and one thing and another."

Now, in those days, I was doing little things for the FBI. You know,

"Neil, we'd like to have you go out and lay in the bushes and take down the car numbers off of the cars that are going to be at this little meeting in Bel-Air. Put it in a brown envelope, no return address. And always remember, if you get caught in the bushes, you can just forget about saying, well, you're doing this for the FBI, because we'll just look him right in the eye and say, 'We never saw the guy in our lives.' Forget it."

I talked to him and talked to him about this organization [HIC-CASP]. One evening he calls me—evening, hell, it was about midnight—he had stopped up at the Nutburger stand (there was a Nutburger stand at the corner of Sunset and Doheny at the time, across the street from the drugstore). He says, "I'm having a cup of coffee, come on up." I said, "Do you know what time it is?" "Yeah." "Well, I've been in bed for three hours. Have your coffee and go home and go to bed." "No, I want you to come up." And I said all right; so I put a pair of trousers on and a shirt and drove up the hill. Here he is parked, I got in and—he's a member of the board—he says, "You wouldn't believe it. It just came to me tonight. We have a rule that if a board member misses two meetings without being excused, you're automatically off the board. There's a gal out at the such-and-such studio," and he says, "I've been a little suspicious of her. All of a sudden, we had one of these cases come up tonight, that so-and-so had missed two board meetings, and so they were off, and now we've got to find somebody else. It suddenly dawned on me that over the last several months, every time one of these cases came up, she had just the individual that would be excellent as a re-placement. I managed to filch the minute books before I left. I can show you the page where her board members became a majority of the board, with her replacements."[15]

If Neil reproduced that conversation accurately, Ronald was exaggerating. The board was split into left, right, and middle, a stalemate that led to a series of unity meetings and the drafting of ever more innocuous statements of joint purpose.[16] The organization was under fire from the Tenney Commit-tee, and the right wing of the board insisted that an anti-Communist state-ment be included in the unity draft.[17] When it was rejected, Reagan resigned along with Dore Schary, Olivia de Havilland, and James Roosevelt, in July of 1946.

Just in time. While Reagan's brother was spying on this organization, other FBI eyes were trained on Reagan himself, and had concluded that he was a Communist. A report from the Los Angeles office dated March 13, 1946, put him among the sponsors and directors, "all of whom have records of Communist activity and sympathies," for the Los Angeles Committee for a Democratic Far Eastern Policy.[18] The "proof" of this seems to have been a clipping from the Communist People's World for February 26, 1946, in-cluded in the file, which lists Reagan among the sponsors calling for a free Indochina and withdrawal of support from Chiang Kai-shek. The FBI was also interested in Reagan's ties to HICCASP, to the American Veterans Committee, the Screen Actors Guild, and a radio show he had narrated attacking the Ku Klux Klan.[19] Even resigning from HICCASP over an anti-Communist vote was not enough in some people's eyes to redeem Reagan. One FBI informant, a movie director whose name is crossed out, said that Reagan had stayed in the organization after the Communists took it over in 1945, and "professions of anti-Communism now" should be looked on with skepticism. "These Johnnies-come-lately raise in me a question as to their basic sincerity."[20]

But after the CSU strike began in September of 1946, the Bureau decided to approach Reagan directly, to question him, warn him against past associates, and ask for future cooperation. He describes rather melodramatically the arrival of three agents by night to propose an exchange of information.[21] Reagan says he told them he would not Red-bait.

> "It isn't a question of that. It's a question of national security. You served with the Air Corps. You know what spies and saboteurs are."
> "We thought someone the Communists hated as much as they hate you might be willing to help us," added the third.
> That got me. It's always a jolt to discover others have been talking you over. "What do you mean?" I asked.
> "Well," he said, "they held a meeting last night." He described the house, gave the address, told me who was there, and what they said. I broke in. "What did they say about *me?*"
> "The exact quotation," he replied, "was: 'What are we going to do about that sonofabitching bastard Reagan?' Will that do for openers?"
> It was enough. We got to talking . . . We exchanged information for a few hours [Hubler, p. 195].

He told them about the drafting session of the HICCASP anti-Communist motion, and they warned him about a man who attended it.

It was from this period, if not from this session, that Reagan hardened forever his belief that the CSU strike was part of a Communist plot. As he put it later: "The conclusion was that other forces were encouraging Sorrell and his forces to continue their unauthorized walkout . . . I will say of the Communists—they were the cause of the labor strike, they used minor jurisdictional disputes as excuses for their scheme. Their aim was to gain economic control of the motion picture industry in order to finance their activities and subvert the screen for their propaganda" (Hubler, pp. 157, 182). That was the version of things he presented to Fr. Dunne when he went to Loyola in the spring of 1947. If the FBI had not convinced him that Sorrell was a Communist, someone had. (He did not know that, only a short time before, the Los Angeles office had concluded he was engaged in "Communist" activities.)

Fr. Dunne, who had come to know Sorrell and his family by then (Sorrell's daughter later became a Catholic), tried to assure Reagan that Sorrell was not a Communist, that he had started his 1945 strike in defiance of the Communists, that some were unhappy with this one, that his grievances were real.[22] Reagan presumably concluded that Dunne was a dupe of the "other forces" Sorrell represented—a charge the Tenney Committee had made, and one taken up in questions submitted to the Kearns Committee.[23] By accident, Dunne and Reagan ended up sitting next to each other while waiting to testify before the Kearns Committee on August 18, 1947. Dunne tried to make small talk; Reagan just gave him a cold stare. He had become the enemy.

Many others close to the strike tried to prevent its reduction to a matter of favoring or resisting communism. Carey McWilliams, the most knowledgeable chronicler of Southern California, said it was wrong even to call it a strike: the producers, by their use of hot sets, had maneuvered the workers into a lockout.[24] The UCLA study of the strike reached a similar conclusion.[25] Archbishop Cantwell, who later succumbed to pressure for Dunne's removal from the area, appointed his own experts to study the situation and make recommendations. The report was written by two priests, John Devlin, the archbishop's representative to the film industry, and Thomas Coogan, a professor of labor relations, who concluded in March of 1947:

> Nor can we becloud the air with cries of Communism, radicalism. It is true that Communists have tried hard to infiltrate into the ranks of the CSU. Probably some have succeeded. But the strike is not Communist inspired nor Communist directed.[26]

No such arguments would ever reach Reagan. He blackens Sorrell's name at every opportunity. Using innuendo that conveniently omits the charges, he says: "Sorrell was put on trial by the Los Angeles courts as a result of *certain activities.* He got an even break—convicted on one count, acquitted on another." (Hubler, p. 166, italics added.) Sorrell had been arrested on the picket line, and the charge he was cleared of was major (rioting), the conviction minor (resisting arrest). Such technical niceties are beneath notice when one is playing for the huge stakes Reagan now saw in the strike:

> The Communist plan for Hollywood was remarkably simple. It was merely to take over the motion picture business. Not only for its profit, as the hoodlums had tried—but also for a grand world-wide propaganda base. In those days before television and massive foreign film production, American films dominated 95 percent of the world's movie screens. We had a weekly audience of about 500,000,000 souls. Takeover of this enormous plant and its gradual transformation into a Communist gristmill was a grandiose one. It would have been a magnificent coup for our enemies. Using the CSU as a vehicle for Communist aims was a first step of admirable directness [Hubler, p. 187].

Reagan answered with a symmetrically grand and simple strategy: he would turn the Guild into as effective a vehicle for anti-communism as CSU had become for communism. This is the real reason he could call himself a "rabid union man." Union details bored him, the closed shop he disliked, the profession of economic goals seemed grubby. But now he had a large cause, for which his union was the perfect weapon and expression.

Bennett (Iowa) baseball team, 1898. Jack Reagan, middle row right, with his Oscar Wilde hairstyle.

Hennepin Canal at Tampico, Reagan's birthplace. Site of Disciple immersions.

Reagan as lifeguard at Lowell Park in Dixon, Illinois.

The stylish Reagans in Chicago. Jack, Neil (with his father's hairstyle), Ronald, Nelle.

B. J. Palmer, Reagan's first professional employer
at radio station WOC (for World of Chiropractic).

"A Little Bit O' Heaven" beside the B. J. Palmer residence. Reagan's radio station was atop the
school shown on the right.

Alpha Epsilon Sigma, Eureka College dramatic society. Reagan (back row, third from left) wearing his youthful trade-mark glasses; Margaret Cleaver, his fiancée, seated first on the left.

Alla Nazimova as Salome. Nancy Davis grew up calling her godmother "Zim."

Ronald Reagan cheesecake, 1937, with Susan Hayward.

Nancy Davis cheesecake, 1948.

Ronald Reagan with his mother.

Reagan "off to war," January 1943 cover of *Modern Screen*.

Reagan and Ann Sheridan in *Kings Row,* 1942. "Happy New Century."

Screen Actors Guild conference call to two of the "three wise men" in 1946. James Skelton and Herb Sorrell of Conference of Studio Unions, Ronald Reagan and Edward Arnold of Screen Actors Guild, Roy Tindall of CSU, George Murphy and Gene Kelly of SAG, October 26, 1946.

Old Governor's Mansion in Sacramento (Lincoln Steffens' home), in which Nancy Reagan refused to live.
Courtesy of Dan Tidwell

AP/Wide World Photo

Hollywood in the White House. The Reagans with Frank Sinatra, 1981.

He had more reason to use the union for patriotic ends as he looked at
what he considered some labor leaders' cynical use of communism for purely
selfish goals. The heart of his objection to the higher command in the A.F. of
L. comes out in this version of an exchange Reagan had with Bill Hutcheson, the carpenters' boss, at the Chicago convention:

> "Tell Walsh" [of the IA] he [Hutcheson] boomed after us, "that if he'll
> give in on the August directive, I'll run Sorrell out of Hollywood and
> break up the CSU in five minutes. I'll do the same to the Commies."
> This too was an admission because up to now he had charged there
> were no Communists involved in any way.[27]

Of course, if the Guild was to serve the purpose Reagan saw for it, it must
be kept pure, absolutely pure, of communism itself. So Reagan secretly gave
the name of suspect people within his organization to the FBI. What good
was an organization whose whole rationale had become anti-Communist for
Reagan if it collaborated with Communists even in part? Jane Wyman, still
on the board of the Guild, was his associate in this effort. Together they
named at least six people on April 10, 1947, one of whom led the support for
Sorrell's strike within the membership, and others of whom belonged to one
of two cliques that "follow the Communist Party line."[28] The agent, in the
Bureau's self-protective way, notes that Mr. and Mrs. Reagan "had requested that they be interviewed" to give this information. But Reagan was
no doubt sincere in his desire to purify the Guild. The records released in his
file are incomplete—there is a notice of pages omitted, and many are blacked
out entirely except for dates and case numbers—but even from the record as
visible, there were at least three meetings with the FBI in 1947 alone.[29]
Reagan dealt regularly enough with the Bureau to be given an informer's
code number, T-10, several times referred to, and be included on a list of
eighteen such informers.[30] The names of the authors are blacked out, but T-9
is identified as a woman. It is natural to suppose this referred to Jane Wyman, since she gave information on the same date as Reagan, but the unnamed woman is quoted in a way that makes this improbable. I cannot
believe the FBI would ask a wife to inform on her own husband, but T-9 is
questioned about Reagan, and is quoted as "of the opinion that RONALD
REAGAN, executive officer of the Guild, had seen the light and was sincere
in his efforts to keep the radical members out of controlling positions."[31]
This may well be Olivia de Havilland, numbered in proximity to Reagan
because she too was on the HICCASP board, and adopting the penitential
language of "seeing the light" because she had to impress on agents her own
break with the noxious organization. Reagan remembers that, at the HIC-
CASP meeting that drafted the anti-Communist motion,

> I kept grinning at Olivia until she asked me what was so funny. "Noth-
> ing," I said, "except that I thought you were one." She grinned right
> back. "I thought you were one," she murmured. "Until tonight, that is"
> [Hubler, p. 192].

With the help of the FBI, he had seen the light. It is a touching reversal of Orwell: under the spreading chestnut tree, she did *not* have to sell him, nor he her.

Those who say Reagan's career suffered, or his marriage did, because he was wrapped up in union affairs in the late forties underestimate the urgency of his mission. He was busy at saving the nation. This was more important than the movies. In fact it was the reality the movies could only hint at. He had been a T-Man in his Bancroft series. Now he was really T-10, a servant of his government against the most dangerous kind of conspiracy. He had not been with Neil during his period of ambush from the Bel-Air shrubbery. But now he, too, was helping the FBI. Both Reagans were once again G-Men.

Reagan received a threatening phone call during the tensest period of the CSU strike, and the police outfitted him with a gun. He knew he was not merely facing petty thugs. An international movement was out to stop him. Later, as President-elect, he would tell three *Time* reporters, in a taped interview, that the Russians were unhappy over his election: "You see, they remember back, I guess, to those union days when we had a domestic Communist problem. I was very definitely on the wrong side for them."[32] This has almost the ring of General MacArthur's claim that the Kremlin had been out to get him since he prevented the Bonus Arm from overthrowing America's government. Reagan proves that such a belief can be held not only sincerely but without megalomania.

CHAPTER 27

MPIC: Rituals of Clearance

Destruction with destruction to destroy.
—Paradise Lost *10.1006*

The founders of the Motion Picture Alliance for the Preservation of American Ideals (MPA) had the courage of their principles in 1944. They were opposing not only communism, but the New Deal, labor unions, and civil rights organizations at a time when others connected with those causes were pulling together for the war effort, postponing their differences for the duration. Through all the time of later blacklisting, these pioneers would say they were the first to be discriminated against, as some of them doubtless were. They were widely disliked. Some, like Walt Disney and Cecil B. DeMille, resisted unions in general. Others had opposed the forming of their respective talent guilds. A large bloc of Alliance founders—John Lee Mahin, Morrie Ryskind, Rupert Hughes, and Howard Emmett Rogers—were involved in Thalberg's attempt to undo the Screen Writers Guild.[1] Others went back to Louis B. Mayer's use of the Academy as an anti-union force. But all were sincere anti-Communists, whatever their other political sympathies.

The first President of the Alliance, Sam Wood, was so obsessed with communism that his daughter says his fatal stroke was brought on by a morning of Alliance controversies. Her opinion may have been colored by the fact that Wood made all his heirs except his widow file court affidavits that they "are not now, nor have they ever been, Communists" as a condition of inheritance.[2] These were dedicated people. A later president of the Alliance, John Wayne, remembered its founding days as the time "while Roosevelt was giving the world communism."[3] The popular front for which Browder would be punished as too cozy with liberals looked, from the other side, like a takeover of the whole war and Roosevelt government by the Communists.

The final touch for completing the early unpopularity of the Alliance was

its call for government investigation of Hollywood.⁴ Producers already resented the intervention of the NLRB in their labor affairs. Liberals feared
censorship. Some conservatives opposed government regulation in the name
of the autonomy of corporations. When the Dies Committee had looked,
briefly, at Hollywood in 1939, that angered almost everyone, including Jack
Tenney and Sam Yorty.⁵ From every quarter, Hollywood let Washington
know it had no trouble it could not take care of on its own. Leaders of the
Alliance were told to keep things "within the family." But they were too
dedicated to go along with that advice.

They say that beaten children grow up to be child beaters. Any mistreat-
ment Alliance members suffered in the organization's early years would be
well repaid. But for three years the Hollywood community held Congress
off. One of the more revealing outbursts in the Reagan FBI file is a note in J.
Edgar Hoover's handwriting on a 1946 report about Communist infiltration
of the Motion Picture Industry. "It is outrageous that House Un-American
Activities Committee got cold feet and dropped Hollywood Investigation."⁶
But Hoover would keep pushing, and so would the Alliance. The very next
year, they got their way.

The Alliance had been growing stronger in the interval, helped not only
by the increasing international tension with Russia but by the petty sectari-
anism and self-defeating shifts of the Communist Party's line in Hollywood.
(The Party was, in these years, disillusioning and driving out some of the
people who would later be imprisoned or blacklisted for belonging to it.) One
of the most important recruits to the Alliance was a man reluctantly accepted in 1945. When Roy Brewer joined, some of those who opposed labor
in general, or the racketeering background of the IA in particular, handed in
their resignations. Besides, Brewer was a Democrat. But he soon demonstrated that few could outdo him in the hot pursuit of Communists, apparent
Communists, or their sympathizers.

Brewer was a union troubleshooter sent to Hollywood on temporary assignment in March of 1945 to cope with the first CSU strike. The A.F. of L.
had found charges of communism useful in dealing with the CIO. They were
just as useful in dealing with another A.F. of L. union, so long as that union
was the CSU. Opportunity seems to have marched with conviction in Brewer's opposition to communism. Indeed, his zeal became self-fueling, growing
merely by going. Jack Dales, the executive secretary of SAG who dealt with
Brewer throughout the strike period and beyond, is an anti-Communist who
calls himself "very conservative," yet he could not match (or approve of)
Brewer's degree of panic. He said in 1981:

> Roy Brewer was very close to Reagan—and I guess he still is to a
> degree—but that was all over the non-Communist thing. Roy Brewer, a
> friend of mine, is a gung-ho anti-Communist. I used to say he saw
> Communists under every bush, you know, that kind of thing. He's not
> uneducated. He's remarkably well educated in that field as in others,
> and he can argue me under the table with respect to it. But I still always

had a little thing in the back of my mind. I don't want to be that involved; I'm not that gung-ho. But he and Reagan were very close.[7]

Brewer succeeded John Wayne as president of the Alliance, and worked with him on a resolution passed during Wayne's presidency that called for the City of Los Angeles to register all Communists within its boundaries.

When Brewer came to Hollywood in response to the 1945 strike, he found Herb Sorrell was not only a professional rival but a convenient target for all his fears of Communism. When he met with the producers in August and September of 1946, to plan the "hot sets" device for driving the CSU from the lots, he undoubtedly meant also to rid the town of what he considered its worst Communist threat. Reagan had joined him in this effort by the end of the year, and their cooperation would continue into a series of anti-Communist activities. In 1948, the two formed the Labor League of Hollywood Voters to vet the anti-Communist credentials of political candidates.[8] In 1949, the two were founding vice presidents of the Motion Picture Industrial Council (MPIC), a producers' public relations organization meant to convince the public that Hollywood had "cleaned house" of its Communists.[9] One of its major functions, in the committee that both Brewer and Reagan served on, was the "clearing" of those charged with Communist ties. Brewer had become the most important man in the "rehabilitation" business, and Reagan was his close associate. As Jack Dales remembered, after Reagan became President:

He [Brewer] and Reagan were very close, and they worked very hard together during the time that I mentioned—'48, '49, early '50—of working with people who were either accused or who had been accused correctly, let alone falsely, of trying to get them to turn around. So, they worked very closely together. Roy, I think, still sees him occasionally.[10]

Reagan's FBI file, which had dark things to say about the organizations he joined in 1945 and early 1946, notes with approval his many anti-Communist activities after that time. Reagan has always denied that he was involved in blacklisting or purging people—he merely helped people who had been accused. But he told a different story to the FBI:

T-10 advised Special Agent [blacked out] that he has been made a member of a committee headed by L. B. MAYER, the purpose of which allegedly is to "purge" the motion picture industry of Communist Party members, which committee was an outgrowth of the THOMAS committee hearings in Washington and the subsequent meeting of motion picture producers in New York City.[11]

Reagan, like the producers in their official statements, said this was not the ideal procedure—that the government should outlaw the Communist Party, and then legal proceedings could be taken against any members. But, pending that, Reagan would participate in the clearings.

Blacklisting had been in Hollywood from the first attempts to prevent raids on stars by banning contract jumpers, and it had always been a bad word, something that was practiced and denied with equal fervor. As Irving Thalberg had responded, when told that Luis Buñuel was being kept out of Hollywood: "We have no blacklist. But I'll see that he is taken off it."[12] The morals clause in studio contracts let producers fire employees for reasons extraneous to their work, and let other producers use that as a "market-place" argument—there is no box-office support for the immoral.

Reagan denies there was ever a blacklist in Hollywood.[13] George Murphy denies there was.[14] The quaintest denial came from John Wayne:

> There was no black list at that time [during his presidency of the Alli-ance], as some people said. That was a lot of horseshit . . . The only thing our side did that was anywhere near black listing was just running a lot of people out of the business . . . I'll never regret having helped run [screenwriter Carl] Foreman out of this country.[15]

It was not till 1953 that Howard Hughes established in the courts that the morals clause could be used to break the contract of a suspected Commu-nist.[16] But the producers had assumed that right since November of 1947 when they suspended the "Hollywood Ten" on "Article 16" grounds. Rea-gan, speaking for the Screen Actors Guild, denied that it supported any blacklist, but informed member Gale Sondergaard after she took the Fifth Amendment before the Committee: "If any actor by his own actions outside of union activities has so offended public opinion that he has made himself unsaleable at the box office, the Guild cannot and would not want to force any employers to hire him."[17] He had taken earlier steps to make such morals-testing easier for the producers. In November, 1947, at the SAG meeting that elected him to his own first full term as president, he supported the resolution that "no one shall be eligible for office in the organization unless he signs an affidavit stipulating that he is not a member of the Party."[18] Reagan also suggested that the Motion Picture Alliance send the dossiers it was collecting on everyone in Hollywood to the subjects so they could "correct" them.[19]

Given the extent of Reagan's involvement in the clearing process, which was run by the blacklisters themselves, it is surprising that he has main-tained the reputation of a moderate during the late forties and early fifties. He is even presented as something of a critic of the House Committee on Un-American Activities. Lou Cannon represents the informed consensus that existed—at least before the release of Reagan's FBI file—on Reagan's 1947 appearance before HUAC:

> In retrospect, Reagan's testimony still looks good, and even liberal crit-ics of him like Phillip Dunne have agreed that he made "a fine state-ment of civil libertarian principles on the stand" . . . Years later he would obscure his own moderate and politically astute conduct by exag-gerating the danger the Communists had posed to the film industry, quoting approvingly from the findings of the committee and denying

that a blacklist really existed. But at the time of his testimony, Reagan was both sensible and restrained, and paying the minimum homage to the committee.[20]

It is true that Reagan did not publicly name names in his testimony—a ritual of humiliation that was intended not for investigative purposes but penitential ones.[21] Reagan had broken his left-wing ties early enough, and cooperated with the FBI enthusiastically enough, to need no further disciplining. As we know now, he had named names in secret, but even there he was careful to say he had no firsthand proof of anyone's Communist membership (he had been to no Party meetings, seen no Party cards). He identified those he named as members of cliques that always voted the Party line.

Like the other "friendly witnesses," Reagan met with committee counsel before his testimony to be told what was expected from him, what he would be allowed to say. Later he complained to his FBI contact that he had not been given as much time to praise the film industry as Robert Stripling had promised him.[22] But there is a set speech on the contributions of the industry in his testimony. On the stand he quoted Hutcheson of the carpenters' union as saying he "would run this Sorrell and the other Commies out"[23]—as close as he came to naming names in public. But he said that the Hollywood community had itself been aware of the menace of communism and had controlled it, so that "I do not believe the Communists have ever at any time been able to use the motion-picture screen as a sounding board for their philosophy or their ideology."[24]

This was the stand agreed on by the producers and impressed on all those who were working with them. Even Sam Wood, who had earlier asked Congress to investigate Hollywood, told the Thomas Committee in 1947 that Washington censorship was not needed.[25] This has been praised as a civil-libertarian position, but it was actually the birth of the blacklist. The purging of suspected Communists was a preemptive move on Hollywood's part to keep the government away. It was free-enterprise censorship. Reagan and others could persuade themselves that they were actually defending freedom as they screened and circulated secret charges, protecting people from government persecution and "only" running them out of the business—for the good of the business. It was voluntarism keeping "govment" out of the regulation of private industry.

The producers had originally tried to keep Washington entirely away. Then, when subpoenas went out to "unfriendly witnesses" in 1947, lawyers were assured by Eric Johnston, the man hired to promote the industry's interests, that there would be no blacklist. But when Congress moved to cite ten of the "unfriendlies" (the Hollywoood Ten) for contempt, there was a meeting with the movies' financiers in New York—the Waldorf Conference of November 24–25, 1947—which issued a statement saying the Ten would be fired, but "we will not knowingly employ a Communist," and "we will invite the Hollywood talent guilds to work with us to eliminate any subversives, to protect the innocent, and to safeguard the free speech and a free screen wherever threatened."[26]

The resounding language of that last phrase described what Reagan, for the Screen Actors Guild, was planning with Louis B. Mayer. This is what he frankly called a "purge" to his FBI contact. Reagan deplored the necessity of doing this, but only as the producers had in their statement:

> The absence of a national policy, established by Congress, with respect to the employment of Communists in private industry makes our task difficult. Ours is a nation of laws. We request Congress to enact legislation to rid itself of subversive, disloyal elements.[27]

This stand was not at variance with Hollywood's desire to keep government away from Hollywood, since the legislation called for would not be Hollywood-specific. It would ban agents of foreign powers, and perhaps Communist Party members, under rules applying to *all* walks of life, presumably both specific enough and vague enough to prevent any special provisions for show business. Once this became the official Hollywood position, Reagan adopted it in his conversations with the FBI:

> T-10 stated it is his firm conviction that Congress should declare, first of all, by statute, that the Communist Party is not a legal Party, but is a foreign inspired conspiracy. Secondly, Congress should define what organizations are Communist-controlled so that membership therein could be construed as an indication of disloyalty. He felt that lacking such a definitive stand on the part of the Government it would be difficult for any committee of motion pictures to conduct any type of cleansing of their own household.[28]

The last part of this statement echoes the thought of the producers: "The absence of a national policy, established by Congress, with respect to the employment of Communists in private industry makes our task difficult." Reagan had some lingering doubts about this matter during his testimony before the Committee on October 23:

> Whether the party should be outlawed, I agree with the gentleman that preceded me that that is a matter for the Government to decide. As a citizen I would hesitate, or not like, to see any political party outlawed on the basis of its political ideology. We have spent 170 years in this country on the basis that democracy is strong enough to stand up and fight against the inroads of any ideology. However, if it is proven that an organization is an agent of a power, a foreign power, or in any way not a legitimate political party, and I think the Government is capable of proving that, if the proof is there, then that is another matter.[29]

When he said that, Eric Johnston was saying the same thing for the producers. A month later, when the producers changed their position, so did he. It is not surprising that another FBI informant, assuring agents that Reagan was keeping Communists out of the Guild, said he "is alleged to be influenced with regard to guild matters by the Warner Brothers motion picture interests."[30] A similar charge was often made against Roy Brewer (who ended up accepting a job from the producers), and Reagan's response to that is instructive: "Roy Brewer was one labor leader who talked as much about labor's responsibility as he did about its privilege. The class warfare boys would try to exploit this as a pro-boss attitude . . ." (Hubler, p. 183).

Most of those who have discussed in print Reagan's "conversion" from conservative to liberal, Democrat to Republican, union to management, date it, as Lou Cannon does, to his period of public relations work for General Electric (1953–62):

> The audiences on Reagan's GE tours usually were of the service club or corporate variety, and the questions thrown at him often focused on inflation or government regulation. In the process of answering these questions in a manner pleasing to the questioners, Reagan became a defender of corporations and a critic of the government that the corporate leaders thought was strangling them. The process was gradual, but pervasive. Reagan believes in what he says, and he wound up believing what he was saying. More than anything, it is his GE experience that changed Reagan from an adversary of big business into one of its most ardent spokesmen.[31]

The problem is misstated from the outset if one conceives Reagan as ever having been "an adversary of big business." He was united with the producers in his attitude toward communism—no special regulation for the industry, but a preemptive blacklist while calling for general legislation. Earlier, he had been united with them in support of the lockout over contrived hot sets—Reagan's principal union ally was Roy Brewer, who planned that operation. In a studio famous for its actors' public fights with management, where Jimmy Cagney, Bette Davis, and Olivia de Havilland were suspended or sued for insubordination, Reagan was never suspended by the irascible Jack Warner. His relations with management were always cozy, while his feelings toward fellow actors were touchy on the idea of having a closed shop in the first place. As Jack Dales, his SAG associate, put it, Reagan "was not one of those who was particularly unhappy with the Warners stock contract."[32] Before the Kearns Committee, Reagan concluded his testimony against Sorrell and the CSU by saying: "I think one of the greatest tragedies as the result of this labor strife that we have been through is the fact that it breaks up this closely knit family unit."[33] The paternalistic Louis B. Mayer could not have put it better.

Though Reagan did not change his party registration until 1962, his world and his views were conservative, business-oriented and actively anti-Communist from 1947 on. His "union period" is as much marked by work with the Motion Picture Alliance and the Motion Picture Industry Council as with the Screen Actors Guild. The MPIC was especially important, as Brewer's main instrument for clearing blacklisted actors. The Council had tried to

pass a loyalty oath for the whole industry.[34] Brewer, a Democrat, used the
MPIC to oppose the campaign of Henry Wallace in 1948.[35] Reagan, a Democrat, used his party registration to run "Democrats for Eisenhower" in 1952.
They were both conservatives all along. One of the clearing channels for
Brewer would be Victor Riesel's column, which could damn or give dispen-
sation to suspect Reds. Reagan's place in the Hollywood "disinfecting" process was assured from the time when he wrote a 1947 "guest column" for
Riesel, dutifully inserted in his FBI file.[36] That was not a column liberals
were writing then.

Reagan is quite right when he says that he did not suffer any conversion
from left to right. His experience held aspects of them both, and he felt a
perfect continuity with his past in the efforts of the forties. On the one hand,
he was a patriot, an admirer of the armed services and the intelligence
agencies of the government, loyally spying on people for national security
reasons. He was Brass Bancroft; he was the FBI's informer T-10. On the
other hand, he was the booster of an ideal community that should not be
tampered with by authority: he was the Eureka freshman expelling the president from a happy faculty-student concord. He was anti-Communist, and
therefore willing to use governmental powers against communism. But he
was antigovernment when it came to the regulation of the movie business, or
any other business. All these personae were always present in him, and were
not felt to be at odds. Like much of America, he contained contradictions,
but never experienced them.

Reagan remains unapologetic about his part in the purge days of Hollywood—unlike his conservative colleague, SAG executive director Jack
Dales. Dales told a SAG interviewer in 1979:

> I was not a Ronnie Reagan or a Roy Brewer . . . I would argue with
> them when it got to be how far we were going, particularly when it got
> to be the clearing people for work. I think of people now who I think
> were terribly mistreated—Larry Parks, Marcia Hunt . . . I talked to
> Ronnie Reagan since, not recently, but since, and he has no doubts
> about the propriety of what we did. I do.[37]

The measure of Reagan's impenitence can be seen in one of his presidential
appointments. In 1984 he appointed Roy Brewer of IATSE, the framer of
the "hot sets" scheme and the father of the Hollywood clearing process, to
the Federal Impasses Panel for adjudicating labor disputes with the government.[38] Reagan had remained, in his own view of things, a "rabid union
man."

PART SIX

COMPANY MAN

CHAPTER 28

MCA: The Deal

*The central fact of MCA's whole rise to power . . .
was undoubtedly the blanket waiver.*

—*Justice Department memorandum*

Reagan not only got along well with management, he did a much rarer thing in Hollywood—he got along with his agent. David Niven has eloquently described the actor's temptation, whether rising or falling, to change agents often and impulsively.[1] It is customary to blame agents for missed opportunities, mistaken role choices, disadvantageous contracts. As Reagan, in a candid moment before a grand jury, said: "Van Heflin is in and out of MCA [his own agency] like somebody going in and out of a department store."[2] Yet Reagan, through all his slow rise and painful decline as a screen star, stayed with the same agent—the very first one he had talked to about an audition. He would be divorced from Jane Wyman, but both would stay true to the same agent. Taft Schreiber, of the agency in question, told Bill Boyarsky: "He only had this one agency. Most actors blamed their agents. He understood. He had a very sound grasp of the situation."[3] Actually, Reagan was taken into the Music Corporation of America along with his first agent, William Meiklejohn, and from then on the fates of Reagan and of MCA were interdependent. He was the first actor for which the agency wrote a million-dollar contract, and he was the actor who did more for the agency than any other during his presidency of SAG.

MCA was the band-booking giant created by Jules Stein in 1924. Stein, an ophthalmologist who played in bands for a hobby, changed the way bands lived after he began scheduling their appearances as a business.[4] His players were kept constantly on the road, doing brief stands to give a new attraction every night or every week to the popular ballrooms of the time. In 1940, Jack Teagarden improvised a farewell to his New York fans, singing he would not be back for many a day "cause I'm on the road for MCA."[5] Stein built a little empire of musicians under exclusive contract to him, coping with nightclub gangsters during the prohibition era in Chicago. In 1936, he hired Lew Wasserman, a public relations man in a casino, to represent clients passing through Chicago. In 1938, he sent Wasserman to Hollywood, just a year after Reagan arrived there. Wasserman soon united Meiklejohn and Reagan with his rise. A portent of that rise was the contract he negotiated for Reagan after *Kings Row*. Warners wanted to change Reagan's contract before the picture was released, to keep his demands low, and Reagan naturally resisted. But Wasserman persuaded him that he would soon be drafted into the military, and it was better to have a sure thing waiting for him when he came out than to gamble on the chances of wartime. Wasserman dearly wanted to write this contract, for a reason Reagan says he did not know about beforehand:

> One thing about the new contract puzzled me. All contracts are for forty weeks a year; mine was for forty-three. This particular demand of Lew's puzzled Jack Warner too. When all the commas were in place, J. L. said to Lew, "Now will you tell me why I've just given in to the only forty-three-week deal in the whole industry?" Lew grinned like a kid with a hand in the cookie jar. "I knew you wouldn't go higher than three thousand five hundred dollars," he said, "and I've never written a million-dollar deal before—so three extra weeks for seven years makes this my first million-dollar sale" [Hubler, p. 123].

It was the quiet beginning of a whole new financial period in Hollywood, that of the modern "deal"—the symbolic big money on paper that means the dealer is moving up (or staying there). Joan Didion described the magical property such numbers had acquired by 1973:

> The action itself is an art form, and is described in aesthetic terms: "A very imaginative deal," they say, or, "He writes the most creative deals in the business." . . . I talk on the telephone to an agent, who tells me that he has on his desk a check made out to a client for $1,275,000, the client's share of first profits on a movie now in release. Last week, in someone's office, I was shown another such check, this one made out for $4,850,000. Every year there are a few such checks around town. An agent will speak of such a check as being "on my desk," or "on Guy McIlwaine's desk," as if the exact physical location lent the piece of paper its credibility . . . the actual pieces of paper which bear such numbers have, in the community, a totemic significance. They are totems of the action.[6]

Reagan's contract was made by the father of all such deals in modern Hollywood, and was a minor step toward the financial heights Wasserman would scale. But there was already an air of unreality about the affair, one that Didion identifies as the presiding mark of the deal: Wasserman was getting money ahead of time for what might come to nothing. In any case, he had set a mark for himself that others must pay attention to. In fact, as things turned out after the war, Wasserman had priced Reagan out of the market he would have preferred. Warners had bought, at its top price for such an item, a light romantic comic lead. The only way for Reagan to retain the value they put on him was to keep playing those parts.

When Reagan grew restive with such casting, by 1949, Wasserman was there to oblige. So long as an actor stays with the same agent, the more he moves studios, the more action there is for the agent. That was the reason the studios tried to break the power of agents in the 1934 code that led to the formation of the Screen Actors Guild. Wasserman first loosened up Reagan's commitment to Warners: one picture a year for half the money, rather than three for full money. (The studio no longer valued Reagan so highly and was willing to write off the financial loss to *avoid* making many pictures with him.) Then Wasserman signed him at Universal (which MCA would later own) for five pictures rather than an exclusive contract for a period of years.[7] Reagan would shop around from studio to studio to make his Westerns, damaging his career as he fulfilled his dreams. Wasserman was there, unable to prevent the stall in his client's professional life but cushioning the glide down. When a crash landing loomed, MCA reverted to its old form of booking, and arranged for him to appear in a Las Vegas act. But it owed him something better than that. Reagan, as President of the Screen Actors Guild, did as much for the agency as it did for him.

His favors for it were performed in 1952 and 1954, and they made MCA's Revue Productions the leading producer of television shows in Hollywood. In the early fifties, the large studios were trying to keep movies off the little screen. Television advertising could not pay, yet, what theaters could, or even the costs of large-scale production. The majors hoped, with lessening conviction, that such a condition could be maintained, making television offer shabby as well as tiny competition to their own more lavish outpourings on the large screen. But minor studios, by 1951, were already trying to release their films to TV. One objection, which would take many forms over the years, came from actors and musicians who wanted new contracts for release of film in this medium. Republic, Monogram, and Lippert were able to release old films only if they made new sound tracks that gave another round of jobs to members of the American Federation of Musicians.[8] They made the new tracks.

Though television had its early center in New York (where Nancy Davis appeared on the infant medium), it was bound to move, as it grew, toward Hollywood, where the supply of actors, directors, and equipment was endless. By June of 1951 Jack Gould was reporting in the New York *Times:*

> Production of films especially for television is a growing business in Hollywood, and seems certain to increase. According to one source, film footage for TV was being produced in May at a rate of 988 hours a year, compared with 855 hours of feature films for theater showing . . . A matter for major speculation has been the possibility of "a marriage" between TV and Hollywood. While many deals have been rumored periodically, the only concrete development has been the contemplated merger of the American Broadcasting Company with United

Paramount Theaters, which is a theatre chain and is not to be confused with the producing concern, Paramount Pictures.[9]

In 1952, the FCC was loosening its restrictions on the number of television stations, advertising revenue was on the rise, and it was getting harder for Hollywood studios to stay out of the game. At this point MCA, which had already produced a number of television shows in Hollywood, planned to form Revue Productions, to go into regular production employing many of its own actors. It would be tailored to television, avoiding the large costs to major studios if they came in. If MCA moved swiftly it could preclude such an entry. The agency did not have, yet, the "residuals" problem of backlogs that tied up studios with actors' claims. This seemed the perfect time for MCA to preempt the field.

There was one problem. The Screen Actors Guild refused, by long-settled policy, to let its actors retain agents who were also movie producers—refused, that is, to let the agents be spokesmen for labor and management at the same time, like lawyers serving both parties. So firm was the Guild about conflicts of interest that Robert Montgomery had to resign as SAG president (allowing the board to replace him with Reagan) because he had become a producer as well as an actor.

Special waivers had been granted in special cases—e.g., to let an agent help put up the money for a movie that would employ his clients. But these had been case-by-case exceptions. Television production had not become extensive enough in Hollywood for the Guild to extend its ban on agents as producers into this new field (which allowed MCA to produce its shows before 1952). But no one doubted that, as the production grew, the same ban would be applied, since the same principle was involved. Anticipating that action, Jules Stein and Lew Wasserman of MCA approached Reagan and Jack Dales of the Guild to confide in them. They would undertake production on an ambitious scale, furnishing employment to Hollywood actors, but they could only do this if the Guild would not undercut the project at some future date by making production an impermissible activity for agents.

This was not the first time MCA had sought a blanket waiver of this sort from a union. Back in his band-booking days, Jules Stein had formed close ties with James Petrillo, who was the founder of the American Federation of Musicians. The AFM's bylaws made it impossible for musicians to use agents who were also producing nightclub acts; but Petrillo granted MCA an exclusive waiver of that rule, along with other special favors.[10]

The MCA men came to SAG with a benefit to offer for services rendered. The Agency's lawyer, Laurence Beilenson, later spelled out the terms under which it sought the waiver: MCA "was willing to sign a contract giving the Guild members reuse fees [residuals] when no one else was willing to do so."[11] The deal was cozily made, and its terms kept secret. Even the lawyer who served as intermediary exemplified the conflict of interest that runs through the acts of the participants like a tune transposed: Larry Beilenson had been the Guild's lawyer in its early days and was now MCA's, the intimate of both sides. Beilenson, in fact, had recruited Jack Dales to SAG in the late thirties.[12]

On July 14, 1952, Reagan signed an unprecedented blanket waiver for MCA to produce an unlimited number of television shows. Each side had reason to keep the terms of the waiver confidential. MCA did not want it to appear that granting actors residuals was the price of a general waiver, since other agencies were undoubtedly willing to pay that price for a similar grant. Also, MCA did not want to be known in the industry as sabotaging the producers' opposition to residuals. The Guild wanted to prevent the appearance of a kickback to its members for the favor granted—an appearance that the Justice Department took very seriously when it discovered, years later, the terms of the grant.

The reason Reagan and Dales gave for the Guild's action was the need for employment in Hollywood. Dales put it this way:

> Lew Wasserman and Jules Stein came to us and said, "Do you know what's happening? It's all going to New York. Your guys are not going to get a whiff of it [television acting]," which we already knew. But the only reason they brought it to us was that "We would like to do it. We'd like to go into it, and we'll guarantee to make lots of filmed television *if* you can work it out with us as an agent." Well, of course, that was a shocking thought then, but we thought about it. I don't know if you've ever looked at the deal that was made, but they could not charge their own clients in a picture [of their own] any commission; if they ever put their client in a picture made by them, he had to get the highest salary he'd ever gotten in any picture in his life. It was just loaded with that kind of thing. We were scared that we were going to lose television [to New York], and that's the way we started.[13]

It is not a convincing statement. For one thing the Guild represented the television actors in New York as well as in California. Admittedly there were fewer actors in New York, but jobs there were not taken from Guild members.[14] Besides, the idea that television was draining away from Hollywood in 1952, rather than drifting toward it, is false. We have seen Jack Gould's report from the preceding year of increased hours of Hollywood filming, studio deals with musicians, impending deals, and studio interest in the medium. Reagan himself had acted on television as early as December 7, 1950, when he starred in an episode of Airflyte Theatre.[15] Finally, if the aim of the waiver was to promote employment, why not encourage as many agents as possible to produce television shows, rather than give a monopoly to one? Reagan would later be asked that question before a grand jury. He answered:

> Well, that is very easy to recall. Screen Actors Guild board and executives met in meetings and very carefully considered these things, weighed them at board meetings. I remember discussions taking place

about it and usually the result of the discussions would be that we felt we were amply protected, that if any harm started from this, if anything happened to react against the actors' interest—we could always pull the rug out from under them [MCA].[16]

That does not answer the questions asked. It also neglects the fact that Reagan and his wife, both Guild board members, were in no position to "pull the rug out from under" MCA after 1953, since his whole new career was based on the success of one of the agency's first major productions, the General Electric Theater. In 1954, while Reagan was appearing on that show, and still serving with his wife on the SAG board, the Guild made its expected formal extension of the ban to agents producing television as well as movies. Partial and specific exceptions were made for projects under way. But twenty-four hours before those partial grants were negotiated, a private session had extended MCA's general waiver, giving it a monopoly on that privilege so far as agencies were concerned.[17] The extension was granted in the form of a revision of the 1952 waiver Reagan had signed.[18]

That act, more than anything else Reagan did in Hollywood—as actor, as labor leader, as anti-Communist—shaped the future of Hollywood. It made MCA the first and biggest of the new breed of superagents, who in time replaced the studios as Hollywood's power center with "the packager." The Supreme Court had taken away the industry's vertical integration of movie production and distribution in 1948. The new entrepreneurs would achieve a kind of horizontal integration denied to the old Hollywood, in which money men from New York, and the stars with their agents and guilds, inhibited the studio chiefs. Raymond Chandler predicted the future of the Hollywood agent in the very year of the waiver, 1952:

He could create packaging corporations which delivered complete. shows to the networks or the advertising agencies, and he loaded them with talent which, sometimes under another corporate name, he represented as an agent. He took his commission for getting you a job, and then he sold the job itself for an additional profit.[19]

That is a precise description of Reagan's first contract with the General Electric Theater. He was technically employed by the advertising agency (Batten, Barton, Durstine and Osborn) to which MCA had sold the show, which allowed MCA to keep collecting its 10 percent from Reagan's salary.[20]

MCA was launched on a dizzying course. Its income from production soon passed that from its agency fees. In 1958 it bought Paramount's backlog of films and the Universal backlot (Hollywood's largest). In 1962, it bought Decca Records and the Universal Studio. Just ten years after the waiver that brought the company into production on a large scale, it controlled 60 percent of the entertainment industry, while the original talent agency accounted for only 10 percent of its income.[21]

The giant was creating many imitators: "By the 1970s most of the major Hollywood studios were run by graduates of these huge enterprises [the agencies], while so many agents had crossed over to produce films with their own clients that it was becoming almost impossible to tell the two functions (of agenting and producing) apart."[22] Some of the most famous packagers of talent are graduates of MCA.

Even its flops helped support MCA. The production team has to rent the studio space, use the talent and equipment, keep Universal City going with its tours and pretentious hotel and expensive restaurants. It is a kind of Disneyland that makes pictures. In his old band-booking days, Jules Stein sold his acts as a package, making dance halls take his chimpanzee act one night to get Guy Lombardo the next week. MCA's flops are its chimpanzee acts. The dealer mixes and matches, keeping the tour up. Joan Didion catches the tone of a Hollywood that had been MCA-ized:

> At the next table were an agent and a director who should have been, at that moment, on his way to a location to begin a new picture. I knew what he was supposed to be doing because this picture had been talked about around town: six million dollars above the line. There was one million for one actor, there was a million and a quarter for another actor. The director was in for $800,000. The property had cost more than half a million, the first-draft screenplay $200,000, the second draft a little less. A third writer had been brought in, at $6,000 a week. Among the three writers were two Academy Awards and one New York Film Critics Award. The director had an Academy Award for his last picture but one.
>
> And now the director was sitting at lunch in Beverly Hills and he wanted out. The script was not right. Only 38 pages worked, the director said. The financing was shaky. "They're in breach, we all recognize your right to pull out," the agent said carefully. The agent represented many of the principals, and did not want the director to pull out. On the other hand he also represented the director, and the director seemed unhappy. It was difficult to ascertain what anyone involved did want, except for the action to continue. "You pull out," the agent said, "it dies right here, not that I want to influence your decisions." The director picked up the bottle of Margaux they were drinking and examined the label.
>
> "Nice little red," the agent said.
>
> "Very nice."
>
> I left as the Sanka was being served. No decision had been reached. Many people have been talking these past few days about this aborted picture, always with a note of regret. It had been a very creative deal and they had run with it as far as they could run and they had had some fun and now the fun was over, as it also would have been had they made the picture.[23]

And Reagan shared in the action. When MCA's Vice President, Taft Schreiber, came to him with the General Electric offer, Reagan admits, "They weren't beating a path to my door offering me parts, and then this television show came riding along. The cavalry to the rescue."[24] His career

had a second springtime. No more Las Vegas acts. "General Electric Theater" climbed rapidly in the ratings—from number nineteen in 1954–55, to
number ten in 1955–56, to number three in 1956–57.[25] It was regularly the
number one show in its desirable prime-time slot, nine o'clock on Sunday
night. It came, in the strong CBS lineup, between "The Ed Sullivan Show"
and "Alfred Hitchcock Presents."[26] Reagan as host was given a vehicle for
becoming familiar to a whole new generation of young people who would
later vote for him. They were the first television generation, being introduced
to the man who would use television better than any other politician. He was
a dignified greeter of the stars, pleasant without being patronizing. He not
only acted in some of the shows, but produced one episode in 1955 ("Seeds
of Hate").[27] Furthermore, Nancy Davis, who had been on the Guild board
when both waivers were given MCA, played the female lead in four episodes
of General Electric Theater.[28] Of the six actors represented by MCA who
served on the SAG board that granted the waivers, four acted on General
Electric Theater—Leon Ames twice and Audrey Totter twice, besides the
Reagans.[29]

In 1959, MCA began paying Reagan directly, which meant dropping his
agent's fee—in effect, a 10 percent raise.[30] This was necessary if Reagan was
to become part owner of the show (and not, as theretofore, a mere employee
of the sponsor's advertising agency). "I had had MCA exploring with General Electric and BBD&O if there wasn't some way I could cut down my
senior partner, the Department of Internal Revenue, and start building for
the future, instead of taking everything in straight income."[31] He says he
asked for a cut in the reruns of shows he acted in, but MCA secured him 25
percent of all the shows' eventual proceeds. "I haven't even read the pictures, and I own 25 percent of them."[32] Admitting that he would not see any
returns from this for a while, Reagan said, "We run a little loss." The Justice
Department interrogator rather testily responded: "Don't say 'we.' You are
running the loss."[33] But Reagan's solidarity with MCA justified the "we."
He explained that the producer does not expect a sponsor to cover all costs
of the first run—he was speaking as a partner to MCA's Revue Productions.

General Electric canceled its television show in 1962, but MCA continued
to take care of Ronald Reagan. It was his agent for Death Valley Days under
another sponsor, and the agency's own Revue Productions starred him in
the made-for-television movie The Killers in 1964. Meanwhile Taft Schreiber, MCA's Republican donor (as Jules Stein was its Democratic donor),
had encouraged Reagan to change political parties in 1962, and to join in
campaign activities culminating in the Goldwater effort. Schreiber, with Cy
Rubel, Holmes Tuttle, and Henry Salvatori, was the mobilizer of the Friends
of Reagan preparing for the 1966 gubernatorial race. And Schreiber did
more than solicit public support for Reagan. With Stein's help, he negotiated
the sale of Reagan's second "ranch," a canyon property in the Santa Monica
mountains, since Reagan said he needed financial security in a political career. Stein and Schreiber sold the land to 20th Century-Fox, the studio of

Richard Zanuck, another Friend of Reagan, for $8,000 an acre, though Reagan had purchased it (fifteen years earlier) for only $293 an acre and the studio would resell it (to the state of California, during Reagan's incumbency as governor) for only $1,800 an acre. MCA officials can be very persuasive when talking to the motion picture industry. As Moldea and Goldberg note: "On an initial $65,000 investment for the 236 acres, after fifteen years Reagan pocketed nearly two million dollars—for more than a 3,000 percent profit."[34]

Reagan told Lou Cannon in 1967 that selling the ranch had been a *prior* necessity for his campaign: "I could not have *run* for office unless I'd sold the ranch" (emphasis added).[35] But the sale was not made to Fox until December 13, 1966 (completed January 31, 1967), when he was already governor.[36] Schreiber had been Reagan's campaign vice chairman. Stein was put in charge of the trust that would handle his money while he was in office. William French Smith, Reagan's lawyer in the transaction, would be intimately involved in his real estate and political life. Nancy Reagan has explained the sale of the ranch as part of the sacrifice her husband made in accepting a low-salaried public office: "Ronnie had taken a large cut in income when he left television to become governor. We simply could not afford the luxury of a ranch."[37]

Yet two years into his governor's term, which was supposed to be exacting such financial sacrifice from him, Reagan bought a far more expensive ranch, of 778 acres in Riverside County, through the trust headed by Jules Stein.[38] As down payment on this purchase, the trustees used fifty-four acres of land left over from the 20th Century-Fox sale, which was accepted by the sellers at five times its assessed value.[39] The partners doing the selling—which included Kaiser Aluminum—were in a mood to be generous to the governor and his MCA spokesman.

There was only one hitch. If the sellers could not unload the fifty-four acres within a year, Reagan would have to buy them back at the inflated price. It was apparently hard to find a buyer for this overpriced hill land, since Stein had to resort to a company of his own—the 57th Madison Corporation—as purchaser, though it never bought other real estate outside New York.[40] Eventually, when Reagan was running for the presidency, he sold his Riverside ranch for well over twice its purchase price, in a secret deal with a developer.[41]

On some of the ranchland, Reagan was given the tax break California has devised to protect landholders against developers. But Stein, a friend of great ingenuity, came up with other tax shelters as well. In 1970 he introduced the governor to Harold L. Oppenheimer of Kansas City, whose cattle-breeding firm welcomed large investors looking for a break with the IRS. In a 1975 interview Reagan vaguely said, "I knew the guy who does this, bought this herd of bulls." He certainly knew the man who owned the firm. It was Jules Stein himself, Harold Oppenheimer's stepfather.[42]

As a result of such expert management of his burgeoning assets, Reagan grew wealthy in office while paying very low taxes on his acquisitions. He steadfastly fought disclosure of his tax returns, but the Sacramento *Bee* finally circumvented his defenses and revealed that he had paid only an average of $1,000 a year in state taxes for the four years preceding 1970, and *no* state taxes in 1970. Reagan's only response was to denounce this illegal "invasion of privacy," but his aides said he had suffered business reversals in 1970.[43] The "business reverses" were his tax shelters.

Some of Reagan's California critics maintain that MCA, in one of its acquisitive fits, simply bought itself a governor in 1966. That is clearly going too far. But the parts played by MCA men and money—by Stein and Schreiber and Wasserman, by the 1952 SAG deal, the General Electric contracts, the Revue Productions partnership, the 57th Madison Corporation, and Harold Oppenheimer, by the political and financial network mobilizable in California through the entertainment industry—should make us look at the conjunction of actor and politician in a new way. It is often said that Reagan's acting career was an advantage to him in politics, since it taught him delivery, timing, and "communication." In California, at least, it was an advantage in some ways more concrete and downright bankable.

Yet it seems that Reagan's political career would not have emerged at all if the circumstances of a 1962 investigation had become known at the time; if an indictment of Reagan, seriously considered for months by the Justice Department, had been brought or even publicly threatened; if a civil suit of conspiracy against the MCA had not been settled by a divestiture. Had any or all of these things turned out other than they did, it would have been hard or impossible for MCA to support Reagan in 1966 without at least the appearance of embarrassing payoffs. The 1966 victory depended, though Reagan was no doubt unaware of it at the time, on the failure of the 1962 investigation to reach the level of public notice.

CHAPTER 29

MCA: The Investigation

And all of this, including the opinions of myself, is vague at the Guild on everything that took place for all those years all the way back including whether I was present or not.

—Ronald Reagan, to Grand Jury

While Robert Kennedy was Attorney General, the Justice Department examined the extent of MCA's control over show business, its possible conflicts of interest, its overlapping relationships with clients, studios, and networks. This was the era of "payola" scandals in the music industry, a form of bribery by preferential treatment. MCA was in a position to get its way in many areas by offering jobs, promotion, recording opportunities, productions scheduled with one studio rather than another. Nat Hentoff explained, in 1961, how ubiquitous was MCA:

> An independent packager trying to sell a new series to a network may discover that the particular stars he wants for that series are represented by MCA, and somehow are not currently available. MCA meanwhile may be trying to sell the same network its own Revue production involving the very stars the independent producer wanted. Whenever possible, MCA prefers to control the whole package . . . On occasion, MCA may produce a series in partnership with one of its leading stars. But since the series is produced at its own Revue Studios, MCA can also collect overhead and studio rental, thereby coming into a larger share of the eventual profit than its partners. When and if the same series is shown as a rerun, either on a network or in local markets, MCA as sales agent for the package takes another forty percent off the top from network reruns, thirty to fifty percent from non-network showings in this country, and fifty percent from sales overseas.[1]

Thus, apart from all its other interests, MCA was producing over 40 percent of all prime-time television by 1961.

Even before the coming of television, the antitrust division of the Justice Department had kept an eye on MCA's aggressive activities. A World War II investigation was suspended because of the international crisis. In 1945 a San Diego dance hall operator won a private suit against MCA for coercive booking practices. The judge in this case gave MCA the nickname that stuck —the Octopus, its "tentacles reaching out to all phases and grasping everything in show business."[2] Eight investigations had been launched by the antitrust division before 1961, but the Justice Department was repeatedly baffled, since "evidence was difficult to obtain; attempts to obtain evidence voluntarily from MCA's files proved [futile]; witnesses exhibited intense fear of reprisal."[3] MCA was secretive about everything, even its list of clients. Taft Schreiber refused, even under subpoena, to give the Federal Communications Commission a list of its television programs unless he was guaranteed a private hearing with sealed transcripts.[4]

Reagan, sharing the attitude of his friend Taft Schreiber, deeply resented the government's curiosity about MCA:

> Feuding is a mild word to use when one is talking of our government's campaign against a private business concern . . . My [Justice Department] inquisitor had spent weeks at the Guild, prying through drawers and files and buttonholing secretaries on their way to lunch, to ask slyly if the Guild didn't have some secret files he hadn't been shown [Hubler, pp. 325–26].

The MCA investigation had led to the Guild because of the waivers in 1952 and 1954. And the Department was, indeed, looking for secrets. Documents released under the Freedom of Information Act to *Daily Variety* show that Reagan's IRS returns were investigated by the FBI, along with those of his wife and the other MCA clients on the board when the waivers were granted. Little over a decade earlier, Reagan had cooperated with such FBI prying and informing when Herb Sorrell was the target. But Sorrell was an uneducated painter who spoke the language of the streets—the kind of "thug" Treasury agent Brass Bancroft beat up in his pursuit of financial malefactors. The neatly dressed and respectable corporate heads of MCA seemed beyond governmental scrutiny, so far as Reagan was concerned.

On the day of his own testimony to the grand jury, February 5, 1962, Reagan had lunch with actress Jeanne Crain and the director of the General Electric Theater episode they were making; they joked about finding out that afternoon whether they were all still working for MCA; Reagan apologized to the grand jury for appearing without a tie (he had been called directly from the set).[5] Though he recalled little for the jurors about the waivers, he was certain about two things, both of which proved false—that other agencies had been given the same kind of waiver as MCA, and that no arrangement about returns had been involved in the granting of the waiver. On both those grounds, Reagan argued, there was nothing special about the treatment of MCA, so he could not be expected to remember much from a period that had been a "kaleidoscope of meetings."[6]

On the first point, Reagan said that "we granted an extended waiver to MCA to be engaged in production, as we had done with other people. Mr. [Charles] Feldman, who was an agent and produced feature pictures, we gave him a waiver also."[7] Besides the difference Reagan himself points out— Feldman's making of feature pictures, as opposed to television—there was another distinction, established when the examiner asked: "That was a limited waiver . . . not a blanket or unlimited waiver?" Reagan answered, "Right." He was asked for another example, and could recall none.[8] Nor has anyone since. Yet Reagan would afterward claim in his autobiography, "We had never withheld such waivers" (Hubler, p. 325). Asked before the grand jury if other agencies would be given such waivers on request, Reagan said, "If all the circumstances were the same as, they would."[9]

Which brings us to the second point—that, in Reagan's view, there were no special conditions involved in MCA's waiver.[10] Reagan denied that getting residuals had been the price for giving MCA the waiver. When his questioner read from Laurence Beilenson's letter to Lew Wasserman about "the special set of circumstances" involved in the 1952 waiver, Reagan tried to say that residuals were not the same as "a bargaining point." Asked if Beilenson's letter did not expressly make them that, Reagan had to retreat: "Mr. Beilenson is a lawyer and in charge of negotiation. It's quite conceivable then if he says it in this letter."[11]

Reagan's strategy was to retreat toward constantly expanding areas of forgetfulness. At first, he thought he could not remember anything from the summer of 1952 because he was married in March of that year, and was on a kind of extended honeymoon.[12] Later, he thought of another reason for his amnesia: "You keep saying in the summer. I think maybe one of the reasons I don't recall was because I feel that in the summer of 1952 I was up in Glacier National Park making a cowboy picture for RKO, Ben Borgeaus Productions, so it's very possible there were some things going on that I would not participate in but I have no recollection of this particularly."[13] *(Cattle Queen of Montana* was made in 1954, not 1952.)

Reagan tried several evasive turns, even though they were at odds with his general line of defense. Most of the time he said there were no special circumstances involved in the waivers, so he could not remember anything about granting them. But sometimes he said he remembered avoiding discussions of them *because* the circumstances were special—he was a client of the agency: "I must tell you that I always told Jack Dales in the Guild that I realized that I felt a little self-conscious about that, lest there might ever be a misunderstanding because of the fact that I had been so long with MCA, and sometimes I kind of ran for cover and was very happy to duck a committee duty in these matters."[14] Later, referring to the *partial* waiver MCA was granted in 1949, Reagan said, "I think I kind of ran for cover and ducked on that," explaining "I was always very conscious of my position in the Guild and also my relationship with Lew and he was very conscious of it."[15]

So his position is that he half-recused himself—enough to be ignorant of the proceedings. To which the normal reaction is: Why not recuse oneself entirely? Reagan was, on his own showing, responsible but uninformed. He signed the 1952 waiver. He and his wife remained voting members of the board throughout this whole transaction, as did the other four MCA clients on the board. Jack Dales, too, showed some uneasiness about Reagan's part in the waiver, and tried to buffer him from it: "I remember talking to him about it and getting encouragement, that's all."[16] The oral-history interviewer wondered if Reagan was only involved at such a remove:

Do you think there was any—
Personal?
—personal conversation between Reagan and Wasserman.
No.
Reagan and Stein?

They were very close for a while, but by that time they had split [sic]. Reagan was really more with Taft Schreiber than with Wasserman.

But Schreiber was also—I mean he was MCA.
I know, but you said between Reagan and Wasserman. No, I don't think there was, and that's the kind of thing that Wasserman—we've negotiated with Wasserman, not Schreiber.
Not with Schreiber. Was Schreiber at that time more involved in agency work than in production work?
Yes.[17]

The picture given, of MCA's top personnel acting in compartments separate from each other, is absurd. Before the grand jury, Reagan said that his personal agent at MCA was Arthur Park in 1962, but: "In MCA, when you have been around this long, you still go to Lew Wasserman on some matters."[18]

It would have been better not to bring up the subject of conflict of interest. The waivers were granted in a maze of conflicts. The Justice Department, despite the wishes of some of its investigators, did not issue criminal indictments, but it did bring a civil suit for conspiracy in restraint of trade, naming the Guild under Reagan's presidency as a coconspirator. MCA avoided having to go to trial by divesting itself of its agency (which was no longer as profitable as production). MCA and the Guild had agreed to end this conflict even before the Justice Department brought its suit.[19] But Reagan blames the government for forcing the company to hasten its divestiture:

The guiding genius of the meat-ax operation issued a pontifical statement to the press that he had "freed the slaves." We, the clients—now without representation, many of us in the midst of negotiations regarding pictures and theatrical work—were the supposed slaves. It's a good

thing this legal emancipator didn't decide to visit the slaves personally
—he'd have been beaten to death with "Oscars" [Hubler, p. 326].[20]

Actually, the agents who handled most clients were able, with MCA's blessing, to continue handling them by setting up their own agency or taking
them to other firms. MCA was able to avoid an embarrassing trial, and
Reagan was not deprived of the agency's later political support.

Reagan's conflict of interest after he went to the General Electric Theater
was compounded. Not only was he now a voting member of the Guild's
board and a client-employee of MCA; he was also a producer. After giving
the corporation permission to act as producer, he became a producer himself, while continuing to speak for labor. From the outset he was listed as
GE's "program supervisor," and he was specifically credited with the production of "Seeds of Hate," starring Charlton Heston, in 1955. Reagan told
the grand jury that he deserved credit for being a producer, but that GE
opposed this: "I wasn't getting credit as being a producer, actually being in
back of the actual productions. They resisted. They didn't want me to ever
have that much authority."[21] This difficulty was resolved in 1959, when
Reagan became part owner of the series, paid directly by MCA.

But the very next year Reagan (and the Guild) found it necessary to hide
his producer's status when he returned to the presidency of the Guild. And
that, too, was brought about by MCA. A crisis over actors' residuals was
forced on the industry by MCA's purchase of 700 Paramount films for
television release. This massive investment in nostalgia—fifty million dollars'
worth—paid for itself by 1960, just two years after the initial outlay. Income
from all future showings would be clear profit for the company—with nothing going to the actors. Some Guild members thought their leaders had sold
them out, or simply been remiss, in not pursuing the matter of residuals
from the onset of television.[22] MCA, with a stake in all aspects of production, wanted to settle on terms as favorable as it could get; but the major
studios, still resisting television on several grounds, maintained the principle
that any distribution of film—to theaters, abroad, or to TV—was their right
once they had shot the product.

Jack Dales was at the center of this controversy, as he had been in the
Communist strike of 1947, when he helped promote Reagan to his first
Guild presidency. He asked Reagan to become president again for the crucial negotiations of 1959 and 1960. Dales calls this Reagan's finest hour as a
labor leader.[23] Others claim he was sympathetic to business interests in general and to MCA in particular. Reagan was disqualified, they say, because he
had become a producer—the very thing that forced Robert Montgomery out
of the presidency in 1947. The Guild, responding to this charge, published
what is now known to be a false statement:

> Members are being told that Ronald Reagan, president of the Guild,
> produced and has an ownership interest in the television series, the
> "General Electric Theater." Ronald Reagan is a contract employee of

the advertising agency Batten, Barton, Durstine and Osborn. Under this contract he is required to appear as an actor, as a master of ceremonies and to make personal appearances. He is paid a weekly salary. He has no ownership interest, precentage participation or otherwise in the "General Electric Theater," or any other picture or series. He is not the producer of the series and he has no voice in the selection or approval of the actors employed.[24]

This was in September of 1959. As Reagan later told the grand jury, he had negotiated in March of 1959 a one-fourth ownership in the show's re-release rights, retroactive for all shows in the year when he signed the agreement.[25] Even before that, he had been "in back of the actual productions," and sometimes in front as well, as when credited with the production of the 1955 show with Charlton Heston.

According to Reagan, it was Jack Dales who asked him to return to the Guild's presidency in 1959. Whether Dales had consulted with MCA is not known. But Reagan's first instinct was to do so:

Convinced as I was that my previous service had hurt careerwise, and feeling the upsurge of success in the GE Theater after the lean period, I didn't want to answer the question at all—I just wanted to hide some place . . . Finally, I called my agent, Lew Wasserman—who else? I know that he shared my belief that my career had suffered. To tell the truth, I was positive he'd reiterate that belief and I could say "no" with a clear conscience. Well, I pulled the ripcord and the chute didn't open. Lew said he thought I should take the job [Hubler, pp. 313–14].

We hear nothing, in this account, of MCA's stake in the coming negotiations. Naturally Wasserman would be glad to have a friendly voice at the helm of the Guild, just as his agency had when the waiver launched it as a television power.

The intransigence of the major studios led to a strike of seven weeks in 1960.[26] MCA settled early with the Guild, and television production was not affected by the withdrawal of actors from seven studios. Some movie producers came over to the Guild position early on—Frank Sinatra's independent operation prominent among them. But even as Reagan was conducting the strike, he was denounced by some actors (notably Glenn Ford) for setting modest goals; Ford later considered the deal that ended the strike a sellout. Even Reagan suggests that his demands were slight. He says the producers and their negotiator were surprised at them: "Do you mean," she demanded, "that this whole thing can be ended for just what you've told me?" And the producers themselves asked with incredulity, "Can you deliver your people on such a basis?" (Hubler, p. 320).

Reagan presents the contract he achieved as a victory on three grounds:

When the strike ended we settled on (1) the principle of extra payment for reuse; (2) a sound pension and welfare plan for the SAG membership; and (3) the sale of all TV rights for the 1948–1959 pictures to the producers for a flat sum of $2,000,000 to get the pension plan moving immediately [Hubler, p. 320].

Critics of the settlement answer, to the first point, that the "principle" was established by surrendering the actual product in question—the vast horde of films made before 1960. On the second point, they claim that the pension was created to disguise the giveaway of earlier films, since—in what Reagan makes his third and separate claim—the studios made a one-time two-million-dollar payment to that fund in lieu of pre-1960 reuse payments.[27] This was a drop in the bucket for films on which MCA alone had made fifty million dollars in reruns over the preceding two years. Bob Hope, who had to say goodbye to any thought of profits from his old films, said, "The pictures were sold down the river for a certain amount of money."[28]

Having performed the task which Wasserman had assigned him, Reagan resigned his presidency before the end of his term. The reason, he says in his autobiography, was the brand-new possibility of a conflict of interests:

> A new deal had been worked out involving GE, Revue, and me—and for the first time I found myself with an ownership interest in the films we were producing for the show. According to SAG tradition, my course was predetermined. I followed in the footsteps of all those other Guild officers who had stepped down when they acquired a financial interest on the other side of the labor-management table [Hubler, p. 521].

The conflict had been there all along, and Reagan apparently did not want to risk its discovery after he had performed the necessary services of the strike period.

Despite his final compliance with the Guild "tradition," Reagan clearly does not sympathize with the principle of raising barriers against possible conflicts of interest—with financial disclosure, the ban on double representation, or the recusing of oneself where one has a stake. This seems odd, at first, since Reagan made such a point, in his inaccurate account of the student strike at Eureka, of the underclassmen's disinterested leadership of the effort where seniors and faculty had an interest. But his emphasis there was on the altruism of his individual effort. In the same way, describing the Guild, he emphasizes the way stars, from their benevolence, gave extras and free-lance actors a helping hand. So reliant is he on such charity that he would make Guild membership entirely voluntary. He is as distrustful of organized social action as he is trusting of the individual. Human motives darken only when they act in conjunction. As individuals, businessmen and officials are to be presumed virtuous, no matter how many different hats they wear. That, after all, is the way Reagan believes he conducted himself. He never spoke "just" for labor in his negotiating:

> Studios can call an actor back after a product is finished for needed closeups and added shots that weren't anticipated during regular shooting. Under such circumstances, they don't have to pay for the interven-

ing period. Some of the "quick buck" producers had developed a nasty habit of deliberately shortcutting and then getting a free ride by pretending they were calling the cast back for "added closeups" not contemplated during the scheduled production. After a bitter battle, we won the producers' consent to no more such free rides. As the negotiations went on to other points, we were uncomfortable among ourselves about our victory. We realized that in blocking the "sharpies" we had made legitimate added "closeups" so expensive that they just wouldn't be made. This violated point three of our code: "Was it fair to the public?" Hadn't we done something to prevent the public from getting as good a picture as it was possible for all of us to make? The last day of the negotiations we brought up the point again, much to the producers' surprise, and we handed it back to them [Hubler, p. 226].

Reagan had been accused before 1960 of writing "sweetheart" contracts, of being a patsy for management. Since the appearance of the Justice Department documents dating from 1961 and 1962, a darker link has been suggested between Reagan and specific MCA interests. I think it more likely that Reagan was generally favorable to business as such, which he contrives to think of as an individual rather than a social activity. He was always prepared to think the best of his own bosses. This was true from the days when he idolized Peter MacArthur as "a saint, but a show business kind of saint" at station WHO (Hubler, pp. 57–58). It remained true of his remarkably smooth relationship with Jack Warner. It would extend to his next boss, General Electric, despite that company's coolness toward him. Why should his attitude toward MCA have been any different?

CHAPTER 30

GE: The Speech

Your face is a company face;
It smiles at executives, then goes back in place.

— *Frank Loesser*

Reagan was given a whole new career when MCA took him to General Electric: "This television show came riding along. The cavalry to the rescue . . . It was Revue through Taft Schreiber who approached me."[1] Reagan was not only made the host, occasional star, and part-time producer of the successful new show; he became a symbol and spokesman for the entire GE endeavor, what a publicist called the company's ambassador of goodwill to the public at large. His very mode of life was turned into an advertisement for living well electrically. GE remodeled his Pacific Palisades home with state-of-the-art conveniences. A three-minute advertisement was filmed of Ronald and Nancy Reagan showing off their technological dream house.

> GE had played with it like a Christmas toy and we benefited no end from their generous intention to give us an electric-powered home. As one department after another got in its licks, the panel where the switches and circuit-breakers are began to outgrow the usual back porch cupboard. One day a truck arrived with a three-thousand-pound steel cabinet, twelve feet long and eight feet high. They mounted it outside one wall of the house on a concrete platform—this is where our electricity comes in. From there I'm sure we have a direct line to Hoover Dam [Hubler, p. 311].

It was now his professional duty to be a conspicuous consumer.

General Electric early realized that its task was not simply to sell appliances but to create a desire for the kind of life that craves such appliances. Reagan's home was the descendant of GE's "House of Magic," a great tourist attraction of the 1930s, and of architectural contests sponsored to develop more "modern" (electricity-consuming) residences.[2] In 1929 GE hired the pioneer publicist Edward Bernays to create a huge cultural event, the Golden Jubilee of Light, honoring Thomas Edison on the fiftieth anniversary of his invention of the light bulb. It was a touchy task for Bernays, since Henry Villard and J. P. Morgan had taken Edison's own company away from him to form General Electric in 1892. Henry Ford, Edison's friend, got his share of the publicity by having the celebration take place in Dearborn, Michigan, rather than at GE's home laboratory, Schenectady, where Bernays had planned it. But Bernays created the publicity, and the nation tuned in by radio to hear the miraculous invention recreated by Graham McNamee, one of Reagan's broadcasting heroes. Bernays persuaded George M. Cohan to write a theme song for electricity that was widely played by bands that year.[3]

Even earlier in the twenties, GE and Westinghouse had helped local utility suppliers sponsor student essay contests that made the schools promote their product:

> In this campaign 1,500 Middletown children submitted essays on how the lighting of their homes could be improved, and upwards of 1,500 families were made immediately aware of the inadequacies of their homes as regards library table lamps, porch lights, piano lamps, and convenient floor sockets. As one of the winning local essays said: "I and all my family have learned a great deal that we did not know before and we intend improving the lighting in our own home."[4]

Besides cash prizes, the companies gave away radios and other electric appliances to encourage consumption of electricity.

As a pioneer at selling whole ways of life, at creating a demand before supplying the demanded items, GE has been a training ground for advertising talent over the decades. It has a long line of alumni in the field of publicity, who have annual get-togethers. Carl Ally, Harry Schachte, and Al Ries went on to lead their own advertising agencies.[5] It is a company acutely aware of its "image" as a symbol of progress, and it protects the sacred monogram that typifies the firm's products. "Outsiders say that the GE monogram is stamped on the rear ends of its people."[6] When any company is absorbed, its own logo yields to the all-important guarantee of quality. "That monogram constitutes a banner and a franchise under which everyone wins or loses—the 'toaster rubs off on the turbine' theory."[7] Reagan himself became an important part of the corporate image, and so did every aspect of his television program. He tells us how carefully it was monitored for any tainting of GE's image:

> Usually the [sponsor's] liaison man is to guard against us show folk innocently embarrassing the sponsor . . . His original task is legitimate and necessary. Take us, for example—the time we came up with an exciting half-hour play based on the danger to a planeload of passengers lost in the fog with all instruments out of whack. We needed someone to remind us GE made those instruments, sold them to the airlines, and said airlines would consider it tactless if GE told umpteen million

potential passengers they might land the hard way [Hubler, pp. 290–91].

The GE world, like Disney's, is a place where everything is neat and clean and safe. The company tries to create the same wholesome, reliable atmosphere in its plants:

> GE is the original Boy Scout company . . . They're not flashy. They tend to be straitlaced engineers devoted to getting the job done . . . In 1983, a sharp-eyed writer for the *Berkshire Eagle* in Pittsfield, Massachusetts (a major GE plant city), noted that if the three-piece suit is back, "you'd never know it" from the General Electric annual report, which featured pictures of 50 male executives, not one of them wearing a vest, all wearing four-in-hands, none showing "a wisp of whisker on a corporate lip, chin, or jowl"—and all 100 corporate ears visible, free of all hair.[8]

Although GE would later have its share of the defense-contract scandals brought on by the spending spree of Reagan's own first term as President, its history has been one of self-dramatizing rectitude. As the New York *Times* noted in its headline on the fraud case in 1985: "GE's Image Makes Conviction More Jarring."[9]

> Conservative comportment in dress and speech (profanity raises eyebrows) is paralleled by marked financial conservatism. "It's a mature company, balanced, sound, solid, one of the most financially conservative companies," [President Reginald] Jones remarked, adding, "A foreign visitor once said, 'The company reminds me of a staid old woman who looks both ways before going across the street.' "[10]

The company encourages a team spirit in its workers, a sense of family. There is a rite of passage for junior managers held every year in a camp atmosphere of inspirational talk with the senior executives on an informal basis. For years these meetings were held at an island GE owned in the St. Lawrence River. Reginald Jones, later the president himself, remembers one such meeting when it was addressed by Charles E. Wilson, the president (1940–1950) who had started at GE as a stock boy in 1899:

> I still remember Charlie Wilson, the very epitome of the inspirational leader. He told us, in the Town Hall, how Westinghouse planned to surpass us in sales and earnings. "They should live so long!" he roared. "Their grandchildren should live so long." And then he got us out behind the marching band, and they led us out to the flagpole playing "Onward Christian Soldiers." At that moment, I would have followed him anywhere on earth—and beyond if necessary.[11]

Another loyal employee put the matter even more emphatically: "There are three great experiences available on earth—the Roman Catholic Church, the Mafia, and General Electric."[12]

The company rewards loyalty—most of its managers have risen from the ranks. But it enforces it as well. Levinson and Rosenthal, in their study of corporate executives, found no company where the employees were more guarded in discussion of their superiors. One rises *from* the ranks by obeying *in* the ranks. "Self-aggrandizement is not tolerated. In fact, some believe that when *Fortune* featured Dr. Thomas A. Vanderslice as a potential successor to Jones, that killed his chances."[13]

Big business, though it speaks the language of individualism, encourages conformism among its employees. A 1984 study of successful executives, found that CEOs regularly think in military metaphors, with the "troops" under them supposed to observe soldiers' discipline. They even prefer to have them in some kind of uniform. Thomas Watson, the legendary leader of IBM, told his interviewers: "I don't really give a damn about a white shirt but, if I wear a nice-looking blue shirt, the next fellow down is going to wear a purple shirt, and then . . . we're going to have an aloha shirt down at the salesman level."[14] Leaders can be bold only if their troops are compliant.

In Ronald Reagan, the Boy Scout company found the perfect Scout. He, too, had loved discipline and the military ever since he joined the Reserves in Des Moines. He came to revere Charles Wilson's successor as president of GE, Ralph Cordiner. He accepted the company's censorship not only of his TV shows about airplanes but of his own speeches about TVA. He even accepted his own overnight dismissal from GE without rancor. Like any graduate of the Association Island jamborees, he continued to assure people that GE is "as human as the corner grocer" (Hubler, p. 293). Big might be bad in government. It was reassuring in business. There, bigger meant better, as conformity meant freedom.

Reagan, the mild-mannered son of Nelle, the model kid who got along with everyone, was always by temperament a company man. Not only did he manage to work successfully for an egomaniac like B. J. Palmer (no matter how buffered by Peter MacArthur); he also worked harmoniously with the most irascible of Hollywood bosses, Jack Warner. James Cagney and Bette Davis broke their contracts with Warner (Davis leaving the country to get beyond his lawyers' range). Olivia de Havilland sued him. Humphrey Bogart and Errol Flynn squabbled with him. Reagan never had a legal dispute or even a public falling-out with Warner. The most he did, after being directly lied to by Warner, was send him an arch private letter saying, "I know you too well to ever think you'd break your word."[15] When, in 1966, a letter went out from "Friends of Ronald Reagan" soliciting support for his entry into the race for governor, Jack Warner was on the list of prominent supporters (the only figure from the film industry who appeared there). Asked before the grand jury if he ever had complaints about his treatment by MCA, Reagan said, "Oh no."[16]

Despite Reagan's praise of the entrepreneurial spirit, he never struck off on bold ventures of his own. The "rebellion" at Eureka that he compares to Paul Revere's ride was a carefully managed affair, run by the faculty, involving a majority of the students, and led by the fraternity he had just joined.

His own most independent career move was, as he admits, an attempt to join the fad for epic Westerns before it faded (Hubler, pp. 233–34). Reagan is a joiner, a cheerleader, the "best friend," not a maverick, not an independent thinker. His virtues are those of the community, of going along to get along. He is reliable rather than innovative. That is his real strength, despite his own misleading praise of enterprise, entrepreneurial risk, difference, competition, and individualism. He was the ideal GE man.

Reagan says he visited all 135 GE plants in the eight years he worked for the company. Since he still would not fly (despite GE's promotion of its own navigation instruments), this involved him in weeks of cross-country railroad travel every year.[17] Paul Gavaghan, a GE publicity director who conducted Reagan on one of his New England tours, described the experience: "There was a formula we always followed. He was taken to meet the top people at the plant, then there was a brief assembly with the workers, in the dining room or some such area. At night we always tried to arrange a banquet with some civic group—the Chamber of Commerce, for instance—where he would be the principal speaker. His speech was always the same, he had it polished to perfection. It was old American values—the ones I believe in, but it was like the Boy Scout code, you know, not very informative. But always lively, with entertaining stories.

"He was very different in private from his public personality, so outgoing. In private he was more restrained, disciplined, careful. He knew what he was doing all the time. He conserved his time and energy. As he said, 'We sell the difference,' and for him the difference was appearance. He took very good care of himself. He was not a nine-to-five man. He needed time off to rest and exercise and keep himself in shape. He was a professional. He never directly hawked GE products at the banquets, but he was a spokesman for the company. He promoted anti-communism and the free enterprise system."[18]

The endurance of these trips is to be gauged not merely from miles logged, plants visited, numbers addressed, rubber chickens eaten or poked at, but from the fact that Reagan was giving the same speech year after year, making it vivid and enjoyable, though its message was apocalyptic: a slow invisible tide of socialism was engulfing America, held back only by a few brave businessmen.

I have already argued that Reagan had to undergo no profound conversion to become a right-wing spokesman by this stage of his career. He had been a believer in the Communist conspiracy as a domestic threat, especially in the labor unions, since 1947. He was in essential sympathy with J. Edgar Hoover's view of America and the world as desperately imperiled and naïvely "soft" on the doctrines of collectivism. In moving among business leaders and polishing the punch lines that brought their warmest response, it took no special effort to sympathize with their grumblings about government regulation, high taxes, and interference with "the private sector." Insurance executives loved it when he told them social security could be voluntary.

Some power distributors liked it when he said the government should turn TVA back to private developers. His father-in-law joined many other doctors in applause for his attacks on "socialized medicine."

As had happened with Reagan ever since his speech as a freshman in the Eureka chapel, his rhetoric carried him away. He sees issues in moral terms, where the choice is clear. This means that the evil is always undiluted, whether that evil be President Wilson of Eureka attacking the whole basis of free speech, or Herb Sorrell's CSU trying to give Hollywood to Russia. Even GE's executives believed in most of the rhetoric used by Reagan. But they also did not like to make waves. No need to be controversial about something just because you are right. And on one point they had a company interest at stake. TVA was a contractor for extensive electrical equipment built by GE. By Reagan's account, he heard of this concern and volunteered at once to remove the offending references: "Dropping TVA from the speech was no problem. You can reach out blindfolded and grab a hundred examples of overgrown government. The whole attempt only served to illustrate how late it is if we are to save freedom" (Hubler, p. 306). He was the company man, even when it meant tailoring his speech as he had changed his TV show's plots.

It is surprising that Reagan, happily saluted in hundreds of GE plants, boardrooms, and banquet tables, endlessly photographed with and posed in front of GE projects (even in the cockpits of the airplanes he disliked), should be dropped by the company on twenty-four-hour notice in 1962. Accounts of the break are confusing, and Reagan tries to smooth the matter over. He says he would not have been fired if Ralph Cordiner, the man he most admired, were still in office at GE—but he was. Even in dismissal, Reagan is a good company man, making excuses for his boss.[19] Reagan says that one reason for the TV show's demise was its loss of the lead on Sunday night to "Bonanza," a color show, while General Electric Theater still ran in black and white. But the show was doing well enough to switch it to a less competitive place on the schedule. Others have brought up the TVA speeches, but Reagan had shown alacrity in conforming to company policy on that. Still others say Reagan's speech was just getting too controversial for the safely middle-of-the-road GE. Perhaps. But the bitterest notes would enter The Speech when Reagan kept delivering it for four years after he left GE.

The timing of GE's decision makes another explanation seem more probable than any of those offered by Reagan. The GE show went off the air in September of 1962. On July 10, 1962, the civil indictment of MCA had been issued for antitrust actions, with the Guild named as coconspirator from the time when Reagan was its president. Reagan's contract, it is true, had already been dropped in March, the regular renewal time.[20] But the possibility of scandal was in the air. Reagan had been summoned by the grand jury in February, along with other MCA clients. Their appearance was publicized, though what they said was not. Meanwhile, as if to confirm the rumors about MCA's monopolistic practices, the company, with Reagan's concurrence, offered this solution to the decline in General Electric Theater's popularity:

> to go to an hour every other Sunday, alternating with the Alcoa Theatre, hosted by that gentle genius, Fred Astaire. Frankly, my mouth was watering *because both shows were Revue productions,* which meant we could have worked out all kinds of co-starring gimmicks and exchanges to keep both shows sparking. [Hubler, p. 309, italics added.]

MCA rotates its chimpanzee acts until they can no longer be peddled. But GE, with its good-guy image and its many government contracts, had to be chary of a team getting so much hostile attention from the Justice Department, with further revelations or even ind.ctments possible. Reagan's own phrasing seems to suggest the real cause of his severance: "Twenty-four hours later the 'GE Theater' was canceled. I don't know—maybe eight years was long enough. I do know that GE stood up against government threats in a day *when government was less prone to use force and coercion*" (Hubler, p. 310, italics added). The threats and coercion of the Kennedy Justice Department seem to be what GE could no longer stand up to. Reagan had another grievance against "govment."

Reagan was financially secure by 1962, and in wide demand as a speaker. He made a couple of guest appearances on other TV shows, shot the TV movie *The Killers* in 1964, and went back to hosting his own program ("Death Valley Days") in 1965. But more and more, in these years, he lived to deliver The Speech. It had become his mission in life. He sought occasions to issue his warning, and audiences were so moved that the performance became a famous one. The public relations adjunct to his plant tours had now become the center of his life. He is a man who likes to be on crusade, at least rhetorically. He had preached the clean life to boys' groups in Davenport, the healthy normality of Hollywood at publicity appearances before Pearl Harbor, the war effort when he was in uniform, the Red menace during his days of union leadership. Now he had a crusade that corporation executives liked to hear him talk about—though they, too, had their government contracts, like GE, and kept their indignation channeled in ways that Reagan could ignore.

In the early sixties, he was reaching a broader audience than businessmen. He was in the place, Southern California, where the New Right was enjoying its most spectacular growth. Reagan had begun delivering The Speech during the Eisenhower years, an era of good feeling presided over by a Republican administration very friendly to business. Yet Reagan asserted through it all that the hour was late and freedom diminishing. He talked in apocalyptic terms about the Soviet Union, but the body of his talk was about *gradual* surrenders of freedom to things like farm subsidization, bureaucratic form-filling, and rural electrification. He was still attacking the New Deal at a time when President Eisenhower had finally given it a Republican sanction.

The New Right rose from the Taft wing of the Republicans, which felt it had been "sold out" by the Eastern establishment of the party when Eisenhower was nominated in 1952. This was part of a pattern by which Eastern money interests bought influence and used slick media advantages. Phyllis Schlafly deplored the way the Republicans were tricked into offering an echo to the Democrats, rather than a choice between alternatives:

> A small group of secret king makers, using hidden persuaders and psychological warfare techniques, manipulated the Republican national convention to nominate candidates who had sidestepped or suppressed the key issues.[21]

The right wing of the Republican party in California was especially angry at the choice of Dwight Eisenhower, suspecting its own senator, Richard Nixon, of persuading the head of the California delegation, Earl Warren, to desert Taft. Robert Welch was briefly influential because he voiced, in more conspiratorial language, resentments widely shared. For Welch, the "betrayal" of Taft was "the dirtiest deal in American political history, participated in if not entirely engineered by Richard Nixon in order to make himself Vice President (and to put Earl Warren on the Supreme Court as part of that deal)."[22] By the time Mr. Welch wrote that, in 1960, he was so dismayed at Eisenhower's unwillingness to undo the Communist work of the New Deal that he came to the conclusion that the President himself was a Soviet agent—as were John Foster and Allen Dulles.[23] In 1958, he had founded the John Birch Society, whose membership was heaviest in Southern California, where two congressmen belonged to the Society.[24]

The public first became aware of the John Birch Society in 1960, two years after its founding. That same year an immensely successful book was published, Barry Goldwater's *The Conscience of a Conservative*. It was an impersonal political argument written by L. Brent Bozell, William Buckley's Yale classmate and brother-in-law, who had also written foreign policy speeches for Senator Joseph McCarthy. It put in politer terms the Schlafly-Welch thesis that the Eisenhower administration perpetuated the statism of the New Deal. "Today, *neither* of our two parties maintains a meaningful commitment to the principle of States' Rights. This, the cornerstone of the Republic, our chief bulwark against the encroachment of [sic] individual freedom by Big Government, is fast disappearing under the piling sands of statism."[25] The book recommended resistance to the school integration ruling of 1954, repudiation of the doctrine of peaceful coexistence, and the aggressive use of tactical nuclear weapons against "vulnerable Communist regimes."[26] Modern "conservatism" was about to enter electoral politics at the national level—as a radical attempt to overthrow not only the New Deal but the Republican establishment that had "surrendered" to it. This was programmatically more radical than the piecemeal war on "security risks" that Bozell's former boss, McCarthy, had ever waged.

Reagan's Speech—folksy in some of its examples, friendly in its delivery, but seeing "statism" everywhere doing the work of the Soviet Union within our borders—was perfectly attuned to the movement of which Reagan would become the principal beneficiary. And the tone of The Speech became more frantic in the early years of the Kennedy administration. Though Kennedy committed the nation to bearing any burden in the fight against communism, and energetically devoted himself to the overthrow of Fidel Castro by any means, his Secretary of Defense, Robert McNamara, used planning methods deeply disturbing to Pentagon routine, to the old-boy network of retired officers and their business contacts. McNamara thought America needed the capacity to respond flexibly to a vast range of commitments— which meant carefully calibrating resources, cutting back on the "massive response" schedule of new bombers, larger bombs, and heavier missiles.[27] Senator Goldwater voiced the Pentagon's fear of such civilian calibration: "Robert S. McNamara and his chorus of whiz kids at the Pentagon were the objects of unrestrained media praise. In my judgment, McNamara should have been punished for his pursuit of a policy calculated to produce parity with the Russians as a satisfactory replacement for our earlier superiority."[28] The claim that America's leaders were digging their country's grave was adopted by the New Right. Phyllis Schlafly, collaborating with retired admiral Chester Ward on *The Gravediggers,* wrote that McNamara was acting on "a pattern of unilateral disarmament," the charge Ronald Reagan would make against the Carter administration in 1980.[29] McNamara was accused of an "emotional monomania against weapons of massive megatonnage."[30]

John A. Stormer published one of the all-time paperback bestsellers for the 1964 campaign, *None Dare Call It Treason,* on Communist control of the American press and government. He used a fake quote from Lenin, taken from Welch's *Blue Book,* which Reagan quickly picked up and has used to this day (most recently in September of 1985): "I .rst we will take Eastern Europe. Next, the masses of Asia. Then we shall encircle the last bastion of capitalism, the United States of America. We shall not have to attack; it will fall like overripe fruit into our hands."[31]

Thus The Speech was part of that body of right-wing rhetoric igniting the grass-roots Goldwater movement of the early sixties. Reagan appeared before anti-Communist and Republican groups more frequently after he left GE, but even before that, in 1961, he had addressed a rally of Dr. Fred Schwarz's Christian Anti-Communism Crusade. In 1962, he spoke to a fund-raising dinner for John Rousselot, one of the acknowledged Birch Society congressmen. Three years later, preparing to run for office himself, he said: "Johnny Rousselot is a terrific fellow," who "would do anything from calling me names in public to endorsement—whatever we want."[32] By then, Rousselot was district governor of the Birch Society, in charge of chapters in California and five other states.[33]

In 1964 Reagan would be involved in both the Goldwater campaign for President and his fellow actor George Murphy's successful run for the Senate. Others had long been asking Reagan to run for office—they had approached him for the nomination that went to Murphy. It is usually said that delivering The Speech for Goldwater brought Reagan into politics. But if that had not done so, something else would. He was obviously preparing for a political career when he dictated his memoirs to Richard Hubler, before his involvement in the Goldwater campaign. In the book, which never refers to Goldwater, Reagan says, "I have my movie hat on again—I hope for some little while" (Hubler, p. 336). It was obviously made while he was preparing or filming *The Killers,* which came out in 1964. But the entire book is arranged as a quest for larger arenas, where he will discover the rest of himself. Parts of that discovery came from acting, from union work, from his family. But they were not enough. For now, giving The Speech is his mission, and he says he will keep performing that as long as it is his greatest service. He knew that, in American politics, the best way to put yourself forward is to seem to be holding back.

> Another hat—a really new one—was displayed recently and, while it had some intriguing features, I decided it wouldn't be completely comfortable. A group of my fellow citizens were the designers and they did me a great honor, for which I am humbly grateful, even though the hat didn't fit. Their hat was the kind you throw into the political ring and they wanted me to do just that, for either governor or senator. One does what he feels he can do best and serves where he feels he can make the greatest contribution. For me, I think that service is to continue accepting speaking engagements, in an effort to make people aware of the danger to freedom in a vast permanent government structure so big and complex it virtually entraps Presidents and legislators [Hubler, p. 336].

But the book itself lays the groundwork for a political career, devoting much of its length to Reagan's union leadership, negotiating sessions, and struggle with Communists in the labor movement. His long association with the Democratic Party is variously explained and tactfully minimized. His membership in liberal organizations—which could turn up to embarrass him with new right zealots (and actually did)[34]—is repented as an emotional moment of postwar hopefulness and naïveté: "I was a near-hopeless hemophilic liberal" (Hubler, p. 160). He admits that he voted Democratic in 1948, but says that was the last time: "Harry S. Truman can credit me with at least one assist—but never thereafter." From then on his life is "the story of my disillusionment with big government" and his defense of the free enterprise system. The book is not a Hollywood memoir but a political confession. As he had in The Speech, Reagan uses show business anecdotes to capture an audience for his political preaching. The last chapter of *Where's the Rest of Me?* was, simply, The Speech. The book, like The Speech, was a political campaign waiting to happen.

CHAPTER 31

BASICO: Behavior Engineering

Temper'd soft Tunings, intermixt with Voice
—Paradise Lost 7.598

The long-term effects of Goldwater's campaign in 1964 were felt principally in the South. In the midst of his defeat everywhere else but in his native state, Goldwater won a majority of white Southern votes and carried five states from the "solid South," even though he was running against a Southerner. This laid the foundation for Richard Nixon's victorious Southern strategy four years later, and provided the most supportive part of the electorate for Reagan's future candidacies of 1968, 1976, 1980, and 1984. But if the future meaning of the race lay in the South, its immediate impact was felt most in California, the site of its climactic Republican primary and of the tumultuous Republican national convention. One of the many things that branded Goldwater an extremist in his bitter fight with Rockefeller was the fact that he clinched the nomination in California, where Republican radicals of the right were most important and visible. They were at the Cow Palace to shout down Nelson Rockefeller, giving the television audience its first (and at the time shocking) sight of convention turmoil. It was to satisfy them that Goldwater made his defiant choice of a running mate and an acceptance slogan.

Such ideological fervor not only looked new to the rest of the nation; it was relatively new for California itself. The Republicans had been a largely moderate and unified party under Governors Earl Warren and Goodwin Knight. The period of change set in when William Knowland tried to replace Knight in 1958 with a hard anti-labor campaign. The divisions that appeared then deepened rapidly. Richard Nixon returned to a quarreling party in 1962. In his primary race for the governor's office, he had a tough struggle with a representative of the party's right wing, Joe Shell, former football star at Southern Cal, then an oil executive backed by the money of his fellow oilman, Cy Rubel.[1] To defeat Shell, Nixon had to associate him with the John Birch Society, denying himself the Society's votes in the general election. As Nixon later told William Buckley: "If Barry showed that the Republicans can't win with just the right wing, I showed in 1962 that we can't win without them."

After his defeat, Nixon left California—permanently, he thought. The 1963 National Young Republicans' Convention held in San Francisco seemed to underline the wisdom of his choice. It was a tempestuous affair controlled by organized crowds of shouting right-wingers—a rehearsal for the party's senior convention the next year.[2] Nelson Rockefeller, from New York, denounced "extremists" who had taken over the Young Republicans, whetting appetites for his descent into their arena.[3] Yet Rockefeller came to California in 1964 with an Oregon victory just behind him and a healthy lead in the polls. He had ample money, shrewd management (provided by Stuart Spencer and Bill Roberts), and the Warren-Knight elders of the party on his side. But Goldwater had an army of true believers who seemed to show up on every doorstep, and a smaller band of zealots willing to capitalize on the fact that a son was born to Rockefeller's new wife just three days before the election, reviving memories of the divorce scandal he was beginning to live down. The Catholic Cardinal of Los Angeles, Francis McIntyre, ordered Loyola University to cancel a scheduled campaign appearance on the campus—as McIntyre's predecessor had ordered Father Dunne off the same campus in the 1940s.[4]

To counter Rockefeller's financial resources, the California Goldwater campaign, with Henry Salvatori as finance chairman, hung onto the money it raised with the help of its actor celebrities, causing friction with the national organization.[5] One of the fund-raising dinners put on by Salvatori and Holmes Tuttle featured Ronald Reagan, and The Speech was a hit as usual. The Californians thought it should be televised nationally. Goldwater's advisers were by this time chary of volunteer suggestions from California, there had been so many wild ones. Goldwater himself had canceled an inflammatory ad made by California's Russell Lawton, a glimpse of America sinking into a pit of sex and violence under the patronage of Lyndon Johnson.[6] Besides, when Californians taped a Raymond Massey appeal for money to be appended to Goldwater's national television ads, the actor gave a Los Angeles address for the contributions to be sent to.[7] And Reagan's views were well known by this time—he sponsored a voluntary social security program, and opposed TVA, subjects that had already burned Goldwater. It seemed better to hear no voices out of Birchland.

The Californians solved the money problem by paying for the national telecast themselves, with funds raised by a prior broadcast of The Speech in their state. The ideological objections were harder to meet. Goldwater's high command, William Baroody and Denison Kitchel, both read the script of The Speech and declared it unacceptable. They prevailed with Goldwater, who called Reagan and asked him to withdraw the tape. Reagan was polite, but not deferential. He asked if Goldwater had seen the film or read its text, and Goldwater had to admit that he had not. Stephen Shadegg, an ally of the Californians in this struggle, says that Reagan asked Goldwater to read or see it before deciding to kill it.[8] One day went by, then a second. Baroody and Kitchel called again to say no to the project, but Salvatori refused to release the money collected for any other use, and the national committee had a half hour of air time to fill *and pay for* if it kept refusing.[9] Reagan took the fact that Goldwater did not call back himself as tacit permission to go ahead. The Californians got their way.

The Goldwater team tried to prevent Reagan's appearance as part of their effort to shake the extremist label; yet Reagan appeared to most of the nation as a more reasonable advocate than Goldwater. The actor's manner and familiar charm, the generality of his warnings, the lack of personal assault or references (even to Goldwater), made the amateur look more statesmanlike than the professional politician. Reagan had been in movies as botched and messy as the Goldwater campaign, and survived by the professional instinct always to underplay his lines. As had often happened before, he was the only thing that looked natural on the screen. At the right-wingers' darkest moment, Reagan was the one light of hope for the future, uncontaminated by the looniness of the Goldwater operation. Say what you would of Ronald Reagan, there was nothing wild-eyed about him.

Reagan lost no time using the flood of adulation (and money) that resulted from his broadcast. David Broder called it "the most successful national political debut since William Jennings Bryan electrified the 1896 Democratic convention with the 'Cross of Gold' speech," one that "made Reagan a political star overnight."[10] Rubel, Salvatori and some other backers of the Goldwater campaign were already convinced they had been working for the wrong candidate. As Salvatori would tell a reporter, after helping Reagan become governor:

> People criticize Ronnie for having no political experience. But he has a great image, a way to get through to people. Look at the Goldwater experience. His philosophy was sound, but he didn't articulate it moderately. The governor has a similar philosophy, but he can express his thought. Look at John F. Kennedy. He didn't have much of a record as a senator. But he made a great appearance—and he had a beautiful wife. So does the governor. Nancy Reagan doesn't have to take a back seat to anyone. And the governor has plenty of time between now and the [1968] nomination to make a record as an administrator. But I don't believe people in other states really care much about what's happening in California.[11]

But in 1964 Salvatori had to care about California. To run his horse at the national level, he would have to reunite the California party, so bitterly riven. That meant reaching out to those who had supported Rockefeller in the 1964 primary, people like Thurston Dart and the public relations team of Spencer and Roberts. Reagan would have to be presented as a peacemaker. The newly elected party chairman for the state, Dr. Gaylord Parkinson, had just promulgated his Eleventh Commandment: "Thou shalt speak no ill of any other Republican."[12]

Reagan had to be wooed first, and was easily won, though it was part of the strategy to keep everything tentative: the wooing of support *for* him would be presented as a joint wooing *of* him. A letter sent out by the "Friends of Ronald Reagan," to "explore the depth of feeling and the possible commitment" for Reagan, said the actor would run "providing a substantial cross section of our party will unite behind his candidacy."[13] Long after Reagan had left "Death Valley Days" and taken up a heavy campaign schedule of speaking appearances, he would claim he was just trying "to determine if I am acceptable to all sectors of the party."[14]

Spencer and Roberts had to be won over early on. They were a Republican team, with a good track record. Though not overtly ideological, they managed the "liberal" campaigns of Thomas Kuchel for Senate and Nelson Rockefeller in the 1964 primary. They had handled the race that won John Rousselot his seat in 1960, but they did not try to repeat the feat in 1962, after it had been discovered that he was a member of the Birch Society. They looked at their material in terms of its political usability—could it be made to win? They were the best in their line of work, and they had doubts about Reagan. "We had reservations about Reagan," Roberts told Lou Cannon. "We had heard that Reagan was a real right-winger and we thought that a right-wing kind of candidacy would not be successful."[15]

In several meetings of mutual reassurance, Reagan convinced them they were convincing him. He must broaden his appeal beyond the hard-core right. Goldwater had won California narrowly in numbers, and even more narrowly in terms of geography and demography. He won only four of the state's fifty-eight counties, clustered around the Los Angeles area.[16] A credible candidate for governing the entire state must not only campaign in the "liberal" north but show some ability to win votes there. Reagan was, as he always is in private, charming, modest, and respectful of advisers' expertise. Spencer and Roberts were not only won over but impressed. They knew they had an extraordinary candidate on their hands.

Reagan's political skills were getting their first big-league test in the heady months that followed Goldwater's defeat. Defiant Goldwaterites were adoring, and many of them called for punishment of the "traitors" to the party who had not campaigned for their man. Reagan was being asked to appear before all kinds of groups, to make statements that would show the cause was not defeated. He restrained himself. He had worked hard to attract a political audience. He now had it, and he showed the innate sense and cool nerves to sit and wait for the money and the talent to come to him, to woo him on what they conceived as their terms and he recognized as winning terms. A measure of his determination was his willingness, finally, to use airplanes. He had kept for almost three decades his pledge not to repeat the harrowing experience of his short trip to Catalina Island. But the men willing to back him now had a big world in mind for him. Not only would he have to campaign throughout a state spread eight hundred miles along the Pacific coastline, he would have to become a national figure in a short time, and acquire some claims to international expertise. He had still, at age fifty-five, never been abroad except for one boat trip to England to make *The Hasty Heart.* But now he would fly. That is how much he wanted his new political career. Governor Pat Brown sized him up as a dilettante, a negligible actor, a lightweight. Others would repeat that mistake as he showed his determination on broader and broader stages, till Reagan could at last relax on Air Force One, the safest airplane in the world.

In line with the healing approach that had been outlined for him, Reagan became the most frequent citer of Parkinson's Eleventh Commandment. Presenting himself as a Republican loyalist helped make amends for his late registration in the party—he had only belonged to it for two years when he gave the Goldwater speech. Yet it was useful, at this juncture, to have no history of association with feuding camps in the party. He could urge Goldwaterites not to be vindictive toward Rockefeller's supporters. More important, being uncensorious on principle gave him a way to handle the touchy problem of the John Birch Society. Unlike Nixon in 1962, he would neither endorse nor denounce the Society as such, but welcome the votes of its members as of "any good Republicans." The riven and bitter party needed the infusion of nice-guyism that was Reagan's specialty. As he wrote to the true believers of *National Review* after Goldwater's defeat, conservatives had to learn more about "the soft sell."[17]

Spencer and Roberts could turn Reagan's weaknesses into strengths. He lacked experience? That made him a citizen candidate. Pat Brown looked and sounded like a politician of the old school. Honest himself, he had to bargain his bills through a Democratic legislature dominated by "Big Daddy," Jesse Unruh, who rejoiced in his reputation as a schemer.[18] Unruh's creed was, "Money is the mother's milk of politics." It might be better to be innocent of such "experience."

The idea of citizen politics was not new in 1966. George Romney had used it in the 1950s to maneuver his way from automobile executive to Michigan's governor. But the concept had special appeal in Hollywood, and special applicability to Reagan. It is, after all, politics as Hollywood plot line. Frank Capra's movies constantly showed the ordinary man straightening out the mess in the capital—Mr. Deeds going to town, Mr. Smith going to Washington. When people despair of politics as usual, John Doe is the hope of the world. As Gary Cooper put it: "He's simple, and he's wise. He's Joe Doakes, the world's greatest stooge and the world's greatest strength." It is true that, in *Meet John Doe,* Capra gives us a glimpse of the ugly side to such naive populism—that it will advance a Huey Long or Father Coughlin to power if he just denounces power. But, as Barbara Stanwyck says, the John Doe movement can be done over again, and done right, after the bad guys are exposed: "We can start clean now . . . It will grow big because it will be honest . . ."

There was never any danger that Reagan would veer into uncontrolled personal domination. Naturally ingratiating, he was being put through inoffensiveness training by Spencer and Roberts. They hired a typically Californian corporation—of behavioral engineers—to retool Reagan for the campaign, coaching him on all points of matter and manner that were likely to arise. BASICO, the Behavior Sciences Corporation of Reseda, California, was established by two clinical psychologists, Dr. Stanley Plog of UCLA and Dr. Kenneth Holden of San Fernando Valley State College. They advised campuses and businesses on improving human relations within their enterprises. This was the first time they had worked on a political campaign, fitting the personality of an unusual candidate to the demands of the political system.[19] Plog remembers how he was called on:

> They were looking for the kind of help that I could give. What really kicked that off was that Reagan in January of 1966, I guess it was, when he made his announcement—for the 1966 campaign it was, I guess— and said, "Would you believe that 15.1 percent of the population of California is on welfare?" Well, the fact is, it was 5.1 at that time, not 15.1. So the guys who really got Reagan going, like Holmes Tuttle and Henry Salvatori, said no more of this. "If he's going after it, he's going to have a professional background. . . ." They didn't want any more goofs like that.[20]

The two men went to meet Reagan at his home, and Holden was shocked at the way Reagan had been preparing himself: "He didn't have a secretary, and he was assimilating stacks of material on state issues, clipping newspapers and magazines."[21] Plog's assessment was even blunter: "He knew zero about California when we came in, I mean zero."[22] The two men told Reagan's managers that drastic action was needed. "They cut his campaign schedule and gave us three days with him down at Malibu. They put him up at a beach cottage and we met with him all day for three days . . . We worked on the whole concept of the man."[23] They had to decide what he was trying to convey to voters, and how he could convey it—translating his personal appeal into a political program. Among other things, that meant avoiding statements that went beyond his personal appeal and cited evidence. "He was overanswering every question."[24]

They organized the intellectual content of the campaign around a concept that had been invented in the spring of 1965, when the Friends of Reagan were looking for a slogan he might run with. A right-wing radio evangelist who had ingratiated himself with Reagan, the Reverend W. S. McBirnie, attended a few of these sessions and came up with "The Creative Society."[25] The tag had entered Reagan's speeches, but now Plog and Holden made it the thematic principle for unifying Reagan's attacks on big government, welfare handouts, and high taxes. All those things blunted the initiative, imagination, and energy of private enterprise, which would be "unleashed" under his administration. Businessmen would be consulted on the best way to streamline government. The private sector, unfettered, would create a more prosperous community. As Plog says of his and Holden's work, "Citizen Politics came from the Spencer-Roberts group; the Creative Society came from us."[26] The slogan was McBirnie's—as Governor Brown insisted through the campaign, citing McBirnie's extremist views on other matters— but the content (what there was of it) was Plog's and Holden's.

The BASICO team assembled simple answers for Reagan, framed in terms of his theme, and arranged them into eight books of five-by-eight cards that would focus his and the voters' minds. From that time on, with one assistant (James Gibson), they became the keepers of the candidate and his cards, updating the cards, supplying him with the appropriate one, coaching him from stop to stop. "We were with him every waking moment during the entire campaign, one of the three of us . . . You'd follow him into the rest room before he goes onstage, giving him a last-minute bit of advice . . . It was divided one-third, one-third, one-third between the three of us, we just took our turns."[27] Goofproofing Reagan was a task that called for eternal vigilance. "He made one other mistake on a statistic, and it was a statistic that someone gave to him in the campaign, unknown to us, just before he went onstage someplace in Berkeley."[28]

Handling Reagan's moods was as important as stocking his mind. In March of 1966, Reagan and his primary opponent, George Christopher, appeared together for public questioning at the state convention of the National Negro Republican Assembly. Ben Peery, a black Los Angeles businessman, asked Reagan how he could ask for black votes after defending Barry Goldwater's opposition to the civil rights bill of 1964. Reagan, as he inevitably does, personalized the issue—he was not a racist, and neither was Barry. "If I didn't know personally that Barry Goldwater was not the very opposite of racist, I could not have supported him." Christopher, a liberal speaking to such an audience, naturally disagreed: "The position taken by Goldwater did more harm than any other thing to the Republican party, and we're still paying for that defeat. This situation still plagues the Republican party, and unless we cast out this image, we're going to suffer defeat."[29]

At this, Reagan rose angrily and shouted: "I want to make a point of personal privilege. I resent the implication that there is any bigotry in my nature. Don't anyone ever imply I lack integrity. I will not stand silent and let anyone imply that—in this or any other group."[30] With that, he left the podium and the hall, saying nothing further to his hosts. Ken Holden, who was the keeper of the cards that day, was left behind. Brown's scouts had predicted that Reagan would come apart in unscripted conflicts, that he could not stand the real world of political give-and-take. This was a potential disaster. Holden sent press secretary Lyn Nofziger after Reagan, saying he must be persuaded to return. Then he called Bill Roberts with the same request. By the time Reagan reached his home, the phones were ringing with assurances that he had to return. Reagan did go back; and, though Christopher was gone by then, Reagan apologized to the sponsors of the meeting for his abrupt exit. Yet he would not apologize for his anger. "Frankly, I got mad. It was the sum total of the afternoon. I'm not a politician. There are just some things you can't take as a man."[31]

Reagan's handlers became even more careful about keeping their man rested. His sunny nature, the winningest thing about him, tends to dim along with his energy level. A regular nap was scheduled in the afternoon, before his evening appearances. Much of the campaign was carried on through television spot commercials made by Neil Reagan, filmed in simple, almost amateur settings, with Reagan just talking at the camera, using no props or gimmicks.[32] For the minimum necessary travel to the north of the state, Reagan chartered a slow, dependable DC-3 whose pilot he trusted. "If [Mervin] Amerine had worked on the Warners lot when Reagan was making B movies, he would have been cast as a pilot. He was tall, calm and handsome, a man who had been flying for twenty-eight of his forty-three years."[33]

In the more populous (and more important) southern section of the state, Reagan had a large bus outfitted for his travel—morning stops, a noon appearance, then rest at a motel before an evening show at the farthermost point of that day's odyssey. Reagan was normally back home in his bed each night; but when he and his wife met on platforms, they embraced as after long separation and often complained that the campaign was keeping them apart.[34] It was like the public appearances with Jane Wyman, during World War II, when Reagan was presented as "on leave." He was commuting to politics, an outsider—and he defeated Brown by a million votes.

The BASICO candidate was leading those who had blamed Goldwater's defeat on the psychological conditioning and "hidden persuaders" of the modern media. The spokesman for rugged individualism was programmed more than any major candidate up to that time, with techniques—psychiatry, conformity-enhancers, group dynamics—that were anathema to conservatives. Social engineering was a swearword on the right. Yet Reagan was the first candidate to be engineered by professionals at that arcane calling. As Herbert Baus wrote in 1968: "A major innovation, of clinical interest as a breakthrough in political technology, was the role played in the Reagan campaign by Behavior Sciences Corporation."[35]

Reagan called for a return to simple human ties, for escape from the social machinery that makes people interdependent. Remembering the blur of acronyms involved in his days of labor dispute, he deplored "a world where initials have replaced titles" (Hubler, p. 154). But the president of SAG, an ardent supporter of MPIC, the pampered client of MCA, the very symbol of GE, was now the proudest product of BASICO. He was "plugged in" to a homogenizing, nonideological, party-unity corporate-relations campaign. It is impossible to imagine Barry Goldwater submitting to the kind of minute-by-minute intellectual baby-sitting that Plog and Holden did for Reagan. For good or ill in electoral terms, Goldwater was an individualist; a maverick, riskily candid; unorthodox in his style, however consistent in his patriotism; going his own way.

There is something typical of the men in their attitude toward flight— Goldwater taking his own plane up as a teenager and loving the challenge of the most advanced and experimental planes he was allowed to fly (including the delicate, hard-to-handle U-2)[36]—and Reagan, spending three decades on the ground after his short flight to Catalina. Reagan was never a convincing cowboy because there was something too cautious, not carefree enough, in his carriage. He is essentially a homebody, not personally adventuresome.

Goldwater flew his own plane to many campaign appearances. Reagan was driven and sequestered to arrive in rested condition. The company man needed a well-policed routine to get him through the day. It was the careful pacing of his GE tours, refined by behavioral scientists. Reagan had to be spared all unnecessary stress—long days, painful staff conflict, the making of critical decisions. Decisions were made by others—the original backers (Tuttle, Rubel, Salvatori), the public relations team (Spencer and Roberts), the advertising man (Neil Reagan), the press secretary (Lyn Nofziger), the campaign managers (Philip Battaglia and Taft Schreiber), the candidate-handlers (Plog and Holden)—in roughly that descending order. Reagan was on the bottom rung of responsibility for strategy and the shaping of issues. But he was on the top of the apparatus for visibility, goodwill, the "soft sell."

Reagan's unusual blend of ambition and unpretentiousness, so important to the success of his presidency, was evident in that first campaign. On the face of it, he was engaged in the most arrogant exercise imaginable. Despite his cosmopolitan surroundings in Hollywood, he was still parochial in his views and tastes. He lived in a small world he had carried with him from Dixon and Eureka, Davenport and Des Moines. He knew only part of America, and practically nothing of the rest of the world. But he was sure his part of America was the best part of the world's best people. Unlike others of his generation, he had not met many foreigners in their own countries, as allies or foes in wars, as hosts or instructors in peace. Yet he was being groomed from the outset for the post of highest political power among and over all those people. Rubel and Salvatori were thinking presidential. Sacramento was always just a way station for them. They had made clear what they expected of Reagan, and he did not feel inadequate to the assignment. His America was up to anything.

Yet while entertaining an ambition that might dizzy the most brazen man, Reagan submitted to a tutoring that would have been insulting to most people of even ordinary pride. He was told to avoid subjects that would reveal his ignorance. He was spoon-fed knowledge in five-by-eight baby spoons. He was told by personality constructors that he had to invent a "total concept" of himself. He took it all with equanimity, and not only because he was a political novice. He would continue to take such handling through his political life. In future campaigns he hired people like John

Sears, who made clear their view of his mental limits. Reagan is not, like most of us, plagued by the little vanities—by jokes about his age, or his being an actor, or the statistics he misquotes. His larger confidence in his capacity is unshakable, because not entirely dependent on his own achievements. He really does believe in the ordinary good person of his background, who can preserve values that are more important than expertise. He *is* Joe Doakes, "the world's greatest stooge, and the world's greatest strength."

CHAPTER 32

Citizen Governor

*We had a kind of watchword [in the governor's office]
we used on each other: "When we begin thinking of
government as we instead of they, we've been here
too long."*

—*Ronald Reagan, 1976*

Ronald Reagan likes to present himself as the restorer of an older America. But he is not really a traditionalist. That bothers even such friendly promoters of his presidency as journalist George Will, who wrote in 1985: "He is painfully fond of the least conservative sentiment conceivable, a statement taken from an anti-conservative, Thomas Paine: 'We have it in our power to begin the world over again.' Any time, any place, that is nonsense."[1] Yet precisely that nonsense was the basis of Reagan's whole approach to the governor's office in California. He was to be the new broom sweeping through, the citizen politician defying the rules, the outsider uncontaminated by past practices. To make the break painfully obvious, his predecessor was excluded from the inaugural ritual—despite Reagan's natural congeniality; there was to be no symbol of continuity, only of disjunction.[2] Furthermore, the custom of being sworn in by the chief justice of the state supreme court was abrogated, since the chief justice was a liberal. A conservative associate justice was promoted to the task, precedent yielding to the new ideology in town.[3]

Even the time of the inauguration was meant to startle: he would begin as soon as possible after midnight of his very first day in office, which entailed a swearing-in at 12:10. But that time had to be changed to one minute after midnight, since astrologers claimed that 12:10 was astrally favorable to him. His staff wanted to show Reagan responding to new winds of inspiration but not to magi.[4]

Reagan had campaigned on a conventional promise, to throw the rascals out. But, unconventionally, he meant it. He was "sick at the sit-ins, the teach-ins, the walk-outs. When I am elected Governor, I will organize a throw-out, and Clark Kerr [Chancellor of the University of California] will head that list."[5] He did. Reagan brought his Southern California style north. Walt Disney studios designed the inaugural program.[6] Reagan's campaign team was so heavily recruited from the south that it even tried, at first, to organize the transition period four hundred miles from the capital in Sacramento.[7]

Northern and Southern California are very different in ethos. Reagan's predecessor, Pat Brown, was a San Franciscan whose electoral strength was in the north. But no one could have been a more typical Southern Californian than "Dutch" Reagan of Iowa. Northern California, for such a recently settled part of our country, has an acute sense of its own history, one seen in the family claims of Steinbeck's *East of Eden,* in Jack London's memories of the wilderness, in Joan Didion's account of growing up in country where her family had lived for five generations. Even Lincoln Steffens, the world traveler, was proud of his father's splendid Sacramento home, and printed a plate of it in his autobiography.[8]

Southern California is a place of quicker turnover. Its taste in history runs to confections like Knott's Berry Farm, the Mission Inn (where Ronald and Nancy Reagan spent their wedding night), and the "reconstructions" of Forest Lawn (where Reagan and Jane Wyman were married). This taste showed itself when Reagan went to Sacramento and moved out of the traditional governor's mansion, which is the splendid home Lincoln Steffens was proud of. Built in 1878, it had been the Albert Gallatin mansion before Joseph Steffens bought it. The state of California acquired it in 1903 and made it the governor's house. In 1917 part of the house was marred by a radical's bomb, causing a statewide "Red scare."[9] But the rich interior, with six Italian marble fireplaces on the ground floor, and a relief of Columbia carved in wood above every door, had served governors from Hiram Johnson's predecessor, James N. Gillett, down to Pat Brown in 1966. Joan Didion, who calls it "my favorite house in the world," remembers staying there with other friends of Earl Warren's daughter, Nina. It is, she writes, "the kind of house in which sixty adolescent girls might gather and never interrupt the real life of the household."[10]

The house was conveniently near the Capitol, a place where the governor could meet people outside his office, entertain legislators, and maintain a symbolic presence at the center of state government. But Ronald Reagan, who likes to escape the workplace after minimal office hours, wanted something remoter, preferably outside town altogether. Besides, the neighborhood had decayed by 1966. Reagan said his son Ron would have trouble finding playmates and schools. But Kathleen, the youngest daughter of Pat and Bernice Brown, had no trouble attending Sutton Junior High School.[11] Nancy, realizing that her husband's words could be taken as a class slur on children of the neighborhood, assured reporters that only safety considerations made it necessary to leave the mansion. It was a firetrap.[12]

Sacramento is full of desirable Victorian mansions made of wood, protected by escape and extinguisher equipment, and the governor's mansion was another of those. It was not hard to keep up. In fact, Bernice Brown recalls that Christmas was a particular joy there, since the Buildings and Grounds division put up three ceiling-high Christmas trees in the front room, and lesser trees in other rooms. The hall carpets were rolled up for dancing. She remembers one Christmas as "the year of the bicycles." The Browns' daughter at Stanford and their grandson both wanted one. "You cannot wrap a bicycle," Mrs. Brown says, "so I put envelopes under the tree, with clues that sent them on separate treasure hunts. There are so many cubbyholes and pantries in that house that they were led upstairs and down and all around the place until the last clue took them to the basement where the bicycles were hidden."

The Reagans wanted a house more like the one General Electric had built for them. Wealthy friends—Taft Schreiber of MCA among them—bought land on the American River and built an antiseptic bunker as forbidding as it was expensive.[13] To add the final touch of historic contempt, the vast low building was laid over a Maidu Indian burial ground. Jerry Brown, the former governor's son, had been elected California's Secretary of State by the time construction was about to begin, and he brought an injunction against the desecration of the site, arguing that the old mansion was not only still usable but preferable.[14] By the time he was elected governor in 1974, he could not return to the house his father had used. It had been converted into a museum.

The new house outside town was not completed in time for the Reagans to move into it. Jerry Brown would not do so, and no other governor—no other family—has ever done so. It has gone unfurnished, unlandscaped, a millionaire's toy never used, a symbol of the rootless desire for "modernity." While the planning and building of the new mansion went on, the Reagans' ever-obliging friends bought them a home they wanted to rent, on Forty-fifth Street. "Forty-fifth Street is isolated from the rest of the city by the high cost of its homes and by tradition, which reserves it for the old, established families of Sacramento. It is a patch of wealth amid blocks of middle-income homes—inward-looking, rich and Republican. No Negroes there."[15]

Reagan had come to town as a transient, just renting, moving on. He would call in outside accountants to catch the bureaucrats at their tricks. He would consult (on a time-donated basis) with businessmen, who had a track record in "real" management, where you have to turn a profit. He swore not to lose his amateur status in office. He would commute to the grubbiness of politics from the homes of "clean" power. The transition team, pried loose at last from Los Angeles, moved into Sacramento's IBM Building.

Reagan had reason to think the politicians had put something over on him. Pat Brown naturally delayed tax increases before the election, which involved some creative accounting by his able finance director, Hale Champion. After the election, Champion offered to explain what problems he was leaving the victors, and to suggest the ways he had planned to retrieve the situation. The new men did not want to hear.[16] They resembled Krook in

Bleak House, who has to teach himself to read rather than be taught by someone who knows. Krook, with his omnidirectional distrust, is afraid that a teacher, while knowing more, might "teach me wrong."

Reagan's chief talent hunter at the time, Tom Reed, had trouble filling the important post of finance director. Professional politicians were ruled out. Several outsiders were offered the job but declined. Others were blocked for ideological reasons—Caspar Weinberger, for instance, was still unacceptable to right-wingers who remembered his support for Rockefeller against Goldwater in 1964.[17] Finally Gordon Paul Smith, the vice president of a management consulting firm, agreed to take the job. Unable to learn the intricacies of the budget in a short time, his response to the crisis in state funds was to adopt an idea Reagan had picked up at a Republican governors' conference —an across-the-board cut of 10 percent in all government spending.[18] This approach cut equally into bare-subsistence programs, efficiently run ones, and padded ones. Like rain falling on the just and unjust, it punished alike the needed and the unnecessary. Naturally, the impact on needed (and needy) programs, especially those having to do with mental health, got most of the publicity, which caused the plan to backfire. Within two years, in fact, Reagan had substantially *increased* spending on mental health, so that "what had begun as a superficial attempt to find a dramatic economy based solely on statistics had ended in an expensive reform."[19] Reagan had eventually to rush compensatory funds to areas that could have been trimmed more modestly over time. Here, as with education, Reagan would create an outcry by threatening draconian reductions, and find he had to give more than was necessary to still the fears he had called up.[20] As for Gordon Smith, he "never seemed to know what the budget of the State of California was all about."[21] Reagan did not get control of the financial process until Caspar Weinberger at last became finance director, and by then Reagan had been forced to make a complex series of deals with the legislature to pass the state's long overdue tax raise.

There was another disadvantage to the outsiders' team Reagan had brought in with him. It had not been sifted by any public testing process, undergone scrutiny, been politically sensitized. Reagan's first chief of staff, the most important job in his administration, was a bright young lawyer brought to the campaign by Holmes Tuttle. Lyn Nofziger, an ex-journalist, suspected that this man was filling a number of posts with homosexual friends, and quietly set about collecting evidence. Reagan had campaigned against the "moral decline" in modern society,[22] and his right-wing backers clearly treated the open homosexuality of San Francisco and other parts of California as symptoms of decay. It would be a damaging political blow if the press discovered—as in time it must—that the old-fashioned righteousness of the Reagan administration was being dealt out by homosexuals.

Nofziger convinced Reagan that the people he had spied on must go, quietly but as quickly as possible. Their departure was bound to be noticed, and would have to be explained as innocuously as possible. The first interpretation by reporters was that an ideological purge had taken place. Reagan's unannounced campaign for President, already being shaped toward the 1968 convention, was thrown badly off stride as tasks were reassigned within the administration. According to Lou Cannon, "the surviving staffers, unable to discuss their story with the outside world, lived in daily worry that the truth would become known."[23] Reagan, normally so trusting with aides, withdrew from the administration of the government, so that "the governorship went into receivership." He had been sufficiently detached beforehand not to know about the problem or about its investigation, though eventually Nofziger recruited Tom Reed, Ed Meese, Arthur Van Court and others before informing Reagan of the results. The governor's first reaction was, "My God, has government failed?"[24] For two months afterward, he acted as if his words had come true.

At last Nofziger decided that the spell had to be broken. The staff was in the position of a person ordered *not* to think of a rhinoceros. It could think of little else. Rumors were now out and being published (first in *Newsweek*). So Nofziger, acting without Reagan's knowledge, as he had done when collecting evidence, leaked the story to newsmen. Reagan denied the story and claimed that Nofziger could not be saying such a thing, on the morally defensible grounds that families had to be protected. Nancy Reagan was so furious with Nofziger that she would not speak to him, and eventually this cost him his job.[25] But the pretense was over. Reagan would have to welcome Nofziger back when he needed his skills in future campaigns.

Amateurism posed another threat that Reagan was peculiarly exposed to —conflict of interest. Soliciting the good offices of businessmen and his millionaire patrons, Reagan praised them for their public spirit, never asking whether they might be expecting or taking something in return. We get a glimpse of *their* attitude from the accident that a reporter was in one movie executive's office during a typical phone call of that period:

> Late one afternoon, Richard Zanuck received a telephone call from Governor Ronald Reagan's office in Sacramento. The caller was one of Reagan's aides, who wondered if the studio had a spare lawyer it could lend the administration to help out the utilities commission during the summer holidays. Zanuck listened politely to the caller and said he would get back to him. When he hung up, he rang Harry Sokolow. "Ronnie Reagan wants to borrow a lawyer," Zanuck said. "They're short-handed in Sacramento with everyone taking vacations up there. Check the legal department and see if we can spare one, and if we can, let's throw him one for four weeks. It never hurts to have a friend in Sacramento."[26]

Zanuck, it should be remembered, was at 20th Century-Fox, the studio that bought Reagan's ranch, just after his election, for such an inflated sum. Zanuck was clearly looking for favors down the road, and he got at least one. In 1968 Governor Reagan signed a state bill, which Governor Brown had vetoed, that gave the major studios—including MCA's Universal—three to four million dollars each in tax breaks on their film inventories.[27]

As we shall be seeing in the next chapter, Reagan followed a routine in his legislative actions, which meant that he rarely considered special pleas outside of channels, or granted favors directly. (Bing Crosby won an exception to this rule when, with a phone call, he got Reagan to override his Secretary of Resources on a matter that concerned duck hunters.)[28] But those around Reagan were clearly taught to admire and help the businessmen who were supposed to be contributing so much wisdom, as well as financial support, to the administration. The results over the years have been registered in the courts.

Tom Reed, who helped Nofziger handle the homosexual scandal in Sacramento, provides a good example of the kinds of scandal that would be common in the Reagan circle. He organized Reagan's national team for the 1968 presidential campaign, and stayed with him through the years. In 1980 he ran a Political Action Committee that raised over a million dollars for Reagan's election. He was appointed Special National Security Assistant to the President, but in his first year was accused of trading on inside knowledge to turn a $3,000 investment, in two days, into a $341,000 sale. The Securities and Exchange Commission would have brought suit over this, but he escaped by surrendering the money in a consent decree. This transaction was attacked as showing favoritism to a member of the administration.[29] Reed resigned, but was later appointed by the President to his MX advisory panel. Then the Justice Department indicted him for the investment that had led to his resignation. Though the prosecution was unable to prove a source of inside knowledge, and therefore to obtain a conviction, Reed was forced on the stand to admit that he had covered the source of the investment by forging documents and diverting the money to two lovers, one of whom he had appointed to a government post while serving as Secretary of the Air Force under President Ford, and the other of whom had been his private secretary in that post.[30]

Reed was the sixth official of high rank in President Reagan's first administration to be indicted on criminal charges. Paul Thayer, Deputy Defense Secretary, went to jail for four years after trading on inside knowledge for his own profit. Criminal proceedings complicated matters that were difficult enough in themselves. When *Challenger*, the NASA space shuttle, exploded, killing its crew, the space agency had trouble responding effectively since its director, James Beggs, was under indictment for defrauding the Army as an executive of General Dynamics Corporation.[31]

Nor can the conflicts of interest in the Reagan White House be measured solely in terms of indictments or convictions. Twenty-five high officials were fired, resigned, or had their nominations withdrawn for allegations of financial misconduct or lax standards.[32] There were famous resignations (Raymond Donovan, Rita Lavelle, Max Hugel, Richard Allen, J. Lynn Helms), and many quieter withdrawals, many cases where the interplay of interests brought no punitive action, or penitence. Richard Perle, the Assistant Secretary of Defense, continued to be the primary planner of the administration's disarmament strategy, unembarrassed by the revelation that he personally recommended to the Secretary of the Army a weapon made by an Israeli firm that had employed Perle as a consultant. Robert Buford, director of the Interior Department's Bureau of Land Management, received a waiver of rules against owning grazing lands administered by his bureau. Minor favors seemed ordinary, even routine—e.g., the removal of Coors factories from health-inspection lists on orders from high in the Occupational Safety and Health Administration.[33]

Through it all, as Laurence Barrett has remarked, "Reagan was astonishingly unconcerned about displaying a keen sense of propriety."[34] Just as he did not recuse himself from SAG actions when they involved his own agent, he has not insisted that his highest appointees live by conflict-of-interest safeguards taken for granted in other administrations. Caspar Weinberger and William Casey, whose departments make contracts in the millions of dollars with companies they have ties to, are not even partially shielded from knowledge of their personal stake in such transactions by having their money in a blind trust.[35] When William French Smith, already appointed Attorney General, made profitable tax-shelter investments on his own, outside a blind trust already set up, Reagan's only response was to tell his staff, "If I find out who's been bad-mouthing Bill, I'm going to kick . . . his ass out of here."[36] When William Casey, the head of the CIA, omitted large items from his financial disclosure forms (required by law), Reagan saw nothing to criticize. When Edwin Meese's confirmation as Attorney General was held up for many months by a web of intersecting favors done and received, including public offices given to those who had lent him money, the President just pushed harder for his confirmation.[37]

This was a pattern set in Sacramento, where Reagan first became truly wealthy while in office. One of the men involved in the real estate sales that accomplished that transformation, William French Smith, was appointed a regent to the University of California (later he became chairman of the board of regents). In this role, he was sued for conflict of interest on several grounds. The university was developing a new campus on property donated by the Irvine Corporation to stimulate growth of its planned community, and French was the Irvine Company's lawyer. He was also an investor in agricultural firms dealing with UC development projects, and with nuclear weapons industries that dealt with the UC laboratory at Livermore.[38] None of these ties—or those to Reagan's private finances—was severed, even temporarily, and French continued serving as regent after becoming President Reagan's Attorney General.

Just as Reagan seems incapable of recognizing anything good about "govment," he is literally blind to the possibility that businessmen may be anything but high-minded when they lend their services to government. Only the rich, he seems to feel, can serve unselfishly—they are above bribes.

(Chesterton answered this old argument for plutocracy by saying the rich are born bribed.) What Reagan calls "citizen politics," though it may involve many community leaders with high motives, is extremely vulnerable to the few who may be plunderers. They go unremarked by Reagan because they are, by definition, nonexistent. Reagan administrations would be a series of failed testimonials to the myth that businessmen do not steal from government.

Reagan, without sordid dealing himself, did not clearly discourage it in those around him. That began with his own readiness to accept so many favors from his wealthy friends while in office, and that began the minute he took office in Sacramento—or, rather, before. Determined to bring some style to the stodgy north, Reagan's friends raised a private fund to throw the most expensive inaugural celebration in California's history. It was a forerunner of the house they would soon build him, and the other house they bought for him to rent; a forerunner of friendly bequests in the White House, like the expensive gowns and furnishings given the First Lady. Reagan accepts these tributes as public-spirited donations to the people, not to him. He admires people like J. Lynn Helms, who offered his government salary at the Federal Aviation Administration to charity—and then had to resign under investigation of business frauds for his own profit.[39]

The inaugural party in Sacramento was a rehearsal for similar occasions in Washington. In fact, the tone for Reagan's presidential administration was set by the private trust established to finance the transition period from his election in 1980 to his inauguration in 1981. Congress allots two million dollars to the winning candidate for this purpose, and President Carter had returned three thousand dollars of that money in 1976. But wealthy friends of Reagan raised almost a million dollars more to pay for consulting and brain-trusting activities, which rewarded Reagan allies and conservative groups. When the trust was set up, it was called tax-exempt (though no application was made for that status), and public accounting was promised. But after the President took office, the trust refused to publish its accounts or even to let any government officials see them—not the Comptroller General, not the General Accounting Office.[40] The three directors of the trust were Edwin Meese, William Casey, and Verne Orr (later Secretary of the Air Force). These were the men who set the rules to be observed by the Reagan administration, and the President who agreed with them was observably the same man who saw no conflict of interest in the SAG-MCA waiver of 1952. The citizen politician, like the Guild president with an agent, lives by standards different from those imposed on mere civil servants. He never has to think of government as "we." Reagan campaigned for the White House with these words: "Unless we elect to the highest office men with no ties to the system, men at the top who are not afraid to tangle with it and take it on head first, we will never change it."[41] By "the system" he means any contamination of merely paid public service. Ties to corporations and banks and intersecting business interests are no disqualification at all. They are the ties that liberate.

CHAPTER 33

Government Man

*We did not go backward under Reagan's regime.
We went forward.*

*—Wilson Riles, California Superintendent
of Public Instruction*

The men who backed Reagan for governor in 1966 had, most of them, been deeply involved in the Goldwater campaign. They wanted to elect a President. While others were certain that Goldwater's crushing loss had discredited his cause, if not his entire party, these men were convinced that the only thing wrong with the 1964 campaign had been its candidate. As Henry Salvatori said of Goldwater, "His philosophy was sound, but he didn't articulate it moderately."[1] Reagan was the right articulator, and the governor's mansion was to be just an out-of-town trial run for a Washington opening in 1968.

Reagan understood this exercise. Stanley Plog, his full-time coach-attendant in the gubernatorial campaign, said his pupil had a clearer view of the ultimate goal than of the immediate one: "The primary thing was to educate him on the politics and issues of California because, all along, that guy has been focused on national politics. He always wanted to be President, not governor."[2] It was a feeling shared by the whole Reagan entourage. "Nofziger had wanted to make Reagan President from the time he first laid eyes on him. Reed's interest was in the national arena."[3] Even before his inauguration as governor in 1966, just ten days after his election, Reagan met with his advisers to plan the presidential campaign—it was only two years off, after all. Tom Reed was made the principal coordinator of the effort, which he would keep in mind as he recruited talent for the state administration. Within two weeks Reed made Clif White, who had captured delegates for Goldwater at the 1964 convention, the campaign counsel.[4] That presidential appointment came before most state offices had been filled.

Reagan's whirlwind early days in Sacramento were meant to accomplish startling things in a hurry, to make a record the very first year, so Reagan would have something to take with him on speaking tours in 1968. That was why so many precedents had to be shattered, so much action taken rapidly—the midnight beginning of the term, the immediate ten percent cut in funds, the demand that government respond to the emergency by working on national holidays, the task forces of outside accountants and management experts set loose on the bureaucracy to scourge it toward reforms.[5] Those who mean to stay in one place have regard for precedent, for long-term relations, for settled methods of operation. Reagan argued that his freedom from this "buddy system" would let him innovate fearlessly.

As soon as Reed had staffed the California administration, he began to tour the nation, formally as a talent scout for conservative ideas on governing California, actually as a booking agent to set up future speeches by the governor. He was forming a network of alliances for 1968, commissioned both to rally the dispirited Goldwater forces and reconcile those Republicans disaffected by Goldwater. This grand strategy ran into a series of obstacles. Hurried actions in Sacramento undid themselves. The recruitment of fresh outside talent led to the homosexual scandal. The uniform cuts led to real and feigned cries of pain from those affected. The tough talk against students led to further campus turmoil. The state legislature, with Jesse Unruh leading its lower house, defied the brash new men in town.

But this local balkiness might not have stopped Reagan in his daring attempt to revive the Goldwater movement had he not run into an unexpected obstacle at the national level: Richard Nixon. In 1962, everyone knew Nixon was through. In 1964, everyone knew it but Nixon. His magic recovery began with the Goldwater campaign. Nixon, who had never really been trusted by the right, stuck doggedly with Goldwater while Rockefeller and Romney moderates deserted the cause. In the depths of the Goldwater loss, only Reagan had seemed to be a winner. But on a larger if quieter scale, so was Nixon. In 1965, the campaign director for the House of Representatives made Nixon honorary chairman of the Congressional Boosters Club to raise money for the 1966 races. In the campaign year itself, Nixon set up three more committees on his own to raise and disburse funds, to keep him on the road speaking for Republican candidates, and to form what became the core of his 1968 campaign team.[6] By 1967 he had so effectively wooed Goldwater himself, and key Southern leaders like Strom Thurmond and John Tower, that Reagan's people were denied support they were taking for granted as their base. This was so unexpected that Reed and Nofziger proceeded as if it had not happened. Republicans, they reasoned, had to go through the motions of repaying Nixon, but would finally let their hearts speak.

Reagan had given one small hostage to fortune in order to reach his first staging area—and that, ironically, was also caused by Nixon. When Nixon ran for governor in 1962, there was such feeling against his using the statehouse as a mere steppingstone that he had to pledge he would not run for President in 1964. In 1966, though Reagan deftly steered around Nixon's disavowal of the John Birch Society, he had to repeat the promise to serve out his first term. Still, that could be finessed, his backers reasoned. Reagan would be granted the traditional governor's prerogative of running as a favorite son, improving the large California delegation's position. When he arrived at the convention, the delegates organized by White were supposed to rise up and demand that he become a real candidate, and the nominee.

By the time Reagan warmed again to his own ambitions, after the homosexual scandal, Clif White found Nixon commitments blocking him everywhere in the South. Reagan was dispatched on speaking tours there, to play on conservative affections. But the only way to do that, by 1968, was to compete with George Wallace for the extremist vote, which Reagan did charily enough to be ineffective.[7] By the time he arrived in Miami in 1968, Reagan still claimed he was not a "real" candidate as he scurried around the delegations, though his people were paying for White's expensive communications van at the convention hall.[8] When the cry for him did not arise, Reagan "responded" to it in the hope of eliciting it, with a late declaration of his open but unadmitted status. Only his impregnable air of candor could have survived so many repeated violations of it in such public circumstances. The exercise was so embarrassing that Reagan people tried resolutely to forget it afterward. As Nancy Reagan wrote in her book: "Ronnie never sought the nomination in 1968."[9]

Despite that claim, the entire first half of Reagan's first term as governor was dominated by presidential considerations. That shows especially in his major achievement, the tax increase. Reagan knew he had to make it a large one, and to make it fast, for several reasons. The quicker it came, the more closely it could be tied to the fiscal crisis inherited from Pat Brown. The larger it was, the less Reagan would have to worry about seeking further grants from a legislature unwilling to raise taxes more than once. Also, the larger amount of money he had at his disposal, the more he could satisfy state needs and free himself for political activity elsewhere as the 1968 convention approached. "Success would give him leisure to travel and participate in national politics. Failure would keep him at home trying to raise money to pay for the running of government, dogged by the local difficulties that overcome other governors."[10]

Thus the candidate who had run against big spenders quickly became the governor who asked for and got the highest tax raise in the history of California (or any other state), one that ran far beyond actual need, so that he had to think, eventually, of ways to return some of it in the form of rebates.[11] And the man who claimed he was above politics was campaigning for the presidency with the state's money. To get what he wanted, he resorted to the very abuse he had come to purge—buying votes with political payoffs:

> In the need for victory, the Reagan men forgot all the old campaign promises of no political deals. Where once the administration scorned legislators' appeals for patronage, they now listened. Through his aides, the governor asked recalcitrant senators if they wanted to make a deal.

Several, rebuffed for months, were delighted, and [Philip] Battaglia, standing quietly in back of the senate chamber, talked to them. One senator was told that Reagan would now sign his appropriation bill, despite the administration's economy goals. Two more were told that, by coincidence, the men they were backing for judgeships would now get the appointments. Power was also used. The legislature's only member of the John Birch Society, John Schmitz, whose conservative constituency provided some of Reagan's most enthusiastic and wealthy supporters, refused to vote for the tax increase. Brought into a side room by Battaglia, Schmitz was told that every one of his bills would be vetoed if he refused Reagan a vote.[12]

All this bargaining was in the Senate, and was part of the price exacted by Jesse Unruh for getting the bill through the Assembly. The other part of the price was that Unruh's aides dictated much of the bill's shape, making the tax highly progressive. But this would have happened in any case, once Reagan decided he needed the raise fast, since his own finance director was ineffectual and "he [Reagan] knew next to nothing about the state tax system."[13] Weinberger had not yet been installed as financial manager. Therefore "the committees in which the bill was written were dominated by bright young staff aides, many of them recruited by Unruh, who were as sophisticated about government as Reagan was unknowledgeable."[14]

It was a spectacular gamble from ignorance—and it was actually helped by the miscalculations involved in the ten-percent spending cut. Even while blaming the tax increase on Democrats' spendthrift ways, Reagan said the cut proved that his administration could be trusted to remain austere. Then, when the unnecessarily high tax resulted in surpluses, Reagan coolly took credit for good management. By wonderful showmanship, he turned a series of blunders, compromises, and broken campaign promises, into the illusion of shrewd control. There in miniature was the pattern for much of his later work as President. No wonder the act would mystify so many experts. He liked to quote General MacArthur's dictum that there is no substitute for victory, yet he early found an acceptable substitute for success, and has continued to repeat the trick, making it clear that this was not an isolated fluke.

Yet, despite all the frisky talk about bold departures with which he began, despite the public support he won with his tough rhetoric against campus radicals, despite the good face he managed to put on the tax bill, Reagan's first term "had been moderate and responsible but undistinguished."[15] He had spent more than his predecessor, though he had balanced the books. He had won token victories in imposing tuition (softened to "charges") at the state university and delaying income tax withholding. At midterm he had gained a Republican majority in the legislature, but the Republicans proved even less amenable to discipline than the Democrats, and Reagan's worst years were the only two in which he had a majority in the statehouse. The main advantage Reagan had, facing reelection in 1970, was the healthy state of the state's finances. But he had just about run through the rebates from his surplus, and the legislature of 1970 was writing the first deficit budget since the tax bill.

It is not surprising, then, that the knowledgeable Lou Cannon wrote *Ronnie and Jesse: A Political Odyssey*, to appear in 1969. He foresaw the 1970 election as a titanic struggle between the new Republican strength in California and the shrewdest state legislator in anybody's memory. Unruh had been maneuvering toward the governor's mansion for a long time. He even helped Reagan pass his tax bill because he thought it would recoil upon its signer when people had to *pay* its high costs. But what should have been a close struggle turned into a comic mismatch. Unruh, driven by whatever personal demons, made a fool of himself early in the campaign. Reagan airily dismissed his calls for a debate between the candidates, his calls for disclosure of their personal finances, his slurs on the manhood of those purged during the scandal. Unruh, like Brown before him and like every political opponent after him, found that Reagan is not merely a good campaigner himself (though he is that), but he is impossible to campaign *against*. Attacks on him always hurt the attacker, so effectively has he preengaged sympathy at many levels. As Falstaff would say, a man knows not where to have him. He is uncome-at-able. He breezed back in.

But now Nixon held the White House, presumably till 1976, two years beyond the end of Reagan's second term. There was no way to govern California by running for President in his second term. Reagan would have to settle for the less glamorous task of governing California. And govern it he did, competently, popularly, routinely. He worked responsibly with Unruh's less flashy successor, Assembly leader Bob Moretti, to pass welfare legislation that raised benefits for recipients (long overdue) while tightening administration and accountability.[16] This was not the result of an overnight spree of influence peddling, as had been the case with the rapid passage of the tax bill, but of patient negotiating and long-term planning.

Reagan was able to accomplish this through an extraordinarily efficient team. It had taken shape in the aftermath of the scandal, when William Clark became chief of staff. It was said that the government went into receivership at the time of the scandal. Clark was the receiver. He took up the tasks that others were too numb to perform, and imposed the pattern that would be followed by his successor, Edwin Meese, throughout the second term. Clark established the centrality of the cabinet meeting. Toward it all recommendations and pleas were directed, paced by a schedule for the submission of one-page memo forms as the basis for discussion. Everything properly filed was discussed in Reagan's presence; decisions were made there. Attempts to "end-run" that process were blocked. Reagan turned a deaf ear to them.[17]

This administrative procedure was similar to President Eisenhower's in the White House—not simply, as one might expect, because Reagan thought of himself as the chairman of a corporation's board, but because corporate

officers like to think of themselves as generals. Ed Meese, who took charge of
the Reagan organization, adjusted it to military models. After his two years'
service in the army in the nineteen-fifties, he remained active in the military
reserve, and retired only in 1976, with the rank of lieutenant colonel. His son
graduated from West Point in 1981.[18] In the White House, he would use his
influence to be reactivated in the reserve at the rank of colonel. He is a
military buff, which made him aspire toward military procedures as the
executive secretary to Reagan's administration. "One of the staff, who
shared Meese's interest in management theory, recalled that they would
spend hours debating such things as whether the Army's general staff system
was superior to the Navy's chain of command system."[19]

This was in accord with Reagan's own fondness for the military. But it sits
strangely with his endless criticism of the bureaucracy. What does he imagine the military branches belong to? As Chesterton remarked in 1926 (showing how old is the "Tory lament"):

> I have never understood, by the way, why Tory debaters are so very
> anxious to prove against Socialism that "State Servants" must be in-
> competent and inert. Surely it might be left to others to point out the
> lethargy of [Admiral] Nelson or the dull routine of [General] Gordon.[20]

Or, one might add, the methodical staffing of Eisenhower.

Clark and Meese brought order to the Reagan administration, which
made it successful. As Reagan later said: "For eight years somebody handed
me a piece of paper every night that told me what I was going to be doing
the next day."[21] That suited Reagan's personality; he is a company person.
He functions best as part of a production team, where his job is clear, limited, and geared toward the public. That was his role at Warner Bros., at the
Guild (where Jack Dales ran the staff in its settled ways), at GE. For all his
claims about creative innovation, he is not a person to upset others' settled
ways, his own are so very placid. This enemy of the planned society cannot
move in his daily life without fixed schedules. There is something almost
touchingly inappropriate in his midnight inauguration—Reagan is often in
bed by ten.

As Gary Hamilton and Nicole Biggart show, in extensive interviews with
the staffs of both ex-governors, Jerry Brown actually lived up to Reagan's
claims about experimenting with a "creative society." Brown brought in
outside opinions and fresh approaches. He shook the bureaucracy, defied
precedent, remained an outsider uncaptured by his office. Though he came
from a political family and had prior political experience, he moved freer of
that background than Reagan ever would. He really did his work (not just
one television appearance) at midnight. Yet he was not as successful at governing as Reagan. "By fighting the system, Brown paralyzed government."[22]

By functioning according to system, Reagan strengthened the government. Reagan "used the bureaucracy in ways consistent with its structure
and, if anything, sharpened such structural attributes as role differentiation,

communication-channels, and chains of command."[23] Needless to say, these are all bureaucratic values. They were Executive Secretary Meese's values, as he was proud to state. "Public management has been a hobby of mine since I majored in Public Administration back at Yale," he told Hamilton and Biggart. "When I was in Sacramento, I spent a lot of time studying management patterns and the staff organization of everybody I could get my hands on."[24] When Jerry Brown's incoming aides were briefed by Meese, they mocked him for his bureaucratic fascinations, from which they intended to remain creatively free. As Anthony Klein told the story: "He showed us a chart of state government in 1930. It had a million lines down to a million agencies. Then he showed us a chart of state government in the last year of the Reagan administration. They had four lines from the governor to their four main agencies and a fifth to Finance. It was all very impressive, but I don't know whether it worked. I don't know what it all meant."[25] And Klein had no intention of learning. He obviously shared a Reagan aide's view: "If anybody were to describe [Meese] to you, they would say that if he's got two things to do, he makes an outline."[26]

Reagan would continue talking like a man on a guerrilla raid as he placidly administered California's huge bureaucracy. He acted on his words at times. But the principal occasion when he did that, he suffered the worst setback of his second term—the failed effort to put a legal limit on state taxes.[27] Though this was inspired by a former member of the John Birch Society, a favorite of Meese's, the executive secretary normally let his penchant for organization overcome his ideological zeal. He and others found that competent administrators had to be people who understood the bureaucracy, believed in the functions they were asked to oversee, and commanded the respect of their workers. Reagan, the good company man, developed genial relations with the heads of the departments and became proud of what his government had accomplished, giving it a magic exemption from the general condemnations he still issued about government-in-general. Thus he compiled excellent records in areas where his rhetoric would not have prompted confidence—areas like education, where the (elected) Superintendent of Public Instruction was Wilson Riles, a Democrat Reagan supported warmly; or in the environment, where his administrator of resources was Norman (Ike) Livermore.

Reagan would later claim too much for his administration of the state, or actually take credit for the opposite of what happened. He spent more, not less, than either of the Browns. He often let the machinery work rather than working it. He delegated widely. He shared the job. But he did the job. He often came in late on decisions.[28] But he made the decisions. Here is the balanced judgment of Hamilton and Biggart:

> A final, ironic consequence of the structured Reagan administration was that it worked well to systematize government. Many of the management reforms and experienced executives that the Reagan adminis-

tration brought to Sacramento in fact made government run better and deliver services more effectively. While the budget more than doubled from $4.6 billion to $10.2 billion, in large part due to inflation, the number of state workers did not grow appreciably. But neither did California shrink and allow private citizens to handle their own affairs. Instead, government entrenched itself in many ways as a strong, effective force in California society.[29]

Reagan had committed the very sin he inveighed against—government.

CHAPTER 34

Unique Selling Intelligence

Is the art of the window dresser a substitute
for copy? Is it going to add persuasion?

—*Rosser Reeves*

Little over a year after his formal entry into politics, Ronald Reagan was running a state that, as he liked to remind people, is larger than most countries in the world. And the challenge of California does not come merely from its size, but from the need for simultaneous effort at restraint and exploitation. The state lives off manufactured lifelines carrying water, at great cost to an environment altered by bringing it in. Joan Didion is fascinated by the complexity of a system that acts like a respirator on a patient who would otherwise die:

> The water I will draw tomorrow from my tap in Malibu is today crossing the Mojave Desert from the Colorado River, and I like to think about exactly where that water is. The water I will drink tonight in a restaurant in Hollywood is by now well down the Los Angeles Aquaduct from the Owens River, and I also think about exactly where that water is: I particularly like to imagine it as it cascades down the 45-degree stone steps that aerate Owens water after its airless passage through the mountain pipes and siphons.[1]

The Water Plan formed under Edmund Brown and completed by Ronald Reagan accomplished a massive moving of waters that entailed the largest engineering works ever undertaken in history—one dwarfing Reagan's hated target of old, the TVA.[2] It is only by virtue of such large-scale coordination that the entirely artificial fertility of California is maintained, making its central valley an outdoor greenhouse, its southern basin a thin veil of vegetation spread over inhospitable soil forever imperiled.

Marx in his youth thought hydraulic societies were naturally despotic.

The central planning needed, to coordinate large regional efforts on a tight seasonal calendar, drains authority from the local community so that irrigation ditches can run on time.[3] The success of the Mormons in bringing water to Utah shows the advantage of an authoritarian community in arid country. California never had a central power of that sort, but it had many economic fiefdoms and interlocking systems of control. Here even less than in the territory that Turner discussed was the idea of "free land" ever a reality.[4] Land barons swallowed the old Mexican ranches and laid claim to huge swaths of northern timberland. Public lands were gobbled up by speculators using dummy agents. Government surveyors sold information about good land for private gain. As in Iowa, government scrip was purchased by third parties and used to buy government land. In Iowa, it was veterans' scrip. In California, it was scrip issued to the various states for agricultural colleges under the Morrill Land Grant of 1862.[5] One fifth of the land in private ownership belonged to the Southern Pacific Railroad, which had been built with the help of federal funds and a corrupt state legislature.

As the railways were built by collusion of public authority and private investors, so were the early water projects. William Chapman Ralston's Bank of California developed the Spring Valley Water Company in San Francisco as part of his vast financial empire.[6] President Theodore Roosevelt, an enemy of Sierra Club founder John Muir, gave permission in 1908 for part of Yosemite National Park to be turned into a reservoir for supplying Los Angeles with water, and helped clear the way for the largest aquaduct in the world by an "extension of the Sierra National Forest eastward to include the prospective right of way, even though the only trees in the region were those planted by the settlers themselves."[7]

The resulting distribution of water led to the characteristic layout and population density of Southern California, neither urban nor rural,[8] and to anomalies like the shape of Los Angeles's legal boundaries. The successively imprinted networks of waterways, railroads, trollies, and freeways created an economic geography not centered, like most major urban areas, around a port or river landing. The result is a profitable but precarious growth so insecurely rooted in nature that Carey McWilliams subtitled his classic book on Southern California *An Island on the Land.*

The state, like the West in general, was born of dependence on the federal government. In other states, federal troops had to take land only from the Indians. California was also taken from Mexico. Then it was developed by federal outlay on railroads, naval operations, and water projects. Ronald Reagan has several times recalled how he mused on what he would put into a time capsule while riding the highway along California's magnificent coast. The freeway system, which is one of California's most characteristic features, was heavily subsidized with federal money.[9] And the state draws even more government money for defense contracts, especially in the realm of aeronautics and microcomputers. In 1980 California alone received a quarter of the Defense Department's prime contracts (44 percent of NASA's).[10]

The myth of Western "independence" is even less connected with reality in California than it was in the Mississippi catchment area where Reagan was born along the hydraulic works of the Hennepin Canal. As Donald Worster has argued: "The West, more than any other American region, was built by state power, state expertise, state technology, and state bureaucracy."[11]

Provisioning the exception that is California takes careful prevision. It is a place of planned communities, of interlocking systems, of extraordinary docility to the rules that make such a juggling act possible.[12] A constant reminder of this is the punctilio with which the rules against jaywalking are observed, traffic screeching to a halt around unauthorized street-crossers. The whizzing of cars in such numbers through and near urban areas would be impossible if people did not develop a compensatory sensitivity to right-of-way rules. Those rules are as important to California life on foot as right-of-way is to ships at sea. The "freewheeling" spirit lives by a consensus on restraints.

It is a state demanding extensive government services, responsive to drought or earthquake, to floods when the arid regions are washed by sudden rainbursts, to fires that whip through chaparral, to mudslides that bury homes and bodies. It must cope with fisheries all but wiped out by shoreline pollution and the inland restructuring of waterways; with shifts in technology that affect a smog created, in part, by the artificial environment; with regional tensions between the extremes of a state that reaches down through more degrees of latitude than any other, and is divided lengthwise by mountain chains. It is a state that grew by waves of immigration and continues to. It must have the social institutions to cope with newcomers *en masse,* the educational tools to socialize them, health facilities to heal them. It is a state with extremes of wealth and poverty rubbed together in irritating proximity, with government as the necessary intermediary.

Ronald Reagan, running for governor, expressed resentment at many of the things such a government must do. He played on the concern of earlier immigrants to the state (like himself) that newcomers will crowd them out of their share. "Great numbers of people are coming to California simply because they know that in twenty-four hours they can be taken care of by the rest of us," he claimed, though only one kind of welfare had no eligibility tests, that to the blind.[13] Even when Reagan passed the generally balanced welfare reforms in his second term, he included a residency requirement that was struck down by the courts.[14] Voters resent the complex government that keeps them suspended above the hostile sites they inhabit. Even more than in other democracies, the trick to politics in California is to get enough people to ask you to govern, and then to do it without earning their resentment for having done it. That is just the trick the Browns failed at, while Reagan succeeded.

The problem can be seen most clearly in the area of education, the largest item on the state's budget. The University of California is among the finest in the world, state or private, and it crowns an extensively tiered system of colleges and junior colleges. The hostility toward student radicals at Berkeley, which Reagan manipulated in his campaign, was fed by the amounts of tax money going into education, and especially into the preferential treatment of students at elite university branches (the top 12.5 percent of their high school classes). The state subsidized students there at $45.16 per credit hour, as opposed to $27.07 an hour at the colleges and even lower rates at the junior colleges (in 1963 figures).[15]

On the other hand, most federal grants—in large amounts—go to the research departments of the elite university, giving the state economic dividends in many forms (contracts for laboratories and producers, prestigious teachers who could not be lured there otherwise, industrial relocations that bring jobs in their wake). This created a conflict of constituencies typical of Reagan's political life, one recognized in his actions but not in his rhetoric. As a populist conservative, he opposed the elitism and intellectual arrogance of Berkeley. But as a friend of business and a beneficiary (both personally and politically) of the state's prosperity, he had to support a goose that could lay such golden eggs. As we have seen, William French Smith, his regent on the university board of trustees, was an investor in agricultural concerns that had contracts with the university, and he was counsel for the Irvine Corporation, which was setting up an ambitious new campus of the university. Thus Reagan, the critic of elitist Berkeley, helped defend it from an Unruh reform that would have reduced the gap between the university and state colleges.[16] Yet the mere existence of that proposal shows that attention to the colleges and junior colleges is the political price of voters' support for the flagship campuses. Overall, Reagan had to defend the system he had scourged on the campaign trail, and he did so more conventionally than Jerry Brown, who entertained radical doubts about parts of the educational establishment, and thought of surgical remedies that the combined branches resisted. The educational system, like much else in California's political ecology, is so edgily balanced that to touch one part endangers the whole. Reagan, for all his verbal roughhousing, never fundamentally challenged it.

It is a commonplace of democratic practice that the office seeker must coax people to yield an authority they are afraid to see him wield; and one might think Reagan was just following an age-old pattern in departing from campaign promises. Franklin Roosevelt had to campaign against large government expenditures, in 1932, before he could use the fiscal powers of government to fight the Depression. John Kennedy sincerely thought there was a missile gap when he was campaigning, but was convinced by Defense Secretary McNamara, on taking office, that there was no such thing. Officeholding sobers one.

But Reagan is different. He not only maintained his campaign views, but he did so sincerely, despite a diverging practice. He did not seem to be affected by the reality of what he was doing. He continued to profess that he had cut government spending when he had raised it drastically. That is the first mystery about the man. The second is that he was (and is) believed.

How explain both mysteries? It will not do to address the first without reference to the second—e.g., by assuming that Reagan is just cynical, or just dumb; that he does not care about contradictions, or that he does not see them. Not only is that contrary to his character and history; it still leaves the problem of people's acquiescence in the performance. Are the American people entirely inured to cynicism? Their reaction to Watergate casts some doubt on that. Are they themselves just dumb? Not in the sense that they cannot see the contradictions between what Reagan says and what he does after these are pointed out. The contradictions have often been demonstrated and admitted, yet people do not care. Why?

To seek an answer one must ask exactly what Reagan's function was as governor and is as President. This is normally explained in terms of "delegation," of his instinctive guidance while avoiding detail, inspiring people while letting his staff handle administration. In fact, Reagan is often compared with Eisenhower. They are the only successful two-term Presidents of the post-Roosevelt era. Both Republicans. Both heavily reliant on their staff. Recent reevaluations of Eisenhower have made people more cautious about dismissing Reagan as an amateur, uninformed, part-time President—all charges that were brought against Eisenhower in the White House. Modern scholars give at least some assent to Fred Greenstein's claim that Eisenhower skillfully compensated for a weakness in the American presidency by playing up the head-of-state role and at least partially disguising the head-of-party role.[17]

Reagan clearly relishes the ceremonial aspects of his office, and multiplies them, finding new occasions to give out medals, awards, presidential congratulations; attending as many banquets and memorial functions as he can fit into a schedule that is notoriously light on desk hours; getting as much television coverage at these events as at political jobs more narrowly defined. To stress the contrast with his predecessor in the White House, Reagan's aides are quick to volunteer that he does not get immersed in details of administration or predecision debate. In all these ways, Reagan's conduct can be compared with the ceremonial, nonpartisan, patriotic performance of Eisenhower.

But it is the thesis of Greenstein and other revisionists that Eisenhower was more involved in partisan and administrative activity than he let others perceive. He actually kept subordinates like Nixon and Dulles on invisible leashes, and succeeded "by keeping the controversial political side of the presidential role largely covert (without, however, abdicating it)."[18] It is clear from Reagan's record in California that he did not engage in such "hidden hand" activity. He was unaware of the presence of homosexual aides in his administration, and of much else as well—though it was easier to keep track of California's governing apparatus, large as that is, than of the federal machinery. Reagan attended all cabinet meetings as governor (without presiding over them), and personally endorsed the decisions made there:

but the staff worked out deals and compromises before the presentation of the mini-memoranda that formed the basis of cabinet discussion.

> The cabinet members worked out their differences alone and, whenever possible, presented him with a *fait accompli* to be ratified. This suited his desire for consensus and preserved him from conflict, which he found distasteful. But it strengthened the position of the cabinet, who knew that Reagan rarely turned down a decision they all supported.[19]

If this was true at the cabinet level, it was bound to be even more so in the departments. Nicole Biggart recorded this interview with a key administrator:

> We instituted for the first time in the history of California, regulation of insurance agents' fee commissions under Ronald Reagan, and he never knew a thing about it. The guy who had been responsible for it said, "I know his philosophy; that's against Ronald Reagan's philosophy, but there are times when you have to overcome philosophy." In that case Ronald Reagan never knew what happened. And had he heard about it, he would have come unglued. But at the end [of the administration] it was "Let's work everything out before it gets to Ronald Reagan."[20]

This was not simply the result of carelessness or inattention on Reagan's part. He temperamentally shies from unpleasant human encounters, and kept himself deliberately removed from the squabbling that was as common in his California administration as it would be in the White House.[21]

This is not a picture of hidden-hand leadership. Nor does it conform to the picture Reagan himself likes to give of his governing method—that he functions like the chairman of the board on a large corporation. Those gentlemen like to claim, at least, that they know what is going on in their companies, and the effective ones do. In fact, it is hard to find a parallel for Reagan's function, in government, business, or any other organization. In some ways, he acts for his own administration as he did for GE, as symbol and spokesman. Yet even that comparison can mislead, because Reagan was a peripheral (and, as it turned out, disposable) adjunct to GE's selling efforts, while he is the indispensable center, as well as the symbol, of his highly personalized government. A little better comparison would be with the advertising manager of a large corporation, who is not responsible for the entire product, but only for getting his account executive at a creative agency to understand the product's best selling points. That, too, is inadequate, since the advertising manager is usually a minor executive compared to those who have responsibility for production and distribution of the product. And Reagan as President (or governor) not only sells the product, he *is* the product.

Here there is the danger of falling into the Joe McGinnis fallacy—the idea that politicians can be simply packaged by shrewd manipulators of public mood; or that, handled with sufficient expertise, a politician can be given a predetermined "image" that will make him irresistible to voters. McGinnis advanced his claim for Harry Treleaven, who is supposed to have "remade" Richard Nixon into a winning product in 1968—though Joe Napolitan was using equal skills on Hubert Humphrey that year.[22] The fragility of the claim can be seen from the fact that Treleaven was given a much more attractive product to sell in 1976—Ronald Reagan—and botched the job so badly he was fired in mid-campaign.[23]

Reagan is very conscious of his image, as any actor must be. But he did not become a skillful debater—as he proved himself against both Robert Kennedy and William F. Buckley even before his presidential debates—merely by good looks. He is a passionate believer in his cause, and one who works hard to present it well. This means that he studies everything he and his government do very closely, but from a selective angle, looking first and most intently at what can be done to make the action or idea as attractive to as many people as possible. This gives him a focus that is admittedly partial, but extremely effective. In advertising language, he thinks less of "image," as ad men like David Ogilvy do, than of Rosser Reeves's Unique Selling Proposition (USP): What is the single strongest claim that can be made for this product in terms of its desirability? Reeves cautions that the USP must be true, though it need not be the whole truth or a truth specific to the product of which it is asserted.[24]

Once the USP is found, the advertiser must not tire of repeating it, or lose faith in its efficacy simply because he has become bored with it; "A great campaign will never wear itself out."[25] Reeves himself became famous for his delivery of the same speech: "His favorite sermon on the virtues of a USP was known around the agency as the Cross of Gold speech. 'Rosser had a way of making the clients agree with him, *out loud,* from the moment he started to talk,' according to his associate. 'The client's intellectual capacity for resisting what Rosser said just seemed to disintegrate as he talked.' "[26] One is reminded of Reagan's ability to give The Speech year after year, making it seem fresh at each hearing, or his gift for retelling the same touching anecdote, always on the verge of tears. But Reeves was just promoting a technique of promotion. Reagan is promoting a set of ideas (the free enterprise system, the Communist menace) with which his career has become synonymous.

Reeves argued that the USP will gain and maintain "penetration" if it is simple and is asserted early and often. Even if it makes a claim that competing products can legitimately echo, a strong USP, advanced early and often, will preempt the claim.

Thus the U.S.P. becomes his property. It is identified with him. Who can steal "STOP HALITOSIS" from Listerine? Dozens of other mouthwashes stop halitosis. Many tried to move in on this great classic U.S.P. until it became almost a source of embarrassment to them, seeking ways to phrase their imitation, so that they did not advertise the leader. This U.S.P., in the public's mind, belongs to Listerine.[27]

Many people discuss modern political advertising in terms of image-manipulation; but the agency leader whose firm was most associated with image ads felt that advertising should play no role in politics.[28] Rosser Reeves, on the other hand, created the first television spot commercials for Dwight Eisenhower, writing them all himself, creating a separate USP for each issue he brought up. Eisenhower chafed at this simplification of his message, and his brother Milton protected him by rejecting a number of the proposed lines.[29]

Ronald Reagan is often accused of thinking in one-liners, but the art is in choosing the right line for each occasion, the one that will speak most directly to the audience's feelings, needs, or ideals. The process of presenting simple slogans is not itself simple-minded, especially when it is done constantly, day and night, over years. Rosser Reeves, though he played only fairly good chess and wrote terrible poetry, was brilliant at his chosen work. Admittedly, he was just selling toothpaste most of the time; but other practitioners of his approach can have more serious goals in mind. Preachers like Norman Vincent Peale and Robert Schuller, with their "positive thinking" and "positivity thinking," cast their teaching almost entirely in slogans. One of the most intelligent candidates of the 1984 presidential race—indeed, the most nimble performer in the Democratic primary debates—was Jesse Jackson, who spoke in jingles.

Jesse Jackson, in fact, more than any other politician now on the scene, resembles Reagan in his appeal and in his use of intelligence to expand that appeal. Both men are believers in a cause they embody, so that self-promotion and ideological commitment are fused. Both think, always, of a way to turn each situation, each event, into a vehicle for increasing the acceptance of their message. Both make claims that are one-sided, partial, over-simple, but deeply felt and almost hypnotically convincing to any listeners not actively determined to resist them (and even to some who are resisting). They both need to believe they are selling something far larger than themselves, but that the only way to do that is *through* themselves. They carry the message. Without them, it does not arrive. Each, indeed, has expressed a belief in a divine appointment to bring the message. Such professions raise the suspicion of fanaticism in others, but these two help defuse such fears with humor, modest admission of their limits, and a recognition of their role's dependence on others. Neither is a manager. They look to others for administrative direction.

Even when taking positions some consider extreme, Reagan and Jackson surprise people with their moderation in person, charming even their foes. Like Reagan with the Birchers, Jackson has extremists among his followers (Black Muslims) he neither renounces nor imitates. When Jackson ran for President in 1984, he had never been elected to political office. Reagan spent two years as governor before running for President in 1968; but if the calendar had been different, there is little doubt he would have attempted the higher office—his real goal in 1966—directly, just as he challenged a sitting

President of his own party in 1976. There is no end to each man's belief in himself and in his ability to mobilize other believers. Chutzpah becomes afflatus.

But the arrogance serves a cause, one constantly (and shrewdly) promoted. Reagan's claim that his administration spent less than his predecessor's in Sacramento was not, on balance, true. It was a claim made early and often, based on real intent and real action, and on certain aspects of his government as seen from a certain angle. That was the working truth he was dealing in, hoping all the while to make it come true by repeating it. The intent might be delayed, run into obstacles, become almost submerged in the labyrinths of administrative necessity (to which Reagan did not much advert), but the intent remained firm in his own mind and in a few programs he presented as symbols through the whole eight years. The intent was recognized even by those who knew very well that taxes had gone up. Jesse Jackson argues with great eloquence and conviction that blacks hold the balance of power in the Democratic Party's future. They do not. But they can become more powerful by saying that they do; it is a truth waiting to happen, if all the things Jackson thinks possible can be brought together (especially the formation of a coalition with other ethnic groups and women activists). It is a USP truth, accepted as such even by many who recognize the low voter turnout in a tenth of the electorate.

Thus, apart from his ceremonial duties, Reagan is *not* a do-nothing President. He is making a public *argument,* not merely a grand appearance. This is not just a matter of window dressing, but of constant analysis and testing *of people's reactions.* He is selling substance, not appearance—just as the advertiser is selling the product, not the slogan. A failure to grasp this has misled those who think that Reagan does not have a good mind. It is not an abstract or speculative mind, nor is it an administrative or managerial mind. But it is a very keen intelligence of the Rosser Reeves sort. After all, anyone who has spent time with Jesse Jackson knows he has a good mind.

PART SEVEN

STATE OF
GRACE

CHAPTER 35

The Sears
Interregnum

Hee, leading swiftly, rowld
In tangles, and made intricate seem strait.

—Paradise Lost *9.631–32*

Reagan ended his time as governor just as he had begun it, campaigning for President. In 1973 he still thought Richard Nixon would end a second term in 1976, and Spiro Agnew would make a strong bid for the Republican nomination, using his conservative base with the help of right-wing speech-writers like Patrick Buchanan and William Safire. But Reagan was deter-mined to run for President and win, this second time, even against a con-servative Vice President of his own party. There was no disorienting recent scandal just behind Reagan, no shaky early period in office as governor, to hamper him. He was completing a successful reign, and would have two years to use his skills on the speaker's tour, as a radio commentator, and as a newspaper columnist.

During Reagan's last year in Sacramento, there was a breakfast meeting every two weeks or so, called Nofziger's Group, to which Robert Walker reported on his travels about the country lining up support for a future campaign.[1] After he left office, Reagan's speaking and travel plans were arranged with that race in mind. Reagan wanted to start fresh, forgetting as much as he could about 1968, so Clif White would not run the search for delegates. Instead, Walker approached John Sears, who had worked against White and for Nixon in the delegate hunt of 1968. Sears was driven out of the Nixon administration by his old law partner John Mitchell; but he had cultivated Spiro Agnew, hoping to run his campaign in 1976.[2] That plan was shattered at the end of 1973, when Agnew resigned in disgrace and fled to the financial mercies of Frank Sinatra. Now Sears was interested in Walker's proposals. He went to California to meet Reagan and his aides in May of

1974. At this meeting, Ed Meese argued that Reagan's plans depended on Nixon's surviving in office. If Gerald Ford took over from a President driven out of office, he would be a fresh incumbent around whom the nation would rally. Sears said they should assume just the opposite—that Nixon would be gone within six months (he resigned less than three months after this meeting), and that Ford would not be up to the job of leading the nation. Reagan was impressed.[3] His determination to run, even against a sitting Republican President, was hardened by Ford's selection of the liberal Nelson Rockefeller as his Vice President. This angered conservatives in the party and disappointed Reagan, who—according to Lou Cannon's perception at the time—had hoped Ford would choose him. As in 1966, his friends set up a Citizens for Reagan operation, this one national in scope.[4]

Sears, a young sage looking prematurely ancient, thus came to the Reagan entourage with an air of wizardry, which he cultivated by keeping his plans secret from Reagan aides and from Reagan himself. Reagan submitted with great docility to Sears's elaborate campaign schemes, even letting him dismiss Lyn Nofziger as press secretary when Sears felt Nofziger had become a rival.[5] Sears said of Reagan: "He knows more about acting than politics; and he knew it. That made him a good listener."[6] Reagan had reasons for this compliance, apart from Sears's demonstrated competence. Stuart Spencer, who had run both Reagan's successful campaigns for governor, was supporting President Ford in 1976. Even Henry Salvatori, who had helped bring Reagan into politics to make him President, was loyally supporting Ford now.[7] Much of the Republican establishment would be giving the new President a fair chance to govern. Even Reagan had doggedly defended Nixon to the very end out of his "reverence for the presidency," calling the investigation of Watergate the work of a "lynch mob."[8] How could the California campaigner, who had always invoked the Republicans' Eleventh Commandment, challenge a sitting President who was pulling his party together after the disgrace of Watergate? It would take a bold approach, and Sears favored high rolling.

Yet Reagan's own experiments in bold ideas had proved spectacularly unsuccessful. The first of these was Proposition One, which Reagan hoped to take out of office with him as the figurehead victory for a nationwide tax revolt—but he could not get his own state to accept it, and had to abandon any hope of reviving its reputation.[9] He tried a new approach to the same idea when he gave a Chicago speech written by a young conservative, Jeff Bell, who had picked up some tax-cutting notions from Jude Wanniski of *The Wall Street Journal.* The Bell speech, delivered to the Executives Club on September 26, 1975, would haunt and almost destroy Reagan's 1976 campaign. It proposed a "transfer of authority and resources" from the federal to the state level, a program of "creative federalism" that would cut the federal budget by ninety billion dollars, balance the budget, and reduce the citizen's tax burden by an average 23 percent. How the transfer was to be made, and how a mere transfer could be a savings, were not spelled out—as

Stuart Spencer, already gathering ammunition for Ford's use in the New Hampshire primary, noticed. New Hampshire is a state without income or sales taxes, where 62 percent of the welfare costs are paid with federal money. Would the transfer of functions mean raising money at the state level, as well as spending it there? If not, how was this either a savings or a transfer? Economist Martin Anderson was called in to invent ingenious answers to these questions; but the answers were so convoluted that no one could follow them, beginning with Reagan. Nofziger said the arguments resembled "pan-unscrambling an egg." "The ninety billion dollar blunder" had to be survived rather than explained. It cost Reagan the first primary, which he had entered as the favorite.[10]

Another Bell speech, delivered two weeks after the one in Chicago, gave Reagan an albatross in his second primary state. Addressing the Southern Republican Conference in Houston on December 13, 1975, Reagan suggested ways to make social security voluntary.[11] The demography of Florida made that as dangerous a position as Reagan could adopt on domestic matters. Stuart Spencer had brought in his old campaign firm's partner, Bill Roberts, to run Ford's Florida campaign against their former client, and Roberts worked the social security issue expertly.[12] Ford beat Reagan again, with 53 percent of the general vote, but with a crushing 60 percent of the voters over sixty-five.

The Sears master plan had fallen apart. He had carefully chosen the three primaries where he thought Reagan could win at the outset, proving Ford was an unelected President unable to draw votes outside Grand Rapids. After New Hampshire and Florida came Reagan's boyhood state, Illinois. Sears had spent heavily on these three states, gambling that victories there would make Reagan look like a winner and draw the funds necessary to complete the campaign. Then he could go back and bargain for spare delegates in the big states—New York, Pennsylvania, Ohio, New Jersey—which were too expensive for anyone challenging an incumbent President.[13] When Reagan lost the Illinois primary on March 16, with the campaign two million dollars in debt, Sears secretly explored the idea of joining forces with the Ford team.[14] Sears expected to lose the next primary, in North Carolina, and on the very day of that election he persuaded Reagan to cancel all further engagements in the Wisconsin primary, where he was campaigning, and go back to California to launch a new campaign with a national television broadcast.[15] This would raise the funds that were supposed to have come in from victories in the three states now lost.

Reagan did not realize till he was about to board his flight for Los Angeles that he had won the North Carolina primary after all, thanks to the hardline compaigning of a Jesse Helms faction at odds with the Sears campaign strategy.[16] Sears wanted Reagan to win on qualities of inspiration and leadership that the lackluster Ford had been unable to supply the nation. An attempt to mobilize the far right could win the nomination but forfeit the election, after a bitterly divisive ideological convention. But the poor showing in the early states made Reagan turn increasingly to strident attacks on the Ford-Nixon policy of détente with the Soviet Union and recognition of China. It was not the most elegant way to win the nomination, but now his ability to win at all was in serious doubt. Sears could and did argue that it was the extremists who had sabotaged his plan with their radical schemes for a ninety-billion-dollar cut in government and voluntary Social Security. But the extremists now had the only victory Reagan could claim to their credit, and they thought the moderate Sears approach should be abandoned.[17] They planned to be vindicated in Texas, where cross-over rules would let Wallace Democrats vote Republican. (Wallace was out of the race after Carter's victory over him in Florida.) Reagan had just the issue for cross-over voters —the Panama Canal. He had tried out in Florida a line that caused a dependably wild reaction: "We bought it, we paid for it, it's ours, and we aren't going to give it away to some tinhorn dictator!"[18]

Reagan did sweep Texas, but playing to the ideologues led him to costly slips—a criticism of TVA that defeated him in Tennessee, a suggestion that he might send American troops to occupy Rhodesia, and praise of President McKinley for "freeing" Cuba.[19] He escalated his assaults on Ford, and especially on Henry Kissinger, whom he had called "almost hysterical" in the Illinois primary.[20] Yet he ended the primary season without the requisite delegates for nomination, his only consolation the fact that he had denied the President that number as well. The two men settled into an intense bargaining for individual delegates in the caucus and convention states, but here President Ford had the advantage of federal largesse on his side, wooing uncommitted delegates with White House favors and attention. Reagan denounced him for trying to buy votes with the taxpayers' money, as if this were something new in presidential politics. Both sides were claiming hidden strengths and secret commitments, but Ford was making the actual gains. His Southern operative, Harry Dent, was even cracking a formally uncommitted delegation in Mississippi which had for months been secretly promised to Reagan. Sears had to buy time and create the impression of momentum just before the convention, so he took the bold step of asking Senator Richard Schweiker of Pennsylvania to let his name be announced, before the convention began, as Reagan's running mate. This step was stunning among other things because Sears had not even discussed it with Reagan when he met Schweiker.

The right wing was furious at the choice of Schweiker, since he was considered a liberal Republican whose votes reflected a labor union constituency. Jesse Helms called the Schweiker announcement "the shock of my life."[21] But Sears was able to convince Reagan that the senator—a member of the German Pietist sect called Schwenkfelders—agreed with him on social issues like abortion and prayer in schools.[22] Reagan put himself entirely in Sears's hands from this point throughout a stormy convention, where the campaign manager became the star of the show, even while his candidate lost. Every day in Kansas City reporters went to the Sears press conference in preference to any candidate's, wondering what new trick he would unveil. Ford had more committed delegates on the first ballot. Sears had to keep enough holdouts believing that delegates pledged to vote Ford only one time around would reveal their true preference on a second vote. One way to do this was to show Reagan sentiment through some procedural vote, on which the bound delegates could act however they wished. The issue Sears chose was proposed rule 16-C, which would oblige all candidates to reveal their running mates before the vote for the top place on the ticket. Ford's team contemptuously called this the "misery loves company" rule, and had no intention of getting into the crossfire Schweiker had caused among Reagan's own people. Sears meant not only to embarrass Ford, but to reveal Reagan sentiment in delegations formally bound or officially uncommitted. He failed, in part because his plan was so devious that even Reagan supporters did not appreciate its real significance. Zealots dismissed such procedural fencing because they were fighting hard for twenty-two platform revisions sponsored by Jesse Helms. These would commit the party to a repudiation of its own Secretary of State and all his policies. The best Sears could do to head off these troublesome allies was submit one plank to the vote, with veiled criticism of the unnamed Kissinger's views. It is a mark of the weakness of President Ford at this point that James Baker, running his strategy, did not fight the plank, and said later he would have admitted much harsher language to avoid any fight that might upset Ford's shaky lead. Asked if there was anything the President would not swallow by then, Baker said there was only one unacceptable plank he could think of: "Fire Kissinger."[23] (As it was, Kissinger was kept semihidden throughout the convention.)

Reagan accepted his defeat with equanimity, campaigned loyally for Ford, and immediately began to plan his own race in 1980, when he would be sixty-nine years old. He did not have to undergo the long decompression many candidates require after a losing campaign, when a certain numbness is the best defense they can muster against bitterness or self-doubt. Sears said with admiration: "I often wondered whether Reagan could really taste defeat, the way Nixon did. Nixon had no inner confidence. But this guy did."[24] Some might think Reagan takes defeat almost too well. He seems best at deferring, as he was the hero's friend in the movies. He is endlessly likable, without the edgy temperament, the touchy pride, that drives some who become superstars. More interesting even than his acceptance of loss was his acquiescence in a supporting role throughout most of his campaign, climaxed by a convention in which Sears was known to be making all the decisions. Reagan can delegate freely because he is so sure of his own appeal that he does not mind if others get credit for management, direction, administration. This is very unusual in politicians (and it forms one valid point of resemblance to Eisenhower, despite the many differences between them). The seeker and holder of political office is acutely conscious of "turf." Logrolling is a cooperative legislative task made possible only by proper accreditation of the log each man has rolled in order to collect return favors.

Unlike many actors, Reagan never wanted to become a director. He took direction well. He carried the same attitude into political performance. Stuart Spencer, who defeated Reagan in 1976, remembered coaching him ten years earlier:

> I don't think we ever had a candidate more easy to work with. He turned out to be probably the best speaker we ever handled and he was a team man—all I could hope for in a candidate . . . It wasn't really a very democratic operation. It was a benevolent dictatorship . . . A candidate hires us for our expertise. And he and his committee either trusts us or they don't. We insist on full authority to make the decisions.[25]

Thus the reign of Sears might not seem anything new to Reagan's campaigning. Spencer and Roberts had run his only two races for governor, and Clif White had been totally in charge of his presidential effort in 1968. But Spencer was a congenial companion to Reagan—so much so that Nancy Reagan dropped her grudge against him for the tactics he used against her husband in 1976 and called him back to service when things got sticky in 1980; and White had been remote from Reagan's Sacramento headquarters during the national delegate hunt in 1968, running the draft campaign from Washington. But Sears had been omnipresent in the 1976 campaign, as jealous of turf as Reagan was yielding of it; and Sears was abrupt with Reagan, not easy company for him. Unlike most in the governor's retinue, he "did not laugh at his old movie jokes."[26] Although Sears understood that Nancy Reagan must be kept personally well disposed, he was high-handed with most members of the California staff, and increasingly brought into the campaign people primarily loyal to him.

Yet Reagan, by accepting instruction from this man half his age, showed he had the political wisdom to prefer a brilliant professional to the ideologues clamoring for his dismissal. The right wing would claim, when they left Kansas City, that Sears had lost the nomination by not "letting Reagan be Reagan." But there was never any hint of regret, much less of recrimination, in Reagan's attitude toward Sears after the loss—or any doubt that he wanted him to lead his campaign over the next four years. Reagan realized that it would have been a hollow triumph to defeat Ford with a right-wing charge at the Kansas City convention. That would have obliged Reagan to campaign against the policies and personnel of a Republican President who would be in office for five months after the convention. Reagan would have been unable to reunite his own (the minority) party, much less to reach out to Democrats and independents, as he knew he must to win a general election.

And he meant to win such an election. He had been running for President for ten years now, and if he was patient in defeat it was because he considered it only temporary. Theodore White dates the beginning of Reagan's 1980 campaign from a lunch at his house held shortly after the 1976 election, when Nancy asked assembled loyalists how many had voted for Ford (only three hands went up), and rival candidates for the next race were assessed.[27] Lou Cannon dates it even earlier, from before the election, a September lunch at which Reagan told his advisers what issues he would be raising in the new year.[28] At any rate, by December of 1976 not only had Reagan set up his own Political Action Committee, but Nofziger had held the first of a series of regional seminars to create a national network which Reagan would cultivate intensely over the next four years. Even some of his warmest supporters were assuming that he would be too old to mount an effective campaign in 1980. He had to be active the whole time, to prevent his own organizers from drifting toward new candidates. That meant, in the first place, retaining Sears.

Sears came back insisting on even more power this time around. He also spent too much money in the early stages of the campaign. He meant to take Reagan in as the front-runner in what promised to be a crowded field (there turned out to be eight Republican candidates, including such minor figures as Philip Crane and John Anderson). He was successful, despite a narrow loss in the Iowa caucus; but by the day of the New Hampshire victory Sears was dismissed. His compulsion to rule exclusively had at last turned Nancy Reagan against him. He had always appreciated her power. He likes to recount Jimmy Stewart's remark to him: "If Ronnie had married Nancy at the time he married Jane Wyman, he would have won an Oscar. She would have *made* him do it." But Sears drove Mrs. Reagan's favorite, Michael Deaver, out of the campaign (after using Deaver to get rid of Nofziger) and was trying to drive out Ed Meese. Reagan had resented the action against Deaver, but put up with it to retain Sears. After Mrs. Reagan saw the depths of bitterness and distrust that had been sown in the staff, she forced her husband to face the issue and fire Sears, along with his two principal associates.[29]

There are always power struggles in a Reagan administration, precisely because he dislikes them so much. He averts his eyes from the first signs of them. He cannot control them because he cannot bring himself to look at them. It is a weakness that goes with complementary strengths—a lack of pettiness himself, of the smaller vanities. As he does not squabble over turf, he does not earn a grudge. He likes to be liked, and usually does what he must to make others like him. He can work pleasantly with people he has no real fondness for, like Sears. He is a company man, even when the company belongs to him. That is how he retains a tranquillity surrounded by strife. He submitted, on unspoken terms, to Sears; but they were his terms all along. His was a captive innocence in charge of things. He never looked better than on the night of his defeat in Kansas City. The way he lost revealed a great deal about his character, as did the way he had fought, and the ways he had refused to fight. It was a defeat he could build on.

CHAPTER 36

War Movies II

Turning our Tortures into horrid Arms Against the Torturer.

—Paradise Lost *2.63–64*

When Reagan, the defeated presidential aspirant, discussed with his staff, in September of 1976, the issues he would be raising in 1977, he could not have hoped for the opportunity which that year would give him to exploit one of the most popular themes from his recent campaign. His attack on the Panama Canal negotiations had been so successful that President Ford not only broke off all effort to reach an agreement, but lied about his progress to that point.[1] The public was clearly against the "loss" of the Canal. The new President, Jimmy Carter, faced polls showing 78 percent of the people opposed to "giving up" the Canal, and only 8 percent in favor of that move (or of that formulation of it).[2] But Carter decided to spend the goodwill of his political honeymoon on a serious campaign to change America's attitude toward the Third World in general. This campaign would include Andrew Young's many trips to Africa, and a human rights policy that softened America's traditional sponsorship of right-wing dictators. Removing America's own colonial outpost in Panama was a necessary preliminary to such a program, yet the very first step was the most difficult one, and Reagan would make it harder.

In his regular broadcasts and newspaper columns, and in personal speeches across the country, Reagan repeated the claims he made during the 1976 campaign season—that the Canal was vital to America's security and domestic economy, that we had sovereignty over the Zone, that we were displaying weakness before the world, that General Omar Torrijos was a Marxist puppet of Fidel Castro. Responsible conservatives denied all these points. During the campaign, Barry Goldwater had said Reagan was "totally deceptive in the way he is raising the issues" on Panama and "telling the American people things that are not true."[3] William F. Buckley visited the Canal Zone for the first time late in 1976, met with General Torrijos, and became convinced of the justice of the settlement being negotiated—he would debate the matter with Reagan on TV.[4] But Reagan's harshest critic in the right-wing camp was his old ally John Wayne, who wrote a series of open letters arguing with Reagan in some detail. One letter said, "I am sure it is quite embarrassing to General Torrijos to be called a 'tinhorn' dictator, and I didn't feel that was your style. I hope they weren't your words. This is more the style of a liberal punk who doesn't have to answer for his words."[5] When Reagan continued the assault, Wayne got angrier: "Now I have taken your letter [to the Republican National Committee], and I'll show you point by God damn point in the Treaty where you are misinforming the people. This is not my point of view against your point of view. These are facts."[6]

After an intense public education effort by the Carter administration and heavy Senate lobbying, with polls still opposed (but only slightly) to what had become a two-treaty process, sixty-eight senators—one more than the required two-thirds—fought their way through a blizzard of adverse mailings to vote confirmation on April 18, 1978. But Carter admits he had to use up a good deal of his power to influence the Senate, leaving him weakened for later encounters: "My sense is that the Republican hierarchy has decided to go along with us on Panama and to fight us on SALT . . . It is almost impossible to imagine how difficult it was for some of the Republicans (and Democrats, too, of course) to vote for the Panama treaties. To support a Democratic President on two such difficult issues would have been almost suicidal for those whose political future depended on rich extremists who finance a lot of Republican campaigns."[7]

Two other issues that would plague the Carter administration were staples of Reagan's radio commentaries and speeches—SALT II limits (ratifying an alleged "decade of neglect" in arms production) and the "window of vulnerability." The idea that America's defense needs had been neglected during the period of détente was first directed against the Nixon and Ford administrations by a group of former Democrats. But the concept was expanded and intensified for use against Carter, who was supposed to be even less dedicated to matching Russia in the military spending race. The most pointed formulation of this view was undertaken in the very year of Reagan's challenge to Ford, 1976, when the Committee on the Present Danger was founded.[8] Some of the principals in this group had launched an earlier protest against détente, under the name of the Coalition for a Democratic Majority. The coalition was formed in 1974 to show that the views of the last Democratic presidential candidate, George McGovern, must be repudiated if the party was to regain power. But two years later the same people were ready to deal with the Republican right if it was willing to attack the policies of Henry Kissinger, its own party's Secretary of State. Eugene Rostow, while setting up the CPD, sent James Schlesinger a criticism of President Ford's address to the American Jewish Committee and suggested "you might pass the enclosed package on to Governor Reagan, perhaps with your own outline of a possible speech."[9]

Though Reagan soon found he had to attack détente to keep his campaign alive among true believers in the South, Sears's original strategy called for his man to observe the Eleventh Commandment and demolish Ford with high-minded inspiration instead of nagging criticism. This prevented formal cooperation with Rostow's nascent Committee in the 1976 campaign.[10] But Reagan helped the cause of the Committee without realizing it. His mounting criticism in 1976 made President Ford retreat on issue after issue. Ford dropped not only the Panama talks, but any further advocacy of SALT II, and even the offensively defensive word "détente." He also let CIA Director George Bush bring in outside analysts to rework CIA estimates of Soviet military strength (realistically low estimates that hard-liners thought understated).[11] In June of the campaign year, Bush appointed "Team B" to go over the figures—and six of its sixteen members, including its chairman, Richard Pipes, were on the still-to-be-announced first list of CPD members.[12] Bush had opened the agency's secret files to a group of outsiders called by the New York *Times* "a panel of members with predictable views"—what former CIA analyst Ray Cline, himself known for hard-line views, called "a kangaroo court of outside critics all picked from one point of view."[13] The aim of these critics was to convince the nation of the Soviet threat; their findings were leaked in order to influence the Carter transition.[14] The estimates of Team B were formed by bias and strange procedure—Pipes, the chairman, is a historian who has little command of scientific matters.[15] But the views of Team B members were often cited during Carter's administration; they played a part in his first move away from the SALT procedure toward deep nuclear cuts—a position favored by the CPD and by Senator Jackson's effective crusader against SALT, Richard Perle.[16] Jackson and Perle led the fight against confirmation of Paul Warnke as President Carter's arms negotiator, boasting that if they could get thirty-five votes against him, it would show their power to keep any treaty he negotiated from confirmation by the necessary two thirds.[17]

The Carter administration even had its own version of Team B, when its hard-liner at the National Security Council, Zbigniew Brzezinski, appointed neoconservative Samuel Huntington to direct an interagency report on military policy (PRM-10, Presidential Review Memorandum Number Ten). People appointed by Huntington told a Washington *Post* reporter they felt their job was to "scare the Carter administration into greater respect for the Soviet menace."[18] Yet, despite PRM-10's recommendation to continue deploying Trident submarine missiles, to upgrade Minuteman warheads, to develop cruise missiles and an MX (all of which the Carter administration would do), the CFD was not satisfied. Paul Nitze said "PRM-10 *tried* to be another NSC-68"—referring to his own report of 1950 that led to the massive defense buildup under Truman.[19]

Carter returned to the SALT process, and to his own attempts at détente, and the ex-Democrats who had criticized Nixon and Ford became far harsher toward one of their own. Carter seemed to be the fulfillment of the fears that made them create the Coalition for a Democratic Majority. Mc-

Govern had merely betrayed the Democratic Party; Carter was destroying it. Carter was McGovern with the added offense of being in the White House. The neoconservatives were now looking to the Republicans, and Reagan was looking back. He quoted Pipes on the need for civil defense, and devoted six broadcasts, titled Rostow I-VI, to Eugene Rostow's criticisms of SALT II.[20]

To Panama and SALT II, a third issue was added in 1978, completing Reagan's arsenal of campaign arguments against Carter's defense policy— the famous "window of vulnerability."[21] This is a catchy slogan condensing a sophisticated argument with three alternatives. *First,* the Soviets are achieving such superiority in ICBMs that they can launch a ground strike taking out all our land-based missiles; after which we cannot use our submarines or cruise missiles to deliver a retaliatory blow, because the Russians would still have enough ICBMs to launch another strike; so we would have to submit to dictated terms of surrender. Or, *second,* the Russians could hit a selected target here or in Europe with nuclear weapons, and threaten the above sequence unless we short-circuited it by surrender. Or, *third,* even without launching an attack, Russia would be in a position to threaten either of the two processes just described, and get the same results without any attack at all. As Reagan summarized the argument in this extreme form, "the Russians could just take us with a phone call."[22]

Reagan liked the phrase "window of vulnerability," though he was never able to explain the argument's stages.[23] Just as well. They form a ramshackle collection of premises, each rickety when taken singly and collapsing on the others in conjunction. The ability to take out all ICBMs assumes a perfectly timed series of launches, to make sure the missiles arrive together rather than in "ragged" flight, which alerts the enemy and allows response by the missiles not struck first. The flight across the North Pole would have to maintain this perfect discipline and timing through untested atmospheric conditions. And the hits would have to be of uniform accuracy to take out hardened silos. It might work, but who would take the multiple risks, knowing that a breakdown in *any* part of the operation could free at least some of the ICBMs to fly rather than remain "sitting ducks," so that the inhibition on our cruise and submarine missiles would be gone?

The variants of the argument are even more fanciful. They assume perfect intelligence, popular discipline, and reliance on Russian promises, in an America reeling from nuclear attack but cool enough to judge (and enforce the judgment) that retaliation, however tempting, would be too dangerous. The Russians would have to believe that Americans are capable of superhuman feats of communication-maintenance in such circumstances, and of angelic freedom from vindictive impulse. Yet why should Americans accept the promise that Russia would refrain from a second strike even if they surrendered? A country seething with hate after such an attack is a deadly peril to the attackers as long as it has any nuclear weapons left. If Russia demanded the surrender of our nuclear weapons (assuming that were logistically feasible), who would turn them over, or enforce the complex task of doing so? Short of that, the war could not really end.[24]

The whole "scenario," to use the appropriate term of dramaturgy favored by war-gamers, is fantastic. The window of vulnerability disappeared by declaration in Reagan's own administration, going the way of Kennedy's missile gap. But Reagan believed in that nightmare long enough to ride it into the White House. What was called America's "window of vulnerability"—supposed to be opening in the eighties and fully open by the middle of that decade—was sometimes called the Russians' "window of opportunity." It was certainly the window of Reagan's opportunity. It brought together the most pointed fears of the old right wing and the articulate criticisms of the CPD. Reagan was not more measured in his comments on nuclear war than Barry Goldwater had been. But when Reagan spoke, he had important parts of the "permanent government" ready to support him, an advantage denied Goldwater, who spoke from outside the national security establishment in 1964. Aside from retired military officers, few figures who had earned reputations in national security posts were willing to back Goldwater's campaign. He might well have had trouble finding qualified people to fill top defense positions in his government if he had, *per impossible,* won the election.

Why had that changed by 1980? Had the country shifted so far to the right that it was willing to accept doomsday scenarios as national policy? What we need to remember is that doomsday scenarios had always been the basis of national policy. The CPD members rightly claim that they have remained consistent over the years. The shift, in the interval between Goldwater and Reagan, had been *away* from their position, dividing the establishment, making parts of it skeptical of the Cold War liberalism that prevailed under Democratic Presidents from Truman to Kennedy to Johnson. The cobweb of argument that created the window of vulnerability may strain credulity. But, as Robert Johnson and Richard Ned Lebow point out, the same kind of argument had in the past created the bomber gap of the middle fifties and the missile gap of the late 1950s—both based on guesses that proved entirely insubstantial.[25] The Team B report differed from NSC-68 (1950), the Killiam Report (1955), and the Gaither Report (1957) only in this: that it had to be filed as a dissident and rival estimate. In other respects it perpetuated the Cold War consensus typified by Paul Nitze. As the author of NSC-68, Nitze was the father of the "bomber gap." He was a consultant to the Gaither Committee that created the "missile gap." As early as 1961 he was using a proto-form of the "window of vulnerability" argument.[26] In the earlier cases, the exaggerated estimates were the official and accepted ones, beyond effective challenge.

Goldwater stood outside the establishment in the 1960s because Republicans had forfeited, in the McCarthy period, the claim to be "responsible" anti-Communists, not because their view of the Russian threat differed very much from that of the Americans for Democratic Action.[27] Democrats in the fifties had a justified suspicion that many Republicans' anti-Communist zeal was aimed as much at purging America of the New Deal as at saving the world from communism. (Men like Robert Welch found the tasks indistinguishable.)

What divided the foreign policy establishment by 1980 was not a defection to the right of people like the CPD members, but a motion to the left of a significant number of original cold warriors who saw their predictions baffled, their plans undone, their confidence misplaced. The journey that Daniel Ellsberg made with such drama was more cautiously and quietly taken by Ellsberg's former mentor Bernard Brodie and his former employer Robert McNamara.[28] The opening to China shook the dogma that communism is monolithic—and, in the process, the fundamental rationale of the Korean and Vietnamese wars. Nuclear proliferation and economic developments made it more difficult to conceive a bipolar power structure as the entire basis of foreign policy. Efforts to make the world safer through nuclear power had made it more dangerous. There were doubters and defectors, even among those who had been "present at the creation" of American Cold War policies and arsenal. But not among the rock-solid members of the CPD.

Yet, while the CPD neoconservatives had kept faith on foreign policy, they too had undergone some change since 1964—in domestic matters, on social issues. Goldwater voted against the civil rights bill in the spring of 1964. That alone would have made it difficult for any Democrat outside the South to join with him, no matter how similar their views on the Russian threat. But precisely because the neoconservatives were unwavering in their view of communism abroad, they became more responsive to calls for "law and order" at home—even to a reduction in democracy, as Samuel Huntington put it—when the nation seemed to be losing its will to fight.[29] In the grand effort that had inspired neoconservatives during their first youth in World War II, they made it their boast, against domestic critics of the Democratic Party, that they were equally anti-fascist and anti-Communist. Indeed, the war feelings generated against one threat were easily rechanneled against the other—in 1945. In this they shared a history with Ronald Reagan, who moved at once from waging the propaganda war against Hitler to denouncing, with the same patriotic fervor, Herb Sorrell. The surrealistic imaginings through a window of vulnerability return us to war movies as a discipline, to hysteria about the enemy as a patriotic duty.

During World War II, citizens had been asked to set aside lesser concerns —labor strikes, racial grievances, college years on campus—to respond to the greater national need. In a time of equal "present danger," against a foe as implacable, the neoconservatives saw the social movements of recent years—from civil rights to women's rights to gay rights—as distractions from, if not downright treasonous disregard of, the country's peril. They read the defection of their former colleagues from the consensus on foreign policy in a context where all things fit together, forming what Norman Podhoretz called "a culture of appeasement." It was time to assert a "new nationalism," Irving Kristol believed—muscle-flexing, being unafraid to say "We're Number One," requiring sacrifices to make that boast come true against increasing Soviet advantage. Thus Midge Decter joined forces with George Gilder or with Phyllis Schlafly against the women's movement, and with her husband (Podhoretz) against the gay rights movement.[30] Both movements, they felt, were literally emasculating the nation. The civil rights movement had gone too far when it lionized people like Muhammad Ali, a draft dodger, and proved itself ungrateful to so many of its earlier benefactors (many of them Jewish).[31] Affirmative action was just another word for quotas, for divorcing rewards from performance, at the very time when the nation must perform at peak efficiency against the present danger.[32]

During the radical moment of the 1960s, harder leftists had criticized the "yippie" aspects of the counterculture as not politically serious, but the neoconservatives were arguing that the "lifestyle" revolution was the more serious because it was the more lasting phenomenon: it changed attitudes toward sex, parents, authority, the police, the military. The Students for a Democratic Society destroyed themselves before they had much chance to injure society. But the more cynical and hedonistic aspect of "the movement" sapped reverence and the foundations of respect for country, family, and morality, creating a coddled "unisex" elite unwilling—indeed, unable—to stand up to America's enemies. It could not even hear the bear's growl over the rock beat.

The fact that so many of the neoconservatives were versed in the thought of Marx made them look for large social explanations behind what might seem to many like minor social irritants. They explained it all with an invention of dissident Marxists, the "new class." One of the principal difficulties in applying Marx's analysis to actual Communist regimes is that he foretold a triumph of the proletariat in the most industrialized portions of the world, which had reached a stage of overcapitalization, yet Communist regimes took hold in underindustrialized countries, among peasants and farm workers, not factory hands.[33] In Czarist Russia, in China, in Cuba, communism had been an *agent* of industrialization rather than its outcome and punishment, and Marxism had been introduced by intellectuals and professionals intent on "modernizing" their backward countries. Some anti-Stalinist Marxists decided that these could not be "authentic" revolutions; they were bastards—not the result of historical determinants, by which the proletariat takes its own destiny in its hands, but created by people who have decided what the historical outcome should be and gained a disproportionate influence in situations of chaos they helped induce. This is the "new class" of revolutionaries who are neither of the proletariat, though they presume to speak for them, nor of the ruling class, which they want to overthrow, but something formed for the special mission of conducting class warfare from outside the contending classes.

The Polish Marxist Jan Waclaw Machajski (1866–1926) was perhaps the first to see this as the path revolution was taking in Russia—though he had drawn some of his ideas from Bakunin.[34] His adherents would be persecuted by Bolsheviks as the evil "Machayevtsi" but other victims or critics of Communist regimes—from Leon Trotsky to Milovan Djilas—took up the idea that revolution had simply created a ruling "new class." This class is conceived as "adversary" to its host environment, and as maintaining a sense of threat to keep itself in power. This adversary role distinguishes it from the more neutral growth of bureaucratic society (Weber) or professionalism (Parsons), of a managerial class (Veblen, Burnham, Berle, Galbraith), of a technocratic elite (Daniel Bell), or of the educated as possessors of "human capital" (Theodore Schulz). Alvin Gouldner differentiates the two by calling the adversary class "intellectuals" and the scientific or managerial elite an "intelligentsia."[35] The two groups use different language systems. One is a "culture of critical discourse," making for social discontent; the other a culture of scientific discourse, based on accepted terms. Thus the neoconservatives have no quarrel to pick with the technocrats of Silicon Valley or Livermore Laboratory, any more than with the professional and managerial elites of the business culture. They concentrate their attack on "the knowledge industry," especially on the media and the academy.

Harold Lasswell, whom we encountered earlier teaching those "symbol specialists," the World War II propagandists, how to put hatred to useful purposes, has been the most active proponent of Machajski's views in English. He calls the new class "symbol specialists," trained to criticize and persuade, finding expression in "agitation" rather than production.[36] Jeane Kirkpatrick used Lasswell's framework to analyze the McGovern delegates at the 1972 convention, expressing in survey form the views of the Coalition for a Democratic Majority.[37]

The neoconservative analysis of the new class allowed ex-Democrats to combine their old anti-communism with the disgust many of them felt for the counterculture of the 1960s. It even allowed intellectuals to join anti-intellectuals of the "moral majority" in condemning the growth of permissiveness, feminism, and environmentalism as "elite" hobbies of the new class. Right-wing Republicans reciprocated the neoconservatives' interest in them by adopting the new-class analysis themselves. Kevin Phillips, for instance, hardly an ex-Trotskyite like Irving Kristol, had long been denouncing "limousine liberals." Now he learned to use the classier denunciation "new class," which had become, as it were, the limousine level in condemnation.[38]

What had been a relatively isolated position in 1964, when Reagan campaigned for Goldwater, was now the rallying ground for old allies and old foes alike, who found they had much to share in the attack on what they considered Jimmy Carter's "surrender" of America to foreign intimidation, new-class doubts, and Democratic McGovernites. Carter had come into office offering amnesty to Vietnam-war draft evaders, and was leaving it at the apparent mercy of the Ayatollah Khomeini. Ronald Reagan, the last of our "second lieutenant" Presidents—that whole line of our rulers who served as junior officers in World War II (Kennedy, Johnson, Nixon, Ford)—was being carried to office on a surge of war morale which gave some people a second youth and offered others their first political vision of hope. The Republicans had put Watergate behind them; many Democrats had put the McGovern reforms behind them; Americans in general had put Vietnam behind them. A window of opportunity was opening for the whole country.

CHAPTER 37

Home Base

So forcible within my heart I feel
The Bond of Nature draw me to my own.
—Paradise Lost 9.955–56

Ronald Reagan, the actor who took up politics in his mid-fifties, confounded expectation in California, where he retained the voters' esteem through two terms as governor. This distinguished him from both his predecessor and his successor, each of whom had been seasoned in California politics—Brown senior by training, Brown junior by birth and domestic influence. But Reagan's success in California was a minor feat by comparison with his sustained popularity as President. He entered the White House when the completion of a second term had come to seem a disappearing art.[1] Nixon had fallen from that office, after Johnson fled it. Ford could not be renominated, nor Carter reelected. The presidency was being called an impossible assignment, just when Reagan came along and treated it as a part-time job—with the public's hearty approval.

This performance rested on the paradox of Reagan's accessible yet legendary status, similar to Eisenhower's—the unintimidating Everyman as hero. But it had more specifically traceable causes as well. One cause was Reagan's shrewd concentration on *domestic* policy. That is the meat and potatoes of our politics, the thing on which most elections hinge. Yet modern Presidents forget or suppress this basic information. There is not only more immediate glamour, but a greater sense of control, when a President deals with foreign powers than when he tries to placate blocs of the American electorate. Ceremony itself seems more substantial at state dinners for foreign rulers than at a reception for high school teachers.

Recent Presidents have immersed themselves in foreign policy, so thoroughly that at last they could not resurface. President Nixon had the patience and determination to thread a devious course toward China, plotting its every turn in long sessions with Henry Kissinger. Welfare reform, by comparison, bored him, and he let it take a shape at odds with his own campaign promises, untroubled by the discrepancies. When it came to tricky planning on the domestic front, he called on the expertise of Tony Ulasewicz. Mao demanded a Kissinger. For Daniel Ellsberg, a Colson would do. Nixon dismissed his own country's internal affairs as "building outhouses in Peoria."[2]

John Kennedy aspired to office with a misconception that it made him "Commander in Chief" of all the American people. He was so fascinated by international relations that he devoted all of his famous inaugural address to the subject, omitting domestic matters entirely. President Carter went to the Oval Office with dreams similar in scale if more pacific in content. He hoped to create an entirely new policy toward Third World countries and the USSR. At first he staked his reelection hopes on a treaty in the Middle East. Then he relied on the first surge of support for him when American hostages were taken by Iran—only to become a hostage to that crisis himself.

The President is blessed with a power that can turn overnight into a curse: the power to change Air Force One from pumpkin to hero's chariot just by taking off from Andrew's Air Force Base on the way to some foreign capital.[3] When Nixon could not land his great plane at civilian airports in America without heckling from demonstrators, he was still given a hero's welcome in Tel Aviv. It has been the desperate ruler's resort, since before the time of Shakespeare's Bolingbroke, "to busy giddy minds/With foreign quarrels."[4] American Presidents have even entertained the softer hope that *composing* foreign quarrels, instead of stirring them up, can distract voters from a humdrum reality like the price of bread. But election results offer little support for that hope. Entirely aside from the Iranian crisis, Carter's chances for reelection were sealed when he entered the election year with an inflation rate running to two digits. That is tantamount to resignation.

It would have been easy and natural for Reagan to compensate for his inexperience in dealing with (or even seeing) other nations by foreign-policy activism. His anti-Communist rhetoric over the years led in that direction, and so did the cries of immediate peril over SALT provisions, Russian advances, allied disorder. Yet all the feverish rhetoric did not produce a hyperkinetic first few months in office, like Kennedy's attempt to forge a "first hundred days" of foreign victories comparable to FDR's domestic onslaught. Reagan was in no hurry to deal with unfamiliar parts of the world. More to the point, he retained a performer's feel for his audience. He knows you cannot leave an audience, to go off and study the arcana of diplomacy, and expect to have it waiting for you when you finish. His first rule is not to lose the crowd—you may never get it back. The electorate does not follow missile counts day by day, but it knows how much it pays for groceries. Reagan's first concern, therefore, remained "the free market system" at home. The grain embargo was hurting the Soviets—which was, for Reagan, a strong argument in its favor. It was also hurting American farmers— which was a fatal consideration. Lifting the embargo was the first decisive thing Reagan did in foreign policy, because he was looking to its domestic effect.

Reagan not only steered clear of the temptation to huddle with fellow princes, he defied another maxim dear to modern presidents—that one must do the hard but necessary things during one's first year in office, a year of honeymoon and bated opposition, before opponents rally with accumulating grudges. The immediate problem to be addressed can be foreign or domestic. In 1916, 1940, and 1964 Presidents who had just taken office or returned to it by promising to keep America out of war felt they had to begin preparing the nation for war. Carter bit the bullet on Panama. Nixon began the difficult process of achieving détente with China and Russia. On the domestic front, Roosevelt tried to pack the Supreme Court right after his 1936 reelection. Johnson used the penitent mood of the nation after his predecessor's assassination to push through a civil rights bill that had been stiffly resisted while Kennedy lived.

Reagan disregarded all this accumulated wisdom about investing political capital at once in order to draw dividends of popularity when they are needed down the road. His was a politics of immediate, not deferred, gratification. The compelling task he set himself in his first year was a large tax cut, something for which there is always a certain popular support, whatever the misgivings expressed by keepers of the nation's books. Jimmy Carter had a core to his political beliefs—the need to seek human rights in a peaceful way with the Soviet Union and in the Third World. He tried to accomplish the difficult preliminaries of this task in his first year. If Reagan had felt a similar commitment to the difficult parts of his moral program—e.g., to the social agenda of the New Right calling for prayer in schools, an end to abortion, and suppression of pornography—he might have spent his early days of popularity working for them. But he made his first assignment the inflation that had plagued Carter. To counter that in a *popular* way meant not only consciously putting off any pledges of return to an older morality— more dangerously, in the eyes of some White House advisers, it meant letting foreign matters wait on domestic.

The first indication of Reagan's priorities was the grain embargo. President Carter had imposed it in response to the Soviets' invasion of Afghanistan. It had severe effects on the Russian economy, primarily by cutting back feed for livestock. Yet Reagan lifted it at a time when Soviet armed forces seemed poised to invade Poland during the height of the Solidarity campaign. The new President's Secretary of State argued that the embargo must be retained, for a while at least, as a bargaining point in that crisis.[5] Instead, new grain contracts were written with promises not to reimpose the embargo —a matter that led to some recrimination when Poland, under Soviet pressure, imposed martial law. Not only were the grain contracts now untouchable; their status gave Europeans an excuse to resist other sanctions suggested by America—steps like shutting down work on the Russians' oil pipeline to Europe.[6]

There were other early signs that Reagan's heart was in domestic affairs rather than foreign. Much of his campaign had been based on the "window of vulnerability," supposed to be opening even as he came into office. The remedy he had campaigned on was a movable MX-missile plan developed and promoted during the Carter administration. But this ran into domestic opposition in a region where Reagan was especially strong, the Southwest. Reagan had already placated this group by the appointment of James Watt, a symbol and spokesman for the "sagebrush rebellion," as his Secretary of the Interior. A movable MX would not only require federal control of huge tracts of the Southwest; it would affect the "water politics" in states most dependent on that precious commodity. Reagan instructed his Secretary of Defense to find another "basing mode" for the MX—which began the slide of that missile into a token program, drastically cut back, one housed in the very silos Reagan had called vulnerable.

Moves like these convinced Reagan's hard-line followers that he had come to preside over an edgier détente, not to end the era of negotiation; that he would use brisker rhetoric while completing some of the things Kissinger had begun. For true believers, Reagan was repeating the defection of Eisenhower, who gave the New Deal its first Republican sanction rather than dismantling it. Their fears seemed confirmed when the limits of the unratified SALT II were observed throughout Reagan's first term, despite his attacks on that "fatally flawed" treaty in the campaign.[7] Relations with the People's Republic of China were continued, though he had attacked Carter for establishing them. Arms control talks were continued, though Reagan had never approved a single arms treaty in the past and his own favored experts shared his view that the Russians cannot be trusted to observe any international agreements.[8] All this was less a surrender of Reagan's campaign positions than a refusal to deal with foreign matters energetically while domestic politics absorbed his time and energies.

The President did not keep his thoughts at home for lack of strong pressures toward activism abroad. The most clamorous demands came from Alexander Haig, appointed in part to placate the Kissinger faction in the party, and resented by cold warriors for that reason.[9] Yet by 1986 Kissinger himself had been cultivating the Reagan camp for some time, backing away from the negotiatory flexibility Reagan criticized in the 1976 campaign. Kissinger distinguished his own form of détente from what he ridiculed as Jimmy Carter's weakness, and called for a show of strength. In April of election year 1980 he was telling the American Society of Newspaper Editors that "somewhere, somehow, the United States must show that it is capable of rewarding a friend or penalizing an opponent."[10]

Haig, fresh from the attempt to mount his own presidential campaign, shared Kissinger's sense that détente could only be revived in conjunction with a bellicose stance; Nixon, after all, had achieved détente on some issues while (and partly because) he was continuing the Vietnam war. And Haig thought he was in a position to use his old mentor's bureaucratic maneuvers to continue his policies. But the balancing act that urges forward tough and conciliatory lines in conjunction can only be performed by one who maintains control of all the "signals" being sent in apparently opposite directions. Kissinger could concentrate decision-making powers in his office at the National Security Council (cutting the Secretaries of State and Defense out of the action) because his President was using him for that purpose. Haig made the mistake of thinking Ronald Reagan would allow a similar concentration, not because Reagan had a Nixonlike devotion to foreign policy, but out of his very inexperience. The whole Haig period in the Reagan administration looks like a dogged attempt to keep performing Hamlet's lines though everyone else was playing *Measure for Measure.*

Kissinger had staged, by inauguration day, a reorganization of the NSC that his critics called a bureaucratic coup d' etat.[11] Haig tried to enact the same revolution-by-memorandum on January 20, 1980. The 1968 "NSDM 2" document drew all lines of policy together under one man at the NSC; Haig's "NSDD 1" ran them to the Secretary's office at the State Department.[12] Reagan was not Nixon, and men close to the President still feared Haig's presidential dreams. Some of these men wanted to run foreign affairs themselves (Richard Allen, for instance, in Kissinger's old office at the NSC). Others did not want them run at all, at least for a while—until the economic program could be passed. The result was that for most of Reagan's first term no one really ran foreign policy. And President Reagan barely noticed the omission. He was not even talking to Haig.[13] Secretary of Defense Caspar Weinberger was buying arms from all directions and discouraging their use in any sector. Eugene Rostow was talking about START negotiations in order to stop all prior negotiations. Senator Helms was monitoring U.S. embassies. Reagan, so different from Nixon, was not himself the Secretary of State—and neither was anyone else.

At first Haig thought he could personify the recovery from Carter's paralysis. He quotes wistfully Senator Paul Tsongas's words at his confirmation: "You are going to dominate this administration."[14] Despite his own disclaimers, Haig agreed. He made it to the cover of newsweeklies as rapidly as Kissinger had. Haig even thought he had his own Vietnam to run, but with a big advantage: it was a miniature replay of that struggle, winnable, to be executed on our terms and on our turf. Kissinger said it was time to win one somewhere, and Haig thought he knew where—El Salvador. In his rare private meetings with Reagan he repeated, "Mr. President, this is one you can win."[15] Haig thought of El Salvador as a "good" Vietnam, one where all the advantages lay with America. Now it was the Communists who had a long and difficult supply line. Their arms came, according to Haig, through Cuba, no longer down a misnamed Ho Chi Minh "trail" which was actually a huge sponge of forest trickling men and arms through numerous pores and capillaries. Haig thought that aid to government troops in El Salvador would make them prevail as soon as we cut off the rebels' support by threatening to "go to its source" in our own backyard, Cuba.

He found surprisingly few allies in the Reagan administration, despite all the anti-Communist appeal of his little war, and despite a shared resolve to reverse Carter's "human rights" approach to Latin America:

> Some advisers, especially his [Reagan's] highest aides, counseled against diluting the impact of his domestic program with a foreign undertaking that would generate tremendous background noise in the press and in Congress. The Secretary of Defense [Weinberger] genuinely feared the creation of another unmanageable tropical war . . . The Joint Chiefs of Staff, chastened by the experience of Vietnam, in which our troops performed with admirable success but were declared to have been defeated, and by the steady decline of respect for the military and of military budgets in the post-Vietnam period, resisted a major commitment.[16]

When the Reagan administration finally found a war small enough to win, it would be in Grenada. America's invasion would be partly justified there on the grounds that so small an island should not have so large an airport.

Even Jeane Kirkpatrick, who was identified with tough Central American policies in many minds, became at first a rival and then a bitter foe of Haig. The two were equally touchy about White House slights, but instead of making an ally of her, Haig (following Kissinger's loner policy) emphasized the irrelevancy of a mere UN Ambassador's role to the formation of policy in the State Department.[17] She, in turn, thought Haig had borrowed her views and then made a mess of them by his bungling procedures.

Kirkpatrick was widely credited with the distinction between "authoritarian" and "totalitarian" governments as a touchstone for American policy. The former are said to be personal in their despotism, corrupt but of limited effect throughout the society, while the latter are programmatic, reaching into the lives and thoughts of every subject. Actually, in her overpraised *Commentary* article on this matter, she had discussed "traditional versus revolutionary autocracies."[18] That was her twist of language on the contrast between authoritarian and totalitarian governments, which is a rather obvious one.[19] It had become popular in neoconservative circles well before her article appeared in November of 1979; Ernest Lefever, who led the administration's first assault on Carter's human rights policy, had put it in the customary language for the Heritage Foundation over a year before Kirkpatrick's article appeared: "In terms of political rights, moral freedom and cultural vitality, there is a profound difference between authoritarian and totalitarian regimes."[20] So Haig was not specifically stealing from Kirkpatrick when he told the Trilateral Commission, shortly after the inauguration, that

> the totalitarian model unfortunately draws upon the resources of modern technology to impose its will on all aspects of a citizen's behavior . . . [But] the authoritarian regime . . . customarily reserves for itself absolute authority in only a few politically sensitive areas.[21]

Mrs. Kirkpatrick was called the discoverer of this doctrine since her article was one of the few citeable works on foreign policy that Reagan had actually read (at the suggestion of Richard Allen).

According to Kirkpatrick, traditional dictatorships are not as onerous as Communist regimes because "maintaining a culture requires less repression than does the effort to radically alter it by administrative decision."[22] On this basis, the Reagan administration supported "constructive engagement" with the government of South Africa—though it was hard to imagine a regime more intrusive into the daily life, marriage, employment, and residence of subjects than the Botha regime with its passbook system. And in time Reagan had to adopt a program of mild sanctions toward South Africa in order to prevent Congress from acting even more harshly. President Carter was attacked by Kirkpatrick for "destabilizing" the regimes of autocratic friends like Somoza of Nicaragua and the Shah of Iran.[23] Yet spontaneous anger of the rulers' own population forced Reagan to withdraw his early support for Jean-Claude Duvalier in Haiti and Ferdinand Marcos in the Philippines—though Kirkpatrick was speaking for both governments to the very end, as she had comforted the generals in Argentina during the Falklands war.[24]

Kirkpatrick's is the classical theme of European conservatism—that maintaining "traditional culture and roles" is less disruptive of ordinary life than ambitious efforts to reform society as well as the state.[25] Yet there is often popular support for such reform efforts, even if they involve hardship and a self-imposed discipline. Example after example of this has presented itself to Americans in the anticolonial movement that swept the globe after World War II. American observers like Kirkpatrick saw all this activity in the "so-called Third World"[26] as an epiphenomenon to Soviet aggression. South Africa was supported on the grounds that black rulers who came to power during anticolonial wars led regimes more intrusive into the lives of ordinary people than had the colonial administrators. The charge is quite true, since colonial rulers did not want to disturb the goose unduly, just take the golden egg from it. Determination to prevent that has led people after people to submit to rigors enforced by their own kind rather than be harvested seasonally by foreigners.

There is nothing surprising or new in the voluntary submission to dictators of a people's choice—even Hitler, Mrs. Kirkpatrick's model of a totalitarian ruler in her first treatment of the theme,[27] was democratically elected. Many less despicable governments have been popularly sustained despite repression of large segments of the population—Andrew Jackson's America, for instance, despite its treatment of black slaves and the "savage" native Americans. Fidel Castro has been more popular with Cubans over the span of his reign than was Fulgencio Batista. One may say this "should" not have been; indeed, Henry Kissinger *did* say that of Chile, where he thought citizens had no right to choose against their own interests, as Kissinger read those interests for them, by voting Communist.[28] But it is hard to distinguish the denial of a people's right to rule themselves, even badly, from any other denials of freedom, especially when the denial is imposed by a foreigner.

In any case, Reagan had to back off from his support for "authoritarian" regimes in Argentina, South Africa, Haiti, and the Philippines. But he did this gracefully, with his gift for declaring setbacks victories. In fact, he tried to use these "democratic" victories as endorsements of his administration, and even drew a parallel he had at first denied. He came into office supporting Marcos because he was authoritarian, and therefore different from Daniel Ortega in Nicaragua, whose regime Reagan was trying to overthrow by aiding the contras. After the fall of Marcos, former supporters of Kirkpatrick like Reagan's communications director Patrick Buchanan said that aid to contras in Nicaragua would be an equivalent to, or continuation of, the democratic "revolution" (actually an election) that had brought down Marcos. Overnight an authoritarian regime had become just like a totalitarian one.

Carter had been mocked as irresolute and wavering in his attitude toward other nations. Yet his positions were not nearly as mutable as Reagan's, who reversed himself on relations with the People's Republic of China, on the European pipeline, on keeping Marines in Lebanon, on holding a summit without an agenda, on swift reprisals against all terrorists, on visiting a death camp in Germany, as well as on sanctions for South Africa and support for Duvalier and Marcos. Yet, far from hurting himself by these reversals, Reagan usually benefited by them, since the original position was often ill-considered. But the astonishing thing was that he was perceived as following a consistent (strong) course through all the zigs and zags. This came in largest part from Reagan's easy way of avoiding accountability for mere facts, for accuracy or consistency. But it also came in some measure from his refusal to become obsessed—or even involved—with the niceties of foreign politics. Secretary Haig was expressing personal grievance when he wrote, "The necessity of speaking with one voice on foreign policy . . . simply never took hold among Reagan's advisers."[29] But many observers with no sympathy for Haig came to the same conclusion during Reagan's first term.

When George Schultz finally established his authority as Haig's successor, he avoided his predecessor's worst personal clashes, the disputes over turf that had doomed the imperious Haig, even as he continued the policies Haig had tried to establish—a retaliatory attitude toward Communist terrorists in Central America and elsewhere, combined with a search for arms control and stable relations with the Soviets. But where Haig's form of détente ran into personal problems with the Arms Control and Disarmament Commission, Schultz found the President's Strategic Defense Initiative blocking all approaches to a treaty; and on retaliation he found Caspar Weinberger as little disposed to send troops for the Schultz State Department as for the Haig one. There were no longer five or six foreign policies, as in the first years of the Reagan administration—more like two or three. But the public tended not to notice this because their President, so close to them in his continuing addresses and ceremonial appearances, did not notice either. He knew that the public mind is not disposed toward foreign quarrels unless it has been kindled to it by a President trying to show off his prowess among other leaders.

Reagan's very provincialism formed a bond with his fellow citizens and a bastion for his office. He had traveled little in other countries before taking office, and he was not going to acquire that taste. Reagan went late and reluctantly to his first summit with a Soviet leader (in the final year of his first term), all the while playing down the meeting's significance, denying it would address substantive issues. (Early in his term, he had made such issues the requirement for a summit, in order to avoid holding one.) When Reagan had to be abroad, he addressed domestic issues even in a foreign land. A trip to Canada became a "Shamrock Summit," played—like his visit to "the ancestral home" in Ireland itself—for American voters. His address at the Normandy beaches provided some of the choicest footage in his 1984 campaign film, as did his worship at a religious service with GIs in South Korea. Even the troubles of his Bitburg visit arose from an initial attempt to find an analogue for Arlington Cemetery abroad and to avoid touchy political issues. Other Presidents experienced an influx of power as they moved farther off from American shores, but President Reagan just felt the distance widening between him and his audience. His instinct proved as useful as it is unusual. Others felt fully "the President" only when away from home. He never really left home.

CHAPTER 38

Silver Bullet

Now wav'd thir fierie Swords, and in the Air
Made horrid Circles.

—Paradise Lost *6.304–5*

Reagan's relaxed approach to foreign matters bothered some cold warriors, but others found uses for it. Neglect could, after all, be translated into withdrawal. In their eyes, America could never be properly interventionist till it was freed from commitments to its partners who are less bold. Some treaties "tied our hands," they felt, and the sooner we were quit of them the more vigorous we could be, undeterred by carping from putative allies.

So, playing on Reagan's lack of interest in complex international processes, these advisers canceled a Law of the Seas Treaty negotiated toward tense but acceptable terms after seven years of bargaining.[1] In his second month as President, Reagan appointed a new delegation to the treaty talks, one that was certain to vote against the treaty a month later. On one level this was just another example of Reagan's yielding to domestic pressures, as he had in lifting the grain embargo—except that businessmen were being placated in this case, instead of farmers. Access to mineral rights in international waters was at issue.[2] But the grain deal had disappointed anti-Communists. Withdrawing from the Law of the Seas treaty—a document that had been denounced in a Heritage Foundation study—was an act that pleased conservatives.[3] It was also the first in a long series of repudiated international agreements.

Many of Reagan's backers supported him on the assumption that the Democratic Party had "gone soft" on communism, but they felt this American form of accommodation was just one sign that "the West" in general was losing its nerve. Henry Kissinger himself denounced "differential détente" among allies in the early 1970s—the readiness Germany and France showed to outrun American efforts (and, he thought, undermine them) in reaching economic agreements with the Soviet bloc.[4] Kissinger's cold-warrior critics had expected no less from "weak" bodies like the United Nations organization. The Reagan administration's attitude could be gauged by the appointment of Jeane Kirkpatrick as Ambassador to the UN. She was a frequent critic of the "anti-Americanism" expressed in General Assembly votes. American distrust and dislike of the UN would be confirmed repeatedly in the Reagan years. The Administration withdrew from UNESCO, cut off America's contribution to the UN Fund for Population Activities, cast the single vote against a World Health Organization code for infant formula, and did not oppose the Kassebaum amendment reducing America's contribution to the General Assembly by 25 percent unless the UN should amend its charter. The Administration encouraged Britain's withdrawal from UNESCO (the objective of a Heritage Foundation campaign), and threatened its own withdrawal from the UN Conference on Trade and Development as well as the Food and Agricultural Organization and the International Atomic Energy Commission.[5]

When Nicaragua took the CIA's mining of its harbors before the International Court, the United States Government refused to recognize the Court's jurisdiction, though America had used and emphasized the Court's authority in the Iranian hostage crisis. Jeane Kirkpatrick, reversing what had been the American position on the Court, declared it "a semilegal, semijuridical, semi-international body"—though America's own representative on the Court's panel of judges voted to proceed with the case.[6]

The Reagan position was that America must uphold freedom around the world, protecting allies everywhere—though this must often be done against the expressed will of those allies, who presumably did not know their own interests. We would, in the Rousseauean formula, "force them to be free." The CIA equipped and supported Nicaraguan contras not only against the government in place, but against the expressed will of all the neighboring states except our own questionable clients, Honduras and El Salvador. The plan of the Central American "Contadora Group" was brushed aside. The invasion of Grenada was undertaken to "save" the American states to our south—yet it violated the treaty of the Organization of American States and the Rio Pact, as well as the UN charter and the United States Constitution.[7]

On the diplomatic level, at least, America sharply changed its position during the first Reagan term. It became unilateralist (if not isolationist) in its attitude toward structures of international accord. Meetings with Soviet representatives were delayed and desultory, a policy the Administration dramatized by depriving Ambassador Dobrynin of his customary private entry to the State Department.[8] Arms control negotiations were put in an induced state of coma. Even NATO, the basic alliance, came into question. All this was supposed to free America for more decisive activity. We would no longer wait on more timorous associates for their concurrence. Yet, even so freed, President Reagan refrained from imaginative swoops of eagle-assertiveness. The cage was open, yet the bird still perched. When the Soviets imposed martial law in Poland, shot down a Korean airliner, backed Syria in the Lebanon war with Israel, and continued building the European pipeline,

Reagan did not "go to the source" of what he called all the world's troubles. He did not even punish weaker intermediaries—by letting Poland go into default, for instance, or mounting a punitive raid in Lebanon after the truck bombing that killed 241 marines. Despite take-no-prisoners rhetoric over Muammar Qaddafi, no overt campaign was launched against him in the first term (though two of his fighters were shot down in a casual encounter). Reagan was praised and blamed, from opposite ends of the spectrum, for what seemed his lack of enterprise. As Jeane Kirkpatrick would write after leaving the administration, "Ronald Reagan resembles Jimmy Carter more than anyone conceived possible."[9]

Those who wanted a Reagan as fierce in deed as in words had to pin their hopes on covert action. After a period of constraint upon the CIA, William Casey was "unleashed" to act in unknowable ways against Qaddafi in Libya, the Soviets in Afghanistan, the Sandinistas in Nicaragua, the insurgents in El Salvador. It could even be argued that Reagan was following the course of the last successful Republican President, Dwight Eisenhower, who pursued an eirenic course in public while overthrowing the governments of Iran and Guatemala in secret. But there were important differences. While Eisenhower expanded the scope of the CIA under Allen Dulles, Allen's brother John Foster was creating, in the domain of open diplomacy, a structure of interlocking alliances for the whole "free world." He threw a flimsy geodesic dome of acronyms over all nations that would align themselves with America.[10] And those are precisely the kinds of pacts and treaties the Reagan administration considers worthless.

Despite criticism from his own right wing, Reagan was not held accountable for the gap between bellicose rhetoric and his measured response (or nonresponse) to what the hawks took as extremely provocative acts. Jimmy Carter, for instance, would hardly have survived the lethargic reaction to Russia's downing of a Korean civilian airliner, with all its passengers dead. Reagan's tepid response was to cancel Aeroflot landings in America—a slap on the wrist with no domestic repercussions, since American airliners do not land in Moscow. Carter, by contrast, had imposed the grain embargo when Russia cracked down on Solidarity, and canceled the American appearance at the Moscow Olympics after the invasion of Afghanistan. Yet the one man was considered weak, despite his actions, and the other strong in his repose. Why? Part of the explanation lay in the two men's symbolic initiatives before any provocation. There was also an assumption that Reagan's heart was in the right (fighting) place, though he was restrained by timorous counselors. These "pragmatists" (the favored swearword for them) prevented "Reagan from being Reagan," though he was presumably on the verge, at any moment, of this catastrophic transformation into himself. This picture of a Clark Kent who would at last strip to the "real" Superman was even less plausible than criticisms from the left, which assumed that Reagan had donned sheep's clothing to lull enemies into his wolvish traps. Few seemed willing to grant that Reagan was always Reagan, trusting more to words than actions, to weapons bought than to weapons used. He actually believed that if one just took a tough stance, then bullies would scatter. When they failed to, he bought a bigger bomb and assumed it would work the next time. His strength lay in his singleness of purpose and simplicity of means.

Meanwhile, those who feared that pragmatists would undermine America's strength at home were not any more indulgent toward weak-kneed allies. For some reason, foreigners should be bellicose even when America is not. European reluctance to accept America's intermediate range missiles on its soil, or to foreclose on the Polish debt, or to suspend Russia's oil pipeline, led to a series of attacks on NATO from the very people who once criticized Senator Fulbright for suggesting that American troops should be withdrawn from Europe. A new line was set in "neoconservative" articles arguing that "the U.S. already is standing alone, but it is an encumbered aloneness that inhibits freedom to develop new policies."[11] During the 1980 campaign, it was claimed that Reagan's rhetoric would reanimate allies. Instead, it now became a touchstone to reveal the cowardice of others. As Melvyn Krauss put it in a New York *Times* Op-Ed piece, "European 'pacifism' has soared under Ronald Reagan."[12] At the moment when Reagan was beginning to call the Soviets' bluff, Europe had chickened out. Even Richard Perle, the Pentagon's hardest liner, decided that deploying missiles in Europe was not worth the Pacific assurances NATO was calling for.[13]

The neoconservative guru Irving Kristol had anticipated this development in a talk called "Does NATO Exist," which he gave at a 1979 Brussels conference. In the first Reagan term, he recycled this talk in a number of journals, encouraging a neoconservative view of NATO that a European conservative like Peregrine Worsthorne found disturbing.[14] By a paradox, the champions of headlong engagement around the world were stripping themselves of potential helpers for the struggle. The only intimacy to be allowed was that of direct wrestling with the foe. Norman Podhoretz's friends wanted to remove the "trip-wire" presence of American troops in Europe, precisely because they would not work as a sensitive hair trigger in response to Soviet moves. Our soldiers should be moved to the Middle East, where they actually could set off hostilities.[15]

At the outset of the Reagan administration, such views found a partial welcome in the State Department. Alexander Haig, while not favoring any withdrawal from NATO (of which he had been Supreme Allied Commander), did support joint military exercises with Israel to implement his policy of "strategic consensus." He thought that the Arab-Israeli conflict could be subordinated to a higher "fear of the Soviet Union" felt by some moderate Arab states as well as by Israel.[16] Science fiction writers have long been able to compose earthly conflicts by introducing a threat from Mars. In much the same way, Haig hoped to solve age-old conflicts in the Middle East by mobilizing the rivals against a numinous alien power, the USSR.

This policy played into the hands of those who believe the health of the alliance between Israel and America depends on the Cold War. That view made Richard Nixon popular in Israel even in his moment of utmost disgrace at home. And it explains some of the Israeli coolness felt toward Jimmy Carter, despite the great effort he expended on the Camp David Accords. Israel does not want to be seen as dependent upon America, but as its stoutest bastion in an area where American interests are at stake against Russia. The Israelis' rapport with Haig, cultivated in a series of missions to him, gave clearer and clearer glimpses of an intent to invade Lebanon. Despite expressions of American displeasure at Israel's bombing of Iraq's nuclear reactor, despite a coolness after the de facto annexation of the Golan Heights, General Ariel Sharon seems to have convinced himself that Haig would support aggressive measures that could be presented as anti-Communist.[17]

This "green light," no matter how accidentally turned on, had calamitous results for Haig personally and for the American government in general. After the Israeli capture of Beirut, American marines were sent to Lebanon, not to join in anti-Communist activities, but to give the PLO safe conduct from the country as a way of extricating Israel. Then, after massacres occurred in the Israeli-controlled camps of Sabra and Shatilla, the marines, sent back with a vague peace-keeping mission, were tethered in an exposed position at the Beirut airport. President Reagan, who had attacked former Presidents for asking troops to fight "with one hand tied behind them" in Vietnam, tied *both* hands behind the marines, not only by restrictions on their activities but by the indeterminacy of their mission. After 241 of them were killed by one terrorist truck bomb (showing how vulnerable was their posting), Reagan first declared an American national interest in the troops' continuing Lebanese service, and then withdrew the troops.

"Strategic consensus" had led to strategic disaster. The Pentagon was confirmed in its opposition to missions with undefined goals and wavering civilian commitment. Reagan was unscathed by the disaster because he launched the invasion of Grenada, already in preparation, the day after the bombing in Beirut. Troops were withdrawn from Lebanon in the afterglow of the Grenada "victory."

Yet even while people were cheering the assault on Grenada, that attack gave military men more arguments for reluctance to engage in "little wars." Almost everything went wrong, in the invasion of Grenada, that could have.[18] The war was won because it could not be lost—the American invaders had a ten-to-one superiority over the defenders, and *all* of the air and artillery weapons used in the "war." Two thirds of American casualties were inflicted by other Americans or by accident. The exclusion of reporters from the scene helped suppress knowledge of these facts, as has classification of some information to this day and the suppression of several court martial complaints.[19]

Yet this was Reagan's kind of war—swift, conclusive, symbolic, clear in cause and outcome.[20] The Army alone (discounting Navy, Marine, and Air Force personnel) issued more medals than there had been assailants, leading

"Doonesbury" cartoonist Garry Trudeau to call Grenada the "Special Olympics" of handicapped military forces.[21] The Pentagon's leeriness of such actions, meeting with Reagan's distaste for anything *but* such quick victories, prevented larger commitments. The withdrawal from Beirut, humiliating as it would have been for President Carter, was taken in stride by Reagan, who genuinely expects quick victory for the virtuous side. When this does not occur, he dismisses the incident by an act less of absolution than amnesia. He knows that one does not try to go on with a routine that is flopping; move to the next one if the first is not reaching the audience. The investment in long-term results is not congenial to a performer attuned to a constant interplay with his audience.

Reagan is sometimes accused of having a short attention span. The truth, more likely, is that he has a good feel for the public's short patience with uncertainties. Investment in long-term gains, across intervening disturbances, is hard to justify if one has that constraint in mind. Being "the great communicator" is a matter of remaining understood, step by step, never breaking the sequence of easy exposition. The Beirut performance, in the ominously appropriate show-business term, had "bombed." Reagan wanted to distract attention from it. On the afternoon between that bombing and the assault on Grenada, an armed man tried to break into the Georgia country club where Reagan was playing golf. The President overruled suggestions that he react to that incident by returning at once to the White House. It was important, now, for the performer to finish his golf round: "I want this weekend to end on an up note."[22]

Reagan took the same approach to the lingering hostage crisis he could not solve, that of five Americans held in Lebanon for periods of a year and more. While doing the inevitable, ineffectual diplomatic things about this, the White House publicly adverted to the matter as little as possible. Reagan had claimed, in his campaign against Carter, that a strong America would not be bearded by terrorists. When terrorist attackers killed marines, and individual kidnappings accumulated hostages, Reagan attributed this to the lingering effects of Carterism and assured others (as well as himself) that it would not happen in the future (though it continued to). In the case of the "invisible" captives, the public's weak powers of concentration were confirmed.

Reagan was consistent, in all such apparent contradictions, with his principled optimism. Even when untoward things happened on his "watch" of responsibility (if not control), he was busy convincing people that the future would be different. That explained the energy with which he campaigned against the government even when he *was* the government. In the area of defense, such hopefulness meant spending a great deal on future possibilities of control (especially from space), prodigally buying weapons whose mere purchase insured (he told us) that they would never be used. Generosity to domestic contractors became a substitute for intervention abroad, in accord with Reagan's preference for domestic rather than foreign affairs. He could have a strong foreign policy by satisfying businessmen at home. The results were a "binge" at Caspar Weinberger's Pentagon, followed by scandals on cost overruns, fraudulently reported expenses, and wasteful planning.[23] In an administration devoted to cutting back "govment," defense remained sacred.[24] Only in defense matters was governmental size an advantage. Here, as he put it, "things *are* cheaper by the dozen."

While Reagan launched a broad rhetorical defense, the details were left to others—to Weinberger's buyers, to the Joint Chiefs in Lebanon and Grenada, to Richard Perle's bureaucrats on missiles. There was one characteristic exception to this, one project for which Reagan took direct responsibility, pushing it forward despite the doubts of some in his own circle. This was the Strategic Defense Initiative. An implausible scheme in itself, it is a perfect expression of Reagan's politics, which are at one with his personality. The weapon's promoters shrewdly appealed to him personally for support, and he made it a point of presidential esteem.[25] "Star Wars," in the conception of it adopted by Reagan, is a "nice" weapons system—defensive, not offensive; killing missiles, not people; finally sharable with others (even the Russians) in an act of American altruism. Reagan—who could not credibly be menacing on the screen as a Western gun hand, who has trouble dismissing anyone or being impolite face to face with others, who cannot be presented as a "bad guy" by his political opponents—feels most at home when preaching a hopeful message. The very intensity of his belief that communism in the abstract is pure evil makes him believe that pure good is the proper response, whatever compromises must be made with counterterrorism and imperfect regimes as a temporary expedient. SDI was a "final solution" in a benign sense, the one answer to all our problems.

Its simplicity of intent was not the least of its charms for a man who felt uncomfortable with the complexities of less absolute weapons systems—the man who confessed, well into his presidency, that he never had understood what "this throw-weight business is all about"; who thought that cruise missiles could only be used defensively, or that submarine missiles could be recalled.[26] Long after his own disarmament scheme, based on heavy cuts in ICBMs, had been offered, debated, and rejected, Reagan told astonished congressmen that he had not realized at the time of its formulation that most of the Russians' missiles were ICBMs.[27] Such technical matters would never plague his rhapsodic discussion of SDI. In the first place, *no one* understood all its multiple if sketchy projections. There were more dreams—and the key parts of those, classified—than tested components to it. It was more an expensive and glamorous wish than a single project, and such wishes are the very stuff of Reagan's leadership.

Once again, Reagan's personality harmonized with deep instincts in the American public. The belief in a technological solution to everything, in the possibilities of "Yankee know-how," resists gloomier prognostications of the sort Jimmy Carter indulged. This tendency has been displayed frequently in the world of defense, where optimism about Vietnam was tied to a belief in the wonders of a new kind of warfare, dependent on wizardry like defoliants, quick-hopping helicopter forces, air control, and even Robert McNamara's electric buffer zone to divide South Vietnam from North Vietnam.[28] In military *buying,* a desire to put many eggs in one basket has led to the invention of all-purpose weapons that are too sophisticated for easy use or repair, or that compromise a basic function by trying to include eighteen others.[29] The same tendency was manifested in the space program, where the shuttle was designed to do in combination things that were better done separately—to carry humans aloft, act as a delivery system for business "payloads," carry on scientific research, and perform military duties. One function tended to cancel out another—e.g., the use of backup equipment for human life-support systems made the whole too large and expensive to compete efficiently for business loads with unmanned missiles like the European Ariane. And the concentration of skill and money on the shuttle precluded separate scientific tasks like the exploration of Halley's Comet in its only passage across this generation's heavens.

But here, as with America's other "frontier" experiences, government inefficiencies translate into business advantages. According to economic theology, "market forces" are best at opening new areas of capital investment, but in fact our government has usually borne the basic first costs in risky new areas, and suffered initial setbacks that would break the coffers or the confidence of individual investors. Early trade in the nation was made possible by internal improvements (especially canals) and external ports and naval facilities, underwritten by the government. The West was opened by railroads heavily subsidized by government loans, land grants, cavalry protection, mail contracts, and naval enticements on the West Coast. After World War II, transportation, housing, and urban economies were shaped around the government's interstate highway system—a direct subsidy to truckers, car manufacturers, oil companies, tire makers and others, and the indirect subsidizer of housing and shopping developments outside city cores. Airline developments have also piggybacked on governmental research, the defense contracts of World War II, safety and airport facilities, and the United States mail. The computer industry and nuclear energy companies also rode on governmental pioneering.

Now space is being opened up for later investors, by government programs that try and fail, that explore new possibilities, using corporate products for which taxpayers bear the cost and officials the responsibility. The fruits of this effort will be turned over to businesses, or seized by them, after the initial costs (in lives among other things) have been accepted by the taxpayers. Any progress in space will be credited to American technology (and, by a non sequitur, to capitalism) as well as to national pride and patriotism. SDI not only encapsulates all these tendencies, but promotes the "American way of life" that Reagan believes in. In 1983 and 1984, forty-five percent of the prime contracts for space weapons went to Reagan's home state of California.[30] This is the kind of government "interference" that pro-

motes, rather than competes with, big business—a phenomenon that occurred most spectacularly in this century during what Reagan thinks of as
"the magic age" for America, the time of our last "good war," World War II,
for which he was a governmental spokesman.[31] All the grumbling about
governmental misuse of money on job training or welfare does not dilute one
bit the nation's enthusiasm for projects that seem to underwrite the future.
What businessmen see as spadework for their own industries, the electorate
watches as a thrilling show and source of vicarious power—moon shots,
laser demonstrations, and a "space shield." We have seen the future, and it is
Disneyland.

SDI also fits Reagan's foreign-policy pattern of aggressive withdrawal. It
is not only a defensive weapon, rather than an offensive one; it is a unilateral
American effort that does not depend on the goodwill or the nervous doubts
of allies. It is true that subcontracts for ancillary products have been dangled
before allies, and there is a "promise" on Reagan's part (though not the
Pentagon's) to share the results once a working "shield" is in place. But in
the long interlude before that roseate outcome, the technology will be protected with the same anxieties we displayed over the atomic bomb when we
thought we had a retainable monopoly on that. The project will depend not
only on American "know-how" but on jealously guarded contracts, fought
for over the years by major defense companies (87 percent of the SDI contracts for 1983 and 1984 went to ten companies, all with many other defense
projects, and 77 percent of the prime contracts went to states or districts
with congressional representatives on the armed services committees).[32] This
is to be America's show, reestablishing a primacy in computerization and
other skills where Japan has challenged Silicon Valley.

The project fulfills Reagan's narrative requirement that a single hero (or
hero-nation) save the day by a decisive act. Raising our "space shield,"
which Reagan describes as impenetrable by enemy missiles, is a life-giving
use of destructive force, much like the Lone Ranger's silver bullet which he
used only to knock guns out of the bad guys' hands.

The problem Reagan poses to all his critics is also exemplified in the SDI
program. It can be urged that Reagan is inaccurate and simplistic; that if his
rhetoric were taken seriously, it would lead to dangerous consequences; that
"govment" acts in ways entirely at odds with his double use of the term (for
vilification when it supports its own citizens and glorification when it cows
other nations' subjects); that his optimism is blind to real problems—yet
these points seem niggling next to the sweep of vision Reagan offers, to his
obvious goodwill, which seems to preclude danger. Similarly, it is clear that
SDI, as described by Reagan, is an impossible project; that it blocks arms
control measures and offers immediate offensive threats while pursuing ultimate defense; that it exploits government for private profit; that real goods
are being sacrificed to illusory hopes. The arguments are sound, and can be
documented at length.[33] But they get no hearing. Others have the arguments,
but Reagan has the audience; and he has it because he reaches its instincts so

instantly, unerringly. SDI, in this light, has a certain inevitability to it; it is not only the most apt symbol of Reagan's presidency, but a perfect expression of Reagan's America. In his 1940 Brass Bancroft movie, *Murder in the Air,* Reagan protected the secret of a wonder weapon against those who would steal it from America—an "inertia projector" that would bring down enemy airplanes by knocking out their electrical systems.[34] Over the years, Reagan himself rode the airwaves as a benign user of technology for human purposes, turning telegraphed codes into sports anecdotes, flickering shadows into abiding human verities, sales pitches for GE into pledges of happiness. The economic and technological realities involved in delivering these benign images were of little interest to Reagan, so long as he could use them to restate an enduring set of values through their maze of rapid changes, convincing himself and others that all inventions and historical changes just offer new ways for saying old things. Movies are just stories, not sprockets and patents and labor troubles. What is Star Wars but another, more complex projector meant to trace, in lasers and benign nuclear "searchlights," the image of America itself across the widest screen of all? It is another premiere, a cosmic opening night.

CHAPTER 39

Reaganomics

How build, unbuild, contrive
To save appeerances, how gird the Sphear
With Centric and Eccentric scribl'd o'er,
Cycle and Epicycle, Orb in Orb.

—Paradise Lost *8.81–84*

Inflation elected Ronald Reagan in 1980. The hostages taken in Iran filled the newspapers during that year's campaign; they were a temporary distraction from the illness that had been draining power from Carter, as it took money from wallets, month after month. The hostages, in fact, had given Carter months of illusory vitality—enough to finish off Edward Kennedy's primary challenge. What may be called "the Mayaguez effect" rallied the nation so fervently, if briefly, to the President that he might have been reelected had the hostages been taken just three or four months before voters went to the polls.

But a second Carter term would have been even more disastrous than the first. Despite the artificial animation that moved him in electric starts and jolts during his last year as President, he was already, politically, a corpse. Reagan's campaign manager, William Casey, said in a frank postmortem: "By 1980, the public had decided they didn't want any more Jimmy Carter. It would have been hard to lose that election."[1] Exit polls at the voting places showed that people rejected Carter more than they approved Reagan.[2] Paul Volcker, of the Federal Reserve, could sum up the Carter presidency this way:

> As Jerry Ford left the White House, he handed Jimmy Carter three envelopes, instructing him to open them one at a time as problems became overwhelming. After a year, Carter opened the first envelope. It said, "Attack Jerry Ford." He did. A year later, Carter opened the second envelope. It said, "Attack the Federal Reserve." He did. Three years later into his term, and even more overwhelmed by the economy, Iran, Afghanistan and so forth, Carter opened the third envelope. It said: "Prepare three envelopes."[3]

Reagan's team knew just where to strike. In August of 1979, adviser Martin Anderson opened "Policy Memorandum No. 1" of the campaign with these words: "By a wide margin, the most important issue in the minds of voters today is inflation."⁴ And by the campaign's end, the candidate who had risen by ideology, the true believer, was asking people to vote their pocketbooks. Over and over Reagan asked, "Are you better off now than you were four years ago?"

What went wrong for Carter, by all accounts one of the most intelligent men ever to hold his office? Bad breaks, no doubt, and the structurally shaky position of the Democratic Party (reflected in its need for him in the first place—to bring the South back, even momentarily, to its old home). But he was also not cynical enough. Admittedly the economy was out of control in the late seventies, but every President since Eisenhower has managed to contrive at least the appearance of economic improvement in election years. Richard Nixon, who felt that Eisenhower's refusal to jigger the economy had cost him the 1960 election, made such blatant use of the devices at a President's command in 1972 that a flourishing economic literature discovered subtler ways the practice had entrenched itself even before Nixon. The basic work, by Edward Tufte, establishes that there are two cycles—one for every second year, when disposable income is moving up by the time of the election, and one for presidential years, when unemployment is moving down.⁵

When Tufte published his book in 1978, Eisenhower was the only exception to this political manipulation of prices and employment. Two years later, Carter became the second. In his third year Carter did not respond to danger signs by pinching in an economy he could relax toward his November deadline the next year. As Emma Rothschild pointed out, he did many of the right things economically, but at the wrong time electorally. He added more jobs than Reagan would do in his first term, but his boom came in his first year, while Reagan's came in his election year.⁶ Cumulatively, Americans would *not* be better off after four years of Reagan than they had been after four years of Carter; but Reagan's recession hurt his party only in the congressional elections, and was forgotten by his own race, when recovery had begun. Since voters judge by their prospects at election time, rather than from the remoter record of preceding years, a slight move up in the indicators brings disproportionate rewards if it is properly timed.⁷ Carter had no economic timing at all.

There were deeper problems than surface manipulation could deal with, and Reagan's campaign addressed these. Not only was there runaway inflation in Carter's years, but a stall in the growth that is supposed to go with an "overheated" economy's high prices. The fiscal attunements that were the pride of the sixties had broken down entirely—the alternate use of bit and spur to rein in or prod on, looking to a steady pace of employment, productivity, and expenditure. The old formula was simple. For inflation, cut back government spending; for unemployment, increase it. But the seventies brought simultaneous inflation and stagnation, defying conventional economic prescriptions. Some blamed this on the long-term effects of Lyndon Johnson's attempt to have a war and the Great Society at the same time, using funds for the one to bribe opponents of the other, back and forth.[8] Some reduced it to the successive "oil shocks."[9] Others blamed it on the growing structure of insurance for credit, employment, retirement, and quality of life, which put a floor under prices but no ceiling above them.[10] Others thought fiscal jitteriness, combined with monetary unsteadiness, was causing the problem by every attempt to cure it.[11] Others thought that the productive base of American industry had been eroded and must be rebuilt.[12] There was little agreement among the experts.

So the amateurs took over. Several editorial writers at *The Wall Street Journal*—Robert Bartley, Jude Wanniski, Norman Ture—had become enthusiasts for the ideas of a weirdly persuasive academic showman named Arthur Laffer.[13] The Laffer theorem was at least as old as Montesquieu, and beyond challenge in itself—the claim that tax revenues can be so high as to dry up their source. Wanniski had Laffer explain this to one of President Ford's aides (who must have been rather dense) by drawing an igloo shape on a napkin to explain the trajectory of tax returns. The drawing was not only simplistic but tendentious—a lopsided igloo, or one melting to collapse in one direction would better describe the irregularities of the curve.[14] Yet, from Jude Wanniski's unparalleled publicity campaign, built around this doodle, the mystique of supply-side economics grew.

The general proposition of supply side is also an obvious one, though discredited in its simpler formulation by Jean-Baptiste Say. Say's Law maintained that supply can never outrun demand, since demand is infinite, being based on human appetites. Supply responds to the demands it first stimulates. So, supply-siders claimed, the answer to stagnation is not to give consumers money to buy with, but to give producers capital to produce with—through lower taxes, faster depreciation, less regulation, and other incentives. If the circular process was frictionless, perfect, the market constantly adjusting supply to demand by its own magic, it would not matter where you entered this chicken-and-egg sequence. But since the circle does not close itself at once, who gets what first—producers or employees—is in fact a crucial question, at least for employees, who have less to begin with.

Why, for that matter, should supply-siders themselves care where one enters the pattern, so long as it completes itself so quickly and surely? Why not give the first boost to the poor rather than the rich? Because they answer, the poor tend to *break* the circle. Given an unearned sufficiency (e.g., by welfare), they tend not to work or not to work efficiently, not to earn beyond sufficiency, not to store money for larger purchases in capital-creating banks.[15] Here was the supply-siders' explanation for the stagflation riddle— benefits had been diverted into many little pools of wasted sufficiency, lost to the joint effort at growth. Prices rise because the money to buy is there, but employment does not rise because the money is not spent in productive ways. Even producers divert their capital to shelters, since the government encourages consumers to limit new purchases. Carter, by dwelling on limits, on shrinking oil use, on cutting back, had effectively paralyzed the growth machine of the American economy.

There was much in the supply-side analysis to appeal to Ronald Reagan. It trusted the market, distrusted government, and believed in growth. But when Jude Wanniski tried to get a hearing from the Reagan camp in 1976, he was not successful. John Sears stood in the way.[16] Reagan had already fallen for a "funny money" speech from Jeff Bell, and Sears wanted no more risky departures from the Republicans' earlier loves—the "old-time religion" of a balanced budget, or Milton Friedman's monetary policy. But by 1980 Sears was looking for something new in the era of stagflation, something that sounded aggressive and hopeful, to strike a contrast with Carter's economic stance, which looked passive when not negative. By that time, Laffer's views had been adopted by congressional Republicans who supported the Kemp-Roth tax cut, and Sears encouraged Congressman Jack Kemp to travel with Reagan, to change his mood as well as his views, stimulating him with Kemp's own hot-gospeler's belief. It was another way of keeping the performer "up."[17]

Reagan himself was a cautious convert. He had years of programmed response to overcome—all those years of denouncing deficits, paying homage to the balanced budget, ridiculing the "Democratic" idea that there is any such thing as a free lunch. But a free lunch is just what Kemp was spreading for Reagan. Tax cuts would pay for themselves, since taxes had reached a point where they drained the economy rather than strengthened it. The tax monies released into private circulation would promote savings (to form new capital) and investment (to use that capital) and growth (the product of that investment). Hastened depreciation and eased regulation would create a wave of new plants capable of cheaper production. Since government was the problem, not the solution, just getting government out of the way would be a solution to every economic ill. The Gulliver of American capitalism, tied down with a thousand strings by Lilliputian bureaucrats, would spring up into boisterous activity. Supply side was inconsistent with much of what Reagan had said over the years about economic theory; but it fit everything he believed about the American saga, about "what made us great" before there was any government to cripple the lone pioneer on the frontier. Supply side was cowboy economics—you get your free lunch by roping and throwing meat on the hoof, lassoing it with the Laffer curve. Any cowboy can do that on his own, so long as he is not obstructed by timid city folk in green eyeshades.

There were aspects of the supply-side story that appealed to every brand of Republican. The monetarist and fiscal-restraint people found aspects of it compatible, and dismissed the rest as campaign rhetoric. The supply-side view was the domestic equivalent of what became Reagan's answer to foreign problems. Like SDI, supply side seemed unthreatening. It would restore the economy without pain, reduce inflation without recession. As Reagan shifted all his emphasis from offense to defense in weaponry, he shifted his rhetoric on the economy from thrift to plenty. The "conservative" position was reoriented from the past to the future, to a bold new world of endless supply.

Engineering the SDI remains a puzzle. But engineering the free lunch has a record, since David Stockman began that task even before Ronald Reagan was inaugurated. Stockman, a young Representative from Michigan, began work on Capitol Hill as part of the expanding congressional bureaucracy.[18] Later, in Congress himself, he became an ally of Senator Jack Kemp, with whom he wrote a presidential-transition report on the economy intended, among other things, to make Stockman become Reagan's Director of the Office of Management and the Budget.[19] This document, called "An Economic Dunkirk," said that Reagan would need to seize the post-election euphoria, temper and challenge it with predictions of disaster ("Dunkirk"), declare a state of emergency, and ram through *simultaneous* measures that would entirely change public expectations.[20] The nerve to cut government revenue while encouraging growth (especially in defense) would falter, on Wall Street and in the Congress, unless confidence was secured by early victories. The budget had to be cut immediately, along with taxes, to ease congressional apprehension about deficits and business anxiety about interest rates. The government had to become less competitive for credit while making the private sector more competitive, or the result would be "Thatcherization," cuts and stagnation.[21] Everything depended on "a hair-trigger market psychology."[22]

All one had to sell was hope—the salesman's basic commodity, as Reagan's father knew. And Reagan would have to be the supreme salesman, confident as he sailed through a Symplegades of rocky traps closing behind and before him at every moment. He would have to forswear "quick fixes" as trouble spots developed, trusting to the resilience of the business community itself.[23] The first budget drawn up by the new administration would "elicit coronary contractions among some" and make them call for "deferral or temporary abandonment of the tax program," but Reagan would have to bash on regardless, true to the faith.[24] It would be his job to keep smiling at the customer, pooh-poohing the problems, while he relied on someone who knew all about the problems and kept finessing them. In short, he needed a sorcerer's apprentice—and Stockman even looked the part, a frowning pixie in aviator glasses.

Stockman promised to give Reagan's dream the substance of things countable. Reagan would sell the program, but he expected others—principally Stockman—to formulate it. The director of OMB had charted the congressional assault before the other economics appointees knew where their offices were.[25] By inauguration, they had little choice but to line up behind his effort. He *was* the President's economic policy. Though Reagan had not declared a state of national emergency, everything else the Dunkirk memorandum asked for was given into Stockman's hands. He was a throwback to the Kennedy years of bustling competence, when Robert McNamara seemed a walking computer, radiating certitude.

But McNamara became acquainted with doubt only far down his particular road toward Vietnam. Stockman quickly found out (but did not show) that he could not square the circle after all, which is what "Reaganomics" had promised to do—not if the President was serious about raising defense expenditures (and he was) and leaving Social Security alone (he almost was). Stockman knew that the "out years," those beyond the immediate budget, were crucial to the supply-siders' gamble on the recuperative powers of business. He had to show that the government would ease up on its competition for credit down the road if interest rates were to drop and private investment soar, enough to balance (at least in part) the drop in government funds caused by tax cuts and a slowed inflation. The projections were, thus, everything. But they were bleak. He had to change them. He abandoned the Wharton School of Economics model for future performance that the OMB had been using, and sought a system with more hope in it—first from Alan Greenspan.[26] When that did not work either, he tried one from the Claremont Economics Institute. He was running out of devices, and none gave him enough yield; so, as he told Laurence Barrett, "We had doctored that one, just the way the previous administration doctored the Wharton model. They're absolutely doctored."[27] But never before doctored on such a scale— one that made Murray Weidenbaum consider resigning as Chairman of the Council of Economic Advisers.[28]

The numbers did not have to be authentic, in the Stockman view. If only people believed them, they would come true as a consequence. Thus faith had to be engendered by whatever legerdemain. And for a while, Congress almost *had* to believe Stockman's numbers, so sure was the Reagan team, all speaking with one voice, and so new were the budget claims, all using methods no one was familiar with. As Stockman told William Greider of the Washington *Post,* "We got away with that because of the novelty of all these budget reductions."[29] Stockman had worked with incredible speed and what seemed a cool efficiency. But soon he was drowning in his own flood of figures, each uncheckable against another, all aimed at fostering confidence rather than meeting tests of probability. The con man finally loses his own confidence when he cannot remember what is true and what is not in his own spiel:

> None of us really understands what's going on with all these numbers. You've got so many different budgets out and so many different baselines and such complexity now in the interactive parts of the budget between policy action and the economic environment and all the internal mysteries of the budget, and there are a lot of them. People are getting from A to B and it's not clear how they are getting there. It's not clear how we got there.[30]

While Stockman was widely perceived as whittling government down to pitiful size, he saw the "real" budget projections mounting dizzily. At last he had to resort to what Senator Howard Baker called the "magic asterisk," a footnote attributing improbable future reductions in the out years to "unidentified savings."[31] The Reagan team was beginning to admit what its own Vice President had charged in the primary campaign, that supply-side theory is "voodoo economics."

What Stockman had come to fear most was his own program's success. With Reagan solidly behind him, and the whole team lined up, Congress had gone along with the first budget bill (Gramm-Latta). Then, after a setback on the attempt to cut Social Security, the Administration came back with a second budget bill (Gramm-Latta II). The impression created was that taxes could safely be cut since government had been reduced. (This was an interesting reversal of Reagan's procedure in California, where he argued that taxes could be *raised* because he had cut government, insuring that new revenue would not be used on extravagances.) But Stockman knew that the budget cuts would come nowhere near offsetting the tax cuts, and that future projections made it unlikely business would fill the gap with a spurt of its own.

By the time the budget cuts were in place, in the summer of 1981, Stockman and Richard Darman toyed with the idea of letting the tax cut lose.[32] But Reagan would not change his mind on the part of his program he loved the most by now, and the two men could think of no credible way of sabotaging their own program without being caught at it. They would have to win and bear it. Reagan's own certitude and charm had made him, scarily, unbeatable.

But the more the White House succeeded politically, the more it failed economically. Business did not revive, nor savings go up. Tax reductions did not make for a broader base of productivity to be taxed. Even the unexpected drop in inflation—itself partly the result of accounting magic—hurt.[33] It reduced the value of government holdings and slowed the revenue from tax "bracket creep." Reagan began to rail, politely, at Wall Street, for not doing its part.[34] He had given them what they wanted, in his eyes, and they were sitting there doing nothing. The people were urged to spend and have faith, even as the recession overtook them.[35] In Reagan's eyes the free lunch was out there, but spiteful people were refusing to eat it.

By the end of Reagan's first year, in December of 1981, 59 percent of those asked by pollsters said no when asked if they were better off than last year; only 36 percent said yes.[36] And the worst was still ahead. In 1982, unemployment rose to 10.7 percent, higher than it had been since the Great Depression, along with the greatest number of bank failures since 1940.[37] Record bankruptcies and farm closures were occurring. It was a world gone crazy. The President who came in to cut spending increased it throughout his first term. He added as much to the national debt in those four years as had been accumulated in our national history to that point, so that one of every seven dollars spent by the government in 1985 went to paying interest on the debt.[38]

No sooner had the Reagan program passed than its creators turned on it —all but one: Reagan still believed it was working.[39] When Stockman's doubts were published in the December 1981 issue of *Atlantic*, Reagan responded the way he usually did when faced with an unpleasant reality. He said it was not there: journalist William Greider had misquoted Stockman (a claim Stockman himself never made). Like Reagan's divorce, the embarrassing quotes had not occurred. The President even compared the press "assassination" of Stockman to John Hinckley's attempt on his own life.[40] It took a major conspiracy of his own White House team to make Reagan believe that "revenue enhancement" measures, to make up for the tax cuts, were not themselves taxes. Businessmen had to be brought in to tell him that the stories he was spreading about their happiness were false.[41] Even that did not register. Laurence Barrett, given extraordinary access to Reagan at this time, marveled at his "absolute refusal to acknowledge the connection between his policies and the major recession of 1981–82."[42]

Reagan felt that everything was on schedule, that night would soon lead to dawn. Not even the theological supply-siders believed that. They felt their program was not working because it had been sabotaged. The tax cuts were modified to get them passed. Or Volcker at the Fed had kept money too tight (though that helped Reagan to his one clear achievement, the drop in inflation). Or Reagan had not understood the full program—it needed to be grounded on a return to the gold standard.[43] Or weak-hearted followers like Stockman had scared people off with his talk of cuts and out-year projections, not trusting to the simple response of the market if one just let go of everything. Also, hard-core supply-siders had a further axiom that Reagan did not mention (if he knew about it) during his campaign: deficits do not matter.[44] True believers will never be convinced by the failure of their system, since they will always claim the system did not get a fair trial—even Reagan chickened out when he let the "revenue enhancers" trick him into disguised taxes in 1982. That alone was enough to destroy the magic. The plan offered *everything* or nothing.

Reagan continued to believe that everything had been not only offered but won, long after most supply-siders had found something to blame for the fact that their scheme had not worked in 1982. He thought it had. He took the later recovery as proof of the matter, though the bounce-back was following a normal pattern after a recession (but at lower and later rates).[45] By the time he ran for reelection in 1984, Reagan said that it was "morning in America" because "America is back." The night had ended, the dark interlude of Carter's indecision and timidity. What America was really coming back from was the Reagan recession, which took more out of the economy in two years than Carter could in four. The idling, total stall, and slow lurch forward brought down inflation, but at a cost of 600 billion dollars in GNP, and about half again as much in diminished capacity over the succeeding years.[46] It cost the average person $1,000 in lost income, and the average family over $3,000, with a very uneven distribution of the suffering—the lower half of society absorbed four to five times as much of the loss as the upper half did.[47]

In the "upbeat" mood of the 1984 campaign, Reagan's followers could talk about an economic miracle wrought by supply-side economics. The promise had been pain-free deliverance from stagflation. The reality had been a quick easing of inflation by the "old-time-religion" remedy of deep recession, followed by a sluggish move away from stagnation. About half of the inflation's drop was the product of recession, another third coming from the adventitious easing of oil and other import prices, and 20 percent from a change in accounting practices (another example of the kind of magic the Reagan administration practiced with numbers).[48]

In the midst of the recession, Reagan's own people had been forced back on the truth. It was not only Stockman who blurted it out, telling the Chamber of Commerce that unemployment is "part of the cure, not the problem."[49] Larry Speakes, delivering the Administration's line, had said three months earlier that unemployment was "the price you have to pay for bringing down inflation."[50] Supply-siders of the purer sort were outraged at this abandonment of the myth. Their only consolation was that the President himself never stopped telling stories that confirmed the myth, even in the darkest times. And though his polls dropped for a while in 1982, people were eager to reward the President for keeping the faith after they experienced a recovery in 1984. By then it seemed that he had believed, against all odds, not only in a theory of economics but in America itself—and that is what we pay him for.

CHAPTER 40

Greenfield Village on the Potomac

Man falls deceiv'd
By the other first.
—Paradise Lost *3.130–31*

Reagan gives our history the continuity of a celluloid Möbius strip. We ride its curves backward and forward at the same time, and he is always there. There is an endlessness of surface that becomes a kind of depth, a self-reflecting omnipresence in the cultural processing of Americans over the second half of the twentieth century. This inescapability of Reagan was a joke in the movie about time travel, *Back to the Future,* which Reagan quoted seriously in his 1982 State of the Union address. Then, to complete the loop, Reagan's real son played Reagan in a television parody of *Back to the Future,* the film with which this sequence began. Reagan's image precedes us as we ride forward or backward in time, anticipating our reactions, reflecting us back to ourselves, stirring "memories of the future." Reagan is part of the process that forged our self-awareness, at a time when movie imagery, broadcast immediacy, and highway mobility entered Americans' lives—or, rather, when Americans entered the new atmosphere created by those inventions. This was the past that most vividly created our future.

In Muncie ("Middletown") during the 1920s, sociologists Robert and Helen Lynd discovered that people were skeptical or hostile toward change in moral terms, but comparatively unquestioning about technological alterations, on the assumption that the latter need not affect the former.

Here, as elsewhere, one thing that determines whether a given change is welcomed or resisted appears to be the fact of its unsettling simply material traits or the personal attitudes, ideals, and values of the population. Changes, such as the adoption of electrical devices, refrigeration, and similar material factors, occur with relatively greater ease and speed than those touching marriage, the relation of parents and children, and other "sanctities" of life.[1]

One could retain one's original goals, but reach them more rapidly, by using new gadgets, mere conveniences of life not touching life's core. The past and present, religion and science, morality and modernity, were not contending but complementary forces.

Yet the Lynds' book tells a far different story. Mere "conveniences" like cars and movies were changing the deepest patterns of family life, generational interplay, and the relation of the sexes. Cars loosened the web of community and neighborhood, changed the conditions of work and leisure time. They affected church attendance. They even changed the appearance of homes and their lawns.[2] Cars indurated a habit of buying on credit that had been restricted, for many, to the single big purchase of a lifetime, that of one's house.[3] Soon more people had to own cars than owned their own homes; yet cars were even more extravagant purchases than houses, if one considered the brisker rate of depreciation and repurchase. The ethos of thrift and saving was already deeply eroded by the 1920s. If one could buy a car "on time," why not such comparatively minor things as washing machines, vacuum cleaners, radios, encyclopedias? The credit card society was being born.

The car changed courtship and dating patterns; it led to pairing before arrival at a dance, and separate paths home afterward.[4] One of the most common sources of domestic conflict, as measured in a high school questionnaire, was children's demand for use of their parents' car—and cars were already being bought to the children's specifications.[5] By allowing young couples to be alone together, unchaperoned, at night, sheltered from the elements and from others' eyes, the car did more over the years for a "sexual revolution" in this century than any other invention, including the contraceptive pill.[6] No wonder the "time machine" in *Back to the Future,* a film tailored to teen audiences, is a car.[7] The automobile changed more than an individual's location, moment by moment. Its users became different people because of this tool. Car construction and car theft had both entered the regular pattern of Muncie living.[8] The new means did not simply take people more swiftly to the same old ends; the means altered the ends. The process of going deflected one from former goals.

The automobile was just one element in the complex of modern life being woven in Reagan's youth by technological development. Radio changed politics, becoming almost as important to Roosevelt's presidency as television would later be to Reagan's. Movies altered reading habits before television supplanted them. Living an alternative life of continuous fantasy by way of radio soap operas, genre films, and TV series became ingrained at earlier and earlier years of childhood. Yet this other-life of dreams, opened up by modern inventions, often celebrated outmoded (rather than innovative) codes of behavior. "Home" images were subtly anachronistic, adapting modern life back toward inherited ideals. The new vehicles bore one away from the past as one gazed backward at it. Grandmothers on television are still taken from the Norman Rockwell casting service of the mind. With all the racetracks in America available for use in a TV spot, an agency had to create an artificial track because the real ones did not "look right"—i.e., did not look like the racetracks from people's "real life" of movie fantasy.[9] Though that particular TV spot was being made for a telephone company, not even the phone booths in use at the time could be filmed; they did not fit people's image of phone booths.[10] The modern convenience had to present itself in reassuringly archaic guise. In order to change our lives, technology has to promise it will not (really) change our lives. We are carried forward under the impression that we are going *back* to our cherished dreams, taking a shorter route there. The telephone will not, as Thorstein Veblen claimed, make one vulnerable to anonymous or unsolicited intercourse—wrong numbers, dunning creditors, advertising "surveys," random messages—but will let one stay in touch with the family that has been dispersed by modern life.[11]

A return to the land of "real" racetracks and phone booths was strenuously undertaken by Henry Ford, who wanted access not only to a vision of the past but to its tangible stuff. When Ford said "history is bunk,"[12] he meant other people's versions of history (especially the scholars'). Toward his own history he was pious, not only personally but in a public way. To his Greenfield Village, in Dearborn, Michigan, he moved not only his own birthplace but—if it was at all purchasable—that of every other American he admired, including the man who taught him what history he knew, William Holmes McGuffey (1800–73), author of the schoolchildren's *Eclectic Readers.*[13]

Ford's tribute to McGuffey was meant not only to remember the past but to resurrect it, to drill its lessons—*by its methods*—into present-day students. He built a one-room schoolhouse at Greenfield Village (using eighteenth-century logs) where children could be taught from the *Eclectic Readers'* pious and patriotic excerpts, abridgements, and adaptations—a kind of education by *Reader's Digest.*[14] Nor was this an isolated experiment. Ford opened other one-room schools near his factories—there were fifteen of them in 1934—where children could be taught the right things in the right way.[15] The schools combined two emphases. The first was a pragmatic, empirical approach toward doing things—the students were to work land, master tools, produce a profit. But this aggressive productivity was paired with an entirely submissive attitude toward the moral precepts embodied in McGuffey texts and the schools' chapel service. As the Village high school paper put it: "Each year sees the expansion of this flexible system to meet new needs that may arise; yet the fundamental precepts as taught from the McGuffey *Readers* are basic to all developments."[16] Ford was trying to restore, at least in part, that union he saw endangered all around him—a union between the "simpler values" of the world that encouraged the development of his gifts and the modern conditions he had brought about with the fruits of those gifts. The significant point is that he knew only one way to maintain this disintegrating unity—by time travel. He must actually take us back to the world of horses and buggies in order to instill the "horse-and-buggy" morality. At Greenfield Village you can still ride the vehicles Ford's own handiwork swept from the highways.

There could be no better (because inadvertent) confession that the hope of "Middletown" was an empty one—the hope that one can change the mere "outward" conditions without affecting the "inner" values of human beings. Ford kept creating new models of his car to replace the old, but he would not allow his schools to admit new readers to replace McGuffey's. He wanted the profit from the new cars to buy back respectability for the old texts; but that proved a bargain he could not strike with time. He could not take his old world with him as he whizzed off in his automobile time machine, which carried him in the wrong direction, *forward* to the future.

Ford's attempt to escape the consequences of his own work was shared by his idol, Thomas Edison, to whose memory much of Greenfield Village is dedicated.[17] Edison thought *education* was bunk, and constructed intelligence tests precisely so college graduates would flunk them.[18] (He also constructed a "genius test," which Einstein flunked.) Edison feared that higher education would undermine the practical "horse sense" to which he attributed his success—though when he could no longer hold educated men (like Nicholas Tesla) he was supplanted by educated men (like Charles Steinmetz). Edison and Ford kept busy acclaiming and erasing the conditions of their own rise. Though Edison deplored the decline of abstemious ways, he kept promoting the pleasure machines he had, by austere application, contrived or promoted—bright lights, phonographs, movies, radios. Edison was hailed as the modern Prometheus, bringer of light. But his own lights blinded him, left him adrift in a dazzling new world he denounced, a baffled Prometheus turned Jeremiah. The world had not listened carefully to *what* he had to say over his new instrument for saying things. The first words he spoke on the machine of the future harked back to the idyllic world of horses and other animal husbandry: "Mary had a little lamb . . ."

Edison could count on Ford, at least, to take his message seriously. As usual, what Ford revered he tried to buy. He purchased and restored the Massachusetts school allegedly attended by the Mary of the poem; he even attended the school's opening day with a lamb in tow.[19] There is, in such an exercise, a touching attempt to make a vanishing world become palpable again, something a "hardheaded Yankee" can believe in by touching it. Greenfield Village was a dream the nation was invited to join, and did. President Herbert Hoover arrived at the dedication in 1929, riding an artfully antiquated train. Eight days after the ceremony, which was broadcast as part of "Light's Golden Jubilee" promoted by Edward Bernays, the stock market crashed—all that overtoppling credit system that had underwritten the cars and power companies and pleasure machines.

Perhaps the best symbol of Ford's attempt to hold in his grasp evanescing things is a phial in the Ford collection that purports to contain "Edison's last breath." Here is the holiest relic in the shrine, one whose value depends entirely on belief, but one contained in a scientist's test tube. The quest for "down-to-earth" reality has ended in credulity. Since Ford preferred real houses to records of them, he read the records so poorly that he ended up buying the wrong houses. The most famous case is that of Stephen Collins Foster. There is no evidence Foster ever lived in or even saw the home Ford bought and displayed as his birthplace.[20]

Ford was buying a dream, the past as he imagined it was or as it should have been. Hanging above the real Model Ts and other treasures, there is a "Spirit of St. Louis," but it is not Charles Lindbergh's airplane (despite Ford's friendship and admiration for another hero of modernity); it is Jimmy Stewart's, the "actual" plane used in the movie. Many viewers would not be more impressed if they were looking at the original plane in the Smithsonian. This, after all, is the only one they *saw* crossing the ocean on film. It is the dream-reality, more reassuring than the messier facts of authentic (bunk) history.

Ford felt America's need for a safer past. We want to "retain" what we never had—a mythical frontier life, an America where merit and hard work were the only paths to success, where the government did not interfere with the workings of the market's invisible hand: the past, that is, as Reagan thinks he lived it, where performing and earning merged, and the part to be performed was always that of the meritocrat. It is a world subtly distorted toward small perfections, like the buildings at Disneyland. Disney, an admirer of Ford, was influenced by Greenfield Village when he planned Disneyland, where you can see a New Orleans that is "real" as the racetrack on the TV spot was—a New Orleans of the mind, preferable to the original, lacking dirt, contradiction, and bunk.

Disneyland presents America's favored version of history in general, and especially of American history, the version accepted by Reagan, who attended an opening of Disneyland. Reagan is a "conservative" who constantly invokes the past, genuinely loves it, judges events in its lights, and thinks he lived through much of it. But it is a Foster-birthplace past he has seen—as he *saw* the black hero end segregation by shooting down planes at Pearl Harbor. It matters to Reagan that he worked in "historic" Lowell Park, even if he does not know which Lowell gave it its name. "To a Waterfowl" is personal to him because of the park, if only because he thinks the Lowell who gave a name to the park gave the poem to the world. Reagan has acquired a vivid and intimate America by emotional purchase, as Ford tried to acquire it with coarser currency.

For others, Reagan offers not only a path of entry into such an America, a relic of its reality, but a guarantee of its continued existence into our time. In several senses, he gives us the past as a present. The dizzier the pace of change, the more desperate is the mind's need for continuity, stability, a guideline through chaos. America's "remembered" self is simplified to resist the endless impingements of disorienting change. Old things, we are assured, do not really change; they are fixed under the blur of mere "externals." There is an orthodox version of the past—of the Founders (freedom fighters against the communism of their day), of the Alamo, of the good times and the good wars, of Everyman as entrepreneur—that scholarship can never touch with its confusing bunk. Reagan has walked straight out of that past, partly by means of the very technological pleasure-machines that seem to threaten it. He even lived in a kind of Disneyland house, the "house of the future" provided by the wizardry of General Electric, with a humming switchbox, almost as big as a house, that stood guard over the house like a robot dog or kindly "droid."

The GE house was an earlier version of the home full of robot gadgets to wake one up, to pour one's coffee, shown at the beginning of *Back to the Future*. Even in the inventor's den of that film there is a shelf of old (black-and-white) pictures, where American heroes of initiative are honored—Benjamin Franklin, Thomas Edison. At one desperate point the inventor picks up Edison's picture and asks, "Tom, how am I going to generate that kind of power?" The past is not only reassuringly present, but is our guide to the future.

There is evil even in the ideal past of Ford, or Edison, or Lindbergh, or Disney. It is the alien, the un-American. Ford would not let foreign languages be taught in his McGuffeyized high schools, and he spent a great deal of money on his own Americanization program to make immigrants forget their un-American pasts.[21] To disseminate the truth about that old world, Ford printed and freely spread the "Protocols of the Elders of Zion," unveiling the aliens' plot, the truth behind all the distracting bunk.[22]

Reagan, of course, is not an anti-Semite. For him, the alien is not the Jew; but every threat to his miniature country of the mind comes from outside, and from one place. *That* is the cause of all the troubles everywhere, "the focus of evil in the modern world."[23] That alone explained the confusing turmoil of Hollywood's union struggles: "Ugly reality came to our town on direct orders of the Kremlin."[24] Anything that contradicted such a reading, in all those congressional records, was so much government bunk. (Besides, who will read it all, or try to understand it?) Government only becomes good when it exposes the enemy by any means (the Thomas Committee, or the McCarthy Committee), not when it is investigating possible greed or failures in America (the Kearns Committee, or the Justice Department's investigation of MCA). One keeps one's own identity by defining it, always, in terms of the alien. Americanism is anti-communism. "The very heart of the darkness is the Soviet Union"[25]—which makes America the only light on a hill for every other country, mankind's best hope against those who adhere to "the ten commandments of Nikolai Lenin"[26] (the Protocols, as it were, of the Elders of Moscow).

The outside threat becomes oddly comforting because it helps *remove* the threatening aspects from those instruments of change that seemed to be eroding old ways. The very technology that altered American mores has been conscripted to the supreme task of resisting the aliens. Only our inventions of death keep the world living, despite the deep schemings of the "evil empire." And Reagan means to remove the last traces of ambiguity from the weapons' benevolent role by making them solely defensive, silver bullets that disarm but hurt not.

Reagan, on a grander political scale than Ford could ever imagine, has erected a technological Greenfield Village on the Potomac. Like the movie *Star Wars* (or *ET* or *Superman),* it combines an infantile regressiveness of story with the utmost sophistication of special effects. But the movies were arch in tone, while Reagan is as soberly sentimental in his cause as Henry Ford. Only a believer could make Reagan's fictive past credible to others. Only a touch of fanaticism can hold out against all kinds of converging evidence. But Reagan is that most disarming of political apparitions, the kindly fanatic—closer, indeed, to the gentle inventor of *Back to the Future* than to well-intended bigots like Ford or Edison. For many, Reagan is not only a comfort but a necessity. He is the demagogue as rabble-soother, at a time when people do not need to be stirred up but assuaged, to have anxieties dispelled, complexities resolved. They need to believe that the simpler past not only perdures but prevails. Its Force is with us. Reagan not only represents the past, but resurrects it as a promise of the future. He has Edison's last breath in his lungs.

CHAPTER 41

Original Sinlessness

how man fell
Degraded by himself, on grace depending.
—Paradise Regained *4.311–12*

At Disneyland, one can meet a real President, real as the racetrack on the TV spot was real, realer than the ordinary world. We enter through an anteroom of old clippings and photographs; curtains are drawn; we find Lincoln sitting at his ease, delivering immortal lines as in conversation; he rises, moves about, stands tall, his voice resonating from speakers around us. Technology has brought us living history, not bunk, its limbs disposed and moved artificially but realistically (under the right light), delivering an ancient and beautiful message. Who would have thought, until recently, that such a President was to be found outside Anaheim?

The Reagan presidency is not a mere exercise in nostalgia. It must be *modern* as well. The message must travel to us by way of complex intermediation, labyrinthine as the electronics that work Lincoln's innards. Reagan must be not merely a *laudator temporis acti,* but a celebrant of the future, both simultaneously and equally insistently. Only in this way can Reagan, simply by being who he is, where he is, alleviate a deep ideological contradiction in American life. According to the American myth he advances, capitalism is both individualistic and conservative, though the terms of that proposition are mutually contradictory.

It is hard to understand why people should think capitalism is identical with, or even conduces to, individualism. The classic exponent of free markets, Adam Smith, argued that accumulation of a "store" (capital) left over from immediate use makes possible vaster projects than the individual can undertake, either as a matter of handicraft or of trade. The way to reach larger markets than the immediate use area is to specialize (making a surplus of, say, pins) by collaborative effort (a number of people dividing up the labor of making pins). After consumption of the first "store" that made possible the specialization in pins, the workers would be deprived of other products (neglected in their concentration on the pin) but for the goods obtained in the larger market reached by the pins' traveling agents (themselves part of the division of labor that makes pins for the multitudes).[1] Increased efficiency in the cooperative specializations, which produce all the traded goods, will produce the "wealth of nations" (not, primarily, of the individual). The leading note of the operation is, at every level, interdependence—of the workers on each other as they make parts of the pin (each useless in itself), of the workers on their factors as the latter peddle the product in ever wider markets, of both makers and distributors on the specialists in other products. The first victim of this system would be the *individual* pin-maker, who tried to compete using his slower process of manufacture and limited range of customers. Making his obsolete pin in the center of a community that turns out the things in quantity, he would be trying to sell coals in Newcastle. That is the story of the demise of individual handicraft (and individualism) before the division of labor based on capital.

Once this operation is under way, individuals in the management, distribution, or ownership of materials and tools can try to get more than their share out of the vast cooperative venture. But that is not capitalism; it is theft (and very common). And even an individual parasite on the joint system must *keep up* the cooperative effort in order to reap an unfair share of its profits. He must keep the workers performing their converging tasks, and keep traders and stockers busy at their interlocking functions. To the extent that individuals try to divert the wealth of nations to their private use, they subvert the process that creates the wealth—Veblen's complaint against the wastefulness of merely pecuniary managers.[2]

It is true that other pin-making groups may try to supplant the first one with a better process. It must, usually, be a *very* much better process, to make up for the advantages the first pin factory has established in patterns of workmanship, supply, and trade, which have also created habits of buying and use in all the pins' customers. Smith's pin factory had "at least eighteen" separate operations. An individual might think of a way to cut the steps to fifteen, thus decreasing labor and lowering price; but he would still need the fifteen people in his plan. It would still be a cooperative project that prevailed, however equitably (or not) the advantages, gained in this way, were afterward divided.

Modern technology has been created by the efforts of people using stores of abundance in increasingly complex patterns of interdependence. Each time we use such a typical product of the system as (say) a jetliner, we are trusting a vast army of unseen collaborators in our journey—all those who designed, built, sold, service, fly, guard, and guide the plane. One slip in the huge operation, and it ends in disaster. We are depending on the social responsibility of others—that the maintenance man was not doped up, the inspector was not lazy, the pilot is not hung over, the air controller is not too harried to see straight (or too tranquilized to resist the harassment). Any breakdown in this web of social links makes us vulnerable, no matter what our individual force of will or play of ingenuity. The self-reliant test pilot, strapped in his seat in the travel section of a jetliner next to the dimmest bureaucrat, will die along with him if the maintenance people have not done their work properly.

In fact, most of us will be happier with the individualistic test pilot sitting next to us in the travelers' section rather than at the controls of the plane. If Tom Wolfe (who spent a good deal of time with them) is to be believed, test pilots love risk, and try to give each flight an individual mark. They also like to drink and fly.[3] Daredevils are needed in the early tests of a product not yet reduced to rule; but the aim of the process that uses them is to make them obsolete as soon as possible, to make the finally tested function performable on a routine basis. After that, in a complex operation, individualism is irregularity, a nuisance and obstruction.[4] That is why the use of test pilots as astronauts was determined partly by a concern for public relations rather than efficiency. Actually, trained monkeys had flown the most dangerous first experiments, and the first astronauts learned (to their frustration) that they were not really flying the capsule into which they were inserted like hams in the oven, to be warmed and basted, their temperature taken, other measurements made. The early satellites had side portholes until the pilots' demand (and the public relations claim that they "flew" the satellites) led to the insertion of a front "windshield." This is another example of the way technology sells the new by imitating the old, making the space capsule (a word the astronauts did not like either, and had changed) resemble a "real" spacecraft—i.e., more like Flash Gordon visualizations of it. The new frontier called for new cowboys, and their horsepower had to *look* as if it had horsepower—as the first automobiles had carriages like those drawn by horses.[5]

As we saw in Chapter 9, the American frontier was not settled by lone cowboys but by federal troops, civic organizations, community posses, and railroad combines, organizations whose first concern was to get guns out of the hands of lone operators (often lone psychopaths). The West was not settled by the gun but by gun-control laws. In our day, the same concerns are evident. If the test pilot in a jetliner's coach section can die because of some maintenance man's error, he can die just as well from a bomb concealed by a single traveler. The maintenance man with a drug problem can sabotage all the other skills and goodwill involved in a flight, simply by inadvertence, with no particular intent of his own. The lone bomber, by contrast, is imposing his or her will, and winning, against the joint wills of all those who lifted several hundred people into the air inside their large tubular capsule. That is why the terrorist is the true individualist of our time, the lone defier (and defeater) of the common will.

A society orchestrated out of the varying specializations that capital makes possible is so dependent on cooperation that it is extraordinarily vulnerable to even one uncooperative person. Like the jet capsule, the Tylenol capsule can be sabotaged, and then the very efficiency of the product's wide distribution becomes a menace—as the telephone's obliteration of space becomes a menace if it is used by an anonymous threatener, unreachable, unlocalizeable. More force of will, more accumulated power, does nothing to remedy this. Executives of large corporations are the private citizens most endangered by kidnappers-for-profit precisely *because* they have resources to pay the ransom. What people call for in a Tylenol scare is more regulation and investigation, more controlled steps in the processes of production and distribution—more cooperative effort. The threat of bombs on planes is answered most effectively by exhaustive search procedures, to which people must submit with good grace in order to achieve mutual protection.

But though these are the workaday realities of life, they do not fit Americans' self-image, nurtured by myth, ideology, and special interests. *We,* not the terrorist, are supposed to typify modern individualism and its success. The truth about our actual behavior, whether on the old frontier or the new, is as threatening to our sense of identity as the terrorist himself. The truth is that the delicate capitalist machinery has lifted itself, like a lumbering jet that overcomes the tug of gravity, by a social discipline of standardization. Yet we fly on, connected to each other, dreaming of a disconnected past—as if each passenger on the jet had floated up independently into the air and settled into the seat he or she aimed for, using separate skill and willpower. In our social dream, the individual passengers are carrying the dead weight of the airplane, rather than vice versa.

Reagan makes this absurdity believable, partly by believing in it so thoroughly himself. He believes that terrorists will stay away from jet planes if America acts like a cowboy. He believes that the moving vehicle has not altered the goal of modern life. He professes and prolongs a mystique of the individual that is obstructive when not destructive in a world of meshing needs, increased as well as satisfied by the growing pleasure machines of our time. He has used his annual messages to institute a cult of "heroes," the extraordinary individuals who redeem modern life, brought before Congress to rebuke mere "govment," which shackles the individual. He would arm the passengers on our national "jetliner" of history, and have them "settle things" on their own. And, like jet passengers intently watching a movie, unaware of their own motion, Americans are determined to retain the individualist fantasy while others are doing the job that keeps them aloft.

If it is strange to see capitalism posing as individualist, it is even odder for it to act as the voice of conservatism. Conservatism, in a minimal definition, wants to conserve; but capitalism is an instrument for change, for expansion, driven toward ever new resources, products, markets. It reorders life drastically. Even at the paradigmatic simplest model, it changes people from providers of self-sufficiency to specialists in a pin factory, whose reward for this odd imposition of uniformity and regularity in their lives is the hope of a richer return from ever more distant parts of an expanding market. If they sop up all the need for pins in the nearest pool, they must have transportation and communication experts who take the pins out to new areas; and this process is never-ending and accelerating, because all the *other* specialists are under the same mutually stimulating pressures. In this flow of products created by a growing surplus, "capital has no home," in the words of Bernard Shaw.[6] It is a roving, restless, innovative force. It must have newer models at shorter intervals. It literally remakes lives in order to have new customers for new models. As we saw in Middletown, residents became different people after they had made, and borrowed for, and driven, and fought with the children over, and learned to update, their automobiles. We are a different people after we have made movies on the scale that we have, and televisions and jet airplanes. We become a different people when we have made nuclear weapons on the scale that we have.

There is nothing less conservative than capitalism, so itchy for the new. It expends, in order to expand; it razes, to rebuild; it destroys, to employ. Whatever merits it may have, conservatism is not among them. In the sixties, when black ghettos were exploding, I talked with some businessmen who blamed it all on radicals. I thought them too modest. I suggested they drive (quickly) through black neighborhoods and notice the forest of TV antennas rising above the most rundown housing. The sets had originally been sold "on time," by aggressive methods that convinced buyers they would share in the good life. But what the dream box told buyers was that they must have this *further* toy or that *newer* product in order to enjoy the good life. The buyers' children were brought up with the imperatives of a consumer society dinning at them day and night, tantalizing them with things withheld. The result was a certain raising of aspirations, some fulfillable, most destined to frustration. There was an inevitable redefinition of needs and demands, one that radicals may applaud. But capitalists deserve the credit for that development.

The most conservative expressions of a society are ordinarily religious. Attitudes toward the divine tend to be stable, as their object is thought to be. They look back to a past revelation. They observe a prescribed ritual, repeat sacred words, replicate the requirements for priests or initiates. They judge the world against some otherworld of the supernatural and find it wanting— this life is but a falling off from, a dim reflection of, or arduous preparation for, a better one.

It is not surprising, then, that the support given Reagan by religious groups should be considered "conservative" in this general sense given to all religion. Reagan himself calls the present time a period of great religious revival, and revival means a return of life; it looks to some prior state which must be reanimated.[7] The leaders of various "moral majority" groups yearn back to the "good old days," especially in matters of sexual morality. They feel uneasy or indignant about what they take to be tolerance (if not encouragement) of homosexuality, heterosexual infidelity, pornography, illegitimate births, abortion, teen use of contraceptives. A dozen or so prominent preachers have become highly visible and affluent deploring these changes. Their very salience, however, is a confession of their failure. They are trying, from a few scattered rooftops, to shout back a flood that was once contained, quietly, by the joint efforts of most preachers and their supportive parishioners. The few now deplore what the many once prevented. The TV evangelist's personal success, as an individual, indicates that his cause is lost.

He is undermined by the very conduit of his jeremiads, television. Changes in moral attitudes have been accomplished with the help of the cameras and other instruments the preachers rely on. Childhood and adolescent appetites undergo perpetual hedonistic solicitings which are, in commercial terms, proofs that capitalism can create ever-new levels of demand to be satisfied. These pressures are inescapable because they are, at the economic level, admirable. In stodgy Middletown, for instance, thinly disguised advertisements for prostitution could not be refused by the newspapers since they were in agreement with the economic belief in profit—unlike the advertisements for cheap labor which *were* refused, because they interfered with profit.[8]

The conservative Christian temperament will find in modern hedonism just a continuing manifestation of fallen human nature. Such a temperament holds, that is, to the doctrine of original sin. But this is a point on which our Lesser Awakening fatally hesitates. Original sin, the belief in shared human corruption, treats religion in what William James called the "sick soul" manner. But America's contribution to the history of Christian practice has been an institutional effort to cure the sick soul, here and now. It has a therapeutic character, moving readily from fundamentalists' faith healing to the more sophisticated mind-cure of positive thinking. Christian Science is the type toward which other American religions are subtly deflected precisely because it is "the most radical branch of mind-cure in its dealings with evil."[9] Only mind-cure, James thought, might rank, in America, with earlier great reforms and awakenings like Luther's or Wesley's: as the century opened, he guessed that mind-cure would "play a part almost as great in the evolution of the popular religion of the future as did those earlier movements in their day," constituting America's "only decidedly original contribution to the systematic philosophy of life."[10] There has rarely been a more accurate forecast of American history. The motion of American religion away from a belief in original sin can be traced, progressively, in the softening of Calvinism, from the belief of Presbyterians in a "moral sense" retained despite depravity, through Barton Stone's rejection of the need for substitute redemption of human nature, to the Disciples' progressive dilution of their one major requirement for cleansing of sin (baptism), and—more rapidly as we pass the year in which James delivered his lectures, 1899—in the vague religiosity traceable, generation by generation, down from Nelle Reagan through Ronald Reagan to the Reagan children. Reagan is an intermediary figure here, easing the transition he seems to deny.

Like most accurate predictions, James's looks almost inevitable when seen in retrospect. The American ethos, as shaped by our history, resists the concept of original sin, which describes not only the Fall of Man but the ruin of Eden. Nature is recalcitrant, after the Fall, since man Adam's act had consequences, an entrainment of progressively crippling circumstances. According to the classic expositor of original sin, St. Augustine, it was the very attempt to be free of constraint—"You will be like gods"—that led to linked sequences of disaster, the *series calamitatis* of history.[11] Defective human choices have multiple consequences, some unforeseen, some unintended; one tries to help one's child by sending him or her to this or that school, and such a choice has effects one cannot be sure of, trammeled up in the consequences of many other acts (by other parents sending children to the same school that year, by educators coming to or staying at or departing from the school, by those educators' educators, and so on). We are involved in each other's miscalculations, inadequate foreknowledge, hasty or regretted acts; minute by minute made part of Augustine's *massa damnata;* hostages to each other in a deadly interrelatedness.[12] There is no "clean slate" of nature unscribbled on by all one's forebears, no neat break from an "old world" to begin again on a "virgin continent." There is no "America" as Americans have often conceived it.

At one time, a woman of unsavory enough experience was delicately but cruelly referred to as "having a past." The doctrine of original sin states that humankind, in exactly that sense, "has a past." And much of American theorizing has been intended to exempt this country from that stigma. Yet the only way to avoid such trammels would be to have no other person's act affect us; and the only way to do that would be to exist in a state where one's own actions were equally inconsequential in others' lives. That would be the perfect triumph of individualism, where "men should be as gods" to themselves, each ruling his own "universe."

If the doctrine of the Fall entangles humans in each others' errors, the doctrine of the Market disentangles each fumbled attempt toward a finally concatenated good. Modern capitalism lives by a counter-myth to the Fall of Man—one where benign nature makes everything go, miraculously, right. We no longer have a reluctant nature made worse by further errors, but a silent machinery of correction that turns private vices to public good, by the ministrations of the invisible hand. Individual greeds add up to general gain. Aimlessness leads straight to the goal, so long as it is unseen; we need no roads. One achieves good only by refusing to intend it or plan it. All the individual's actions are good until they are interfered with. The Market thus produces a happy outcome from endless miseries, a sinless product of countless sins and inadvertencies. Eden was lost by free choice in the Fall of Man. It rises again, unbidden, by the automatic engineerings of the Market.

The earlier myth called for a repenting awareness of sin. The later one calls for a dutiful innocence and optimism. As James noted, mind-cure prohibits sad thoughts. It is the psychic concomitant of laissez-faire economics:

> Give up the feeling of responsibility, let go your hold, resign the care of your destiny to higher powers, be genuinely indifferent as to what be-

comes of it all, and you will find not only that you gain a perfect inward relief, but often also, in addition, the particular goods you sincerely thought you were renouncing.[13]

James is describing, in religious terms, the free lunch. The very preachers who deplore certain modern developments are celebrators of the greatness of America, its way of life, its capitalist system, its moral claims on the world. A happy Jeremiah is not a convincing scourge of sin. Optimism accepts; it blesses what is; it transmutes initiative into acquiescence—one rides the process and thinks one is guiding it.

In Reagan's campaign and presidency, the principal accusation against Democratic predecessors and rivals has been that they were guilty of pessimism. Reagan, speaking at a Notre Dame graduation as Jimmy Carter had before him, lamented that "little men with loud voices cry doom." The alternative Reagan offers is a discipline of cheer. As he said in the 1980 campaign: "Our optimism has once again been turned loose. And all of us recognize that these people who keep talking about the age of limits are really talking about their own limitations, not America's."[14]

Reagan can never be accused of a failure to know his audience; and it was precisely the religious part of his audience that heard echoes of many sermons in Reagan's words, echoes of all the happy Jeremiahs. In 1980, even Southern evangelical voters deserted a President who, in most ways, reflected their background better than Reagan did. Jimmy Carter was more devout by ordinary standards (like church attendance), better acquainted with the Bible, far more active in church affairs (like doing missionary work), more willing to talk about his born-again experience. Despite all these discrete points of contact between his experience and theirs, religious voters found that Carter lacked the higher confidence in man, man's products, and America. He talked of limits and self-denial, of tendencies toward aggression even in a sacred or "saved" nation like America. He believed in original sin.[15]

Ronald Reagan, by contrast, is so energetic a believer in the counter-myth to the Fall that, when he was asked to discuss his religious experiences as President, every instance he could think of was a matter of seeing the bright side to death or disaster. In the first three cases, the President was comforting relatives of the deceased—of the 101st Airborne Division soldiers (276 of them) who died in a plane crash, of the seven astronauts killed in the shuttle accident (whose families told him "it was all worthwhile"), and of casualties on the D-Day beaches. The President hesitated, till "a fourth recollection was prompted by White House chief of staff Donald Regan," who said of the visit to the death camp at Bergen-Belsen: "I know it affected you almost in a religious experience." Reagan agreed ("Oh my, yes!"), and said the change from camp to museum proved that Germans are a good people: "This Germany of today is not trying to cover up." Like all his stories, this one ends on an "up" note, with 10,000 German teenagers singing the American national anthem for him in English. "I had a tennis ball in my throat. I couldn't have [sung along]. It was just wonderful."[16]

It can be argued that the myth of the Market, like the myth of the Fall, contains elements of truth (or makes its own truth in the minds of believers). But why should believers in the Market call themselves conservatives? Laissez-faire means letting go—of the past, among other things. It is nontenacious of the old, from a trust in good to come. Yet capitalists, like Ford and Edison, do not want to be held responsible for some of the things they have produced: for restiveness in Harlem or Africa, for youthful hedonism or rebellion, for modern discontents. Change is disturbing even to its celebrants; it provokes, of itself, a countereffort to hang on to something—to one's self, at the least; to identity. A sense of identity is based on the experience of perdurance through shifting circumstances; and since all actual situations up to the present were, by definition, *past* situations, identity always has to be sought in the past. That is why continuing scrutiny of the real past is so important to human growth.

If one settles, instead, for a substitute past, an illusion of it, then that fragile construct must be protected from the challenge of complex or contradictory evidence, from any test of evidence at all. That explains Americans' extraordinary tacit bargain with each other not to challenge Reagan's version of the past. The power of his appeal is the great joint confession that we cannot live with our real past, that we not only prefer but need a substitute. Because of that, we *will* a belief in all his stories. His team, sure enough, won the football game during Eureka's strike, and lost it when he told the referee about a foul. He *saw* the black navy man end segregation, just as he *heard* the dying colloquy of the pilot and his tail gunner. He photographed the death camps. He found the Kremlin in Hollywood and defeated it. SAG struck no deal with MCA, and the Justice Department was just "anti-business" (like govment in general) when it thought so. Reagan cut welfare costs and raised welfare benefits as Governor of California. He has been to Nicaragua. All these things are "true to life" in Reagan's America since they help people live their lives. When I asked a group of American businessmen assembled abroad what they thought of Reagan's claim to have photographed the death camps, they supported the President for expressing a "higher truth" of concern for the persecuted. Heads nodded when one executive's wife said, "Even Jesus spoke in parables." That was a "conservative" use of religion very like Reagan's own. We support each other's belief in the performance, much like Disney World workers ("cast members") handling a mix-up in Stanley Elkin's *The Magic Kingdom:*

> The others follow, hustled along by the remaining cast members, openly winking, not at each other but at the children, at the two adults, flashing secret agreement, doling these out somehow—the winks—managing the delicate choreography of their high-sign arrangements so that no one is winked at twice by the same person or is even observed to have winked.[17]

It is a difficult assignment, after all, to hold the components of illusion together—a Greenfield Village past, a space-bliss promised in the future, and a present that obliterates the former while demanding belief in the latter's inevitability. There are so many contradictions in this larger construct that one cannot risk entertaining serious challenge to any of its details. In Reagan, luckily, all these clashes are resolved. He is the ideal past, the successful present, the hopeful future all in one. He is convincing because he has "been there"—been almost everywhere in our modern American culture—yet he "has no past" in the sinister sense. He is guilelessly guiltless. If, to recognize that miracle, one must reject historical record for historical fantasy, fact for parable, it is a small price to pay. One had to pretend to think Disneyland's Lincoln did not jerk at all when he moved. There is no such effortful make-believing with Reagan. Indeed, he has made pretending the easiest thing we do.

What Irving Howe said about Emerson's importance in the nineteenth century applies to the positive *need* for Reagan in wider circles now:

> He starts from where people actually are—slipping away from but still held by religious faith—and helps them move to where, roughly, they want to go: an enlightened commonality of vision justifying pride in the republic, a vision akin to, yet distinct from, religious faith. The remains of religious sentiment—ideality, yearning, spiritual earnestness— thereby become the grounding for a high public culture.[18]

Substitute "broad" for "high" in that passage and you get Reagan. We look at him and see the singleness we lack. He "skins and films the ulcerous place" where disparities open between what we think of ourselves and what we do. He casts a surface unity over elements that have long been drifting apart—religious beliefs away from religious posturing, conservative nostalgia from capitalist innovation, interdependence from nonconformism. He spans the chasm by not noticing it. He elides our cultural inconcinnities.

Even young people who did not grow up with Reagan, or grow up hearing him on the radio or watching him at the movies, have accepted his version of the past as their own best pledge of the future. That is not as surprising as it might seem. A visit to his past is always a pleasant experience. Visiting Reaganland is very much like taking children to Disneyland, where they can deal with a New Orleans cut to their measure. It is a safe past, with no sharp edges to stumble against. The more visits one makes to such a past, the better is one immunized against any troubling incursions of a real New Orleans, a real racetrack, the real American West. If capitalist "conservatism" cannot be rooted in the real past it works to obliterate, then it will invent a deracinating past, a nostalgia for the new, a substitute history to lull us in the time machine that travels on no roads, reaching goals no one could plan.

An older model of conservatism (to be replaced in the market by "new models of the old") held that the past is necessarily a guide to the future.

Since the future has not happened, it is not knowable by the tests we apply to things that have occurred. Driving forward, we see nothing ahead through the windshield. To steer at all, we must go forward looking into the rearview mirror, trying to trace large curves or bending forces in prior events, to proceed along their lines. But what happens if, when we look into our historical rearview mirror, all we can see is a movie?

It is appropriate that the teenage hero of *Back to the Future*, when he reached the time when his parents met, should find a Reagan Western at the local theater. The aim of *Back to the Future* is to unite the generations, to make the hero see his parents with new eyes, as not outmoded but still young. Here is the most optimistic imaginable completion of the anti-myth to the Fall. Parents redeemed erase the sins of the past and become Paradise regained. As the economic Market remedies private faults, because money inserted anywhere into the economic circle courses quickly around and benefits people everywhere, so *Back to the Future* closes a temporal cycle, making efforts (even mistaken ones) exerted at any time conduce to a happy outcome for all times. At the final eucharistic table of the free lunch, Ronald Reagan is the rehabilitated parent par excellence, the faded idol as reachable ideal.

Innocents Abroad

AN AFTERWORD

The legacy Reagan would leave behind as President seemed to many a bright one, until the trading of arms for hostages and the diversion of secret funds to the contras was revealed late in 1986, just as this book was about to be published. Were those scandals merely blots on an otherwise creditable record, isolated events that should not affect Reagan's larger legacy and his standing in history? Or did they open lines of sight into the very structure of the Reagan presidency, into its inner workings, the multiple mutual deceptions that had always energized it? An argument for the latter view can be made from the Reagan team's performance at Reykjavik, the Iceland summit meeting held over a month before the Iran sales were first published to the world. In fact, that mysterious meeting can only be understood, in retrospect, now that we know about the hostage deals that were being made before and during it. And when the full meaning of Reykjavik is riddled out, the great puzzles of the Reagan presidency are solved.

The Iran and contra scandals, coming in quick succession to Reykjavik, did not leave time for the summit to "sink in," though diplomats around the world were giving it horrified attention. After October 12, 1986, no other country could know precisely where the Reagan government stood because no one within that government could say where it might, at any next moment, be standing. Reykjavik is the black hole of Reagan diplomacy, where all its meanings converge and disappear.

The summit had all the major elements of the Reagan presidency encoded within it—a public relations life of its own, maintained apart from what really went on; a confusion, even among those most central to the event, about what *had* gone on; a fight by Reagan's attendants for the prize of his attention, and a horror at what he finally attended to; contradictory urges, afterward, to deny and to defend what happened; a juggling of prior secrets in the race to catch up with breaking troubles. This was the culmination of Reagan's entire time in office, the summit toward which all the conflicting tendencies of his administration had been laboring upward from different directions.

It will take us years to sort out the levels of activity in and around that complex event. But even on the surface, going just by first reactions, it was astonishing enough—a summit hastily called, with no agenda but to call a later summit; a "pre-summit," presented as a non-summit, which blossomed overnight into a super-summit, with stakes that dwarfed those of earlier, better-prepared meetings between the superpowers; a feverish nightlong session during which aides improvised offers that became more generous or reckless, according to one's view, reaching finally to half the nations' ballistic arsenals; followed by an extra session on Sunday afternoon where the leaders themselves topped each other's boldest bids and, for a dizzying moment, saw the elimination of all nuclear weapons lurch into view; only to have things collapse more rapidly than they had ballooned, all the expanding hopes pricked (apparently) by a single word, a quibbling on the meaning of "laboratory" in the terms for testing the Strategic Defense Initiative.

The summit closed without a formal statement, with scowls and gallows humor and a static of emotions hard to read around the edges of the drama. Some were sad that one or other heady new opportunity had been missed. Others were relieved that such "opportunities" had been escaped. All wondered exactly what had come to pass. Dan Rather, excited by a rumor of success, broke into a football game promising good news; then, shortly after, introduced an obviously grieving George Shultz. Moments later, the President was seen at a nearby military base doing an almost manic Bob Hope routine for the soldiers. The plane back to America throbbed with baffled team-spirit urges, deprived of channels for expression: had this been a loss, a victory, or one of the above snatched from the jaws of the other? Perhaps only Philip Marlowe's response could do justice to the bewilderment over who won: "I don't even know what teams are playing today."

There were instant hints of disappointment with the President, who had subordinated every other consideration to SDI, the ultimate "bargaining chip" that was not played. Alerted in midair to these dissatisfactions, the President's men had established their line by the time they reached Washington. The summit had been a great success: the Russians' flamboyant bids showed they were willing to do anything to sabotage the SDI, but Reagan had been too shrewd to fall into that trap. Thus, with their own heads still spinning, Reagan's aides began their greatest all-out effort at "spin control." Every high official of the government, even the reclusive John Poindexter, was sent sprinting from network to network, calling reporters whose calls he had not answered, asking for interviews he had previously refused. Later, when the Iran scandal broke, Donald Regan would labor under the understandable illusion that he could "spin" anything in a desirable direction after he had "turned Reykjavik around."

But Reagan was one of those who, setting the tune, fluffed the words. Larry Speakes and other voices of the administration were intent on minimizing what was put up for bargain in the ultimate Sunday session. They said only *ballistic* missiles were to be eliminated—half of them certainly, perhaps even all—and only over a ten-year period. But Regan was positive (as ever) when he gave his undoctored version of what happened: "President Reagan was the one who volunteered that we would give up all of these weapons. We made the proposal, not the Soviets. We said to the Soviets, we will do away with all nuclear weapons—nuclear bombs, nuclear shells for field artillery. Everything was on the table. We'll give it away if you will agree to let us continue our search for this defense." Few could be found who would agree with Regan's account. But, unfortunately for those who denied it, one of those few was the President himself. In a briefing for congressional leaders, he said that *all* nuclear weapons would have been abolished if the Russians had only allowed full SDI testing to go forward. Senator Sam Nunn of Georgia, who took careful notes on points that fall within his area of special expertise, quotes the President as saying: "We put on the table a proposal to eliminate within ten years all nuclear ballistic missiles, everything else, including bombs." Speakes insisted that the President had "misspoke," then corrected that to "had been misquoted," then corrected that to "had been misunderstood." It is true that the President is not precise about the peculiarities of weapon systems (he would later describe TOW missiles as shoulder-held devices), and the grand offers at Reykjavik came after two days of long negotiations, labyrinthine in their earlier stages however simplified toward the end, negotiations tiring everyone concerned, not least the President, who was ending an extended work day through the four-hour final session. Could he have misunderstood his own offer? And if so, what were the Russians expected to make of it? And, in any case, the version he gave to Senator Nunn and others was not produced in the heat of a long session with foreigners, but after time for deliberation and coaching. What, then, was the position of the United States government, and who can pretend to know what it will be, from moment to moment, when this President is speaking?

The evidence is that President Reagan offered to trade *all* of America's nuclear weapons for all those of Russia. We must accept this on the *lectio difficilior* principle that so odd a thing would not have occurred to anybody as an even remotely possible version of the event unless it had, improbably, happened. It is the version Gorbachev, as well as Reagan, endorsed. What higher authority can we find under normal diplomatic rules (little as they may apply to this event)? Not the least Reaganesque aspect of Reykjavik is that it slides toward an epistemological abyss: the one thing we can know about it is that what one can know about it will be forever in dispute.

The effort at "spin control" was successful, in the short run, because the unthinkability of the proposal made it relatively easy to deny. How *could* the President have tried to bargain away all nuclear weapons, the basis of our entire defense policy, and that of our allies, without even consulting those allies, or the Congress, or the Joint Chiefs of Staff? What about nuclear weapons in other than Russian or American hands? What of the drastic realignment in force that would result when nuclear weapons were subtracted from conventional forces? It was hard enough for Reagan's people to justify the lesser offers they admitted to—abolishing all of our ballistic missiles (or, according to one story, half). Criticism of such a hasty jump, taken on a sudden inspiration, came from surprisingly ecumenical sources—from right and left, friend and critic, Europeans and Americans. If some deplored the fact that SDI had prevented a breakthrough into new areas of arms control, more people were delighted that it—or anything— blocked the deal that was shaping up. As James Schlesinger put it, "We must accept the astonishing irony: it was the impasse over SDI that saved us from the embarrassment of entering into completed agreements from which subsequently we would have had to withdraw." Congress would never have endorsed an offer only it was authorized to make in the first place.

Despite the brief success of spin control, sophisticated workers for the President had to search their souls. They resembled a crew of absentminded mini-Frankensteins who had fiddled at separate parts of a monster for benevolent but widely varying purposes, only to see him break the clasps and rear himself up off the table in a weird compulsion to do some monstrous Good Thing that none of them had ever believed possible. The President told aides what had happened during the long last session at Hofdi House. After days of touchy maneuver, of trying to score points and hold to staked-out positions, when hope soared at last past confusing details and endless frustrations, "my dream" popped out of Reagan—his dream of a missile-free world, realizable by the one thing that could guarantee it, the Strategic Defense Initiative, Reagan's favorite scheme ("I thought of it myself"). All his supporters paid lip service to that dream; but none took it with the fundamentalism of Reagan, who believed it was solely and simply a defensive device, not a weapon at all, a shield instead of a sword. It and it alone would make nuclear weapons so useless that no one would want to go to the expense of building another one. He believed that. Why not say it? Why continue niggling at Reykjavik over little things while that one thing was the obvious answer?

Whatever the deal being offered at Reykjavik—whether all nuclear weapons, all ballistic weapons, or some lower gesture of almost equal drama—everyone admits that the reason Reagan turned it down was not based on calculations of the stategic balance throughout the world. Those considerations had disappeared from his view, replaced entirely by the great Defense, which must be mounted as soon as possible, for the good of everyone, not merely of the United States. Reagan had promised to give the Russians all the SDI technology as soon as it was perfected—to give it to everyone; why not? What harm can be done to us by another's possession of a purely defensive device? He had been saying that all along, but it still came as a momentarily disabling shock to find that he *believed* it. Sure, he had believed lots of strange things in the past, and those had been smiled on with differing degrees of condescension or suspended criticism. But surely not even he could believe that space lasers, satellites, and "interceptor" technology could not be used in any offensive manner. If he did believe that, why had they all been talking and bargaining about balanced numbers and detailed trade-offs that made Saturday night a torture of calculations? All bets were now off. Budgets and strategies were flimsy playthings at the mercy of that Belief.

The whole Reagan presidency involved the *use* of his beliefs by people who only partly shared them, or barely conceived them as shareable. The sophisticates around Reagan could indulge his rhetorical visions, since they knew they were impracticable, however attractive. They set people in motion to do the attainable things his aides had in mind, while he gave the glowing account of what it would all lead to—someday safely off in the clouds, it was fatally assumed. Lip service to SDI was useful to many people with their own agenda. It allowed them to take the next step in weapons technology, to establish supremacy in space, to frighten the Russians, to force them into overspending, to weaken their economic system, to please American contractors and entice those in other countries, to keep America number one in science, and, as a last resort, perhaps, to use SDI as a bargaining chip for something even more desirable on the conventional scale of things. All these motives were jostling along together under the cover of the Reagan fairy tale, each gaining advantages so long as the fairy tale was neither questioned *nor taken seriously*. Aides showed their loyalty to Reagan by not questioning, but he broke the tacit compact they thought they had struck with him when he took his own words seriously. He had indeed believed the cover story, as he believed other cover stories—that David Stockman did not say the things he did (though he did), or that Nicholas Daniloff was not traded for Gennady Zakharov (though he was).

It was a great strength of the Reagan presidency, at the outset anyway, that he believed so deeply in what he said. It allowed him to arrange moral energies in an unambiguous way while those dealing with daily ambiguity directed such energies to their own purpose. "Reaganomics," for instance, was something that Reagan could present to the world with a straight face, claiming that tax cuts would result in private savings, form a capital pool, and return even more money to the government as a smaller levy on a larger product. Under the umbrella of that myth David Stockman and Donald Regan and James Baker could cope with intractable fiscal realities, with the help of some true-believers at the staff level (the economic equivalents of Oliver North), and Reagan would not himself notice that government income was dropping, deficits growing, private savings shrinking. The Reagan economy was what was done in the shadow of "Reaganomics," and the President, up in the sun, never looked under the umbrella. In this area, at least, the Frankensteins seemed to have their monster under control.

The overarching belief was not only useful to those who channeled its energies; it was pleasing to the American people. For several years, while doing the research for this book on Reagan, I tried out on many different kinds of audiences the story Reagan has told of his filming the death camps at the end of World War II. I asked for their reactions, as a gauge of Reagan's appeal. No one, to my surprise, ever said, "He could not have said such a thing." They were all willing to believe he made that claim, though they knew it was false. Yet this willingness to suspect the accuracy of the story went blithely along with a willingness to forgive, even to praise, the imagination that would concoct it. The story was meant to make its hearers (including an Israeli prime minister) feel good about a depressing thing, and Reagan had meant to perform that service to others, not primarily to boost himself. In fact, the achievement most people put first in Reagan's presidency is that he made Americans feel good about themselves again. What can be bad about feeling good? Only a few carpers said that a President should not indulge such fantasies in dealing with other heads of state. Most went along with the woman who told me, "Even Jesus spoke in parables."

The argument for Reagan's fantasies was that they did no harm. They were pleasant for everyone involved, uplifting, morally illustrative. Some people were helped by them—e.g., those who profited from the tax cuts, those who wanted no arms control anyway, those who were desperate to get Daniloff back no matter what cover was given the operation. These people had the most realistic reasons for supporting Reagan's idealism. They, of all people, thought it was most harmless, since they knew that the stated goals were so far out of reach that even Reagan was only gesturing at them, not really reaching for them.

Till Reykjavik. There the President enunciated his dream with a straight face, not to the American electorate, not to a staff that humored him and went about its real work, not to a leader of Israel wondering about Reagan's attitude toward his people, but to the head of the only other superpower in the world, while trying to make the most important decision about dooms-day weapons short of the decision to use them. Reagan's dream popped out there, a little ghost to haunt all later foreign policy negotiations by this man or his representatives. Who could say for sure that such dreams were bottled up for good? When and where might they pop out once more? Who would cram them down, bottle them up, the next time?

For Reykjavik was not an isolated event, the one time when Reagan's jaunty belief bred terror among his followers. It was part of a sequence that crippled the Reagan presidency, making it disjunct, at odds with itself in its most intimate workings, ignorant of what was done here or there under the several umbrellas of Reagan optimism. Reagan could believe the swap for Daniloff was not a swap, since he had already (secretly) been paying a ransom for hostages which he believed was not ransom. In fact, Reykjavik itself, the calling of that hasty summit and the giddying pressures at work on it, cannot be understood unless we see it played out against the hostage crisis that was "unraveling" (in the phrase of William Casey) a full month before it broke the surface in a Lebanese newspaper. Oliver North was already stoking the shredders when Reagan set off for Iceland.

The Russian invitation to Reykjavik emerged in the flurry of open and secret bargaining for Daniloff's return. At the time, one might have questioned the almost hysterical concern for one man's arrest in Russia. Daniloff was in no danger, as the Iran captives were. He had been taken in a cruel but fairly conventional tit-for-tat after a Russian spy was arrested in New York—an American "spy" on one side was framed for a spy on the other side arrested. Some trade would be worked out eventually; it was just a matter of time.

But the Reagan administration was extremely touchy over the concept of hostages. Elected to change Jimmy Carter's bad luck with captives, Reagan had said no hostages would be taken if America only stood tall. Unfortunately for that promise, hostages were not only taken but killed during his time in office, and their ordeal was prolonged far beyond the year's time Carter suffered the indignity of pleading for mercy from the Ayatollah Khomeini. Pleading was not Reagan's public mode. Reagan's hostages, fewer than Carter's, less visible, taken sporadically, killed selectively, had become permanent facts of life, if background facts, not a defined and single embarrassment. But that did not make them less an irritant or long-term danger.

The policy of the administration was to keep public attention off the hostages (Carter had focused on them obsessively, to his detriment). But that meant keeping their relatives reasonably quiet, and that meant convincing them that something was being done in secret to get them back. Even to hide the hostages, then, one had to be doing *something* to get them out. Besides, the hostages presented Reagan with so many stories, the misadventures of concrete individuals—just the kind of thing President Reagan finds it easiest to think about, to envisage, to empathize with. There was nothing he loved about his presidency more than the opportunity to be photographed with released hostages. That is how he came into office, posing with the hostages of Carter's time. He meant to face the camera with each and every one taken in his time, too.

Thus ingenuity in dealing with the "LebNaps" (Colonel North's word for those kidnapped in Lebanon) became a highly tradeable item in the White House power market. The President wanted something, anything, done; the situation required it; the relatives were restive, quieted only to the extent that some convincing scheme seemed to be taking shape; the CIA director had an agent among the captives, and a reputation for ingenious secret operations. The President, of course, would have to believe a cover story he could tell the world with a straight face, in order to rally the nation to whatever course became necessary. He would have to be convinced that any money or authority extended would be for "rescue," not "ransom"— as he was convinced that his "revenue enhancement" measures were not really taxes. He would have to sign, at some point, a "finding" that emergency action had been authorized. The details of the finding would matter less than the cover story he believed and the real resources that could be mastered to achieve the simultaneous release of all hostages.

Ultimately, Reagan signed too many findings and too few—and remembered signing only some: one was retroactive, one was a draft, and he did not read the rationale attached to the third. The first audience to be addressed by the documents was any squeamish or resisting people in the CIA or Defense or State departments who might (and eventually did) question the standing of freebooters assembled from various pools for the operation—Israeli intelligence agency in-and-outers, arms merchants, ex-CIA adventurers, NSC staffers, and down into the nether world. The realities of the hostage trade would be as different from the cover story (all the stuff made up in the second-draft finding about a strategic overture to Iranian moderates) as the economic facts of 1980–1987 differed from the myths of "supply side." Those working under the "rescue" umbrella were mainly concerned with one question: would it *work?*

It did not. The first two arms shipments, shuttled through Israel, funded by shadowy intermediaries (Saudi businessman Adnan Khashoggi later admitted he made up some Canadian partners to the deal), on terms hazily relayed through too many filters, produced only one hostage. The freebooters thought they could do better working directly and not through Israel, but their effort broke down in Portugal, and their arms, when finally delivered, were rejected as obsolete. One of the many disadvantages built into the trade was Iran's ability to be finicky about the quality of what it was receiving. We could not send back a hostage, no matter how bad his condition—in fact, we bargained for the dead CIA agent's body. After the fifth arms delivery, a second hostage was released—but one had also been killed in that period, and three were about to be taken. Former national security adviser Robert McFarlane had soured on the operation, though he kept running its errands. Even Oliver North was tempted to cut his losses. By the end of October 1986, he was telling Admiral Poindexter: "Wd. very much like to give RR two hostages that he can take credit for and stop worrying about these other things." (North liked to "give" the President things in his PROF notes—even, prematurely, a Nobel peace prize.)

But the process, once begun, was almost impossible to stop. If one could buy one hostage, or two, then the principle was broken for them all. What could one ultimately say to the relatives about refusal to pay, whatever the price, for the rest of the captives? What price does one set on a life, once one has started bartering for it? The more Reagan's men put into the venture, the more desperately they wanted to have something to show for their effort. The original plan, which its originators kept trying to revive at later stages, called for a sequence of payments leading to release of *all* the hostages. But by the end, Colonel North had lowered his hopes and sharpened his calculations to the formula of hundreds of missiles for "one and a half hostages." Getting something from the effort—other than the spare hostage parsimoniously doled out on an excruciating timetable—became a relief: at least some of the money created by the intermediaries' overpricing policy could be sent to the contras (Colonel North's other great concern). "Stroking" the relatives and inspiring contra supporters were intensely satisfying activities for North, despite the evident frustrations that were making McFarlane and Poindexter and Shultz all express concern for North's stability.

But North had made himself essential to the project, and however others might waver, one person, at least, maintained his optimism through this whole ordeal. The President is never known to have spoken against any aspect of the trade, and McFarlane says that when he updated him on Israeli doubts about his commitment to it, "his reaction was always, well, cross your fingers or hope for the best, and keep me informed." After another setback, McFarlane recalled: "The President was always very hopeful, optimistic, and on almost every issue, and I think on this one that day, was disappointed that he [sic] hadn't turned out so far, but always looking for the bright side or the possibility that it could be salvaged."

The President never wavered. Testifying in the hospital after his suicide attempt, McFarlane looked back to the first arms sales and said, "The President had no hesitancy about it at all, *nor did he when he called me about it last week here in the hospital* . . . [He said] words to the effect that gee, that sounds pretty good." (italics added). On an occasion when McFarlane worried, the President assured him "I will be glad to take all the heat"—an expression he also seems to have used with (or got from) Casey.

The heat was getting intense by October 7, three days before Reykjavik, the day when North got back from a meeting in Frankfurt that promised, once again, to free all the hostages, or at least one. By that day William Casey was hearing from within his agency (from Charles Allen) and from outside (from attorney Roy Furmark) that word had spread of the arms trades for hostages, and even of the diversion of funds to the contras. Casey told this to North, who started shredding. But the pressure to keep working for one more release in the immediate future was as great as that to efface all tracks of what had been done in the past. The activities were at odds with each other, but had to go forward forcibly yoked.

One reason for this was that, one month earlier, Daniloff had been imprisoned in Moscow. The press, it was said, treated his captivity more seriously than it had others because he was one of their own. But he was an especially challenging case for the White House as well. The government had to repeat, with histrionic emphasis, its routine about never dealing for hostages, even while insisting that Daniloff was a hostage and not a criminal. But Reagan's insiders knew something the press did not—that they had already been paying for hostages, for over a year, and were on the verge of getting at least one more hostage out (Jacobsen was released November 2). How could they refuse to deal for Daniloff? On the other hand, if a trade *were* worked out for Daniloff, the hostages' relatives would demand the same kind of open trade for their own captives, even the trade for terrorists being held in Kuwait that the captors were demanding. Jacobsen and another hostage, Terry Anderson, were made to release a videotape supporting that demand. North reported the pressures being exerted.

> Some, like Jacobsen's son Paul, accused us of being callous to the LebNap victims—and unwilling to pressure the Kuwaitis because the issue has "slipped from the public eye and that we are willing to make deals for Daniloff because it was more important to the President because of the visibility." All indicated that they are planning to hold a press conference later this week to "turn the heat on" the Administration. My rejoinder that no deal for Daniloff was in the mill was, because of earlier press coverage to the contrary, not taken seriously.

Of course a deal for Daniloff was "in the mill," and had to be. For one thing, the administration could not let the Soviets start a whole new pool of hostages disturbingly similar to the fluctuating supply of LebNaps. And, precisely *because* of their similarities, Colonel North had to argue that the cases were different, claim that no deal was being made for Daniloff, to cover up the fact that one was being made (and perpetually unmade and remade) for those in Lebanon. Daniloff's freedom had to be bought, because Weir's and Jenco's had been. Yet that just made it more pressing that the Daniloff trade not *look* like a trade, because the relatives were being told no trade was possible (though by some magic other than trading two hostages had come home). The open deal had to be accepted, despite the flimsiness of the pretense that it was not a deal, to keep all the fictions of the secret deal in place. Reagan was put into this absurd position: he had to bargain for Daniloff to prove that he had not struck any bargains for Weir or Jenco. Deviousness was doubling back and back upon itself. No matter which way it turned, the administration met itself coming the other way. The two hostage crises were running on parallel tracks, one secret, one public, and the secret one determined in large part how the public one had to be managed—i.e., by dealing while denying any deal; which meant the public one had to be turned into a secret one as far as possible; the deal had to be disguised or made at least formally deniable. Was Daniloff hostage to the other hostages, by this point, or was the government hostage to them both?

This situation became more complex, just five days before Reykjavik, when Eugene Hasenfus was shot down in Nicaragua, opening the possibility of a *third* tier of hostages to be dealt with, all three interacting, *therefore* to be treated as separate. Once again North laid out the dangers, in a memo to McFarlane written on the very day Ronald Reagan was offering to do away with all nuclear arms at Hofdi House:

> We urgently need to find a high powered lawyer and benefactor who can raise a legal defense for Hassenfus [sic] in Managua. If we can find such persons we can not only hold Gene and Sally Hassenfus together (i.e., on our side, not pawns of the Sandinista propaganda machine) but can make some significant headway of our own in counterattacking in the media. Obviously, there is the added benefit of being able to do something substantive in the legal system to defend this young man. I know that this is a tall order and that many U.S. lawyers will not want to step to this task, but for the man (or woman) who does, there will be a fair bite of history made in the next few weeks. . . . Believe this to be a matter of great urgency to hold things together. Unfortunately RR was b;iefed [sic] that this plan was being contemplated before he left for Iceland and am concerned that along about Wednesday when people begin to think of things other than meetings in cold places, he will remember this and nothing will have been done.

So this third tier of hostage dealing had to be treated like the second one, under pressure from the first—turning the public scandal back into a secret one. The entanglement of large issues with limited instruments is seen in the fact that the marital troubles of a man no one had heard of twenty-four hours earlier had become a possible determinant of one superpower's credibility at the very moment of its most vulnerable jockeying with the other superpower.

Hasenfus the forlorn adventurer is not a mere sidelight to this story. Only by looking down, tier below tier, at what was happening in the government during Reykjavik can we answer the first mystery of Reykjavik: how did we get there? The meeting was hastily called, remember; unexpected; unprepared for. The timing of the meeting was set during the September flurry of negotiation over Daniloff's imprisonment. The Reagan people wanted any figleaf of deniability about "buying" Daniloff out of prison. The Russians went along with the fiction that there was no trade-off for Zakharov, refraining from pressing their advantage against Reagan, uncharacteristically accommodating him, releasing the dissidents, Uri and Irina Yurov, to confuse the symmetry of a straight man-for-man exchange. Why should they do that? What was the *hidden* quid pro quo for thus partially effacing the overt quid pro quo?

The answer: Reykjavik. In September Reagan badly needed Russian help with his multiple hostage crises. At the same time Mikhail Gorbachev badly wanted an early meeting with the President to push forward his popular European initiative on arms control and limitation of SDI. Reagan, against the wishes of his own right-wingers, accommodated that demand in the spirit of the Daniloff exchange. Iceland had been called to discuss Daniloff. Reagan announced the summit in the same statement that dealt with the Daniloff release.

The cover story for the hostage exchange with Iran was that larger strategic interests were being established for the long run. Part of the cover story for the Daniloff affair would be that the Russians and the Americans were being mutually accommodating as part of a longer-view adjustment in the arms race to be discussed at a time agreed on, quickly, at Reykjavik. To emphasize that the talks would not be serious, Reagan's team included only two of the Defense Department's hardline critics of arms control, and sixty-seven of the "soft" State Department's men. It was to be a meeting full of atmospherics, not specifics; of good feeling, not rigid accords. That was the spirit in which Zakharov had been given our version of a quick show trial in Brooklyn, sparing Reagan the embarrassment of an exchange, which violated his stated principles.

But it is always dangerous to give Ronald Reagan a cover story. Show it to him, however briefly, and, before it can crumble, he will have believed it. He believed the cover story about moderate Iranians. He went to Reykjavik prepared to believe the cover story about long-term goals to be broached at Reykjavik. The stories were connected in his mind. That is why, in its way, Reykjavik was the biggest arms-for-hostage deal ever envisaged in history. Our incremental shipments of Hawks and TOWs, to this port and that, had led circuitously to the moment when Reagan offered our entire nuclear arsenal to the man who had just returned Daniloff (thereby helping cover up the Iran trade). The Daniloff trade had needed a cover story, and the cover story touched on the SDI dream that eventually popped out of Reagan. George Will cannot have appreciated the full meaning of his own words on the hastily called summit: "The signal sent by dithering on the Daniloff affair is a thread in a seamless web of events" (*Newsweek*, September 29, 1986).

Of course, only some in the White House knew about the hostage trades at the time when Reykjavik was agreed to and engaged in—but they were the few that mattered. Casey knew that Roy Furmark and Charles Allen were talking about the trades. McFarlane knew that certain people might crack—one of the many Hasenfuses; perhaps North himself; maybe even McFarlane himself—under the pressure of failure after failure, each riskier than the last and demanding greater risks ahead. Only the sunny optimism of the President, confident of final success and credulous of his own cover story, kept the rickety succession of complex and shady exchanges going. He believed in "freedom fighters" (he had been a Yank in the RAF, volunteering for another country's wars, in two movies). He believed in rescue raids (he had filmed those too). He believed in the magic of private money working behind the scenes (his friends had made him a millionaire by such maneuvers). He liked to use the powers of government to alleviate individual hardship—calling stricken children he read about in the news. What greater hardship case was there than that of the Reverend Weir or the Reverend Jenco? He believed he was rescuing men of the cloth (and inscribing a Bible to do it). He believed in all these things—just as he believed he could look Mikhail Gorbachev in the eye and convince him that SDI is entirely and only a defensive device.

Donald Regan employed a man to supply him with a joke a day for catching the President's attention and giving an upbeat opening to the morning's work. Casey, McFarlane, and Poindexter employed Colonel North and his colleagues to supply the President with an adventure a day. The adventures were not necessarily more reputable or reliable than the locker-room jokes the President loved. But each new adventure gave promise of a photograph in the Rose Garden with a returned hero standing beside the President, even more exciting and inspiring than the invited heroes he put on display at his State of the Union speeches. (The first time he omitted that ceremony was in January 1987, when his use of the term "hero" for Colonel North had made the term ambiguous). The adventures were never completely satisfactory in their outcome (though the President was still preparing to be photographed with Jacobsen), but they were enough to give him that fatal thing for Reagan, hope. Besides, even the disappointments came to him in narrative form—they were at least stories, though not yet happily ended. Those who came to him with doubts were disarmed before they began, wielding mere arguments against the strength of anecdotes.

The difficulty of dealing with Reagan in the grip of a vivid hope was made clear by George Shultz in his testimony before the joint congressional committees investigating the Iran-contra affair. He had argued against the hostage scheme, repeatedly; he had fended off, barely, Casey's delivery of perjured testimony before a committee; he had tried to reach the President on a Saturday to keep him from relaying falsehoods in his speech; he had called after a press conference to tell the President he had not been telling the truth; he went to the White House and specified all the errors in an extraordinary session, "bark off all the way," the kind of talk he never thought he would conduct with a President of the United States—and all with what effect? He told his aides afterward: "I don't think I made a dent."

Others found Reagan's visions of the raids and rescues and freedom fighters and bright moderate future for Iran an undissipatable complex of convictions. Nothing is more durable in Reagan than his dreams, his optimism, his religious-tinted hopes. Even after the Tower Commission said there had been an arms-for-hostage trade, and after many aides other than Shultz tried to get Reagan to admit the obvious, and speech writers worked out a careful formula that he would accept, Reagan could only arrive at this carefully negotiated entente with reality:

I told the American people I did not trade arms for hostages. My heart and my best intentions still tell me that is true, but the facts and the evidence tell me it is not.

Translated into Reaganesque, that sentence means: "I will try to believe for limited purposes what I don't really believe." But the dream will come back, you may be sure. With him, it always does. A truth of the head that resists his hoping heart can only be treated stiffly, as a stranger, when he is forced briefly into its presence. The Tower Commission was ushered even more summarily into and out of his mind than the donor groups cycled through the White House to be photographed with him.

Some wonder why Shultz did not resign at some point in his long protest over the foolish hostage scheme—if not when it was first raised, then when it was pursued so dangerously beyond its first design, or lied about by the administration, or misrepresented by the President himself. After all, Shultz tells us he threatened to resign three other times, once for the loss of executive plane privileges. Was that less important than the undermining of America's entire credibility in foreign affairs?

But we miss the point if we think of Shultz's threats to resign as intended for anything but catching the President's attention. On the Iran affair, he got the President's attention, over and over again, and had been baffled before the surreal nature of Reagan's beliefs. We misconceive his situation if we imagine this was the only time that had happened to him or other top Reagan aides. They all had to cope with the private realities of Reagan's world, the myths of filming death camps (which led, circuitously, *away* from death camps toward Bitburg), the dream of a "supply side" cure-all, the various cover stories that aides found sometimes useful and helped promote. If the only rudder by which to steer the ship of state was the commanding popularity of Reagan's dreams, then responsible statesmen took it as their duty to share those dreams so far as possible, feign belief in them if necessary, correct for their ill effects, get close enough to help steer them away from the most dangerous consequences (and Reykjavik was just the closest sheering off from the rocks in this unsteady navigation of the state). One had to flatter the dream in order to direct it, to deflect threats from it, to use it in promotion of one's own narrower ("realistic") purposes. This was each side's way of saying, "Even Jesus spoke in parables," and it was the order of the day around Reagan. It was the way to rub some of Reagan's popular magic off onto one's own program or faction or priorities of the moment. In this way all the Reagan people were engaged in rolling up a large thin balloon of roseate optimisms, a balloon far bigger than the White House, eased up a rocky hill, tenderly guided over outcroppings of resistant fact, none of the toilers sure of what was going on around the disappearing curves of the balloon he had to guide over a particular snag or troubling spot.

Just as Reagan had to be brought to a touchily phrased entente with reality, so each of his principal aides had to work out his own particular treaty-terms with pretense. That led to rather tricky uses of language on each aide's part, and to endless gradations of misunderstanding, intended or unintended, in their exchanges with each other, even before or apart from any specific deceptions being practiced. If one did not fully share Reagan's dream, it was better to be silent about it, if not ignorant, rather than lose the power others gained by humoring it. Thus McFarlane, playing with dangerous doubts about the hostage scheme's later developments, could not voice them for fear that "Bill Casey or Jeane Kirkpatrick would call me a communist." The truly crippling charge any Reagan advocate could make against another was that he was not a true believer, one working to "let Reagan be Reagan," to have the *full* dream come true. And even Casey was subject to the same pressure he could put on others, according to CIA operations chief, Clair George: "The way to handle Bill Casey was to outflank him to the right." Guarding one's flanks against one's colleagues was always difficult in such a world. So Poindexter tells North not to tell Casey what Casey is telling North not to tell Shultz—which was easier than might be expected, because Shultz did not want to know. Not speaking, or not speaking before others, was sometimes less effective than simply not knowing at all. Shultz thought that if he just knew little enough about the hostages he might not be blamed for leaking, and so might keep his job, or his influence, or his relevance, or whatever. It was important not to pretend to knowledge when one could not pretend to believe. Shultz's hope to avoid being blamed for leaks was feckless. North was ready to blame him no matter what he knew or pretended not to know: "I protested [to Casey] that experience showed that Shultz would tend to talk to——or——who would in turn talk to——and that——could well be the source of the Jack Anderson stuff we have seen periodically." Even pretending ignorance was no defense against those who demanded total belief in the pretense.

The kinds of pretense could vary, from level to level of any operation, not necessarily diminishing as they receded from the center. McFarlane, with some misgivings, carried the cake to Teheran; but it was his former subordinate, Colonel North, who invented its icing-iconography. The President inscribed the Bible, but Colonel North chose the text. The President, in whatever haze he thought appropriate for his role in such matters, signed some findings he remembered and at least one he forgot; but Messrs. Casey, Sporkin, and others confected their surreal motivations. Out at the ends, where the true "residuals" were—the leftovers from failed CIA missions, legendary Bay of Pigs exploits, Green Beret bravos turned arms profiteers—we cannot assume less fidelity to reality than at the center. Khashoggi, as we have seen, made up a set of Canadian financiers. Colonel North made up long conversations with the President about the Bible. Here is North presenting the President's Bible to the Iranians:

We inside our Government had an enormous debate, a very angry debate inside our government whether or not my president should authorize me to say "We accept the Islamic Revolution of Iran as a fact . . ." He [the President] went off one whole weekend and prayed about what th [sic] answer should be and he came back almost a year ago with that passage I gave you that he wrote in front of the Bible I gave you. And he said to me, "This is a promise that God gave to Abraham. Who am I to say that we should not do this?"

This was the major leagues of pretending.

The Reagan administration, in short, combined a maximum of overt trust and candor, matching its chief's, and a maximum of covert distrust and protective skepticism about part of that chief's dreams and all of his minions' attempts to use those dreams, altering while "implementing" them, extending them to exotic places and bizarre results. Each had to know enough about the other's schemes to avoid getting entangled in any unacceptable consequences of them, and yet know little enough to deny responsible implications. So Shultz would run errands to the Sultan of Brunei, as McFarlane would give lip service to Kirkpatrickism in the pursuit of hostages; but Shultz was careful not to know where the money he had raised was going, and McFarlane at least tried to have North recommitted to the hospital. The President himself had to be kept in what Fawn Hall called a "protective mode," not seeming to know why he was congratulating the donors who were brought into the White House for his thanks. They, too, were heroes, but it would not do for him to know too much about their heroism. The bright world of Reagan's sonorous clarities hid a dimmer world of burrowers who had each lost the thread to the others' labyrinths (and often to his own), busily churning past and around the others in the dark, protecting projects, and protecting himself from projects, and protecting the President from his own projects, and turning the projects over to even shadier figures farther off from the central muddle, all in the name of the simple dream that had empowered each of them in the first place.

Only in such an atmosphere can we explain an event like Reykjavik, the uncertainty of all concerned about what really was going on, the schemings around a central vision, everyone trying to use that dream and being tripped up by it, rejecting and reaffirming it, with the President smiling approval over it all. What else but such a world of deliberate feigning and inadvertent ignorance could explain the unthinkable things done and denied, approved and repudiated, regretted but unforgettable, at Reykjavik?

NOTES

Chapter 1

[1]"The United States of Lyncherdom," in *Mark Twain on the Damned Human Race*, edited by Janet Smith (Hill and Wang, 1962), pp. 96–104.

[2]Martin Green, *Dreams of Adventure, Deeds of Empire* (Basic Books, 1979), p. 246.

[3]Tampico *Tornado*, April 20, 1906.

[4]*Life on the Mississippi*, Ch. 56. For "the contrast between Southern backwardness and Northern enlightenment and prosperity as a basic structure" of the book, cf. Henry Nash Smith, *Democracy and the Novel* (Oxford, 1978), p. 119.

[5]Charles Bent, *History of Whiteside County, Illinois* (Morrison, Illinois, 1877), pp. 163, 166–67; Wayne Bastian, *Whiteside County*, pp. 219–21.

[6]Whiteside County Census, 1880, Fulton, p. 29.

[7]Henry Nash Smith, op. cit., p. 124: "The outcome of *A Connecticut Yankee* reveals a loss of faith in the doctrine of progress that was central to the American sense of identity. The experience was so shocking that Mark Twain's critics and even the writer himself were at first unable to admit to consciousness the pessimistic implications of the ending of the fable." Cf. Richard Slotkin, *The Fatal Environment: The Myth of the Frontier in the Age of Industrialization* (Atheneum, 1985), pp. 523–30.

[8]For the transition from "eager promotion" to "outraged disappointment," see Robert Wiebe, *The Search for Order, 1877–1920* (Hill and Wang, 1967), p. 85; William H. McNeill, *The Great Frontier: Freedom and Hierarchy in Modern Times* (Princeton, 1983), pp. 27–28; and Richard Hofstadter, *The Age of Reform: From Bryan to F.D.R.* (Vintage, 1955), p. 58.

[9]Whiteside County Census, 1880, Fulton, p. 29.

[10]Fred A. Shannon, *The Farmer's Last Frontier: Agriculture, 1860–1897* (New York, 1945), pp. 292–94; Richard Hofstadter, op. cit., pp. 50–59.

[11]Wiebe, op. cit., p. 102.

[12]Joseph Dorfman, *Thorstein Veblen and His America* (Viking, 1934), p. 105.

[13]Roy V. Scott, *The Agrarian Movement in Illinois, 1880–1896* (University of Illinois, 1962), p. 20.

[14]For the demographer's use of "ritualist" and "pietist" as categories, see Paul Klepper, *The Cross of Culture: A Social Analysis of Midwestern Politics, 1850–1900* (Free Press, 1970), pp. 69–91. For the claim that the Democrats lost in 1896 because of their attempt to absorb pietistic agrarianism, ibid., pp. 279–315, and James L. Sundquist, *Dynamics of the Party System* (Brookings Institution, 1973), pp. 144–46.

[15]Whiteside County Census, 1900, Fulton, p. 11. Mary Chapman was the other sister known to be alive, along with Margaret and their mother (Jack's grandmother). Another sister, Clementine, is buried in Fulton Township Cemetery, under an undecipherable married name. It is not recorded when she died.

[16]Verl L. Lekwa, *Bennett, Iowa and Inland Township* (Marceline, Missouri, 1983), pp. 95–96.

[17]Cedar County Census, 1900, Ward 2, p. 11.

[18]Lekwa, op. cit., pp. 86, 93.

[19]Ibid., p. 99.

[20]Interview with town historian, Verl L. Lekwa, now living in Columbus Junction, Iowa.

[21]The recently made microfilm of the sole file of early *Tornado*s, a film kept in the Illinois Historical Society at Springfield, shows that part of the "Local News" column for Feb. 9, 1906, has been torn out. But earlier viewers of the file quoted it, including the man who had custody when the damage seems to have occurred. My source is Myron S. Waldman, *Newsday,* Jan. 18, 1981: "H. C. Pitney has hired J. E. Reagan of Fulton to clerk in his store. Mr. Reagan worked for eight years in Broadhead's big store at Fulton and comes highly recommended."

[22]Fulton City Directory, 1905–6, "on the corner of Wall and Locust Streets."

[23]Interview with county historian Wayne Bastian.

[24]Lekwa, op. cit., p. 96.

[25]Ibid., p. 99.

[26]"John Reagan has been calling thirty-seven inches a yard and giving seventeen ounces for a pound this week at Pitney's store [because] he has been feeling so jubilant over the arrival of a ten-pound boy on Monday," Tampico *Tornado,* Feb. 10, 1911. H. C. Pitney was one of the *Tornado*'s principal advertisers. There was usually a large ad for his store on the front page of each issue, and the publisher, George Isherwood, found many ways to plug the store in his "Local News" column.

[27]For Reagan at the Fair Store, cf. Dixon *Daily Telegraph,* Feb. 4, 1984. At Colwell's, Galesburg *Register-Mail,* Nov. 21, 1975. At Johnson's, Monmouth *Review-Atlas,* Nov. 11, 1980. For pictures and article on the O. T. Johnson store, see the Galesburg *Prairie Journal,* Winter 1983.

[28]The Fair Store became Montgomery Ward's on State Street, Johnson's is the Social Security Building, and Colwell's is the Bowman Furniture Store. For the expansion of Pitney's to fill two contiguous stores (which it has again been reduced to), see the Tampico *Tornado,* Jan. 6, 1905.

[29]Tampico *Tornado,* Aug. 15, 1903.

[30]*The Confidence-Man* (1857), Ch. 16.

[31]Carl W. Condit, *The Chicago School of Architecture* (University of Chicago, 1964), pp. 90–91; Robert Hendrickson, *The Grand Emporiums: The Illustrated History of America's Great Department Stores* (Stein and Day, 1979), pp. 399–400. The Fair was the first store to buy full-page ads in Chicago newspapers. In 1914 it was being run by E. J. Lehmann, Jr., son of the flamboyant and erratic founder.

[32]Loyal Davis, a Galesburg man who became Ronald Reagan's second father-in-law, was attending Northwestern University's medical school while Reagan lived in his town as a boy.

[33]The house is at 218 S. Seventh Street, the address given on his school application, and one he revisited during his 1976 presidential campaign. In July of 1966 the Monmouth *Review-Atlas* found that the "1917 directory shows Dr. Charles T. Gallop was living there, and a 1919 directory shows the house was occupied by the Rev. John Acheson. Apparently the Reagan family was here only about a year."

[34]Interview with Vernon Denison in Tampico.

[35]Dixon *Daily Telegraph,* Feb. 28, 1921.

[36]Robert S. Lynd and Helen Merrill Lynd, *Middletown: A Study in American Culture* (Harcourt, Brace & World, 1929), p. 191.

[37]Dixon *Daily Telegraph,* Feb. 28, 1981; Dixon City Directory, 1927–28. Interview in Dixon with Helen Lawton, the Reagans' next-door neighbor on Lincolnway (as it was then spelled). Why was he working at the hospital? Nelle's church group regularly entertained patients at the hospital. Perhaps she was able to get Jack an office job when he had exhausted his selling opportunities in Dixon.

[38]Ibid., Aug. 13, 1929.

[39]Ibid., Jan. 7, 1930.

CHAPTER 2

[1]Tampico *Tornado*, April 13, June 21, July 13, 1906.

[2]Ibid., Sept. 20, June 21.

[3]Ibid., April 12, 19, 26; July 5, 1907.

[4]I have seen the record of the baptism of "Reagan, Mrs. Nellie" on p. 19 of the "Church Record Begun Oct. 21. 1900 by J. S. Clements" in the Christian Church. Mr. and Mrs. Warren Anderson are custodians of the church documents during a period when the Christian Church (at present the Church of Christ) had no pastor. Unfortunately, there is no date for the baptisms of the first decades in that book, and once again the relevant Tampico *Tornado*s are missing from the file microfilmed for the Illinois Historical Society. But the late Reverend Gordon Gardiner, who for years made it his hobby to do research on the religious background of presidents' mothers, had access to the paper's information in 1980. We know the Hennepin Canal was used by the Christian Church in Tampico immersion services *(Tornado,* July 13, 1906). Easter was a normal time for baptism. If March 27 seems a cold date for total outdoor immersion, we should remember that James A. Garfield was baptized in Ohio's freezing Chagrin River on March 3, 1850. Cf. Allan Peskin, *Garfield* (Kent State University, 1978), p. 17.

Mrs. Reagan comes sixth in the list of those whose names began with R and were baptized after the church's founding in 1900. It should have taken about ten years to reach that point in a church that started in 1900 with thirty members, and had only sixty by 1915. Cf. Nathaniel Haynes, *History of the Disciples of Christ in Illinois, 1819–1914* (Cincinnati, 1915), p. 441. And the 1910 date would accord with Nelle Reagan's differing attitudes toward the Catholic baptism of her two sons, Neil born in 1908 and Ronald in 1911. Cf. Gordon Gardiner, "Nelle Reagan," in *Bread of Life* (monthly published from the Ridgewood Pentecostal Church), May 1981.

[5]Interview with Mrs. Kirk Snydor in Fulton.

[6]Gordon Gardiner, *Bread of Life.* For the Methodist Episcopal Church, built in 1872, see Wayne Bastian, *Whiteside County* (Henry, Illinois, 1960), p. 162.

[7]Haynes, op. cit., p. 439.

[8]*Tampico Church Record,* p. 27 entry: "Sept. 29 1919 [Mrs.] J. E. Reagan, Letter (Mar 17–21 Dixon C. Ch)."

[9]John Neil Reagan was baptized Sept. 16, 1908, by the Rev. F. X. Du Four. Du Four had been in Tampico four years, according to the county history published the year of Neil's baptism, and was reputed to be a professor as well as a preacher, but he makes a mistake in the Latin of the baptism form (putting Jack's name in the vocative rather than the nominative). William W. Davis, *History of Whiteside County, Illinois* (Chicago, 1908), p. 204. One of Neil's godparents was A. C. Burden, from the most prominent Catholic family in town, which owned the Opera House in which Nelle put on her plays. A. C. Burden at some point became a bartender. There is a picture of him at work in Tinks Tavern on p. 64 of the centennial volume *Tampico 1875–1975: Historical Record.*

[10]The First Christian Church records kept in Dixon by the Rev. Ben Cleaver show that Neil and Ronald Reagan are listed for confession (of faith) and baptism on June 21, 1922.

[11]Interview in Fulton with Florence Johns, who also worked in Mrs. Baldwin's store.

[12]According to her birth record, on file in the county seat of Morrison, Illinois, Nelle was actually born on the river, in Albany township, which stretches along the river south of Fulton; but the record was not made at the time of her birth. It was filed in 1943, and seems to have the wrong birth date, July 18, 1882, which would

have made her a year older than her husband, rather than two years younger, as she claimed on her wedding license of November 7, 1904. (Just to confuse matters further, Jack claimed to be twenty-two on that certificate when—according to his birth certificate, filed at the right time—he was twenty-one.)

[13]For Disciple churches in Chicago's Hyde Park area (where the Reagans lived in 1914), Galesburg, Monmouth, and Dixon, see Haynes, op. cit., pp. 160, 243, 258-9, 426.

[14]Interview with Ben Cleaver's daughter, Helen, now living in Columbia, Missouri.

[15]Stone studied from Witherspoon's notes under David Caldwell, of Princeton, at Guilford, N.C. Cf. William Garrett West, Barton Warren Stone (Nashville, 1954), p. 4. For Madison's use of the notes, see Garry Wills, Explaining America (Doubleday, 1981), p. 16.

[16]West, op. cit., p. 36. On the Cane Ridge services, cf. Charles A. Johnson, The Frontier Camp Meeting: Religion's Harvest Time (Southern Methodist University, 1955), pp. 62-67, and Bernard A. Weisberger, They Gathered at the River (Quadrangle, 1966), pp. 31-37.

[17]West, pp. 7-10; Johnson, op. cit., pp. 32-38; Weisberger, op. cit., pp. 23-26, 30, 41-42.

[18]West, op. cit., pp. 84-96.

[19]John Boles, The Great Revival (University of Kentucky, 1972), pp. 157-58; Johnson, op. cit., pp. 73-76.

[20]Winfred Ernest Garrison, The Sources of Alexander Campbell's Theology (St. Louis, 1900), pp. 231-34.

[21]Lester G. McAllister, Thomas Campbell: Man of the Book (Bethany Press, 1954), pp. 72-95.

[22]Winfred Ernest Garrison and Alfred T. DeGroot, The Disciples of Christ: A History (Bethany Press, 1958 revised edition), pp. 158-61.

[23]West, op. cit., pp. 136, 142, 163, 169.

[24]Haynes, op. cit., table between pp. 108 and 109.

[25]West, op. cit., p. 219. Dixon Wecter, Samuel Clemens of Hannibal (Houghton Mifflin, 1952), pp. 86-89.

[26]Boles, op. cit., pp. 27-34. Cf. Ernest Lee Tuveson, Redeemer Nation: The Idea of America's Millennial Role (University of Chicago, 1968), p. 218. "The Campbellite theology might be called socioreligious; abstract issues of 'justification,' 'calling,' and the like yield to practical preparation for rational and social happiness."

[27]Wecter, op. cit., p. 88.

[28]Reagan was mature enough to recall, for the California pastor of his Disciples church (Myron C. Cole), what words were said over him as he came from his immersion: "Arise, and walk in newness of faith." Interview with Reverend Cole, now living in Hawaii.

[29]The four were Abington, Berean, Southern Illinois College, and Eureka (Haynes, op. cit., pp. 33-67). There are currently eighteen Disciple colleges or universities, not counting seminaries. They are listed in Kenneth L. Teegarden, We Call Ourselves Disciples (Bethany Press, 1975), p. 109.

[30]For Disciple publications, see William E. Tucker and Lester G. McAllister, Journey in Faith: A History of the Christian Church (Disciples of Christ) (Bethany Press, 1975), pp. 327-30.

[31]Robert Frederick West, Alexander Campbell and Natural Religion (Yale, 1948), pp. 66-89; Tuveson, op. cit., pp. 79-82.

[32]Harold Adams, History of Eureka College (Henry, Illinois, 1982), p. 25.

[33]California Oral History Project, 1981, UCLA Special Collections, p. 11.

[34]Dixon Daily Telegraph, Jan. 21, 1922, Feb. 28, 1981.

[35]Interview in Tampico with Frances Aldrich Rakow.

[36]Hubler, p. 20. When Tampico put on a weekend revue honoring the President in

1982, a young woman of Nelle's age in her Tampico days, wearing period dress, recited "Levinsky." I quote from a photocopy of the text she used.

³⁷Tampico *Tornado,* June 3, June 10, 1920.

³⁸Ibid., Sept. 2, 1920.

³⁹Ibid., Nov. 18, 1920.

⁴⁰Quoted by permission from the original, whose possessor prefers not to be named.

⁴¹Haynes, op. cit., p. 70. Actually, the debate lasted eight days. In the sketch of Protestant origins given as an introduction to his book, Haynes traces these to *"the denial of the Pope's arrogant claim to the universal headship of the church on earth"* (p. 14, italics of the original).

⁴²Harold L. Lunger, *The Political Ethics of Alexander Campbell* (Bethany Press, 1954), p. 158. The climactic proposition drawn up by Campbell for defense in his debate with Bishop Purcell was this: "The Roman Catholic religion, if infallible and unsusceptible of reformation as alleged, is essentially anti-American, being opposed to the genius of all free institutions, and positively subversive of them . . ." (ibid., p. 157). In his debate with Owen, Campbell held that the *mysterium iniquitatis* in Scripture was the Catholic Church (Tuveson, op. cit., p. 218). In the 1940s and 1950s, the Disciples' International Convention actively opposed United States representation of any kind at the Vatican (James A. Crain, *The Development of Social Ideas Among the Disciples of Christ,* Bethany Press, 1969, pp. 295–98). A book used for a long time as the standard history of the Disciples dates the modern church from Reformers' break with a Catholic Church that had "set up bishops' courts and inquisitions as vigilant and ruthless as any Gestapo" (Winfred Ernest Garrison and Alfred T. DeGroot, op. cit., 1958 revised edition of 1948, third printing, 1969, p. 32). The attitude changed only in the 1970s, after the Second Vatican Council (William E. Tucker and Lester G. McAllister, op. cit., p. 458).

⁴³Verl L. Lekwa, *Bennett, Iowa, and Inland Township* (Marceline, Missouri, 1983), pp. 26–27.

⁴⁴In 1905, licensing (under strict controls) barely won—129 to 119. In 1907, it lost. Tampico *Tornado,* Jan. 6, 1905, April 19, 1907.

⁴⁵For temperance meetings at the Christian Church, see the Tampico *Tornado,* Nov. 23, 1906, Feb. 15, 1907.

⁴⁶James A. Crain, *The Development of Social Ideas Among the Disciples of Christ* (Bethany Press, 1969), pp. 250–55. "Illinois Disciples seem to have become prohibition activists somewhat later but perhaps more fervently than their brethren in any other midwestern states. The state convention passed a prohibition resolution in 1884 and Disciples were locally active in promoting the cause in the 1880s. But not until the 1880s did militant prohibitionists dominate the church. In the last decade of the century Disciple ministers went everywhere in Illinois lecturing, building temperance hotels, and crusading for the Prohibitionist party in the state." (David Edwin Harrell, Jr., *The Social Sources of Division in the Disciples of Christ, 1865–1900* [Atlanta, 1973], p. 239.)

⁴⁷The son of a minister from a neighboring congregation played the drunkard in Nelle Reagan's play, and that, too, was the subject of joking comment for years.

⁴⁸On the righthand page following Ronald Reagan's baptismal notice, the only entry is: "May 12, 1940 Hollywood Beverly Christian Church, Hollywood CA."

⁴⁹San Francisco *Chronicle,* Aug. 27, 1980.

⁵⁰Henry Bellamann, *Kings Row* (Simon and Schuster, 1940), p. 69. A "Morris Reagan" once lived in Kings Row, but he was hanged before the novel's action begins (p. 106).

⁵¹Ibid., pp. 367–68. Cf. pp. 13, 370. Campbellites were respectable in Kings Row, unlike the Catholics: "The Presbyterian was the 'high-toned' church. The Campbellite ranked second, though a good many newcomers had somehow become enrolled

there. The Baptist and Methodist graded equally, but certainly much lower than the first two. Of course there was the Catholic church, but that didn't figure in any way" (p. 30). Bellamann grew up in Fulton, Missouri, another city named, like Jack Reagan's birthplace in Illinois, for the patron of steamboats in the West.

CHAPTER 3

[1]California Oral History Project, 1981, UCLA Special Collections, p. 2. Neil went to pool halls, but Ronald "would never do anything like that. He would rather be up there, just gazing at his birds and eggs, and no such thought of going into a pool hall" (p. 9).

[2]Tom Bates, "The President's Brother," *California*, July 1982.

[3]California Oral History Project, 1981, UCLA Special Collections, p. 38.

[4]Ibid., pp. 20, 31. He also taught Ronald's first child how to swim (ibid., p. 37).

[5]Ibid., p. 10.

[6]Facsimile of letter reprinted with permission of its owner in the Ashton (Illinois) *Gazette*, Nov. 20, 1980.

[7]Interview with Howard Short, the 1928 football team manager, now living in St. Louis, Missouri.

[8]Eureka *Pegasus*, Nov. 16, 1929.

[9]E.g., the AP dispatch run in the Sacramento *Daily Enterprise*, Aug. 6, 1971: "He was a good two-way tackle. But I was the star end who made the touchdowns." Cf. Bates, op. cit.: "He wasn't first-string when I was."

[10]Neil Reagan, who attended grades one through four in Galesburg's Silas Willard School, was promoted from fourth grade in 1918, the same year Ronald finished first grade (March 1, 1918), according to the records kept by William Abel, superintendent of schools. Ronald entered the Central School in Monmouth to begin second grade Sept. 9, 1918, but was promoted from third grade on June 6, 1919, the same year that Neil spent in the fifth grade (information from Donald R. Jenkins, Superintendent). During the year he skipped a grade, the school was closed for several weeks by a flu epidemic, the one mentioned at Hubler 18 (interview in Monmouth with Monmouth classmate Gertrude Crockett Romine, and letter from Reagan to Mrs. Romine).

Ronald's fourth-grade records (1919–20) I have seen in Tampico, courtesy of Larry E. Wilcoxen, Tampico superintendent, along with Neil's *sixth*-grade records. The distance between the two boys has narrowed by a year. Ronald, two and a half years younger than Neil, could have started school when he was five; he would have turned six in February of that year. Instead, he was held back until he was the normal age—six—for starting first grade, when he had already learned to read (Hubler, p. 17). Kindergarten was not normally available then.

[11]Bates, op. cit.

[12]Oral History Project, p. 29.

[13]Galesburg *Register-Mail*, May 2, 1966. Reporters saw these grades before authorities stopped releasing them.

[14]See note 10 above.

[15]James Russell Lowell reached Illinois on a lecture tour in 1851 and "detested it" (Martin B. Duberman, *James Russell Lowell*, Houghton Mifflin, 1966, p. 143). But he did not take revenge by writing the "Ode to a Waterfowl." William Cullen Bryant did that, with no help at all from Illinois.

[16]For early pictures of Reagan at the YMCA, which stood next to the Nachusa Hotel, see Dixon *Daily Telegraph*, Feb. 28, 1981.

[17]"After two days' hard work we got over the rapids of Rock River . . ." From

the memoirs of J. W. Spencer, in *The Early Days of Rock Island and Davenport* (Chicago, 1942), p. 54.

[18]Dixon *Daily Telegraph*, Sept. 3, 1929.

[19]Ibid., July 23, 1932.

[20]Ibid., May 1, 1941, Feb. 28, 1981.

[21]Ibid., June 18, 1931.

[22]"Meditations of a Lifeguard," *Dixonian*, 1932.

[23]*Daily Telegraph*, July 23, 1932.

[24]Ibid., May 1, 1941.

[25]"Easter Week Services," facsimile printed in First Christian Church booklet, *Ronald Reagan's Boyhood Church.*

[26]Bill Boyarsky, *The Rise of Ronald Reagan* (Random House, 1968), p. 198.

[27]Robert Dallek, *Ronald Reagan: The Politics of Symbolism* (Harvard, 1968), pp. 16, 52.

[28]Ibid., p. 86; and pp. 140, 194. Another psychobiography that explains political views from childhood revulsion against a drunken father should prompt our caution, since it is devoted to an architect of the welfare state—Graham White and John Mazo, *Harold Ickes of the New Deal* (Harvard, 1985). The authors find an Oedipal attachment to trees behind Ickes's interest in forestry programs (pp. 18, 157). Reagan, it is well known, once expressed doubt that you can see with profit more than one redwood tree.

CHAPTER 4

[1]Ashton (Illinois) *Gazette*, Nov. 20, 1980.

[2]Harold Adams, *History of Eureka College* (Henry, Illinois, 1982), p. 81.

[3]Ibid., p. 82.

[4]Ibid., p. 222.

[5]Ibid., p. 162.

[6]*The Pegasus*, Nov. 6, 1930.

[7]Adams, op. cit., p. 230.

[8]Ibid., p. 41.

[9]Ibid., pp. 29–30.

[10]Winfred Ernest Garrison and Alfred T. DeGroot, *The Disciples of Christ, A History* (Bethany Press, 1948), p. 331; Harold L. Lunger, *The Political Ethics of Alexander Campbell* (Bethany Press, 1954), pp. 75–93.

[11]Adams, op. cit., pp. 207, 214–18.

[12]David Edwin Harrell, Jr., *The Social Sources of Division in the Disciples of Christ, 1865–1900* (Atlanta, 1973), pp. 323–50; Alfred T. DeGroot, *The Grounds of Divisions Among the Disciples of Christ* (Chicago, 1940), pp. 90–134; William E. Tudor and Lester G. McAllister, *Journey in Faith: A History of the Christian Church (Disciples of Christ)* (Bethany Press), pp. 244–54, 361–82.

[13]Adams, op. cit., pp. 138–39.

[14]Ibid., pp. 58, 61, 65.

[15]Ibid., pp. 143, 174–75.

[16]Ibid., p. 173.

[17]President Wilson's report, printed in the Bloomington *Daily Pantagraph*, Nov. 24, 1928, p. 2.

[18]Adams, op. cit., p. 187.

[19]*The Pegasus*, Nov. 19, 1928.

[20]Eureka College Catalogue, 1928–29, "News Writing and Editing," Professor Wiggins.

[21]Bloomington *Daily Pantagraph*, Nov. 21, 1928.

[22]Adams, op. cit., p. 179.
[23]Bloomington *Daily Pantagraph*, Nov. 24, 1928.
[24]Adams, op. cit., p. 173.
[25]Ibid., p. 184.
[26]Ibid.
[27]E.g., Charles McCabe, "How to Dump a Prexy," San Francisco *Chronicle*, May 5, 1967.
[28]*The Pegasus*, Nov. 19, 1928.
[29]Adams, op. cit., pp. 76, 78. Interview with Burris Dickinson, Peoria *Star*, Dec. 3, 1928.
[30]Woodford County *Journal*, Nov. 29, 1928: "The *Journal* did not mention the affair last week, deciding to let the papers on the west and southeast give Mr. Wilson the daily publicity he says Eureka College has lacked."
[31]Bloomington *Daily Pantagraph*, Nov. 25, 1928.
[32]Ibid., Nov. 27.
[33]Ibid., Nov. 24.
[34]*The Pegasus*, Nov. 19.

CHAPTER 5

[1]Interview with the other journalistic footballer, Howard Short. Team record from *The Pegasus*, Nov. 26, 1928.
[2]Bloomington *Daily Pantagraph*, Nov. 28, 1928.
[3]After the demand for Wilson's resignation was made, Leslie Pierce's organization had to issue a statement that "emphatically denied that they [the students] were making charges against President Wilson on moral grounds and the alleged misappropriation and mismanagement of college funds as had been previously stated." Bloomington *Daily Pantagraph*, Nov. 23.
[4]Indeed, two of the faculty reported the joint committee's findings to the board, along with Wilson. *The Pegasus*, Nov. 19, 1928.
[5]*The Pegasus*, Nov. 26.
[6]Bloomington *Daily Pantagraph*, Nov. 22.
[7]*The Pegasus*, Nov. 26. Reagan pauses in his account of the student strike to tell how Eureka *won* the game against Illinois "with a dropkick of better than fifty yards" made by "a colored boy" (Hubler 34). He also has the game take place on a Saturday, with a board meeting going on simultaneously. He claims no one was watching the moment of victory because of the newspapers, so "it was one of the best games no one ever saw." It is true that no one ever saw the game he describes.
[8]Bloomington *Daily Pantagraph*, Nov. 24.
[9]Ibid., Nov. 25.
[10]Ibid.
[11]*The Pegasus*, Nov. 26. The students dutifully organized this recruiting for "immediate" success after Wilson's departure: *The Pegasus*, Jan. 8, Jan. 15, April 23, 1929. But freshmen enrollment dropped the next year by twenty students (ibid., Sept. 28, 1929). This was before the stock market crash of the same year, so that did not cause the drop. The strike apparently gave the school more "bad publicity" than had the gloomy statement it protested.
[12]Bloomington *Daily Pantagraph*, Nov. 27.
[13]Ibid., Nov. 24.
[14]Ibid., Nov. 29.
[15]Ibid., Nov. 28.
[16]*The Pegasus*, Dec. 11.
[17]Ibid.

[18]Bloomington *Daily Pantagraph,* Nov. 29.

[19]Ibid., Nov. 22.

[20]Ibid., Dec. 4.

[21]*The Pegasus,* Dec. 11.

[22]Peoria *Journal-Star,* Dec. 8.

[23]Adams, op. cit., p. 192.

CHAPTER 6

[1]Reagan class biography, *The Pegasus,* May 12, 1932. Reports on plays are in the issues of April 9, 1929; April 19 and Nov. 16, 1930; Mar. 19, April 30, and Oct. 22, 1931; April 21, 1932.

[2]Interview in Eureka with Burrus Dickinson.

[3]*The Pegasus,* Oct. 16, 1930.

[4]Ibid., Oct. 5 and Nov. 23, 1929.

[5]Ibid., April 3, 1930. Reagan gives the team a second place in Hubler, p. 53.

[6]Eureka College Catalogue, 1928–29.

[7]*The Prism* (Eureka Yearbook), 1930, p. 24.

[8]Hubler, p. 48. For the date of the production, cf. *The Pegasus,* April 9, 1929.

[9]*The Statistical History of the United States, From Colonial Times to the Present,* prepared by the U.S. Census Bureau (Basic Books, 1971), p. 126.

[10]Ronald's appeared in the May 12, 1932, *Pegasus,* Neil's in the February 21, 1933, issue.

[11]Harold Adams, *History of Eureka College* (Henry, Illinois, 1982), p. 201.

[12]Community feelings were both expressed and aroused in the Dixon *Afternoon Telegraph* for May 10, 1985, in which Norman Wymbs was quoted attacking the "myths" of Reagan poverty. The subject comes up in debates over the accuracy of the restoration of Reagan's "boyhood home," which seems furnished with more and better furniture than the Reagans could have accumulated in their Illinois days.

[13]The best account of MacArthur's disobedience is Roger Daniels, *The Bonus March: An Episode of the Great Depression* (Government Publishing Corporation, 1971), pp. 162–72.

[14]Douglas MacArthur, *Reminiscences* (McGraw-Hill, 1964), p. 97.

[15]Arthur M. Schlesinger, Jr., *The Crisis of the Old Order* (Houghton Mifflin, 1957), p. 302.

[16]James MacGregor Burns, *Roosevelt: The Lion and the Fox* (Harcourt, Brace and World, 1956), p. 139. Edie Luckett Davis, Chicago's actress-socialite, attended the opening of the convention that nominated Roosevelt, accompanied by her eleven-year-old daughter, Nancy. The Chicago *Daily Times* ran a picture of them on the front page of its June 28, 1932, edition, with the caption "THAT'S THE WAY IT GOES, NANCY: another experience entered the life of a metropolitan young lady today when Nancy Davis, ably tutored by her mother, Mrs. Loyal Davis, learned what conventions were like." Cf. Washington *Post,* April 26, 1981. In 1932, Sarah Jane Fulks, an eighteen-year-old later known as Jane Wyman, was already singing and dancing in the chorus of Hollywood musicals. Cf. Dixon *Daily Telegraph,* Sept. 12, 1941; Joe Morella and Edward Z. Epstein, *Jane Wyman* (Delacorte, 1985), pp. 9–10.

[17]Dixon *Daily Telegraph,* Oct. 28, 1932.

[18]Doris Carothers, *Chronology of the Federal Emergency Relief Administration* (U.S. Government Printing Office, 1937), p. 3.

[19]Ibid. Records of the Reagans' early family life are confused since Nelle's collection of materials perished in Neil's house during a California fire of 1961. California Oral History Project, 1981, p. 4.

[20]Ibid., p. 27.

[21]Dixon *Daily Telegraph*, Feb. 10, 1933.

[22]Ibid., Nov. 23, 1933.

[23]Since the Illinois FERA was one of the first established, and Jack Reagan was in it from the outset according to Reagan (a claim his later record supports), the newspaper's "several months" should be read expansively, as four or five months.

[24]Ibid., Dec. 13, 1933.

[25]Arthur Burns and Edward A. Williams, *Federal Work Security and Relief Programs* (U.S. Government Printing Office, 1941), pp. 131–32.

[26]Dixon *Daily Telegraph*, Oct. 29, 1934.

[27]Washington fought back with federal investigations and indictments of state and local administrators. Cf. Searle F. Charles, *Minister of Relief: Harry Hopkins and the Depression* (Syracuse University, 1963), pp. 58–59.

[28]Dixon *Daily Telegraph*, Jan. 27, 1934. Cf. Bonnie Fox Schwartz, *The Civil Works Administration: The Business of Emergency Employment in the New Deal* (Princeton, 1984), pp. 88–94.

[29]Dixon *Daily Telegraph*, Dec. 10, 1933. Other towns sent delegations to study the hangar's parabolic-arch structure.

[30]Burns and Williams, op. cit., pp. 29–35.

[31]Dixon *Daily Telegraph*, Dec. 15, 18, 21, 1933; Jan. 11, 25, 1934.

[32]Ibid., Jan. 3, 1934. For the project-approval system, cf. B. F. Schwartz, op. cit., pp. 55–69.

[33]Dixon *Daily Telegraph*, Jan. 5, Jan. 8, 1933.

[34]Ibid., Dec. 10, 1933.

[35]Ibid., Nov. 20, Nov. 29, 1933. Burns and Williams, op. cit., p. 34.

[36]Ibid., Oct. 29, 1934. For airport projects of the CWA, cf. B. F. Schwartz, op. cit., p. 183.

CHAPTER 7

[1]Jordan A. Schwarz, *The Interregnum of Despair: Hoover, Congress, and the Depression* (University of Illinois, 1970), pp. vii–viii, 230–38.

[2]Rexford G. Tugwell, *The Democratic Roosevelt* (Doubleday, 1957), pp. 256–62; William E. Leuchtenburg, *Franklin D. Roosevelt and the New Deal* (Harper & Row, 1963), p. 39.

[3]David L. Lewis, *The Public Image of Henry Ford: An American Folk Hero and His Company* (Wayne State University, 1976), pp. 238–39, 524; Richard Norton Smith, *An Uncommon Man: The Triumph of Herbert Hoover* (Simon and Schuster, 1984), pp. 155–56.

[4]Ibid., pp. 157–61; Leuchtenburg, op. cit., p. 39; Arthur M. Schlesinger, Jr., *The Crisis of the Old Order* (Houghton Mifflin, 1957), pp. 480–81.

[5]Philip S. Klein, *President James Buchanan* (Pennsylvania State University, 1962), pp. 365–67, 381–86.

[6]Allan Nevins, *The Emergence of Lincoln II: Prologue to Civil War, 1859–61* (Scribner, 1950), p. 277; Klein, op. cit., p. 365.

[7]Ibid., p. 395.

[8]Ibid., pp. 355–57.

[9]Klein, op. cit., p. 378.

[10]Nevins, op. cit., p. 451.

[11]Alfred Haworth Jones, *Roosevelt's Image Brokers: Poets, Playwrights, and the Use of the Lincoln Symbol* (National University Publications, 1974), p. 65. The three Lincoln celebrants coaxed to write for or about Roosevelt were Carl Sandburg, author of *Lincoln: The Prairie Years*, and *Lincoln: The War Years*, Stephen Vincent Benét, author of *John Brown's Body*, and Robert Sherwood, author of *Abe Lincoln in*

Illinois. Raymond Massey, the Lincoln impersonator who performed the works of all three authors, also campaigned for Roosevelt. Op. cit., pp. 38–62, 97–111.

[12]Tugwell, op. cit., p. 265. He continues: "It was the result of panic. With matters in complete chaos, the congressmen ran from responsibility. If anyone else wanted to accept it under such circumstances, let him."

[13]R. N. Smith, op. cit., p. 136. For Hoover's attitude toward broadcasting, ibid., p. 137.

[14]For *Gabriel* as a vigilante film, see Andrew Bergman, *We're in the Money: Depression America and Its Films* (Harper & Row, 1972), pp. 115–18; Carlos Clarens, *Crime Movies from Griffith to the Godfather and Beyond* (Norton, 1980), pp. 107–8; Richard Gid Powers, *G-Men: Hoover's FBI in American Popular Culture* (Southern Illinois University, 1983), pp. 31–32.

[15]William Tryon, "Fascism over Hollywood," *The Nation,* April 26, 1933.

[16]Bosley Crowther, *Hollywood Rajah: The Life and Times of Louis B. Mayer* (Holt, Rinehart and Winston, 1960), pp. 178–81. Crowther saw Hearst's speeches in the papers of the movie's scriptwriter, Carey Wilson. Samuel Marx, *Mayer and Thalberg: The Make-Believe Saints* (Random House, 1975), pp. 204–5. Marx dates Mayer's later suspicion that Wilson was a Communist from the *Gabriel* project (ibid., pp. 237–38).

[17]W. A. Swanberg, *Citizen Hearst* (Scribner, 1961), p. 431.

[18]Crowther, op. cit., p. 179.

[19]New York *Times,* March 17, 1933: " 'Gabriel' Film Sent Back to Hollywood."

[20]Walter Lippmann in his column, Mordaunt Hall in the New York *Times* (April 1), Stark Young in *The New Republic* (April 19), and William Troy in *The Nation* (April 26), all remarked on the Lincolnesque presentation of the film's dictator-president.

[21]Crowther, p. 180. In fact, Roosevelt appropriated a wisecrack from the movie for his own use. Mordaunt Hall says that Huston, as President, appoints a crony as ambassador to Greece, with the hope "he has good legs for wearing the court knickerbockers." Roosevelt told his sons how he made Joseph P. Kennedy pull up his pants before appointing him to the Court of Saint James's, so he could tell him he did not have the legs for the job. Cf. Michael R. Beschloss, *Kennedy and Roosevelt: The Uneasy Alliance* (Norton, 1980), p. 154.

[22]Lippmann's column is quoted and discussed in an article on the movie in *The Literary Digest* for April 22, 1933, "A President After Hollywood's Heart." Lippmann was understandably concerned about the support Hearst had given Roosevelt in the 1932 campaign, in part through the mediation of Joseph Kennedy. Cf. Ronald Steel, *Walter Lippmann and the American Century* (Little, Brown, 1980), pp. 292–94.

[23]Mordaunt Hall, New York *Times,* April 9, 1933.

[24]Ibid. Tweed's book appeared anonymously in America (published by Farrar and Rinehart) during February 1933, with some correction of Americanisms by a *Time* writer, John Billings. In March it was published in England as *Rinehart: A Melodrama of the Nineteen-Thirties* (A. Barker, Ltd.). Tweed tried unsuccessfully to follow up his success with *Destiny's Man* in 1935, the story of a "benign" dictator for a federated Europe. As a movie, *Gabriel* had been one of the top six box office draws in 1933 (Bergman, op. cit., p. 118).

[25]The President is led into his well-meant breaches of the Constitution by head injuries suffered in a car accident. An attempted gangland assassination brings him back to his mind at the end of the novel. Cabinet members had considered a coup when he went idealistically "mad," but rejected the plan. They act on their earlier plan when he returns to "normal" at the end. The ironies of this situation were beyond Hollywood, which has the President die a natural death after working his extralegal miracles.

[26]Bruce Bliven, "Four Films: Art and Propaganda," *The New Republic,* April 19, 1933.

[27]For the Army's study of the CWA's rapid formation, see Irving Bernstein, *A Caring Society: The New Deal, the Worker, and the Great Depression* (Houghton Mifflin, 1985), pp. 39–40. For the Blue Eagle as war emblem, see Leo Rosten in *Harpers* for June of 1935: "We are waging a war, a war against unemployment, against social insecurity, a war for social justice. There was in the Blue Eagle, the codes, the honor rolls, the public stigmatizing of the New Deal, all the panoply of a military campaign and a holy crusade." Also William Leuchtenburg, "The New Deal and the Analogue of War," in John Braeman et al., *Change and Continuity in Twenti-eth-Century America* (Ohio State, 1964), pp. 81–143.

[28]Henry H. Adams, *Harry Hopkins* (Putnam, 1977), p. 22.

[29]William E. Leuchtenburg, *Franklin D. Roosevelt and the New Deal, 1932–1940* (Harper & Row, 1963), p. 121.

[30]Ibid., p. 125.

[31]Robert Sherwood, *Roosevelt and Hopkins: An Intimate History* (Harper, 1948), pp. 30, 49. Cf. Bonnie Fox Schwartz, *The Civil Works Administration: The Business of Emergency Employment in the New Deal* (Princeton, 1984), pp. 24–26.

[32]Ronald always refers to Jack's New Deal services as performed for the WPA. The local paper does not mention him in connection with any WPA projects—only FERA and CWA ones. But the FERA was the basis for both the CWA and the WPA, and one would expect Jack to continue into the WPA when it absorbed the FERA in 1935. Yet he could not have been with it for long, since Ronald says Jack's heart trouble kept him from employment before the parents moved to Hollywood (Hubler, p. 99), and that was in 1937 (Dixon *Daily Telegraph,* Sept. 1, 1937).

[33]Hubler, p. 64. The original text is: "To dole out relief *in this way* [omitted part in italics: Roosevelt is referring to his preceding passage on *direct* relief] is to minister a narcotic, a subtle destroyer of the human spirit . . . The Federal Government must and shall quit this business of relief." Fred L. Israel, editor, *The State of the Union Messages of the Presidents, 1790–1966* (Chelsea House), Vol. 3, p. 2815.

[34]Arthur W. McMahon, John D. Millett, and Gladys Ogden, *The Administration of Federal Work Relief* (Social Science Research Council, 1941), p. 23. Arthur M. Schlesinger, Jr., *The Coming of the New Deal* (Houghton Mifflin, 1958), p. 276; B. F. Schwartz, op. cit., pp. 218–20.

[35]Tugwell, op. cit., p. 449.

[36]Marriner S. Eccles, *Beckoning Frontiers: Public and Personal Recollections* (Knopf, 1951), p. 311.

[37]Some of Hopkins's worst problems with local interference were with the governor of Illinois and the Chicago Democratic establishment. "In Chicago it became neces-sary, as it did in several cities and states, to place an engineer in each CWA office, and to use army engineers as CWA state administrators, since they were relatively free from the need to play politics" (Searle F. Charles, *Minister of Relief: Harry Hopkins and the Depression,* Syracuse University, 1963, p. 57). In the Tweed novel, the narra-tor reports a discussion with the radical bureaucrat: "We discussed for a long time some of our difficulties—the limited powers of Congress in getting the State govern-ments to assent to remedial schemes on a national scale; the legal constrictions of working within the Constitution if it was suspected that such Amendments might affect the selfish interests of a small group of States" (p. 60).

[38]Israel, op. cit., p. 2815.

[39]Josephine Chapin Brown, *Public Relief, 1929–1939* (Henry Holt, 1940), pp. 159–60. Cf. B. F. Schwartz, op. cit., pp. 43, 257–59.

[40]Dixon *Daily Telegraph,* Nov. 13, 1933, Nov. 29, 1933.

[41]There were serious objections to the means test under the WPA. It forced people to sign up for welfare who did not want to. See Eccles, op. cit., pp. 185–86; H. H.

Adams, op. cit., p. 91. But the means test was an important bureaucratic tool for Hopkins in his competition for funds with Harold Ickes of the PWA: "His requirement that people on the relief rolls be given employment first was a major stumbling block to Ickes, because if Hopkins estimated there was insufficient unemployed labor in a community, its project would not be approved." Graham White and John Maze, *Harold Ickes of the New Deal: His Private Life and Public Career* (Harvard, 1985), p. 153.

CHAPTER 8

[1]William E. Leuchtenburg, *In the Shadow of FDR: From Harry Truman to Ronald Reagan* (Cornell University, 1983), pp. 209–17.

[2]Richard Gid Powers, *G-Men: Hoover's FBI in American Popular Culture* (Southern Illinois University, 1983), p. 217.

[3]Ibid., pp. xii–xiii, 293, and *The Challenge of Crime in a Free Society: A Report by the President's Commission on Law Enforcement and Administration of Justice* (Avon, 1968), pp. 101–5.

[4]Sanford Ungar, *The FBI* (Little, Brown, 1976), pp. 41–54.

[5]New York *Times*, June 3, 1933, quoted in Powers, op. cit., p. 39.

[6]Powers, op. cit., p. 44.

[7]Ibid., pp. 86, 173; Ungar, op. cit., pp. 55–56.

[8]Max Lowenthal, *The Federal Bureau of Investigation* (William Sloane, 1950), p. 380. Hoover, who had worked as a card-indexer at the Library of Congress while attending law school at night, became a master of files when he compiled the records of radicals for A. Mitchell Palmer in 1919. His campaign to fingerprint everyone in the United States established a basis for opening files on people without criminal records—a policy adopted in conscious defiance of legal precedent (ibid., pp. 173–84 and 375–77).

[9]Carlos Clarens, *Crime Movies: From Griffith to the Godfather and Beyond* (Norton, 1980), pp. 60, 81; Powers, op. cit., pp. 66–69.

[10]Jack Warner, *My First Hundred Years in Hollywood* (Random House, 1964), pp. 196, 208, 215–16, 285, 290–92; Michael Freedland, *The Warner Brothers* (St. Martin's, 1983), pp. 64–65, 116–17, 150–53.

[11]Andrew Bergman, *We're in the Money: Depression America and Its Films* (New York University, 1971), p. 102.

[12]Powers, op. cit., pp. 69–72.

[13]Ibid., pp. 51–73; Clarens, op. cit., pp. 124–27.

[14]Homer Dickens, *The Films of James Cagney* (Citadel, 1972), p. 100. There were seven G-Man pictures in 1935 (ibid., p. 65).

[15]Nick Roddick, *A New Deal in Entertainment: Warner Brothers in the 1930s* (British Film Institute, 1983), p. 109.

[16]Ibid.

[17]Ibid., pp. 73, 173–74, 252–54; Bergman, op. cit., pp. 96–109.

[18]Roddick, op. cit., pp. 128–29.

[19]Clarens, op. cit., pp. 134–35.

[20]Op. cit., pp. 135–36; Powers, op. cit.

[21]*Who's Who, 1936–1937.*

[22]Warner Bros. scripts in the Wisconsin Center for Film and Theater Research, temporary screenplay dated Nov. 9, 1938, final draft Nov. 23, 1938.

[23]Tony Thomas, *The Films of Ronald Reagan* (Citadel, 1980), photograph at p. 72.

[24]Ted Sennett, *Warner Brothers Presents* (Arlington, 1971), p. 380.

[25]*Murder in the Air* began as an anti-fascist film, first called *Uncle Sam Awakens,* then *The Enemy Within* (screenplays of Sept. 5, 1939, Sept. 9, 1939, and Sept. 13,

1939). The opening scenes were to be of goose-stepping Germans. But the Foy assembly line brought the villains back within the range of stereotype—foreign bolshies who call each other "Comrade."

[26]In fact, Clive Hirschhorn calls the Bancroft films an FBI series in *The Warner Brothers Story* (Crown, 1979), p. 212. In the film as shot, Bancroft gets his mission from a congressional committee investigating "un-American activities." This was seven years before he worked with the real thing.

CHAPTER 9

[1]Tampico *Tornado,* March 16, 1906.
[2]William W. Davis, *History of Whiteside County* (Chicago, 1908), p. 204; Tampico *Tornado,* Aug. 5, 1904.
[3]Wayne Bastian, *Whiteside County* (Henry, Illinois, 1968), pp. 439–43; Moline *Dispatch,* Aug. 9, 1968; Tampico *Tornado,* Sept. 19, 1903; Hubler, p. 15; Neil Reagan, California Oral History Project, 1981, UCLA Special Collections, p. 10.
[4]Cannon, p. 23; Davis, op. cit., p. 209; Harry Terry, the doctor who delivered the Reagan boys, was a Catholic *(Tampico Centennial Book: 1875–1975,* pp. 66–69).
[5]Bastian, op. cit., p. 432; Tampico *Tornado,* April 26, 1906. The monument cost the town seven hundred dollars.
[6]Ibid., p. 429
[7]Carter Goodrich, *Government Promotion of American Canals and Railroads, 1800–1890* (Columbia University, 1960), pp. 6–7. For Washington's and Jefferson's hopes for a canal system, see ibid., pp. 1, 32, 89, 299. John Quincy Adams hoped to see "the surface of the whole Union . . . checkered over with railroads and canals" before the middle of the century, and deplored the Jackson administration's withdrawal of support for the canals. Ibid., pp. 17, 41–42. For Lincoln's use of the "internal improvements" issue against Jacksonian Democrats, see Roy P. Basler, editor, *The Collected Works of Abraham Lincoln* (Rutgers, 1953), Vol. 1, pp. 503–6.
[8]Goodrich, op. cit., pp. 13, 41.
[9]Ibid., pp. 28–36. Henry Adams wrote of Albert Gallatin's plan: "Few persons have now any conception of the magnitude of the scheme thus originated." It was one "in comparison with which all the others were only fragments and playthings." *The Life of Albert Gallatin* (Lippincott, 1879), pp. 350–51.
[10]*Canals and Railroads of the Mid-Atlantic States, 1800–1860* (Regional Economic History Research Center, Wilmington, Delaware, 1981), unpaginated cumulative mileage tables in Appendices B and D. The system of federal land grants developed for the canals became the model for the later railroad grants. Cf. John Bell Rae, "Federal Land Grants in Aid of Canals," *Journal of Economic History,* Nov. 1944, pp. 167–77; Paul W. Gates, *History of Public Land Law Development* (Public Land Law Review Commission, 1968), pp. 350, 353, 358.
[11]Goodrich, op. cit., pp. 37, 142; James W. Putnam, *The Illinois and Michigan Canal: A Study in Economic History* (University of Chicago, 1918), pp. 1–29.
[12]Putnam, op. cit., pp. 17–18; Goodrich, op. cit., pp. 42, 230; Davis, op. cit., pp. 282–83. The quote is from Putnam, p. 155.
[13]Francis Parkman, *La Salle and the Discovery of the Great West* (1869), Ch. 5.
[14]Ibid., Ch. 7.
[15]Putnam, op. cit., pp. 38–42; Bastian, op. cit., pp. 138–41; Davis, op. cit., pp. 281–89.
[16]Davis, op. cit., p. 284; Dixon *Daily Telegraph,* June 9, 1881, June 30, 1886.
[17]Bastian, op. cit., 142.
[18]Yeater, op. cit., 142; Jim Arpy, *Quad-City Times,* May 26, 1980.
[19]Verl L. Lekwa, *Bennett, Iowa, and Inland Township* (Marceline, Mo., 1983), p.

11. Cf. Gates, op. cit., pp. 274–76, on Iowa as the leading state for military bounty land.

²⁰Cecil Eby, *"That Disgraceful Affair," The Black Hawk War* (Norton, 1973), p. 101. For Lincoln's applications to the Land Office for his successive warrants, see Basler, op. cit., Vol. 2, pp. 223, 319.

²¹Anthony F. C. Wallace, "Prelude to Disaster: The Course of Indian-White Relations Which Led to the Black Hawk War of 1832," the introductory essay to Ellen M. Whitney, *The Black Hawk War, 1831–1832,* four consecutive volumes (XXXV–XXXVIII) of *Collections of the Illinois State Historical Library* (Springfield, 1970–1978), XXXV, pp. 13–21. The 1804 treaty was not considered valid by the Sauks since women had not ratified it as tribal procedure required (ibid., pp. 6–7).

²²For an eyewitness account by one of the white settlers, see J. W. Spencer, *Reminiscences of Pioneer Life in the Mississippi Valley* (Davenport, 1872), reprinted in *The Early Day of Rock Island Davenport* (Chicago: Lakeside Press, 1942), pp. 23–25.

²³Wallace, op. cit., p. 36; Spencer, op. cit., p. 49, on the militia "doing me ten times as much damage [by stealing his crops] as the Indians had ever done." The comings and goings of volunteers in the militia, authorized and unauthorized, was so casual that even the steady Lincoln served in three different companies in less than three months as a militiaman—first as an elected captain, twice as a private after successive musterings out of his fellows. See Frank E. Stevens, *The Black Hawk War* (Chicago, 1903), p. 286.

²⁴Wallace, op. cit., p. 51.

²⁵Ibid., p. 39.

²⁶Francis Paul Prucha, *The Sword of the Republic: The United States Army on the Frontier, 1783–1846* (Macmillan, 1969), pp. 225–26; Charles W. Elliot, *Winfield Scott: The Soldier and the Man* (Macmillan, 1937), p. 262.

²⁷Ibid., p. 226; Wallace, op. cit., pp. 2, 51.

²⁸Ibid., pp. 228–29.

²⁹Colonel Zachary Taylor and Lieutenant Jefferson Davis were both serving at Fort Crawford (Prairie du Chien) at the end of the Black Hawk War and, though the men disliked each other, the future President of the Confederate States fell in love with a daughter of the future President of the United States, and married her. Cf. Brainerd Dyer, *Zachary Taylor* (Louisiana State University, 1946), pp. 96–98.

³⁰*Wisconsin Historical Collections,* Vol. 12, pp. 260–61.

³¹For his registry before service in the militia, and loss of the election after, see Basler, op. cit., Vol. 1, pp. 5, 13.

³²In an 1848 campaign pamphlet, reproduced from a speech in the House, Lincoln mocked the depiction of candidate Lewis Cass as a military hero: "He *in*vaded Canada without resistance, and he *out*vaded it without pursuit." Cass's war exploits were so absurd that "speaking of Gen: Cass' career, reminds me of my own," and Lincoln hopes that if, *per impossible,* he should ever run for President, his friends "shall not make fun of me, as they have of Gen: Cass, by attempting to write me into a military hero." Basler, op. cit., Vol. 1, pp. 509–10.

³³W. M. Hummel, *Positive Knowledge and a Personal Opinion of Wabokieshiek* (privately printed at Prophetstown). Wabokieshiek was the Prophet's name.

³⁴In the 1832 war, Lincoln was at Dixon's Ferry for a week as a captain (May 12–19), three more times as a private (for a day each on June 8 and June 13, then for the week June 21–27), and for a day in mid-July as a newly mustered-out civilian on his way home. Stevens, op. cit., pp. 284, 286–88—Stevens chronicled the affairs of Dixon with special attention, since he was born there (cf. Hudson Strode, *Jefferson Davis, American Patriot: 1808–1861,* Harcourt, Brace & World, 1955, p. 66).

³⁵"It is quite certain I did not break my sword, for I had none to break, but I bent a musket pretty badly on one occasion." Basler, op. cit., Vol. 1, p. 510.

³⁶On Dixon, see Whitney, op. cit., Vol. 2, pp. 60–61; Stevens, op. cit., pp. 291–92;

Frank E. Stevens, *History of Lee County* (Chicago, 1914), Vol. 1, pp. 253–56. For the land rush to the area after the Black Hawk War, cf. Malcolm Rohrbaugh, *The Land Office Business: The Settlement and Administration of American Public Lands, 1789–1837* (Oxford, 1968), pp. 238–40.

[37]Another founder of Davenport used his rewards as interpreter for the Army during the war: cf. Charles Snyder, "Antoine LeClaire, the First Proprietor of Davenport," *Annals of Iowa,* Series 3, No. 23 (1941–42), pp. 79–117.

[38]Albert J. Beveridge, *Abraham Lincoln, 1809–1858* (Houghton Mifflin, 1928), Vol. 1, pp. 597–605.

[39]Ibid., p. 25: "No one member of the General Assembly had done more than Lincoln to fasten upon the State the Internal Improvement scheme, and, now [1839] that it was beginning to crumble, he came forward with a plan to strengthen and continue it." Also pp. 196–98, 251–57.

[40]Ibid., pp. 684–97. For Jackson's opposition to improvements, cf. Gates, op. cit., p. 352.

[41]For Douglas and the first railway land grant, cf. Gates, op. cit., pp. 350, 357. For the importance of the Illinois Central in the Lincoln-Douglas campaign, cf. Gates, *The Illinois Central Railroad and Its Colonization Work* (Harvard, 1934), pp. 243–45.

CHAPTER 10

[1]John D. Unruh, Jr., *The Plains Across: The Overland Emigrants and the Trans-Mississippi West, 1840–1868* (University of Illinois, 1979), p. 201.

[2]*The Education of Henry Adams* (1906), Ch. 15: "On this new scale of power, merely to make the continent habitable for civilized people would require an immediate outlay that would have bankrupted the world. . . . The field was vast, altogether beyond its power to control offhand; and society dropped every thought of dealing with anything more than the single fraction called a railway system. This relatively small part of its task was still so big as to need the energies of a generation, for it required all the new machinery to be created—capital, banks, mines, furnaces, shops, power-houses, technical knowledge, mechanical population, together with a steady remodeling of social and political habits, ideas, and institutions to fit the new scale and suit the new conditions. The generation between 1865 and 1895 was already mortgaged to the railways, and no one knew it better than the generation itself." The large-scale corruption of government involved in financing the railroads sullied the reputation of two leading Disciples of Christ, James Garfield and former Attorney General Jeremiah Black (John Noonan, *Bribes,* Macmillan, 1984, pp. 446–98).

[3]Carter Goodrich, *Government Promotion of American Canals and Railroads, 1800–1890* (Columbia University, 1960), pp. 183–204.

[4]For the Civil War's annihilation tactics, cf. Russell F. Weighley, "American Strategy from Its Beginnings Through the First World War," in Peter Paret, *Makers of Modern Strategy from Machiavelli to the Nuclear Age* (Princeton, 1986), pp. 424–36.

[5]John S. Hutchins, "Mounted Riflemen: The Real Role of Cavalry in the Indian Wars," in *Probing the American West: Papers from the Santa Fe Conference* (Museum of New Mexico Press, 1962), pp. 79–85. Francis Parkman's *Oregon Trail* of 1843 vividly records problems with horse supply, maintenance, protection, loss, and injury in the West.

[6]Cf. Frank Gilbert Roe on Indians' treatment of "the horse as a dragoon's transport asset rather than a cavalry arm": *The Indian and the Horse* (University of Oklahoma, 1955), pp. 229–31.

[7]Hutchins, op. cit., p. 82.

[8]Unruh, op. cit., p. 201. On civilian longing for dragoon escorts along the Oregon Trail in 1843, cf. Parkman op. cit., Ch. 5.

⁹Ray Allen Billington, *Westward Expansion: A History of the American Frontier,* 3rd ed. (New York, 1967), p. 678.

¹⁰Robert R. Dykstra, *The Cattle Towns* (Knopf, 1968), p. 146. Dykstra compiled his figures from the newspapers of the territory.

¹¹Ibid., p. 123. There was a rapidly growing set of regulations for law officers (ibid., pp. 123–24), and when the cattle drivers were not in town, the police officials were often given menial chores like street maintenance—a job the Wichita city council assigned to Wyatt Earp in 1873 (p. 124).

¹²For the numbers of herd tenders, cf. William W. Savage, Jr., *The Cowboy Hero: His Image in American History and Culture* (University of Oklahoma, 1979), p. 8. For the gun laws in Kansas, cf. Dykstra, op. cit., p. 121.

¹³Dykstra, op. cit., pp. 142–43.

¹⁴Ibid., pp. 269–74.

¹⁵Ibid., pp. 116, 289.

¹⁶The form for legally declaring anyone "outlaw" can be seen in Jefferson's revision of the Virginia statutes—e.g., the one for a white woman who, having borne a black man's child, refused to "depart the commonwealth" within a year: "the woman shall be out of the protection of the laws" Julian Boyd, editor, *The Papers of Thomas Jefferson* (Princeton, 1950), Vol. 2, p. 471. Frederick Jackson Turner made Jefferson his first great type of the frontier man (*The Frontier in American History,* Henry Holt, 1920), pp. 93–94, 105. On this point, at least, Turner was unintentionally right. For his intended errors, cf. Richard Hofstadter, *The Progressive Historians* (Knopf, 1968), pp. 133–34.

¹⁷This bears a remarkable resemblance to a passage in Parkman that Twain was not only reading as he worked on *Huckleberry Finn* but actually quoted in *Life on the Mississippi* (Ch. 2)—a European's first sight of a buffalo: "the fierce and stupid look of the old bulls, as they stared at the intruders through the tangled mane which nearly blinded them" *(La Salle and the Great West,* Ch. 5). In his next novel, too, Twain would describe "brawny men, with long, coarse, uncombed hair that hung down over their face and made them look like animals" *(A Connecticut Yankee in King Arthur's Court,* Ch. 1). The fastidious man in the white suit hated the dirt of the frontier, as of the middle ages. He wrote that soap alone would be the greatest challenge to the medieval church's despotism *(Connecticut Yankee,* Chs. 16, 24).

¹⁸The Santa Fe line for instance, supported the reform party in Dodge City (Dykstra, op. cit., p. 274).

¹⁹Ibid., p. 253. In Caldwell, Kansas, a man who persisted in selling liquor was lynched by the Vigilance Committee (ibid., p. 289).

²⁰Ibid., p. 278.

²¹Aileen S. Kraditor, *The Ideas of the Woman Suffrage Movement, 1890–1920* (Anchor, 1971), p. 3.

²²Alan P. Grimes, *The Puritan Ethic and Woman Suffrage* (Oxford, 1967), p. xi. Mormon women were the first to vote, to give their group more weight than that of "gentiles" in Utah. But similar pressures gave women the vote in other states, to protect territorial communities from "unrespectable" types, gentility playing a role like religion's as the *communal* bond.

²³Ibid., p. 131.

²⁴William H. McNeill, *The Great Frontier: Freedom and Hierarchy in Modern Times* (Princeton, 1983), p. 20. Cf. Hofstadter, op. cit., pp. 130–32, on the "social stratification" that rapidly asserted itself on the frontier, so that "egalitarianism actually lost ground." Also, Francis S. Philbrick, *The Rise of the West, 1754–1830* (Harper & Row, 1965), pp. 366ff.

²⁵McNeill, p. 26. For frontier tendencies to shelter behind military guards and to accept emergency authorities, cf. Owen Lattimore, "The Frontier in History," *Studies in Frontier History, 1928–1958* (Oxford, 1962), pp. 476, 487.

[26]Hofstadter, op. cit., p. 144. Cf. Mody C. Boatright, "The Myth of Frontier Individualism," in Hofstadter and Lipset, *Turner and the Sociology of the Frontier* (Basic Books, 1968), pp. 43–64. Contrast this with Turner's belief that westerners were so "atomic" that they showed a consistent "antipathy to control" or "impatience of restraints" (op. cit., pp. 30, 212, 306).

[27]It is interesting that Black Hawk was one of the Indians who realized the danger of liquor to an imperiled people, and became a Sauk version of Carrie Nation, tomahawking whiskey barrels whenever he could. Cf. J. W. Spencer, *Reminiscences of Pioneer Life in the Mississippi Valley* (Davenport, 1872), p. 27.

[28]Charles A. Johnson, *The Frontier Camp Meeting: Religion's Harvest Time* (Southern Methodist University Press, 1955), pp. 41–66, 208–28.

[29]Ibid., pp. 8–18.

[30]McNeill, op. cit., pp. 42–43; Donald Worster, *Rivers of Empire: Water, Aridity, and the Growth of the American West* (Pantheon, 1985), pp. 74–83. Set apart from other settlers in many ways, the Mormons shared their intense hatred of American Indians. Cf. A. Irving Hallowell, "The Backwash of the Frontier," in *The Frontier in Perspective* (ed. Walker D. Wyman and Clifton D. Droeber, University of Wisconsin, 1957, pp. 244–45).

[31]Grimes, op. cit., p. 30: "The Mormon settlement of Utah was probably the most successful experiment in large-scale social planning and social engineering in American history."

[32]Henry Nash Smith, "Mark Twain as an Interpreter of the Far West: The Structure of *Roughing It,*" in Wyman and Kroeber, op. cit., p. 225.

[33]Fernand Braudel, *The Perspective of the World,* translated from the French by Sian Reynolds (Harper & Row, 1982), pp. 207ff.; Immanuel Wallerstein, *The Modern World-System* (Academic Press, 1974), Vol. 1, pp. 301ff. Donald Worster argues that the imperial expansion has reached the point, now, where the West has "become a principal seat of the world-circling Empire" (op. cit., p. 15).

[34]For technological superiority along the frontier, cf. McNeill, op. cit., pp. 11–13; Howard Lamar and Leonard Thompson, *The Frontier in History: North America and Southern Africa Compared,* p. 9. McNeill includes among technical skills the facilities for travel that made the intruders acquire an immunity to many of the diseases they carried. Cf. Lamar and Thompson, pp. 26–27, 189–90. For slave labor on the frontier, cf. Braudel, op. cit., pp. 392–99; Wallerstein, op. cit., Vol. 2, pp. 171–75; McNeill, pp. 50–51. Since North American Indians proved hard to enslave, America's first frontier was worked by imported slaves, forming the capital base for expansion of later frontiers. Also, the railroads in California were built by coolie labor, as were those of western Canada. (Coolie labor also played a role in the Peruvian guano trade and the Australian gold rush.)

[35]Hofstadter, *The Progressive Historians,* p. 134.

[36]On Turner's neglect of the frontier as a conflict with American Indian cultures, cf. Robert F. Berkhofer, Jr., "The North American Frontier as Process and Context," in Lamar and Thompson, op. cit., pp. 43–75. Turner's picture of the West as offering "free land" neglects the fact that it first became government land by conquest or purchase or treaty, not only from Indian chiefs and tribes, but from Napoleon and Alexander III, from General de Santa Anna and Queen Liliuokalani. Heavy speculation in the government lands, through literal "land office business," created land "barons," cattle barons, and railroad barons, with a wage-earning work force more common than the freeholder or yeoman of myth—and even that storied character, when he did exist, was "a little capitalist, often by necessity a rather speculative one operating in the new and uncertain Western world along with big capitalists like the land speculator and the railroader" (Hofstadter, op. cit., p. 159). Cf. Paul Wallace Gates, *Frontier Landlords and Pioneer Tenants* (Cornell, 1954), and Leslie E. Decker,

"The Great Speculation: An Interpretation of Mid-Continent Pioneering," in *The Frontier in American Development* (ed. David M. Ellis, Cornell, 1969), pp. 357–80.

[37]Lattimore, op. cit., p. 490. Cf. Benjamin F. Wright, "Political Institutions and the Frontier," *Sources of Culture in the Middle West: Backgrounds Versus Frontier* (ed. Dixon Ryan Fox, D. Appleton-Century, 1934), pp. 15–38. Cf. James O. Steffen, *Comparative Frontiers: A Proposal for Studying the American West* (University of California, 1980), pp. xiii–xvi, 12, 19, 29, 31, 73.

[38]Lattimore, op. cit., pp. 490–91. And there was more differentiation in western Canada than Lattimore estimated. Cf. Marvin W. Mikesell, "Comparative Studies in Frontier History," in Hofstadter and Lipset, op. cit., pp. 157–60.

[39]Lattimore, op. cit., p. 489.

[40]Hofstadter, op. cit., p. 160: "We must think of the West as a magnificent area for the rapid expansion of middle-class society, and remember that the 'pioneer' went westward not to be a self-sufficient yeoman but to find a stronger position in the market, not to live forever in a log cabin or a sod house but to build as soon as possible a substantial frame house, not to enjoy a primitive or wilderness environment but to recreate for himself the American standard of living as he had seen it in the East, not to forge a utopian egalitarian society but to re-order the social differences of the older world—with himself now closer to the top."

[41]Albert Bigelow Paine, editor, *Mark Twain's Letters* (Harper, 1916), Vol. 1, p. 289. Twain's view of small towns is suggested by his claim that the Gadarene swine were content to be used in an exorcism if it got them out of places like Capernaum and Tiberias: "The swine of the miracle ran down into the sea, and doubtless thought it was better to swallow a devil or two and get drowned into the bargain than to have to live any longer in such a place." *Innocents Abroad,* Ch. 48.

CHAPTER 11

[1]Details about B. J. Palmer's life are taken, unless otherwise annotated, from his son's book *The Palmers* by Dave Palmer (Bawden Bros., 1977), available in the Palmer Collection of the Palmer College, pp. 16–20, 29–32, 38–39, 48–49, 75–78, 86, 95, 102, 107–10, 133, 138–40, 153–56, 168–69, 173.

[2]Joseph Maynard, *Healing Hands* (Mobile, Alabama, undated), p. 118.

[3]Ibid., p. 123. This page also gives the price of admission to "A Little Bit O'Heaven."

[4]Lecture titles from Palmer School Lyceum advertisement, Davenport *Democrat,* Aug. 16, 1914.

[5]From WOC promotional tour pamphlet of the twenties.

[6]Palmer School Yearbook, 1929.

[7]WOC tour pamphlet.

[8]Mimeographed account of the station from B.J. files at the Palmer School.

[9]History of the station from B.J. file and from the Davenport *Daily Times,* Oct. 8, 1931, May 11, 1933, and Jan. 2, 1938.

[10]*The Confidence-Man* (1857), Ch. 19.

[11]*History in the Making,* "by B. J. of Davenport—philosopher, scientist, artist, builder, hobbyist, musician, author, lecturer, publisher, art connoisseur—a bit of a moral human being whom Innate Intelligence developed" (Davenport, Iowa, 1957), p. 22.

[12]Jeane J. Kirkpatrick, "Politics and the 'New Class,'" from *Dictatorships and Double Standards* (Simon and Schuster, 1982). This essay sharpens the analysis made of 1972 McGovern delegates as a "new breed" in Kirkpatrick's *The New Presidential Elite: Men and Women in National Politics* (Russell Sage Foundation, 1976).

[13]Jack Dales, California Oral History Project, Special Collections, UCLA, pp. 8, 48.

[14]*The New Presidential Elite,* p. 356.

[15]Ibid., p. 252.

[16]Ibid., pp. 65, 65–69. Kirkpatrick calls her new breed "rectitude specialists" (p. 116). Cf. *Dictatorships and Double Standards,* p. 195.

[17]*The New Presidential Elite,* pp. 9, 65, 72, 295.

[18]Ibid., pp. 5, 356.

[19]Hubler, p. 57. Dave Palmer tells no stories about Reagan's days working for the Palmer family in Davenport or Des Moines in his book, *The Palmers.* He lists Reagan among those who visited the mansion (p. 13)—certain broadcasts, especially those using B.J.'s beloved organ, originated from the mansion, so Reagan's could have been a working "visit." He also says Reagan used the family tennis court (p. 39) —though Reagan, with his poor vision, did not play much tennis. Finally, he reproduces on p. 61 a picture of Reagan, who appears about the age of his GE years of service, uneffusively inscribed, "To Dave, With Warm Regard, Dutch" (p. 81).

[20]Dixon *Daily Telegraph,* Feb. 10, 1933; Davenport *Daily Times,* May 11, 1933.

[21]Davenport *Times,* May 25, 1980, article by Bill Wundram.

[22]Richard M. Sudhalter and Philip R. Evans, *Bix: Man and Legend* (Arlington House, 1974), p. 39.

[23]Ibid., p. 334.

[24]Davenport *Times,* Mar. 15, 1981, article by Jim Arpy. Daniel J. Czitrom, *Media and the American Mind: From Morse to McLuhan* (University of North Carolina, 1982), pp. 79–80. A good example of the drift from vaudeville to sound *film* was the pioneering career of Bryan Foy, one of the "Seven Little Foys" stage act. He made the early Warner Bros. sound shorts of 1927 and 1928. Douglas Gomery, "The Coming of Sound: Technological Change in the American Film Industry," in *Film Sound, Theory and Practice* (Columbia University, 1985), pp. 14–15. This experience prepared Foy for the Warner Bros. B unit that put out the Brass Bancroft series, where another "Little Foy," Eddy, Jr., Bryan's brother, played Reagan's "stooge."

[25]H. G. Wells, *The New America, The New World* (Macmillan, 1935), p. 25.

[26]Davenport *Daily Times,* May 11, 1933.

[27]Des Moines *Dispatch,* March 31, April 21, May 12, 1933.

[28]Interview with Harold Risser in Des Moines.

[29]Des Moines *Tribune,* interview with Walter E. Shotwell, June 6, 1980.

[30]Dixon *Daily Telegraph,* Sept. 4, 1934, Jan. 21, 1936.

CHAPTER 12

[1]Francis Paul Prucha, *Great Father: The United States Government and the American Indians* (University of Nebraska, 1984), Vol. 1, p. 257.

[2]In the seventeenth century, the whimsy of French explorers had turned ill-understood Indian sounds into "La Rivière des Moines," the Monks' River. Charles H. Keyes, "Des Moines River, and the Origin of the Name," *Annals of Iowa,* Vol. 3, pp. 553–59.

[3]Benjamin F. Gue, *History of Iowa* (New York, 1903), Vol. 4, pp. 236–37. *Iowa: A Guide to the Hawkeye State: Compiled and Written by the Federal Writers' Project* (Viking, 1938), pp. 229–30.

[4]Gue, op. cit., Vol. 1, p. 237.

[5]Will Porter, *Annals of Polk County, Iowa, and City of Des Moines* (Des Moines, 1898), pp. 177–79. Daniel Blue not only lost but ate his brothers on the trip, according to his own sensational account: *A Thrilling Narrative of the Adventures, Suffering and Starvation of Pike's Peak Gold Seekers on the Plains of the West* (Morrison, Ill.,

1859). The brothers, lost and starving, bound each other to live off the flesh of the first to die. Alexander died first, and Charles and Daniel fulfilled the agreement. Then Charles died, and only Daniel lived to tell this tale of consensual and fraternal cannibalism when he returned to normal family life and the notoriety of his own pamphlet. Cf. Charles Bent, *History of Whiteside County, Illinois* (Morrison, 1877), pp. 145–46; Wayne Bastian, *Whiteside County* (Henry, Illinois, 1968), p. 161. Daniel was the brother of Nelle Reagan's grandmother, Jane Blue Wilson.

[6]Gue, op. cit., Vol. 4, p. 237.

[7]*Federal Writers' Project*, pp. 231–32.

[8]Ibid., pp. 227, 233, 246.

[9]Rexford G. Tugwell, *The Democratic Roosevelt* (Doubleday, 1957), pp. 424–25.

[10]Interview in Des Moines with Mrs. Moon.

[11]Des Moines *Dispatch*, May 21, 1937.

[12]Gene Raffensberger, "Reagan Saved Woman in '33 From Robber," Des Moines *Register*, Jan. 28, 1984.

[13]Interview in Des Moines with Mrs. King. *Sports Afield*, Feb. 1984.

[14]Des Moines *Tribune*, Sept. 22, 1980. This is one of a series of valuable articles on Reagan's days in Des Moines by Walter E. Shotwell of the *Tribune*.

[15]*Federal Writers' Project*, p. 228.

[16]Ibid., p. 246.

[17]Interview with Mrs. Moon.

[18]California Oral History Project, June 25, 1981, UCLA Special Collections.

[19]Charles J. Ritchey, *Drake University Through Seventy-Five Years, 1881–1956* (Drake University, 1956), pp. 27–35.

[20]Drake (1830–1903) had twice gone to California seeking gold before he distinguished himself in the Civil War, from which he emerged a Brigadier General of Volunteers. After his business successes, he was elected Governor of Iowa in 1896. His father, who served in the Iowa legislature, had been a friend of Disciples founder Alexander Campbell. *A Memorial and Biographical Record of Iowa* (Chicago: Lewis Company, 1896), pp. 11–13.

[21]It was disturbing, however, that the first fall registration date occurred on the day Garfield died of his assassin's wounds. Ritchey, op. cit., p. 36.

[22]Des Moines *Dispatch*, Sept. 16, 1934.

[23]Interview with Mr. Johnson, now living in Escondido, California.

[24]Interview with Mr. Claussen, now living in San Marcos, California.

[25]Interview with Mrs. Moon.

[26]Interview in Monmouth, Illinois, with Mrs. Gertrude Romine, about her cousin, Mrs. Mildred Brown, on whose dates with Reagan see Monmouth *Review-Atlas*, Feb. 24, 1976.

[27]Carey McWilliams, *Southern California Country: An Island on the Land* (Dell, Sloan & Pierce, 1946), pp. 162–64.

[28]Josephine Kingsbury Jacobs, "Sunkist Advertising—The Iowa Campaign," in *Los Angeles: Biography of a City*, edited by John and Laree Caughey (University of California, 1976), pp. 215–18.

[29]For the Iowa Club as the most influential of the important state clubs of California, see McWilliams, op. cit., pp. 166–75. For the Iowa Day picnic, *Los Angeles, the Ultimate City* (Oxford, 1967), pp. 136–38.

[30]Des Moines *Register*, April 4, 1937.

[31]Ibid., Feb. 5, 1937.

[32]Interview with Glen Claussen, now living in San Marcos.

[33]Walter E. Shotwell, Des Moines *Register*, June 6, 1980; Myron Waldman, *Newsday*, January 18, 1981.

[34]Des Moines *Dispatch*, April 16, 1937.

[35]Letter from Reagan to his agent, George Ward, in April 1937, quoted from Ward's copy by Hugh Sidey, *Time,* June 17, 1985.

[36]Des Moines *Register,* April 4, 1937.

[37]Des Moines *Dispatch,* May 21, 1937; Dixon *Daily Telegraph,* May 20, 1937.

CHAPTER 13

[1]"Dutch Debates Rose Bowl Versus Sugar Bowl Games," Des Moines *Dispatch,* Dec. 18, 1936. Unfortunately, I have not been able to find a complete edition of Des Moines's short-lived "third paper" of the 1930s, the *Dispatch.* The Des Moines Public Library has a volume of the first year (1933–34), and the Iowa Historical Building has microfilms of 1938–39. But Reagan's column—"Around the World of Sports with Dutch Reagan"—was made a regular feature after his first appearance in the paper on June 2, 1935, and he wrote until he was given his Hollywood contract in 1937. Myrtle Williams Moon remembers finishing some columns for Reagan when he had to go on the road to cover teams, but she kept no samples. The few *Dispatch* columns and clippings I have were turned up in B. J. Palmer's own file of newspaper items about his radio stations. That file is at the Palmer School in Davenport.

[2]Des Moines *Dispatch,* Feb. 5, 1937.

[3]Grantland Rice, *"The Final Answer" and Other Poems* (A. S. Barnes, 1955), p. 69.

[4]*The Dixonian,* 1927.

[5]Des Moines *Dispatch,* Dec. 18, 1936.

[6]Ibid., Feb. 4, 1937. Reagan's attitude is that of Grantland Rice's poem "A Sporting Epitaph" (op. cit., p. 66): "And when the bell gave out its ringing call,/He had not much to give—but gave it all."

[7]Thorstein Veblen, *The Theory of the Leisure Class* (1899), Penguin, 1981, pp. 256–57.

[8]Benjamin G. Rader, *In Its Own Image: How Television Has Transformed Sports* (Free Press, 1984), p. 20.

[9]Ibid., p. 25. Oliver Pilat, *Pegler: Angry Man of the Press* (Beacon, 1963), p. 101.

[10]Rader, op. cit., p. 29.

[11]Ibid., p. 30.

[12]Ibid., p. 28.

[13]Garry Trudeau, *The Doonesbury Chronicles* (Holt, Rinehart and Winston, 1975), Introduction.

[14]Philip Roth, *Portnoy's Complaint* (Simon and Schuster, 1984), p. 254.

[15]Des Moines *Dispatch,* Aug. 24, 1934.

[16]Rader, op. cit., p. 22.

[17]Ibid., p. 30. Stern was heaping further myth on the mythical in this case, since no contemporary record shows any connection between baseball and its supposed "inventor," Abner Doubleday.

[18]Grantland Rice, *The Tumult and the Shouting: My Life in Sport* (A. S. Barnes, 1954), p. 182.

[19]Michael R. Steele, *Knute Rockne, A Biblio-Biography* (Greenwood, 1983), p. 33. This, the only scrupulously researched book on Rockne, is written by a Notre Dame alumnus who admirably combines affection for his material with objectivity in judging it.

[20]Coles Phinizy, *Sports Illustrated,* Sept. 10, 1979, pp. 106–7. Steele (op. cit., pp. 189–91) discusses the Phinizy articles as the best magazine treatment of Rockne.

[21]Ibid., pp. 107–8.

[22]Ibid., p. 107.

[23]Steele, op. cit., p. 20.

[24]Coles Phinizy, *Sports Illustrated,* Sept. 17, 1979, p. 42; Rice, op. cit., p. 176.

[25]Steele, op. cit., p. 20.

[26]Ibid., p. 196.

[27]Michael Steele extenuates Rockne's lifelong "embellishment of the truth" (p. 10) by saying "he sincerely believed in the moral core of the anecdotes while attending very little to the actual vehicle that carried his message" (p. 190).

[28]Ibid., p. 23.

[29]Ibid., p. 40.

[30]Since the movie postdates the shift, Gipp is not allowed to run from it on film, as he did in life; he is changed from a halfback to a tailback. Steele, op. cit., p. 195. The movie also has the team undefeated before the "Win one for the Gipper" game (they were 0 for 2 in fact), and scoreless till the last minutes (Chevigny scored the first touchdown in the third quarter). Steele was unable to see Pat O'Brien's plea to "Win one for the Gipper" while writing his book, since that was cut from all prints of the film as it was released to television, in order to avoid a possible plagiarism suit. Even Notre Dame stopped showing its uncut print for a while (though the archivist showed it for me in 1984). The scene has been restored on videocassettes. One speech in the movie rings especially hollow for those who know about Gipp's heavy bets on Notre Dame games. O'Brien as Rockne warns a gambler away from his team with the words: "You've done your best to ruin baseball and boxing. This is one game that's clean and it's going to stay clean."

[31]Reagan complained to Father Hesburgh, the university's president, that he could not find an uncut version of the film. Hesburgh had a copy of Notre Dame's print made and delivered to the White House.

[32]Lou Cannon, *Reagan* (Putnam, 1982), p. 55.

[33]Warners did not want to use O'Brien for the Rockne role. He looked too soft and tubby. But Notre Dame University vetoed the studio's choice, James Cagney, since Catholic organizations were boycotting Cagney for his support to the Loyalist cause in the Spanish Civil War. The university insisted on O'Brien, and got him. Then O'Brien helped Reagan get the Gipp role. Cf. Rudy Behlmer, *Inside Warner Bros. (1935–1957)*, Viking, 1985, pp. 113–16.

[34]The first Notre Dame player to become an All-American was Gipp.

[35]Since Reagan admits elsewhere (Hubler, p. 109) that Rockne may have made up the deathbed request, one cannot say he refrained from using it for eight years. He could not use it until he had invented it. If he made it up under pressure the day before the game, as he did material for his other pep talks, he did not even wait until the day was over before using it—on Grantland Rice.

[36]Cf. Hubler, p. 110: "As in every picture based on real-life exploits, truth was stranger than fiction. There were scenes that couldn't be photographed because an audience wouldn't accept the truth, or it would appear too melodramatic. For instance it is told that Jack Chevigny, who carried the last touchdown over the goal line in that game and then was carried off the field himself with a broken leg, looked up from the stretcher and said, 'That's the last one I can get for you, Gipper.' " In fact, the movie correctly showed Jack Chevigny shouting, "That's one for the Gipper" when he made the first (not the last) touchdown. Removed from the game by an injury (but not a broken leg), Chevigny continued to shout from the sidelines, "One for the Gipper," according to Frank Carideo, the game's quarterback (Phinizy, *Sports Illustrated,* Sept. 17, 1979, p. 47). Cf. Steele, op. cit., p. 40. For the Warner studio's own boast that "many scenes in that picture never actually occurred as we showed them," cf. Behlmer, op. cit., p. 182.

[37]Cannon, *Reagan,* pp. 55–56. On the opening day of the 1984 Olympics, July 28, Reagan told a radio audience, "Today I find my thoughts turning from politics to something equally important . . ."

[38]For the role of his pep talks in winning Rockne a lucrative position at Studebaker, cf. Steele, op. cit., p. 41. Rockne was good in school plays as a Notre Dame under-

graduate (Phinizy, *Sports Illustrated*, Sept. 10, 1979, p. 101), and Grantland Rice says Rockne was theatrical, not only in his use of his voice but in the timing of his entrances *(The Tumult and the Shouting*, p. 188). This theatrical bent was about to get full expression, in a Hollywood movie, when Rockne died of a plane crash at age forty-three.

[39]Roger Simon, *Simon Says* (Contemporary Books, 1985), pp. 36–37.

[40]William A. Henry, III, *Visions of America: How We Saw the 1984 Election* (Atlantic, 1985), p. 39. Beatty's story is confirmed precisely because he could not get its point. Reagan regularly pairs the tale of the American airman, who wins a posthumous Congressional Medal of Honor, with the story of Russia giving Trotsky's murderer the Stalin Medal: "That explains the difference between our societies." For the repeated use of these twinned stories, cf. Paul D. Erickson, *Reagan Speaks: The Making of an American Myth* (New York University, 1985), pp. 5–7. After Reagan's use of the unverifiable tale in the White House, his aides finally got him to drop it (for a while, at least). Cf. New York *Times*, Sept. 20, 1984 ("Briefing"). Though Reagan continued to claim the pilot was real and received a Medal of Honor, he seems to have come from the 1944 film, *A Wing and a Prayer*, where Dana Andrews says, "We'll take this ride together."

CHAPTER 14

[1]Coles Phinizy, *Sports Illustrated*, Sept. 17, 1979, p. 47.

[2]Michael R. Steele, *Knute Rockne, A Biblio-Biography* (Greenwood, 1983), p. 191.

[3]Thorstein Veblen, *The Theory of the Leisure Class* (1899), Penguin, 1981, pp. 268–69. The need to justify athletics in extraathletic terms is so standardized that coaches' admonitions fall into outline form in Don DeLillo's *End Zone* (Houghton Mifflin, 1972), p. 19: "(1) A team sport. (2) The need to sacrifice. (3) Preparation for the future. (4) Microcosm of life."

[4]John Updike, *Rabbit, Run* (Fawcett, 1966), p. 24.

[5]Jeremy Larner, *Drive, He Said* (Bantam, 1971), pp. 3, 49.

[6]Ernest Hemingway, *The Old Man and the Sea* (Scribner, 1952), p. 75.

[7]Bob Slosser, *Reagan Inside Out* (Word Books, 1984), pp. 38, 48.

[8]Sinclair Lewis, *Elmer Gantry* (1927), Signet, 1971, p. 43: "He had them stretching with admiration as he arched his big shoulder-muscles and observed that he would knock the block off any sneering, sneaking, lying, beer-bloated bully who should dare to come up to *him* in a meeting and try to throw a monkey-wrench into the machinery by dragging out a lot of contemptible, quibbling, atheistic, smart-aleck doubts!"

[9]Veblen, op. cit., pp. 254–55.

[10]Benjamin G. Rader, *In Its Own Image: How Television Has Transformed Sports* (Free Press, 1984), p. 30.

[11]Grantland Rice, *"The Final Answer" and Other Poems* (A. S. Barnes, 1955), p. 76.

[12]Rader, op. cit., p. 19.

[13]Lou Cannon, *Reagan* (Putnam, 1982), p. 36, quoting Reagan's account from the Rockford *Morning Star*.

[14]Ibid.

[15]Grantland Rice, *The Tumult and the Shouting: My Life in Sport* (A. S. Barnes, 1954), p. 181.

[16]Terry Ramsaye, *A Million and One Nights: A History of the Motion Picture* (Simon and Schuster, 1926), Vol. 2, pp. 408–11.

[17]Robert Conot, *A Streak of Luck* (Seaview, 1979), pp. 329–30; Matthew Josephson, *Edison* (McGraw-Hill, 1959), pp. 392–96; Ramsaye, op. cit., Vol. 1, p. 110.

[18]Rader, op. cit., p. 24.

[19]Ibid., pp. 27–28.

CHAPTER 15

[1]Walter E. Shotwell interview with Mr. Jerrel, Des Moines *Tribune,* June 6, 1980.

[2]Donald Day, *Will Rogers* (David McKay, 1962), p. 307.

[3]Daniel J. Czitrom, *Media and the American Mind: From Morse to McLuhan* (University of North Carolina, 1982), pp. 75–76.

[4]Alexander Walker, *Shattered Silents: How the Talkies Came To Stay* (Morrow, 1979), p. 101.

[5]Ibid., p. 94.

[6]Anita Loos, *The Talmadge Girls* (Viking, 1978), p. 2: "Actually, Norma's voice was not in the least disagreeable and she had no trace of a Brooklyn accent. But the heroines she played were noble creatures, and Norma's intonation lacked nobility."

[7]Donat Gallagher, editor, *The Essays, Articles and Reviews of Evelyn Waugh* (Little Brown, 1984), p. 326.

[8]Parker Tyler, *Chaplin, Last of the Clowns* (Horizon, 1972), pp. 116, 154–58.

[9]Walker, op. cit., pp. 167–72; Kevin Brownlow, *Hollywood: The Pioneers* (Knopf, 1979), pp. 193, 202; Leatrice Gilbert Fountain, *Dark Star* (St. Martin's, 1985), pp. 178–81, 190–9.

[10]Walker, op. cit., p. 77.

[11]Ibid., pp. 161–62.

[12]For the importance of sound to the classic horror films, cf. Leo Braudy, *The World in a Frame* (Doubleday, 1976), p. 228.

[13]Gangster shows and films "came on like gangbusters"—i.e., opened with a blaring sound montage, according to the formula Phillips Lord used for his successful radio shows (including "Gangbusters"). Cf. Richard Gid Powers, *G-Men: Hoover's FBI in American Popular Culture* (Southern Illinois University, 1983), pp. 208–15; Thomas Schatz, *Hollywood Genres* (Temple University, 1981), p. 85.

[14]Louise Brooks, *Lulu in Hollywood* (Knopf, 1982), pp. 62, 64: "Cagney, in *The Roaring Twenties,* threw him [Bogart] into confusion, splitting him between Bogey and Humphrey. Cagney's swift dialogue and his swift movements, which had the glitter and precision of a meat slicer, were impossible to anticipate or counterattack. . . . Bogart was trying ineffectually to emulate the dynamic style of most successful actors [of the time]." As late as 1941, Warners producer Hal Wallis was still trying to make Bogart more "brisk," more "stoccato." Cf. the June 12, 1941, memo in Rudy Behlmer, *Inside Warner Bros. (1935–1951)* (Viking, 1985), p. 15.

[15]John Russell, editor, *Graham Greene on Film* (Simon and Schuster, 1972), p. 221.

[16]*Cagney by Cagney* (Pocket Books, 1977), p. 67.

[17]Ibid., p. 66.

[18]Walker, op. cit., pp. 1–3. Warner Bros., the sound pioneer, even set up its own Los Angeles radio station, KFWB, to promote its movies. Douglas Gomery, "The Coming of Sound: Technological Change in the American Film Industry," in *Film Sound, Theory and Practice,* edited by Elizabeth Weis and John Belton (Columbia University, 1985), p. 11.

[19]MacDonald, op. cit., p. 51.

[20]Louella Parsons, *The Gay Illiterate* (Doubleday, 1944), pp. 154–59.

[21]Jack Warner, *My First Hundred Years in Hollywood* (Random House, 1964), p. 315.

[22]Parsons, op. cit., p. 160.

[23]Dixon *Evening Telegraph,* Sept. 15, 1941. Warner Bros. gave Dixon's Lee Theater

the "international premiere" of Reagan's new film, *International Squadron*, during this visit.

[24]Hubler, p. 90. Alexander had made his last film, *Ready, Willing, and Able*, released the month Reagan reached Hollywood, with Jane Wyman.

[25]Alex McNeil, *Total Television: A Comprehensive Guide to Programming From 1948 to the Present* (Penguin, 1984), pp. 232, 245, 735, 161.

[26]The scene is included in a videotape of Warner Brothers out-takes released commercially as *Presidential Bloopers* (Hollywood Home Theaters, 1980).

CHAPTER 16

[1]Des Moines *Register*, April 4, 1937. Des Moines *Evening Telegraph*, May 20, 1937, Sept. 1, 1937.

[2]Interview with Walter B. Scott, now living in Scottsdale, Arizona, about his brother Will's decision to leave Drake and follow Dutch.

[3]Neil Reagan's only screen credit was as "Rex Olcott" in Ronald's 1940 film with Wyman, *Tugboat Annie Sails Again.* Cf. Tony Thomas, *The Films of Ronald Reagan* (Citadel, 1980), p. 107.

[4]James Q. Wilson, "The Political Culture of Southern California, *Commentary,* May, 1967 (reprinted in *The California Dream,* edited by Dennis Hale and Jonathan Eisen, Collier Books, 1968, p. 222). Cf. Carey McWilliams, *Southern California Country: An Island on the Land* (Duell, Sloan & Pierce, 1946), p. 149, on the old report that in Los Angeles "snooping is the popular pastime, gossiping the popular practice, privacy is impossible."

[5]McWilliams, pp. 171–72.

[6]Ibid., pp. 214–17, 230.

[7]Wilson, op. cit., pp. 218–20; Reyner Banham, *Los Angeles: The Architecture of Four Ecologies* (Harper & Row, 1971), pp. 75–76, 137–60. Donald Worster, *Rivers of Empire: Water, Aridity, and the Growth of the American West* (Pantheon, 1985), p. 130: "The ecological situation demanded group effort."

[8]Dixon *Evening Telegraph,* Aug. 22, 1950.

[9]Mary Jane Manners, "Making a Double Go Of It," *Silver Screen,* August, 1941.

[10]Ida Zeitlin, "Jane Wyman's Life Story," *Modern Screen,* July 1947.

[11]Interview with Pastor Myron C. Cole, now living in Hawaii.

[12]Interview with Hubert Johnson, now living in Escondido, California.

[13]Burrus Dickinson, *History of Eureka, Illinois* (Eureka, 1985), p. 149.

[14]John Baxter, *Sixty Years of Hollywood* (Barnes, 1973), p. 18.

[15]Katharyn C. Esselman, "From Camelot to Monument Valley: Dramatic Origins of the Western Film," in *Focus on the Western,* edited by Jack Nachbar (Prentice-Hall, 1974), p. 17.

[16]Sergei Eisenstein, "Dickens, Griffith, and Film Today," in *Film Form: Essays in Film Theory,* translated by Jay Leyda (Harcourt, Brace, 1949), p. 197.

[17]André Bazin, *What Is Cinema?,* Vol. 2, translated by Hugh Bray (University of California, 1971), p. 140.

[18]Anita Loos, *The Talmadge Girls* (Viking, 1978), p. 45.

[19]Alexander Walker, *The Shattered Silents* (Morrow, 1979), p. 31.

[20]Jon Tuska, "The American Western Cinema: 1903–Present," in *Focus on the Western,* edited by Jack Nachbar (Prentice-Hall, 1974), pp. 40–41. Tuska argues that Carl Laemmle was "probably the single most important figure in the history of the silent Western" (ibid., p. 29)—i.e., of the most archetypically American film form.

[21]Hortense Powdermaker, *Hollywood: The Dream Factory* (Little, Brown, 1950).

[22]Frank Capra describes his invention of Langdon's third take in *The Name Above the Title* (Macmillan, 1971), pp. 62–63, 65.

[23]André Bazin, *What Is Cinema?*, translated by Hugh Grey (University of California, 1967), p. 151.

[24]Walter Kerr, *The Silent Clowns* (Knopf, 1975), p. 264.

CHAPTER 17

[1]Hortense Powdermaker, *Hollywood: The Dream Factory* (Little, Brown, 1950), p. 209: "In 1946, Humphrey Bogart received $432,000; Bette Davis $328,000; Bing Crosby $325,000; Deanna Durbin $325,477; Betty Grable $299,333; Ann Sheridan $269,345; Robert Montgomery $250,000; Errol Flynn $199,999; Rosalind Russell $190,104; Ronald Reagan $169,750; Rita Hayworth $94,916."

[2]Alexander Walker, *Stardom: The Hollywood Phenomenon* (Stein and Day, 1970), pp. 34–35.

[3]Reproduced in Walker, op. cit., pp. 371–76.

[4]Ibid., p. 37.

[5]Alexander Walker, *The Celluloid Sacrifice: Aspects of Sex in the Movies* (Hawthorn, 1966), p. 50.

[6]Mary Pickford, *Sunshine and Shadow* (Doubleday, 1955), pp. 137–38.

[7]Adolph Zukor, *The Public Is Never Wrong* (Putnam, 1953), p. 175.

[8]Walker, *Stardom*, p. 55.

[9]Pickford, op. cit., p. 139.

[10]Cecil B. DeMille, *Autobiography* (Prentice-Hall, 1959), p. 149. Louis B. Mayer courted Cardinal Spellman of New York so obsequiously that there were repeated rumors he would convert from the Jewish faith. Cf. Bosley Crowther, *Hollywood Rajah: The Life and Times of Louis B. Mayer* (Holt, Rinehart, and Winston, 1960), pp. 256–57.

[11]David Pirie, *Anatomy of the Movies* (Macmillan, 1981), pp. 108–11.

[12]Walker, *Stardom*, p. 259.

[13]Richard Schickel, *His Picture in the Papers: A Speculation on Celebrity in America Based on the Life of Douglas Fairbanks, Sr.* (Charterhouse, 1973), p. 54.

[14]Alistair Cooke, *Douglas Fairbanks: The Making of a Screen Character* (Museum of Modern Art, 1940), p. 30.

[15]Carlos Clarens, *The Crime Movie: From Griffith to the Godfather and Beyond* (Norton, 1980), p. 27.

[16]Molly Haskell, *From Reverence to Rape: The Treatment of Women in the Movies* (Penguin, 1974), pp. 81–82.

[17]Gloria Swanson, *Swanson on Swanson* (Random House, 1980), Kennedy, when he took over Swanson's career, said he wanted to rescue her from roles like that of the prostitute Sadie Thompson (ibid., p. 330): "he refused to identify me with the image I projected in it even though he was attracted to that image" (p. 374). Kennedy "took a heavily sentimental view of the family" (p. 338) and insisted that Swanson's child by another man be baptized a Catholic (p. 359–60).

[18]Crowther, op. cit., pp. 235–43; Lillian Ross, *Picture* (Avon, 1952), pp. 25, 170.

[19]Ben Hecht, *A Child of the Century* (Simon and Schuster, 1954), p. 479.

[20]Powdermaker, op. cit., p. 55: "The Hollywood taboos embodied in the self-imposed production Code have the same psychological origin as do those of primitive man, fear. But they differ in that they do not represent the actual beliefs, values, or behavior of the people practising them."

[21]Schickel, op. cit., p. 31. Cf. Pickford, op. cit., p. 237: "In some ways Charlie Chaplin's early life reminded me of my own."

[22]Walker, *Stardom*, p. 200.

[23]Pickford, op. cit., pp. 192–94.

[24]Clarens, op. cit., p. 27.

[25]Aljean Harmetz, "Old and New Hollywood," New York *Times,* Aug. 8, 1985.

[26]Evelyn Waugh, *The Loved One* (Little, Brown, 1948), pp. 8–9, 25.

[27]*The Essays, Articles and Reviews of Evelyn Waugh,* edited by Donat Gallagher (Little, Brown, 1984), p. 330.

[28]Powdermaker, op. cit., p. 63. In order to solve the problem of portraying people who have "been around," while observing the letter of the Code, Hollywood invented a whole new genre, the "remarriage" film, in which sexual references to a lover's past are all to *married* relationships. Stanley Cavell has written a very clever book *(Pursuits of Happiness)* on this genre, finding in it great depths of literary and philosophical meaning, without fully admitting that it began as a maneuver around the censors. (The Code did give visual life to a very ancient poetic genre, the classical *paraklausithyron,* or lover's plaint by a closed door. One of Cavell's favorite "remarriage comedies," *The Awful Truth* (1937), ends with the most sustained (and tedious) *paraklausithyron* in all of film.)

[29]Hecht, op. cit., p. 495.

[30]Goulding wanted Reagan to say "You're the one *man"* for Bette Davis. Reagan wanted to say "You're the *one* man." Reagan fudged the emphasis, and Goulding played the line down by shooting Reagan from behind during it. Bernard Dick, *Dark Victory* (University of Wisconsin, 1981), pp. 29, 169, 209.

[31]Charles Chaplin, *My Autobiography* (Pocket Books, 1966), pp. 174, 457.

[32]W. A. Swanberg, *Citizen Hearst* (Bantam, 1963), p. 590.

[33]Pauline Kael, *The Citizen Kane Book* (Little, Brown, 1971), p. 6.

[34]James Robert Parish and Don E. Stanke, *The Forties Gals* (Arlington, 1980), p. 374. Reagan and Wyman may in fact have been engaged before the Parsons tour, but that could not be revealed since Wyman was not yet divorced from her first husband, Myron Futterman.

[35]Mary Jane Higby, *Tune in Tomorrow* (Cowles, 1968), pp. 60–65.

[36]David Niven, *Bring on the Empty Horses* (1975), Octopus Edition, 1984, p. 369.

[37]Louella O. Parsons, "Last Call For Happiness," *Photoplay,* April 1948.

[38]Cannon, *Reagan,* p. 65.

CHAPTER 18

[1]He was still a Yank in the RAF for *Desperate Journey* (1942), when Americans no longer had to join English forces in order to fight. The standard plot had not been retooled yet, but Errol Flynn was given a last line as he and Reagan flew a captured bomber out of Germany: "Now for Australia and a crack at those Japs." Reagan was the turret gunner on this flight. Richard R. Lingeman, *Don't You Know There's a War On? The American Home Front, 1941–1945* (Putnam, 1970), p. 203.

[2]William Safire, an experienced presidential speech writer, remarked of Reagan's second inaugural address: "Inside the Rotunda, he read the line prepared before the sub-zero cold snap: 'We stand against the steps of this symbol of our democracy. . . .' He looked up and seemingly ad-libbed: 'or we would've been standing at the steps if it hadn't gotten so cold.' That drew a smile, but caused old speech writers to wonder: Didn't anybody check his reading draft that morning? How could that mistake slip by? The answer, I think, shows the Old Pro at work. Of course he checked the draft at the last minute, as the comparison of before-and-after delivery texts reveals. He left the standing-at-the-steps mistake in so that he could 'ad lib' a correction, drawing that smile and relieving the tensions before launching on his peroration . . ." New York *Times,* Jan. 24, 1985. In classical rhetoric, this is called *captatio benevolentiae.* In the deliberate clowning before a television show goes on the air, it is called "warming up the audience." Sometimes Reagan has taken this kind of "mistake" too far, as with the tension-releasing jokes before beginning his Saturday

radio broadcasts, the most famous of which promised an attack on Russia in five minutes. Some pompously analyzed that comment as a Freudian mistake, revealing repressed ideological desires. This demonstrates how necessary it is to understand Reagan in terms of his performer's background. The comment was meant exactly as seriously (because it was said in the same context) as "break a leg."

³OWI quoted from John Morton Blum, *V Was For Victory: Politics and American Culture During World War II* (Harcourt Brace Jovanovich, 1976), pp. 37–38. Another reason for using advertising in propaganda was that the Germans and Japanese were doing it—an early instance of the need to ape the enemy.

⁴Blum, op. cit., p. 26.

⁵Ibid., p. 27.

⁶Allan M. Winkler, *The Politics of Propaganda: The Office of War Information* (Yale University, 1978), pp. 63–65.

⁷Blum, op. cit., p. 42.

⁸Ibid., p. 28.

⁹Winkler, op. cit., p. 91.

¹⁰New York *Times*, Jan. 17, 1943, quoted from *Values Americans Live By* (Arno Press, 1974), pp. 124–25.

¹¹Blum, op. cit., p. 27.

¹²Cynthia Miller, "So Long, Button-Nose," *Modern Screen*, July 1942.

¹³For the legend of Captain Kelly, see Lingeman, op. cit., p. 301. Kelly may have contributed to Reagan's story of the bomber pilot going down with his plane, though Kelly had no belly gunner to cradle. For the supposed comment of the officer at Wake Island, ibid., pp. 197–98, and Blum, op. cit., pp. 54–55.

¹⁴Lingeman, op. cit., p. 184.

¹⁵For the riots in Detroit, Mobile, Beaumont, Harlem, and Los Angeles, ibid., pp. 326–35; Blum, op. cit., pp. 205–6.

¹⁶Ibid., pp. 207–8.

¹⁷*Time*, Dec. 22, 1941. *Life*, on the same date, claimed that the exceptional tall Japanese (like Admiral Nomura) was part "hairy Ainu."

¹⁸Cannon, *Reagan*, p. 20.

¹⁹Lingeman, op. cit., p. 204.

²⁰New York *Times*, June 7, 1984.

²¹John Dower, *War Without Mercy* (Pantheon, 1986), p. 141. Lingeman, op. cit., pp. 333–35; Blum, op. cit., pp. 204–5.

²²Ibid., p. 169.

²³Miller, loc. cit.

²⁴Ida Zeitlin, "My Soldier," *Modern Screen* cover story, Jan. 1943.

²⁵*Movie Life*, Nov. 1943.

²⁶Los Angeles *Examiner*, Jan. 4, 1944.

²⁷*Movie Life*, Feb. 1944.

²⁸Cal York, "Inside Stuff," *Photoplay*, Sept. 1942.

²⁹"Hollywood's Furlough Fashions," *Movie Picture*, June 1943. Elizabeth Arden brought out a patriotic lipstick called "Montezuma Red" in honor of the Marines (Blum, op. cit., p. 20).

³⁰"Walt Disney, Great Teacher," *Fortune*, Aug. 1942, p. 94.

³¹Interview with Ms. Omang.

³²He was never out of California. Reagan's first trip abroad (by boat, he was still not flying) was to make *The Hasty Heart* in 1949 (Hubler, p. 218) and his only excursion on the continent was a quick drive along the coast of France (241).

³³Interview with Mr. Cannon.

³⁴Cannon says the various White House corrections were themselves contradictory. Sometimes Reagan showed the film to a group, sometimes to one person.

³⁵Lou Cannon, "Germany, Take One; Roll 'Em," Washington *Post*, April 29, 1985.

[36]President Reagan's claim that he had not included a visit to a death camp because he did not want to embarrass Chancellor Kohl so embarrassed the Kohl government that it had to release a letter in which Kohl reminded the President that "I suggested that you visit the Dachau memorial." James M. Markham, from Bonn, New York *Times*, April 17, 1985. Deaver "repeatedly ruled out a concentration camp stop," at the President's instruction, a White House official told Lou Cannon (Washington *Post*, April 16, 1985).

[37]Chicago *Tribune*, May 9, 1985.

CHAPTER 19

[1]Laurence Leamer, *Make-Believe: The Story of Nancy and Ronald Reagan* (Harper & Row, 1983), pp. 130–31.

[2]Richard R. Lingeman, *Don't You Know There's a War On? The American Home Front, 1941–1945* (Putnam, 1970), p. 174.

[3]Leila J. Rupp, *Mobilizing Women For War: German and American Propaganda, 1939–1945* (Princeton University, 1978), pp. 143–66.

[4]Cannon, *Reagan*, p. 63.

[5]Ibid., p. 57.

[6]The audit chart is reproduced on p. 159 of Ogilvy's 1983 book, *Ogilvy on Advertising* (Crown). It covers the period from October 1941 to January 1952, and breaks down the respondents into fifteen categories. This was the kind of market research being done by studios in the period described by Lillian Ross in her classic *Picture* (Avon, 1952).

[7]Bosley Crowther dismissed Reagan's acting of Drake McHugh's role (New York *Times*, Feb. 3, 1942). The critics of *Time* (Feb. 2) and *Newsweek* (Feb. 16) did not even mention it.

[8]André Bazin made this scene a pivot of history for cinéastes by his famous description in *Orson Welles, A Critical View* (translated by Jonathan Rosenbaum, Harper & Row, 1972, pp. 77–81). He thought it was a case of deep focus, but it was a process shot (cf. Robert L. Carringer, *The Making of "Citizen Kane,"* University of California, 1985, pp. 72, 82). For the reciprocal influencing of Toland and Howe, see Pauline Kael, *The "Citizen Kane" Book* (Little, Brown, 1971), p. 75.

[9]This scene, with Cummings's overwrought reaction to the hypodermic needle, is one of those that relied on the public's knowledge of the novel. The mystery around the death of Parris's grandmother comes from his complicity in her euthanasia. Later in the novel, Parris helps Randy put Drake out of his suffering.

[10]Tony Thomas, *The Films of Ronald Reagan* (Citadel, 1980), p. 131. For Menzies, see Ephraim Katz, *The Film Encyclopedia* (Putnam, 1979), pp. 799–800.

[11]Parker Tyler, *The Hollywood Hallucination* (Simon and Schuster, 1970), p. 162.

[12]Erich Wolfgang Korngold had been a concert pianist, and he performs whenever a character in his movies goes to the piano—Robert Cummings, in the case of *Kings Row*. Henry Bellamann, whose fifth novel, *Kings Row*, made him the Margaret Mitchell of 1940, had been music professor at the Juilliard School and Vassar, and Dean of the Curtis Institute of Music; but when studio publicists suggested that Bellamann might collaborate on the music for *Kings Row*, Korngold put an end to such talk. Cf. Rudy Behlmer, *Inside Warner Bros. (1935–1951)* (Viking, 1985), pp. 41–42. Cf. *Current Biography*, 1942, pp. 63–65.

[13]Reagan sat in the first row in school for some time to be near the blackboard, and still could not see it (Hubbard 25)—which tells us not only how bad his eyesight was but how long it went uncorrected.

[14]Cannon, *Reagan*, p. 64.

CHAPTER 20

[1]Dore Schary, *Case History of a Movie* (Random House, 1950), p. 164.

[2]Ibid., p. 3.

[3]Ibid., p. 33.

[4]Ibid., p. 43. On Schary's devotion to *The Next Voice You Hear,* see Lillian Ross, *Picture* (Avon, 1952), p. 92.

[5]Cannon, *Reagan,* pp. 89, 141. Asked by Chris Wallace which date is correct, 1921 or 1923, Mrs. Reagan said, "I haven't made up my mind yet," then laughed: "That's a pretty good answer, isn't it?" NBC Special, "The First Lady: Nancy Reagan," 1985.

[6]Christine Edwards, *The Stanislavsky Heritage: Its Contribution to the Russian and American Theatre* (New York University, 1965), pp. 214–15; Daniel Blum, *A Pictorial History of the American Theatre: 1860–1970,* 3rd ed. (Crown, 1971), pp. 94–95, 99–101, 117, 168–69.

[7]Alexander Walker, *Rudolph Valentino* (London: Hamish Hamilton, 1976), pp. 32–43, 51–57, 85–107.

[8]Ibid., p. 34. Sumiko Higashi, *Virgins, Vamps and Flappers: The American Silent Movie Heroine* (Eden, 1978), pp. 63–71; Thomas R. Adkins, *Sexuality in the Movies* (Indiana University, 1975), p. 39. Rambova's art-deco *Salome* seems to have been based on the contemporary cubist one performed by the Kamerny Theatre. Cf. Oliver M. Sayler, *The Russian Theatre* (Little, Brown, 1920), pp. 152–62. Both designs were under the influence of Diaghilev's sets for *L'Après-midi d'un Faune.* Rambova had Valentino pose for private pictures in her approximation of Nijinsky's costume for that production (cf. Sayler, op. cit., p. 160, and Walker, op. cit., pp. 51–52). For the look of a Rambova production *(What Price Beauty?* in 1928 for Pathé), see Lawrence J. Quirk, *The Films of Myrna Loy* (Citadel, 1980), pp. 66–67.

[9]Nancy Reagan, with Bill Libby, *Nancy* (Morrow, 1980), p. 57.

[10]Ibid., p. 23.

[11]Ibid., pp. 91-92.

[12]Ibid., p. 23.

[13]Interview with Studs Terkel, another actor on the show, which originated from World Record Company in Chicago.

[14]Nancy Reagan, op. cit., p. 69.

[15]Ibid., pp. 66–72.

[16]Ibid., p. 93.

[17]Ibid., p. 96.

[18]Schary, op. cit., p. 42. The Screen Actors Guild file on Nancy Reagan shows a concern on her part about being confused with a supporter of the Hollywood Ten; but this was *after* her marriage to Reagan. Cf. letter from B. B. Kahane of Columbia Pictures, Jan. 7, 1953, sent at request of SAG official, Jack Dales. Ironically, this minor "clearance" problem arose because of the loyalty system Reagan helped set up.

[19]Laurence Leamer, *Make-Believe: The Story of Nancy and Ronald Reagan* (Harper & Row, 1983), p. 156.

[20]Joan Didion, *The White Album* (Washington Square, 1980), p. 156.

[21]Cannon, op. cit., p. 143.

[22]Ibid.

[23]Thorstein Veblen, *The Theory of the Leisure Class* (1899), Penguin, 1981, p. 96.

[24]Richard Nixon, *RN* (Grosset and Dunlap, 1978), p. 536.

[25]Reagan, op. cit., p. 94.

[26]For Bitzer, see Richard Schickel, *D. W. Griffith: An American Life* (Simon and

Schuster, 1985), p. 146. For Daniels, see Alexander Walker, *Garbo* (Macmillan, 1980), p. 41.

[27]Roland Barthes, *Mythologies* (Éditions du Seuil, 1957), pp. 70–71.

[28]Charles Affron, *Star Acting: Gish, Garbo, Davis* (Dutton, 1977), pp. 103–4.

[29]Arthur C. Miller tells how he lit Miss Temple in *One Reel a Week* (University of California, 1967), pp. 183–84. Mary Pickford describes how she learned, early on, the flattering capacity of lights aimed from below in *Sunshine and Shadow* (Doubleday, 1955), p. 179.

[30]Alexander Walker, *The Celluloid Sacrifice: Aspects of Sex in the Movies* (Hawthorn, 1966), p. 116.

[31]Robert L. Carringer, *The Making of "Citizen Kane"* (University of California, 1985), p. 129.

[32]Parker Tyler, *The Hollywood Hallucination* (Simon and Schuster, 1970), p. 83.

[33]Mauritz Stiller slowed Garbo down by having G. W. Pabst run film through the camera at extra speed, eliminating all twitchiness from the goddess (Walker, op. cit., p. 102). Josef von Sternberg also talks of restraining Dietrich's natural exuberance to create poise *(Fun in a Chinese Laundry,* Macmillan, 1952, p. 231).

[34]Tyler, op. cit., p. 94. Tyler is the first to admit that the somnambule is in danger, always, of lapsing into mere narcolepsy—like Hedi Lamarr (ibid., pp. 93–95), Lauren Bacall *(Magic and Myth of the Movies,* Simon and Schuster, 1970, pp. 21–26), or Veronica Lake (ibid., pp. 83–84, 256).

CHAPTER 21

[1]New York *Times,* Aug. 15, Aug. 19, 1984.

[2]Ibid., Aug. 19, 1984.

[3]Washington *Post,* Aug. 22, 1984.

[4]Elizabeth Drew, *Portrait of an Election* (Simon and Schuster, 1980), p. 112.

[5]New York *Times,* March 24, 1985.

[6]Laurence Olivier, *Confessions of an Actor* (Simon and Schuster, 1982), p. 262.

[7]Lillian Ross, *Picture* (Avon, 1952), p. 100.

[8]Ibid.

[9]Ibid., p. 103.

[10]A grim instance is given in a late interview with Groucho Marx by Roger Ebert, *A Kiss Is Still a Kiss* (Andrews, McMeel, Parker, 1984), pp. 43–60.

[11]Alex McNeil, *Total Television* (Penguin), 2nd ed., 1984, pp. 899–900.

[12]Jack W. Germond and Jules Witcover, *Wake Us When It's Over: Presidential Politics of 1984* (Macmillan, 1985), p. 523.

[13]Cannon, *Reagan,* p. 256 on Sears's "contempt for his own candidate's capacity." Germond and Witcover, *Blue Smoke and Mirrors: How Reagan Won and Why Carter Lost the Election of 1980* (Viking, 1981), p. 132 on Reagan as "patronized" by Sears. Reagan later told Theodore White, "There was . . . a feeling that I was just kind of a spokesman for John Sears." *America in Search of Itself: The Making of the President, 1956–1980,* Harper & Row, p. 251.

[14]Cannon, op. cit., p. 255; Germond and Witcover, op. cit., p. 136.

[15]Cannon, op. cit., pp. 254–56. Germond and Witcover, *Blue Smoke and Mirrors,* pp. 135–38.

[16]Cannon, op. cit., pp. 274–79.

[17]For "reinforcing" Reagan, see Stuart Spencer memo reprinted in Peter Goldman and Tony Fuller, *The Quest for the Presidency* (Bantam, 1985), p. 416.

[18]Germond and Witcover, *Wake Us When It's Over,* p. 526.

[19]Ibid., p. 503. Peter Goldman and Tony Fuller, op. cit., p. 311. The twenty-five-page briefing book dealt with twelve big issues "in an untaxing page apiece," and had

pages of "RR WINNERS culled mainly from his speeches—one liners like 'Why is your crystal ball so cloudy?' "

[20]Goldman and Fuller, p. 311.

[21]Ibid., pp. 321–22, 337–39. *Newsweek* had a team of people covering the President on a confidential basis—unable to print anything it gathered till after the election—which obtained the quotes from Ailes and others.

[22]Donnie Radcliffe, "First Lady," Washington *Post*, Aug. 6, 1985; Lou Cannon, "Aides Acknowledge Confusion," ibid., Aug. 7; Lawrence K. Altman, M.D., "Questions About Care of President," New York *Times*, Aug. 13.

[23]Gerald M. Boyd, "Speakes and the Press," New York *Times*, Aug. 8, 1985.

[24]Olivier, op. cit., p. 254.

[25]Eureka *Prism*, 1930, p. 22.

[26]Cannon, *Reagan*, p. 49.

[27]Bob Slosser, *Reagan Inside Out* (Word Books, 1984), pp. 14–15.

[28]Ibid., p. 20.

[29]William James, *The Varieties of Religious Experience: A Study in Human Nature* (1902), Collier Books, 1961, pp. 114–42. For the classical nature of sick-soul religion, see pp. 141–42: "The completest religions would therefore seem to be those in which the pessimistic elements are best developed. Buddhism, of course, and Christianity are the best known to us of these. They are essentially religions of deliverance: the man must die to an unreal life before he can be born into the real life."

[30]Ibid., pp. 78–113. For the displacement of sin by misery, see p. 92: "Whereas Christian theology has always considered *frowardness* to be the essential vice of the lower part of human nature, the mind-curers say that the mark of the beast in it is *fear;* and this is what gives such an entirely new religious turn to their persuasion."

[31]James refers to the changes made in America's brand of Calvinism by theological unitarianism, liberalism, and meliorism (op. cit., pp. 87–88). We have considered one step in that process—the way the Disciples of Christ promoted the Scottish Enlightenment's moral-sense view of human nature over the doctrine of total depravity.

[32]James, op. cit., p. 93: "The 'misery-habit,' the 'martyr habit,' engendered by the prevalent 'fearthought,' get pungent criticism from the mind-cure writers." The *religious* resentment of any belief in national limit is expressed in Slosser, op. cit., p. 72: "As you read his [George Gilder's] ongoing work, you are struck with the conviction that *we need not succumb to our problems*—poverty, disease, pollution, hatred, war, and the like. Using different words, he convinces you that [TV evangelist Pat] Robertson, in *The Secret Kingdom*, was on the mark in arguing that it is possible to live in such a manner as to *overcome shortages*, deprivation, poverty, meanness. Robertson calls for living out, as individuals and as nations, the laws or principles of the kingdom of God and thus experiencing now that condition in which there is *no diminishing of resources*, but rather abundance." Italics added.

[33]Elizabeth Drew, *Campaign Journal: The Political Events of 1983–1984* (Macmillan, 1985), pp. 602–3.

CHAPTER 22

[1]Parker Tyler, *Magic and Myth of the Movies* (Simon and Schuster, 1970), p. 4.

[2]Bosley Crowther, *Hollywood Rajah: The Life and Times of Louis B. Mayer* (Holt, Rinehart, 1960), pp. 68–69.

[3]Lillian Gish, *The Movies, Mr. Griffith, and Me* (Prentice-Hall, 1969), p. 136.

[4]Richard Schickel, *D. W. Griffith, An American Life* (Simon and Schuster, 1984), pp. 270, 298.

[5]Edward Bernays, *Biography of an Idea* (Simon and Schuster, 1965), pp. 340–41.

The White House visit is described in Ishbel Ross, *Grace Coolidge and Her Era* (Dodd, Mead, 1962), pp. 164–65.

[6]Crowther, op. cit., pp. 127–28, 136–37.

[7]Richard Whalen, *The Founding Fathers* (New American Library, 1964), pp. 122–26.

[8]Philip French, *The Movie Moguls* (Weidenfeld and Nicholson, 1969), p. 115. Cf. Larry Ceplair and Steven Englund, *The Inquisition in Hollywood* (University of California, 1979), pp. 89–93.

[9]Bob Thomas, *Thalberg: Life and Legend* (Doubleday, 1969), p. 269.

[10]Whalen, op. cit., pp. 83–84, 98–99.

[11]Richard B. Jewell with Vernon Harbin, *The RKO Story* (Arlington, 1982), p. 10.

[12]Whalen, op. cit., p. 81.

[13]Ibid., p. 95.

[14]Herbert Parmet notices that the dates Judith Campbell gave for her White House visits—which have not been found to conflict with other evidence of events there—coincided with Kennedy's severe back pains, for which he was taking procaine shots from Dr. Janet Travell, injections that disturbed her fellow physicians. Parmet, *J.F.K. The Presidency of John F. Kennedy* (Dial, 1983), pp. 118–28.

[15]Arthur M. Schlesinger, Jr., *Robert Kennedy and His Times* (Houghton Mifflin, 1978), pp. 495–96.

[16]William F. Buckley, Jr., "The Way They Are," *Vanity Fair,* June 1985, p. 52.

[17]Laurence Leamer, *Make-Believe* (Harper & Row, 1983), p. 374.

[18]Crowther, op. cit., pp. 122–23, 185–86, 200–1.

[19]Op cit., pp. 117, 145, 268–69.

[20]Donald Spoto, *The Dark Side of Genius: The Life of Alfred Hitchcock* (Ballantine, 1984), pp. 162, 374, 432, 433, 531.

[21]Ibid., p. 483.

[22]Ibid., p. 429.

[23]Ibid., p. 477. For Hitchcock's finicky supervision of his actresses' wardrobes, see ibid., pp. 367, 372, 378.

[24]Ibid., p. 402.

[25]Ibid., p. 436.

[26]For the exploitative nature of these films, see Garry Wills, "The Assassination Madness," *The Movies,* November 1983.

[27]Jack and Jo Ann Hinckley, with Elizabeth Sherrill, *Breaking Points* (Chosen Books, 1985), p. 21.

[28]Ibid., p. 49.

[29]Ibid., p. 84.

[30]Lincoln Caplan, *The Insanity Defense and the Trial of John W. Hinckley, Jr.* (David R. Godine, 1984), p. 35.

[31]Hinckleys, op. cit., p. 298.

[32]Caplan, op. cit., p. 38.

[33]Ibid., pp. 35–41.

[34]Hinckleys, op. cit., pp. 150, 237.

[35]Ibid., p. 341.

[36]*The New Republic,* May 27, 1985.

[37]Caplan, op. cit., p. 16.

CHAPTER 23

[1]Arthur M. Schlesinger, Jr., *The Coming of the New Deal* (Houghton Mifflin, 1958), pp. 96–98.

[2]Rexford G. Tugwell, *The Democratic Roosevelt* (Doubleday, 1957), pp. 281–86.

³Ibid., pp. 311–12, 327.

⁴Ibid., pp. 310, 314.

⁵Murray Ross, *Stars and Strikes: Unionization of Hollywood* (Columbia University, 1941), pp. 64–88; Louis B. Perry and Richard S. Perry, *A History of the Los Angeles Labor Movement, 1911–1941* (University of California, 1963), pp. 344–45. Despite David Niven's personal resilience and outside prospects during his period as an extra, he offers the reader a vivid glimpse of the extras' way of life *(Bring on the Empty Horses,* 1975, Octopus Edition, 1984, pp. 493–97).

⁶Donat Gallagher, *The Essays, Articles and Reviews of Evelyn Waugh* (Little, Brown, 1984), p. 331: "the idol Oscar—sexless image of infertility."

⁷Grace Heilman Stimson, *Rise of the Labor Movement in Los Angeles* (University of California, 1955), pp. 366–89.

⁸Bosley Crowther, *Hollywood Rajah: The Life and Times of Louis B. Mayer* (Holt, Rinehart and Winston, 1960), pp. 173–74. Perry and Perry, op. cit., pp. 319–20; Ross, op. cit., p. 41: "An examination of the Academy constitution supplies ample proof that a small number of influential 'foundation members' guided the Academy ship. The foundation members were charter members and a select few who were elected to the sacrosanct circle. Other Academy members were not eligible for election to the board of directors and could not amend the bylaws. The Academy was obviously never meant to be a thoroughly democratic organization."

⁹Perry and Perry, op. cit., p. 339; Ross, op. cit., pp. 28–29.

¹⁰Ross, pp. 29–30.

¹¹Perry and Perry, p. 342.

¹²Ibid., p. 348; Ross, pp. 90–92.

¹³Perry and Perry, p. 348; Ross, p. 149. Boris Karloff was the best-known of the original members. Reagan's account of his own Guild's founding (Hubler, p. 152) gets the date wrong (June 30 for July 12) and gives the wrong number of founding members (twenty-one).

¹⁴Perry and Perry, p. 349; Ross, p. 105. Larry Ceplair and Steven Englund, *The Inquisition in Hollywood: Politics in the Film Community, 1930–1960* (University of California, 1979), p. 29.

¹⁵Perry and Perry, p. 350; Ross, pp. 152–58.

¹⁶Perry and Perry, p. 351; Ross, pp. 159–61.

¹⁷Perry and Perry, p. 351; Ross, pp. 115–17.

¹⁸Frank Capra, *The Name Above the Title* (Macmillan, 1971), p. 188.

¹⁹Richard Schickel, *D. W. Griffith: An American Life* (Simon and Schuster, 1984), pp. 582–84. Ford later took his Oscar, but Nichols stayed true to his first stand.

²⁰Rexford G. Tugwell, *The Democratic Roosevelt* (Doubleday, 1957), p. 416.

²¹William E. Leuchtenburg, *Franklin D. Roosevelt and the New Deal* (Harper & Row, 1963), pp. 150–52.

²²Ross, p. 161.

²³Perry and Perry, pp. 351–52.

²⁴Ross, p. 162; Perry and Perry, p. 352.

²⁵Ross, p. 163.

²⁶Reagan remembers being appointed to the board in 1938 (Hubler, p. 153), but the earliest item in his Guild file shows that he was first appointed as an alternate to Heather Angel in July of 1941. By that time Reagan was married to Jane Wyman, who was on the board. He claims he was admitted simply because he fit a category ("new, young contract player"), but the long-time Executive Secretary of the Guild, who was closely associated with both actors, claimed: "He [Reagan] was urged upon the board, as I recall, by Jane Wyman." John L. Dales, California Oral History Project, 1981, UCLA Special Collections, pp. 4–5.

²⁷Ibid., p. 174.

²⁸Dales, op. cit., p. 48.

CHAPTER 24

[1]Hubler 146. Cf. Larry Ceplair and Steven Englund, *The Inquisition in Hollywood: Politics in the Film Community, 1930–1960* (University of California, 1979), p. 207: "Between 1941 and 1945, 6.7 million strikers participated in 14,471 strikes in this country, far more than in the CIO organizational surge of the late thirties; indeed, far more than in any comparable period of United States history."

[2]Richard R. Lingeman, *Don't You Know There's a War On? The American Home Front, 1941–1945* (Putnam, 1970), p. 187.

[3]"Jurisdictional Disputes in the Motion Picture Industry," Hearings Before the House Special Subcommittee on Education and Labor, Eightieth Congress, Reagan testimony of August 18, 1947, p. 222. Jack Dales, California Oral History Project, 1981, UCLA Special Collections, p. 5. SAG Reagan file.

[4]Dales, op. cit., pp. 1–3.

[5]Louis B. Perry and Richard S. Perry, *A History of the Los Angeles Labor Movement, 1911–1941* (University of California, 1963), p. 321.

[6]Murray Ross, *Stars and Strikes: Unionization of Hollywood* (Columbia University, 1941), p. viii.

[7]Andrew Laskos, "The Hollywood Majors," in *Anatomy of the Movies,* edited by David Pirie (Macmillan, 1981), pp. 16–19.

[8]Ross, op. cit., p. ix.

[9]Perry and Perry, op. cit., p. 325; Ross, op. cit., pp

[10]Perry and Perry, pp. 328–29; Ross, pp. 132–38.

[11]Perry and Perry, p. 330; Ross, p. 192.

[12]Perry and Perry, p. 336; Ross, pp. 194–95.

[13]Perry and Perry, pp. 351–52; Ross, pp. 198–202.

[14]Many people had a hand in Bioff's undoing, including Bioff. The California legislature was investigating him, and a Sacramento grand jury (Ross, p. 197), and the United States Treasury Department. Carey McWilliams had written attacks on him, and so had Arthur Ungar. Pegler was his best-known critic, but neither the only nor the earliest one. Cf. Oliver Pilat, *Pegler: Angry Man of the Press* (Beacon, 1963), p. 169; John Cogley, *Report on Blacklisting, I: Movies* (Fund for the Republic, 1956), pp. 51–52. There were dissenters even within the IA, calling themselves IATSE Progressives, who worked against Bioff. Cf. Eugene Mailes oral history, tape 2, Wisconsin Center for Film and Theater Research.

[15]Ross, pp. 199, 201–2.

[16]Perry and Perry, pp. 335–36.

[17]Richard Schickel, *The Disney Version: The Life, Times, Art and Commerce of Walt Disney* (Simon and Schuster, 1968), pp. 249–62.

[18]Perry and Perry, p. 336.

[19]"Jurisdictional Disputes," pp. 2040–47 (War Board decision), and pp. 2053–57 (NLRB decision).

[20]Nancy Lynn Schwartz, *The Hollywood Writers' Wars* (Knopf, 1982), p. 223.

[21]Ross, p. 9.

[22]"Jurisdictional Disputes," p. 221.

[23]Ceplair and Englund, p. 221.

[24]The final NLRB decision, written by Stewart Meacham, was delivered on October 16 (Schwartz, op. cit., p. 229).

CHAPTER 25

[1]For Father Dunne, I rely on my own interview with him in 1985, the UCLA oral history interview of 1981, Dunne's testimony to the House Subcommittee on Education and Labor in 1947, an article he wrote about the forties in *Commonweal* (June 2, 1972), and clippings from the "Hollywood Studio Strike" file (three boxes) in the UCLA Special Collections. Dunne also lent me a copy of his play and of a pamphlet he wrote on the unions in 1948.

[2]"Jurisdictional Disputes in the Motion Picture Industry," Hearings Before the House Special Subcommittee on Education and Labor, Eightieth Congress, Dunne testimony of August 22, 1947, p. 404.

[3]Ibid., p. 406.

[4]"Jurisdictional Disputes," p. 463.

[5]Ibid., p. 1119, pp. 300–1, 1030.

[6]Ibid., p. 1119. The committee sat from Dec. 3 to Dec. 10 inclusive. Those eight days become "a whirlwind four days" in Reagan's account (Hubler 164).

[7]"Jurisdictional Disputes," pp. 1262–65.

[8]Ibid., p. 14.

[9]Ibid., pp. 463–65.

[10]Ibid., 1117–32.

[11]Ibid., p. 33.

[12]Reagan accepted this argument from the producers. Ibid., p. 223.

[13]Ibid., pp. 900–5.

[14]Interview with Fr. Dunne, who discussed the whole strike with Casey after it had been settled.

[15]This was the "Treaty of Beverly Hills," as *Time* magazine called it (ibid., 1278–81). Reagan mistakenly thinks this was called in response to a CSU machinists' local strike ("Jurisdictional Disputes," 222, 227, Hubler, pp. 167–68). The machinists' grievance was settled by the NLRB on June 28, 1946. The "Treaty of Beverly Hills" of July 2, 1946, was addressed to grievances of *both* the CSU and the IA. See UCLA study of the strike, conducted by Professor McMahan ("Jurisdictional Disputes," pp. 527–28), and John Cogley, *Report on Blacklisting, I: The Movies* (Fund for the Republic, 1956), p. 67. Reagan exaggerates the importance of the role played by SAG in that "treaty," and misrepresents the issues when he says it was solved by finding out "who is lying" (Hubler 168).

[16]"Jurisdictional Disputes," p. 911.

[17]Ibid., pp. 1283–85.

[18]Ibid., p. 908.

[19]Ibid., p. 911.

[20]Ibid., p. 971.

[21]Ibid., p. 913. But the UCLA study of the strike did not find any willingness to bargain manifested by the studios (ibid., p. 529).

[22]Ibid., p. 910.

[23]Ibid., p. 912.

[24]Ibid.

[25]Ibid., p. 913.

[26]Reagan made a gingerly admission that he knew of Brewer's threat to use a projectionists' strike: "We told him [Brewer] that the studios would close, and he said, no, that if the studios just closed with virtually no excuse, without making an attempt to continue production, that they would consider not to show the films" (ibid., p. 226). When committee counsel asked if this was a threat that "didn't sound very nice," Reagan answered: "Nothing in the strike sounded very nice to us." Pat

Somerset then obviously whispered instructions to Reagan, who said: "Mr. Somerset refreshes my memory on that—that they [the IATSE] were going to prevent a lockout if they could." That was the IA line.

[27]Ibid., pp. 230–31.

[28]Ibid., p. 234.

[29]Ibid., p. 236. One member of the committee says he might have mentioned something vague about resigning in a private meeting with some of the actors, but not when they met as a group; and he never expressed a firm intention of resigning, much less wrote a letter of resignation. Since Reagan was present in the hearing room, the three men offered to submit to his cross-examination, though that was not Committee procedure. Ibid., pp. 294–95.

[30]Ibid., p. 248 (also Hubler, p. 177).

[31]Ibid., p. 248.

[32]Ibid., p. 249.

[33]Ibid., pp. 279–80. Text of the telegram is on pp. 161–62.

[34]Ibid., pp. 292–94.

[35]Ibid., p. 222.

[36]Clippings from "Hollywood Strike" boxes in UCLA Special Collections: The Tidings (Catholic archdiocesan paper), Dec. 30, 1946; Mar. 21, 1947; Los Angeles Times, Sept. 2, 1947.

[37]"Jurisdictional Disputes," p. 355.

[38]Ibid., pp. 419–22.

[39]Ibid., pp. 260–62.

[40]Ibid., p. 282.

[41]Ibid., pp. 516–17.

[42]Ibid., pp. 412–13.

[43]Fr. Dunne went on to render distinguished service to his church and order. When his social apostolate had been blocked, he turned back to his original missionary interests. Working in the Jesuit archives in Rome, he wrote a history of early Jesuits in China (Generation of Giants, Notre Dame University, 1962), noting that their efforts were misunderstood and resisted even by their coreligionists: "They were accused of being innovators, of compromising the faith. Actually, they were attempting to restore the genuine ideal of Christianity as the leaven of the world" (p. 13). After six years at Georgetown's School of Foreign Service, he became the Vatican representative to the World Council of Churches Committee on Social Development.

[44]Fr. Dunne was not sent to "the other side of the country" from Loyola but to northern California.

CHAPTER 26

[1]"Jurisdictional Disputes in the Motion-Picture Industry," Hearings Before the Education and Labor Subcommittee, Eightieth Congress, p. 228.

[2]Larry Ceplair and Steven Englund, The Inquisition in Hollywood: Politics in the Film Community, 1930–1960 (University of California, 1979), p. 89.

[3]Ibid., pp. 37–39. Nancy Lynn Schwartz, The Hollywood Writers' Wars (Knopf, 1982), pp. 64–65, 71–72, 74–75, 291–92. Samuel Marx, Mayer and Thalberg, The Make-Believe Saints (Random House, 1975), pp. 218–19.

[4]Schwartz, op. cit., p. 291.

[5]John Cogley, Report on Blacklisting, I: The Movies (Fund for the Republic, 1956), p. 50.

[6]Ceplair and Englund, op. cit., p. 157.

[7]Schwartz, op. cit., pp. 158–60. Variety Music Cavalcade, 1920–1961 (Prentice-Hall, 1962), p. 397.

[8]David Caute, *The Great Fear: The Anti-Communist Purge Under Truman and Eisenhower* (Simon and Schuster, 1978), pp. 77–78.

[9]"Jurisdictional Disputes," p. 1589. For Sorrell's response to the card accusation, ibid., pp. 1959–61. Reagan says some were misled by Sorrell because "we didn't know . . . that the House Un-American Activities Committee in 1947 had received testimony about the card" (Hubler, p. 185)—but the charge was public from 1941, often repeated by Roy Brewer and others. Jack Dales, in his oral history interview for SAG files, called Sorrell "as radical and interesting a man as I've ever met . . . He always introduced himself as 'I'm just a dumb painter,' but he was far from dumb."

[10]Harry Bridges and others opposed the 1946 strike. Ben Margolis and David Robinson thought Sorrell handled it poorly because he "lacked leftist grounding." Cf. Schwartz, op. cit., p. 245.

[11]Cogley, op. cit., pp. 54–55.

[12]Ibid., p. 61. There is a 1971 interview of Sorrell by Eugene Mailes, an IATSE Progressive who sided with the Communists against the 1945 strike; Sorrell restates his independence of the Communists. Mailes, tape 7, Wisconsin Center for Film and Theater Research.

[13]Ceplair and Englund, op. cit., p. 218.

[14]Murphy interview with Robert Scheer, Los Angeles *Times*, April 8, 1982.

[15]Neil Reagan, California Oral History Project, 1981, UCLA Special Collections, pp. 30–31.

[16]Ceplair and Englund, op. cit., p. 238.

[17]Schwartz, op. cit., p. 261. For a similar anti-Communist statement in SAG, see Anne Revere's oral history tape from 1979 in SAG files.

[18]The Reagan FBI file was obtained in 1985, under the Freedom of Information Act, by the San Jose *Mercury-News*. I am grateful to the paper for a copy of its 156 pages.

[19]Summary of Reagan's memberships made by the Bureau on May 23, 1951.

[20]Ibid.

[21]This was not Reagan's first confidential dealing with the FBI. An agent had received permission before the war to interview him for a reason crossed out in the file, and he was questioned about a Hollywood party he attended in November of 1943, where a man made anti-Semitic remarks critical of the war effort. "REAGAN became highly incensed and withdrew from the conversation. He said that he almost came to blows with the subject, although he emphasized that considerable drinking had been done by all persons involved." Reagan told them a French model at the party might know the suspect man's whereabouts. Report of Dec. 27, 1943.

[22]Dunne described visiting Sorrell's home as particularly interesting, since his wife was a devout Jehovah's Witness. "While he went to union meetings every night, she went to church meetings."

[23]"Jurisdictional Disputes," pp. 425–33.

[24]Carey McWilliams, California Oral History Project, 1978, UCLA Special Collections.

[25]The UCLA study decided the carpenters who refused to touch the hot sets were involved in a work stoppage, but the supportive CSU unions were locked out. "Jurisdictional Disputes," pp. 528–29.

[26]*The Tidings*, Mar. 21, 1947. The report also concluded that "The Producers have taken a most negative attitude in their relationship to the strike."

[27]Hubler 175. In 1947, under oath, Reagan had made no mention of the Communist charge, which does not mean he did not believe it by 1965: "He [Hutcheson] said to us, 'If Dick Walsh will give in on the August directive, I will run Herb Sorrell out of Hollywood and in five minutes break up the Conference of Studio Unions" ("Jurisdictional Disputes," p. 240).

[28]Report numbered LA 100-15732. The list of names is blacked out, but the suc-

ceeding list "of the individuals mentioned by REAGAN and his wife . . . known to the Los Angeles office to be members of the Communist Party" has six (blacked out) entries.

[29]The 1947 dates are April 10, Dec. 3, and Dec. 19. The 1946 meeting described in Hubler (presumably in fall of 1946) is not identifiable from the partial record released. Nor is the subject matter of several 1948 reports.

[30]The list is in the document LA 100-15732, referring to the Dec. 3 interview with T-9 as well as T-10. The designation is used in a report on the Dec. 19 interview summarized on May 23, 1951. In *Murder in the Air*, Reagan had posed as terrorist agent No. 685. As so often with Reagan, life and fiction blend in the matter of being a numbered secret agent.

[31]LA 100-15732.

[32]Laurence I. Barrett, *Gambling with History: Ronald Reagan in the White House* (Doubleday, 1983), p. 58. In 1951, Reagan told a reporter for the Los Angeles *Times* (July 17): "The Russians sent their first team, their all-string, here [to Hollywood] to take us over . . . We were up against hard-core organizers."

CHAPTER 27

[1]Nancy Lynn Schwartz, *The Hollywood Writers' Wars* (Knopf, 1982), pp. 61–72, 203–7.

[2]Larry Ceplair and Steven Englund, *The Inquisition in Hollywood: Politics in the Film Community, 1930–1960* (University of California, 1979), p. 209.

[3]*Playboy* Interview, April 1971, p. 91.

[4]Schwartz, op. cit., p. 209. Ceplair and Englund, op. cit., p. 212.

[5]Ibid., pp. 158–59.

[6]LA 100-138754-472. Even the 1947 investigation by Parnell Thomas's committee would not satisfy Hoover, who appended to a March 3, 1949, report in the Reagan file: "The picture industry still continues to be a stinking mess." LA 100-138754-513.

[7]California Oral History Project, 1981, UCLA Special Collections, p. 47.

[8]Reagan FBI File, Mar. 3, 1949, report LA 100-138754-513: "Ronald Reagan was the chairman and Roy Brewer the vice chairman of the group."

[9]Ceplair and Englund, p. 359.

[10]Dales, op. cit., p. 47. For Brewer's central role in clearing, cf. Cogley, *Report on Blacklisting, I: The Movies* (Fund for the Republic, 1956), pp. 155–60.

[11]Reagan FBI File, Office Memorandum of Nov. 14, 1947, LA 100-138754-314.

[12]Samuel Marx, *Mayer and Thalberg: The Make-Believe Saints* (Random House, 1975), p. 247. There was good reason to deny the practice of blacklisting in California—it was against state law (Cogley, op. cit., p. 89).

[13]Cannon, *Reagan*, p. 85.

[14]Victor S. Navasky, *Naming Names* (Viking, 1980), p. 87.

[15]Wayne, op. cit., pp. 88, 90. Wayne added that his running Foreman out of the country was meant as "a figure of speech." But Foreman publicly told Wayne (when he went to England, where Foreman had run) that the language was very real indeed (*Punch*, Aug. 14, 1974). Reagan, who denied there was a blacklist, boasts in the same way that Fr. Dunne was run out of town.

[16]Navasky, op. cit., pp. 182–84.

[17]Walter Goodman, *The Committee: The Extraordinary Career of the House Committee on Un-American Activities* (Farrar, Straus & Giroux, 1968), p. 300.

[18]Reagan FBI File, with clippings from the Nov. 17, 1947, issues of the Washington *Evening Star* and Los Angeles *Herald-Examiner*.

[19]Navasky, op. cit., p. 90.

[20]Cannon, *Reagan*, p. 84.

[21]"Friendly witnesses" had often given the names to government authorities and were told, if they needed persuading, that others had already named those people (Navasky, op. cit., pp. 281–83). The testimony was to establish the witness's conformity to correct attitudes. The Committee resembled the Party it opposed in this machinery of orthodoxy. Men like Alfred Maltz and Budd Schulberg, who had already faced the cultural exactions of V. J. Jerome, had to repeat their ordeal for Parnell Thomas.

[22]Reagan FBI File (LA 100-15732): "one incident which lessened his respect for the Committee involved the Committee's Chief Investigator, STRIBLING [sic]. T-10 advised that the night before he was scheduled to testify, STRIBLING came to his hotel room and asked him numerous questions, some of which led T-10 into a 'pretty good defense of the motion industry,' although by no means a defense of the Communist element therein. However, the following day when he was on the stand STRIBLING failed to ask him any of these questions which would have enabled him to get in a good word for the motion picture industry as a whole." Reagan found frequent occasion to "get in a good word." For instance: "I, like Mr. Montgomery, would like at this moment to say I happen to be very proud of the industry in which I work . . . I would also like to say that I think we can match the record of our industry in the contribution to the social welfare against that of any industry in the United States." "Communist Infiltration of the Motion-Picture Industry," Hearings of the House Committee on Un-American Activities, Eightieth Congress, 1947, p. 217.

[23]"Communist Infiltration," p. 216. As we have seen, Reagan did not use the word "Commies" earlier, before the Kearns Committee.

[24]Ibid., p. 217.

[25]Ibid., pp. 60–65.

[26]Schwartz, op. cit., pp. 277–80. Ceplair and Englund, op. cit., pp. 328–31. Johnston's reliance on the advice of ex-Secretary of State James Byrnes, who attended the Waldorf Conference, is described in Dore Schary, *Heyday* (Little, Brown, 1979), pp. 164–5.

[27]Schwartz, op. cit., p. 279.

[28]Reagan File (LA 100-15732). Reagan, obviously praising the real FBI to its agents, asked: "Do they expect us to constitute ourselves as a little FBI of our own and determine just who is a Communist and who isn't?"

[29]"Communist Infiltration," p. 217.

[30]Reagan FBI File (LA 100-15732).

[31]Cannon, p. 94. Others attribute Reagan's "conversion" to the influence of Nancy Reagan, daughter of the conservative surgeon Dr. Loyal Davis. But his activities with Brewer preceded his meeting her. Indeed, she claims to have met him through the clearing procedure he was already running.

[32]Dales, op. cit., p. 2.

[33]"Jurisdictional Disputes in the Motion-Picture Industry," Hearings Before the House Subcommittee on Education and Labor, Eightieth Congress, p. 358.

[34]Ceplair and Englund, op. cit., p. 367.

[35]Ibid., p. 370.

[36]The Riesel column (New York *Post,* June 24, 1947) is quoted in a *Current Biography* article included in Reagan's file on May 23, 1951. For Riesel's role in clearing people for employment in show business, see Navasky, op. cit., pp. 89, 152, 219, 347, 371.

[37]SAG oral history interview, 1979.

[38]The Brewer appointment runs till 1989. Union defenders protested when President Reagan appointed the known anti-unionist, J. Lynn Helms, as Administrator of the Federal Aviation Administration. Cf. Ronald Brownstein and Nina Easton, *Reagan's Ruling Class: Portraits of the President's Top 100 Officials* (Presidential Accounting Group, 1982), pp. 318–23). When Lynn broke the air controllers' strike,

there was a move to take away Reagan's honorary membership in SAG. Cf. SAG files and Will Tushman, *Daily Variety*, Aug. 26, 1981. The millionaire Helms was forced to leave the FAA under multiple investigations for business fraud.

CHAPTER 28

[1]David Niven, *Bring on the Empty Horses* (1975, Octopus Edition, 1984), pp. 630–33.

[2]Federal grand jury hearing, Los Angeles, Feb. 5, 1962, p. 78.

[3]Bill Boyarsky, *Ronald Reagan: His Life and Rise to the Presidency* (Random House, 1981), p. 52.

[4]Information on Jules Stein and MCA from *Current Biography* 1967, pp. 400–3; Nat Hentoff, "The Octopus of Show Biz," *The Reporter*, Nov. 23, 1961, pp. 39–43; Axel Madsen, *The New Hollywood: American Movies in the '70s* (Crowell, 1975), pp. 8–12; David Pirie, *Anatomy of the Movies* (Macmillan, 1981), pp. 42–43; David Robb, "JD Eyed with Suspicion SAG, Reagan, MCA Deal That Made TV History," *Daily Variety*, April 18, 1964; Dan E. Moldea and Jeff Goldberg, "The Deal's the Thing," *Los Angeles Reader*, Nov. 2, 1984; Susan Deutsch, "It's Lew!" *California*, March 1985; Geraldine Fabrikant, "A Movie Giant's Unfinished Script," New York *Times*, Oct. 20, 1985.

[5]Hentoff, op. cit., p. 39.

[6]Joan Didion, *The White Album* (1979, Pocket Books, 1980), pp. 158–59.

[7]Lou Cannon, *Reagan* (Putnam, 1982), pp. 67–68.

[8]Jack Gould, "TV Transforming U.S. Social Scene: Challenges Films," New York *Times*, June 24, 1951.

[9]Ibid.

[10]Moldea and Goldberg, op. cit., p. 8.

[11]Letter of Larry Beilenson to Lew Wasserman dated June 7, 1954, cited by Justice Department attorney John Fricano in examination of Ronald Reagan before the grand jury, Feb. 5, 1962, p. 74.

[12]Jack Dales, SAG oral history interview, June 1979. Beilenson was also a friend of Reagan, who often quoted in his radio commentary a book Beilenson wrote as an old negotiator *(The Treaty Trap)* to show the futility of dealing with Communist nations, Peter Hannaford, *The Reagans: A Political Portrait* (Coward, McCann, 1983), pp. 76, 159, and radio broadcast texts at the Wisconsin Center for Film and Theater Research.

[13]Jack Dales, California Oral History Project, 1981, UCLA Special Collections, p. 45.

[14]In 1979, Dales remembered most Guild members in New York as extras. SAG oral history tape.

[15]James Robert Parish, *Actors' Television Credits* (Scarecrow Press, 1973), p. 696.

[16]Grand jury testimony, p. 72.

[17]Ibid., p. 82.

[18]Ibid., p. 74, where Beilenson argues that the 1954 waiver should take the form of an amendment to the 1952 one, rather than a superseding letter, to take advantage of the "special set of circumstances" established in 1952.

[19]Raymond Chandler, "Ten Per Cent of Your Life," *Atlantic Monthly*, Feb. 1952, p. 51.

[20]Grand jury testimony, pp. 96, 104–5.

[21]Deutsch, op. cit., pp. 120–22.

[22]Pirie, op. cit., p. 42.

[23]Didion, op. cit., p. 42.

[24]Grand jury testimony, pp. 99–100.

[25]Alex McNeil, *Total Television* (Penguin, 1984), pp. 899–900.

[26]Ibid., pp. 786–92.

[27]Moldea and Goldberg, op. cit., p. 10.

[28]Parish, op. cit., p. 206. On Nov. 23, 1958, Reagan and Davis played an Indian husband and wife on a Thanksgiving show, "A Turkey for the President." McNeil, op. cit., p. 245.

[29]Parish, op. cit., pp. 17, 804–5.

[30]Grand jury testimony, p. 109.

[31]Ibid., pp. 104–5. Reagan again calls the IRS his "senior partner," p. 113.

[32]Ibid., p. 111.

[33]Ibid., p. 112.

[34]Moldea and Goldberg, op. cit., p. 14. Cf. "Film Company Paid the Candidate a Steep Price for Some Steep Land to Make Him a Millionaire," *The Wall Street Journal,* Aug. 1, 1980.

[35]Cannon, *Reagan,* p. 354.

[36]Moldea and Goldberg, p. 14.

[37]Nancy Reagan, with Bill Libby, *Nancy* (William Morrow, 1980), p. 127.

[38]Cannon, *Reagan,* p. 354. Moldea and Goldberg, op. cit., p. 14.

[39]Moldea and Goldberg, p. 14.

[40]Ibid.

[41]Cannon, *Reagan,* p. 354. He bought the land in 1968 for $347,000 and sold it in 1976 for $856,000.

[42]Moldea and Goldberg, p. 14.

[43]Cannon, *Reagan,* p. 356. After the *Bee*'s disclosure, Cannon says, Reagan instructed his aides to make sure he always paid some minimum tax every year. But he did not let zeal push him too far. He continued to take a tax break from his Rancho del Ciel (which became the Western White House) as a working ranch, though he kept only a token two dozen cattle there. Ibid., p. 355.

CHAPTER 29

[1]Nat Hentoff, "The Octopus of Show Biz," *The Reporter,* Nov. 23, 1961, p. 41.

[2]Dan Moldea and Jeff Goldberg, "The Deal's the Thing," *Los Angeles Reader,* Nov. 2, 1984, p. 8.

[3]Ibid., p. 11.

[4]Hentoff, op. cit., p. 39.

[5]Reagan testimony to federal grand jury, Feb. 5, 1962, p. 55.

[6]Ibid., p. 66.

[7]Ibid., p. 67.

[8]Ibid., p. 69.

[9]Ibid., p. 73.

[10]Ibid., p. 58.

[11]Ibid., pp. 74–75.

[12]Ibid., p. 67.

[13]Ibid., p. 82.

[14]Ibid., p. 81.

[15]Ibid., pp. 91–92.

[16]Jack Dales, California Oral History Project, 1981, UCLA Special Collections, p. 46.

[17]Ibid.

[18]Grand jury testimony, p. 56. Elsewhere Reagan describes the settling of another sticky problem: "So Art Parke, who is a vice-president [of MCA], and Taft Schreiber, who is a vice-president in charge of Revue went and took the problem to the

head school teacher, Lew Wasserman, who is the president of the whole works" (ibid., p. 99).

[19]Hentoff, op. cit., p. 39.

[20]As we shall see, Reagan was himself looking for new contracts in the summer of 1962, after General Electric dropped its television theater.

[21]Grand jury testimony, p. 104.

[22]Jack Dales, in his 1979 interview for SAG's oral history program, admits that West Coast actors and their representatives had been slow to respond to the challenge of TV reruns, by contrast with New York actors; but he blames that on the different working conditions in the two places—Hollywood actors trying to receive ever larger salaries, New York actors settling for work at "scale" but depending on long runs or on reruns. Also, the major commercials were first made in New York, and they posed the residual problem in a very pointed way.

[23]Jack Dales, California Oral History Project, 1981, Special Collections, UCLA, pp. 36–41.

[24]*Screen Actor* editorial, December 1959.

[25]Grand jury testimony, p. 118.

[26]Reagan makes the strike last six months (Hubler, p. 316). It ran from March 7 to April 18, 1960. Reagan resigned as president on June 7, having taken office on November 7, 1959.

[27]The exact terms were for $2,250,000 to be paid in installments over ten years. New York *Times,* April 9, 1960, p. 16.

[28]Moldea and Goldberg, op. cit., p. 10.

CHAPTER 30

[1]Ronald Reagan, testimony before federal grand jury, Feb. 5, 1962, pp. 95, 100.

[2]David L. Lewis, *The Public Image of Henry Ford* (Wayne State University, 1976), p. 514, n.2. *The House for Modern Living, 197 Small House Designs Including 54 Prize Winners in the General Electric Architectural Competition* (Harcourt, Brace, 1935).

[3]Edward L. Bernays, *Biography of an Idea* (Simon and Schuster, 1965), pp. 444–60. McNamee's "recreation" of the historical event on radio not only resembles Reagan's later baseball games but anticipates the Walter Cronkite radio show "You Are There."

[4]Robert S. Lynd and Helen Merrell Lynd, *Middletown: A Study in American Culture* (Harcourt, Brace, 1929), p. 82.

[5]Robert Levering, Milton Moskowitz, and Michael Katz, *The 100 Best Companies to Work for in America* (Addison-Wesley, 1984), p. 115.

[6]Harry Levinson and Stuart Rosenthal, *CEO: Corporate Leadership in Action* (Basic Books, 1984), p. 20.

[7]Ibid.

[8]Levering et al., op. cit., 117.

[9]New York *Times,* July 5, 1985. The company had admitted defrauding the government of $800,000 in work on the Minuteman missile. (Ibid., July 19, 1985.)

[10]Levinson and Rosenthal, op. cit., p. 21.

[11]Ibid., p. 46. Charles E. Wilson, president of General Electric, who became Truman's Director of the Office of Defense Mobilization during the Korean War, was a contemporary of Charles F. Wilson, Jr., the president of General Motors who became Eisenhower's Secretary of Defense. The latter was called "Engine Charlie" to distinguish him from the former. *Current Biography,* 1951, pp. 663–65.

[12]Levering et al., p. 115.

[13]Levinson and Rosenthal, p. 20.

[14]Ibid., p. 204. In the book, the CEOs become "warriors" (p. 9), their companies "armies" (18), their lead executives a "combat group" (78). IBM's staff system is praised for resembling that of the German army (189). We are assured that "Selling is by definition a vanquishing activity" (150). This is all in a scholarly book. Popular tracts on salesmanship descend to the level of *Patton's Principles: A Handbook for Managers Who MEAN IT!* (by Porter B. Williamson, Simon and Schuster, 1979).

[15]Louis Cannon, *Reagan* (Putnam, 1982), p. 67. For other actors' stormy relations with Warner, see the files reprinted in Rudy Behlmer, *Inside Warner Bros. (1935–1951),* Viking, 1985, pp. 28, 44, 234–5, 305–7.

[16]Grand jury testimony, p. 116.

[17]At first, GE demanded twenty weeks on the road, but that was soon cut to sixteen—two tours of eight weeks. Reagan, after one round of that, argued that "No man lives to do the eight-week tour, and not give snarling lessons," so the total was cut to twelve weeks, made up of three-week or four-week tours. Later he won a further reduction, to eight weeks, in two-week installments. Grand jury testimony, p. 115.

[18]Interview with Gavaghan, now working in the District of Columbia.

[19]Cannon, *Reagan,* p. 97. Reagan the loyalist is never fired by a boss he likes. He says Peter MacArthur could have had nothing to do with his dismissal from the radio station in Davenport (Hubler, p. 68).

[20]Grand jury testimony, p. 105.

[21]Phyllis Schlafly, *A Choice Not an Echo* (Père Marquette Press, 1964), p. 25. Jonathan Martin Kolkey notes that "choice" became a shorthand for the New Right program in 1964. Reagan's televised speech for Goldwater was titled "A Time for Choosing," and the controversial law-and-order commercial Goldwater himself killed was called "Choice." Kolkey, *The New Right, 1960–1968, With Epilogue 1969–1980* (University Press of America, 1983), p. 255.

[22]Robert Welch, *The Blue Book* (John Birch Society, 1961), p. 123. Barry Goldwater thought Herbert Brownell and Henry Cabot Lodge, not Nixon, made the convention deal with Warren *(With No Apologies,* Berkley, 1980, p. 64).

[23]Robert Welch, *The Politician* (John Birch Society, 1963), pp. 223, 227.

[24]The best surveys agree that California membership made up at least a quarter and perhaps a third of the entire John Birch Society, and that as much as four fifths of the California members were in the south of the state. Seymour Martin Lipset and Earl Raab, *The Politics of Unreason: Right-Wing Extremism in America, 1790–1970* (Harper & Row, 1970), pp. 305–6.

[25]Barry Goldwater, *The Conscience of a Conservative* (Hillman, 1960), pp. 26–27.

[26]Ibid., pp. 34–37, 102–5, 124–25.

[27]Fred Kaplan, *The Wizards of Armageddon* (Simon and Schuster, 1963), pp. 248–57.

[28]Goldwater, *With No Apologies,* p. 150.

[29]Phyllis Schlafly and Chester Ward, *The Gravediggers* (Père Marquette Press, 195, 1964), p. 19.

[30]Ibid., p. 92.

[31]John A. Stormer, *None Dare Call It Treason* (Liberty Bell Press, 1964), p. 26. Stormer offers the words as a quotation, but introduces them: "Summarized and paraphrased, Lenin's plan stated:" Welch, in the *Blue Book* (p. 10), introduced the same words in quotation marks with this formula: "It [Lenin's plan] has been paraphrased and summarized as follows:" Reagan regularly offers it as a quote from the works of "Nikolai" Lenin—he seems to have taken Lenin's first name from Stormer's book, too (p. 23). Cf. Karl E. Meyer, "The Elusive Lenin: Where Ronald Reagan Read of the Plot to Conquer America," New York *Times,* Oct. 8, 1985.

[32]Ronnie Duggan, *On Reagan: The Man and His Presidency* (McGraw-Hill, 1983), p. 14.

[33]J. Allen Broyles, *The John Birch Society: Anatomy of a Protest* (Beacon, 1964), pp. 66–67.

[34]George Christopher, Reagan's opponent in the Republican primary race for governor in 1966, tried to use Reagan's membership in Communist front organizations against him. Lou Cannon, *Reagan* (Putnam, 1982), p. 107. The matter cropped up again only on the creepymost right (e.g., Kent H. Steffgen, *Here's the Rest of Him* (Foresight Books, 1968), Intro. and p. 137.

CHAPTER 31

[1]Robert Novak, *The Agony of the G.O.P. 1964* (Macmillan, 1965), p. 86.

[2]Theodore White, *The Making of the President, 1964* (Atheneum, 1965), pp. 118–19. The Goldwater movement had been begun by a network of former Young Republican activists maintained by F. Clifton White. For White's version of the 1963 YR convention in San Francisco, see his book, *Suite 3505.* By contrast, even the generally conservative Robert Novak called the convention a gathering of "well-scrubbed young monsters," where "Silver-haired Robert Gaston, the mercurial leader of the Birch-infested California delegation, paced in and out of the convention hall as he directed the tactics of disruption" (op. cit., pp. 196–201). Every prospective GOP candidate for the next year's election was invited to this convention, but Rockefeller, Romney, and Scranton stayed away, fearing the reception they would get. Only Goldwater went, to a rapturous response.

[3]Novak, op. cit., pp. 202–18.

[4]Barry Goldwater, *With No Apologies* (Berkley, 1980), pp. 180–81.

[5]John H. Kessel, *The Goldwater Coalition: Republican Strategies in 1964* (Bobbs-Merrill, 1968), p. 212.

[6]Jonathan Martin Kolkey, *The New Right, 1960–1968, With Epilogue, 1969–1980* (University Press of America), p. 213.

[7]Kessel, op. cit., p. 212.

[8]Stephen Shadegg, *What Happened to Goldwater?* (Holt, Rinehart and Winston, 1965), pp. 252–53.

[9]Lee Edwards, *Reagan: A Political Biography* (Viewpoint Books, 1967), pp. 78–79.

[10]David S. Broder and Stephen Hess, *The Republican Establishment* (Harper & Row, 1967), pp. 253–54.

[11]Interview with Doris Klein of AP, quoted in Bill Boyarsky, *The Rise of Ronald Reagan* (Random House, 1968), pp. 158–59. Even more bluntly, Salvatori told Joel Kotkin and Paul Grabowicz: "We knew then, as we know now, that Reagan didn't have any depth. But he was sure good on his feet." *California Inc.* (Rawson, Wade, 1982), p. 53.

[12]Lou Cannon, *Ronnie and Jesse: A Political Odyssey* (Doubleday, 1969), pp. 76–77.

[13]Boyarsky, op. cit., p. 106.

[14]Shana Alexander, *Life,* August 13, 1965.

[15]Lou Cannon, *Ronnie and Jesse,* p. 73. To show that Reagan's campaign was not radical, Goldwater and Nixon—respectively the hero and the ogre of the Birch Society—were pointedly not asked for help, endorsement, or appearances. Totton J. Anderson and Eugene C. Lee, "The 1966 Election in California," *Western Political Quarterly,* June 1969, p. 542.

[16]Kessel, op. cit., p. 8.

[17]*National Review,* December 1, 1964.

[18]Though generally honorable, Brown indulged in one political dirty trick during the 1966 campaign that not only made him look bad but demonstrated his underestimation of Reagan. Thinking Reagan would be the weaker candidate in the general

election, Brown helped him in the Republican primary by sabotaging his rival, George Christopher. He hired detectives to confirm a past indictment over a technical violation of the law and gave the information to Drew Pearson for use in his column. Brown was also clumsy enough to leave tracks, and the public soon knew of his role in the matter. Cannon, *Ronnie and Jesse,* pp. 78–79.

[19]Boyarsky, op. cit., pp. 142–45.

[20]Stanley Plog, Oral History Project, 1981, UCLA Special Collections, p. 2.

[21]Boyarsky, op. cit., p. 143.

[22]Plog, op. cit., p. 6.

[23]Ibid., pp. 3, 5.

[24]Ibid., p. 6.

[25]Boyarsky, op. cit., pp. 108–10; Cannon, *Ronnie and Jesse,* p. 77.

[26]Plog, op. cit., p. 12.

[27]Ibid., pp. 5, 10.

[28]Ibid., p. 13.

[29]Boyarsky, op. cit., p. 148.

[30]Ibid., p. 149.

[31]Plog, op. cit., p. 7, Boyarsky, op. cit., p. 149, Cannon, *Ronnie and Jesse,* p. 84.

[32]Boyarsky, op. cit., pp. 149–50.

[33]Ibid., p. 151.

[34]Ibid., p. 152.

[35]Herbert M. Baus and William B. Ross, *Politics Battle Plan* (Macmillan, 1968), p. 260.

[36]Goldwater, op. cit., pp. 73–74.

CHAPTER 32

[1]George F. Will, "Fresh Start?" Washington *Post,* Oct. 31, 1985.

[2]Walton Bean, *California: An Interpretive History* (McGraw-Hill, 1973), p. 559.

[3]Ibid.

[4]Bill Boyarsky, *The Rise of Ronald Reagan* (Random House, 1968), p. 14.

[5]Bean, op. cit., p. 561.

[6]Boyarsky, op. cit., p. 164.

[7]Lou Cannon, *Ronnie and Jesse: A Political Odyssey* (Doubleday, 1969), p. 131, quoting Lyn Nofziger: "We were so innocent that we tried to run government from Los Angeles during the interim and discovered that we couldn't."

[8]Lincoln Steffens, *The Autobiography of Lincoln Steffens* (Harcourt, Brace & World, 1931), p. 128.

[9]Justin Kaplan, *Lincoln Steffens* (Simon and Schuster, 1974), p. 17.

[10]Joan Didion, *The White Album* (Pocket Books, 1980), p. 71.

[11]Interview with Mrs. Brown, now living in Los Angeles.

[12]Boyarsky, op. cit., p. 18.

[13]Didion, op. cit., p. 69: "The place [built by Tuttle et al.] has been called by Jerry Brown, a 'Taj Mahal.' It has been called a 'white elephant,' a 'resort,' a 'monument to the colossal ego of our former governor.' It is not exactly any of these things. It is simply and rather astonishingly an enlarged version of a very common kind of California tract house, a monument not to colossal ego but to a weird absence of ego, a case study in the architecture of limited possibilities, insistently, malevolently 'democratic,' flattened out, mediocre and 'open' and as devoid of privacy or personal eccentricity as the lobby area in a Ramada Inn."

[14]Interview with former governor Jerry Brown, now living in Los Angeles.

[15]Boyarsky, op. cit., pp. 193–94.

[16]Cannon, *Ronnie and Jesse,* p. 134.

[17]Ibid., pp. 132–33.

[18]Boyarsky, op. cit., pp. 169–70.

[19]Cannon, *Ronnie and Jesse*, p. 149. Cf. Dale Everett Carter, "The Government and the Budget: The Case of Mental Hygiene," in Eugene C. Lee and Willis D. Hawley, *The Challenge of California* (Little, Brown, 1970), pp. 129–40.

[20]In the case of higher education, Reagan raised the state's spending one-third more than his overall budget increases, which were considerable. Cannon, *Ronnie and Jesse*, p. 154. "The Reagan budget did even more for elementary and secondary schools than it had done for higher education, increasing spending by 89 percent during Reagan's eight years compared to 71 percent during Brown's two terms. These figures are all the more impressive considering that elementary and secondary enrollment rose 37.6 percent during the Brown years and only 2.6 percent during Reagan's terms. Reagan backed a program for early childhood education and a master plan for special education advocated by Wilson Riles, the progressive state Superintendent of Public Instruction." (Ibid., p. 184.)

[21]Ibid., p. 134.

[22]Reagan delivered a verbal equivalent of the canceled Goldwater ad called "Choice" in his 1966 speeches, proving that "the morality gap is so great that we can no longer ignore it" by describing orgies at Berkeley where giant screens were filled with "pictures of men and women, nude, in sensuous poses, provocative, fondling." As Boyarsky, covering the campaign, wrote: "It was heady material for the women's club." Boyarsky, op. cit., pp. 22–23.

[23]Cannon, *Ronnie and Jesse*, p. 184.

[24]Ibid., p. 183. Long after, Reagan could joke about the matter. He told William F. Buckley that, when Truman Capote visited his office to discuss the plight of those on Death Row, the governor joked with his aides about Capote's effeminate manner saying, "Perhaps we should trawl him through the halls to see if there are any of them left."

[25]Cannon, *Ronnie and Jesse*, pp. 185–88. Buffalo Bills quarterback Jack Kemp worked briefly for the Reagan administration during its first year, became a friend of one of those purged by Nofziger, and bought a house with him in Lake Tahoe—though he never visited it. This connection would come back to plague Kemp when he ran for Congress. Marie Brenner, "Jack the Jock," *Vanity Fair*, January 1986, p. 102.

[26]John Gregory Dunne, *The Studio* (Farrar, Straus & Giroux, 1969), pp. 126–27.

[27]Joel Kotkin and Paul Grabowicz, *California, Inc.* (Rawson, Wade, 1982), p. 68. Ronald Brownstein and Nina Easton, *Reagan's Ruling Class: Portraits of the President's Top 100 Officials* (Presidential Accountability Group, 1982), p. 350.

[28]Gary G. Hamilton and Nicole Woolsey Biggart, quoting Secretary of Resources Norman Livermore in *Governor Reagan, Governor Brown* (Columbia University, 1984), p. 259.

[29]Ronnie Duggan, *Reagan: The Man and His Presidency* (McGraw-Hill, 1983), pp. 40–41.

[30]Howard Kurtz, Washington *Post*, Dec. 13, 1985; Mary Thornton and Howard Kurtz, ibid., Dec. 17, 1985.

[31]New York *Times*, Feb. 26, 1986.

[32]Laurence I. Barrett, "The Sleaze Factor," Ch. 27 of *Gambling with History: Ronald Reagan in the White House* (Doubleday, 1983), pp. 455–66.

[33]Larry Maegasak, "Reagan Ties Aided Coors, Official Says," Chicago *Sun-Times*, April 13, 1984.

[34]Barrett, op. cit., p. 465.

[35]Ronald Brownstein and Nina Easton, *Reagan's Ruling Class: Portraits of the President's Top 100 Officials* (Presidential Accountability Group, 1982), pp. 438, 632–33.

[36]Barrett, op. cit., p. 465.

[37]"The Reagan 45," *New Republic,* April 16, 1984.

[38]Brownstein and Easton, op. cit., pp. 353–54. Kotkin and Grabowicz, op. cit., pp. 67–68.

[39]*The Wall Street Journal,* Oct. 7, 27, 1983; April 30, Sept. 25, 1984.

[40]Leslie Maitland Werner, "Reagan '80 Group Rebuffs Inquiry by Congress on Transition Books," New York *Times,* April 15, 1984.

[41]Peter Hannaford, *The Reagans: A Political Portrait* (Coward-McCann, 1983), p. 84.

CHAPTER 33

[1]Bill Boyarsky, *The Rise of Ronald Reagan* (Random House, 1968), p. 158.

[2]Stanley Plog, California Oral History Project, 1981, UCLA Special Collections, p. 6.

[3]Lou Cannon, *Reagan* (Putnam, 1982), p. 158.

[4]Theodore H. White, *The Making of the President 1968* (Atheneum, 1969), p. 40.

[5]The idea of management consultants to criticize government remained attractive to Reagan over the years, though it was a consultant of this type who gummed up the works as his first director of finance in Sacramento. One Washington task force would be the Grace Commission, the familiar title for the President's Private Sector Survey on Cost Control. The commission's report, issued in January of 1985, accused the bureaucracy of bungling, but was itself bungled in its numbers and procedures. See Steven Kelman, "The Grace Commission: How Much Waste in Government?" *The Public Interest,* Winter 1985, pp. 62–82.

[6]Jules Witcover, *The Resurrection of Richard Nixon* (Putnam, 1970), pp. 113, 123–24, 168–70.

[7]Ibid., pp. 338–39; Cannon, *Reagan,* pp. 162–63.

[8]Garry Wills, *Nixon Agonistes* (Houghton Mifflin, 1970), p. 254.

[9]Nancy Reagan with Bill Libby, *Nancy* (Morrow, 1980), p. 165.

[10]Boyarsky, op. cit., p. 178.

[11]Reagan "sponsored a tax increase far beyond anything the state needed to balance its books . . . Partly this was because Reagan lacked an accurate estimate of the deficit from his own director of finance [Gordon Paul Smith]." Cannon, *Reagan,* p. 156.

[12]Boyarsky, op. cit., 156–57. Cannon adds other uses of "political muscle" in the Senate, once Assembly leader Unruh was appeased. Bills important to the Senators languished in Assembly committees until the tax bill was voted through. One man was given two judges for his vote—Senator Alfred E. Alquist. Cannon, *Reagan,* p. 156. Getting Unruh's concessions on this and other matters cost four judgeships to men of his choice. Cannon, *Ronnie and Jesse* (Doubleday, 1969), p. 305.

[13]Cannon, *Reagan,* p. 155.

[14]Ibid., p. 156. Cf. Rowland Evans and Robert Novak, *The Reagan Revolution* (Dutton, 1981), pp. 31–32: "Thus it was that Ronald Reagan, having preached for a generation about the ills of high taxation, became the greatest taxer in California's history . . . When he left office, the California tax system was far more progressive than he had found it, with upper-income individuals, corporations, and banks paying a markedly higher share of the state's revenue than they had under Pat Brown."

[15]Cannon, *Reagan,* p. 167.

[16]Evans and Novak, op. cit., p. 32: "Welfare reform, the pride of his governorship, was also a surrender to the conventional wisdom . . . [which] increased by 43 percent benefits for the 'truly needy'—that is, those who could meet the new, more rigorous qualification standards."

[17]Gary G. Hamilton and Nicole Woolsey Biggart, *Governor Reagan, Governor Brown: A Sociology of Executive Power* (Columbia University, 1984), pp. 186–94.

[18]Ronald Brownstein and Nina Easton, *Reagan's Ruling Class: Portraits of the President's Top 100 Officials* (Presidential Accountability Group, 1982), p. 646.

[19]Hamilton and Biggart, op. cit., p. 189.

[20]G. K. Chesterton, *The Outline of Sanity* (Methuen, 1926), p. 27.

[21]Lou Cannon, "Reaganisms of the Year," Washington *Post,* December 30, 1985.

[22]Hamilton and Biggart, p. 214.

[23]Ibid.

[24]Ibid., p. 1.

[25]Ibid., pp. 1–2.

[26]Nicole Woolsey Biggart, "Management Style as Strategic Interaction: The Case of Governor Ronald Reagan," *Journal of Applied Behavioral Science,* 1981, p. 300.

[27]For Proposition One's defeat in 1972, see Boyarsky, *Ronald Reagan,* pp. 160–64, and Cannon, *Reagan,* pp. 189–90. After this defeat, the legislature overrode Reagan's veto for the first and only time (after sustaining 797 vetoes for him). Proposition One was produced by ex-Bircher Lewis Uhler, on one of those task forces Reagan is fond of.

[28]Reagan's late involvement in the 1967 abortion bill left him hesitant over, critical of, and yet acquiescent in measures that made abortion in California far easier to obtain than before. "For the first time on an important measure, Reagan had to make the decision himself. Left to his own devices, he didn't know where to turn." Cannon, *Reagan,* p. 131. Cf. Boyarsky, *Reagan,* pp. 121–24. But Reagan could not avoid a happy outcome even by the most strenuous bungling: the increase in abortions helped diminish the number of mothers and children on the relief rolls, for which he gave credit to his welfare reforms. Evans and Novak, op. cit., p. 33: "Thanks to the Reagan-signed law, California's state-financed abortions increased from 518 in 1967 to 135,762 in 1974; the total during his eight years was 276,000. Since most if not all of those abortions prevented additions to the welfare rolls, they are responsible for a large share—perhaps half or more—of the 200,000 to 300,000 fewer state welfare cases during Reagan's tenure."

[29]Hamilton and Biggart, op. cit., p. 214.

CHAPTER 34

[1]Joan Didion, "Holy Water," in *The White Album* (Pocket Books, 1979), p. 59. See, in the same collection, "At the Dam," for California's dependence on artificial supplies of water. The state has 1,200 major dams, 1,250 major reservoirs. Cf. Marc Reisner, *Cadillac Desert: The American West and Its Disappearing Water* (Viking, 1986), pp. 3, 9.

[2]For Reagan's role in the final stages of this process, see Irwin E. Farrar, California Oral History Project, 1974, 142ff. Reagan's remarks at the opening of the 600-mile system's completion are reprinted at pp. 335ff.

[3]Karl Marx, New York Daily *Tribune,* June 28 and Aug. 8, 1853. For Marx's more nuanced later view of Oriental societies' immobilism, see *Capital* (Fowkes translation, Vintage, 1977), I, pp. 477–79. Karl Wittfogel rebuked Marx for backsliding from his original position: *Oriental Despotism: A Comparative Study of Total Power* (Yale, 1957), pp. 380–82. Cf. Donald Worster, *Rivers of Empire: Water, Aridity, and the Growth of the American West* (Pantheon, 1985), pp. 22–60.

[4]"According to the theory pronounced in 1893 by Frederick Jackson Turner, then a young professor of American history at the University of Wisconsin, 'the existence of an area of free land, its continuous recession, and the advance of American settlement westward, explain American development.' This 'Turner hypothesis' was an

oversimplification and exaggeration even as applied to the upper Mississippi Valley, the region Turner knew best. As applied to the development of California, the Turner theory of the significance of the frontier is worse than worthless." Walton Bean, *California: An Interpretive History,* Second Edition (McGraw-Hill, 1973), p. 224. Cf. Worster, op. cit., pp. 98–104.

⁵Ibid., p. 225. Carey McWilliams, *California: The Great Exception* (Current Books, 1949), p. 98. One purchaser who used scrip, Henry Miller, owned a million acres of California, a realm the size of Belgium.

⁶Bean, op. cit., p. 231.

⁷Ibid., p. 351. For the "wholesale juggling of the public domain" involved, see Remi A. Nadeau, *The Water Seekers* (Doubleday, 1950), pp. 36–39. For the fraud and violence, and the artificial water famine created in Los Angeles to create a sense of emergency, see Carey McWilliams, op. cit., pp. 297–99. For Theodore Roosevelt "national forest without trees," cf. Reisner, op. cit., pp. 84–87.

⁸Carey McWilliams, *Southern California Country: An Island on the Land* (Dell, Cloan & Pearce, 1946), pp. 12ff.

⁹The first freeway (the Pasadena) was built in the Depression by the WPA and the PWA. H. Marshall Goodwin, Jr., "The First Freeway," in John and Laree Caughey, *Los Angeles: A Biography of a City* (University of California, 1976), p. 351. Federal money has supplied as much as 90 percent of later freeways; Christopher Rand, *Los Angeles: The Ultimate City* (Oxford, 1967), p. 55.

¹⁰Joel Kotkin and Paul Grabowicz, *California, Inc.* (Rawson, Wade, 1982), p. 9.

¹¹Worster, op. cit., p. 131. California's "original sin" is water control in the 1974 Roman Polanski movie, *Chinatown.*

¹²For the history of the all-important supervision of the state's irrigation districts, see Nadeau, op. cit., pp. 10–11. This involved a defense of the constitutionality of the Wright Act of 1887 declaring communal rights in water (Worster, op. cit., pp. 108–9). California is preeminently the land of planned communities, including the largest planned community ever undertaken, Irvine—a project Reagan's administration fostered. Cf. Rand, op. cit., pp. 11–12, 22–26; Reyner G. Banham, *Los Angeles: The Architecture of Four Ecologies* (Harper & Row, 1971), pp. 77–81. For Irvine developers as contributors to Reagan's reelection campaign in 1970, see Kotkin and Grabowicz, op. cit., pp. 67–68. For Irvine's irrigation history, cf. Wright, op. cit., p. 352.

¹³Bill Boyarsky, *The Rise of Ronald Reagan* (Random House, 1968), p. 206.

¹⁴Lou Cannon, *Reagan* (Putnam, 1982), pp. 182–83.

¹⁵Lou Cannon, *Ronnie and Jesse: A Political Odyssey* (Doubleday, 1969), p. 246.

¹⁶Ibid., pp. 247–48.

¹⁷Fred Greenstein, *The Hidden-Hand Presidency: Eisenhower as Leader* (Basic Books, 1982), pp. 5–6.

¹⁸Ibid., pp. 57–92.

¹⁹Gary Hamilton and Nicole Woolsey Biggart, *Governor Reagan, Governor Brown: A Sociology of Executive Power* (Columbia University, 1984), p. 198.

²⁰Nicole Woolsey Biggart, "Management Style as Strategic Interaction: The Case of Governor Ronald Reagan," *Journal of Applied Behavioral Sciences,* 1981, p. 305.

²¹Ibid., p. 306. Hamilton and Biggart, op. cit., p. 48. As one staff member put it: "We didn't like each other . . . There was just no friendship there."

²²Joe McGinnis, *The Selling of the President 1968* (Trident, 1969). See, for instance, the Treleaven memorandum on humanizing Nixon's image, quoted on p. 179.

²³Peter Hannaford, *The Reagans: A Political Portrait* (Coward-McCann, 1983), pp. 84, 102, 111; Jules Witcover, *Marathon: The Pursuit of the Presidency, 1972–1976* (Viking, 1977), p. 412.

²⁴Rosser Reeves, *Reality in Advertising* (Knopf, 1961), pp. 55–61.

²⁵Ibid., p. 32.

[26]Stephen Fax, *The Mirror Makers: A History of American Advertising and Its Creators* (William Morrow, 1984), p. 189. Reeves, like Reagan, was not interested in the office management of his enterprise, and left that to his partner Ted Bates, while he did the creating and inspiring (ibid., pp. 190–91).

[27]Reeves, op. cit., p. 57.

[28]David Ogilvy, *Confessions of an Advertising Man* (Atheneum, 1981), pp. 159–60, and *Ogilvy on Advertising* (Crown, 1983), pp. 209–13.

[29]Martin Mayer, *Madison Avenue, U.S.A.* (Harper, 1958), pp. 293–304.

CHAPTER 35

[1]Peter Hannaford, *The Reagans: A Political Portrait* (Coward-McCann, 1983), p. 32.

[2]Rowland Evans and Robert Novak, *The Reagan Revolution* (E. P. Dutton, 1981), pp. 45–46. Sears had been assigned to Agnew's campaign plane in 1968 when it became obvious that someone from the Nixon camp had to control his indiscreet remarks: Jules Witcover, *The Resurrection of Richard Nixon* (Putnam, 1970), p. 367.

[3]Jules Witcover, *Marathon: The Pursuit of the Presidency, 1972–1976* (Viking, 1977), p. 66.

[4]Lou Cannon, *Reagan* (Putnam, 1982), pp. 194, 200.

[5]Evans and Novak, op. cit., pp. 56–57.

[6]Witcover, *Marathon,* p. 399.

[7]Cannon, *Reagan,* p. 200.

[8]Ibid., p. 188.

[9]Evans and Novak, op. cit., pp. 37–38.

[10]The best treatment of the Bell speech and its impact is Witcover, *Marathon,* pp. 373–97. See also Cannon, *Reagan,* pp. 202–6.

[11]Evans and Novak, pp. 50–51.

[12]Spencer and Roberts used their knowledge of Reagan's weaknesses—and their grudge against some of his staff—to hurt him, describing his "lazy" campaigning and governing habits in California, and ridiculing his lack of thoughtful response on subjects like sending American troops to Rhodesia. Cannon, *Reagan,* pp. 204, 213, 220.

[13]Witcover, *Marathon,* pp. 416–17.

[14]Ibid., pp. 410, 413–14.

[15]Hannaford, op. cit., pp. 107–8.

[16]For the local campaign's flirtations with racism in North Carolina, see Witcover, *Marathon,* pp. 411–12; Cannon, op. cit., p. 206.

[17]Cf. Evans and Novak, op. cit., p. 57: "Sears never truly understood the genius of the Reagan campaign—the ideological fervor that led Phil Crane to defy his state party leadership and Tom Ellis [the North Carolina campaign manager] to defy not only his president and governor but to confront Reagan's own campaign manager on strategy questions."

[18]Hannaford, op. cit., pp. 76–77.

[19]Witcover, *Marathon,* pp. 427–32.

[20]Ibid., p. 405.

[21]Evans and Novak, op. cit., p. 55.

[22]The American Schwenkfelders are confined almost entirely to Pennsylvania, and in 1950 numbered only 2,400 members, though they arrived there in the 1730s. Sidney E. Ahlstrom, *A Religious History of the American People* (Doubleday Image, 1975), I, pp. 305–6.

[23]Witcover, *Marathon,* p. 500.

[24]Ibid., p. 398.

²⁵Spencer quoted by John C. Waugh, "Packaging Politics: The Campaign Managers," in Eugene C. Lee and Willis D. Hawley, *The Challenge of California* (Little, Brown, 1970), pp. 78, 81.

²⁶Cannon, op. cit., p. 239.

²⁷Theodore White, *America in Search of Itself: The Making of the President, 1956–1980* (Harper & Row, 1982), p. 245.

²⁸Cannon, op. cit., p. 229.

²⁹Ibid., pp. 245–55. Among other things, Sears had come increasingly to show his own disregard for Reagan's intellect, something Reagan could overlook, but not his wife. Ibid., pp. 239, 244, 246, 256. Cf. Jack W. Germond and Jules Witcover, *Blue Smoke and Mirrors: How Reagan Won and Why Carter Lost the Election of 1980* (Viking, 1981), pp. 132–38.

CHAPTER 36

¹William J. Jordan, *Panama Odyssey* (University of Texas, 1984), p. 319.

²Jimmy Carter, *Keeping Faith: Memoirs of a President* (Bantam, 1982), p. 159.

³Jordan, op. cit., p. 320.

⁴Ibid., pp. 458–59. Reagan, who had refused to participate in a public debate on the Canal being promoted by Norman Lear, preferred the friendlier forum of Buckley's *Firing Line*, taped before a Southern audience with Senator Sam Ervin as moderator, on Jan. 13, 1978. Peter Hannaford, *The Reagans: A Political Portrait* (Coward-McCann, 1983), pp. 150–51, 157–58.

⁵Jordan, op. cit., p. 488.

⁶Ibid., p. 489.

⁷Carter, op. cit., p. 224. Secretary of State Vance questions this view, saying Carter's trouble with SALT II came from a "rightward shift" in the country that accelerated during 1979 and 1980. Vance, *Hard Choices: Critical Years in America's Foreign Policy* (Simon and Schuster, 1983), pp. 156–57. But that shift was partly organized and energized by the heated Panama controversy. Richard Viguerie claimed that the Panama Canal debate added 250,000 to 400,000 new names to his computer file of mobilizable conservatives. Jerry W. Sanders, *Peddlers of Crisis: The Committee on the Present Danger and the Politics of Containment* (South End Press, 1983), pp. 216–17.

⁸Sanders, op. cit., pp. 152–54.

⁹Ibid., p. 154. Norman Podhoretz spoke for the Democratic neoconservatives when he said later: "In Ronald Reagan, a former Democrat, we thought we had discovered a more legitimate heir to the mainstream Democratic tradition in foreign policy—the commitment to containment running from Truman through Kennedy, Johnson and Senator Henry M. Jackson—than Jimmy Carter, let alone Mr. Carter's leading Democratic rival, Senator Edward Kennedy. Whereas the Democrats of 1980 seemed to have lost the heady faith in American power expressed by Senator Kennedy's older brother John in 1960, Mr. Reagan wanted to 'get the country moving again.' " *Foreign Affairs*, Vol. 63, No. 3 (1984), p. 448.

¹⁰Reagan's principal liaison to the CPD in the 1980 campaign, Richard Allen, played only a minor role in the 1976 race, supplying Reagan with information on Rhodesia that had caused him trouble during the California primary. Hannaford, op. cit., pp. 118–19. But Allen, a founding member of the CPD who was an early member of the Reagan team for 1980, regularly worked CPD material into Reagan's preparation, and Reagan became a member of the CPD during his visit to Washington in January, 1979 (Sanders, op. cit., p. 217). After that, Reagan was regularly briefed by CPD personnel, and the Committee became the research branch of the

Reagan campaign, according to its director, Charles Tyroler II. Robert Scheer, *With Enough Shovels: Reagan, Bush, and Nuclear War* (Random House, 1982), pp. 41, 48.

[11]The CIA had itself upped the figures on Soviet military costs, some retired agents say because of reports from a defector (Andrew Cockburn, *The Threat: Inside the Soviet Military Machine*, Random House, 1983, p. 81). But the Agency could not see where all the extra money was going, since the same numbers of men and weapons were involved as in the earlier estimates. They concluded that inefficiency of production was eating up the percentage of GNP that military costs are stated in. Hardliners, refusing to accept this explanation, wanted to show that Russia was actually *producing* twice the former threat.

[12]Sanders, op. cit., pp. 198–99.

[13]New York *Times* editorial, Jan. 19, 1977. Murray Marder, "Carter to Inherit Intense Dispute on Soviet Intentions," Washington *Post*, Jan. 2, 1977.

[14]Stansfield Turner, *Secrecy and Democracy: The CIA in Transition* (Houghton Mifflin, 1985), p. 251. Richard Pipes also used the classified Team B report as the basis for his *Commentary* article of July 1977, "Why the Soviet Union Thinks It Can Fight and Win a Nuclear War." Pipes found one source of fear in the Soviet civil defense program—a program traditional since the early days of the nuclear age, when the Russians had no atomic bomb, and carried on in large part to maintain a sense of crisis and militaristic discipline in their own society; hardly effective, in any case, since they have never done a practice evacuation of a single city, and the first move in the direction of mass evacuations would be a clear tipoff of any "surprise" attack being mounted. Cf. Scheer, op. cit., pp. 62–64, 106, 117–19.

[15]Scheer, op. cit., p. 55. Cf. the analysis of Team B by former CIA analyst Arthur Macy Cox, "The CIA's Tragic Effort," *New York Review of Books*, Nov. 6, 1980.

[16]For Perle's impact on the first Carter position on arms reduction, cf. Ronald Brownstein and Nina Easton, *Reagan's Ruling Class: Portraits of the President's Top 100 Officials* (Presidential Accountability Group, 1982), pp. 499–500.

[17]Ibid., and Sanders, op. cit., pp. 209–10.

[18]Robert G. Kaiser, "Memo Sets Stage in Assessing U.S., Soviet Strength," Washington *Post*, July 6, 1977.

[19]Sanders, op. cit., p. 244.

[20]Ronnie Duggan, *On Reagan: The Man and His Presidency* (McGraw-Hill, 1983), pp. 534–35.

[21]The phrase, derived from the Pentagon, was taken up and popularized in 1978 by the CPD. Cf. Robert H. Johnson, "Periods of Peril: The Window of Vulnerability and Other Myths," *International Security*, Spring 1983.

[22]Scheer, op. cit., p. 66.

[23]Ibid., pp. 67–68.

[24]I have sketched too briefly the throng of technical problems involved in "taking out" America's entire ICBM system. Cf. James Fallows, *National Defense* (Random House, 1981), pp. 148–57.

[25]Johnson, op. cit., pp. 950–70. Richard Ned Lebow, "Windows of Opportunity: Do States Jump Through Them?" *International Security*, Summer 1984, pp. 147–86.

[26]Brownstein and Easton, op. cit., p. 520.

[27]The ADA was practicing its own form of McCarthyism before McCarthy when Arthur Schlesinger, Jr., circulated a warning about the suspect loyalty of a man whose only offense was opposing the ADA. Cf. Penn Kimball, *The File* (Harcourt Brace Jovanovich, 1983), p. 225.

[28]For Bernard Brodie's travel from the "father of deterrence theory" to disillusionment with the whole arms race, see Fred Kaplan, *The Wizards of Armageddon* (Simon and Schuster, 1983).

[29]Michael Crozier, Samuel P. Huntington, and Joji Watanuki, *The Crisis of Democracy: A Report on the Governability of Democracies to the Trilateral Commission* (New

York University, 1975), p. 113. For Huntington's importance in the neoconservative movement, see Peter Steinfels, *The Neoconservatives: The Men Who Are Changing America's Politics* (Simon and Schuster, 1979), pp. 262–69.

[30]For George Gilder, see *Sexual Suicide* (Quadrangle, 1973). For the assault on lavender soldiers and leather-bar anti-Americanism, see Podhoretz, "The Culture of Appeasement," *Harper's*, Oct. 1977, and Decter, "The Boys on the Beach," *Commentary*, Sept. 1980. Dorothy Rabinowitz attacked the "unmanly fraudulence" of radicals in "The Radicalized Professor: A Portrait," *Commentary*, July, 1972, p. 64, and Podhoretz denounced in the New York *Post* any emergency funds to study Acquired Immune Deficiency Syndrome, which particularly affects homosexuals. Such funds would, he said, amount to "a kind of AIDS in the moral and spiritual realm," which would "allow them to resume buggering each other with complete medical impunity." G. Jonathan Liebersohn, "The Reality of AIDS," *New York Review of Books*, Jan. 16, 1986.

[31]Glenn C. Loury, "Behind the Black-Jewish Split," *Commentary*, Jan. 1986.

[32]Bernard Rosenberg and Irving Howe, "Are American Jews Turning Right?" in *The New Conservatives: A Critique From the Left*, edited by Lewis A. Caesar and Irving Howe (New American Library, 1976), pp. 84–87.

[33]For the thesis that modern speculation about "the new class" arises from this "repressed problematic of Marxist history," cf. Alvin W. Gouldner, "Prologue to a Theory of Revolutionary Intellectuals," *Telos*, Winter 1975, pp. 3–4, and the same author's *The Future of Intellectuals and the Rise of the New Class* (Seabury, 1979), pp. 9, 53–58, 75–82.

[34]For English excerpts from Machajski's three-volume major work *The Intellectual Worker* (first published under the pseudonym A. Vol'skii), see *The Making of Society: An Outline of Sociology*, edited by V. F. Calverton (Modern Library, 1937), pp. 427–36, and sections quoted in Marshall Sharon Shatz's 1969 doctoral dissertation (Columbia University), "Jan Waclaw Machajski and 'Machaevschina,' 1861–1926: Anti-Intellectualism and the Russian Intelligentsia." Cf. Paul Avrich, *The Russian Anarchists* (Princeton, 1917), pp. 102–6. It is a sign of the anomaly of Marxism in peasant Russia that Machajski uses "white hands" and "black hands" as the class terms for what the English called horny-handed (vs. soft-handed) labor. In Russia, it was still the farmer's hand black with the soil that was the sign of labor. For a short biographical essay see Max Nomad's "The Saga of Waclaw Machajski," in *Aspects of Revolt* (Bookman Associates, 1959), pp. 96–117. Nomad became something of a disciple of Machajski, as he admits in *Rebels and Renegades* (Macmillan, 1932), p. 4. See also his *Political Heretics: From Plato to Mao Tse-tung* (University of Michigan, 1983), pp. 238–41. For a criticism of Machajski's thought, see Gouldner, "Prologue to a Theory," pp. 29–31.

[35]Gouldner, *The Future of Intellectuals*, pp. 28–49.

[36]Harold D. Lasswell, "The World Revolution of Our Time: A Framework for Basic Policy Research," in *World Revolutionary Elites: Studies in Coercive Ideological Movements*, edited by Harold D. Lasswell and Daniel Lerner (M.I.T. Press, 1965), esp. pp. 85–93. The education of people beyond productive *uses* for their education leads to the critical nature of the adversary culture: "When the social process creates an unbalanced supply of symbol manipulators, it prepares more than an excess of symbolic expression; it disposes toward *destructive* expression" (p. 91).

[37]Jeane Kirkpatrick, *The New Presidential Elite: Men and Women in National Politics* (Russell Sage Foundation, 1976). Kirkpatrick deplores the decline in union and business representation at the Democratic convention, interests served by broker-politicians. These have yielded to cause-oriented symbol specialists more interested in being right (or claiming to be) than in governing. Cf. pp. 252–53, 351–53.

[38]Kevin Phillips, *Mediacracy* (Doubleday, 1975), pp. 31–38. William Rusher of *National Review* accepted the new-class analysis in *The Making of the New Majority*

Party (Sheed & Ward, 1975). The neoconservatives' alliance with the "moral majority" against the counterculture is ironic, since one of Jeane Kirkpatrick's grievances against McGovernites in 1972 was their "rectitude," a moralism at odds with the brokering mentality (op. cit., pp. 208, 245, 253–55).

CHAPTER 37

[1]Godfrey Hodgson expressed the general view in his 1980 book, *All Things to All Men: The False Promise of the Modern American Presidency* (Simon and Schuster). Though Hodgson is a perceptive critic of modern American politics, his judgment—like that of most experts—was about to be confounded by Reagan even as he came to conclusions like this: "My own hunch is that the presidency will never again be at the center of the national consciousness in quite the way it was between 1933 and 1973" (p. 206). In the year that would elect the most skillful wielder of television in our political history, he could say: "[Presidential] television appearances have yielded reliable dividends in the past. They are likely to yield diminishing returns in the future."

[2]Ibid., p. 105.

[3]Cf. Thomas E. Cronin, *The State of the Presidency* (Little, Brown, 1975), p. 13: "Twelve miles offshore a President virtually is the United States."

[4]"King Henry IV, Part II," iv 5, 213–14. Cf. John E. Mueller, *War, Presidents and Public Opinion* (Wiley, 1973).

[5]Alexander M. Haig, Jr., *Caveat: Realism, Reagan, and Foreign Policy* (Macmillan, 1984), pp. 111–16.

[6]Haig, op. cit., pp. 251–56.

[7]The SALT adherence continued, in fact, into Reagan's second term: "In June 1985, the President surprised both critics and supporters by deciding that the United States would dismantle rather than dry-dock an aging Poseidon submarine in order to remain within the limits set by SALT II" (Charles William Maynes, "Lost Opportunities," *Foreign Affairs*, Vol. 64, No. 3, 1985, p. 413). Not till 1986, five years after the original treaty would have expired if ratified, did the President back off from it, tentatively.

[8]Maynes, op. cit., p. 413.

[9]Rowland Evans and Robert Novak, *The Reagan Revolution* (Dutton, 1981), pp. 191–92.

[10]New York *Times*, April 11, 1980.

[11]Cf. Seymour M. Hersh, *The Price of Power: Kissinger in the Nixon White House* (Summit, 1983), pp. 28–36. Kissinger's own version is in his *White House Years* (Little, Brown, 1979), pp. 40–48.

[12]Evans and Novak, op. cit., pp. 179–80. Haig's account of his efforts for "NSDD I" resembles Kissinger's defense of his own "NSDM 2" (Haig, op. cit., pp. 54–55, 74–75 and Kissinger, op. cit., pp. 40–48). He even compares the two documents (pp. 59–60). The principal difference is that Haig could not, despite repeated efforts, get his authorizing document signed by the President (pp. 83–85, 147–48, 355).

[13]Haig, op. cit., pp. 53, 80–84. It is rare for a presidential appointee to admit in print that "neither Allen nor I had direct, regular access to the President" (p. 84). For Haig, "the White House was as mysterious as a ghost ship; you heard the creak of the rigging and the groan of the timbers and sometimes even glimpsed the crew on deck" (p. 85).

[14]Haig, op. cit., p. 54.

[15]Laurence I. Barrett, *Gambling with History: Ronald Reagan in the White House* (Doubleday, 1983), p. 207.

[16]Haig, op. cit., pp. 127–28.

[17]Barrett, op. cit., pp. 168, 222, for the Haig-Kirkpatrick wrangling that had become public by June of the inaugural year and would reach a peak of acrimony during the Falklands war (pp. 237–42). Compare Haig, op. cit., pp. 268–70.

[18]Jeane J. Kirkpatrick, "Dictatorships and Double Stands," the famous article *(Commentary,* November 1979), reprinted in a collection with the same title (Simon and Schuster, 1982), p. 49. In a 1963 article she made a similar distinction between "Communist elites and other antidemocratic elites" (ibid., pp. 133–34), saying "Communist elites are more repressive than traditional dictatorships" (134).

[19]I can vouch for the fact that the distinction is obvious even to one who is beginning to think about politics, from the fact that I wrote in 1961, almost two decades before the Kirkpatrick essay: "Society is ultimately hurt less by individuals who catch at instant advantage than by the messiahs who undertake great missions with long-range planning, ingenuity, patience, endurance, and conviction of ultimate triumph . . . Power arms itself for the long pull, invades the mind, and gives structure to human effort, not when it is a spasm leading to dissolution, but when it is summoned up by a false god, with rights over the whole man and all men. Nero is personally more despicable, but politically less destructive, than Robespierre or Lenin." ("The Convenient State," reprinted in *Did You Ever See a Dream Walking,* ed. William F. Buckley, Jr., Bobbs-Merrill, 1970, p. 22.) I neglected some of the realities mentioned in the text of this chapter.

[20]Ernest Lefever, "The Trivialization of Human Rights," *Heritage Foundation Policy Review,* Winter 1978. Lefever was nominated to replace President Carter's human rights specialist, Patricia Derian, in the State Department's Bureau of Human Rights, but could not be confirmed because of compromising corporate ties.

[21]Bernard Gwertzman, "Haig Favors Stand Against Violations of Rights Abroad," New York *Times,* April 21, 1981.

[22]Kirkpatrick, op. cit., p. 134.

[23]Ibid., pp. 48, 63.

[24]Haig, op. cit., 268–70.

[25]Kirkpatrick, op. cit., p. 135.

[26]Ibid., p. 35.

[27]Ibid., pp. 106–14.

[28]In the minutes of a crisis group dealing with Chile, Kissinger said on June 27, 1970: "I don't see why we need to stand by and watch a country go Communist due to the irresponsibility of its own people" (Hersh, op. cit., p. 265).

[29]Haig, op. cit., p. 269.

CHAPTER 38

[1]Allen Sultan, "The International Rule of Law Under the Reagan Administration," *University of Dayton Law Review,* Winter 1985, pp. 246–50.

[2]Rowland Evans and Robert Novak, *The Reagan Revolution* (Dutton, 1981), p. 181: "The opposition stemmed from a consortium of U.S. mining concerns: Lockheed, Kennecott Copper, U.S. Steel and International Nickel. All had serious objections to the mining provisions of the proposed treaty that would limit their exploratory operations and deliver part of the profits to the underdeveloped countries."

[3]Sultan, op. cit., p. 248. The Reagan administration rejected the Law of the Seas Treaty even though one of its economic effects was an economic boost for Jamaica, which became the worldwide center for administrating the treaty's terms, and President Reagan had made Jamaica the showcase for America's "Caribbean Basin" program, to show the effects of "free market" prosperity. (Author's interview with Prime Minister Edward Seaga of Jamaica, March 1981.)

[4]Henry Kissinger, *Years of Upheaval* (Little, Brown, 1982), p. 138.

⁵Charles William Maynes, "Lost Opportunities" *(Foreign Affairs,* Vol. 4, No. 3, 1985), pp. 421–22.

⁶Sultan, op. cit., p. 258.

⁷Boyle, Chayes, Dore, Falk, Feinrider, Ferguson, Fine, Nunes, and Weston, "International Lawlessness in Grenada," *American Journal of International Law,* Vol. 78 (1984). The President claimed America could break all these agreements, to which it was signatory, in order to observe a treaty which it had not signed, that of the Organization of Eastern Caribbean States, though the cited articles (Number 6, par. 5 and No. 8) were inapplicable, and the Caribbean countries most active in the invasion, Jamaica and Barbados, were not even members of the OECS (formed in 1981 at the instigation of Grenada itself). Cf. Anthony Payne, Paul Sutton, and Tony Thorndike, *Grenada: Revolution and Invasion* (St. Martin's Press, 1984), pp. 89–101, 156–57; Hugh O'Shaughnessy, *Grenada: An Eyewitness Account of the U.S. Invasion and the Caribbean History That Provoked It* (Dodd, Mead, 1984), pp. 156–57.

⁸Alexander M. Haig, Jr., *Caveat: Realism, Reagan, and Foreign Policy* (Macmillan, 1984), pp. 100–2.

⁹For praise of Reagan's restraint, see for instance Coral Bell, "From Carter to Reagan," *Foreign Affairs,* Vol. 63, No. 3, 1984, pp. 490–510 and Terry L. Deibel, "Why Reagan Is Strong," *Foreign Policy,* Spring 1986, pp. 108–25. For blame, cf. Jeane Kirkpatrick's acerbity on the lack of counterterrorism, "Reagan's Puzzling Strategy," Chicago *Tribune,* Jan. 19, 1986, or Norman Podhoretz's attack on Reagan for not following Haig's "strategic consensus" policy in the Middle East by stationing American troops there as a "trip wire" ("The Reagan Road to Détente," *Foreign Affairs,* Vol. 63, No. 3, 1984, p. 460).

¹⁰Townsend Hoopes, *The Devil and John Foster Dulles* (Little, Brown, 1973), on the overlapping three pacts in the Pacific (p. 109), on SEATO (241–44), and on EDC (187–90).

¹¹Ronald C. Nairn, "Should the U.S. Pull Out of NATO?" *The Wall Street Journal,* Dec. 15, 1981.

¹²Melvyn B. Krauss, "De-Americanize European Defense," New York *Times,* Dec. 11, 1983.

¹³Cf. Strobe Talbott, *Deadly Gambits: The Reagan Administration and the Stalemate in Nuclear Arms Control* (Knopf, 1984), pp. 178–79.

¹⁴Irving Kristol, "What's Wrong with NATO?" New York *Times Magazine,* Sept. 25, 1983 and *Current,* Dec. 1983; "NATO Needs Shock Treatment," *Reader's Digest,* Feb. 1984. See also Eliot A. Cohen, "Do We Still Need Europe?" *Commentary,* Jan. 1986. Peregrine Worsthorne paraphrased the argument this way: "Everybody interested in freedom should put America's security interests first, and if they don't, then they can't be interested in freedom" ("A Tory Critique of Neoconservatives," *American Spectator,* Oct. 1985).

¹⁵Podhoretz, op. cit., p. 460.

¹⁶Haig, op. cit., pp. 169–70.

¹⁷For the secret meeting of Haig with Israeli chief of military intelligence Yehoshua Saguy, see Zeev Schiff, "Green Light, Israel Lebanon?" *Foreign Policy,* Spring 1983, and Zeev Schiff and Ehud Ya'ari, *Israel's Lebanon War* (Simon and Schuster, 1984), pp. 67–68. Haig plays down that meeting (op. cit., p. 332), but admits that Menachem Begin and Ariel Sharon gave him clear indications of their Lebanese intentions (pp. 327–31).

¹⁸Edward N. Luttwak, *The Pentagon and the Art of War* (Simon and Schuster, 1984), pp. 51–58, 266–68; Richard A. Gabriel, *Military Incompetence: Why the American Military Doesn't Win* (Farrar, Straus & Giroux, 1985), pp. 149–86.

¹⁹Casualty and other basic information has been suppressed to protect special operations ("black") procedures used in the early stages of the Grenada invasion. Cf. Gabriel, op. cit., pp. 164, 170, 180–84.

[20]In Reagan's treatment of Grenada, the country's internal politics could be ignored, for the most part, since the contending factions were both Communist, therefore equally evil. The invasion was given ancillary justification as a punishment for the murder of Maurice Bishop by Bernard Coard's followers, despite the fact that Bishop was Reagan's original villain, the recipient of Fidel Castro's support. Castro was not backing Coard at the time America attacked him.

[21]"Medals Outnumber G.I.'s in Grenada Assault," Associated Press, Mar. 29, 1984 (front page in New York *Times);* Jeffrey Record, "More Medals Than We Had Soldiers," Washington *Post,* April 15, 1984; "Doonesbury," Dec. 1, 1985. The Pentagon issued 152 Purple Hearts, though it had only reported 115 wounded (Gabriel, op. cit., p. 182).

[22]O'Shaughnessy, op. cit., p. 163.

[23]Richard Stubbing, "The Defense Program: Buildup or Binge?" *Foreign Affairs,* Spring 1985, pp. 848–72. Secretary Weinberger—fulfilling Reagan's campaign pledge to increase spending over Carter's own campaign-induced boost in expenditures—added thirty-two billion to the defense budget on entering office, without any clear plan for what the money would be spent on or why (ibid., p. 849).

[24]David Stockman, the director of the budget, admitted: "The defense numbers got out of control . . . They [the Pentagon] got a blank check . . . they got so goddam greedy" (William Greider, *The Education of David Stockman and Other Americans,* Dutton, 1982, pp. 37, 41).

[25]Edward Teller, the principal elder sponsor of SDI, cultivated the President in a series of four meetings that promised great things for the project. Cf. William J. Broad, *Star Warriors* (Simon and Schuster, 1985), pp. 16, 89, 122.

[26]Strobe Talbott, *Deadly Gambits: The Reagan Administration and the Stalemate in Nuclear Arms Control* (Knopf, 1984), pp. 132, 237, 273.

[27]Ibid., p. 263.

[28]For the American Army's cautious ground tactics, prompted by reliance on technology to disable the enemy, see Gabriel, op. cit., pp. 175–77.

[29]Luttwak, op. cit., pp. 174–75; James Fallows, *National Defense* (Random House, 1981), pp. 22–24, 76–106.

[30]E. P. Thompson, *The Nation,* March 1, 1986, p. 236. Cf. Jeff Gerth, "Reagan Advisers Received Stock in Laser Concern," New York *Times,* April 28, 1983.

[31]Cf. Bruce Catton, *War Lords of Washington* (Harcourt, Brace, 1948); John Morton Blum, *V Was for Victory* (Harcourt Brace Jovanovich, 1976), pp. 117–46.

[32]Thompson, op. cit., p. 236.

[33]See, for instance, Hans Bethe et al., *Space-Based Missile Defense,* Union of Concerned Scientists, Cambridge, 1984; Sidney D. Drell, Philip J. Farley, David Holloway, *The Reagan Strategic Defense Initiative: A Technical, Political and Arms Control Assessment,* Center for International Security and Arms Control, Stanford, 1984.

[34]Brass Bancroft's leader in the Secret Service describes the inertia projector in the very terms Reagan would use for SDI: "It not only makes the United States invincible in war, but in so doing promises to become the greatest force for world peace ever discovered."

CHAPTER 39

[1]Casey quoted from symposium at the John F. Kennedy School of Government, *The Campaign for President: 1980 in Retrospect,* ed. Jonathan Moore (Ballinger, 1981), p. 253.

[2]Kathleen A. Frankovic, "Public Opinion Trends," in *The Election of 1980: Reports and Interpretations,* Gerald Pomper et al. (Chatham House, 1980), pp. 113–17.

[3]Volcker quoted in *The Hidden Election: Politics and Economics in the 1980 Presi-*

dential Campaign, ed. Thomas Ferguson and Joel Rogers (Pantheon, 1981), p. 141. William Wimpisinger, president of the International Association of Machinists, made the same point in a gruesome monosyllable: asked if there was any way Carter could redeem himself with the electorate, he answered, simply: "Die." Ibid., p. 65.

⁴Theodore H. White, *America in Search of Itself: The Making of the President, 1956–1980* (Harper & Row, 1982), p. 161.

⁵Edward R. Tufte, *Political Control of the Economy* (Princeton, 1978), pp. 15–27. For Nixon's manipulation of the economy in 1971, see Herbert Stein, *Presidential Economics: The Making of Economic Policy from Roosevelt to Reagan and Beyond* (Simon and Schuster, 1984), pp. 176–87, who conceded this was not a new thing in kind, despite its scale: "[It] was an old FDR trick, to combine expansionism [in the election year] with the appearance of fiscal prudence by making this year's deficit so large that future deficits would look moderate by contrast."

⁶Emma Rothschild, "The Job Boom Is Carter's," Op-Ed article, New York *Times,* Oct. 28, 1984. Even in 1984, unemployment ran higher than the average for any year of the Carter administration.

⁷Roderick Kiewiet, *Macro-economics and Micro-economics: The Electoral Effects of Economic Issues* (University of Chicago, 1983).

⁸Lester Thurow, *The Zero-Sum Society: Distribution and the Possibilities for Economic Change* (Basic Books, 1980), pp. 42–47.

⁹Felix Rohatyn, "The New Chance for the Economy," *New York Review,* April 24, 1986.

¹⁰Robert L. Heilbroner, *Beyond Boom and Crash* (Norton, 1979).

¹¹Milton Friedman's works are most often associated with this view; for a more moderate monetarism see Stein, op. cit., pp. 349–52.

¹²Robert Reich, *The Next American Frontier* (Penguin, 1981).

¹³The voluble Laffer is so persuasive that he managed to lure the faculty of the University of Chicago into making him a tenured professor under the impression that he had a Ph.D. (though, at the time, he did not). Cf. *Contemporary Biography,* 1982, p. 212.

¹⁴Stein, op. cit., pp. 246–48.

¹⁵George Gilder, *Wealth and Poverty* (Basic Books, 1981), pp. 111–18. Business can be trusted with tax breaks and other favors because Gilder finds a superior morality in the capitalist, whom he considers the ideal religious figure (pp. 259–69).

¹⁶Rowland Evans and Robert Novak, *The Reagan Revolution* (Dutton, 1981), pp. 68–69.

¹⁷Ibid., pp. 70–72. Cf. Stein, op. cit., pp. 256–57 on Sears's campaign use of the "economics of joy."

¹⁸The Reagan administration, which attacks the federal bureaucracy (usually meaning the executive branch's agencies), has been staffed by key people like Richard Perle and David Stockman, who are products of the growing congressional bureaucracy. Cf. William Greider, *The Education of David Stockman and Other Americans* (Dutton, 1982), pp. 83–86, and Godfrey Hodgson, *All Things to All Men: The False Promise of the Modern American Presidency* (Simon and Schuster, 1980), pp. 134–35.

¹⁹Greider, op. cit., pp. 87–90. The memorandum is reprinted by Greider on pp. 139–59. Stockman calls it "my résumé" *(The Triumph of Politics,* Harper & Row, 1986), pp. 71–73.

²⁰Greider, op. cit., pp. 148–50.

²¹Ibid., pp. 139–40.

²²Ibid., p. 140.

²³Ibid., pp. 140–41.

²⁴Ibid., p. 141.

²⁵Laurence I. Barrett, *Gambling with History: Ronald Reagan in the White House* (Doubleday, 1983), pp. 138–39. Stockman, op. cit., pp. 82–84, 95.

²⁶Isabel V. Sawhill, "Economic Policy," in *The Reagan Experiment,* ed. John L. Palmer and Isabel V. Sawhill (Urban Institute Press, 1982), p. 496.

²⁷Barrett, op. cit., pp. 141–42.

²⁸Ibid., p. 142.

²⁹Greider, op. cit., p. 28.

³⁰Ibid., p. 33.

³¹Barrett, op. cit., p. 143; Greider, op. cit., p. 36; Stockman, op. cit., pp. 167–68.

³²Stockman, op. cit., pp. 262–63. Barrett (op. cit., p. 65) has Stockman plotting with James Baker; but he was brought into the abortive scheme after Darman (Stockman, op. cit., pp. 313, 317, 320–21).

³³John L. Palmer and Isabel V. Sawhill, *The Reagan Record* (Ballinger, 1984), p. 7.

³⁴Barrett, op. cit., p. 348.

³⁵The 1982 State of the Union Address included the plea: "Tonight, I am urging the American people: seize these new opportunities to produce, to save and to invest . . ."

³⁶Barrett, op. cit., p. 337.

³⁷Palmer and Sawhill, *The Reagan Crowd,* pp. 7, 289.

³⁸Ibid., p. 9.

³⁹Paul Craig Roberts, of the Treasury staff, presents himself as one of the few supply-siders who stayed true even when his own boss, Donald Regan, deserted the faith *(The Supply-Side Revolution: An Insider's Account of Policymaking in Washington,* Harvard, 1984, pp. 213–14). Cf. Stockman, op. cit., p. 239.

⁴⁰Reagan told a *People* magazine interviewer (Dec. 28, 1981): "Very frankly, I liken it to another assassination attempt—which I hope will be as unsuccessful as the first." He told Stockman, "You're a victim of sabotage by the press" (Stockman, op. cit., p. 3).

⁴¹Barrett, op. cit., pp. 348–50.

⁴²Ibid., p. 413.

⁴³Jude Wanniski, *The Way the World Works* (Touchstone, 1983), pp. 120–25, 234–35.

⁴⁴Stockman, op. cit., pp. 322, 331.

⁴⁵Palmer and Sawhill, *The Reagan Record,* pp. 93, 289.

⁴⁶Ibid., p. 82.

⁴⁷Ibid., p. 83.

⁴⁸Ibid., pp. 80–82.

⁴⁹Roberts, op. cit., p. 235.

⁵⁰Ibid., p. 200. Stockman (op. cit., p. 97) admits he had to settle for "suffering the dislocations of recession in order to purge out the monetary cancers of inflation."

CHAPTER 40

¹Robert S. Lynd and Helen Merrell Lynd, *Middletown: A Study in American Culture* (Harcourt, Brace & World, 1929), p. 178.

²Ibid., pp. 95, 104, 259–60.

³Ibid., pp. 46–47, 105, 254–57.

⁴Ibid., pp. 137–40.

⁵Ibid., pp. 257, 522.

⁶Ibid., p. 258.

⁷The movie begins with a family crisis because the hero cannot take his parents' car for a weekend with his girlfriend.

⁸Lynds, op. cit., pp. 42–43. There were 154 car thefts in one year the Lynds studied (p. 258). Ford thought the social impact of cars would be wider circles of acquain-

tance, making people give up war: Robert Lacey, *Ford: The Men and the Machine* (Little, Brown, 1986), p. 132.

[9] Michael J. Arlen, *Thirty Seconds* (Farrar, Straus & Giroux, 1980), pp. 51–52.

[10] Ibid., pp. 104–5.

[11] For Veblen on the telephone, cf. *The Instinct of Workmanship* (Augustus M. Kelley, 1964), p. 316: "Its ubiquitous presence conduces to an unremitting nervous tension and unrest wherever it goes."

[12] Allan Nevins and Frank Ernest Hill, *Ford: Expansion and Challenge, 1915–1933* (Scribner, 1957), p. 138. In 1916 Ford was quoted by a Chicago *Tribune* reporter: "History is more or less bunk . . . That's the trouble with the world. We're living in books and history and tradition." Asked about this on the witness stand in 1919, he said: "I did not say it was bunk. It was bunk to me . . . I did not need it very bad." Cf. Carol Gelderman, *Henry Ford: The Wayward Capitalist* (Dial, 1981), p. 177. He later explained, "I thought that a history which excluded harrows and all the rest of daily life is bunk, and I think so yet." *Greenfield Village Herald,* 1984, No. 2, p. 149.

[13] An interest in McGuffey made Ford start collecting things (Gelderman, op. cit., p. 275). His devotion to the books that taught him reading was in no way impaired by the fact that he read slowly and with difficulty (ibid., p. 183).

[14] For an example of the reconstructive "editing" of McGuffey texts, see what was done to Parson Weems's (already fictitious) tale of Washington and the cherry tree (Garry Wills, *Cincinnatus: George Washington and the Enlightenment,* Doubleday, 1984, pp. 39–53, 248–51).

[15] David L. Lewis, *The Public Image of Henry Ford* (Wayne State University, 1976), p. 281.

[16] Geoffrey C. Upward, *A Home for Our Heritage: The Building and Growth of Greenfield Village and Henry Ford Museum, 1929–1979* (Henry Ford Museum, 1979), p. 78.

[17] During Reagan's childhood and early manhood, Edison often came in first in the lists of men most admired in America—though sometimes he came in second to Henry Ford. Cf. Lewis, op. cit., pp. 232, 290, 481, and Wyn Wachhorst, *Thomas Alva Edison, An American Myth* (MIT, 1981), pp. 5–7.

[18] Wachhorst, op. cit., pp. 144–49. Edison liked to tell interviewers that "College men don't know what's going on" (ibid., p. 135).

[19] Lewis, op. cit., p. 225.

[20] Ibid., pp. 278–79.

[21] For the banning of foreign languages from Ford's high schools, see Lewis, op. cit., p. 282. For the Ford Americanization movement, see Olivier Zunz, *The Changing Face of Inequality* (University of Chicago, 1982), pp. 312–14.

[22] For Ford's and Edison's anti-Semitic campaigns, see Lewis, op. cit., pp. 138–54; Lacey, op. cit., pp. 205–19.

[23] Address to National Association of Evangelicals, March 8, 1983.

[24] Address to Phoenix Chamber of Commerce, March 1961.

[25] Address delivered in 1977 under the title "Reshaping the American Political Landscape."

[26] Press conference, Jan. 20, 1983.

CHAPTER 41

[1] For the key role of a geographically extended market in the genesis of Smith's thought, see Garry Wills, "The Benevolent Adam Smith," *New York Review of Books,* Feb. 9, 1978.

[2] Thorstein Veblen, *The Instinct of Workmanship* (Augustus M. Kelley, 1914), pp. 192–94, 222–24; *The Theory of Business Enterprise* (Scribner, 1904), pp. 27–34.

³Tom Wolfe, *The Right Stuff* (Farrar, Straus & Giroux, 1979), pp. 21–43.

⁴Cf. Veblen, *The Theory of Business Enterprise,* p. 10: "Modern industry has little use for, and can make little use of, what does not conform to the standard. What is not competently standardized calls for too much of craftsmanlike skill, reflection, and individual elaboration, and is therefore not available for economical use in the process. Irregularity, departure from standard measurements in any of the measurable facts, is of itself a fault in any item that is to find a use in the industrial process, for it brings delay, it detracts from its ready usability in the nicely adjusted process into which it is to go; and a delay at any point means a more or less far-reaching and intolerable retardation of the comprehensive industrial process at large. Irregularity in products intended for industrial use carries a penalty to the nonconforming producer which urges him to fall into line and submit to the required standardization."

⁵Wolfe, op. cit., pp. 187–93. For the advance of industry under protectively obsolete guises, cf. Veblen, *The Instinct of Workmanship,* pp. 239–40. The time machine in the movie *Back to the Future* has the obsolete "futurism" of a DeLorean car, taken from the decade preceding the movie's appearance.

⁶George Bernard Shaw, *The Intelligent Woman's Guide to Socialism and Capitalism* (Brentano's, 1928), p. 140.

⁷"There's a great spiritual awakening in America, a renewal of the traditional values that have been the bedrock of America's goodness and greatness," Reagan told the National Association of Evangelicals on March 8, 1983. The superiority of Reagan's "new conservatism" (an interesting concept) is, in the view of its adherents, the fact that it shows "Republicans ridding themselves of the albatross of 'negativism'" (Paul Craig Roberts, *The Supply-Side Revolution: An Insider's Account of Policymaking in Washington* [Harvard, 1984], p. 7.)

⁸Robert and Helen Lynd, op. cit., pp. 268, 475.

⁹William James, *The Varieties of Religious Experience: A Study in Human Nature* (Macmillan, 1961), p. 99.

¹⁰Ibid., pp. 91, 100.

¹¹St. Augustine, *The City of God,* 13.14.

¹²Ibid., 21.13.

¹³James, op. cit., p. 101.

¹⁴Paul D. Erickson, *Reagan Speaks: The Making of an American Myth* (New York University, 1985), p. 100. Cf. similar statements on pp. 2, 46, 60, 61, 64, 90, 92, 93, 98, 103, 107.

¹⁵Unlike her brother, Ruth Carter Stapleton was a mind-cure therapist, of the sort she described in her own book: "The deepest healing comes through persons who have moved beyond condemnation, beyond forgiveness [What is there to forgive?], into unconditional acceptance," like the Divine Comforter himself: "The Holy Spirit is a gentleman." Cf. *The Gift of Inner Healing* (Word Books, Waco, Texas, 1976), pp. 105–9.

¹⁶Reagan was asked, in connection with the Easter season, to discuss "moments of profound reverence" in his White House years for a Jack Anderson and Dale Van Atta column, "Revered Moments," Washington *Post,* March 30, 1986.

¹⁷Stanley Elkin, *The Magic Kingdom* (Dutton, 1985), p. 114.

¹⁸Irving Howe, *The American Newness: Culture and Politics in the Age of Emerson* (Harvard, 1986), p. 19.

ACKNOWLEDGMENTS

My principal debt is to John C. Wills, for research in Dixon and other forms of assistance. Tom Shepherd also helped me in Dixon, Bill Major in Eureka, and David Robb in Los Angeles. I was given generous assistance by the archivists at the Illinois State Archives, the Illinois Historical Society, the Whiteside County Records Office, the Chicago Historical Society, Eureka College, the Palmer School of Chiropractic, Drake University, Notre Dame University, the University of California at Los Angeles, and the Wisconsin Center for Screen and Theater Research. Also by the librarians of the Galesburg *Register-Mail*, the Monmouth *Review-Atlas*, the Woodford County *Journal*, the Dixon *Telegraph*, the Bloomington *Daily Pantagraph*, the Peoria *Journal-Star*, and the Des Moines *Register*. My agent, Ted Chichak, helped me with this as with ten preceding books. Like all students of Reagan, I am indebted to the meticulous reporting of Lou Cannon over the years. Very helpful suggestions and corrections were offered by those who read parts of the book: Alfred Appel, Jr., John S. Bushnell, W. Clark Gilpin, Frederick E. Hoxie, William E. Leuchtenburg, Francis Paul Prucha, Fannia Weingartner, Rudolph H. Weingartner, and Robert Wiebe.

INDEX